HAMILTON I
(1757–1789)

By Alonzo Chappell: Museum of the City of New York

Eager to advance his fortunes, Hamilton quickly volunteered for duty when the New York State Congress ordered the recruitment of an artillery company. He is shown above in his uniform as Captain of the Provincial Company of Artillery.

HAMILTON I
(1757–1789)

Robert Hendrickson

MASON/CHARTER

NEW YORK 1976

Library of Congress Cataloging in Publication Data

Hendrickson, Robert A   1923–
    Hamilton.

    Bibliography: p.
    Includes index.
    CONTENTS: 1. 1757–1789.
    1. Hamilton, Alexander, 1757–1804.
E302.6.H2H44   973.4′092′4 [B]   75–45436
ISBN 0–88405–139–0

For
Alex and Rob

CONTENTS

List of Illustrations ix

Foreword: The Grange and Monticello xi

1. Restless Love in the Lesser Antilles 1

2. Island Propaedeutics: Mr. Cruger's Countinghouse and Dr. Knox's Prescripts 20

3. The Importance of Strict College Entrance Requirements 37

4. To Free the Slaves Held Thrall by the *Asia*'s Guns 57

5. Covering the Beaten Retreat of an Essential Aegis to Be 91

6. Headquarters Intelligencer 118

7. The Idol of America Governed by One of His Aides 134

8. Valley Forge 173

9. Misbehavior at Monmouth 190

10. Emancipation—or a Golden Chain? 211

11. Elizabeth Schuyler Comes to Morristown 236

12. Treason! 260

13. Reconciled to His Being Shot, but Not to His Being Hanged 279

14. I Am No Longer a Member of the General's Family   294

15. Fix Bayonets! Follow Me!! To the Last Yorktown Redoubt!!!   313

16. After the Battle Comes the Lawgiver   338

17. A Few Months More in Public Life   356

18. Forfending Mutineers   373

19. Judicial Supremacy   398

20. Annapolis Apostrophe: The Exigencies of the Union   424

21. An Invisible Hand Guided All toward the General Good   451

22. We the People of the United States   480

23. *The Federalist Papers* and Other Poughkeepsie Persuaders   496

24. The Secretary of the Treasury Wept   529

     Hamilton Chronology 1757–1804   560

     A Note about Sources, Notes, and Bibliography   577

     Notes   580

     Bibliography   593

     Acknowledgments   617

     Index   621

LIST OF ILLUSTRATIONS

Captain of the Provincial Company of Artillery (by Alonzo Chappell) — Frontispiece

Plate

The Grange — I
Island of Nevis — II
Nicholas Cruger — III
Cruger's shop; newspaper advertisements — IV
New York City map 1775 — V
Elias Boudinot; William Livingston — VI
Myles Cooper; Alexander McDougall — VII
Horatio Gates; Charles Lee (by John Trumbull) — VIII
Comte d'Estaing; George Clinton — IX
Washington's Morristown headquarters; Hamilton — X
Elizabeth Schuyler; home of General Schuyler — XI
Philip Schuyler; Catherine van Renssalaer (by John Trumbull) — XII
Angelica Schuyler; Cornelia Schuyler (by John Trumbull) — XIII
The Schuyler home near Saratoga; Hamilton's wedding reception — XIV
Benedict Arnold; John André's sketch of the *Vulture* episode near Haverstraw — XV
Margaret Shippen; John André, self-sketch — XVI

Hamilton (by Prud'homme)   XVII
Elizabeth Schuyler (by Ralph Earl)   XVIII
John Laurens; *The Battle of Monmouth* (by Emanuel
    Leutze)   XIX
Washington's triumph at Yorktown (by Charles Willson
    Peale)   XX
Surrender of Cornwallis at Yorktown (by John Trum-
    bull)   XXI
John Jay; James Duane   XXII
James Madison; Robert Morris   XXIII
Maryland State House   XXIV
Washington presiding over Constitutional Convention   XXV
Hamilton's "ship of state" in a New York parade   XXVI
Federal Hall, New York City   XXVII
Frederick W.A.H.F. von Steuben   XXVIII
Philip Hamilton   XXIX
Elizabeth Schuyler Hamilton (by Eastman Johnson)   XXX
"The Farmer Refuted" pamphlet   XXXI
James Rivington   XXXII

FOREWORD: THE GRANGE AND MONTICELLO

Of all the Founding Fathers and Framers of the Constitution of the United States of America, Alexander Hamilton, one of the two or three most important, remains the most enigmatic, controversial, and mysterious. The mere mention of his name provokes violently differing reactions. It always has. Thomas Jefferson's name is honored, along with Andrew Jackson's, at dinners and conventions of the modern Democratic party each year as a patron saint of the party, but no similar homage is paid to Hamilton's name by the modern Republican party. Yet the acknowledged patron saint of the Republicans, Abraham Lincoln, stands for the policies of preserving the Union and emancipating slaves that are in their essence, and their precedents, Hamiltonian. But the name of Alexander Hamilton is not only ignored; it is all but unmentionable. Professor Clinton Rossiter has written that "Alexander Hamilton is the least known and most misunderstood major figure in American history."[1] Why such neglect of such a great man?[2]

Hamilton's name still suffers from Jefferson's apparently immutable indictment that he was a monarchist and an elitist. He is forever the man who was uncivil to Washington in 1781; who tolerated the outburst of speculation that attended his first financial measures; who manipulated the members of Adams's cabinet; who subverted and gratuitously attacked the second president; who had a tasteless affair with Mrs. James Reynolds; who exhibited impatience, immoderation, and inordinate ambition; who had a tendency to glorify the military, to exalt the wealthy, and to affect an unpardonable hubris.[3] Even during Republican administrations no proposals are heard to erect a marble monument to Hamilton beside the Potomac, nor even to appropriate a few thousand dollars to repair the decrepitude of his last home, Hamilton Grange, in New York City's Harlem.[4]

Other memorials to Hamilton more important than monuments remain. *The Federalist Papers* of Hamilton's authorship are root authority when it is necessary to resolve the gravest issues concerning the meaning of the Constitution, as in debates over presidential impeachment and clemency. His face in John Trumbull's portrait reproduced on the ten dollar bill is frequently seen, too frequently of late, partly as a result of the inflation of the currency that has occurred because of departure from rules he laid down for national economic policy management to maintain public credit.

The Bank of New York, which he helped to found, was the first bank in the modern world's financial capital. *The New York Post*, which he also founded, is the oldest surviving newspaper in the nation's communications capital. The Society for Establishing Useful Manufactures—The SUM Corporation—America's first large-scale conglomerate manufacturing corporation, was planned, established, and for a while largely managed by Hamilton in a 38-acre industrial park in the exurbs of the modern world's principal headquarters of conglomerate corporations.

For the SUM he selected the ideal site in the New York area—beside the Great Falls of the Passaic River near what is now Paterson, New Jersey. The acronym he chose for its name has a twentieth-century clang. There is a Hamilton statue in Central Park and a small bust on the Palisades at Weehawken above the ledge where he received his mortal wound in the duel. In Trinity Churchyard on lower Broadway is the sarcophagus where he and his wife Elizabeth Schuyler Hamilton are interred, a short block's walk west from 57 Wall Street, where they made their first home in the city.

If the rather short life of Alexander Hamilton—he was 47 when his body stopped Burr's bullet—remains contemporary, controversial, and mysterious, it is also one of the most dramatic and romantic, and tragic, lives in American history. If such qualities were not yet enough to compel attention, his life is also the story of a poor boy who made good that ranks with Benjamin Franklin's and Abraham Lincoln's—and Richard Nixon's. It seems more of an inevitability than an accident that the author of the Horatio Alger stories chose Hamilton as one of his pen names.

But by contrast to what Erich Fromm would call the marketing orientation and interchangeable character of the typical Horatio Alger hero,[5] Hamilton's deeds and words have a bite and style that are Shakespearean in their individuality and intensity. At the same time, the drama of his life bestrides a hemispheric stage with Marlovian sweep: it is the story of an illegitimate orphan boy from a speck of a cloud-capped isle in the Lesser Antilles who came to the continent, fought to overthrow its royal master, yoked the former colonies together into a new nation, and became the first prime minister of a continental empire. Its unique framework of political, social, and economic order for individual freedom during the following two hundred years would owe as much to his ideas, energy, actions, and precepts as to any other man's.

If the drama, romance, tragedy, upward—and downward—mobility, flame-like intensity, and epic sweep of Hamilton's life were not yet enough to arrest a reader's attention, it may also be argued that Alexander Hamilton was the greatest American who ever lived who was not one of the presidents. Not even the presidential qualification would be necessary except for the one or two, or possibly three, presidents whose greatness was certified by actions—leading the Revolution, preserving the Union and emancipating the slaves, arranging the purchase of the Louisiana Territory—that carried out precepts that Hamilton had always urged, fought for, and fostered. It is not particularly surprising that no biography has succeeded in capturing the greatness of his life between two or four covers.[6]

Hamilton's is one of those multifaceted lives about which the last word can never be said, no matter how multivolumed the work. For as long as the history of the United States will be written and rewritten, his life and works will demand restudy and reevaluation. Within the limits of two volumes neither a complete narrative of his public career nor a thorough analysis of his private affairs, nor the critical interrelation between the two, nor a satisfying overview of the scholarly disputes of fact, opinion, and philosophy that have always raged around his name is possible.

One further submission: Hamilton was the greatest New Yorker who ever lived, notwithstanding rival claims of the likes of Theodore, Fiorello, and Franklin Delano. A useful prelude to Hamilton's story is to pay a visit to what is left of Hamilton's presence in the city at his last home, Hamilton Grange. It is the house in Harlem he began building four years before his death, which became the first and only permanent home he and his family ever had. The street address is 267 Convent Avenue, New York, New York. It is well to have the number firmly in mind because all routes and approaches to it are singularly barren of directional arrows, enscrolled plaques, trail blazes, or other indicia of landmark significance. A site so sacred to American history, at least as far as conservatives are concerned, remains one of the better-kept secrets of a city most of whose millions take pride in calling themselves liberals, and conservatives a misguided minority.

Not much about the physical aspect of the 50-foot lot on which Hamilton Grange stands in a more or less ruined state is calculated to call attention to its presence. On some days, at least when the weather is good, a dirty American flag is flown from a stunted flagpole in the muddy little front yard. For many visitors the trip uptown on the West Side line of the IRT subway to West 142 Street in search of Hamilton's Grange has about it the feeling of a foray into a dangerous faintly hostile foreign country. The visitor is in one of the dirtiest and most dangerous and crime-ridden areas of Manhattan Island. On subway car sides, station walls, advertising placards, and building cornices are graffiti of lurid colors and obscure symbolism—LSD, Kendo, Kool Red and Sniper—sprayed from aerosol paint cans in psychedelic fury. The skins of the Harlem natives of this asphalt turf are black or one of innumerable other polychrome hues of mahogany, brown, beige, orange pekoe, and café au lait. Puerto Rican Spanish and drug culture jive talk are only two of many native tongues. A West Indian immigrant feels more at home here than a WASP—Hamilton was both.

Suddenly there he is!

On a granite pedestal near the stunted flagpole is the grimy bronze statue of a man in greatcoat and knee pants who seems to be striding purposefully westward toward the river. His back is to the muddy little weed patch of yard in front of a foursquare frame house set back about 25 feet from the sidewalk building line. His head is turned slightly southward, and his eyes look across the river past the Weehawken palisades toward the continental empire beyond. His distant view is completely shut out now by a row of brownstone tenements across the street.

On his pedestal appears the name of the sculptor, W. Ordway Partridge; the date, 1892; and HAMILTON, 1757–1804. On the granite are graven the following quotations:

> The name of Hamilton would have honored Greece in the age of Aristides.
>
> *—Ames*

> Model of eloquence and most fascinating of orators.
>
> *—Story*

> His rare powers entitled him to the fame of being the first intellectual product of America.
>
> *—Stevens*

> He smote the rock of the national resources and abundant streams of revenue gushed forth.
>
> *—Webster*

> There is not in the Constitution of the United States an element of order or force or of duration which he has not powerfully contributed to introduce and cause to predominate.
>
> *—Guizot*

Beside the granite pedestal is a small freestanding plaque that reads:

> Hamilton Grange. General Alexander Hamilton, one of the Framers of the Constitution, First Secretary of the Treasury, built this house in 1802.

Anyone who had lived there might well turn his back rather than gaze at the dilapidated two-and-a-half-story clapboard house. It appears more wretched than it otherwise might because it is wedged endwise between two bulky structures that abut and loom above it on either side: on the south, the red brick, Victorian, colonnaded pile of St. Luke's Episcopal Church; on the north, a nondescript tenement building whose dirty brick shoulder is jammed flush against the almost 200-year-old clapboards of The Grange.

From Hamilton Terrace, which runs along the back of The Grange's lot, the visitor who looks up the rise can see a door hanging from broken hinges; laundry drying on a clothesline strung across the sagging back porch; and rusty fencing overgrown with jimson, ragweed, kudzu, and other indomitable weeds indigenous to the city's desolate vacant lots. Cigarette and chewing-gum wrappers, broken gin bottles, empty beer cans, pieces of a plastic doll—the same sort of banal detritus of twentieth-century industrial civilization that fills countless other vacant city lots—litter the grounds of the last home of the author of the "Report on Manufactures" and the prophet of modern industrial America.

The only way to enter the house is up a rickety stoop across what was originally built as a side porch. The structure's once handsome facade and front entrance are now turned sideways on the lot and mashed against the abutting church wall. New York real estate is valuable, and this Procrustean treatment manages to wedge the old house onto a 50-foot strip, thus taking the minimum amount of land out of the hands of free enterprising Harlem slumlords for purposes of a nonprofit-making national monument.

A plaque affixed to the dirty clapboards beside the entrance door reads:

Hamilton Grange. The Home of Alexander Hamilton, 1757, A.B., A.M., L.L.M., 1804.

Statesman
Soldier Administrator Lawyer
Captain
Lt. Col. Staff of General Washington
Major General
Member of Congress
Member New York Legislature
Delegate to Constitutional Convention
First Secretary of the Treasury
Leader of the Federalist Party
He built this house in 1802.

An impressive enough list of offices, but many other men whose names are all but forgotten could match or better it. Offices did not make the man.

The visitor is not welcome to walk in the entrance door unattended. For reasons obvious to urban dwellers, The Grange's front door is kept locked and opened only when a visitor rings the doorbell. For many years the caretaker was a courtly gentleman named Raleigh Henry Daniels, who would warn visitors with old-timey phrases in a southern drawl to "Be very careful walkin' around here" in the neighborhood and to "Watch out for pocketbook snatchers and footpads." He meant the muggers and thieves and drug addicts who occasionally rip off visitors and vandalize this part of Harlem. The visitor is admitted and signs his name in the register. If he should ask, he would be told that in the 1970s ten or fifteen people visited The Grange during a typical day, perhaps 5,000 in all during a busy year.

A neat, smallish man with skin the color of soft cordovan and a tiny patch of white beard on his lower lip, Mr. Daniels would usually be seen in a well-worn overcoat over his blue tick butler's apron. Sometimes when he referred to the former owner, it was just "Hamilton," but more often it was "The General." Leading a visitor into the parlor he would step carefully over a loose board, saying, "They pop up as fast as I nail them down," perhaps adding, "The old wood don't hold the nails like it used to."

The room, almost bare of furnishings, is dominated by the marble portrait bust of the general done from life by Giuseppe Ceracchi. The nose is long and Roman, deeply indented at the bridge. The plane of his high forehead juts out over the recesses of penetrating yet genial eyes, seemingly thrust forward by the power of the mind behind it. His chin is prominent; the curve of his jaw, smooth and strong; his mouth, firm and moderately large. It is rather thin-lipped and set in a confident line. Its expression is warm and only a thought short of a smile. The head has a classical character that suggests one of the Caesars, but that is a quality common to many portraits in marble of subjects less classical than Hamilton. He had not ordered the bust—Ceracchi had asked to be allowed to carve it, ostensibly without obligation on Hamilton's part. When the bill came, Hamilton gracefully paid it anyway. His expense book records the payment of $620.00 on March 3, 1796, and his mild, ironical objection: "For this sum through *delicacy* paid upon Ceracchi's draft for making my bust on his own importunity, and 'as a favour to me.' "

Mr. Daniels would sometimes point through the window to the small patch of weed-covered dirt beside the front stoop and say, "I threw a bit of seed around." He might add respectfully, "It's not the kind of grass the General likes, but it was the best I could buy around here. He likes red clover, too." Only a few shreds of hedge grow at the margins of the yard, and no flowers. "The General likes laurel, you know," he would add. And "He likes hyacinths and tulips and lilies, too. And honeysuckle." Mention of the honeysuckle would sometimes lead to a story about Aaron Burr and an earlier visitor to the Hamilton Grange.

Five hundred thousand tourists, schoolchildren of all ages, troop through Thomas Jefferson's Monticello each year, and more thousands troop through its marble counterpart, the Jefferson Memorial on the banks of the Potomac in Washington. Hamilton's Grange, decaying of urban blight on its 50-foot Harlem lot, its front door locked against vandals, is a far cry from Jefferson's lordly chateau, with its graceful dome, its 35 rooms, its colonnades, porticos, palatial cupolas, hidden stairways, French antiques, and sprawling warrens for quartering more than 150 slaves. From the isolation of the top of its little mountain, Monticello looks down over what were 2,500 and more of its master's acres toward Charlottesville and the rest of mankind from magnificence on high.

Nor did Hamilton's Grange offer a challenge in impressiveness to Aaron

Burr's long since demolished mansion Richmond Hill in what is now Manhattan's West Village area, a sort of city man's Monticello. When New York was the nation's first capital and John and Abigail Adams lived there, Abigail called Richmond Hill "majestic and sublime." When Aaron Burr took over, he made it grander still, filling its rooms with imported objets d'art and rare books and its grounds with elaborately landscaped gardens.

Burr, like Richmond Hill, has long since been demolished as a significant factor in American history, although his story is as strangely fascinating as that of any other man of the period except Hamilton's. The present state of Hamilton's Grange, all but forgotten in Manhattan's Harlem, and Jefferson's Monticello on its Albemarle hilltop and its marble idealization in Washington correspond roughly to the contrasting places that the greater two of the three who were rivals in life seem to hold in the hearts of their countrymen almost two hundred years later. "Monticello," said one perceptive historian, is "a chateau high above contact with man." It bears no relation to the way people in the United States and the world live now. Hamilton's Harlem Grange, for better or worse, is integrated with the thick of modern life. The image of Jefferson that Monticello evokes may be the image of what we wish we were, but the image of Hamilton, as evoked by The Grange, is what we are.

In the days when Hamilton, Jefferson, and Burr waged their struggles like demigods on the plains of the federal Troy, there was a Holy Roman Emperor, Venice was a Republic, France had a king, China an emperor, Japan a shogun, Russia a czar, and Britain, where fewer than 2 percent of the people enjoyed voting representation, was a monarchy tempered by only the barest beginnings of democracy.

Written constitutions are no guarantee of a free people under law. The most repressive governments, like that of Soviet Russia have often boasted the most impressive sounding declarations of independence and written constitutions. Much more is required to achieve what the United States achieved: a sound economic underpinning for free representative government, a decent standard of living for its people, a tradition of adherence to legal and administrative precedent against arbitrary exercise of power, energy in administration, a free press, and appeals to reason and argument more often than emotion and coercion to enlist the people in support of a party or cause.

Among the major nations of the modern world, the only government under which people enjoy freedom in a form that stands unchanged in essentials since 1787 is the federal union of 50 states that grew out of the thirteen former British colonies on the East coast of North America. I submit that the structure, character, and tone of the union that evolved owe more to Alexander Hamilton than to any other man. What follows is an examination of his rise and fall to discover insofar as is possible why any of this should be so.

Hamilton I is a necessarily selective effort to substantiate the rather sweeping assertions that are respectfully suggested above for the first part of Hamilton's life up to the time of his appointment at age 32 as first secretary of the treasury. The notes at the end, as well as the bibliography, index, and chronology of his whole life should be regarded as roots and branches of the story told in the text but leading beyond it to encompass the whole amazing story of Hamilton's rise from 1757 to 1789. The separate but obviously related story of the kaleidescopic, darkening, manic and tragic years ending in Hamilton's fall is told in the soon to be released *Hamilton II* (1789–1804).

1

RESTLESS LOVE IN THE LESSER ANTILLES

[SHE HAD] SHOWN HERSELF TO BE SHAMELESS RUDE AND UN-
GODLY . . . COMPLETELY FORGOTTEN HER DUTY . . . LEFT HER
HUSBAND AND CHILD . . . AND GIVEN HERSELF UP TO WHORING
WITH EVERYONE.
    —*John Michael Lavien's petition for divorce from
Alexander Hamilton's mother, Rachel Fawcett
Lavien, April 18, 1759*

Alexander Hamilton was born on the island of Nevis, on the eleventh of January, seventeen hundred and fifty-seven. No birth certificate, baptismal record, or other contemporaneous document of any kind has been found to substantiate the statement of the time and place set forth in this sentence.[1]

Gertrude Atherton,[2] author of the celebrated fictional biography of Hamilton, *The Conqueror*, published in 1902, like many after her searched island archives and records diligently for such a document but failed to find one. On at least one occasion she describes a precious record that might have provided at least circumstantial evidence that crumbled into dust and disintegrated in the searcher's fingers and cannot now be found or resurrected.[3] No contemporaneous document earlier than a 1766 signature as a witness to a legal paper has been found to corroborate Alexander Hamilton's existence.[4]

Hamilton's name appears in a document for the second time on February 22, 1768 in the record of transaction No. XXIX of the probate court of Christiansted, St. Croix, Danish Virgin Islands of the Lesser Antilles. He is named as one of three sons of a "Madame Rachel Lewine," who had just died there on February 19. Rachel Lewine's three sons were "Peter Lewine, born in the marriage of the decedent with John Michael Lewine who, later, is said for valid reasons to have obtained from the highest authorities a divorce from her (according to what the probate court has been able to ascertain), also two other sons, namely James Hamilton and Alexander Hamilton, the one 15 and the other 13 years old, who are the same illegitimate children born after the decedent's separation from the aforesaid Lewine. The above mentioned Peter Lewine has resided and still resides in South Carolina and according to reports is about 22 years old."

Alexander Hamilton here makes his bow on the stage of history as a bastard child born to an impoverished white woman who had spent most of the previous eighteen years living on the demimonde fringes of white society on the nearby islands of Nevis and St. Christopher, known as St. Kitts, under British, not Danish, sovereignty. It is hardly surprising that no official notice should have been taken of Hamilton until after his mother's death when, as the probate court's record states, he had reached the age of thirteen.

Thirteen? How could he have been thirteen in 1768 if, as stated in the opening sentence of this book, he was born in 1757? This would make him only eleven in 1768.

The opening sentence giving the year of Hamilton's birth as 1757 is the same simple, flat declarative sentence with which Hamilton's son John Church Hamilton begins Chapter I of Volume I of the first official life of his father. This was published in 1834, thirty years after Hamilton's death, at a time when Hamilton's widow, Elizabeth Schuyler Hamilton, six other children of theirs, and many friends—and enemies—who had known him were still alive. There is no record that any of them disputed his son's statement of the facts of the time and place of his birth.

By all accounts Hamilton had a warm, close, and loving family life that must have included the celebration of many a birthday. John Church Hamilton was an honorable and distinguished man and a conscientious biographer, although his biography, like all others, is not free from errors. Yet it is typical of the history of Hamilton's history that on this point even sympathetic later biographers of Hamilton like John C. Miller and Broadus Mitchell reject his son's unqualified statement in favor of the passing reference to his age as thirteen in the St. Croix probate court paper that declared him illegitimate and disinherited him as an heir of his mother's estate. They take Hamilton's son's word for it that the month was January, the date was the eleventh, and the place was Nevis. They thus score John Church Hamilton three quarters right and one quarter wrong for factual accuracy on the opening sentence of his life of his father.

This seemingly rather unimportant dispute over the year of Hamilton's birth illustrates an important point about the nature of the evidence used for writing Hamilton's life in this book and, indeed, most biography and history. Most events of two centuries and more ago went unnoted, unrecorded, unexamined, and unsworn to at the time. Contemporaneous accounts of them found in court papers or letters or other documents were often set down after lapses of time and memory, or recorded only for self-serving purposes or to support a thesis or argument of the maker. Such contemporaneous documentary evidence is often no more than oral misstatements preserved in more misleadingly persuasive written form. This, of course, is to some extent true of all historical and biographical evidence. In the case of a life as caught up in controversy as Alexander Hamilton's from beginning to end, it seems necessary to emphasize this point at the outset and get it out of the way so that the reader will not be in doubt about it later.

Different eyewitnesses to the same remarkable events testifying shortly afterward under oath to expert questioning on television tell sharply conflicting tales about them with great conviction. Courtroom visitors and viewers of television close-ups watching the same person give the same testimony will disagree among themselves about whether he is telling the truth or lying and, indeed, about what the truth is. Tape recordings and wiretaps of the same conversations about which later testimony is given fail to resolve all conflicts. Sometimes they increase the ambiguities. We know from such experiences better than any generation before us how difficult it is to establish ultimate truth beyond a reasonable doubt or even by a preponderance of the evidence.

Most historical evidence consists of unsworn hearsay testimony, self-serving statements, inexpert opinions, and documents for which no foundation for admissibility has been laid. It is often an unclassifiable farrago of inferences from unsurprising similarities of names, unremarkable coincidences of time and place, and sets of circumstances that hardly deserve to be called circumstantial evidence of the fact sought to be proved. Most evidence that is perfectly acceptable as historical evidence would not be legally admissible in a courtroom. Much would not even be admissible at a televised congressional hearing—except possibly under the heading of smear tactics. None of it is subject to the ultimate test of truth in a courtroom: a searching cross-examination.

Many facts of Hamilton's story remain in doubt. Such historical evidence of them as exists is confusing, contradictory, nonexistent, missing or lost. A judge in a civil lawsuit must reach a conclusion on what he finds to be the preponderance or weight of such legally admissible evidence as is brought before him, incomplete or unsatisfactory as it may be, and issue a decision of the case. In this book much that is set forth as a statement of fact is no more than the writer's conclusion as to the preponderance of the evidence after weighing such legally inadmissible but historically admissible evidence as exists. Although it is possible to speak solemnly of the preponderant weight of historical evidence, it cannot be gainsaid, by a lawyer at least, that a preponderance of historical evidence is often lighter than a feather or even than a gust of hot air.

On the question of Hamilton's birth date, John Church Hamilton's statement is at least triple hearsay—Hamilton's mother, Rachel, presumably told him, Hamilton told his son, and his son tells the reader. But based as it purports to be on personal knowledge and standing as it does uncontradicted by other family members or contemporaries, such triple hearsay evidence directed to the point at issue—the year of Hamilton's birth—seems to this writer to outweigh the circumstantial hearsay of an unknown multiple contained in the 1768 St. Croix probate court paper, which did not relate to the question of the year of Hamilton's birth at all. It was of no significance there except to show that he was under twenty-one and so needed a guardian *ad litem* to appear in the proceeding for him, just as a minor would in such a proceeding today. Such misstatements of children's ages occasionally occur in court papers where the exact age is not in issue and of no importance when a small-town scrivener or clerk fills in a blank on a form with whatever number is told him that is not too unreasonable. By such a clerk an eleven-year-old as precocious as Alexander Hamilton might easily have been taken for thirteen.

Although the St. Croix probate court paper that makes the year of Hamilton's birth 1755 may be sufficient to raise a reasonable doubt about his son's statement that the year was 1757, it does not prove beyond a reasonable doubt that the year was 1755. Nor, in my opinion, does it even serve to shift the preponderant weight of the historical evidence based on his son's testimony. Therefore, although it must be recognized that reasonable men, including leading Hamilton scholars, might reach a different conclusion, and have done so, January 11, 1757, is the date used in this book. Having thus illustrated the problem of historical evidence and the imperfect method I intend to use in dealing with it, I will hereafter spare the reader full presentation of the array of evidence on both sides of most disputed points by simply giving my own conclusion. The array of conflicting opinion and argument can be extracted from the references in notes and bibliography at the end, where they do not further check or break the stride of the story of Hamilton's rise—after being born on Nevis on January 11, 1757.

Lack of evidence that is admissible even by the easygoing standards applicable to historical evidence turns almost any statement about the first sixteen years of Hamilton's life on the islands of Nevis, St. Kitts, and St. Croix in the Lesser Antilles into a problem of proof that will probably always remain unresolved. Even the term *Antilles* is one of obscure origin and meaning. It was a name assigned to semimythical lands shown on medieval charts sometimes as an archipelago, sometimes as a continent, uncertainly located in mid-ocean between the Canaries and India. The Lesser Antilles comprised all of the islands east and southward of Puerto Rico. In view of the rather pitiful and embarrassing nature of the few facts that are accepted as true about Hamilton's early years and the glee with which his enemies later retailed morsels of scandal about his sex life and misdeeds with money, it is hardly surprising that neither Hamilton nor his son would relate much about them. Like the Lesser Antilles themselves, Hamilton's early years in the islands will always remain in a semimythical state.

Charlestown on Nevis, where Hamilton was born, was and is a town of a few hundred people, mostly black, on a round volcanic island of an area less than 50 square miles and nowhere more than seven miles across.[5] Seen from the sea across blue green waves that break up into white spray over barrier coral reefs, Nevis is a more or less symmetrical cone. Bright green sugarcane fields slope upward from palm-fringed beaches to the darker green, forest-clad declivities of Nevis peak 3,232 feet high. Mount Lily, Butler's Mountain, and Saddle Hill, form shoulders of Nevis peak at north, east, and southerly points of the compass. A cap of white cloud usually hovers over the central peak, which is a quiescent but smoldering volcano. Its flat top and cloud cap would remind people still living in Hamilton's boyhood of the catastrophe that had occurred in 1680, when the top of the peak blew off, spreading brimstone, lava, fire, and ashes over Jamestown, the former capital. The eruption killed thousands and submerged the whole area off the southeast coast of St. George's Gingerland parish, where the former capital had flourished, beneath the unchanging blue green waves.[6]

The house in Charlestown where Rachel Fawcett Lavien and James Hamilton lived when Alexander was born is believed to have stood at the north edge of the town where the main street ends and the rough, dusty road circling the island turns inland. All that remains of the house today are two coral block walls and a flight of steps descending from the road toward the pinkish gray white beach. Out their west windows through palms and palmettos the family would have had a view of quick tropical sunsets as nightfall dropped a fast curtain on brilliant days, each one almost exactly like the one before it the year round, except for an occasional hurricane.

Today the site is marked by a sign next door saying "Hamilton House" and a plaque which quietly emphasizes the serendipitous quality of his later career as seen from Nevis:

> At this site on January 11, 1757 was born Alexander Hamilton who subsequently went to the North American colonies in search of education and who became one of the Founding Fathers of the United States of America.

The site is next to the present-day meeting place of the Nevis YWCA and the Lions Clubs of Charlestown. It remains like the Harlem Grange in the thick of contemporary life of a predominantly black community.

Geography is fate. The paradigm of the American work ethic, whose favorite word was *energy*, spent the first fifteen years of his life on Nevis and two other tropical West Indian islands, whose temperature varies little from a year-round mean of 82 degrees Fahrenheit. Their white minority colonial populations then typically lived in oleandered ease as proprietors of sugarcane and tobacco plantations, on which all heavy work was done for them by darker skinned slaves.

The white minority always lived in fear of slave revolts on the one-crop islands. It was also unsettling to live in the shadow of a quiescent volcano, but the Hamiltons shared these insecurities with the rest of the white minority. A source of insecurity special to the Hamiltons was the fact that Alexander's father was not married to his mother. While she lived with him, she was married to John Michael Lavien or else, after he had divorced her *in absentia* in 1759, forbidden by the decree of the Danish divorce court in St. Croix to remarry anyone else. To the vestry of white slave owners and prosperous artisans of St. George's Gingerland parish on Nevis she would not have been particularly welcome to celebrate the sacrament of baptism for her illegitimate children. So it is not particularly surprising that no baptismal certificate for a James or Alexander Hamilton has been found there.

John Adams writing to Thomas Jefferson later called Hamilton "the bastard brat of a Scotch pedlar."[7] Little is known of his father, James Hamilton, except that he was the obscure father of a famous son and the ne'er-do-well son of a prosperous father. He was indeed Scotch. He was the fourth of nine sons of Alexander Hamilton, laird of The Grange in the Parish of Stevenston, Ayrshire, Scotland. The laird's wife was Elizabeth, the eldest daughter of Sir Robert Pollock. The Hamiltons of Grange belonged to the Cambuskeith branch of the great House of Hamilton. Though not of the ducal branch, they had possessed the same land for centuries. Their seat in Ayrshire had belonged to the earl of Glencairne as far back as the twelfth century. The fourteenth-century founder of James Hamilton's branch was Walter de Hamilton, the son of Sir Gilbert de Hamilton, who in turn was the common ancestor of the dukes of Hamilton, the dukes of Abercorn, the earls of Haddington, the Viscounts Boyne, the Barons Belhaven, several extinct peerages, and practically all the other Hamilton families of Scotland and Ireland. It was a burden of lineage top-heavy enough to crumple the morale of a much stronger man than a fourth son of nine like Hamilton's father, James.[8] His three older brothers had been born in 1712, 1715, and 1717, and James was probably born in 1718, but the exact date is not known. James's brothers remained in Scotland, and two of them and a nephew succeeded in time to lairdship of The Grange. There was obviously not much patrimony left at Ayrshire for a fourth son, and when James was about 19 he set out for the Leeward Islands to seek the fortune he would never find. He was a handsome, well-liked gentleman without much talent for handling money. His son Alexander would markedly resemble him only in physical appearance and personal charm. James Hamilton was not even noted for being much good as a "pedlar."

Upon arrival on St. Kitts, James Hamilton would find many bearers of the name Hamilton already well established there before him. In fact, the royal governor was William Leslie Hamilton, who with his wife, the former Lady Isabelle Erskine, lived in state at Olivees. Their mansion, a more imposing version of the present-day Nisbet Plantation House on Nevis, was said to be the finest great house and estate in all the West Indies. James Hamilton could expect to receive no special favors in the islands because of his name and notable Ayrshire pedigree. On the contrary, he would find in his way there many a Hamilton who had started life in a lower station than a Hamilton of The Grange, yet who had succeeded notably in making his own way on his own.[9]

At various times in his later life, Alexander Hamilton sent sums of money totaling more than a thousand dollars back to his father and his brother in the islands for their support—at times when Hamilton himself was hard pressed for money. Years later, Hamilton asked his friend Robert Troup, in case of his own death, to see that his father's drafts were paid so that they should not "return upon him and increase his distress." By way of explanation Hamilton added that "Though as I am informed, a man of respectable connections in Scotland, he became, as a merchant, bankrupt at an early day in the West Indies and is now in indigence." To his cousin, the laird of The Grange and head of the Hamilton family in Scotland, Hamilton wrote in 1797 that "my father's affairs at a very early day went to wreck; so as to have rendered his situation during the greatest part of his life far from eligible." Hamilton added, "My heart bleeds at the recollection of his misfortunes and embarrassment." James Hamilton signed a letter written to Alexander from St. Vincent on June 12, 1793, when he was about 75, in a literate but shaky hand, "Your very affectionate father."

Hamilton's mother, Rachel (or Rachael) Fawcett Lavien, was probably born on Nevis probably in 1729, but no birth record has been found to prove it. Her father, Hamilton's maternal grandfather, was Dr. John Fawcett, or Faucett or Faucette, a French Huguenot who had fled to the islands sometime after the revocation of the Edict of Nantes in 1658. Rachel's mother, Dr. Fawcett's second wife, was Mary Uppington Fawcett, of whose background nothing is known. John and Mary Fawcett had been married in St. George's Episcopal Church, Gingerland, Nevis, on August 21, 1718, and lived at Gingerland Estate in the southeastern quadrant of the island which looked across the drowned former capital toward Antigua. John Fawcett was a physician and a man of means, had been married before, was reputedly of a flinty disposition, and 20 years or more older than his wife Mary. He was, as the years passed, of declining fortune. Hamilton thought of him as "a man of letters and of polished manners."

Dr. John Fawcett's first wife's first name had also been Mary. By her he had had a child named Ann, fifteen years older than her half-sister, Hamilton's mother Rachel, who would be Hamilton's only maternal aunt. About 1730 Ann Fawcett married James Lytton, and after three or four children, they moved from Nevis to St. Croix, where Lytton, Hamilton's uncle by marriage, bought Grange plantation in the Company Quarter near Christiansted in 1738.[10]

Hamilton's mother, Rachel, was the sixth of seven children of Dr. John Fawcett's second marriage to his second Mary. The first of the seven was born two months before John and Mary were married, and all of them but Rachel died in infancy or childhood. After twenty-two years of such birth and death pangs, Mary left John, alleging "diverse disputes and controversies," as the formal allegations in their separation papers put it. She applied to the chancellor ordinary and in chief in Nevis "to be relieved against the said John Fawcett" of the harrowing obligation to go on living and procreating young corpses with him. On February 5, 1740, the court issued her a writ of supplicavit for separate maintenance, thus relieving her of the legal duty of living with him and permitting her to live separate and apart. Freedom was more important to her than hanging on to her share of his money or property. She bargained away her one-third dower rights to all of Fawcett's still apparently extensive lands and tenements for his agreement to pay her an annuity of fifty-three pounds four shillings annually. Upon the granting of her writ, she is reputed to have moved briskly with her only surviving and all the more beloved child, Rachel—now about eleven—to the neighboring island of St. Kitts.

The historical evidence for her custody of Rachel is little more than the persuasive intuition of Gertrude Atherton plus the fact that upon the complaint of a mother for separate maintenance, the custody of a young daughter of the union is usually awarded to the mother.

Hamilton thought of his maternal grandmother, Mary Uppington Fawcett, as a woman of beauty and charm, and ambitious and masterful as well. She owned three slaves and eked out her and Rachel's separate maintenance payments from Fawcett by hiring the slaves out to others and by working as a seamstress herself. Her flight with Rachel from Fawcett's estate on Nevis to strike out on her own on St. Kitts showed the family pattern of restlessness within conjugal bonds. It set a precedent for similar restlessness after periods of varying lengths of time in such bonds that would recur in the lives of Hamilton's mother, Rachel; his father, James; and in Hamilton's life as well.

Sometime after Dr. Fawcett's second Mary had won her freedom from him in 1740, he may have moved to St. Croix and died a resident there by 1745. More likely he remained on Nevis but left real estate that he owned on St. Croix. In any event, his will was probated in Christiansted in 1745, leaving everything to Rachel and appointing her as his sole executrix.[11] His will left nothing to his other surviving daughter, Ann, or to any of his Lytton grandchildren. The number of these had reached a total of about six by the time Dr. Fawcett died and would eventually reach eight. Of these maternal first cousins of Hamilton's only Ann Lytton, named for her mother, Ann, born August 23, 1743, fourteen years older than Hamilton, would remain close to Hamilton all his life. Indeed the last document he ever wrote would acknowledge a lifelong obligation to Ann Lytton, later Ann Venton Mitchell, that he would never be able to repay as he felt he ought.

Rachel's appointment as her father Dr. John Fawcett's executrix by the probate court in Christiansted is surprising if, in fact, she had been born in 1729, because in most jurisdictions a minor of 16 is ineligible for such an appointment. It may be only another unsurprising example of how scriveners in drowsy tropical island offices ignore niceties of chronological age and status when it is a matter of no practical importance. The 16-year-old Rachel, no doubt, already exhibited the same executorial talents observable in her mother and soon to be seen in her third son, Alexander.

By 1745 Mary Uppington Fawcett and her daughter, Rachel, had made another change of island, this time from St. Kitts to St. Croix, perhaps for the express purpose of permitting Rachel to assume her executorial duties and collect her inheritance. On November 21 Mary served as a godmother at the christening of Ann and James Lytton's seventh child, Josia.

There on St. Croix in 1745 shortly after coming into her father's estate, 16-year-old Rachel married 28-year-old John Michael Lavien. He had been in business earlier as a merchant on Nevis and undoubtedly knew of the Fawcett family and their Gingerland estate there. At the time of his marriage to Rachel, he owned property on St. Croix, was involved in business dealings with James Lytton, whose business affairs were prospering, and was widely reputed to be rich. Lavien is the most widely accepted spelling of his name, but in island records and by Hamilton and others it is also spelled Levine, Lavine, Levin, Lavin, Lewine, Lawin, Lawien, Lewien, Lowine, Lovien, Lovine and Lavion. His first name was often spelled Johan or Johann as well as John. He wrote to a Danish-speaking attorney in German, kept his accounts in English, and also apparently understood Dutch. Hamilton's grandson, the noted alienist Allan McLane Hamilton, wrote of him, probably expressing his grandfather's belief, that "attracted by Rachel's beauty, and recommended to her mother by his wealth, he received her hand against her inclination." He further described Lavien as "a rich Danish Jew . . . who treated her cruelly."

Lavien is not identified as a Jew in St. Croix records although other Jews were labeled as such, but it may be that he had disavowed Judaism by the time of his marriage to Rachel.

Rachel may have cost Lavien a fortune in dowry. The same year they were married, he increased his debt to the Danish West India Company to 1,930 rigsdalers, two reals—twice the cost of a sugar plantation he had given up the year before. Or perhaps it was the other way round, that he married her hoping to bail himself out of a disastrous loss he had suffered from a crop failure. Each probably had rising expectations that the other was richer than he was or she was, which neither did anything to dispel before the wedding day. It would not be the first or last marriage to founder on rocks of disappointed greed.

They named the son born to them the year after their marriage—Hamilton's half brother to be—Peter Lavien. The first home of Rachel and John Michael Lavien and their only child, Peter, was an imposing plantation southwest of Christiansted just off the main road that runs across the island named Contentment. Contentment proved temporary, however. Three years later they moved to a lesser estate called Beeston Hill, which now buzzed with their strife.

By now Lavien owed the Danish West India Company the large sum of 2,432 rigsdalers. From this time on, Lavien's various efforts as an independent planter were marked by trouble, failure, and decline, as was his and Rachel's marriage. It became a "hateful marriage," and she began to consort openly with other men. Lavien complained to the police of her whoring, swore out a complaint, and in 1750 had her arrested and thrown into jail in the old fort on the quay at Christiansted. She was charged with having "twice been guilty of adultery." When released, according to the complaint Lavien later swore out against her for divorce, instead of changing her "unholy way of life," she ran away from St. Croix to "an English island." There she begot several whore children; she had "shown herself to be shameless, rude and ungodly," had "forgotten her duty," abandoned their child, Peter, and "given herself up to whoring with everyone."

It is only tradition, and Gertrude Atherton's intuition, that after Rachel had served her term for whoring and been released from the Christiansted fort, she fled with her mother in 1750 to St. Kitts. The circumstantial evidence of their move is lighter than air. It would be less embarrassing for them to live for a while at least till scandal died down on any available island but St. Croix. The same year Mary gave notice to her St. Croix creditors by publication that she intended to leave the island. St. Kitts was "an English island" next to Nevis, where she and Rachel had lived for most of their lives.

Gertude Atherton described the place on St. Kitts where she decided that Rachel Fawcett Lavien and Mary Uppington Fawcett had lived together after running away from their husbands as a "Great House, with spacious open galleries and verandahs" surrounded by stone terraces "overflowing with the intense red and orange of the hybiscus and croton bush" and "sensuous tints of orchids." In Mrs. Atherton's account, this mansion of Hamilton's mother and grandmother commanded distant views of cane fields sloping down to the sea, of the palm-thatched huts of a village where the Negro slaves lived, and of the huge fortress on Brimstone Hill to the north with the tall peak of the island of Saba jutting up out of the sea beyond it. In the distance the other way was the cloud-capped cone of Nevis.

With all due respect to Mrs. Atherton's intuition, it seems certain that wherever it was that Rachel and her mother lived on St. Kitts after 1750, such terraced verandahs and distant views of picture post card splendor were not part of the scene they saw except from the same more or less respectful distance kept by the slaves in the village. Dr. John Fawcett's decline and death had meant the end of Mary's annuity and hopes of dower. In 1754 a notice published in St. Croix announced that Mary Uppington Fawcett's debts to the estate of one John Roach were uncollectible "as she is not here, but in poverty has left the island."

Mary Uppington Fawcett soon redisplaced again from one saint-named island flag and legal jurisdiction to yet another. By July 1755 she was living on the Dutch island of St. Eustatius, describing herself as late of the island of Nevis, but now of the island of St. Eustatius, and a widow. A British subject on a Dutch-ruled island even smaller than Nevis, she remained an alien there. She loyally insisted on holding fast to her old allegiance to "our sovereign Lord George II." Her death probably occurred shortly after her move, but the date is not known, nor anything else of probative value about her, except that she had deeded her three slaves to her friend Archibald Hamm, directing that on her death they should pass to her daughter, Rachel, and not long after this Rachel took possession of them.

Rachel did not make the last island hop with her mother because by now she was living with her lover, James Hamilton. She was moving back to Nevis with him to round out the circuit of islands that restless loves and lack of money had compelled them both to run.

No one knows exactly where or when Hamilton's mother, Rachel, and his father, James Hamilton, met, or when they began living together, or when they parted. It is little more than tradition that they met on St. Kitts or Nevis about

1750 or a year or two later when he was 32 or 33 and she was ten years younger, began living together on Nevis not long after they had met, lived together for fifteen years at most, on Nevis till about 1760, back on St. Kitts from then until 1765, and on St. Croix for a few months at the end of that year before parting forever. After parting, each swung again into a separate circuit, his taking him back to St. Kitts then to Tobago and St. Vincent to the southward, hers confining her to the town quarter of Christiansted until her death only three years later on February 19, 1768.

The only documentary evidence of their status and whereabouts during the entire fifteen years they are supposed to have lived together finds them on St. Eustatius, of all places, on October 1, 1758. On that date the official Baptismal Record there shows that "James Hamilton and Rachel Hamilton his wife" stood as godfather and godmother at the christening of Alexander, the four-month-old son of "Alexander Fraser and Elizabeth Thornton his wife." The recorder put down James Hamilton and Rachel Fawcett Lavien, who were not married to each other, and had different legal surnames, as man and wife with the same surname. He put down Alexander Fraser and Elizabeth Thornton, the proud parents of the child as man and wife, but gave them different surnames. This may be another example of the easygoing practicality of island record-keeping authorities in avoiding factual exactitude to avoid embarrassing a man, a woman, or a child by troubling them about their living together without the benefit of a marriage ceremony.

Back on St. Croix the failing fortunes of Rachel's husband, John Michael Lavien, did not take a turn for the better with her out of the way. He continued to fail, first as an overseer for others, then as a renter who complained of the small earnings out of which he had to support their son, Peter. Toward the end he became superintendent of the hospital at Frederiksted and still later an inmate there, where he died February 28, 1771, leaving an estate of 172 rigsdalers, 8 reals, and a few gold buttons in pawn. He seems never to have held an office of public honor or trust. Rachel's brother-in-law, James Lytton, and her other relatives continued to have friendly dealings with him even after he had imprisoned her in the old fort for whoring and even after he had secured his divorce from her on the grounds of her adultery.

Fourteen years after their 1745 marriage, ten years after she had deserted him and he had imprisoned her and she had left St. Croix to return with her mother to St. Kitts, two years after Alexander Hamilton had been born to her and James Hamilton on Nevis, John Michael Lavien filed suit against her on February 26, 1759, in the Temperret, or matrimonial court, of Christiansted for absolute divorce.

In the suit he summoned Rachel and three witnesses to her lewdness that had begun at least nine years earlier to appear at a hearing on April 18 in Baron von Proeck's house. Rachel was served with the summons *in absentia* on March 2 by service on her two last-known addresses: (1) the plantation owned by the town captain, and (2) the Christiansted jail in the fort where she had been locked up. Rachel, of course, failed to respond to this cheerless rehash of her ancient

adultery since she was not on St. Croix at all or even within the range of the writ
of the Danish court. She had by now settled down on Nevis with her lover, James
Hamilton, and their four- and two-year-old children, James and Alexander. This
was the petition in which Lavien alleged that when she had abandoned him and
their four-year-old son, Peter, in 1750, Rachel had already "twice been guilty of
adultery."

Gossip and scandal traveled more quickly and reliably from island to island
than court writs from Danish to British jurisdictions. The number of whites in
the islands was not so large that those on any one would be unaware of scandal
involving those on others. Rachel was a beauty whose repute would nowhere
remain unremarked. Although Lavien had named the name of no corespondent
in his pleadings, Rachel's fertile cohabitation with James Hamilton on Lavien's
former home island of Nevis must have become so open and notorious by now
that there was no need of his naming names. Since the time period covered by
Lavien's allegations was the entire decade from 1750 to 1759, his charge that
Rachel had been whoring with "everyone" seemed to mean on its face at least
that a wider public had enjoyed her favors than James Hamilton alone.

These allegations of Lavien's complaint lent vivid color to later charges
made by John Adams and Thomas Jefferson that Hamilton was a "bastard brat"
and a "foreign bastard." It also gave rise to public speculation that any one of
many men other than James Hamilton was his father: Lavien; the planter
Thomas Stevens of Antigua and St. Croix, the father of Hamilton's friend Edward Stevens; William Leslie Hamilton; and George Washington, who happens
to have been visiting in Barbados around the time of Rachel's conceiving Hamilton. Washington could have met Rachel there, of course, and serviced her, but
only if she had strayed a couple of islands southeast of her customary four-island
circuit. There is no evidence that he did or that she did. Some said that Hamilton
was the son of John Michael Lavien and a Jew whose right name was Alexander
Levine. Others said that Negro blood flowed in Hamilton's veins. Rachel's name
is listed among the whites on the St. Croix tax lists. No other evidence aside from
his later solicitude for blacks and oppressed minorities generally and his opposition to slavery lends support to these possibilities.[12]

Lavien was suing Rachel for divorce at this late date, he alleged, because
she "ought not to have" anything from his "little" estate if he should die, to
"give to her whore children" James and Alexander. Without a divorce, an abandonment that would disqualify a wife from inheriting from a husband is hard to
prove; the surviving wife can claim that the husband, now silenced by death,
drove her out of the marital home. There is a presumption in the law of evidence
that any child born to a married woman is the child of the man to whom her
marriage ties her. This legal fiction holds even if the children, like Rachel's
James and Alexander, are born to her while she has been living apart from her
nominal husband for ten years with another man on an island fifty miles away.
It is not surprising that the presumption of legitimacy is often said to be the
strongest presumption known to the law and one of its most egregious pieces
of nonsense. In any event, Lavien wanted to make sure that none but Peter

Lavien, the only son he was sure of, would get his hands on whatever might be left of his failing fortune.

Rachel, probably still with James Hamilton on Nevis, ignored Lavien's summons. Having obtained jurisdiction of her *in absentia*, the Temperret found that Lavien's case against her was proved. It dissolved their marriage with the declaration that "said Rachel Lewin shall have no rights whatsoever as wife to either John Michael Lewin's person or means. . . . Also, Rachel Lewin's illegitimate children are denied all rights or claims to the plaintiff's possessions." Lavien was judged free to marry again, but Rachel, being the guilty party, was not. She was warned that "you are to be further punished (if seized) in this country." Lavien seems to have married again and had another son and a daughter who died in infancy. Peter Lavien did not stay with him long to look out for his expectancy. He was living in South Carolina by the time he was 19, less than five years after Lavien had brought his suit.

Life on Nevis had always been bound up with the life of St. Kitts, its larger twin island to the northwest across a shallow channel two miles wide. At an unknown date two or three years after Hamilton's birth, in 1760 or thereabouts, James Hamilton's family moved across this channel to St. Kitts, where they remained until about 1765 before taking their last trip together to the still larger island of St. Croix, fifty miles further to the northwest across the Saba bank. But on St. Kitts there are not even ruined walls by the side of the road that can be pointed out as the place where Rachel and James Hamilton and their two children lived during their supposed five-year sojourn there.

On the perimeter of Nevis there had been Fort Charles and Ashby Fort, but on the margins of St. Kitts at all points of the compass were forts, fortifications, fortresses, ruins of forts, and scars of battlefields. In young Hamilton's time there these marked scenes of earlier battles, massacres, naval raids, uneasy truces, traitorous betrayals, and occasions of cannibalism. Kaleidoscopic combinations of Caribs and Arawaks, Spaniards and English, French and Dutch, aborigines and colonists, pirates, freebooters and raiding parties, and invading armies and naval armadas had kept themselves occupied with such activities during the previous two and a half centuries and more going back all the way to Columbus's second voyage of discovery in 1493. It was said that the Caribs, having eaten the flesh of all nationalities, adjudged the French to be the most delicate and the Spanish the hardest to digest. Among the European masters of St. Kitts it was conventional wisdom that the Indians, having once eaten a friar who from much fasting lacked succulence, had lost all taste for men of the cloth. Accordingly, the whites invariably sent priests when it was necessary to parley with Caribs and Arawaks. On one occasion after a French victory in 1666 at Sandy Point, afterward renamed Point de Sable, of course, 8,000 English loyalists who refused to take an oath of allegiance to King Louis XIV had been driven off or fled or been deported to Nevis, Jamaica, and Virginia. On the British colonial twin islands of St. Kitts and Nevis, tall tales of savage conquests and massacres, cannibalism among the aboriginal blacks, slave revolts among the imports, and ruthless and bloody repressions by white minority masters remained common coin of conversation and old wives' tales that a bright boy like Alexander Hamilton would linger among his elders to overhear and ponder.

On the shoulders of a tight little volcanic cone of an island like St. Kitts, a larger model of Nevis not 25 miles long, 150 years of the hot and cold war that Britain and France had been waging across the whole world came down to the harsh practical fact that the 25 miles had been raggedly partitioned between the two powers into three hostile strips. The French were partly on the north end at Dieppe Bay, where Fig Tree Fort marked the frontier, and partly on the southeast end at Basseterre guarded by Stone Fort and Fort Charles. The British were sandwiched into an uncomfortable strip in the middle anchored on the huge fortress on Brimstone Hill, the most formidable structure ever built by Europeans in the Western Hemisphere up to that time. Eternal vigilance of all inhabitants had been necessary for safety from the inscrutable skirmishing back and forth between the two great powers which had invested the cramped little island. When Britain and France were officially at peace elsewhere in the world, their forces on St. Kitts would sometimes try to change the borders peacefully by transplanting back and forth in secret at night the stand of fig trees that marked the western boundary line of the northern strip. The placing of fig trees reflected in island microcosm the ebb and flow of the fortunes of war and diplomacy in the unending struggle around the world between the eighteenth century's two greatest powers. In the corridors of the ministries in London and Paris, the ministers cared little for what any of this meant to the people of St. Kitts.

Although St. Kitts was larger and of more commercial importance than Nevis, it was, of course, less secure, even though the British liked to call it the "Gibraltar of the British West Indies," perhaps to help secure it psychologically. Throughout the eighteenth century Nevis remained the seat of British colonial government. It came to be called "the mother of the English Leeward Caribbees." From there a captain general ruled in the name of the king. The Council and House of Assembly there were modeled in miniature upon the Houses of Peers and Commons in London. Nevis was further distinguished as possessing a chancellor and the only court in the English Antilles where a pirate could be taken for trial.

Nothing much except an occasional hurricane ever occurred in these lush tropical island paradises to displace vivid memories of volcanic catastrophes or traumatic intrusions of great power war and politics. A pirate's trial or a council's parliamentary session would have meant excitement enough to lure a precocious boy like Alexander Hamilton to make the two-mile ferry passage back from St. Kitts to Nevis to watch models of a British court and parliamentary establishment in operation in island microcosms. An alert young Leeward Islander like Hamilton would come early to the conviction that insularity was no guarantee of safety in the unending worldwide clash of European empires. Brimstone Hill loomed as a symbol of their power, of the dangers of invasion, and of the need for self-defense for survival in a world perpetually engaged in hot and cold wars.

Throughout his continental career, Hamilton would manifest a more acute sensibility to such geopolitical concerns than any of his distinguished coadjutors.

In 1765 Archibald Ingram, the St. Kitts merchant who was James Hamilton's employer, sent him to St. Croix as his representative to collect a debt due him from the firm of Moir & Gordon of Christiansted: the large sum of £ 807 11s. 11d. James Hamilton took Rachel and sons James, now ten, and Alexander, now eight, with him on the trip to Christiansted but failed to collect the debt immediately. He arranged for attorneys to institute suit, collected the money early in 1766, and returned to St. Kitts, but left Rachel, James, Jr., and Alexander in Christiansted behind him.[13]

Lavien had remarried by this time and started his new family. When James and Rachel and their two sons arrived in St. Croix, memories of Rachel's imprisonment there fifteen years earlier, revived by Lavien's public charges of adultery against her of six years earlier, would not yet be forgotten. When she appeared on the quay with her consort and two sons of just the right ages, all the old scandal would take on a new life. Lavien's complaint had threatened her with seizure and further punishment if found. The Temperret's final decree had confirmed her guilt and forbidden her to remarry. Some question might exist about what her legal relationship to her traveling companion, James Hamilton, might be, but there could be no question that young James and Alexander were their sons. With his fair complexion, ruddy cheeks, dark blue deep-set eyes, finely textured brown hair with a trace of red, and his regular well-proportioned handsome features, Alexander in particular strongly resembled his father.

For James Hamilton the social pressure of the St. Croix scene may have become too embarrassing for words by the time he slunk back to the calm of St. Kitts in 1766, with Ingram's £ 807 11s. 11d., but without his family. Rachel and the boys stayed behind and took up residence in Christiansted.[14] After the fifteen years with a charming loser like James Hamilton that followed three or four with a cruel loser like Lavien, Rachel, like her mother, Mary Uppington Fawcett, had become restless in conjugal bonds. Fifteen years of living together in the cramped ambit of British colonial islands was the functional equivalent of a long marriage like her mother's, even though Rachel and James had technically been living in sin. In Rachel's family, after fifteen years, living in sin lost its savor.

The conventional notion is that James Hamilton callously abandoned Rachel and their sons on St. Croix. It seems at least as likely, or more likely, that she abandoned him. In the tonic air of the larger, bustling world of Christiansted, whose Danish colonial masters ruled with a hand that was not so much light as simply absentminded, Rachel decided to liberate herself from free love and refused to return to St. Kitts with James Hamilton. She resumed her maiden name of Fawcett for purposes of the tax rolls, used that name or Lavien's for other dealings, and never again called herself by the name of Hamilton. Neither she nor her sons ever saw their father again.

Hamilton always afterward spoke and wrote to and about his seeming failure of a father with tenderness, warmth, and kindness. He never reproached him for deserting the family, although he noted the fact that his having deserted them had thrown him "upon the bounty of my mother's relatives," the Lyttons, "some of whom were then wealthy. . . ."

Alone now with her two boys and no support from their father, Rachel would not have an easy life unless she could find an important sponsor or an aegis for protection. She did. She briskly joined St. John's Anglican (Protestant Episcopal) Church. She rented a house at No. 34 Kompagnietsstrade (Company's Street) from the prominent merchant Thomas Dipnall for 12 rigsdalers a month. At various times, and certainly for some months in 1767 and 1768, she lived across the street at No. 23 at the house of Captain William Egan; whether she did so for business or social reasons, or both, is not known. According to the poll tax lists, there were with her the two white boys, her sons; three slaves, Rebecca, Flora, and Esther, whom she had inherited from her mother; and four slave children under 12 years of age.

She opened a small provision store in the Dipnall house and dealt in pork, beef, flour, fish, rice, apples, and other plantation staples that she bought from him as well as from the firm of Beckman and Cruger just down the street. Alexander Hamilton's experience in political economy and fiscal policy began in this little store of his mother's when he was eight or nine years old as he helped out her, his brother, and the slaves by waiting on customers, posting her ledgers, paying her consignors, and collecting from her debtors.

Around 1767 or 1768 at the age of ten or eleven, he placed a foot firmly on the second rung of the ladder of his rise by moving out from under her wing to go to work for the two young merchants from New York, David Beckman and Nicholas Cruger, who had opened up a new store in St. Croix at Nos. 7 and 8 King's Street.

In February 1768, Rachel was taken ill with a terrible racking fever that Alexander soon caught too. Ann McDonnell took care of Rachel for a week before Dr. Herring was called on February 17. He bled her and gave her fever medicine, and the following day he administered an emetic and gave her more fever medicine. He gave a stiff dose to her son too. "A chicken for 'Elicks' [Alexander?]" was ordered from Thomas Dipnall. On the nineteenth Rachel was given still more fever medicine and also valerian and alcohol for her head. So was Alexander. In the afternoon she was given a decoction, whereas Alexander was bled and given an enema. Rachel died at nine in the evening; Alexander survived.

The official burial record at St. John's Church gives her age at death as 32. If this is correct, it would mean that when she had given birth to her son Peter, a date also officially recorded, she was only ten years old. In fact, if she had been born in 1729, she was 39 when she died. The recorder's action in making her seven years younger than she really was is consistent with the reputation for seductive youthful beauty that remained with her until the end. It is also consistent with local recorders' seeming carelessness about chronological truth when it came into conflict with emotional or physiological reality.

Ann McDonnell laid out Rachel's body. The court reduced her overcharge for this service from 25 to 10 rigsdalers. For the funeral Dipnall billed for eggs, French bread, and cakes. Peter Lytton was paid 40 rigsdalers for eleven yards of black material to cover the coffin; James Towers, the town judge, advanced some money to pay for a pair of shoes for James and black crepe veils for both the children, but billed the estate for reimbursement. This indicates that Alexander was well enough by now to attend her funeral, though probably still shaky from his siege of fever and feelings of loss. The parish clerk of the English church summoned her friends to the ceremony and assembled the pallbearers. Rachel's body was taken in a hearse to James Lytton's family plot on Grange plantation and buried there on February 20 by the English minister, the Reverend Cecil Wray Goodchild. Beside the grave at the interment surely stood James and Ann Lytton; their son Peter, Rachel's sons' guardian *ad litem;* their daughter Ann and others of the Lytton children; and thirteen-year-old James and eleven-year-old Alexander Hamilton. James and Alexander must have listened in awe as the Reverend Goodchild intoned the Anglican Order for the Burial of the Dead from the Book of Common Prayer over their mother's body:

> I am the resurrection and the life, saith the Lord: he that believeth in me, though he were dead, yet shall he live: . . . we brought nothing into this world, and it is certain we can carry nothing out.

In that age of enlightenment the conventional religion of most intellectuals was a deityless deism exhumed from David Hume. All the rest of his life Hamilton was notable for his observance of Episcopalian forms of worship, although he never joined or was confirmed or became an official communicant of any organized church until moments before his own death.

The probate court inventory of the little that Rachel had left behind her in this world was taken in the room where she had died and a court seal placed on her effects for subsequent recording. Her personal effects, a trunk, and so forth, were few; there were some pots and other small things "which remained unsealed for use in preparing the body for burial, among them being six chairs, two tables, and two washbowls." Her room was broken into, the court seal was broken, some of the inventory was probably lost, but the court did not pursue the thief.

The inventory listed five women slaves, Rebecca, Flora, and Esther, and two of their twelve offspring who had matured. Others of the twelve had disappeared. The daughter of one of them, also named Rachel, and three Negro boys remained. The judge had appointed Peter Lytton to act as guardian *ad litem* for the two Hamilton boys to protect their interests, but on the day of the hearing he was inexplicably, probably irresponsibly, absent; so his father, James Lytton, stood in for him. The judge was told, perhaps by quick thinking on James Lytton's part, that before her death Rachel had made gifts of one of the Negro slave boys, Ajax, to her son Alexander, and another, Christian, to her son James. The other slaves were hired out to Rachel's good friend and associate Captain William Egan. There was also what was left of the stock-in-trade of her store, some salt pork, butter, and flour; but most of this belonged to the various merchants who had let her have it only on consignment.

There were left six silver spoons, seven silver teaspoons, one pair of sugar tongs, and two chests. There were four dresses, one red skirt, one white skirt, and one black silk sun hat—perhaps for reading in the sun or promenading on the beach on days when she would leave her Alexander to mind the store. There was one bedstead with a voluptuous eiderdown comforter and bolster.

There were 34 books, which seemed an unusually large number for a woman who supported herself in the grocery trade, although not for one who also pursued a more womanly calling. Peter Lytton, the boys' guardian, bid in her 34 books at the auction for himself. They must have been the source of much of Alexander's book learning up to this time and for the next four years. His grandson Allan McLane Hamilton wrote of Hamilton's deep "familiarity with Virgil's bucolics, especially the First Eclogue." This staple of early education in the days when children were not kept childish with "children's" books may have been one of Rachel's 34. All told, her assets came to 1,700 rigsdalers, 3 reals, 3 styvers; debts and funeral and administration expenses were 1,067 rdl., 4 r., 3-1/2 st.

John Michael Lavien appeared, brandished his 1759 divorce decree, demanded that the court disinherit the two illegitimate Hamilton sons, and claimed the entire inheritance for his son, Peter Lavien, age 22. Peter Lavien had just returned from South Carolina, but he did not appear to sign for his inheritance without first readying himself for accession to Rachel's property by undergoing an adult baptism at St. John's Church a day or two before appearing. His half brothers, James and Alexander, were duly declared to be illegitimate and held to be entitled to take nothing from their own mother's estate. The distribution decree described them as the "one 15 and the other 13 years old, the same illegitimate children born after the deceased person's divorce from said Lewine." Here was the second official notice to the world that Alexander Hamilton was a bastard, and as poor a one as it was possible to be.

This is the record that is supposed to fix Hamilton's birth date in 1755. If it is wrong in this, it is wrong in other particulars as well: either 1755 or 1757 puts Alexander's birth before, not after, Rachel's "divorce from said Lewine," which was not until 1759. Lavien obtained the divorce from her, not she from him.

In any case, James and Alexander, the "bastard children," were cut off with nothing of their mother's whereas their half brother Peter Lavien, who had hardly known her, received all, which amounted to 632 rigsdalers, 6 rigals, 5-1/2 styvers. He returned with it all to South Carolina. Years later, in 1782, writing to his wife, Elizabeth, after learning of Peter's death, Hamilton would wryly write: "You know the circumstances that abate my distress, yet my heart acknowledges the rights of a brother."

The Hamilton boys' cousin Peter Lytton had failed to appear to speak up for them at the distribution hearing, and Peter's father, James Lytton, had stood in for him, failing to obtain anything for them except Ajax and Christian.

He put in a claim of his own for 23 rigsdalers, 4 reals for six walnut chairs with leather seats he had sold Rachel three years earlier, demanding three years' back interest. The Hamiltons now were orphans alone in the world with no father or any other known relatives except the Lyttons. Hamilton's son John Church explained that "indigence" had thrown his father "upon the bounty of his mother's [Lytton] relatives."

The Lyttons' family fortunes had reached a zenith in 1760, but now were failing. There is no evidence that any of the Lyttons gave Hamilton money, other than the lifelong gratitude he always expressed toward Ann Lytton, later Ann Venton Mitchell, for her help to him, extending to the last document he ever wrote. Peter Lytton probably let Alexander read the 34 books of Rachel's that he had bought from her estate. This would not mislead a bright boy into believing that kinship or friendship often overrode economic interest, or that windfalls or free gifts were to be looked for from life.

Years later, Hamilton would recall the disasters that now began to befall his mother's relatives to dispel any misplaced hopes of bounty from them. His cousin Ann's husband went bankrupt. James Lytton, Jr., having stolen some slaves that belonged to his first wife's estate, became insolvent and ran away from the island with them and a second wife. Peter Lytton became increasingly unstable and irresponsible, lost all his money, and committed suicide within the year following Rachel's death. James Lytton died insolvent.

The Lytton family's plantation on St. Croix, where Rachel Fawcett Lavien was buried, like James Hamilton's family seat in Ayrshire, was always known as The Grange. A grange is a barn or granary for laying away produce for later use. The burial ground where Rachel lies is now discovered only with difficulty in the woods a few hundred yards downhill from the old plantation house. One of the dozen or more brick-mounded graves there is probably Rachel's, but identifying slabs have been carried away. Some have been built into copings; others serve as doorstones. Rachel's grave is lost. Broadus Mitchell wrote that "This lost spot is part of America's story. For here lies the original of Alexander Hamilton's peculiar ardor."

Hamilton's son John Church wrote that although his grandmother, Rachel, had died when his father was only a child, the "traces of her character remained vividly impressed upon his memory." Hamilton almost never spoke of his mother to outsiders, but within his family, to his wife, Elizabeth, and their children, Hamilton always "recollected her with inexpressible fondness, and often spoke of her as a woman of superior intellect, highly cultivated, of elevated and generous sentiments, and of unusual elegance of person and manner."

Under the ancient mahogany trees in a glade below the St. Croix hilltop where what remains of the old Lytton Grange house still stand, Gertrude Atherton erected a monument to Rachel. Her inscription says much by saying only, "She was the mother of Alexander Hamilton."

2

ISLAND PROPAEDEUTICS:
MR. CRUGER'S COUNTINGHOUSE
AND DR. KNOX'S PRESCRIPTS

MY AMBITION IS PREVALENT . . . I CONTEMN THE GROV'LING CONDI-
TION OF A CLERK . . . TO WHICH MY FORTUNE CONTEMNS ME AND
WOULD WILLINGLY RISK MY LIFE THO NOT MY CHARACTER TO
EXALT MY STATION.
                                    —*to Edward Stevens, November 11, 1769*

When the Hamiltons lived there, St. Croix rivaled Barbados as the largest
sugar-producing island in the West Indies. Today the ruins of the great plantation houses—with their double stairways and round sugar mills and haunting
names like Anna's Hope, Peter's Rest, Upper Love, and Lower Love, Jealousy,
Sally's Fancy, and Whim Great House—recall the long-gone days of an era only
a little short of glory.[1]

Black slaves were sold at auction along with mules and lived in a state of
degradation. The white minority's strict attitude toward marriage and casual
attitude toward sex produced a large and handsome cash crop of mulattos who
inherited nothing but the slave status of their dusky mothers. Strict ordinances
governed curfew, militia duty, and the obligations of whites to answer alarms.

In their solid stone mansions filled with mahogany furniture, imported cheeses, silver sconces, Chinese silks, and Belgian laces, the white planter aristocracy lived in luxury that contrasted sharply with the comparative poverty of other whites like Rachel's sons, who existed on the fringes of the social order, close to the slaves but not of them, yet shamefacedly unequal with the ruling class of their fellow whites. Of the population of about 24,000, only 2,000 or so were white; almost eleven out of every twelve were black or mulatto slaves. In this social system the status of marginal whites like the Hamiltons, who were neither plantation owners nor slaves, was the most equivocal, precarious, dependent, and insecure of all.

It was a closed system: 381 plantation estates covered almost all of the island's 50,000 arable acres with cane fields stretching in all directions from the tops of the hills down to the sea. There were no open untamed frontiers with open land at the edges of this mature colonial economy. In the event of a loss of economic foothold through crop failure, market glut, lack of shipping, tight money, piracy, foreign seizure, or bad luck or bad judgment, there was no place for a man to move on to make a fresh start. There was no walking away from clearly defined conditions of boom and bust and success and failure. The cost of a long sea passage to the open social and economic conditions of the continent required more liquid capital than practically any one who was not a plantation owner could scrape together in a year.

The rich whites, of course, lived in mortal fear of slave revolts. It was no wonder that having lived with slaves in their quarters and having never enjoyed the life of luxurious ease that slavery made possible for the white aristocracy, Hamilton was an active foe of slavery throughout his later career.

In Christiansted even today Cruzan women with their heads bound in kerchiefs may occasionally still be seen walking alongside a donkey cart loaded with avocados. The thick stone walls of the houses serve as an eighteenth-century form of air conditioning, and colonnaded arcades keep the sidewalks cool in the midday heat with the evening's air. Some of the same red-roofed buildings were new when Hamilton was a clerk. They are still washed pale blue, yellow, pink, and ochre in subtle pastel combinations of high brilliance and low saturation that produce a bright patina in the tropic sun. Everywhere the pale pastels are punctuated by blazes of bougainvillea and hibiscus, some glimpsed only through the wrought-iron gates of a secluded patio or a garden. The old fort on the quay built on the ruins of the one where Rachel was imprisoned is an ominous reminder of lust close by, and a war-wracked world beyond the peaceful-seeming harbor.

A shower of Carib Indian arrows welcomed Columbus when he landed at Salt River in 1493, and the flags of Spain, England, Holland, France, and the Knights of Malta had already flown over St. Croix before Denmark first ran up her ensign in 1733. Though in Hamilton's time St. Croix's official political allegiance was still to Denmark, Dutch bankers were dominant in financing commercial transactions. Almost all manufactured wares, as well as much fish and meat, had to be imported from Denmark; and the island's exports of sugar, cotton, coffee, molasses, and rum had to be exported chiefly to Denmark, in accordance with the governing statute rather than in accordance with the dictates of any rational free market or free enterprise economic system. It was a good place to study at firsthand the economic and political lessons of what it meant to be a colony. The island of St. Croix provided a sharp intensity of focus for such lessons impossible to come by in the spacious, sprawling, diffused colonies on the continent to the northward. Hamilton was a quick learner and a slow forgetter.

Hamilton's older brother, James, became apprenticed to the carpenter Thomas McNobeny.[2] Alexander stayed on as a clerk with Beckman and Cruger. The firm carried on export of island products, especially raw sugar, and importation of plantation supplies. It was one of the few export-import firms in Christiansted with a permanent store and warehouse and a stock-in-trade regularly on hand.

The firm also owned some small vessels that traded among the islands and occasionally made voyages to the continent. Nicholas Cruger, Hamilton's first employer, was born in New York in 1743, died in St. Croix in 1801, and remained Hamilton's friend, patron, and sometime client all his life.[3] Cruger came from a family of merchants that produced two early mayors of New York City and brothers who were, variously, a delegate to the Stamp Act Congress, a senator from New York, and a member of the British Parliament. Cruger's family members were proprietors of related firms with which the St. Croix firm did business in Curaçao; Bristol, England; and New York. In later years Cruger became an enthusiast for the American revolutionary cause; suffered capture, imprisonment, and condemnation of a cargo on this account; and served as chairman of a committee of New Yorkers who escorted Washington triumphantly into the city in 1783 after the war had been won. It was Cruger who gave Hamilton his invaluable early apprenticeship in his firm, who made it financially possible for him to go to the continent to seek his fortune, and who steered him toward New York.

After his partner, David Beckman, or Beekman, ten years older than Cruger, retired in 1769, the firm continued for a time under Cruger alone and then was joined by another prominent merchant, Cornelius Kortright. In 1771, "Messrs. Kortright & Cruger" advertised for sale at Cruger's yard "Three Hundred Prime Slaves." The firm was still making money in the slave trade the next year when they wrote to Henry Cruger, Jr., that "We have a Danish Guinea man Just arrived with 250 Gold Coast Slaves They will sell well . . . for half produce and half Cash or bills." In another transaction, a letter from Nicholas Cruger to John H. Cruger of March 19, 1772, partly in Hamilton's hand, requests "Two or three poor boys" from him, and instructs him to

> Have them bound in the most reasonable manner you can. I fancy you cant fail of getting them by applying at the Poor-House. I want them to put on plantations.

No alert but poor orphan boy who had grown up with slaves in the slaves' quarters on a white-minority-ruled, one-crop colonial island could write orders for such a deal without comparing his own fate—working late, but unbound, in Cruger's store—with that of those other poor boys who were fated to slash sharp-edged cane under the blazing sun for the rest of their lives—for no better reason, seemingly, than that their skins were darker than his. This was business he had to do for his employer, but it was bound to seem a dirty business to him. Still, if there was not much hope for the bound boys from the poorhouse ever to get off the plantations, there did not seem to be much more hope for him of rising out of the groveling condition of being one of the rich slave trader's clerks.

Nicholas Cruger left St. Croix for New York on October 16, 1771, "By reason of a very ill state of health," leaving the 14-year-old Hamilton in full charge of the business. Hamilton proved himself to be capable of managing it in all its aspects. He dealt with ship captains, planters and merchants, customers, and suppliers and kept Cruger informed of all developments. He consulted Cruger's attorneys. Like a good proxy, he took care to save his principal unnecessary trouble and worry. Although Hamilton just then was himself suffering from another spell of sickness, perhaps caught from his employer or perhaps brought on by the tension of his load of new responsibilities, he reported that he had "sold about 30 bbls flour more & Collected a little more money from different people."

But less than a month later, on November 12, 1771, he could not forbear being critical. He had checked and found that

> Your Philadelphia flour is . . . of a most swarthy complexion—& withal very untractable; the Bakers complain that they cannot by any means get it to rise . . . I have observ'd a kind of worm . . . about the surface—which is an indication of age—it could not have been very new when shipped.

It was not a total loss, however; a practical solution could be found: the market was overstocked; so he was considering accepting eight pieces of eight from any buyer of good credit who would take as many as 40 or 50 barrels. Otherwise, he might be obliged "in the end to sell it at a much greater disadvantage."

Not satisfied to rest the business decision on this sound general proposition, as anyone less thorough than Hamilton would have done, he proved the wisdom of the proposition arithmetically; he shows that New York flour of the same weight "is gladly sold by everybody at [eight pieces of eight] at retail, and a great part of your Philadelphia weighs but little more, so that 8-1/2 by the quantity is more than a proportionate price for the difference of weight." Already he had become a merchant sharper than most of any age.

Two weeks later, on November 27, Philadelphia flour remained a serious problem because "Mr. Neall's brig is daily expected with a quantity of superfine . . . so that I must endeavor at all events to get your flour off soon, or it will be unsaleable. Every day brings in fresh complaints against it."

But just when things seemed darkest, the market turned, and by January 10, 1772, Neall's superfine was sold out, and Hamilton was raising the price of wormy Philadelphia flour to the bakers who had been complaining so bitterly against it. He added to Cruger, "Believe me, Sir, I dun as hard as is proper."

He also congratulated his employer on his improved health, reported delivery of a present from Cruger of plate and stockings to Cruger's fiancée, Miss Nancy De Nully, and a cheese to her mother. He thanked Cruger for a present of cheese and apples to himself. He had sold candles, hoops, codfish, and, hard as it is to believe, a consignment of alewives. He had rectified "a small error in . . . addition" in an account of Messrs. Willing & Taylor. He had his employer's business well in hand and was letting him know it.

Getting rid of flour was a continuing problem, and Cruger's business ethics did not rule out some tax evasion. There were useful lessons here for any future secretary of a treasury.

A letter of Nicholas Cruger's of May 25, 1772, in Hamilton's hand, explains one kind of deception tax collectors must be aware of:

> Rye flour will sell for ps 7 a barrel here readily, but the duty is 25 ct. However, we enter it as cornmeal and give the weighter a fee, which hint you must give the Capt, if you send any down, and tell him to see me before he enters. . . .

Captain William Newton of the *Thunderbolt* hove into port with a cargo of sick mules. Hamilton admitted to having problems with them, but wrote Cruger's brother Tileman of how he had coped:

> Two days ago Captain Newton delivered me . . . 41 Mules in such order that I have been obliged to send all of them to pasture, . . . I expect at least a third will die. . . . The highest offer made me for 20 of the best was 70 ps [pieces of eight], whereas if they had been in good order, I could readily have obtained £40 round.
> They were starved skeletons.
> A worse parcel of mules never was seen; she took in at first 48 and lost seven on the passage. I sent all that were able to walk to pasture, 33. The other 8 could hardly stand for 2 minutes together, and in spite of the greatest care, four of them are now in limbo. The surviving four, I think, are out of danger."

The heavy traffic in human skeletons went on too. Hamilton wrote Henry Cruger in New York on June 6, 1772, that 250 Gold Coast slaves arrived in the Danish Guineaman *Venus* "very indifferent indeed, sickly and thin, they average about £30." On the St. Croix market sickly humans thus were worth £10 less apiece than healthy mules.

Hamilton dispatched Captain Newton in the *Thunderbolt* to Tileman Cruger at Curaçao, warning him against the dangers of the *Guarda Costas*— the Spanish revenue patrols. Privately to Tileman the 15-year-old Hamilton expressed disappointment that Captain Newton was not more sophisticated at the dangerous game of smuggling: "You cannot be too particular in your instructions to him. I think he lacks experience in such voyages."

Hamilton's attention to duty and efforts to produce profits for his master did not go unobserved by Nicholas Cruger. Of Hamilton's management of store personnel, he wrote to Hans Buus March 18, 1772, that he was "glad to find my Clerk in my absence has desired you to take all my affairs in your hands that were in Mr. Hassell's, who I am confident has been very negligent in them, and trifled away a good deal of money to no purpose."

After Cruger returned, resumed control of his business, and saw his fiancée, he waxed euphoric in general about the way things had been going: "We are making good crops, praised by God, and have noble seasons of rain that give us every assurance of great crops the ensuing season." He carefully said nothing that his valuable clerk might use to pry himself upward out of his place or even to demand a raise.

The St. Croix Hamilton saw was not the rich and luxurious eighteenth-century world of the white planters in their stone mansions, nor was it the dependent island subsisting on tourist dollars that the visitor sees today. Hamilton saw from the underside a self-sufficient crossroads of commerce where businessmen turned a profit by evading customs duties, cut prices on wormy flour and shrewdly offered it by volume instead of weight, took their losses when there was a glut, gritted their teeth and held on till there was a shortage, and gleefully sold when short commodity markets turned up in their favor. They went bankrupt if they could not hold on long enough or read the future wrongly or put too much at risk in the way of hurricanes, blockades, pirates, or seizures by hostile powers.

Hard choices between right and wrong had to be made on all ventures. No one who received an education in such a school could slide into financial corruption unwittingly or plead lack of *scienter*, or guilty knowledge, if he did.

Alexander Hamilton's education on St. Croix included some study of books and languages, but Cruger's countinghouse served as the most significant part of his schooling for the great world to the northward. Apprenticeship here gave him practice in commercial correspondence and business and personnel management. Those who say that Hamilton, twenty years later, entered upon management of the United States Treasury with no previous practical experience forget that before his service as continental receiver of taxes, he served terms for his mother and Cruger as a young merchant banker in Christiansted.

Hamilton's son John Church perceptively noted that Cruger had left him in charge of the business while away in New York because of his rapid advancement in Cruger's confidence and "his aptitude in conforming himself to his situation." Hamilton's son added that "Foreign as such an avocation was to his inclinations, he nevertheless gave to it all his habitual assiduity, and soon mastered its details; but the inward promptings of his mind looked far beyond it."

John Church Hamilton, a close observer of the father he and all of his brothers and sisters adored, added this insight:

> He thought of immortality, and fondly contemplated from his island home, those fields of glory and summits of honour which displayed themselves to his imagination from beyond the deep.

However, Hamilton's "aptitude in conforming himself to his situation" would not have kept him at Cruger's countinghouse indefinitely because, according to his son, "his aversion to commercial pursuits, and his aspiring temper, leave little reason to suppose that he could have conformed his life to the sphere in which it commenced."

Less than 20 years later, Hamilton would write in *The Federalist:* "There are strong minds in every walk of life that will rise superior to the disadvantages of situation, and will command the tribute due to their merit, not only from the classes to which they particularly belong, but from the society in general."

The choice of callings of the two Hamilton boys—James apprenticed to a carpenter, Alexander to a merchant—pointed up the difference in their aptitudes. Alexander averred that he "always had a strong propensity to literary pursuits." There is only sketchy evidence to explain the early proficiency in writing and accounting that qualified him for the peculiar business of a St. Croix merchant. But his son recalled that Hamilton felt that this "avocation" was of great and lasting benefit to him because it taught him "method" and "facility." He was amply rewarded for his labors by the experience, and in after years he often "adverted to it as the most useful part of his education."

To his son Hamilton also mentioned having "been taught to repeat the Decalogue in Hebrew, at the school of a Jewess, when so small that he was placed standing by her side on a table." His son adds that "the circle of his early studies was very limited, probably embracing little more than the rudiments of the English and French languages, the latter of which he subsequently wrote and spoke with the ease of a native." His knowledge of mathematics seems largely self-taught, and although his proficiency in chemistry was small, "he often urged it as a pursuit well adapted to excite curiosity and create new combinations of thought."

Beyond this, we do not know where or whether Hamilton went to school before coming to the continent in his sixteenth year. He may have studied with one of the schoolmasters in Christiansted who would offer what was beginning to be called an English, as opposed to a classical, education: mathematics and its applications, geography, and perhaps some elements of the natural sciences, but with the omission of Latin and Greek, although Hamilton had a lifelong fondness for Vergil's *Eclogues.* Among his favorite authors were Pope and Plutarch. Whatever his formal schooling, he must have supplemented it by wide miscellaneous reading, including all of Rachel's 34 books.

Throughout the rest of his life, Hamilton would produce a torrent of sentient thought. The first undisputed example written in his own hand is his letter from St. Croix to the close friend of his earliest boyhood and of all his life, Edward Stevens, who had recently been sent abroad for further study at King's College in New York.

The letter is datelined St. Croix, November 11, 1769, when Hamilton was two months short of being thirteen years old. Edward Stevens was the son of Thomas Stevens, who, like Nicholas Cruger, was a successful merchant on St.

Croix. Edward, or Neddy, had been Hamilton's schoolmate, and after Rachel's death, Hamilton probably lived in the Stevens home. The letter is stilted, funny, and rather touching. Young Alexander's feeling of now being left behind in a backwater by the boyhood friend who has already sallied forth to the great world of the continent is transparent.

St. Croix, November 11, 1769

Dear Edward

This just serves to acknowledge receipt of yours per Cap Lowndes. ... The truth of Cap Lightbourn & Lowndes information is now verified by the presence of your father and sister for whose safe arrival I pray. ... As to what you say respecting your having soon the happiness of seeing us all, I wish, for an accomplishment of your hopes provided they are Concomitant with your welfare, otherwise not, tho doubt whether I shall be Present or not for to confess my weakness, Ned, my Ambition is prevalent that I contemn the grov'ling and condition of a Clerk or the like, to which my Fortune, etc. condemns me and would willingly risk my life tho' not my Character to exalt my Station. Im confident, Ned, that my Youth excludes me from any hopes of immediate Preferment nor do I desire it, but I mean to prepare the way for futurity. Im no Philosopher you see and may be jusly said to Build Castles in the Air. My Folly makes me ashamd and beg youll Conceal it, yet Neddy we have seen such Schemes successfull when the Projector is Constant I shall conclude saying I wish there was a War.

I am Dr Edward Yours

Alex Hamilton

P.S. I this moment receivd yours by William Smith and am pleased to see you Give such Close Application to Study.

Here, in this first of Hamilton's many thousands of letters, is laid bare the ambition we recognize as the mainspring of the inner Hamilton that drives him all his life. The record of Hamilton's life after this letter is remarkable by comparison with that of other public men in that almost nowhere else does he admit to a personal ambition or vanity not associated with what he conceives to be the public good. Its open and candid quality also prefigures the frank and indiscreet private manner that would win him undying friendships and mortal enmities all the rest of his life.

The rigidly stratified social and economic structure of the island put a ceiling without an opening above the way up for a poor orphan boy in Hamilton's condition of place. One of the last things a realistic youth like Hamilton would expect a hardheaded employer like Cruger to do, except in dreams, would be to promote him upward out of the condition of a clerk in which he had proved himself to be so valuable, if not entirely indispensable.

What was the way out? Ambition, preparation for futurity, constancy, willingness to "risk my life tho not my Character" might take him nowhere forever, without an opening through the ceiling of society to thrust a ladder through. There was another possibility: "I wish there was a war."

Like Captain William Newton's *Thunderbolt,* Captain Lowndes' and Captain Lightbourn's ships always sailed at risk of seizure by the *Guarda Costas.* Hence Hamilton's prayers for Stevens's father and sister. France and Britain and Spain and Holland had been at war in the West Indies on and off for more than two centuries, and the Arawaks and the Caribbees had been at war for centuries before that. The most imposing works of man on the islands where he had grown up were fortresses like Ashby Fort and Charles Fort on Nevis, and Forts George and Londonderry and the incredible, looming bastion of Brimstone Hill on St. Kitts, not to mention all the forts that protected St. Croix. Wars and rumors of wars and memories of wars were the normal surroundings of Hamilton's youth. Although for the moment Denmark and her Virgin Island colonies like St. Croix were officially neutral and at peace, when invited to dine with the ruling whites at the great plantation houses even the most junior Danish officers wore brilliant uniforms and sat in places of honor.

In the eighteenth century, of course, war meant something very different from the mindless mechanical mass butchery of nonprofessional volunteers and draftees that nineteenth- and twentieth-century improvements have brought to the state of the art.

To Hamilton and most men of the eighteenth century, a war was a series of positionings of professionals, a thing akin to chess or modern professional football, with many time-outs and only occasional brief clashes of armies or fleets to test out the validity of the opposing generals' theories. These tests usually occurred in out-of-the-way places a few days at a time stretched over periods of years. They produced a very moderate number of casualties considering the forces involved—one could see a cannonball coming through the air and duck. Masses of medals and gloriously self-serving memoirs could be issued by all sides from time to time without much risk of contradiction. Such wars, though from time to time involving a few moments or even a day or two of intense unpleasantness and some risk of becoming a casualty, had opened trapdoors upward through stratified societies to worldwide fame for many of Plutarch's ambitious lower middle class youths. His reading would have shown him that this could be true even for those with a turn of mind more literary than military, like Julius Caesar, for example. All in all there is more of humor and high spirits than bloody-mindedness in Hamilton's close of his letter to Neddy, confiding, "I wish there was a war." This is not to say that in this first known letter of Hamilton's his critics cannot find it the first of a life of egregious indiscretions. They do. Still what Hamilton and his friend already knew of the nonsense of war did not oblige them to pretend to the solemn awe in which their elders professed to hold the pursuit.

If Nicholas Cruger gave Hamilton his avocation, Dr. Hugh Knox fostered what Hamilton himself, as his son understood him, saw as his true vocation.[4] As

John Church Hamilton put it, "with a strong propensity to literature, he early became a lover of books." His education was deficient in the classics because "The time which other youth employ in classical learning was by him devoted to miscellaneous reading, happily directed by the advice of Dr. Knox, a respectable Presbyterian divine." Thirty years older than Hamilton, born in the north of Ireland of Scottish blood, learned in the classics and with a "remarkably prepossessing . . . personal appearance and manners," Hugh Knox had spent a few years teaching school and preaching in Pennsylvania and Delaware and a decade in splendid isolation that would powerfully concentrate any mind on the nearby Dutch island of Saba, a 2851 foot volcanic cone only five miles square 16 miles northwest of St. Kitts. Its only town, Bottom, could be approached from the shore 800 feet below only by steps cut into solid rock known as "The Ladder." Knox had visited St. Croix in 1771 and began preaching there regularly in 1772 as minister of the newly established Presbyterian church. "Delighted with the unfolding" of Hamilton's mind, John Church Hamilton wrote, Hugh Knox "took a deep interest in his welfare."

Knox supplied young Alexander with books; directed his miscellaneous reading; contributed to his lifelong piety and religious feeling, his disapproval of slavery, and probably, being a Scot and a Presbyterian, to his rebellious feelings against England. From the rector of Rachel's old church, St. John's Anglican, Hamilton would have received no such nudge in the direction of colonial freedom.

Knox himself, as a 24-year-old newly arrived in America before being called to the cloth, had come under the patronage of the Reverend Francis Alison at New London, Pennsylvania, and of the Reverend John Rodgers of the Presbyterian churches at Middletown and St. George's in the presbytery of New Castle, Delaware. Rodgers had found Knox jobs there as a schoolteacher. One Saturday afternoon in the Middletown Tavern, while hoisting a few seidels with friends who already were calling Knox "parson" and joking about his notable religious zeal, he was asked to preach a sermon. After twice refusing, he yielded and then delivered practically word for word the same sermon that the Reverend John Rodgers had delivered from the pulpit the Sunday before. Not content with merely plagiarizing content, he also mimicked Rodgers's voice, intonations, and gestures—so well that "his profane hearers were deeply affected." Listening from the next room, the tavernkeeper thought Rodgers himself had set up pulpit in his tavern to convert the drunkards. The story goes that next day, full of shame (or perhaps self-impressed by the profound effect his sermon produced on the drunkards), Knox decided to atone for such blasphemy by converting to the ministry. He went to Rodgers, implored him for forgiveness, and won Rodgers's endorsement for admission to The College of New Jersey at Princeton and theological school.

Knox read widely, carried on an extensive correspondence, and published moral tracts and sermons to the world beyond the islands. He admired a man who could unlock the genius that lay hidden in the minds of others. In one of his sermons he had praised Maecenas, the patron of Livy, Horace, and Hamilton's favorite poet, Vergil, for "drawing these incomparable geniuses out of obscurity, and cherishing and developing their parts. . . ."

In his ordination sermon, Knox had preached of the obligation of a pastor like himself to go from house to house, "to be particularly acquainted with every Person under his Care . . . to know their principal Weaknesses and Dangers," and to give special attention to children. Sermonizing on "The Value and Importance of a Child," Knox said that one should "instill into [his] tender opening mind the principles of piety and integrity. . . ." He went on: "Who can conceive the good of which such a child may be made the instrument, or the degrees of happiness and of glory to which it may be advanced." Knox would urge on young Alexander the value of understanding and education, saying, "The mind is as much . . . delighted by the discoveries of knowledge and truth, as the body is with animal refreshments. . . ." To his friend, the Reverend Jacob Green, Knox had written from Saba in the same vein, "When our Lord looked upon the *young man* in the gospel, and *loved him*, can we suppose that he saw nothing in him morally good, which was a motive of his *love?*" So it is not surprising that the difference of thirty years in their ages was no barrier to the 44-year-old Hugh Knox's becoming the chief patron and discoverer of the 14-year-old Alexander Hamilton in the hours the one could spare from ledgers and mules and trading in slaves, and the other from sermons and baptisms. Knox was only practicing what he preached.

Another of Knox's sermons contained the vivid sentence "our duty is written, as it were, with sunbeams." The same phrase gleams through one of Hamilton's finest passages written three years later in New York in 1775: "The sacred rights of mankind are not to be rummaged for among old parchments . . . they are written, as with sunbeams, in the whole volume of human nature, by the hand of Divinity itself."

Having risen from the groveling condition of a schoolteacher to pastorship of his large new St. Croix Presbyterian church, Hugh Knox would open Hamilton's eyes in directions beyond the narrowly religious, particularly to the uses of journalism. Knox was also a licensed apothecary, a part-time medical practitioner, and a contributor of articles to the local newspaper, *The Royal Danish American Gazette*. He also served as its editor when the regular editor was away.

Under the wide-spreading aegis of Dr. Knox, Hamilton tested his emerging literary skills by writing highly derivative pieces for newspaper publication in many different literary forms. On April 6, 1771, he broke into print in *The Royal Danish American Gazette* with a pastoral. Its sources of literary inspiration blotted out the demographic reality of the tropical Antilles that he knew with a verbal Arcadia he had never seen except in print. *The Gazette* ran it below the following apologia:

> Sir,
> I am a youth about seventeen, [he was 14] and consequently such an attempt as this must be presumptuous; but if, upon perusal, you

think the following piece worthy of a place in your paper, by inserting it you'll much oblige

Your obedient servant,

A. H.

> In yonder mead my love I found
> Beside a murm'ring brook reclin'd:
> Her pretty lambkins dancing round
> Secure in harmless bliss.

His "yonder mead," "murm'ring brook," and "pretty lambkins" of conventional pastorals are laughably foreign to the Antillean reality of sudden rainstorms, torrents crashing down deep-scoured ghauts from sharp peaks to gray volcanic sand beaches pounded by blue green waves under blazing tropical suns. Goats and pigs and donkeys, cocoanut palms and slaves in the cane fields were the reality that talk of "yonder meads" and "lambkins" refused to acknowledge. In his imagination Hamilton was as far from the reality of his groveling condition of a clerk as it was possible for him to be. He turned his hand to another antithetical form.

Four days later there appeared in *The Royal Danish American Gazette* of April 10, 1771, a piece entitled "Rules for Statesmen," ostensibly from a correspondent in London, but containing the same thoughts from the same sources that Cruger's clerk would later put to work yoking together the United States of America. From "some years gleaning from Machiavelli, Puffendorff, etc." he wrote, he would endeavor to advise "by what means a Premier may act most to the honor of his Prince, and the enlargement of his own power." He praised the British system of setting over all the departments "a Prime Minister like a Commander-in-Chief; . . . I think this wise regulation a wholesome restraint on the people, whole [whose] turbulence, at times, . . . require[s] a Dictator. . . ."

At the end of August 1772, one of the most devastating hurricanes in the history of the West Indies struck St. Croix, sweeping across the island at dusk without warning. The sea rose 12 or 14 feet. Flood tides parted anchor chains of vessels in the harbor and drove them ashore. Gales blew for six hours, the eye of the hurricane passed, and gales blew again. At least 30 persons were killed—in reports published in *The Gazette* only white casualties were counted—and many more were seriously injured. While it blew, the air reeked with a sulfurous smell. Water in the cisterns was left tasting of niter.

The Sunday following the hurricane, the Reverend Hugh Knox uncorked a ripsnorting sermon to a meeting of survivors and drew powerful moral lessons from the disaster. Young Alexander was surely in the audience, listening carefully, if not taking notes. A week later, in Knox's finest uplifting style, Hamilton addressed some powerful preachments to his father, under date of September 6, 1772. Hamilton had not seen his father since James Hamilton had drifted back to St. Kitts six years before, and James had never evinced susceptibility to religious exhortation. The honor of being the addressee of Alexander's famous

Hurricane Letter seems to have befallen James more as a requirement of the
literary form his son had adopted than as a belated effort of Alexander to reform
a ne'er-do-well father:

> Honoured Sir,
>   I take up my pen just to give you an imperfect account of one of
> the most dreadful hurricanes that memory or any records whatever can
> trace, which happened here on the 31st ultimo at night.

After a vivid description of the hurricane, he gives his father the benefit of
the sermon:

> Where now, O! vile worm, is all thy boasted fortitude and resolu-
> tion? What is become of thine arrogance and self-sufficiency? Why dost
> thou tremble and stand aghast? How humble, how helpless, how con-
> temptible you now appear.

If James Hamilton had cared to read further after such a reproof, he would
find that the accusation was directed upon the author of the letter himself, not
the addressee. It is rhetorical self-accusation in sermon form:

> Hark—ruin and confusion on every side. 'Tis thy turn next; but one
> short moment, even now, O Lord help, Jesus be merciful!
>   Thus did I reflect, and thus at every gust of the wind did I conclude,
> till it pleased the Almighty to allay it. . . .

There was remarkable emotional intensity and a feeling for social injustice
in the contrast Hamilton found between the rich at their ease, who had escaped
harm, and the sufferings of the poor, who had lost everything. His advice to the
rich was to "succour the miserable and lay up a treasure in Heaven." He admonished the white masters of the island who "revel in affluence" to "see the afflic-
tions of humanity, and bestow your superfluity to ease them."

He was apologetic that this preaching by his son might sound a little silly
to his father, or any father: "I am afraid, Sir, you will think this description more
the effort of imagination than a true picture of realities. But I can affirm with
the greatest truth, that there is not a single circumstance touched upon, which
I have not absolutely been an eyewitness to."

With an early eye for good administration and practical solutions, Alexander
wound up his account by noting that despite all the heaven-inflicted rumpus and
tumult, the man in charge down below on the ground, the Danish governor
general, Ulrich Wilhelm Roepstorff, was efficiently putting the pieces back together again:

> Our General has issued several very salutary and humane regula-
> tions, and both in his public and private measures, has shewn himself
> *the Man*.

When Knox's secondhand sermonizing is edited out of Hamilton's letter, what remains is a precise, exciting, almost heart-stopping description of a terrifying natural disaster:

> It began about dusk, at North, and raged very violently until 10 o'clock. Then ensued a sudden and unexpected interval, which lasted about an hour. Meanwhile, the wind was shifting round to the South West point, from whence it returned with redoubled fury and continued so 'till near three o'clock in the morning. Good God! What horror and destruction. . . . It seemed as if a total dissolution of nature was taking place. The roaring of the sea and wind, fiery meteors flying about in the air, the prodigious glare of almost perpetual lightning, the crash of the falling houses, and the ear-piercing shrieks of the distressed, were sufficient to strike astonishment into Angels.

Their "ear-piercing shrieks" were not the only signs of distress. Hamilton felt deeply the tragedy the people had suffered:

> A great part of the buildings throughout the Island are levelled to the ground, almost all the rest very much shattered; several persons killed and numbers utterly ruined; whole families running about the streets, unknowing where to find a place of shelter; the sick exposed to the keenness of water and air without a bed to lie upon, or a dry covering to their bodies; and our harbours entirely bare. In a word, misery, in all its most hideous shapes, spread over the whole face of the country. A strong smell of gunpowder added somewhat to the terrors of the night; and it was observed that the rain was surprizingly salt. Indeed, the water is so brackish and full of sulphur that there is hardly any drinking it.

Reading over a copy of Hamilton's letter, perhaps full of admiration for its religious sentiments that coincided so remarkably with those of the sermon he had delivered the Sunday after the hurricane, Hugh Knox may have remembered his own derivative mock sermon in the Middletown Tavern twenty years before and the Reverend John Rodgers's surprising and benevolent reaction. It had changed his life and started him upward on his religious rise in the secular world. Knox liked Hamilton's letter so well that he arranged to have it printed, perhaps after some personal editing, in *The Royal Danish American Gazette* a month later with the suspiciously overelaborate explanation that it

> was written the week after the late Hurricane, by a youth of this Island, to his Father; the copy of it fell by accident into the hands of a gentleman, who, being pleased with it himself, showed it to others to whom it gave equal satisfaction, and who all agreed that it might not prove unentertaining to the Publick. The Author's modesty in long

refusing to submit it to Publick view, is the reason of its making its appearance so late as it now does.

Hugh Knox did not struggle to keep the letter's authorship secret, and the "hurricane letter" was soon traced to Hamilton. Although the hurricane caused destruction in St. Croix estimated at one million pounds sterling, it is an ill wind that blows nobody good. It has been said that the hurricane blew Hamilton into history, as if by divine intervention. But the human assist from the Reverend Hugh Knox was also indispensable.

A dozen years later, on July 28, 1784, from St. Croix Dr. Knox wrote Hamilton in New York, "I have always had a just & secret pride in having Advised you to go to America, & in having recommended you to Some of my old friends there." No doubt he had also recommended Hamilton to his friends on St. Croix and asked them to aid him with contributions toward the money he would need for his education in America. A period of preparation and three years of college would probably cost no less than £400 pounds sterling.

Hamilton's cousin, Ann Lytton Venton, could help only a little with remittances which were hard-won advances from her father's estate. Besides her, Hamilton's chief benefactors probably were Nicholas Cruger, who was grateful for Alexander's services and knew New York, and his partner Cornelius Kortright, who must have observed Alexander's efficient management of the business in Cruger's absence. The firm consigned some West Indies produce to New York, "to be sold and appropriated to the support of Hamilton." The merchant Thomas Stevens, the father of Alexander's young friend Edward, already at King's on the continent, may also have helped.

Hugh Knox surely, and perhaps some of these and others, saw Hamilton off, possibly from the wharf by the fort in Christiansted or more likely from the deeper harbor at Frederiksted, when he set sail for the continent late in the fall of 1772. In his letter of a dozen years later, Hugh Knox recalled his affectionate pleasure at having recommended that his friends help send their young prodigy on his way:

> You have not only *Answered*, but even far *Exceeded*, our most Sanguine hopes & Expectations. I am glad to find that your popularity increases, & that your fine talents are coming into play, in a way that Contributes so much to your own honour & Emolument, & to the Good of the public.

Knox may have remembered Hamilton's sometimes saying out loud, "I wish there was a war." In light of Hamilton's later serious problems of physical health and "nervous derangement," the healer's comments about his early frailness are worth noting:

> Perhaps Camps & marches & the hardy deeds of War, may have a little fortified & Steel'd your Constitution (which used to be rather

delicate & frail). But beware you do not enfeeble & impair it again, by plunging into intense Studies & the anxieties of the Bar: For I know your laudable Ambition to Excell & that you will Strain Every Nerve to be among the first of your profession. And, great as your talents are, I should imagine that the accurate Study of So Complex & Voluminous Science as the law, & Acquireing all the habits of a pleader, would cost you a deal of Labour.

A delicate and frail constitution, an ambition to excel, a desire that would strain every nerve to be among the first in his profession, clerkship, or army command were the essential baggage that Hamilton took aboard with him when he embarked. He embraced his friends, walked toward the ship, *The Waters of St. Croix*, marched up the gangplank, and was still waving good-bye as she weighed anchor and sailed out of sight.

He had lived in a remote corner of the world, but he had learned some of the most valuable lessons of the world's business. His duties as Cruger's clerk and deputy had thrown him in with the principal figures of the island's private and public life: businessmen, governors, ship captains, merchants, soldiers, masters and slaves, men of property, men of action, men of ambition and guile, Frenchmen, Spaniards, Dutchmen, Britishers, and, of course, many American colonials. He had known and dealt with men in authority. His attitude toward them was deferential but appraising and not diffident. He would arrive in America with the aura of personage rubbed off. He had already lived under two colonial political sovereignties, the British on Nevis and St. Kitts and the Danish on St. Croix. Loans from Amsterdam were familiar parts of the business of island sugar planters. Boston, New York, and Philadelphia were more to him than cities on a map. He had worked for a living at a place that was at the heart of business, commerce, and international politics and an important hub of trade of the world of his age.

Alexander Hamilton would never return to the West Indies or, once arrived, ever leave the North American continent. He had enjoyed his success as Cruger's clerk, and much satisfaction from having known the Reverend Hugh Knox. Deprived of any inheritance from his mother's estate, disturbed by malicious gossip about her past imprisonment and adultery, abandoned by his father, publicly branded a bastard by the court, beholden to his well-to-do Lytton relatives, shocked by their financial collapse and Peter Lytton's suicide, discouraged in the groveling condition of a clerk on the fringes of the closed and stratified white planter society, as the beautiful tropical sugar islands dropped out of sight astern and *The Waters of St. Croix* pointed her prow toward the pole star, the fifteen-year-old Hamilton must have been full of poignant sadness, but few regrets. When John Adams called Hamilton "The bastard brat of a Scotch pedlar," he was wrong about the boy and man on nearly every significant count, except the bald facts.

A three-week trip up the North Atlantic in late fall on a sailing vessel of shallow enough draft to use St. Croix harbors was not a restful and easy pleasure cruise. Hamilton later recalled that as the vessel approached the continent, a fierce fire broke out on board and all hands were in mortal peril. All this, and his frail constitution, must have made him an unusually happy and thankful young man of almost sixteen as he walked down the gangplank onto a Boston wharf and the firm soil of North America late that early winter of 1772.

As a sort of going-away present to St. Croix and Hugh Knox, Hamilton had published in *The Royal Danish American Gazette* of October 17, 1772, in still another literary mode, probably after his ship had sailed. It was a hymn whose title might fancifully be thought to have described his own feelings on embarking for a new world: "The Soul Ascending into Bliss. . . ." or, as the full title admits, "In Humble Imitation of Pope's *Dying Christian to his Soul*":

> Ah! whither, whither, am I flown,
> A wandering guest in worlds unknown?
> Ethereal glories shine around;
> More than Arabia's sweets abound.

Some lines from the concluding stanza would express his gratitude for a safe arrival:

> Translated to this happy place,
> My soul shall all thy steps attend
> In songs of triumph without end.

Rarely, if ever, have more exalted sentiments served to mark a mere debarkation in Boston.

3

THE IMPORTANCE OF STRICT COLLEGE ENTRANCE REQUIREMENTS

DON'T LISTEN TO HIM, GENTLEMEN, HE IS CRAZY, HE IS CRAZY.
—*President Myles Cooper of King's College as Hamilton harangues an angry mob trying to break into the college entrance gates the night of May 10, 1775*

Hamilton's letter to his friend Neddy Stevens in New York, written three years before his arrival in Boston, had confided, "I wish there was a war." Now Hamilton must have read the New England papers, listened to the speeches, and reveled in the revolutionary ferment. The excitement in the crisp autumn air would tell him that it would not be long before his half-joking wish came true. None of his letters of introduction was addressed to anyone in Boston; so he moved on to New York, where, in an age of good manners, he might be properly introduced.

He would have boarded Nicholas Green's stagecoach at the Royal Exchange Tavern, or at Mr. John Boardman's, opposite the Three Doves in Marlborough Street. As the stage trundled south and westward over the rutted post road on the regular New York run through forests of oak and maple turning brilliant hues of orange and yellow and red and brown in New England autumn, past the stone fences of small farms worked by white men who were free, and through the little villages each with its chaste white clapboard meeting house and church, there would be more than enough contrasts with St. Croix to engage his eyes and mind.

According to the American history most of us dimly recall, the United States of America sprang into nationhood out of a continental wilderness around 1776 from the minds of a few patriots like Patrick Henry, James Otis, Samuel Adams, and Nathan Hale, with some military assistance from Washington, Hamilton, and Lafayette, shortly after Paul Revere dismounted from his steed.

Such an opening scene skips the first 150 years and more of the story. The American union evolved slowly and painfully out of separate independent colonial settlements planted on the continent by Britain, France, Holland, and Sweden. After each separate colony had enjoyed a long history of separateness and independence from all others, to persuade them to cut the cords that bound them to their founders and, once free, to yoke them together again into a new union with each other was anything but an automatic and inevitable result of the Signers' and Framers' putting their signatures to parchments in Philadelphia's Independence Hall in 1776 and 1787.

During the same 150 years, Britain and France and Holland and Spain and Denmark and Sweden had been establishing colonies on West Indian fortress-ringed islands like those Hamilton had just left behind. By 1772 these island colonies were approaching the limits of their possibilities for further economic development and growth. The 381 estate plantations and two towns on St. Croix were all that the island had space for. Each island colony he had left behind had its own natural limits at the point where the waves broke over its beaches. The seas between them provided quick and cheap means of carrying on trade and commerce with the mother country, as well as with other colonial islands. By contrast the forests and farms and rutted roads of this vast, empty continental country that Hamilton was passing through on Nicholas Green's stagecoach stretched endlessly on with no or few natural barriers between Massachusetts and Rhode Island, Rhode Island and Connecticut, Connecticut and New York, and all the rest. Still, it was easier to carry on commerce by land between one continental colony and another than by sea between each separate colony and its mother country.

As Hamilton well knew from the business of Cruger's store, the import and export trade of British colonies was required to be carried in English ships manned and commanded by Englishmen. The policy of the staple enumerated the chief products that could be raised in the colonies. Exports had to be brought to England and duties on them paid there. Imports from the colonies were admitted to England at lower rates than the same products from foreign countries. If not needed for the English market, they could then be transshipped from England to foreign countries, but all trade from the colonies had to pass through English ports. Some commodities could not even be shipped direct from one colony to another without passing through an English port first. Other laws were designed to prevent manufacturing from being established in the American colonies. Compensating measures forbade the raising of tobacco in England and Ireland, where it would never have grown in any event, thus preserving by legislation monopolies that the colonies had been given by nature.

British colonization had originated chiefly in private initiative and free enterprise, though it acted in half conscious, half unconscious obedience to certain principles that seemed to be general. Discoverers and would-be colonizers, acting individually or in groups, would collect the ships, men, and money necessary for the enterprise and procure a charter from the Crown by which the king would convey a claim to the soil valid in English law and give the colonizers the right to move Englishmen there, to trade with England and the natives, and to govern the colony, subject to the conditions of allegiance and of British sovereignty in general. The charters typically prohibited the grantee from passing laws or issuing orders that were repugnant to the laws of England and guaranteed the rights and liberties of the colonists as British subjects, without attempting to define what such rights and liberties were. In some colonies, corporate colonies like Virginia, the individual colonist might have no more voice in political matters than a small stockholder has in a large modern corporation. In others, like Massachusetts, his rights might be more like those of a voting member of a cooperative or a church congregation, whereas in still others, proprietary colonies like New York, the colonist might in theory have no more political rights than an employee or tenant farmer of a large landowner. It was the process of a century and a half to change colonists from thinking like purchasers of building lots from a faraway developer into free men thinking politically and to change what began as the real estate ventures they inhabited into free political states.

The indefiniteness of most colonial charters on the matter of political rights made such charters valuable as objects of appeal when colonists sought to uphold local rights and liberties. Hamilton throughout his career would appeal to preexisting rights supposedly created or preserved by the original charter grants and through them to the great traditions of English liberty—the Magna Charta, the Glorious Revolution, and the common law.

The Industrial Revolution in Great Britain was increasing the population of the British Isles rapidly and causing excess people to overflow to less densely peopled regions of the globe. Hamilton's father, James, had been pushed out of Ayrshire to Nevis. As time progressed, colonies became more and more important to Britain as homes for surplus population, sources of food and raw materials, and markets for manufactured goods.

New Netherlands on Manhattan Island and New Sweden in Delaware had soon been absorbed by the British. But until recently it had seemed possible, even likely, that the English colonies would in the end be bottled up on the strip along the coast, just as they had been for much of the previous century and a half by the French at both ends of St. Kitts. Though the thirteen British colonies stretched north to south from Maine to Georgia along the Atlantic seaboard, the

French through their explorers, soldiers, missionaries, and fur traders had until a decade earlier encircled all thirteen by an empire that stretched from Canada on the north, south, and west to the region of the Great Lakes, to the Ohio and Mississippi rivers, and down their courses and westward into regions far beyond across the heart of the continent.

But the French and Indian War and the Treaty of Paris of 1763 had taken this vast territory from France and made it a British dominion as far west as the Mississippi. Although this at first removed the thirteen coastal colonies' old sense of dependence on Great Britain for military aid and protection, their sense of relief was soon replaced by the new fear of being bottled up by the British and, to a lesser degree, by the Spaniards beyond the Mississippi in the Louisiana Territory, and in Florida to the south. The partitioning of the continent among the great European powers in widening concentric rings north, west, and south of the thirteen English-speaking colonies, whose own territorial claims extended inland from their East coast charter grants, would remain a fact of great geopolitical importance for all the rest of Hamilton's life.

Here on the North American continent, Britain, an island herself, ruled over territory and potential resources infinitely richer than she had ruled in St. Kitts and Nevis. Hamilton could not have missed the contrast between the tiny, separate, dependent West Indian island entities under British, French, Dutch, Spanish, and Danish flags, separated by the sea and too weak for anything but colonial subordination to remote European kings, and the restless, powerful mainland colonies separated only by imaginary lines drawn by charter grant title deeds but all part of a single continental land mass. Such lines were arbitrary and artificial divisions of the single continental nation that was waiting for Hamilton and his war to help it discover itself.

As his stagecoach rumbled the last mile down York Island, now Manhattan, toward the little city clustered at its southern tip, Hamilton would put away large thoughts like these to focus on immediate practicalities. Late in 1772, when Hamilton clambered down the stage's steps, New York's population was between 15,000 and 20,000 people, but this was enough to make it, with Boston and Philadelphia, one of the three most populous and important cities of the continent. It was already well known throughout a world whose cities were still small —even in England there were only a few that were larger.

Because part of Hamilton's expenses had been provided for by proceeds of sale of West Indian produce consigned by Nicholas Cruger to Lawrence Kortright in New York, it seems likely that Hamilton's first call would be at the firm's New York store. There Hugh Mulligan, Kortright's partner, may have turned Alexander over to his bachelor younger brother, Hercules Mulligan, who had a haberdashery, tailor shop, and home in Water Street "next door to Philip Rhinelander's china store, between Burling's Slip and the Fly Market." Alexander would lodge there before moving over to Elizabethtown, New Jersey, for the winter. At later times he would again board with Mulligan's family, where, according to Mulligan, he was "always amiable and cheerful" when he sat down with them, sometimes composing doggerel verses for their entertainment.

Alexander Hamilton had been an unusually alert, eager, and energetic boy on tropical islands where one day's and one season's warm weather varied little from the next, except for the punctuation of an occasional hurricane. The crisp tang of bright blue December days in a smog-free New York must have charged Hamilton's nerves on his first few days in the city with the excitement of a lifetime burning in every moment.

The Reverend Hugh Knox had given Hamilton a letter of introduction to the Reverend John Rodgers,[1] now pastor of of the Wall Street Presbyterian Church. It was his sermon that Knox had impersonated in the Middletown Tavern years before. Other letters of Hugh Knox's brought Hamilton to the Reverend John Mason, minister of the Cedar Street Church, and to Elias Boudinot and William Livingston of Elizabethtown. Hamilton's name and abilities would already be well known to Kortright through their correspondence for the firm; so when he presented his letter to the head of the firm at his country house, it would be a reunion with an old friend from the world of commerce and trade. By comparison, his first encounters with the two great divines would seem more like audiences with avenging angels arisen up off Old Testament pages.

As he walked about the city his first few days there, the new arrival from smaller but more cosmopolitan Christiansted would not have looked or allowed himself to appear as any sort of a bemused or confused outlander. To make a good impression in these first important meetings, he would wear his best black coat, white linen knee breeches, black silk stockings, and a lawn shirt beruffled with lace. His eyes, large and gray with a violet tint, would probably have sparkled with ardor and merriment even when first confronting the great divines. His mouth seemed chiseled from a delicate fullness down to a curving line. It was firm even then, but his expression was genial and humorous except on occasions when a fresh experience of the duplicity or fatuousness of mankind would darken the geniality toward mordacity. His nose was long, sharply cut, hard and strong in the nostrils. His head was large, the brow full above his eyes. His whole countenance was of a ruddy, boyish, and sunburned fairness, recalling his Scottish father. He could fetch a smile that lit up his face with an irresistible warmth and charm. His figure was supple and well-knit and proud in its bearing, so that few men, nor any woman, then or later would find fault with, or even take note of, its rather inconsiderable five feet seven inches of height.

Whenever Hamilton was sufficiently in funds to permit him to pay for elegant attire, which he always contrived to be, despite other pressing exigencies, his friend Hercules Mulligan could always supply him, as he would furnish a "resplendent black velvet suit" to President Washington for appearances at his levees. As Mulligan prospered, he offered Hamilton gold and silver lace, with some half laces for hats, "gold and silver buttons and loops," and gold and silver treble French chains.

If Hamilton had walked up the Broad Way to take his first look at King's College, of which he must have heard much in correspondence from his old St. Croix friend Ned Stevens, and perhaps to check on current entrance requirements, he must have noticed how the medieval Dutch architecture of the old city below Wall Street was giving place in the upper town to the Renaissance styles popular in England at the time.

Among the most conspicuous houses would be those of men he would come to know well—Philip Livingston's, with its two-stepped gable, Dutch-style dormers, Tobias Ten Eyck's mansion beyond the fish market shed at Coenties Slip, Robert Livingston's house with its enormously tall chimneys. It had formerly belonged to Captain Kidd, who was the only one of the New York aristocrats who would admit to being a pirate. Within the gardens around it, Colonel Abraham de Peyster's villa just north of the French church seemed sequestered like a grange.

If it were late and the afternoon were sunny, the fashionable world of the city would be promenading on the Battery in front of Fort James, the new name for the old Dutch Fort Amsterdam. Most New Yorkers tended to follow English fashion in dress as well as architecture, but some of the ladies especially were beginning to adopt French modes. Hamilton would see much evidence of New Yorkers' love of luxury and ostentation in dress. *The New York Gazette* of a few years later would describe one beauty who wore a "celestial blue satin gown" with a white satin petticoat, a large Italian gauze handkerchief with satin border stripes at her neck, and a white satin headpiece in a double wing form, trimmed with a wreath of artificial roses over four artificial curls hanging down on each side, and a floating chignon behind. In passing, he may have eyed warily the statue of King George III, rising tall on its pedestal above the Bowling Green, not covered by the cannons of the fort behind. Their muzzles poked seaward out of its portals ready to fire on any invader who might dare to sail up the harbor from the Narrows. In 1776, when the invaders would be King George's own men, these guns could not be turned around in time to prevent this statue from being pulled down and hacked to pieces by a rebellious mob.

To Hamilton, his fellow New Yorkers must have appeared animated, high-bred, and intelligent. The beautiful, chic, proud women walked about with their heads held high. Their eyes usually looked straight ahead, but sometimes they would glance boldly straight into the eyes of a newcomer like Hamilton, sending a thrill through his soul he would never forget.

Looking southward from King's College, the highest pinnacle of the city's skyline would be the steeple of Trinity Church at the corner of the Broad Way and Wall Street, flanked by the steeple of the Dutch church. To the east was the new City Hall at the corner of Wall and Broad Streets, across from what is now the New York Stock Exchange. At the ends of the streets south, east, and west would be glimpses of wharves and piers, the waters of the East River, the Lower Bay, and the Hudson, all filled with busy flotillas of barks, frigates, sloops, and men-of-war from all over the world, as well as lighters and tenders and ferryboats shuttling to and fro between Staten Island and Governor's Island and Brooklyn and Manhattan.

King's College itself was an imposing four-gabled, three-story structure with a balustrade, a cupola, and a steeple on the roof. It rose on the northern outskirts of town on the site now bounded by Murray, Barclay, Church, and

Canal Streets. It looked west over the Hudson to the Jersey Palisades across spacious grounds shaded by ancient sycamores and elms.

Although Hamilton's knowledge of geography, history, natural and moral philosophy, and, indeed, the Decalogue in Hebrew were important qualifications for admission to King's College, he was deficient in formal learning: he lacked the classical languages, Latin and Greek, and mathematics beyond the quick arithmetic of commerce and the double-entry bookkeeping he had picked up at Cruger's countinghouse. More and different book learning was needed for admission to King's. It was not ready to admit him yet. The next rung up would have to be Francis Barber's preparatory school in Elizabethtown, New Jersey.

But after the sights he had seen and the excitement he had felt, he would remain a New Yorker forever. Only fifteen years later his friends, acquaintances, admirers, and strangers, and his enemies as well, with an ironic shrug at the seeming inevitability of having to do so, would be calling the great city Hamiltonopolis in honor of his name.

A week or so after having arrived in New York, Hamilton ferried across the Hudson to New Jersey and rode through the forest to the village of Elizabethtown, now Elizabeth, to present his last two letters of introduction from Hugh Knox to two remarkable and well-selected addressees: William Livingston[2] and Elias Boudinot.

During that winter of 1772–1773, Alexander would live mostly in the household of William Livingston while attending Francis Barber's grammar school. As he solemnly told his son John Church Hamilton, in the immemorial manner of all fathers polishing up images of youthful years to rally the younger generation out of slackness and sloth, he "was accustomed to labour until midnight" over the work he brought home. It must have further depressed the son that his father did not slack off when summer came on. "In summer, it was his habit to retire at dawn to the quiet of a neighboring cemetery, where he was often seen preparing his lessons for the day."

William Livingston, with his wife and four daughters, not only furnished Hamilton with a more cheerful place than the cemetery to live and study, but he probably also helped Elias Boudinot arrange a scholarship for Hamilton at the Academy as one of "a Number of Free Scholars in this Town." Like so many others of Hamilton's earliest acquaintances, both Livingston and Boudinot became and remained his faithful patrons, mentors, friends, and followers throughout the rest of his life. Hamilton's gift for forming deep lifelong friendships with remarkable men of all ages is as striking, if less often noticed, than his gift for making great enemies.

Francis Barber's school, at the time Alexander was racing through the course in 1772 and 1773, was the best in the area. Besides offering Latin and Greek, the Academy's curriculum was adapting to the growing demand for English literature and composition, elocution, mathematics, and geography. It prepared boys for any college, but especially Princeton, whose entrance requirements included the ability to translate Vergil and Cicero, to write Latin prose, and to sight-read the gospels in Greek. The first-year curriculum included Horace, Cicero, Greek testaments, Lucian, and Xenophon.

A two-story, cupolaed wooden building, the Academy was located on the grounds of the Presbyterian church near the upper end of Burial Yard Lot. This location easily explains the oddness of the place Hamilton picked for quiet matutinal cramming. Omission of this key fact from the tale he told his son would give it more vividness and cautionary inspirational force.

Francis Barber, born at Princeton, New Jersey, in 1750, the eldest of four children of an upwardly mobile Irish immigrant, holder of A.B. and A.M. degrees from Princeton, was another of Hamilton's early mentors who became a fast friend for a short life. If a classical curriculum more systematic than Hugh Knox's were required to qualify him for the honor, then he was Hamilton's first teacher. Hamilton must have spent more hours in the company of Barber than any other person at Elizabethtown, and master must have been a model for pupil in ideals and conduct. When Barber had taught in a Latin school at Hackensack, all "those of his Pupils who have been sent to the Colleges, were found well fitted for Reception."

Hamilton's son described Barber as "a man of strong sense, considerable attainments, and respectable connections. Fired by the prospect of distinction, and by his love of country, he broke up his school at the commencement of the revolution—entered the army, soon rose to the rank of colonel, and in the course of the contest was often and much distinguished." Wounded three times, he would be with Hamilton again in a number of the same battles, lastly at the Battle of Yorktown, where columns each of them were leading converged on the last British redoubt to clinch the greatest victory of the war. Near the army's last headquarters at Newburgh, just as the final peace was about to be proclaimed, Barber was killed by a falling tree.

As tuition the young West Indian paid Barber five pounds sterling a year, plus one pound, ten shillings for "wood and cost of house cleaning" and another pound for "Entrance light money." No doubt most of this came through remittances from sales of his St. Croix patrons' sugar and rum through Kortright & Company. Room and board were furnished through the hospitality of the Livingstons and the Boudinots, who also supplied some intangible advantages whose value was beyond any tuition fee.

Both William Livingston and Elias Boudinot were men of parts, position, and the Presbyterian patrimony that linked them to Dr. Knox and his young protégé. They became proud foster parents of the young West Indian. Far from remaining a waif cast up on an alien shore to make his own way unaided, Hamilton quickly became a welcome familiar in their great houses. Both men were deliberate by training and habit and conservative by economic interest. When young Hamilton was their protégé at Elizabethtown, they were watching the rise of the revolutionary storm but hoping that it might be averted with reason and honor. Their Presbyterian heritage left them more open to the emotional appeal of independence than most of their Anglican friends. By opinion, profession, and argument, and, more important, by being the men they were, their influence on their young guest was incalculable.

A younger son of Philip Livingston, the second lord of Livingston Manor,

New York, and his wife, Catherine Van Brugh, William Livingston was born to the best of Scottish and Dutch patrician and patroon traditions. Although his vagrant wish had been to study painting in Italy, he instead studied Logic and Latin paradigms at Yale. After graduating at the head of his class in 1741, he read law with James Alexander and married Susannah French of Albany, whose father's landholdings in New Jersey brought with them enough complications to keep his law practice a busy one in a new colony. His growing Wall Street law practice across the river in New York did not prevent him from indulging a literary bent by publishing verse, such as "Philosophic Solitude, or the Choice of a Rural Life," and contributing opinions, in regular columns, to New York newspapers, advocating civil liberties, the separation of church and state, and the value of representative government.

As a Whig and a Presbyterian spokesman, he was a leader of the party that opposed the ruling Tories, who were mostly Episcopalians. A tall, lanky man with a large nose, he brought mental integrity, blunt candor, and a perverse contentiousness to arguments over the political and religious issues of the day. He vigorously opposed using funds raised from public lotteries to help support King's College because it was an adjunct of the Church of England, and, like all good Presbyterians, he favored strict separation of church and state.

More emotional, more whimsical and satirical than Livingston, but like him in principles, was Elias Boudinot. Hamilton was as indebted to Boudinot as host and patron as he was to Livingston. Like Hamilton's mother, Boudinot's father was of French extraction; the parents of both men had lived in the West Indies, and Boudinot's father had been married in Antigua. Elias and his brother, Elisha Boudinot, were "two brothers, lawyers, elegant men, tall, handsome and every way prepossessing," who "used to attend the court . . . and whenever they spoke, crowds were attracted to hear them. . . ." A devoted gardener and horticulturist, Elias Boudinot planted seeds in young Hamilton's mind that would flower 30 years later in the gardens of The Grange.[3]

Boudinot had just bought a large new mansion known as Boxwood Hall which still stands. It was only a few minutes' walk across Horse Hollow from Elizabethtown Academy. When he was not a guest of the William Livingstons of Liberty Hall, Hamilton stayed with the Boudinots of Boxwood Hall. The Boudinot girls were younger than the Livingston daughters—Susanna Vergereau Boudinot was only eight—and Anna Maria Boudinot was the baby of seven months upon whom all the family doted.

The Presbyterian piety that Hamilton had learned from Hugh Knox was intensified in the Presbyterian environment of Elizabethtown. Elias Boudinot's preoccupation with theology either put a guest on his knees or else turned him into a rebellious blasphemer. About this time Hamilton assiduously wrote out a set of notes, quotations, and paraphrases of the first three chapters of Genesis and Chapters I to XIII of the Book of Revelation. He maintained secular balance by also translating some of Homer's *Iliad* and composing the prologue and epilogue for a play, which was performed by a company of British soldiers stationed near Elizabethtown.

Like Hamilton in personality, Boudinot was a warm, friendly man without

much reserve. When his pastor, the Reverend James Caldwell, was later killed
by a British sentry (after Caldwell's wife had earlier been slain by a stray shot
from the Battle of Springfield that came through her window), Caldwell's coffin
was rested on Boudinot's broad doorstone. Boudinot ranged the nine orphaned
Caldwell children around it, called the attention of the mourners to their pitiful
plight, and demanded that the mourners come forward and adopt and provide
for them all. When Colonel Antil, one of Hamilton's comrades-in-arms during the
Revolution died, leaving his young daughter an orphan, the Hamiltons would
take the child into their own home and raise her as one of their own.

When the Boudinots' darling baby, Anna Maria, died in September 1774,
Hamilton sat up all night with the body before its interment and wrote some
consolatory verses for Mrs. Boudinot:

> For the sweet babe, my doating heart
> Did all a Mother's fondness feel;
> Carefull to act each tender part
> And guard from every threatening ill.
> . . . .
> Thou'st gone, forever gone—yet where,
> Ah! Pleasing thought; to endless bliss.
> Let reason silence nature's strife,
> And weep Maria's fate no more;
> She's safe from all the storms of life,
> And wafted to a peaceful Shore.

Hamilton's preparatory schooling at Elizabethtown Academy did not begin
and end with poring over Vergil through winter midnights or retiring at dawn
to the quiet of Burial Yard Lot. In "idle" hours he would absorb from William
Livingston his polemic skill, his straightforward, driving writing style, his habit
of publication, and his zeal for civil liberties. Later on, as one of Hamilton's
strongest supporters, Livingston would join him in condemning the weakness of
the Confederation, urging adoption of the Constitution, and firmly backing
Hamilton's economic program.

Hamilton and Boudinot would later work together on bargaining with the
British over prisoner exchanges and join in opposing a mutinous threat of the
unpaid soldiers against Congress. On all critical votes on Hamilton's most important measures in Congress, Boudinot, like Livingston, would unfailingly come
forward to support him.

It is not as remarkable as it might seem that Livingston, 34 years older than
Hamilton, and Elias Boudinot, 15 years older, would follow for the rest of their
lives as their political leader a man so much their junior. Hamilton's political
views and style reflected their own because, after all, they were the patterns on
which his were now being significantly modeled.

Susannah Livingston was as strong a Presbyterian patriot and foe of kingly
rule as her husband, William. Their brilliant son Brockholst was Hamilton's

schoolmate at Elizabethtown and King's. Their daughter Sarah, beautiful, sweet, and clever, was perhaps already, by 1773, pensively in love with young John Jay. Sarah's handsome and dashing sisters, Kitty, Susan, and Judith, were still heart-whole and free. All had grown up in a heady atmosphere of political discussion and honor for a lively intellect over the dining-room table. They eagerly welcomed Hamilton for more than the fact that he was male. The handsome, delicate-looking orphan from the exotic tropical islands, with his fair Scottish complexion, charming Gallic manners, and gay good humour, affected no false humility. Before becoming a prep school boy, he had already served as a busy man of the merchant world. He was an exciting addition to a table seating that up to then had consisted of only a patriarch, a brother, and five awestricken women.

Five years later, from the army's winter headquarters at Morristown, Hamilton would write to Kitty Livingston in the tone of an old and dear intimate, "I challenge you to meet me in whatever path you dare . . . in the flowery walks and roseate bowers of Cupid. You know, I am renowned for gallantry, and shall always be able to entertain you with a choice collection of the prettiest things imaginable."

As if remembering their evenings together at Liberty Hall, when he was the cynosure of her whole adoring family, he added, "I fancy my knowledge of you affords me a tolerably just idea of your taste." But he admits that he may be mistaken—a rare admission for Hamilton. He makes it to her only to compel belief in the rest of what he has to say. He asks her what she really thinks, because if she does not tell him herself, it will not be easy for him to guess. "Contrary to the vulgar," he realizes that "woman is not a *simple*, but a most complex, intricate, and enigmatical being." If she will tell him her thoughts and whether she is "of a romantic, or discreet temper, as to love affairs," he will regulate his conduct toward her by it. "If you would choose to be a goddess, and to be worshipped as such," he adds, "you shall be one of the graces, or Diana, or Venus."

But if Kitty, a dashing twenty-two-year-old beauty, six years older than he, and being fervently wooed by Gouverneur Morris at the time of that first winter of his in Elizabethtown, would come down off her goddess's pedestal, she would become "something surpassing them all." If so, he would offer poems "at your Goddesship's shrine."

History does not record whether Kitty and Alexander became lovers that winter in Elizabethtown. For what it's worth, the novelist Gertrude Atherton's powerful intuition told her that Kitty "was the first to reveal to him the fascination of her sex," however much or little that cryptic phrase may mean, if less than all. However, it is unlikely that Kitty was the very first "to reveal to him the fascination of her sex." It would be ridiculous to assume that a handsome teen-ager growing up in the tropics, where many took him to be older than his years, would spend every waking hour ambitiously preparing for futurity and war.

All through his life, to a greater extent than any other framer or founder, and more notoriously than any other public figure except Aaron Burr, Hamilton seemed to excite the hopes and fears aroused by what later times might call the image of the sensuous man. He played the role early with panache, but later with embarrassment. It would lead to his penultimate disgrace. The poems Hamilton promised to write for Kitty have not been found, but they must have been improvements, or at least refinements, on the two he had published in *The Royal Danish American Gazette* of April 6, 1771. After he complied with the conventions of the lyric form by substituting a cool, dreamy Arcadian landscape for the hot and vivid colors of St. Croix, and told of how he "stole a silent kiss," his poem shifted to a down-to-earth description of observed reality:

> She wak'd, and rising sweetly blush'd,
> By far more artless than the dove:
> With eager haste I onward rush'd,
> And clasp'd her in my arms;
> Encircled thus in fond embrace
> Our panting hearts beat mutual love—
> A rosy-red o'erspread her face
> And brighten'd all her charms.

After this account of her climax, Hamilton characteristically went on to insist on following an orderly legal procedure. It comes as a distinct anticlimax to his poesy that

> Silent she stood, and sigh'd consent
> To every tender kiss I gave;
> I closely urged—to church we went,
> And hymen join'd our hands.

Hamilton rather unconvincingly adds that

> Believe me love is doubly sweet
> In wedlock's holy bonds.

Wedlock, he claims, did not even spoil his nightly fun: Even afterward,

> We fondly sport and fondly play,
> And Love away the night.

Not having been married, he was, in fact, here only exercising poetic license about married license.

Kitty Livingston of Livingston Manor was not the same sort of girl as the island conquest of the night that his poem recalled. Nor was she a coquette like one Coelia, whose type he had described in another St. Croix verse:

Coelia's an artful little slut;
Be fond, she'll kiss, et cetera—but
She must have all her will;
For, do but rub her 'gainst the grain
Behold a storm, blow winds and rain,
Go bid the waves be still.

So, stroking puss's velvet paws
How well the jade conceals her claws
And purrs; but if at last
You hap to squeeze her somewhat hard,
She spits—her back up—*prenez garde;*
Good faith, she has you fast.

Having known Kitty Livingston so well at Elizabethtown that winter, he could offer her something better than such doggerel: "If, conformable to your usual discernment, you are content with being a mere mortal, and require no other incense than is justly due to you, I will talk to you like one [in] his sober senses."

Amidst such "amorous transports" while thinking about Kitty, he rounded off his letter to her with a slap and a tickle of self-confident laughter: ". . . and, though it may be straining the point a little, I will even stipulate to pay you all the rational tribute applicable to a fine girl."

When Kitty's sister Sarah Livingston married John Jay at Liberty Hall in the spring of 1774, Hamilton was no doubt on hand. The groom's name would be allied with Hamilton's in like purposes throughout the rest of their lives. Other memorable men and women Hamilton would likely have met at the Livingstons or Boudinots with whom he would always be closely identified were Livingston's brother-in-law William Alexander and his wife, Catherine, also known as Kitty and as Lady Kitty. He was called Lord Stirling because of his claim to a Scottish title. Hamilton came to know him better as a major general in the Revolution. There was William Duer, who was soon to marry Lord and Lady Stirling's daughter Catherine. She was still another Lady Kitty, and Duer would become Hamilton's first assistant in the Treasury. Hamilton's friendship with Duer would be one of the two or three most disastrous of his life.

Still others he would have met at Elizabethtown whose lives would afterward be interwoven with his were Jonathan Dayton, afterward Speaker of the House of Representatives; James Duane, later mayor of New York; other members of the Livingston, Morris, Schuyler, Ogden, Clinton, and Stockton families; and Dr. John Witherspoon, the president of the College of New Jersey at Princeton.

All the Presbyterian elders he met at Elizabethtown, as well as his headmaster Francis Barber, and most of his other friends urged Hamilton to plan to go on to Princeton. Among its 85 students, many were from the West Indies.

President Witherspoon was actively recruiting more, but not because they were boys of supposedly lower orders of race and economic status, unable to meet regular academic standards, who would enjoy a superior ambiance at Princeton. He recruited West Indians for the opposite reason: boys from that prosperous quarter often brought with them both higher skills and more tuition money than local boys.

Hamilton's New York City friend Hercules Mulligan urged him to come back to King's College in New York, but Hamilton insisted on applying first to Presbyterian Princeton, which was less royalist and "more republican" than Anglican King's. But the former young man of the world now confined to preparatory school did not think he needed as much time there as his less privileged fellow students might. When he went to see President Witherspoon in his study, a small room somber with mahogany furniture in the southwest corner of the house that is now the residence of the dean of the college, he took his friend Hercules with him. As Mulligan recalled,

> I went with him to Princeton to the house of Dr. Witherspoon . . . with whom I was well acquainted, and I introduced Mr. Hamilton to him and proposed to him to Examine the young gentleman which the Doctor did to his entire satisfaction. Mr. Hamilton then stated that he wished to enter either of the classes to which his attainments would entitle him but with the understanding that he should be promoted to advance from Class to Class with as much rapidity as his exertions would enable him to do. Dr. Witherspoon listened with great attention to so unusual a proposition from so young a person and replied that . . . he would submit the request to the trustees.

Who is too old to fail to recall the anxieties Hamilton must have suffered that spring waiting for his acceptance notice from the college of his first choice, Princeton?

Witherspoon had explained to other prospective students from the West Indies that "the regular course of instruction is in four classes, exactly after the manner and bearing the names of the classes in the English universities. . . ." An applicant might be admitted to any class year for which he qualified. By dint of "doubled labor," James Madison had received his A.B. from Princeton in the autumn of 1771, after only two calendar years, on much the same kind of speedup program Hamilton had proposed two years later.

Hercules Mulligan's story goes on. There was a crushing disappointment: "In about a fortnight after a letter was received from the President stating that the request could not be complied with because it was contrary to the usage of the College." President Witherspoon had been impressed, but he had not been able to prevail on the admissions office to waive the usual standards. His letter turning Hamilton down for the college of his first choice went beyond the merely perfunctory. "He was convinced that the young gentleman would do honor to any seminary at which he should be educated."

Hamilton's second choice, King's College, accepted him for the spring of

1774 in the sophomore class, with the same privileges of flexible choice of courses and optional acceleration that Princeton had refused him.

In contrast to Princeton, which had been established by Presbyterian dissenters who tended to lean toward the cause of independence, King's College was fostered by Anglicans firmly attached to the British Crown. The president, Myles Cooper, was born in the Church of England, bred at King's College, Oxford, and had become a deacon and priest in his early twenties. In accordance with King's charter, he was a member of, and "in communion with the Church of England, as by law established." Morning and evening, Cooper or his deputy intoned liturgical prayers, and the students chanted responses. The archbishop of Canterbury himself, Thomas Secker, had chosen Cooper to head the college as a man "very well affected to the government." A published attack on the Continental Congress attributed to Cooper called Bostonians who were leading the movement for independence "rebellious Republicans, . . . hair-brained fanaticks, as mad . . . as the *Anabaptists of Munster. . . ."*[4]

Hamilton's Presbyterian friends like William Livingston called Cooper "a Tory and an obnoxious man." To them, King's, unlike Princeton, was "a partycollege" which "will put a new face upon the religion, and in consequence . . . affect the politics of the country." Livingston assailed Cooper and the rest of the royalists who dominated King's for "tincturing the minds of the students with the . . . sentiments of that sector." Such politics would lead them after graduation to "fill all the offices of the government" with royalists.

Hamilton matriculated at this New York bastion of bishops and Books of Common Prayer late in the fall of 1773. He did not lose his ascetic Presbyterian piety there all at once. His roommate, Robert Troup, marveled somewhat that Alexander "was attentive to public worship, and in the habit of praying upon his knees both night and morning." Hamilton's student life was full of the perfunctory ups and downs. He did not confine his prayers to public observances. Robert Troup added:

> I lived in the same room with him for some time, and I have often been powerfully affected by the fervor and eloquence of his prayers. He had read many of the polemical writers on religious subjects, and he was a zealous believer in the fundamental doctrines of Christianity.

The communicative power of Hamilton's religious zeal that winter still cast a spell that helped make a believer of his lifelong friend Robert Troup. "I confess," Troup wrote, "that the arguments with which he was accustomed to justify his belief, have tended in no small degree to confirm my own faith in revealed religion."

The example of Edward Stevens, his boyhood friend, and the Reverend Hugh Knox, who was also a physician and apothecary, helped to inspire Hamilton to early emulation of them. He "originally destined himself to the Science of Physic" and "was regular in attending the anatomical lectures, then delivered in the college by Dr. Clossey."

Hamilton also studied as the private pupil of Robert Harpur, a professor of mathematics and natural philosophy, beginning in September 1774. He paid four pounds, four shillings per quarter. The subject matter of the course included commercial applications in discount, partners' shares, "simple interests," and the exchange of currencies. It probably did not carry either student or professor into the more complicated realms of mathematics like astronomical calculations, of which Harpur was a master. Though most of Harpur's students paid promptly, Hamilton seems to have left his account unpaid until 1783. Harpur's account book notes receipt from Colonel Hamilton that year "as a present at the close of the war 5 Guins. $= 9£ - 6$ s $- 8$ d." Harpur was known as a tough grader, and Troup and others of Hamilton's classmates abused him "by *calling names* in the Dark. . . ." but there is no record of Hamilton's ever having done so.

The college penalized petty offenses such as tardiness and failure to appear in "proper academical habit," but by Hamilton's time the parietal rules no longer expressly condemned fornication, cursing, cockfighting or "maiming any person," as they once had. President Cooper patterned the college's *Book of Misdemeanours* after those of the Oxford colleges, which carried with them such grim penances as translating one of Dr. Chandler's sermons or a chapter of Pufendorf or a number or two of *The Spectator* into Latin. Lists of the students guilty of offenses still exist, but Hamilton's name does not appear on any of them. To sustain this pettily repressive regime, which, however, left no apparent damage on the brains of a remarkable group of graduates, the college steward served the scholars for the midday meal, "roast beef and pudding" on Sundays, "corned beef . . . and mutton pye" on Thursday, and "leg mutton and soup" on Fridays. Substantial midday dinners on other days filled the chinks left by breakfasts of bread and butter and coffee or tea and by suppers that bettered breakfasts only by the addition of cheese.

Hamilton made good use of the college library. There is no complete list, but works he refers to in pamphlets he published in 1774 and 1775 while he was at King's were no doubt there. His published writings flash a knowledge of Grotius, Pufendorf, Locke, Montesquieu, Berlamaqui, Hobbes, Blackstone, Postlethwayt, Hume, the *lex mercatoria*, records of recent debates and acts of the British Parliament, colonial charters, acts of the General Assembly of New York, Samuel Johnson's dictionary, and an account of the wars of Charles XII and Peter the Great. Some of Hamilton's sources may also have been books and journals that he borrowed from the library of another remarkable man who would be his early patron, mentor, and lifelong friend, Alexander McDougall.

Robert Troup recalled that Hamilton, Edward Stevens, Samuel and Delancey Nicoll, Nicholas Fish, and himself were "particular associates . . . in college." They formed themselves into a club that met weekly for mutual self-improvement in writing and debating, "until we were separated by the Revolution." He remembered Hamilton's performances at the club as "displays of richness, of genius, and energy of mind." Nicholas Fish recalled that Hamilton occasionally and confidentially read parts of political pieces to the club before he submitted them to the newspapers for publication. In these pieces Hamilton displayed a bent for practical idealism. No sooner had he become well acquainted with a problem and settled his conclusions upon it than he set out to persuade by force of argument first the members of his club, and then a wider circle, to adopt his point of view. All his life Hamilton read swiftly, remembered much, learned quickly and profoundly, and speedily brought his quick study to bear on a point that would lead to action. Other young men of his circle were still uncertain of themselves; he would leap at a bound from their quiet circle to the court of public opinion. Troup recalled one occasion when John Holt, who then published a Whig paper, *The New York Journal*, had "by his zeal in the American cause, drawn upon himself the invectives of all the ministerial writers," that is, loyalists like President Cooper. Hamilton burlesqued the king's men "in doggerel rhyme, with great wit and humour." As one example of his many experiments with different literary forms, Hamilton presented Troup with "a manuscript of fugitive poetry." To Troup this was "strong evidence of the elasticity of his genius." Troup preserved it, and lamented that it had been "lost with my books and papers during the war."

Political pamphleteering, doggerel verse, mathematics, medicine, mutton, and prayers were not the whole of Hamilton's life at King's. Opposed political loyalties were drawing men to opposite poles of the revolutionary split that was widening, but these did not keep Hamilton from becoming a friend of President Myles Cooper. Though twenty years older, Cooper shared with Hamilton good looks, a gift for expression in many literary modes, and a sense of elegance.

Cooper was a much different man from his notable predecessor as president of King's, Dr. Samuel Johnson. Johnson, at first a Congregationalist, had become "dubious of the lawfulness of [his] ordination," and was posted back to England for priest's orders. By contrast with Cooper, who flaunted his formal learning, Johnson had got his learning mostly by himself, and it was burned deep; whereas Johnson had wrestled with his soul, Cooper enjoyed life. When Johnson had lost one wife, he married another to obtain "a careful and disinterested housekeeper." Cooper, with his handsome looks and graceful ways, remained a bachelor all his life and kept a garret well stocked with wine and a table so richly laden that he often reeled from overindulgence. Whereas the somber Johnson had confined his pen to prose, Cooper the year he was ordained published *Poems on Several Occasions*, most of it polite love verse to Sylvia, Cynthia, and Delia, but some of it scornful and carnal, not so different from Hamilton's verses to Coelia, that wilful little slut. Alumni more gruff than Hamilton granted that Cooper's "moral character was without any serious reproach," but grumbled that "grave men were occasionally offended by the . . . conviviality of his social habits." It was small wonder that a student like Hamilton became "greatly attached" to such a college president or that such a president would court so remarkable a student.

Cooper was a member of a circle of prominent New York Tories that included the Reverend T. B. Chandler, Isaac Wilkins, and Samuel Seabury. When the time came for Hamilton to write such papers as *A Full Vindication of the Measures of Congress* and *The Farmer Refuted*, in opposition to Tory pamphleteers, he had already heard and marshaled his replies to their arguments over sherry and port and Madeira at President Cooper's table. He would then retest them by writing them out and reading them to the more intimate circle of his revolutionary student friends at the gatherings of their club.[5]

Deep differences of political principle in no way affected Hamilton's loyalty to his personal friendship for President Cooper. In May of 1775 the rising revolutionary ferment in the outside world burst in upon the tranquil disputations of scholars beneath the sycamores and elms of King's. A revolutionary mob tried to seize President Cooper and kill him. Hamilton and Troup saved their president's life by arranging his rescue from a mob.

A widely published letter had brought news of the electrifying events of April at Lexington and Concord. It had roared, "the crimson fountain was opened, and God only knew when it would close." Another, datelined Philadelphia, April 25, 1775, addressed to Dr. Myles Cooper and four other "obnoxious gentlemen of New York," blamed the strong attachment of the city to the king on them. It assailed "all the hostile proceedings of England," called them parricides, and warned them that Americans "will no longer satisfy their resentment with the execution of villians [sic] in effigy." It threatened: "Fly for your lives, or anticipate your doom by becoming your own executioners," and was signed "Three Millions."

A surly mob gathered to carry out the threat of the "Three Millions." Angry men raged toward the King's College gates on the night of May 10, 1775, shouting their intention of tarring and feathering Dr. Cooper and riding him out of town on a rail or killing him.[6]

Troup and Hamilton feared that if such a bloody-minded mob caught Dr. Cooper, it might well kill him by accident in the uproar, if not by design. Dr. Cooper feared the same. The mob was 400 strong and, excited by the flickering glare of crackling pine knot torches, was in a murderous temper to wreak dark and vicious violence. They swirled against the college gates. They tried to smash them down. Hamilton jumped up on one of the stoops and began to harangue the mob.[7] Violence to Cooper would bring disgrace to the cause of liberty, of which they claimed themselves to be champions. President Cooper, in his nightshirt, peered down from an upper window of the college on the terrifying scene: the mob, with their swirling torches blazing, and Hamilton on the stoop facing them down, with his stout friend Robert Troup there by his side.

As Cooper's frightened eyes searched the lurid night scene, he at first misunderstood what Hamilton and Troup were trying to do. He would remember the arguments he and his Tory circle had had with Hamilton and Troup over port and cigars, Hamilton's vindication of Congress against the king, his refutation of Samuel Seabury[8] in the homespun guise of the Westchester Farmer, his obstinate refusal to take up the pen for the loyalist side, and his alliance with the party of liberty, of which the mob below now claimed to be sons.

Dr. Cooper cried out to the mob, "Don't listen to him gentlemen; he is crazy! he is crazy!" But they kept on listening to Hamilton anyway—long enough at least for Cooper to start putting on his clothes. Cooper soon realized that Hamilton was not trying to stir them up; he was trying to calm them down.

Hamilton left Troup alone on the stoop to carry on the diversionary harangue and ran into President Cooper's house. The mob was still rattling the "groaning gates" to break into the college grounds. Hamilton breathlessly reassured Cooper that he and Troup had been trying to distract the crowd from killing him. He then hustled Cooper out by the back way just as the mob broke through the front gates and the leaders rushed up the stairs to force the door into his rooms. While Troup continued to try to divert the crowd, Hamilton led Dr. Cooper, still only partly dressed, over the college fence and down to the bank of the Hudson. Cooper's account described how he, with "my faithful pupil by my side" worked his way northward along the Hudson under cover of darkness until by morning they had reached "The good Palemon's cot," which was apparently the house of Cooper's friend Peter Stuyvesant.[9] Inasmuch as King's was near what are now Church and Barclay Streets, and Stuyvesant's "cot" was in his mansion at what is now Fifteenth Street and First Avenue, Dr. Cooper and his faithful pupil had made a long hard flight that night. On the next night, Dr. Cooper boarded the British ship *Kingfisher* under command of Captain James Montague, which sailed for Bristol on May 25. On the first anniversary of his deliverance by Hamilton, Dr. Cooper celebrated the "heaven-directed youth's" exploit in a poem published in the *Gentleman's Magazine of London:*

STANZAS WRITTEN ON THE EVENING OF THE
10TH OF MAY, 1776.
By an Exile from America.

The mob was at the gate
When straight, a heaven-directed youth,
Whom oft my lessons led to truth,

And honour's sacred shrine,
Advancing quick before the rest
With trembling tongue my ear addresst,

Yet sure in voice divine,
Awake! Awake! The storm is high,—
This instant rouse,—this instant fly,—
The next may be too late. . . .

Some say that the education available at one good Ivy League college is much like that of another. Others, Princeton alumni, may insist that Hamilton might have made more of himself if like themselves he had not been turned down at Old Nassau. But aristocratic flexibility at King's had made the special exception for him that Princeton denied, thus setting a precedent for wise exercises of discretion for particular cases that college registrars still ignore at their peril.

If Princeton's trustees had agreed with President Witherspoon and admitted Alexander to Princeton, his after-career would probably have been quite different, as would the history of New York and that of the United States.

Princeton early caught and sustained the revolutionary spirit; but there, fifty miles away from the metropolis, Hamilton would have missed the stirring public events in New York City, in which, as a student at King's, he would play a spectacular part. He would have made valuable friends at Princeton, but not of the same men who became his faithful corps of allies throughout all his later life. After Princeton he might have settled down as a successful New Jersey lawyer, perhaps commuting to New York City like his Elizabethtown friends Livingston and Boudinot, returning home at night to a squire's slippered ease. Instead, New York City became his home for life, both night and day. Another quarter century of intense, sometimes feverish activity centered on New York City would pass before he could finally settle at The Grange as a would-be squire to imitate the Livingstons of Liberty Hall and the Boudinots of Boxwood Hall. But he did not build The Grange as a visible monument to success. It was among other things a consolation for disappointment that the presidency would forever be beyond reach of his efforts, no matter how intense and feverish they might be.

Princeton's refusal to allow Hamilton to enter upon a speeded-up course of study after King's entrance requirements had sent him to Elizabethtown for a year of preparation had turned him back again to New York City. While he was an honor student at King's, his first recorded public speaking engagement was facing down the angry mob in the blazing torchlight, with Robert Troup at his side, to hold back the mob trying to force the college's entrance gates. He agreed with the revolutionary political goals of the mob whose violence he resisted, and he opposed the politics of Cooper and the college he sought to protect. King's College was spared an early trashing. Not long afterward, King's quietly changed its name to Columbia and aligned its political stance to reflect more closely the politics of its students Troup and Hamilton.

All of which shows the vital importance of strict college entrance requirements.

4

TO FREE THE SLAVES HELD THRALL BY THE *ASIA*'S GUNS

ALL MEN HAVE ONE COMMON ORIGINAL . . . ONE COMMON RIGHT.
NO REASON CAN BE ASSIGNED WHY ONE MAN SHOULD EXERCISE
ANY POWER OR PREEMINENCE OVER HIS FELLOW CREATURES
MORE THAN ANY OTHER; UNLESS THEY HAVE VOLUNTARILY
VESTED HIM WITH IT.

—*A Friend to America,* 1774

The restless surging revolutionary mobs like the one Hamilton[1] and Troup
had faced down at the King's College gates while President Myles Cooper made
good his escape to the safety of the British sloop of war *Kingfisher* were
running down an enemies' list known as the "odious six." Another member of
the "odious six" was James Rivington, the publisher of the New York *Gazetteer,*
the best-written and most widely read New York newspaper of the time. He
published the views of both loyalists and revolutionaries, but his loyalist, or at
least conservative, leanings were not in much doubt. To New York revolutionary
mobs, as with mobs in general, anyone who was not enthusiastically with them
in all circumstances was against them and an enemy. Cooper having eluded

them, the mobs threatened to break in to Rivington's print shop and London bookstore on Hanover Square and seize the odious publisher. Rivington fled and joined Cooper for a while as a refugee aboard the *Kingfisher*. Just before she sailed, he returned ashore to try to keep his free press publishing for as much longer as the zealots of the revolutionary mobs would let him—this was only as long as the mobs' fear of British naval guns could preserve his press from destruction when it published opinions that differed from the revolutionary party line.

As long as British naval guns kept Wall Street and Hanover Square covered, there would be reasonable assurance of order and security for Rivington's press to continue to publish the views of citizens like Cooper and the Reverend Samuel Seabury, who criticized the idea of independence, the Continental Association, the Continental Congress, and all who favored them. Rivington would also remain free to publish the views of collegians like Hamilton, who favored independence, the Continental Association, and the Continental Congress. Cooper, Rivington, and Hamilton agreed on only one thing: they deplored the mob violence stirred up to a large extent by the powerful pamphlets that each of them wrote and Rivington published.

Unlike King's College on the western ridge of the island, Rivington's print shop and bookstore in Hanover Square were well within range and under cover of British naval guns mounted on warships moored in the East River. The sailing of the *Kingfisher* with President Cooper aboard did not much weaken this domination. The huge British battleship *Asia* remained at anchor just off the foot of Wall Street. Her high-riding, thick-planked hull and her skyscraping masts and spars towered above all the other vessels that could be seen at the ends of the streets that ran down to the margins of the island.

Sixty-four cannons, 32 on each side, glowered from even rows of gunports that punctuated the *Asia*'s high sides. New Yorkers knew that their wood-framed city was fatally vulnerable to fire and that the *Asia*'s spacious ammunition lockers were well stocked with powder and shot. They were also painfully aware that they had sent almost all of their own powder and shot—a thousand pounds of gunpowder—to Boston in June to help rearm the revolutionary cause there after the battles of Lexington, Concord, and Bunker Hill.

An even more important purpose of New York's gift to Boston was symbolic —it was an attempt to overcome the suspicions that prevailed throughout the other 12 colonies that New Yorkers lacked deep commitment to the revolutionary cause. Leaving themselves without powder and shot of their own also made it easier for New Yorkers to excuse themselves for offering so little effective resistance to remaining in thrall like slaves to the threat of the *Asia*'s guns. It helped to explain why they confined their noisy and spectacular revolutionary heroics to popular but nondangerous targets like the college president and the publisher of a free *Gazetteer*.

To the king and his ministers in Whitehall, to the other imperial powers of Europe, and to everyone else in the world abroad whose views were of any consequence, British domination of New York City by naval and military power based on a battleship or two and a few support vessels in New York harbor symbolized continuing effective British dominion and control over all 13 North American colonies.

Occasional British setbacks at less strategic points on the colonial periphery like Lexington, Concord, and Bunker Hill chipped away at, but did not destroy, the overriding significance of the imperial fact and symbolism of control of New York City. During the year and a half before Hamilton faced down armed revolutionary mobs at the King's College gates and Rivington's print shop in May of 1775, his efforts had contributed as much as any man's to undermining British control of New York and to whipping up the passions of the mobs he tried to face down.

When he sailed up New York Bay in the *Half Moon,* searching for the Northwest Passage and dreaming of a vast fur trade with the Iroquois the summer of 1609, Henry Hudson claimed the newly discovered empire extending beyond Fort Orange at Albany for the United Netherlands and his employers, the Dutch East India Company. In 1626, Peter Minuit bought Manhattan Island from "the wild men" for "the value of sixty guilders." But these realities did not prevent Charles II from claiming New Netherlands as a British province and granting it to his brother James, the duke of York and Albany, as lord proprietor. The lord proprietor appointed Richard Nicolls to organize an expedition to conquer New Amsterdam, and when Nicolls had sailed up the harbor and trained his guns on the little city huddled below what is now Wall Street, Peter Stuyvesant, under the British guns, surrendered the city without a fight on September 8, 1664. New Amsterdam became New York, and Fort Orange became Fort Albany. From then on a British expeditionary force based on New York harbor had commanded all continental reaches and marches between and beyond.

Although a Dutch fleet briefly recaptured New York in 1673, the Treaty of Westminster in February 1704 extinguished Dutch title. The English retook possession, having relearned the lesson that a shipborne expeditionary force in New York harbor could control the city and make possible dominion over the heart of the whole continent, if not the straits leading to China.

For more than a century and a half Britain had made a heavy investment in winning and holding New York as the centerpiece and strategic key to all her American colonial possessions. At New York City she would demonstrate her celebrated imperial tenacity by holding on longer than anywhere else in the colonies.

Long afterward, writing to Thomas Jefferson on August 24, 1815, John Adams said that the real revolution in America occurred "in the minds of the people" between 1760 and 1775, before a drop of blood was shed at Lexington. In 1761, when Paxton, the collector of customs at Boston, had petitioned the court for "writs of assistance" that would enable customs officers to enter homes and warehouses in the exercise of their duty, James Otis made a dramatic plea based on the English legal axiom that "an Englishman's house is his castle." John Adams said that "Then and there the child independence was born."

The year 1763 had seemed to be another pivot point in relations between England and its American colonies. Up to then the colonies had, in effect, enjoyed home rule, with no cause for complaint, but the end of the Seven Years' War against France brought an enormous increase in the British war debt and the feeling in Parliament that the colonies should help pay it. The ministers of George III began taxing the colonies as never before. There was outrage in America.

The Sugar Act of 1764 prohibited trade with the French and British West Indies, and the Stamp Act of 1765 forced colonists to buy stamps to affix to papers, legal documents, printed material, licenses, and other material, even packs of cards and dice. Colonials as different in viewpoint as James Otis of Massachusetts, Christopher Gadsden of South Carolina, and John Dickinson of Pennsylvania and also various colonial legislatures denounced it. John Adams raised the issue of taxation without representation: "We have always understood it to be a grand and fundamental principle of the Constitution that no free man should be subject to any tax to which he has not given his own consent." Radicals and conservatives were united on this point. The Sons of Liberty marched to protest the outrages, tarred and feathered collectors, and burned down their houses. At the climax of the uproar, delegations from nine of the colonies had met in New York in 1765 at the so-called Stamp Act Congress, the precursor of the First Continental Congress. There it was resolved that people not represented in Parliament could not be taxed by Parliament because such a tax was against natural law. In those days New York had been the leading colony in the revolutionary cause.

A boycott against British goods led to the repeal of the Stamp Act in 1766; the next year the Townshend Acts put taxes on glass, lead, paints, paper, and tea; British troops were sent in to quiet the unrest; and in 1770, when a platoon of frightened British soldiers, taunted by a Boston mob, fired into it and killed five people, the outrage lived in infamy as the Boston Massacre. Another boycott led to a repeal of most of these acts—except for the tax on tea—and all of a sudden tea became the symbol of British tyranny. The colonists drank tea, cup upon cup a day, until Benjamin Franklin wondered if the cheap tea being brought in by the East India Company "is sufficient to overcome the patriotism of an American."

During the decade leading up to the Boston Tea Party, New Yorkers had worked with colleagues in the other 12 colonies in raising objections to British policy through the Continental Association. As in the other colonies, a Provincial Congress had sprung up in New York, which served both as a provincial legislature and a provincial executive parallel to, in competition with, and often in defiance of the established royal government, which consisted of the royal governor, the lieutenant governor, the governor's appointed Council, and the elected New York Assembly.

After the repeal of the Stamp Act, the English had requested New York to provide supplies for British troops quartered in the city, but the Assembly at first refused to do so. Parliament answered in 1767 by imposing economic reprisals until New York agreed, and in the elections of 1768 and 1769 Tories gained control of the Assembly and passed an act approving the providing of supplies.

From then on the majority of New Yorkers tended to agree that loyalty to the king and loyalty to the Continental Association were not mutually exclusive positions. Some leaned one way; some, the other. Most, like Hamilton, who had heard all sides in the several circles he frequented at King's College, agreed that the extremists on both sides were wrong. The Provincial Congress, which leaned toward independence, was dominated by merchants, lawyers, and men of property like William Livingston and Elias Boudinot. Such men had become active in the radical movement for independence partly for conservative reasons: they thought it would be wiser and safer to serve as delegates and look out for their interests than to sit back and leave them to the irrational mercies of the Sons of Liberty and mobs like those that attacked King's College's gates in May of 1775.

John Church Hamilton confirmed that his father had previously formed and entertained "strong prejudices on the ministerial side" of the controversy, "until he became convinced by the superior force of the arguments in favor of the colonial claims." The catalytic event that drove home the superior arguments was the pretended violence of a peaceful symbolic act. Hamilton's son writes that the enthusiasm that finally led Hamilton to make a public stand in New York for independence was "kindled by a visit to Boston a short time after the destruction of the tea" on December 16, 1773.

At a public meeting on that day, Samuel Adams had urged that three ships bearing cargoes of tea moored at Griffin's Fort in Boston harbor be made to return without landing the tea. At the close of the meeting he cried, "This meeting can do nothing more to save the country!" Whereupon a group of proper Bostonians, disguised unconvincingly as Indians, went to the wharf, boarded the vessels, opened their tea chests, and threw the tea into the waters of Boston harbor. The group was entirely orderly. They carried out a radical act in a conservative manner so that it could not be passed off by the royal government as an isolated act of a violent minority. Such a deliberate provocation would force the royal government to act unless it were prepared to forfeit all pretence to authority. The British were not prepared to do so. They closed the port of Boston in May of 1774 and sent in more troops to preserve order, fully aware that this would mean the commercial ruin of the city.

The peaceful and orderly symbolic mode of expressing protest and the avoidance of meaningless violence were what impressed Hamilton most. His son writes, "Excited by the high tone" that prevailed in Boston, Hamilton "directed his attention to the leading topics of this great controversy." On his return to New York, his son points out, Hamilton "enlisted warmly on the side of America" and gave "early and public pledge of his devotion to her cause. A short time only elapsed before he hastened to redeem it."

During the decade before Alexander Hamilton arrived in New York, men like Samuel Adams and Patrick Henry in Massachusetts and Virginia had become famous for publicly advocating an immediate revolutionary confrontation with Britain. They had remained at large, but their counterpart in New York, Alexander McDougall, who would become Hamilton's patron in revolutionary politics, had been jailed by the British as a revolutionary firebrand. Under the *Asia*'s guns, it was much more risky and dangerous to be a revolutionary in New York than elsewhere.

Of all the colonies, New York, as a result of her geography, history, commercial ties to Europe, and exposure to the fiercest of the Indian tribes on her frontiers, was the colony where popular resistance to the idea of revolution against British rule would persist most naturally. All this was so even without the immediate possibility of being burned to death if revolutionary demonstrations brought on a conflagration ignited by interdicting cannonfire from the *Asia*'s big guns.

By 1774 in any of the other 12 colonies, a 17-year-old like Alexander Hamilton would have been too late to make much of a mark as a writer and speaker for the revolutionary cause. But in New York loyalists to England were numerous, and the Anglican church, and the *Asia*, remained powerful influences. The Sons of Liberty and other activist revolutionary groups like those that had sought to break down the college gates and seize President Cooper were still a minority. A large group of moderates favored the revolutionary cause, but dissociated themselves from the violent tactics of the Sons of Liberty. Another large group was undecided and ready to swing whichever way the political winds might blow. There remained a vacuum into which a young man like Hamilton, who had recently tasted the revolutionary ferment in Boston, would not be too late to stride.

Though the Boston Tea Party had kindled his revolutionary enthusiasm, the spark had been struck in him earlier.

"A Defense of the Destruction of the Tea" is the way Hamilton described to his son two pieces of his authorship, which were published in Holt's *The New York Journal,* or *General Advertiser,* one on December 16, 1773, over the pen name of Monitor, and the other on February 24, 1774, under the pen name of Americanus. With characteristic energy, force, and wide range of allusion, his "Defense" combines a reasoned argument and citation of authorities with a staccato, impassioned, emotional appeal.

Americanus cried that "the British *Parliament* has no more right of legislation here than it has in the empire of the Great Mogul." However, the case as to His Majesty is widely different;[4] . . . the very charters which confirm our liberty reserve to him a sovereign authority." The British colonies in America are "distinct independent states," and admitted to be so by Charles II. The Acts of Parliament are "an unwarrantable exercise of . . . arbitrary power unknown to the British Constitution" insofar as they are intended to bind persons "out of the realm" like the colonists.

Hamilton's arguments were basic to the thinking of the American Revolution. Many of them came from John Locke. Happiness and pleasure is the pursuit of all people, Locke had written in his *Essay concerning Human Understanding* (1690). In the original state of nature, all men were equal and independent.

The state was formed by social contract and should be guided by natural law. Each man has a right to the product of his labor. One of the natural rights to which man is born is the right of private ownership of property. If a government abuses its power, it forfeits its legitimacy. Revolution is then justified.

Jean-Jacques Rousseau, who had insisted that "Man was born free," was also concerned with the doctrine of human rights. He had pointed out that the general will of the majority was the paramount factor in establishing reciprocal rights, duties, privileges, and responsibilities. And Montesquieu, in his *Spirit of Laws* (1748), said that natural laws derive from man's being, whereas positive laws are decreed by legislatures; so laws must be adapted to the nature of a country, and no country should be forced to obey arbitrary laws.

In this cause Alexander Hamilton demonstrated that his true literary medium was not satirical doggerel nor fugitive Arcadian lyrics, but the now all-but-lost art of political pamphleteering. The greatest years of this now extinct genre probably coincided with the period of Hamilton's political career.

Americanus applauded the proposal of the Virginia Burgesses to form a union of counsel for opposition. He recommended "an annual congress, as tending to greater intimacy of union." Such a congress, he said, should meet in the metropolis of the most central colony, Hamilton's own New York.

Pamphlets like those of Hamilton and many others raised clouds of political steam that condensed and rained not only on New York but also on the most distant colonies to the north and south. They conjured up heady visions of rebellion, freedom, tax-free commercial profits, and an occasional whiff of anarchy. All contributed to rousing the passions of the revolutionary mobs to the anger that Hamilton himself had to face to head off violence.

They also helped rouse New York to reenact her own versions of the Boston Tea Party only a few months later. On April 18, 1774, when Captain Lockyer's ship *Nancy* arrived with tea at Sandy Hook, a New York citizens committee would not permit her to unload. Captain Chambers of the *London* at first denied that he had eighteen boxes of fine tea aboard his ship and claimed that they were his own private venture. Not to be put off, citizens dressed as Mohawk Indians gathered "to do their Duty at a proper Hour." Before they could put on their masquerade and makeup, other more riotous citizens in mufti broke open the cases and dumped the tea into the river, leaving Captain Chambers glad to escape tealess and taxless with his life.

Parliament and the king's ministers retaliated with escalating harshness. Lord North pushed five bills through Parliament in 1774 that became known as the Intolerable Acts or the Coercive Acts. The charter of Massachusetts was all but revoked. British troops could be quartered without provincial consent. Agents acting for the Crown could be taken to England for trial. The Quebec Act, aimed at keeping Canada loyal to the Crown, gave the Catholics religious freedom and Canada all British territory north of the Ohio River, confirming the westerly encirclement of the seaboard colonies. The Boston Port Bill closed the harbor until such time as the city paid for the tea destroyed at the famous party.

Boston refused to pay. But would the other colonies support her? On June

17, 1774, Samuel Adams called for a meeting of all the colonies. On June 20, Pennsylvania called for a colonial congress to procure relief "for our suffering brethren." On July 6, New York called for a boycott of British goods. On July 26, Virginia decided to stop all British imports. The town of Windham, Connecticut, sent 258 sheep to Boston's relief. South Carolina sent 200 barrels of rice and promised 800 more. In Virginia, Colonel George Washington headed a subscription list, which sent £50.

New York's "honest, loyal and prudent" Committee of 51 insisted that it had the exclusive right to nominate New York's delegates to the First Continental Congress in Philadelphia and that no candidates were to be put up by popular nomination. But this did not satisfy Captain Alexander McDougall and the Sons of Liberty. Some of them organized themselves into a rival Committee of Mechanics, whose membership in fact included Whig-minded citizens of all callings and persuasions. They claimed to be acting in concert with the "true sons" of liberty in Boston. They insisted on taking a much stronger stand for independence than the Committee of 51 would countenance. The Committee of Mechanics demanded a voice in the nomination of delegates to the Continental Congress, but the Committee of 51 voted down the Mechanics' resolution calling for a different slate of nominees, one of whom was Alexander McDougall himself. The Committee of 51 called a meeting of the freeholders to rubber-stamp its nominations for July 7, 1774, at City Hall.

Angered by this direct rebuff to the true sons of liberty, as they felt themselves to be, Alexander McDougall and his Committee of Mechanics called a "Great Meeting in the Fields" for July 6, the day before the public meeting of freeholders. "The Fields" is now City Hall Park, where New York's tallest liberty pole then stood, only three blocks away from King's College.

It is related that Hamilton as a collegian often walked alone under the large trees in Batteau Street, now Dey Street, talking to himself in an undertone while apparently engaged in deep thought, a habit he would continue throughout his life. Perhaps he was rehearsing his lessons for King's, or perhaps he was composing arguments for new pamphlets in behalf of revolution. In any event, one of his friends, Robert Troup, or perhaps Nicholas Fish, fell into conversation with him as the Great Meeting in the Fields was gathering, was struck by the pertinence of his thought and aptness of speech, and urged him, on the spur of the moment, to mount the platform as a speaker that afternoon. Hamilton at first is said to have recoiled. But he began to listen more attentively to the speakers at the meeting. Captain Alexander McDougall, the chairman of the meeting, "fully explained" its purpose. He condemned "the dangerous tendency of the numerous vile arts used by the enemies of America to divide and distress her councils, as well as the misrepresentations of the virtuous intentions of the citizens of this metropolis." He cried that "The liberties of America are in an alarming state."

As a man born among common people at a time when aristocrats tended to prevail, McDougall had become the idol of the patriots, and his revolutionary role made a deep impression on Hamilton's mind. When the British garrison cut down the liberty pole the people had put up eight years before to commemorate repeal of the Stamp Act, the patriots put up a second, and the garrison had cut that one down too. Under McDougall's leadership, citizens held mass meetings and denounced the British soldiers as enemies of the people and put up another new liberty pole, clad and clamped with iron, as a stronger symbol of resistance. This now marked the place where McDougall was addressing the people with Hamilton listening thoughtfully on the fringes of the crowd.

When the Townshend Acts had imposed new taxes on the colonies and given British officers new powers of search and seizure, the New York Assembly under loyalist domination had meekly approved. McDougall was the patriot who published a scornful address contrasting their weakness with the boldness of their predecessors of Stamp Act Congress days, who had refused to accept such indignities, and with their similarly bold counterparts in Massachusetts and South Carolina. When the assembly had voted that McDougall's address, entitled "Son of Liberty to the Betrayed Inhabitants of New York," was "an infamous and seditious libel," only one man had stood up and voted "Nay." It was Philip Schuyler, who five years later would become yet another of Hamilton's great patrons. And when the royal governor, William Tryon, had seized McDougall and arrested him for the libel, McDougall had declared, "I rejoice that I am the first sufferer for liberty since the commencement of our glorious struggles." Tryon had thrown him into prison.

Though no texts of the speeches made at the Great Meeting in the Fields have come down to us, the several speakers would almost certainly have retold the story of McDougall's imprisonment and Schuyler's lone stand in his support for inspirational effect while the great throng and Hamilton listened.

A leading member of the assembly had proposed that McDougall be tortured to extort a recantation from his lips. He refused to be intimidated and replied, "rather than resign the rights and privileges of a British subject, I would suffer my right hand to be cut off at the bar of the house."

Now the charismatic figure of Captain Alexander McDougall was out of prison and presiding as chairman of the Great Meeting in the Fields, near the foot of the new iron-bound liberty pole. Suddenly, he looked in Hamilton's direction and beckoned the young collegian standing at the fringes of the crowd with some of his friends to come to the rostrum to speak. His gesture summoned Alexander Hamilton from the fringes of the crowd into the mainstream of revolutionary history.

Present at The Fields that day to hear and remember the performance of the ardent young champion of colonial liberty were many other men whose names would figure prominently in Hamilton's story: John Lamb, Marinus Willett, John Jay, Isaac Low, James Duane, Philip Livingston, Peter Livingston, John Morin Scott, and many others. Also on hand were hundreds or perhaps several thousand nameless mechanics, students, tradesmen, sailors, blacksmiths, longshoremen, loafers, and drunkards—in short, a whole spectrum of possible New Yorkers. They probably stared in amazement at the boy who sprang to the speaker's stand. His slight frame, fine-featured face, reddish curling hair tied loosely with a ribbon, delicate lawn shirt, lace cuffs and broad-cloth coat, and quick, supple gestures made him look even younger than his 17 years.

From the elevation of the speakers' platform, Hamilton could look out over the three-cornered hats and bare heads and powdered wigs and women's bonnets of the crowd, past the step-gabled houses and church steeples behind them down the cobbled streets, past the cannons on the Battery to the tall masts and spars of men-o'-war like the *Asia* riding at anchor in the harbor.

Overawed a little at first by the panorama before him, he hesitated. But as he began to speak the observations on freedom for the colonies that he had polished and refined in anonymous pamphlets and dinner table argument with like-minded friends like Troup and Fish and opposite-minded friends like President Myles Cooper, his mind warmed to the theme and his confidence returned. His concern was not confined to the New Yorkers before him who listened with curiosity and amazement, but extended to all the people of all the colonies.

No text of his address survives, but he no doubt made use of the same arguments that he was making in the pseudonymous broadsides he was publishing during the same period. He denounced the Boston Port Bill under which "our brethren" are "now suffering in the common cause of these colonies" and called for unity of all America in resisting unconstitutional parliamentary taxation. He urged an agreement "to stop all importation from, and exportation to, Great Britain" till Boston's harbor was unblocked. This "will prove the salvation of North-America and her liberties"; otherwise, "fraud, power, and the most odious oppression, will rise triumphant over right, justice, social happiness, and freedom." There should be a subscription for relief of the port of Boston, and the resolves must be given the widest publication. In the coming congress the deputies from New York must consent in these and "all . . . other measures . . . the congress shall . . . judge advancive of these great objects. . . ." The right to vote for deputies should be broadened, and the counties must choose their own delegates, or else have the right to authorize the city deputies to act for them. Pointing to the oppressions of the mother country, he insisted on the duty of resistance. His manner was impassioned, intense, and fiery, yet contained, clear, and cogent. His matter was pointed, logical, and balanced. Following the admired style of Addison's *Spectator*, he did not use a needless word.

The prospect of a British embargo or even a war with Britain did not alarm him, but his good cheer at the prospect of such a war did not come across as reckless bravado. It was based upon a realistic, Metternichian appraisal of British strengths and weaknesses, faith in the long future of America, and belief that the human desire for freedom was bound to succeed in the end.

Hamilton would point out, as he wrote five months later as the Vindicator of Congress, that the supposed "omnipotence and all sufficiency of Great Britain is altogether visionary. It is notorious that she is oppressed with a heavy national debt, which it requires the utmost policy and economy ever to discharge. Luxury has arrived to a great pitch; and it is a universal maxim that luxury indicates the declension of a state. Her subjects are loaded with the most enormous taxes: all circumstances agree in declaring their distress. The continual immigrations, from Great Britain and Ireland, to the continent, are a glaring symptom, that those kingdoms are a good deal impoverished."

By contrast, the colonies were strong: "these colonies, as they are now settled and peopled, have been the work of near two centuries: they are blessed with every advantage of soil, climate and situation. They have advanced with an almost incredible rapidity. . . . The total and sudden loss of so extensive and lucrative a branch, would . . . produce the most violent effects to a nation that subsists entirely among its commerce."

The colonies would be a military match for the British: "Our numbers are very considerable; the courage of Americans has been tried and proved. Contests for liberty have ever been found the most bloody, implacable and obstinate. The disciplined troops Great Britain can send against us, would be but few, our superiority in number would overbalance our inferiority in discipline. It would be a hard, if not an impracticable task to subjugate us by force.

"We can live without trade of any kind. Food and clothing we have within ourselves."

Indeed, a war could be a blessing in disguise, which would help foster the American domestic manufacturing that Britain's mercantile policy had up to now suppressed: "If by the necessity of the thing, manufacturers should once be established and take root among us, they will pave the way, still more, to the future grandeur and glory of America, and by lessening its need of external commerce, will render it still secure against the encroachments of tyranny."

Looking defiantly out toward the lowering gun ports of the British warships in the harbor, he roused the crowd to applause as he shook his fist defiantly toward them. He called for "waves of rebellion sparkling with fire washing back on the shores of England the wrecks of her power, her wealth and her glory!"

If he wished to find a war, he would do his best to find it here by the side of Captain McDougall and the ironclad liberty pole.

To some in the crowd here was a bolt of revolutionary lightning flashing out of the warm blue evening sky to strike contact with their minds. There was a breathless silence; then murmurous whispers rose from the crowd:

> It is a collegian!
> A collegian!
> It is a collegian!

Not only was he young, but he was also from Dr. Myles Cooper's bastion of loyalist sentiment at King's College. There was a roar of applause. After Captain McDougall had quieted the crowd, nine resolutions going far beyond what the Committee of 51 had proposed were twice read and "being separately put . . . they were passed without one dissentient." The favorable votes owed much to the fervor and reasoning of the young collegian. Next day the Committee of 51 briskly voted to rebuke McDougall and the resolutions adopted at his rump meeting of the day before. The Committee criticized "all such proceedings

... calculated to throw an odium on this committee."

But from this time on, Alexander Hamilton would be publicly identified as one of the more radical champions of liberty from the king for all the colonies. He would win the respect and admiration of all who had heard him at the Great Meeting in the Fields and the active support of most.

No one who had seen and heard Hamilton that day calling for freedom from the platform beside Alexander McDougall as he looked out over the heads of the crowd toward the muzzles of the warships' guns could afterward help feeling much but contempt for charges like those incessantly reiterated by men like Thomas Jefferson that Hamilton was a "monarchist."

From this beginning Hamilton would make the countrywide, continent-wide, American-wide outlook distinctively his own. Never the provincial champion of New York alone, the West Indian, as his friends sometimes called him, rendered his greatest services for the Empire State by putting the interests of the United States of America ahead of hers.

Patrick Henry, George Clinton, and Samuel Adams, in some ways Jefferson too, and others with great ability who played creative roles in the resistance of the colonies placed sectional loyalty first, national unity and constitutional government second, and resisted progress toward Hamiltonian goals. Because the springs of his action did not belong first to New York or the middle states, Hamilton became the first acknowledged leader of a national party.

John Adams described the membership of the first Continental Congress as it convened in Carpenter's Hall in Philadelphia on September 4, 1774 as "one third Whig, another Tory; the rest mongrel." The members moved slowly and carefully. Rebellion against the Crown was not a thing to be taken lightly. Their lives could be at stake. What if General Thomas Gage, commanding the British forces in the colonies, took it into his head to send troops to Philadelphia and arrest the entire Continental Congress for sedition?

Edmund Pendleton and Richard Henry Lee of Virginia argued that the rights of the colonists arose from the law of nature. John Rutledge, on the other hand, insisted that their rights were founded on the British Constitution. John Jay maintained that their rights devolved both from the law of nature and the British Constitution. James Duane of New York agreed with Rutledge, as did Joseph Galloway of Pennsylvania.

Galloway presented a plan calling for the union of the colonies with Great Britain, a thing that had been suggested earlier by William Penn in 1697 and by Benjamin Franklin in 1754. When Duane, Jay, and Rutledge supported the Galloway plan, activists for independence were aghast. Clever backroom maneuvering by Adams and his supporters defeated the proposal by the narrowest of margins—one vote.

But by this one-vote margin the activists for independence seized control. England was notified that unless relief were given, the colonies would boycott all English imports starting December 1, and forbid exports after December 10, 1775. An association was to be formed "in every county, city and town in America ... whose business it shall be attentively to observe the conduct of all persons touching this association." Violations were to be publicly denounced.

A ten-point petition to the king was drawn up, starting with the statement that the colonies "are entitled to life, liberty and property, and they have never ceded to any sovereign power whatever, a right to dispose of either without their consent." Obviously, many ideas from this petition would figure in the Declaration of Independence of the following summer.

Many in New York and elsewhere who were counted as loyalists found much to criticize in British policy toward the colonies. But they sought to limit colonial resistance to petitions and remonstrances to Parliament through established channels to avoid provoking open war. A leading spokesman for such critical loyalists was President Myles Cooper's good friend Samuel Seabury, a missionary and physician who had graduated from Yale in 1748, completed medical training at Edinburgh, been ordained a priest at Fulham Palace, and thereafter filled several assignments before settling in Westchester County as an Episcopal rector. As a physician, minister, and teacher, Samuel Seabury ministered to bodies, minds, and souls in many different roles. Still another of his roles was that of the rustic country bumpkin who is shrewder than city folk, a perennial American favorite. On November 16, 1774, assuming the name and style of a Westchester farmer, Seabury issued a pamphlet called "Free Thoughts on Congress," which provided Hamilton with an occasion to spread his revolutionary views to a wider audience than he had commanded from the platform beside Alexander McDougall at the Great Meeting in the Fields.

He had many friends and mentors who helped him, but one of Hamilton's special talents was his ability to make use of opponents' efforts to put him down, as platforms or stepping-stones from which to spring to some of the most spectacular successes of his rise. The pamphlets he wrote as the self-appointed refuter of the Westchester Farmer are two of the earliest and best examples of this talent in action.

The Episcopal clergy looked to the monarch as the head of both church and state, opposed every attempt to impair the royal prerogative, and had long been conspicuous as Britain's most zealous supporters in the colony. They were accomplished scholars and able writers like Dr. Myles Cooper, and of this able group Samuel Seabury was probably the ablest.

As A. W. Farmer from rural Westchester, Seabury sought, with much sly art, to turn the revolutionary turmoil on itself to save the status quo.

The full 90-word title of his pamphlet "Free Thoughts on Congress" gives the flavor of the performance and the occasion: "Free Thoughts on the Proceedings of the Continental Congress, Held at Philadelphia Sept. 5, 1774: Wherein Their Errors are exhibited, their Reasoning Confuted, and the fatal Tendency of their Non-Importation, Non-Exportation, and Non-Consumption Measures, are laid open to the plainest Understandings; and the Only means pointed out for Preserving and Securing our present Happy Constitution: In a letter to the Farmers and other inhabitants of North America in General, and to those of the Province of New York in particular. By a Farmer. Hear me, for I Will speak!" It is signed A. W. Farmer.

Seabury subtly identified freedom of the colonists with the rights of each individual province. He urged all colonists to put their trust in the magnanimity of Great Britain rather than in colonial union and attempts at economic coercion. He ridiculed the "confounded combustion" caused by resentment of a trifling tax on tea. The Continental Congress was the real enemy of farmers: Farmers "had better trust to the mercy of a Turk" than rely on the honor of merchants not to exact unconscionable profits in a restricted market. Will you submit to them, Seabury asks, and answers: "By him that made me, I will not. No, if I must be enslaved, let it be by a king at least, and not by a parcel of upstart lawless committee men. If I must be devoured, let me be devoured by the jaws of a lion, and not gnawed to death by rats and vermin." He knows enough about sheep to remind Congress that the breed cannot be improved by keeping wethers. He raises the loyalist-dominated New York General Assembly to a higher plane than either the informal, poorly attended Continental Congress or New York's revolutionary Provincial Congress. Peace may be restored if farmers will "renounce all dependence on Congresses, and committees . . . Your constitutional representatives . . . are the true, and legal defenders of your rights. . . ."

He anticipates, as a fearful consequence of Congress's actions, the closing of the port of New York, and the suspension of justice. He ridicules the inconsistency of a Congress that, pretending to protect the liberties of the people, has sanctioned the invasion of private rights and assigned inquisitorial powers to committees to enforce fruitless agreements.

Too shrewd to take a stand forthrightly by the side of king and Parliament across the water, Seabury used the tactic of trying to divide, divert, and set the revolutionaries to squabbling with one another. "Free Thoughts on Congress" became the textbook of Tory arguments. Friends of the provincial government extolled its wisdom, circulated it widely, and let it be known that it had official sanction, all of which enraged the Whigs. They resented the clergy's devotion to the Crown and their efforts to introduce an episcopacy to America. Some demanded that the author and publisher of "Free Thoughts" be indicted for treason. At a meeting in one county Seabury's pamphlet was tarred and feathered and nailed to the pillory amid shouts of rage from the mob.

Revolutionary excitement rose. Here was Hamilton's biggest target of opportunity. On December 8, 1774, Rivington's New York *Gazetteer* announced the first publication of one of the great pamphleteer's earliest and greatest pamphlets:

> In the Press, and in a few Days will be published, By James Rivington, A Full Vindication of the Measures of the Continental Congress . . . To the Farmers of the Province of New York.

Rivington presumed that this answer "will meet with a gracious reception at the hands of every reader who has expressed disapprobation to the Free Thoughts of Farmer A. W."

The full title of Hamilton's pamphlet is "A Full Vindication of the Measures of Congress, from the Calumnies of their Enemies: In Answer to A Letter, Under the signature of A. W. Farmer. Whereby his Sophistry is exposed, his Cavils confuted, his Artifices detected, and his Wit ridiculed; in a General Address to the Inhabitants of America, and a Particular Address to the Farmers of the Province of New York. Veritas magna est. & proevalebit. Truth is powerful, and will prevail." Dated December 15, 1774, Hamilton's "Vindication" appeared only a month after Seabury's "Free Thoughts on Congress."

Hamilton saw beneath Seabury's homespun shrewdness the same deep purpose that underlay British policy as formulated by Lord North, the prime minister: to break up and prevent union of the colonies, to divide and conquer, and continue to rule.

With a sure instinct for the marrow of an argument, Hamilton as the Vindicator of Congress plunges straight to the heart of the matter, summarizing his opponent's arguments in a way that destroys them. Anticipating a device of Thomas Paine's, he appeals strongly to the "Common Sense" of his readers:

> Whence arises that violent antipathy they seem to entertain, not only to the natural rights of mankind; but to common sense and to common modesty. That they are enemies to the natural rights of mankind is manifest, because they wish to see one part of their species enslaved by another. That they have an invincible aversion to common sense is apparent in many respects. They endeavor to persuade us that the absolute sovereignty of parliament does not imply our absolute slavery; that it is a Christian duty to submit to be plundered of all we have, merely because some of our fellow subjects are wicked enough to require it of us; that slavery, so far from being a great evil, is a great blessing; and even, that our contest with Britain is founded entirely upon the petty duty of 3 pence per pound on East India tea; whereas the whole world knows, it is built upon this interesting question, whether the inhabitants of Great Britain have a right to dispose of the lives and properties of the inhabitants of America, or not.

Hamilton knew the slave trade well. His eloquent words about slavery were echoed a year and a half later in the Declaration of Independence and three-quarters of a century later in a famous speech of Abraham Lincoln's:

> The only distinction between freedom and slavery consists in this: in the former state, a man is governed by the laws to which he has given his consent, either in person, or by his representative; in the latter, he is governed by the will of another. In the one case his life and property are his own, in the other, they depend upon the pleasure of a master. No man in his senses can hesitate in choosing to be free, rather than a slave.

A man has no right to be master of another, any more than any man was born to be a slave, said Hamilton as the vindicator: "All men have one common original; they participate in one common nature, and consequently have one common right. No reason can be assigned why one man should exercise any power, or preeminence over his fellow creatures more than another; unless they have voluntarily vested him with it."

As Hamilton saw it, this profound truth applied directly to the dispute with Britain: "Since then, Americans have not by any act of theirs impowered the British Parliament to make laws for them, it follows they can have no just authority to do it."

This elevated the dispute from a tax evasion case over three pence per pound duty on tea to a question of the fundamental rights of man. His formulation of the issue leads straight on to the opening words of the Declaration of Independence.

Having known human chattel slavery intimately, Hamilton did not leave his condemnation of slavery at the abstract, metaphorical level. With his usual prescience, he spoke of it in human terms, the way a fervent abolitionist might have seen it three-quarters of a century later; he foresaw that it would lead to the "hideous train of calamities" that it did:

> Were not the disadvantage of slavery too obvious to stand in need of it, I might enumerate and describe the hideous train of calamities, inseparable from it. I might show that it is fatal to religion and morality; that it tends to debase the mind, and corrupts its noblest springs of action. I might show, that it relaxes the sinews of industry, clips the wings of commerce, and introduces misery and indigence in every shape . . . The life of the subject is often sported with; and the fruits of his daily toil are consumed in oppressive taxes, that serve to gratify the ambition, avarice and lust of his superiors. Every court minion riots in the spoils of the honest laborer, and despises the hand by which he is fed. The page of history is replete with instances that loudly warn us to beware of slavery.

Imperial Britain was like Imperial Rome before her. "Rome was the nurse of freedom. She was celebrated for her justice and lenity; but in what manner did she govern her dependent provinces? They were made the continual scene of rapine and cruelty." This demonstrated "how little confidence is due to the wisdom and equity of the most exemplary nations."

To Hamilton, religious freedom went hand in hand with personal and political freedom. He denounced "that unparalleled stride of power" by which "popery" had been established in Canada as a result of the Quebec bill: "How can any of you be sure you would have the free enjoyment of your religion long? Would you put your religion in the power of any set of men living? Remember civil and religious liberty always go together, if the foundation of the one be sapped, the other will fall. Reflect upon the situation of Canada . . . The Romish faith is made the established religion of the land, and his majesty is placed at the head of it. The free exercise of the Protestant faith depends upon the pleasure of the governor and council."

Besides freedom of person and religion, another indispensable safeguard of true freedom was the right of trial by jury and habeas corpus, rights that were now denied in Canada: "The subject is divested of the right of trial by jury, and an innocent man may be imprisoned his whole life, without being able to obtain any trial at all." And military encirclement now threatened the colonies: "The Parliament has annexed to it the vast tracts of land that surround all the colonies . . . They may as well establish popery in New York and the other colonies as they did in Canada. They had no more right to do it there than here.

"Your lives, your property, your religion are all at stake."

Hamilton foresaw, finally, a continental union of much greater extent than the original 13 colonies. Indeed, his vision went beyond the reality of our own time 200 years later: "The Farmer, I am inclined to hope, builds too much upon the present disunion of Canada, Georgia, the Floridas, the Mississippi, and Nova Scotia from other colonies. A little time, I trust, will awaken them from their slumber. I please myself with a flattering prospect, that they will, ere long, unite in one indissoluble chain with the rest of the colonies."

At the close of *A Full Vindication*, Hamilton steps down from the patriot's platform and puts his arm around his countrymen's shoulder to speak in a folksy political style that matches A. W. Farmer's. He addresses himself in particular to the farmers of New York, as "My good countrymen," saying disarmingly that "I am one of your number, or connected with you in interest more than with any other branch of the community. I love to speak the truth and would scorn to prejudice you in favor of what I have to say, by taking upon me a fictitious character as other people have done. I can venture to assure you, the true writer of the pieces signed A. W. Farmer, is not in reality a Farmer. He is some ministerial emissary, that has assumed the name to deceive you."

The Vindicator stooped to no such cheap deception:

> I do not address you in particular, because I have any greater connection with you, than with other people. I despise all false pretensions, and mean arts. Let those have recourse to dissimulation and falsehood, who can't defend their cause without it. 'Tis my maxim to let the plain naked truth speak for itself; and if men won't listen to it, 'tis their own fault; they must be contented to suffer for it. I am neither merchant, nor farmer . . . 'Tis the farmer who is most oppressed in all countries where slavery prevails . . . are you ready to own the English farmers for your masters? . . . You had rather die, than submit to it.

He opposes Parliament's levying a carriage tax on unrepresented taxpayers: "Would you not think it very hard to pay 10 sterling per annum, for every wheel of your waggons and other carriages, a shilling or two for every pane of glass in your houses, and two or three shillings for every one of your hearths?

"The people of England would pull down the Parliament house, if their present heavy burdens were not transferred from them to you. Indeed there is no reason to think the Parliament would have any inclination to spare you: the contrary is evident."

Sweethearts and farmers' daughters played a large part in a farmer's pleasures: "Nay, I don't know but they would find means to tax you for every child you got, and for every kiss your daughters received from their sweethearts, and God knows, that would soon ruin you."

Hamilton ridicules A. W. Farmer for a jest he had made about sheep, when he cries "Let me ask you brother farmers, which of you would keep a flock of sheep, barely, for the sake of their wool?" He answered himself, "Not one of you. If you cannot sell your sheep to advantage, at a certain age, you cannot keep them to any profit." Hamilton snorts, "he thinks, because he calls you brother farmers, that he can cajole you into believing what he pleases; but you are not the fools he takes you for."

The Farmer had cried, "tell me not of delegates, congresses, committees, mobs, riots, insurrections, associations, a plague on them all. Give me the steady uniform unbiassed influence of the courts of justice." Hamilton roars back in rebuttal, rising to his rhetorical climax: "I say, tell me not of the British Commons, Lords, ministry, ministerial tools, placemen, pensioners, parasites. I scorn to let my life and property depend on the pleasure of any of them." Hamilton then enumerates some foundation stones for the constitutional republic he will later help construct: "Give me the steady, uniform, unshaken security of constitutional freedom; give me the right to be tried by a jury of my own neighbors, and to be taxed by my own representatives only."

Regard for law and orderly legal processes was one of Hamilton's ruling passions, but his most basic one was the cause of human liberty: "I would die to preserve the law upon a solid foundation; but take away liberty, and the foundation is destroyed." Then "The shadow may remain, but the substance will be gone."

Having risen to this florid climax, Hamilton subsides again to a homespun mode: "When a man grows warm, he has a confounded itch for swearing. I have been going, above twenty times, to rap out an oath, *by him that made me*, but I have checked myself, with this reflection, that it is rather *unmannerly*, to treat him that made us with so much freedom."

He closes with a benediction that the Reverend Samuel Seabury himself could hardly have improved upon. Indeed Hamilton may have heard it from Seabury himself at daily services at King's or at President Myles Cooper's dinner table:

> May God give you wisdom to see what is your true interest, and inspire you with becoming zeal for the cause of virtue and mankind. Signed,
>
> A Friend to America

As the vindicator of Congress, Hamilton expresses strong suspicion that he knows who the Westchester Farmer is and that he is no farmer. As every lawyer knows, the best way to sharpen, bone, and polish arguments is to play devil's advocate with an opponent as long as he will permit it. Hamilton had probably met Dr. Seabury's arguments and Dr. Seabury himself over wine glasses or teacups at Myles Cooper's apartment at King's. Hamilton's son reports that Dr. Cooper had tendered Hamilton "a most liberal offer" if he would "consent to write in behalf of the ministery," instead of for its opponents. "It is unnecessary to add," his son adds, "that it was rejected." But the extraordinarily high quality of the vindicator's reasoning and writing must owe much to the polishing and honing that went on in the rooms at King's.

The Tories could not let *A Full Vindication of Congress by a Friend to America* stand unanswered; so Samuel Seabury took up the ministerial pen once again. His reply to *A Full Vindication* is known as "A View of the Controversy." Dated December 24, 1774, it was not published by James Rivington until January 5, 1775.

Hamilton, in turn, replied to Seabury for the second time on February 23, 1775, in Rivington's *Gazetteer* with "The Farmer Refuted, or A More Impartial and Comprehensive View of the Dispute between Great Britain and the Colonies, intended as a further vindication of the Congress: In answer to a letter from A. W. Farmer, entitled 'A View of the Controversy'. . . ."

Hamilton's reply to Samuel Seabury, now commonly called *The Farmer Refuted*, pours an even more powerful torrent of pith and vinegar on enemies of the revolution than *A Full Vindication* had done. Hamilton begins what he calls his "More Impartial and Comprehensive View of the Dispute" at a less impartial, more narrowly partisan pitch: "Notwithstanding, I am naturally of a grave and phlegmatic disposition, your curious epistle has been the source of abundant merriment to me. The spirit that breathes throughout is so rancorous, illiberal and imperious: the argumentative part of it so puerile and fallacious: the misrepresentation of facts so palpable and flagrant: the criticism so illiterate, trifling and absurd: the conceits so low, sterile and splenetic, that I will venture to pronounce it one of the most ludicrous performances, which has been exhibited to public view, during all the present controversy."

He compliments his adversary on having "every accomplishment of a polemical writer" which may "serve to dazzle and mislead superficial and vulgar minds; a peremptory dictatorial air, a pert vivacity of expression, an inordinate passion for conceit, and a noble distain of being fettered by the laws of truth." When the occasion called for it, Hamilton himself knew how to deploy all these same skills except possibly the last when writing in the polemical genre. This passage can stand as a self-critique as good as any other to describe Hamilton's own accomplishments, and failings, in the form.

He lashes the Farmer with iambic pentameters supplied by Alexander Pope:

> Fools and witlings "will" ev'ry sentence raise
> And wonder, with a foolish face of praise.

The "Farmer" had stung Hamilton by writing of him that "If you seldom sink into meanness of diction, you never soar into that brilliancy of thought; nor, even with the help of Johnson's dictionary, into that classical elegance of expression which is absolutely necessary for the arduous attempt of ridiculing wit."

Hamilton lamely fired back that "I aimed at nothing more than justness of thought. I addressed myself to the judgment, not to the imagination. In works, where fancy is predominant, as is the case with yours, there is a better opportunity for displaying brilliancy of thought, than where reason presides and directs." Hamilton rarely admitted to lack of proficiency in anything. Here as he admits to lack of "imagination" to write "works where fancy is predominant," there is little reason to doubt the accuracy of his self-assessment. A lack of "imagination" for writing "where fancy is predominant" is an important clue to the answer to the deepest mystery of the story of his tragic life.

Twentieth-century minds blurred by picture images experience strain following the kind of close-grained argumentation over abstract political issues that the American public followed avidly in Hamilton's day. It was an age when the printed word was the most popular and exciting form of public communication. Nonetheless it is still worth the extra effort to follow the intense, precise, carefully wrought linear arguments of this Founding Father to the reward of a deeper understanding of the great issues that divided the colonists. To fail to make the effort when reading the story of a great political man in a great political era would be like trying to understand a fish without understanding the sea he swims in.

For example, Hamilton attacked the Farmer for the heresy of denying the existence of natural law. Most eighteenth-century men like Hamilton shared a common belief in natural law, something that is unknown to most men today. "There is so strong a familitude between your political principles and those maintained by Mr. Hobbes that, in judging from them, a person might very easily mistake you for a disciple of his," Hamilton charged. Hobbes held, as the Westchester Farmer did, that man in a state of nature "was, then, perfectly free from all restraint of *law* and *government*. Moral obligation," according to Hobbes, "is derived from the introduction of civil society; and there is no virtue, but what is purely artificial, the mere contrivance of politicians, for the maintenance of social intercourse. . . . He disbelieved the existence of an intelligent superintending principle, who is the governor, and will be the final judge of the universe."

Hamilton believed the contrary. He was certain that most other enlightened men of his century agreed with him: "Good and wise men, in all ages," Hamilton averred, "have supposed, that the deity, from the relations we stand in, to himself and to each other, has constituted an eternal and immutable law, which is, indispensably, obligatory upon all mankind, prior to any human institution whatever."

"This is what is called the 'law of nature,' which, being coeval with mankind, and dictated by God Himself, is, of course, superior in obligation to any other. It is binding all over the globe, in all countries, and at all times. No human laws are of any validity, if contrary to this; and such of them as are valid, derive all their authority, mediately or immediately, from this original." For this sweeping proposition Hamilton cites no theologian or philosopher. His source is the lawyers' Bible: Blackstone's *Commentaries on the Laws of England.*

Using phrases that recalled Dr. Hugh Knox's Hurricane Sermon, Hamilton drove home the idea in one of his most striking passages:

The sacred rights of mankind are not to be rummaged for, among old parchments, or musty records. They are written, as with a sunbeam, in the whole *volume* of human nature, by the hand of the divinity itself; and can never be erased or obscured by mortal power.

In this source, Hamilton finds, by logical processes, his hatred of slavery and his insistence that the colonies must be free, but free under law: "Upon this law, depend the natural rights of mankind . . . the supreme being gave existence to man, together with the means of preserving and beatifying that existence. He endowed him with rational faculties, by the help of which, to discern and pursue such things, as were consistent with his duty and interest, and invested him with an inviolable right to personal liberty, and personal safety."

Here was the irrefutable argument for freedom and against slavery: "Hence also, the origin of all civil government, justly established, must be a voluntary compact, between the rulers and the ruled; and must be liable to such limitations, as are necessary for the security of the absolute rights of the latter; for what original title can any man or set of men have, to govern others, except their own consent? To usurp dominion over a people, in their own despite, or to grasp at a more extensive power than they are willing to entrust, is to violate that law of nature, which gives every man a right to his personal liberties; and can, therefore, confer no obligation to obedience."

The form of government was dictated by these principles:

The principal aim of society is to protect individuals, in the enjoyment of those absolute rights, which were vested in them by the immutable laws of nature; but which could not be preserved, in peace, without that mutual assistance, and intercourse, which is gained by the institution of friendly and social communities.

The Farmer had argued that the colonists could not claim to be liege subjects to the king of Great Britain, while they disavowed the authority of Parliament, because "The king of Great Britain was placed on the throne, by virtue of an act of Parliament; and he is king of America, by virtue of being king of Great Britain."

Hamilton meets this argument incisively:

Admitting that the king of Great Britain was enthroned by virtue of an act of Parliament, and that he is king of America, because he is king of Great Britain, yet the act of Parliament is not the *efficient cause* of his being the king of America: It is only the *occasion* of it. He is king of America, by virtue of a compact between us and the king of Great Britain. These colonies were planted and settled by the grants, and under the protection of English kings, who entered into covenants with us for themselves, their heirs and successors; and it is from these covenants, that the duty of protection on their part, and the duty of allegiance on ours arise.

To disclaim the authority of a British Parliament over us, does by no means imply the dereliction of our allegiance to British monarchs. . . .

The law of nature and the British Constitution both confine allegiance to the person of the king; and found it upon the principle of protection.

When we ascribe to the British House of Commons a jurisdiction over the colonies, the scene is entirely reversed. No ties of gratitude or interest remain. Interest indeed may operate to our prejudice. The British patriots may, in time, be heard to court the gale of popular favor, by boasting their exploits in laying some new imposition on their American vassals, and, by that means, lessening the burthens of their friends and fellow subjects.

Hamilton then opens up to view the glorious future of a free America: "There seems to be, already, a jealousy of our dawning splendor. It is looked upon as portentous of approaching independence . . . and though it may have chiefly originated in the calumnies of designing men, yet it does not entirely depend upon adventitious or partial causes; but is also founded in the circumstances of our country and situation."

Hamilton sees that, unlike the small, tropic slave islands whence he had come, "The boundless extent of territory we possess, the wholesome temperament of our climate, the luxuriance and fertility of our soil, the variety of our products, the rapidity of our population, the industry of our countrymen and the commodiousness of our ports, naturally lead to a suspicion of independence, and would always have an influence pernicious to us. Jealousy is a predominant passion of human nature and is a source of greatest evils."

Hamilton had already thought deeply about the problem of creating a functioning representative government and the need for checks and balances; he quotes from one of David Hume's essays an idea that would always be basic to his creative political thought: "Political writers have established it as a maxim, that, in contriving any system of government, and fixing the several checks and controls of the Constitution, every man ought to be supposed a knave; and to have no other end in all his actions, but private interest. By this interest, we must govern him, and by means of it, make him cooperate to public good, notwithstanding his insatiable avarice and ambition. Without this, we shall in vain boast of the advantages of any Constitution, and shall find in the end, that we have no security for our liberties and possessions, except the goodwill of our rulers: that is, we should have no security at all." Great political commentators from Edmund Burke to Alexander Solzhenitsyn have always said much the same thing.

Hamilton had many warm friends; he loved people in particular, but he sharply distinguished friendly personal relations with individual people from beliefs about people in mobs or the abstract, which political realism taught him: "It is therefore a just political maxim, that every man must be supposed a knave." Hamilton admits that it appears strange that a maxim should be true in politics that is false in fact. The reason is that

> men are generally more honest in private than in a public capacity; and will go to greater lengths to serve a party than when their own private interest is alone concerned. . . . Honor is a great check upon mankind. But, where a considerable body of men act together, this check is in a great measure removed; since a man is sure to be approved by his own party, for what promotes the common interest, and he soon learns to despise the clamors of adversaries. To this we may add that every court, or senate is determined by the greater number of voices; so that if self-interest influences only the majority (as it will always do) the whole senate follows the allurements of this separate interest, and acts as if it contained not one member who had any regard to public interest and liberty. What additional force do these observations acquire, when applied to the dominion of one community over another!

Throughout almost his entire career, Hamilton's political thought and action tended to follow in a straight line leading out of these observations. There are few public men in history whose careers present to careful analysis fewer deviations from their own first political principles than his.

Hamilton anticipates another Lincolnian formulation about popular government:

> The foundation of the English Constitution rests upon this principle, that no laws have any validity, or binding force, without the consent and approbation of the *people*, given in the persons of *their* representatives, periodically elected by *themselves*. This constitutes the democratical part of the government.

Anarchy and revolution are not things good in themselves, but are good only if they lead to something better. The people of despotic kingdoms have an inherent right, whenever they please, "to shake off the yoke of servitude (though sanctified by the immemorial usage of their ancestors) and to model their government, upon the principles of civil liberty." But even when this happens, the revolution may fail, because "Men, like nations, have a tendency to abuse power when they gain it." Hamilton saw that "A fondness for power is implanted in most men, and it is natural to abuse it, when acquired. This maxim drawn from the experience of all ages makes it the height of folly to entrust any set of men with power, which is not under every possible control: Perpetual strides are made after more, as long as there is any part withheld."

The Westchester Farmer had said that the colonists should have tried the mode of petition and remonstrance to obtain removal of their grievances. But Hamilton was suspicious of this and replied, "The hand of bribery might have been stretched across the Atlantic, and the number of domestic vipers increased among us . . . How great an influence places, pensions and honors have upon the minds of men we may easily discover, by contrasting the former with the present conduct of some among ourselves. Many, who at the time of the Stamp Act were loudest in the cause of liberty, and the most ardent promoters of the spirited proceedings on that occasion, have now from patriots of the first magnitude dwindled into *moderate men*, friends to order and good government, dutiful and zealous, servants to the ministry."

In Hamilton's analyses economics always underlay politics. The Westchester Farmer had sneered that Britain with her vast resources would not be affected by nonimportation measures of the colonies. In refutation, Hamilton pointed out that Britain's national debt "is now about 140 million sterling; a debt unparalleled in the annals of any country . . . So that, with all their present resources, they would not be able to discharge the public debt in less than 112 years, should the peace continue all that time . . . Most of the necessaries of life are, at present, heavily taxed . . . The common people are extremely impoverished, and find it very difficult to procure a subsistence."

The Farmer had argued that "the first winter after our English goods are consumed, we shall be starving with cold" because enough wool to clothe the inhabitants of this continent could not be obtained in 20 years. "As to cotton, it must come from the southern colonies, and the expense of bringing it by land would be too great for the poor. Besides, we have nobody to manufacture our materials after we have got them."

Hamilton disagreed. "Nature has disseminated her blessings variously throughout this continent: Some parts of it are favorable to some things, others to others; some colonies are best calculated for grains, others for flax and hemp; others for cotton; and others for livestock of every kind." He urged one great national domestic market in America: "By this means, a mutually advantageous intercourse may be established between them all. If we were to turn our attention from external to internal commerce, we should give greater stability and more lasting prosperity to our country, than she can possibly have otherwise. We should not then import the luxuries and vices of foreign climes; nor should we make such hasty strides to public corruption and depravity." We could make do with what we had and wear it out: "The clothes we already have in use and the goods at present in the country, will, with care, be sufficient to last three years . . . A suit made of skins, would not be quite so elegant as one of broadcloth, but it would shelter us from the inclemency of the winter, full as well."

There were intangible psychological benefits to be derived from liberty that were real and important. "There is a certain enthusiasm in liberty, that makes human nature rise above itself in acts of bravery and heroism . . . the pulse of Americans beats high, in their country's cause."

To the Farmer's argument that the colonies would have no chance in a war with Britain, Hamilton replied confidently as a military strategist:

Great Britain can never force us to submission by blocking up our ports;
. . . the consequences of such a procedure to herself, Ireland, the West

Indies, would be too fatal to admit of it. If she is determined to enslave us, it must be by force of arms; and to attempt this I again assert it would be nothing less than the grossest infatuation, madness itself.

Much British treasure and blood would be expended in effecting our ruin . . . Her public debt would be augmented several millions . . . Her manufacturers would stagnate and decay, and her revenues would be considerably diminished.

The ancient rivals and enemies of Britain would [not] be idle, at such a conjuncture of this. The French . . . never could have a fairer opportunity, or a greater temptation to aggrandize themselves, and triumph over Britain than would be here presented. Let us imagine England immersed in a war with France, Spain or any other potent neighbor, with her public debt increased, some of her best springs dried up, and America ruined.

Hamilton had the demographic statistics of America at his fingertips. Britain could not spare the army of 15,000 at least that it would need to send against the colonies. If the number of men capable of bearing arms in any nation is a fifth part of the whole people, the fifth part of three million Americans was 600,000. But even if there were only 500,000 fighting men in the colonies, there would still be upwards of 30 Americans to one British soldier, a disparity that could never be compensated by superior British discipline or skill: "It will be objected, that these 500,000 cannot act together. I grant it; nor is there any occasion that they should: 40,000 will be a sufficient number to make head at a time."

Hamilton anticipates the strategy and tactics that George Washington would follow in the war: "There are no large plains, for the two armies to meet in, and decide the contest by some decisive stroke where any advantage gained, by either side, might be prosecuted till the complete victory was obtained." Hamilton matter of factly anticipates the military strategy of the next ten years: "The circumstances of our country put it in our power to evade a pitched battle. It will be better policy to harass and exhaust the soldiery, by frequent skirmishes and incursions, than to take the open field with them, by which means, they would have the full benefit of their superior regularity and skill. Americans are better qualified, for that kind of fighting, which is most adapted to this country, than regular troops."

As the reader grows weary of polemical exposition, even the most expert and pointed, Hamilton winds up 78 pages of *The Farmer Refuted* with an apology that can scarcely be improved upon: "The parts I have left unattended to, are such as cannot operate, materially, to the prejudice of the cause I espouse; but I should not have neglected them, had it not been that I have already taken a very ample range; and it would, perhaps, be imprudent to delay a conclusion."

He politely laments the unnatural quarrel between the parent state and the colonies and avows "that I am a warm advocate for limited monarchy, and an unfeigned well-wisher to the present royal family."

But more important, and overriding this pious sugarcoating, he would accept no British limit on the autonomy of the colonies: "I am inviolably attached to the essential rights of mankind, and the true interest of society. I consider civil liberty, in a genuine and unadulterated sense, as the greatest of terrestrial blessings. I am convinced that the whole human race is entitled to it; and, that it can be wrested from no part of them, without the blackest and most aggravated guilt."

Here, at last, was the supreme paradox in his argument: "The best way to secure a permanent and happy union, between Great Britain and the colonies, is to permit the latter to be as free as they desire."

He signed off as "a Sincere Friend to America."

A close reading of Hamilton's *A Full Vindication* and *The Farmer Refuted* will provide the modern reader who has had the tenacity to follow his eighteenth-century political prose a rewarding reading experience on many levels. He will be reminded of the narrowness of the issues in dispute between Great Britain and her American colonies; of the subtle distinction between the colonies' early acknowledgment of allegiance to the British king, but their refusal to acknowledge the supremacy of the British Parliament; and of the exact meaning of the phrase "no taxation without representation."

A Full Vindication and *The Farmer Refuted* created a sensation. At first, Dr. Myles Cooper thought John Jay was the author, "it being absurd to imagine that a man so young as Hamilton could have written it." Once Cooper found out the truth, it is not surprising that when he had looked out his window and seen Hamilton haranguing the mob at the college gates, he would think he was stirring up their passions, instead of trying to calm them. Others attributed the pamphlets to John Adams or to Governor William Livingston of New Jersey, but the secret that the pseudonymous Friend to America was indeed Hamilton did not remain a secret long. It is too much to expect of the young Hamilton that he would deny his own authorship if asked about it. He was talked of as a surprising prodigy of colonial intellect surprisingly nurtured within the gates of the loyalist bastion at King's. Of New York's revolutionary leaders, Marinus Willett wrote, "Sears was a warm man, but with little reflection; McDougall was strongminded, and Jay, appearing to fall in with the measures of Sears, tempered and controlled them; but Hamilton, after these great writings, became our oracle."

From being known to a few in New York as the eloquent young collegian after the Great Meeting in the Fields that summer, Hamilton now became known throughout the other colonies as "The Vindicator" of the First Continental Congress at just the time when the Second Continental Congress was preparing to convene in Philadelphia on May 5, 1775. Both fiery, ardent leaders of the Sons of Liberty like Isaac Sears and Alexander McDougall and careful moderates like William Livingston and John Jay could now proudly cite as their own the facts and arguments for revolution that had been marshaled so forcefully by their own brilliant protégé. Hamilton had made himself New York's most articulate spokesman for the continental revolutionary cause.

Not the least remarkable thing about the position in which he suddenly found himself is how easily it might have turned out to be the opposite one. Dr. Cooper had sought to win him over, and he knew all the loyalist arguments well. Hamilton could have been as effective a spokesman for the loyalist side as he was for the revolutionary. The question is why he was not. An advertisement published with *The Farmer Refuted* stated that its author's revolutionary views were "the genuine offspring of sober reason." Indeed, it added, "he remembers the time when HE had strong prejudices on the side HE now opposes." It adds that "his change of sentiment [HE firmly believes] proceeded from the superior force of the arguments, in favour of the American claims."

Hamilton contributed no new principles to the controversy. He elaborated doctrines that were being advanced in the Continental Congress and other colonies by men like John Adams, Thomas Jefferson, and others. John Locke's writings, particularly his *Two Treatises of Government*, were his political Bible, like theirs, but Hamilton did more than reduce Locke to everyday terms for the benefit of New Yorkers. His unique contribution to the cause were the facts and figures he marshaled to show the commercial relations between Britain and the continental colonies, the West Indies, and Canada. From them he showed that the colonies would be economically and militarily invincible in their struggle with Britain. He demonstrated that America formed an economic whole in which the various sections complemented each other in such a way as to make clear that providence had planned a great nation—an empire—upon the American continent.

Hamilton's vision of a union of Britain with English-speaking peoples on the North American continent came to pass in a way entirely different from that which he had foreseen, when the British Statute of Westminster made the citizens of Canada and all other British dominions coequal with citizens of Great Britain. But by then it was 150 years too late to include the 13 American colonies as leading members. That same spring of 1775 the battles of Lexington, Concord, and Bunker Hill would replace his early vision with the lesser but large enough vision of a union of the 13 colonies where all men would be free. And Hamilton misread, if perhaps only for rhetorical effect, the attitude of most of the common people of England toward the colonists. Far from sympathizing with the colonists against their own king and Parliament in a way that would allow the colonies to win an easy, quick, and bloodless victory over Great Britain, the majority of Britons would support the claims of king and Parliament against the colonists until the bitter end of eight years of hostilities in 1783.

In their time *A Full Vindication* and *The Farmer Refuted* were not just public statements—they were great events. They struck and stunned the public consciousness, in somewhat the same way that word of the Boston Tea Party had done. Hamilton's pen was a mighty weapon, one of the mightiest in an age when such a pen could accomplish more than any other weapon. Writing to James Madison two decades later in 1795, about the impact of some of Hamilton's later pamphlets, Thomas Jefferson said, "Hamilton is really a colossus to the anti-Republican party. Without numbers, he is an host within himself."

With *A Full Vindication* and *The Farmer Refuted*, Hamilton riveted public attention upon himself in the first of the host of roles he was destined to play
in creating the nation: guidon carrier leading the ranks of constitutional revolutionists.

Political pamphleteering was only one of the extracurricular activities
Hamilton and his remarkable circle of King's College classmates were carrying
on that winter and spring of 1774 and 1775. Every morning in St. George's
churchyard, Hamilton, Fish, Troup, and a number of their other friends turned
out to practice close order drill. Major Edward Fleming, a disciplinarian who had
been an adjutant of a British regiment, but who was now attached to the American cause, was their drillmaster. Hamilton's attendance was eager and constant
and "he became exceedingly expert in the manual exercise." His company of
volunteers was called The Corsicans and later The Hearts of Oak. Short green
coats were their uniforms. On the front of their leather caps was the ominous
motto Freedom or Death. They marched to a song, "The Glorious Seventy-Four,"
sung to the tune "The Hearts of Oak" as they learned to stay in step, counting
cadence as they marched.

Conditions were such in New York that spring that a shooting war for
independence was not to be lightly undertaken, notwithstanding Hamilton's
optimism in *The Farmer Refuted*. New York's war debt from earlier wars was
heavy, and sufferings from French and Indians were still fresh in memory. The
port city remained under the *Asia*'s guns, the northern borders were wide open
to attack from the British and their Iroquois allies, many loyalist and commercial
interests were determined to aid the British, and the New York Assembly was
still controlled by loyalists who had refused to approve the commercial sanctions
against British trade that the First Continental Congress had recommended or
even to appoint state delegates to the Second.

On March 5, 1775, the patriots called a meeting to demand representation
in Congress. The loyalists tried to break it up by violence and dispersed the
patriots. The patriots rallied, collected arms, drove off the loyalists, held the
meeting, and voted to send city delegates to the New York Provincial Congress.

The shooting war actually began on April 19, 1775, with the shot fired near
Concord Bridge whose report was heard round the world. The first blood of the
American war of independence had been shed. Less than a month later, on
May 10, Ethan Allen and his Green Mountain Boys and a fiery Connecticut officer
named Benedict Arnold surprised and seized Fort Ticonderoga in upstate New
York. In June, British Generals William Howe, Sir Henry Clinton, and John
Burgoyne landed in Boston with reinforcements for General Gage, assaulted
Breed's Hill, and lost more than 1,000 men in the Battle of Bunker Hill. Full of
overoptimistic enthusiasm after these successes, Congress launched a military
invasion of Canada under General Philip Schuyler which sallied forth from Fort
Ticonderoga in August only to suffer one of the most tragic disasters of the war.

New England yeomen abandoned their farms and rushed into arms; New
Jersey farmers seized the provincial treasury there; Philadelphia embargoed all
shipping. In New York, Marinus Willett and Isaac Sears organized patriot pa-

trols to stand guard through the night, as if British landing parties were already sailing up the harbor. Dr. Cooper fled aboard the *Kingfisher*. Mobs assembled, seized the keys to the custom house, broke open the royal armory, and forced the royal troops to surrender their weapons and abandon the city. A state of war now existed in New England and on the Canadian border. New Yorkers' fears ran high that new British reinforcements would soon be landed to crush them.

On May 26, 1775, the Continental Congress had ordered that the New York militia of Colonel Lasher's battalion, including Hamilton's Hearts of Oak company, be trained and armed and kept in the city for protection against British troops. New York's Provincial Congress responded with its usual feebleness and merely recommended in notices and handbills that citizens furnish themselves with arms and "use all Diligence to perfect themselves in the Military Art, and if necessary form themselves into Companies." Philip Schuyler was nominated for major general of all New York troops in case a Continental Army should be raised. George Washington was named commander in chief and dispatched to Cambridge to take command of the Continental Army facing the British forces there. On June 25, one of Colonel Lasher's companies was dispatched with Gouverneur Morris and Richard Montgomery and a subcommittee of the Provincial Congress to welcome George Washington and his party to New York, see him through the city on his way north, and prevent his party from colliding with that of Royal Governor William Tryon, who was returning to New York from England after more than a year's absence on the same day. Another of Lasher's companies was dispatched to welcome Tryon and prevent him colliding with Washington. It is not known which of the two parties, Washington's or Tryon's was greeted by the honor guard of Hamilton's Hearts of Oak.

While perfecting their close order drill and manual of arms with the Hearts of Oak at St. George's Churchyard in the early mornings and the King's College curriculum the rest of the day, the recently acclaimed "oracle" of the patriots focused his attention on another British outrage that he had touched on in his replies to the Westchester Farmer. This led to still more extracurricular activity, two pamphlets published in Rivington's *Gazetteer* in June 1775 known as "Remarks on the Quebec Bill."

In the first of these pamphlets, Hamilton defined an established religion as one "which the civil authority engages, not only to protect, but to support." Hamilton found that the Quebec Act made provision not only for the protection, but for the permanent support of "popery," which he strongly opposed. "The characteristic difference between the tolerated and established religion consists in this," he explained, "with respect to the former, the law is passive and improvident; leaving it to those who profess it, to make as much, or as little provision, as the circumstances may require. In this manner, the Presbyterians and other sects are tolerated in England. They are allowed to exercise their religion without molestations; and to maintain their clergy as they think proper."

He points out that "No Protestant Englishman would consent to let the free exercise of his religion depend upon the mere pleasure of any man, however great or exalted. The privilege of worshipping the deity in the manner his conscience dictates, which is one of the dearest he enjoys, must in that case be rendered insecure and precarious."

By August 1775 the New York Provincial Congress and the patriot Committee of Safety had taken over direction of the restless city. To the royal governor, William Tryon, and his lieutenant governor, Cadwallader Colden "it was extremely disagreeable . . . to remain as Spectator of the . . . confusions in Town, when I had it not in my power to prevent." By the night of August 23, Tryon had retired for safety to a retreat in Flushing.

The New York Provincial Congress, meeting in the city, ordered the British cannon to be hauled away from beneath the fort at the Battery. With his Hearts of Oak, Hamilton and the rest of the infantrymen of Colonel Lasher's battalion marched to the Battery at eleven that night but drew no fire from the fort. Earlier in the summer the main British garrison that manned it had been taken off to the safety of the *Asia* to avoid incidents. Captain Vanderput of the *Asia* received advance word that Colonel Lasher's militia intended to seize the cannons from the Battery. He launched one of the *Asia*'s sloops carrying a full complement of armed men to stand in close to shore to see what the Americans would do. Hamilton, with his fellow Hearts of Oak militiamen, was part of the guard detail that formed a semicircle at the fort facing the harbor while others were hauling away the cannon. They spotted the *Asia*'s sloop lying offshore. They loaded, primed, and cocked their muskets. Then they waited for the British to make the first move. Other units of Colonel Lasher's men broke into the fort, made ropes fast to the gun carriages, and began dragging the cannons out of their portals, off the ramparts, out toward the Bowling Green, and up the Broad Way toward the Fields, where the ironclad Liberty Pole stood. There were 21 naval guns in all, an assortment of nine-, 12-, and 18-pounders weighing a ton or more apiece. Their small-wheeled, slow-rolling gun carriages, designed to absorb recoil by friction aboard ship by rolling a few feet backward after discharge, were not designed for a mile-long uphill trek over rutted cobblestones. Manhandling them up the Broad Way at night was hard, sweaty, noisy work. The August night's sounds included much loud confused cursing and swearing.

Suddenly, shortly after midnight, from the *Asia*'s sloop offshore a muzzle flash and musket report blazed out in the darkness. Hamilton's tense guard detail instantly returned the fire on the sloop. No one ashore could be certain whether the fire from the *Asia*'s sloop was an aimed shot, an accidental discharge, or a signal to the *Asia* to open up with all her guns. Under fire from Hamilton's company, the sloop's crew bent to their sweeps and moved out of range, but the armed detachment aboard her continued to fire on Hamilton's guard detail. One of the militia's shots fatally wounded a British crewman aboard the sloop.

The exchange of musket fire between land and water continued as the sloop pulled away. Then, suddenly, from a thousand yards away, there was a flash, an enormous orange ball of flame, then a thunderous "boom!" The *Asia*'s main batteries had opened fire! First came a single, targeting round of solid grapeshot, then several in a salvo. Seen and heard from the business end of the cannons' muzzles by the targets on shore, the flash and boom of such a salvo reverberating across the night sky like thunder and lightning would be the most fearsome sight and sound that Hamilton or any other New Yorker had ever seen in their lives. The sleeping city roused itself in panic! Alarm drums began to beat! Militiamen groped and stumbled and rushed through the darkness to find their assigned posts, blinded by the glare! Householders ran into the streets or down into cellars or fled to the countryside or sought to find a boat for New Jersey. Some thought the British invasion had begun!

Lasher's men went on dragging the cannon out of the fort up Broad Way. As the *Asia*'s sloop pulled out of range of his and his men's muskets, Hamilton decided he could be more useful helping to manhandle the big guns. He seized a rope from the hand of his friend Hercules Mulligan and handed Mulligan his empty musket to hold for him. He put his shoulder to the rope to help haul a cannon off up the Broad Way.

Having lodged the cannon near the Liberty Pole at the Fields, he was running back down toward the Battery for another when he met Mulligan running up the street toward him. Hamilton demanded that Mulligan give him back his musket. Mulligan apologized. He had thrown it down in panic back at the Battery. Hamilton brushed past him and continued on back toward the Battery to find his musket. According to the timorous Mulligan's admiring later account, he did so, "notwithstanding the firing continued, with as much concern as if the vessel had not been there." Elias Boudinot also reported that the soldiers, "regarded the Shot, but little more than if they had been stones thrown by Boys, and never desisted till they got every mounted Cannon away."

As the confusion, disorder, and panic in the city reached a crescendo at about three in the morning, the *Asia*'s guns opened up again. She unleashed an assortment of nine-, 18-, and 24-pound shells in a full, blinding, 32-gun broadside on the defenseless city. The muzzle blasts of her cannon formed a sheet of white orange fire stretching all the way from the foot of Wall Street to the very ceiling of the August night sky. Reverberations of the blasts shook the whole city and filled it with a sickening thud and crumple and crunch: cannon shot crashing through walls and roofs of houses. Citizens' nostrils and lungs burned with the acrid odor of powder and smoke. No one who saw or heard or felt or smelled the broadsides the *Asia* laid on New York that night could ever forget them.[2]

The *Asia*'s awesome display of firepower had not been intended to destroy the city, but was meant as a warning. Captain Vanderput's gunners had aimed generally toward Fort George, not the city itself. They had used solid lead and iron shot, not fire bombs. But most of the shot fell short of Fort George—one struck Roger Morris's townhouse, and another fell through the roof of Fraunces Tavern. Others damaged smaller buildings in Whitehall Street. Three or four New Yorkers were wounded, but no one was killed. When the panic died down and the wreckage was surveyed by the cool morning light, it seemed remarkable that so little actual damage could have been done.

Like his fellow students who had helped haul away the British cannon and had fired their muskets into the muzzles of the *Asia*'s guns that night, Hamilton always afterward was identified in the public's mind as one of the men who had been on the firing line against the enemy's guns on the first night of New York's armed resistance to the British. By surviving without too much trouble, he had also demonstrated the truth of his published thesis that the royal masters were not omnipotent. Although his musket fire was four months too late to be a shot heard round the world like the one fired at Concord, it reverberated throughout New York because it marked the night when de facto control of the city and state passed from the British Crown and the loyalist-dominated Assembly to the revolutionary Provincial Congress.

The practical demonstration that the *Asia*'s guns were not as fearsome as they looked and sounded had weakened, not reinforced, the hitherto awesome strength of the ultimate symbol of British imperial control. When Governor Tryon bustled back from his Flushing retreat the next day, he asserted no royal authority in his own right. Instead, all he could do, or try to do, was make an appeal to the members of the Provincial Congress to do what they could to restore order.

In a time of mounting revolutionary passion and ferment that summer and fall, Hamilton's actions continued to be marked by a concern for order and fairness that risked personal unpopularity and physical violence. On one occasion, a patriot gang known as the Travis mob threatened to kill loyalist merchants Ralph Thurman and Robert Harding for sending military supplies to Boston to help General Gage against the Americans there. According to John Church Hamilton, his father "interposed" with the mob, "diverted their rage," and saved the loyalists.

In November, Captain Isaac Sears, the radical leader of the Sons of Liberty, still furious that Dr. Cooper, the president of King's, and James Rivington, the publisher of his pamphlets as well, had slipped away from the mobs of May to safety aboard the *Kingfisher*, gathered a gang in New Haven to march on New York and root out loyalist rot.[3] While on their march westward, after being joined by 80 horsemen under three captains, they captured Samuel Seabury, the Westchester Farmer himself, and packed him off back to New Haven, where he was jailed for five weeks. Riding on in triumph, Sears's gang clattered into New York City at noon on November 23 and drew up in close order with fixed bayonets in front of Rivington's bookstore and print shop in Hanover Square. Rivington had fled. They broke in and wrecked his establishment, filled their sacks with his precious imported type and threw it away, spilled his files and smashed his presses. A crowd of spectators stood and watched from a wooden platform nearby called the Coffee House Bridge. Most seemed to enjoy the spectacle and from time to time cheered on Sears and his Sons of Liberty. Hamilton's son reports that Hamilton appeared here "as the advocate of order, and relying on his former success, renewed his appeals to the discretion of the citizens." Besides, he was "indignant at the encroachment of unlicensed troops from another colony" coming in and destroying his publisher, who had published Seabury as well. "He offered to join in opposition to the intruders and check their progress."

No other reporter of the event records Hamilton's resistance to Sears's mob, and Hamilton's son admits that "His exhortation was unsuccessful. The outrage was perpetrated."

The day after the Sons of Liberty destroyed Rivington's press, Hamilton, not mentioning his own role in physically attempting to prevent it, but writing with all the authority of an angry eyewitness, sent a long letter to John Jay, then sitting in the Second Continental Congress in Philadelphia. He entreated Jay to use his influence to send some continental troops to New York to help keep a check on patriotic mob violence. A more important reason for sending troops was to meet the British invasion and the loyalist counterinsurrection that he foresaw coming soon.

"You will probably ere this reaches you have heard of the late incursion made into this City by a number of horsemen from New England, under the command of Captain Sears, who took away Mr. Rivington's type and a Couteau or two," Hamilton wrote. Hamilton deplored Rivington's generally anti-Association and loyalist tendencies, saying

> I am fully sensible how dangerous and pernicious Rivington's press has been, and how detestable the character of the man is in every respect, yet I cannot help disapproving and condemning this step.
>
> Men coming from a neighboring province to chastize the notorious friends of the ministry here, will hold up an idea to our enemies . . . that the New Yorkers are totally . . . disaffected to the American cause, which makes the interposal of their neighbors necessary.
>
> Moreover, New England is very populous and powerful . . . I like not to see potent neighbors . . . making inroads at pleasure into this or any other province. . . .

Hamilton's analysis here was subtle and cut in several directions. "If your body gently interposes a check for the future, Rivington will be intimidated & the Tories will be convinced that the other colonies will not tamely see the general cause betrayed by the Yorkers. A favorable idea will be impressed of your justice & impartiality in discouraging the encroachments of any one province on another."

Here is the plan: "Let your body station in different parts of the province most tainted with the ministerial infection, a few regiments of troops, raised in Philadelphia, the Jerseys or any other province except New England. These will suffice to strengthen and support the Whigs, who are still, I flatter myself, a large majority, and to suppress the efforts of the Tories. . . ."

"In times of such commotion as the present," he concluded to his friend John Jay, "there is great danger of fatal extremes. The same state of the passions which fits the multitude, who have not a sufficient stock of reason and knowledge to guide them, for opposition to tyranny and oppression, very naturally leads them to a contempt and disregard of all authority . . . When the minds of these are loosened from their attachment to ancient establishments and courses, they seem to grow giddy and are apt, more or less, to run into anarchy.

"In such tempestuous times, it requires the greatest skill in the political pilots to keep men steady and within proper bounds." Then Hamilton asserts the great theme that undergirds all his political thought: "I am always more or less alarmed at everything which is done of mere will and pleasure without any proper authority."

Hamilton's failure to save Rivington's press from the mob now served to bring him to the active notice of this popular, upright, older leader in action in the context of a complex situation calling for high standards of order, rectitude, moderation, and political acumen that matched Jay's own. Hamilton's son concluded that the failure of his father's efforts to save his publisher's press "elevated him still more in the estimation of the patriots, who saw in his love of order and respect for the authority of the laws assurances of those high qualities which, rising above the wild uproar of the times, disdained to win popularity from popular delusion."

5

COVERING THE BEATEN RETREAT OF AN ESSENTIAL AEGIS TO BE

AFTER ESCAPING THE GRASP OF A DISCIPLINED AND VICTORIOUS
ENEMY, THIS LITTLE BAND OF PATRIOTS WERE SEEN SKILLFULLY
AVOIDING AN ENGAGEMENT UNTIL THEY COULD CONTEND WITH
ADVANTAGE, AND THEN BY THE MASTERLY ENTERPRISES OF TREN-
TON AND PRINCETON, CUTTING THEM UP IN DETACHMENTS, RALLY-
ING THE SCATTERED ENERGIES OF THE COUNTRY, INFUSING TER-
ROR INTO THE BREASTS OF THEIR INVADERS, AND CHANGING THE
WHOLE TIDE AND FORTUNE OF THE WAR.
   — *"Eulogium on General Nathanael Greene," July 4, 1789*

John Jay sent back a warm reply to Hamilton's report of Isaac Sears's raid. Hamilton should continue to keep him informed of the state of the province— "any matters of importance that may arise." So on December 31, 1775, Hamilton wrote back to warn Jay that "the tories have it in contemplation to steal a march upon us." Royal Governor Tryon hoped that by playing down the upcoming elections to the Provincial Assembly scheduled for February 14, the turnout vote would be kept small, conservatives could pack the Assembly with supporters of the Crown, and it could continue to serve as a counterweight to the revolutionary Provincial Congress to keep the politics of New York in confused suspension between independence and loyalty. Hamilton and Jay went to work. They put up a strong New York County pro-independence slate for their pro-Continental Association party: Jay himself, Philip Livingston, John Alsop, and Hamilton's old friend Alexander McDougall. All of them but McDougall, who was considered more radical than the others, were already delegates to both the Continental Congress and the Provincial Congress as well. Hamilton and Jay campaigned to turn out a large vote and elected their entire ticket, including Alexander McDougall.

Not long after Captain Alexander McDougall had summoned Hamilton from the fringes of the crowd to the platform to speak at the Great Meeting in the Fields, he had been appointed colonel of the First New York Regiment, which made him the highest ranking military man in the city. He was soon promoted again to Continental brigadier and in 1777 to major general.

On February 23, 1776, a week after his successful campaign for the assembly, it was recorded in the journals of the New York Provincial Congress that "Col. McDougall recommended Mr. Alexander Hamilton for captain of a company of artillery." McDougall nominated two men with more experience, at the same time but Hamilton would outrank them both. Quick thinking and hard work in political campaigns that succeed bring rewards more quick and tangible than applause for youthful eloquence.

Early morning practice of close order drill and the manual of arms in St. George's churchyard with the militia company Hearts of Oak under Major Edward Fleming had already made Hamilton a well-drilled infantryman.[1] Being under the business end of the *Asia*'s broadsides had given Hamilton an unusually strong impression of the power of big guns, at least if properly aimed. Manhandling them on their carriages up Broadway had demonstrated that they need not rust unused in fixed emplacements but could be more useful if moved along with the infantry to protect and cover their movements. He became acquainted with a British army bombardier from whom he learned how to apply abstract principles of mathematics and trigonometry from Robert Harpur's course at King's to practical matters like calibrating elevations and deflections to aim cannon. So when the New York Provincial Congress on January 6, 1776, ordered that an artillery company be raised for the defense of the colony, Hamilton was ready with the technical expertise to be an artilleryman, as well as the necessary political qualifications. Thus he won his commission as a captain in a preferred branch of the service only a month after turning nineteen.

Hamilton's friend Robert Troup wrote that John Jay, as a member of the Provincial Congress, had pushed the commission through "at McDougall's request." To be certain no mistake was being made in awarding a captain's commission to such a youth, Captain Stephen Badlam conducted an examination; he judged him qualified to command a company of artillery. On March 14, his certificate being read and filed, the Provincial Congress "Ordered that Alexander Hamilton be, and he is hereby appointed captain of the Provincial company of artillery of this Colony."

There was more to being captain of the Provincial company of artillery than accepting congratulations, ordering uniforms, marching out to confront waiting troops, doing a right about face, clicking heels, and commanding the batteries and platoons of bombardiers, gunners, drummers, fifers and matrosses to snap to attention. It was a volunteer army, and officers had to recruit their own men. Hamilton first had to find them, then inspire them to join him as volunteers, scrounge uniforms for them, and persuade the province to pay them as well. In the Provincial army, more than the usual concomitant burdens went with the privileges and honor of an officer's rank.[2]

Hamilton's commission could not even be issued to him until he had fulfilled the condition of raising at least 30 men for his company. Typical strong-arm recruiting tactics stopped not far short of physical abduction. One afternoon he took his gigantic friend Hercules Mulligan with him and came back with the report, "and we engaged 25 men." To help buy uniforms and equip and arm his men before his requisitions for reimbursement were approved by the Provincial Congress, Hamilton advanced the second and last of the money remittances he had received from St. Croix to help pay for his education at King's.

For his men as recruiting proceeded, Hamilton ordered 75 pairs of buckskin breeches, had worn-out breeches repaired, and made use of breeches "half-worn" out.

For his own breeches Hamilton paid 64 shillings. His unpaid account with Curtennies, the commissary of clothing of New York, came to £188.16.9 for such items as "blue Strouds" (a coarse fatigue uniform), "blue Shalloon" (a twill dress uniform), "oznabugs," and eight dozen buttons. He promised to send the money along as soon as he was in cash again.

The men of Hamilton's Provincial company wore blue coats with buff facings and cuffs, following the same style set by Captain John Lamb for his own company, which was in the service of the Continental Congress. By their articles, Hamilton's Provincial company were subject to the same regulations as the Continental artillery, but the pay scale for Continental troops was higher. This caused "many marks of discontent" among Hamilton's men. It was easier for Captain Sebastian Baumann to recruit men to his Continental artillery at the higher pay scale, and according to Hamilton, "this makes it difficult for me to get a single recruit." His appeal to the Provincial Congress on behalf of his men for the same higher pay as the Continentals spelled it out for them in economic terms: "Men will naturally go to men who pay them best." He also asked the Provincial Congress to furnish them with the same kind of "frock" given to other troops as a bounty because "this frock would be extremely serviceable in summer, while the men are on fatigue; and would put it in their power to save their uniform much longer."

The Provincial Congress granted the pay increase and the frock the same day Hamilton made his appeal. For good measure it threw in as an award to

Hamilton himself a bounty of ten shillings per man for every additional recruit he could enlist up to 100.[3]

Hamilton and his formidable friend Hercules Mulligan may have been over-strenuous strong-arming "volunteers" to earn it. Some of their new recruits deserted after a short hitch and took refuge on one of the ships in the harbor. On May 31 the Provincial Congress authorized Hamilton or any of his officers to go on board any vessel in the harbor to make a strict search for any deserters.

Hamilton's company drilled with some of the same cannons Hamilton and Mulligan had retrieved from Fort George under the *Asia*'s guns. In his care for the health, discipline, accoutrements, uniforms, and record keeping of his command, Hamilton anticipated the precepts von Steuben laid down in the pamphlet of "Instructions for the Captain," published by Congress three years later. Mulligan and others often spoke of the zeal with which Hamilton trained his men; "he proceeded with indefatigable pains, to perfect [his company] in every branch and duty; and it was not long before it was esteemed the most beautiful model . . . in the whole army."

With characteristic foresight Hamilton had written to Jay in November 1775 that it would not be long before the British Ministry would attempt to seize New York. The forty-gun frigate *Phoenix* had joined the *Asia* in the East River, lying a little to the north of her, about where Brooklyn Bridge now spans the East River. In February Sir Henry Clinton arrived from Boston aboard the twenty-four-gun frigate *Mercury*, accompanied by a transport ship said to carry five or six hundred armed troops. By April of 1776 there was no doubt that still more British were on their way in force and likely to heave into view at any time.

General Charles Lee moved down from Boston under orders from General Washington and began deploying Continental troops for defense of the island. All this touched off a "convulsion" in the city. Fearful residents tried to flee in a panic that matched the uproar created by the *Asia*'s broadsides of the previous August.

Fearing a British armed incursion at any time, the Provincial Congress resolved to move all the colony's official records out of danger up the Hudson to Kingston. While the records were still in the city before the move, they had been under the guard of New York City's First Regiment of Infantry. The Provincial Congress, finding that "Capt. Alexander Hamilton's company of artillery raised for this Colony, now consists of so many men as that they may safely and easily perform that duty," ordered the infantry to be relieved of this guard duty and replaced by Hamilton's spruce company.

This fact is sometimes cited by Hamilton enthusiasts for the proposition that a single company of artillerymen under his command was worth a whole regiment of another commander's infantry. It may as easily be cited for the proposition that the infantry was more usefully deployed elsewhere. In any event, the Provincial Congress manifested its awareness that Hamilton's company had attained the highest level of readiness for important spit-and-polish duty.

Hamilton gave intense personal attention to the physical needs of each of his men. William Douglass, a matross, or cannoneer, who had enlisted only two weeks earlier, had been firing at newly arriving British ships moving up the harbor on June 12 when its breech exploded in the emplacement. Besides suffering terrible powder burns, Douglass's leg was broken and his right arm blown off. Hamilton petitioned the Provincial Congress to provide disability pay for Douglass, arranged for his transfer to the Corps of Invalids and his eventual discharge.

Hamilton did not disagree with the general army rule that officers' promotions should be made on the basis of seniority, a general rule to which his own promotions were a striking exception all his life. Tradition was also strong, that officerships be conferred on the basis of family and schooling and social rank and that an enlisted man was somehow a different breed of humanity from an officer. Only rarely could one aspire to become "an officer and a gentleman."

Hamilton was among the first, if not the first, to recommend to the Provincial Congress the advantage of a policy of promoting worthy enlisted men to officerships from the ranks. A First Lieutenant Johnson was transferred out of his company, creating a vacancy. In filling the vacancy, seniority should prevail. Hamilton wrote the Provincial Congress in August that "It would be productive of much inconvenience should not the inferior officers succeed in course . . . I doubt not you will think it proper to advance Mr. Gilleland and Mr. Bean, and fill up the third lieutenancy with some other person." But then, Hamilton urged, Congress should promote an enlisted man, Thomas Thompson, the first sergeant, to be an officer. He "has discharged his duty in the present station with uncommon fidelity . . . and expertness . . . his advancement will be a great encouragement . . . to my company in particular, and will be an animating example to all men of merit to whose knowledge it comes."

Hamilton's proposal to commission enlisted men from the ranks seemed sufficiently novel to the Provincial Congress to warrant its directing Colonel James Livingston to "call on Capt. Hamilton & inquire into this matter & report to this house." After Livingston had confirmed Hamilton's facts, Congress duly promoted Sergeant Thompson to lieutenant. It announced as a general policy that "this Convention will exert themselves in promoting from time to time such privates and non-Commissioned Officers . . . as shall distinguish themselves by their Sobriety, Valour and Subordination. . . ." To it, Hamilton's idea seemed such a good one that it went further. It "Ordered, that this Resolution be published in the newspapers of this State," to make it widely known as an animating example to all men of merit in the province.

Hamilton's citation of Thompson make explicit his own standards of excellence for an officer, in ascending order of importance: "He has discharged his duty in his present station with uncommon fidelity, assiduity and expertness. He is a very good disciplinarian." Like many later American veterans, he possessed "the advantage of having seen a good deal of service in Germany." Most important of all, he "has a tolerable share of common sense, and is well calculated not to disgrace the rank of an officer and a gentleman."

Not long after obtaining Thompson's promotion from the ranks, Hamilton obtained another promotion for him, this time to a captain lieutenancy over the heads of senior officers who outranked him. As a captain lieutenant, at the head of Hamilton's old company, Thompson vindicated Hamilton's high regard. He was killed at the Battle of Springfield gallantly fighting off a desperate British charge.

Most of the raw troops pulled together for the defense of New York City were put to work like gangs of laborers, throwing up crude defensive earthworks. Parties of 800 or 900 reported for tools and orders at 5:00 A.M. and worked until sunset. Every morning at 6:00 after reveille, men not working on fortifications would parade. Insubordination, absence from roll calls, neglect of drill, and desertions in most of the units contrasted unfavorably with a sharp, well-disciplined company like Hamilton's.

But even a crack artillery company has its problems of discipline. "Wanted" notices and cash rewards were posted for deserters; when caught, they were firmly dealt with. In September, John Little of Hamilton's company struck and abused one Adjutant Henly. For such an offense the company court martial tribunal would ordinarily consist solely of Hamilton, the company commander. John Little was sentenced to a punishment of 39 lashes.[4] The commander of a crack unit more often runs it as a taut ship than a happy ship.

King George III's grand strategy was to secure maximum advantage from the British fleet. To break the Continental Association of the colonies, royal operations were directed against points of least resistance. An invasion southward from Canada and seaborne assaults to capture Boston, Charleston, Philadelphia, and New York as strategic points along the coast would best fulfill the grand strategy of the king and his ministers. Unlike Hamilton's company, most American units were ill-organized, poorly trained, and scantily clothed and equipped for a war against the world's greatest naval and military power. It was a war that might easily have been lost.

To counter British strategy, the Continental Congress concentrated all its strongest defenses around New York, the strategic hub and finest harbor of all the colonies. By the spring of 1776 the Continental Army based in New York had grown to a number of about 9,000 strong. Congress also fitted out privateers to prey on British commerce, sought to disarm loyalists and loyalist sympathizers in the colonies, declared American ports to be open to the trade of all countries not subject to the British Crown, and established independent governmental relations directly with France. By the spring of 1776, from Montreal and Quebec on the north to Charleston in the Carolinas far to the south, American regulars and Provincial militia units had already been seeing much action against the enemy while Hamilton and his men were still drilling, sprucing up New York's Provincial Artillery Company, throwing up earthworks, and firing futilely at British reinforcements moving up New York harbor out of backfiring cannons.

The summer before on July 2, 1775, two and a half months after the battles of Lexington, Concord, and Bunker Hill, George Washington had arrived in

Cambridge to take command of all that was left of the Continental Army there. Immediately under him in the command structure were three brigadier generals who figured importantly in Hamilton's later life: Charles Lee, formerly of the British army, who claimed to hold a general's commission from the king of Poland; Israel Putnam, a gnarled and scarred old Indian fighter from Connecticut; and Philip Schuyler, a Hudson River patroon of large holdings and influence. Like Washington himself, Schuyler was a hero of the French and Indian Wars. He was also, with George Clinton, a staunch leader of the minority in the Crown-dominated New York Provincial Assembly who stood forthrightly for independence. He became Hamilton's father-in-law and a man whose importance in Hamilton's life was second only to Washington's. In August of 1775, Schuyler had set out from Fort Ticonderoga with New York City's General Richard Montgomery on the ambitious, ill-fated expedition to conquer Quebec "If it will not be disagreeable to the Canadians." But Hamilton's revolutionary ideology, including his call for religious freedom for all sects, was anathema to most of the 80,000 French Canadians dominated by the Catholic clergy. In November the expedition had taken Montreal, after a siege in which the Americans routed the Seventh Royal British Fusiliers and captured a great many prisoners, including a young British officer by the name of John André. A bloody, futile assault on the looming citadel of Quebec in a swirling snowstorm the night of December 31 fell back in a crushing defeat. Richard Montgomery was killed; American morale was broken. A disastrous retreat by the frostbitten survivors to refuge at Fort Ticonderoga ended the pitifully overoptimistic dream of conquest of Canada. Failure of the Canadian expedition changed the whole aspect of the war. With Canada securely in British hands, New York lay wide open to an invasion down the Hudson-Champlain corridor that would cut the American colonies in two.

Like his future son-in-law, General Schuyler enhanced his fame by moving big guns around. Later that same winter of 1775 and 1776, he helped Colonel Henry Knox haul heavy cannons out of Fort Ticonderoga, across Lake Champlain, over the the snowy Berkshire hills, across the breadth of Massachusetts, all the way to the fortifications on Dorchester Heights overlooking Boston harbor. The sudden appearance of cannon muzzles poking out of gun emplacements commanding the harbor reaches suddenly rendered the British fleet's anchorage in the roadstead tactically untenable. Sir William Howe's battle flotilla was forced to sail out and away, beyond the range of the looming guns Schuyler and Knox had manhandled all the way from Fort Ticonderoga through the worst of a New England winter.

On March 18, 1776, Dorothy Dudley exulted to her diary, "Boston is free at last. Today George Washington entered the town accompanied by Mrs. Washington. . . ." After this spectacular exploit, Schuyler was as entitled to boast, as Henry Knox did, that he was the man whom "Washington loved."

As Sir William Howe's battle fleet sailed away past Nantasket Roads, the commander in chief knew that its next appearance would be below the Battery at New York, where artillerymen of Hamilton's company were anxiously keeping watch for its spars and hulls. Dorothy Dudley added that Washington had "ordered five regiments and a portion of artillery . . . to march immediately to New York."

Washington himself arrived from Boston in mid-April. Brushing aside General Charles Lee's doubts that the city could be defended, he insisted that New York be held. It was a political decision that recognized the supreme strategic importance of New York. He charged William Alexander, Lord Stirling, who had taken over command at New York from General Lee early in March, that "It is the place that we must use every endeavor to keep from them. For should they get that town, and the command of the North River, they can stop the intercourse between the northern and southern colonies, upon which depends the safety of America." The British withdrawal from Boston would enable them to concentrate an army of at least 25,000 regulars at New York against Washington's 10,000, and about 13,000 militia.

As part of New York City's elaborate fortifications, Captain Alexander Hamilton's Provincial company helped John Lasher's City Battalion of Independents construct a heptagonal fort on Bayard's Hill, which was located at what is now the intersection of Canal and Mulberry Streets.[5] From high ground, overlooking the city of about 4,000 houses and 25,000 people to the south, Hamilton's guns could command the lower end of Manhattan Island below what is now Chambers Street.

When the men had completed building the fortification on May 16, Washington thanked them "for their masterly manner of executing the work." Seeing its twelve six-pound cannons and its garrison of two commissioned officers, four noncommissioned officers, and 20 privates, Nicholas Fish with ill-founded optimism, called the fort on Bayard's Hill "a fortification superior in strength to any my imagination could ever have conceived."

It was a key strong point in a chain of earthworks on lower Manhattan that stretched across the island from the Jersey Battery on the Hudson side to Horn's Hook on the East River. Spencer's Redoubt on the lower East Side was the southeast anchor of the line. There was another gun position far to the north, near where East 89 Street now runs, and still another fortress named Fort Washington was hacked out of the solid schist near what now is West 180 Street. Across the East River, on the Brooklyn end of Long Island, Generals Rufus Putnam and Nathanael Greene threw up other earthworks along Brooklyn Heights and eastward to the flatlands and down to the beaches beyond Brooklyn village. From an engineering standpoint, these were splendid fortifications, but militarily the whole system was nothing but a trap. Washington and his generals, except for Nathanael Greene, were making the beginner's mistake of trying to protect far wider reaches of territory than could possibly have been held by the available troops.

All speculation ended on June 29. The first waves of the greatest seaborne expeditionary force that Britain had ever sent abroad, eventually swelling to about 34,000 strong, hove into view sailing up the Narrows. Daniel McCurtin gasped as he peered out at sunrise from his Staten Island house with a view of the water: "I . . . spied as I peeped out . . . something resembling a wood of pine trees trimmed . . . the whole Bay was full of shipping as ever it could be. I . . . thought all London was afloat." An enemy fleet of more than one hundred sail dropped anchor in the Lower Bay.

British troops splashed ashore, occupied Staten Island, and scouted the Jersey shore across the narrow Kill van Kull, but made no move just yet toward Manhattan and Long Island. Toward the end of July, still more transports and warships down from Halifax joined the earlier fleet. Admiral Richard Howe, known as Black Dick, brought still more heavy reinforcements directly from England to back up his brother William's efforts. With him came regiments of Hessians that George III had hired from the German princely States.

Still another British fleet arrived in New York harbor in early August from Charleston, ready for revenge after suffering a defeat off Sullivan's Island at the hands of a gallant provincial force under the command of Colonels Christopher Gadsden and Charles Cotesworth Pinckney.

On August 8, 1776, Washington warned of the impending British attack in a portentous general order:

> The movements of the enemy, and intelligence by deserters, give the utmost reason to believe, that the great struggle, in which we are contending for everything dear to us, and our posterity is near at hand.

The British troops had been prepared to disembark for some time. Only bad weather had delayed the grand assault. For the nervous Americans watching this armada burgeon in the harbor, the signal for all to rush to their posts would be "A flag in the daytime, or a light at night in the fort on Bayard's Hill, with three guns from the same place fired quick, but distinct." All drums would beat a tattoo. Hamilton's men kept two days' victuals ready dressed and all their canteens filled. Hamilton drilled his men in firing the warning signal and his drummers in beating the alarm. New York's first Provincial Company of Artillery could not have been more prepared for action—or untested by disaster.

As he kept his company's cannons nervously ready to aim and fire while the seemingly endless enemy buildup in the harbor continued, Hamilton read and heard with growing excitement the news coming back from Philadelphia. On July 4 the Continental Congress had formally adopted a Declaration of Independence, which echoed many of the things he had shouted from the platform in his speech in The Fields and published in pamphlets like *A Full Vindication* and *The Farmer Refuted.*

Unlike Hamilton's published charges, the Declaration's grievances were not focused primarily on the sins of the British Parliament; they did not exempt the king himself. Earlier arguments of the patriots' case had repudiated the authority of Parliament; now, in the Declaration of Independence, the last tie to Britain was severed when blame was laid on King George III himself as well as his Parliament. It proclaimed that "He [the king] has combined with others to subject us to a jurisdiction foreign to our Constitution, and unacknowledged by our laws; giving his assent to their acts of pretended legislation." The Declaration linked the king with the Americans' grievances against Parliament by the clever literary device of including Parliament among the unidentified "others" who were in conspiracy with the king. It did not even mention Parliament as an unindicted coconspirator. The Liberty Bell pealed in Philadelphia. A courier rushed the text to New York where George Washington himself came down from his headquarters house at Richmond Hill to hear the Declaration formally read at another great July meeting in The Fields where Hamilton had cried out for revolution two years earlier.

Almost any American who has spent a few years in the armed service of his country during the many wars it has fought since 1776 less glorious than the Revolution has found that the experience leaves an indelible impression on his mind for the rest of his life. The experience remains most powerfully intense for a veteran of combat, as Hamilton was. It is all but impossible to imagine the strength of the impression that the onset of such an ideologically unexceptionable war must have made on the mind of the nineteen-year-old captain. In later life he would avoid all parade of war stories except to audiences of fellow combat veterans.

The impression on his mind would be made all the more indelible by beginning with a debacle. General Washington, like General Nathanael Greene and Colonel Rufus Putnam in Brooklyn, had contrived to place the backbone of America's outnumbered army in positions that were too widely extended and manned by too few troops too thinly deployed. The British had given the Americans all the time they needed in which to spread out, dig in, and commit themselves fully to their folly.

Still, the fortifications on Manhattan gave credibility to a defense system that caused Admiral Lord Richard Howe and his brother, General Sir William Howe, to decide against a frontal attack on Manhattan Island. The opposite decision might have led to their bottling up the entire American army, and destroying it, and crushing the Revolution then and there. Instead, they made an amphibious landing on Long Island on August 22 through 27.

The British, deploying about 10,000 troops and 28 pieces of artillery, attacked westward toward the Continentals, who dug in to defend Brooklyn Heights. First, General von Heister with his Hessians attacked General John Sullivan at the Flatbush pass. Then, while these diversionary attacks were going on, Howe, General Charles Cornwallis, and Lord Percy swung east to the Jamaica pass, and at 3 o'clock on the morning of August 28 they routed the few Americans posted there as guards, including Hamilton's friend Robert Troup. They stopped briefly for breakfast, then continued marching west to attack Washington's defensive line from the rear. A drenching northeaster soaked the Americans' ammunition, but helped hold the enemy off for three days before they resumed the attack.

General Nathanael Greene had fallen sick three days before the assault began, leaving General John Sullivan as a replacement who was not his equal.

Colonel Rufus Putnam, who replaced Sullivan, was even less so. The sectors they commanded were not clearly marked. The British made the most of all the weaknesses of the unblooded American command.

A large question was whether New York City itself was to be razed to the ground. Washington asked Congress on September 2, "If we should be obliged to abandon the town, ought it to stand as winter quarters for the enemy? . . . If Congress should resolve upon destruction of it, the resolution should be kept a profound secret."

Congress resolved to try to save the city, but the inhabitants sensed that the defense effort would be futile. Women and children with heaps of furniture gathered to seek transportation to the New Jersey shore. One citizen reported that only fascines, small bundles of sticks, were extended across Broadway near the Bowling Green, "where the statue of Chatham was thrown down." On the west more substantial barricades were built out of a ship's cargo of mahogany. One knowing New Yorker scoffed, "but all this was a show to keep up the spirits of the people; for I myself heard General Wooster laugh at the idea of a defense."

The decision to evacuate Long Island and try to defend Manhattan, York Island as it was then called, was a sudden one. Washington had only just notified the New York Provincial Congress that he had troops enough to hold the fortifications on Brooklyn Heights. Young Captain Hamilton recommended the evacuation of all the positions on Long Island. Hercules Mulligan reported that before the battle he had seen Hamilton, who had been dining at Mulligan's house, draft the plan, read it aloud to himself and the Reverend John Mason, write it into an anonymous letter to Washington, and give it to Colonel Webb of Washington's staff. Mulligan was certain that Washington had followed Hamilton's specific directions "because my impression at that time was that the mode of drawing off the army which was adopted was nearly the same as that pointed out in the letter." No doubt, the same idea occurred at about the same time to many good military minds besides Hamilton's. A council of general officers on Long Island late on August 29 agreed that "under all circumstances it is . . . eligible to leave Long Island . . . and remove to New York."[6]

Whether or not Hamilton was with Washington at the time the plan was carried out, it represented a masterful American escape from a self-constructed trap.[7] John Glover's sailors and fishermen from Marblehead Cape brought every skiff, dinghy, dory, and other kind of small boat they could find to the Brooklyn side of the East River and, under cover of rain and darkness, took all the troops, guns, horses, and baggage off to Manhattan without interference from Lord Howe's warships. The few hundred soldiers left in the Brooklyn Heights fortifications built smoky bonfires to help screen the escape, and a dense fog also helped cover them. Washington, hardly out of the saddle for 48 hours, supervised every aspect of the withdrawal and was the last to step into a boat. Hamilton's son indicates, rather vaguely, that the precocious young grand strategist was with Washington on Long Island. His report reads that "In the retreat, Captain Hamilton brought up the rear, having lost his baggage and a field piece." American casualties were about 1,000, with 200 killed. British casualties were fewer than 400. A British historian called the evacuation "a master stroke by which Washington saved his army and his country."

Washington's narrow escape across the East River the night of August 29 and 30, without loss of his army, was a master stroke that preserved a good part of it for the disasters that were still to come.

Major Baurmeister, a Hessian officer, wrote to his patron, Baron von Jungkenn, back in Hesse-Cassel, "We had no knowledge of this [move] until four o'clock in the morning of the 30th." Then, he wrote, "The entire American army has fled to New England, evacuating also New York. . . ."

He was wrong. Congress and Washington still stubbornly insisted on trying to defend Manhattan Island. On the morning of September 15, British warships opened up a cannonade "to scour the ground and cover the landing of the troops." The Howes struck at the thin line of green and panicky American militia cowering in carelessly dug earthworks at the weakest sector of Manhattan's defenses—in the middle, at Kip's Bay, near what is now East 30 Street—and fanned out over the woods and meadows of what is now midtown. An observer reported, "On the appearance of the enemy, not more than 60 or 70 in number," the militiamen "ran away in the greatest confusion without firing a single shot."

Hamilton's Provincial company was part of the army's artillery command under Henry Knox. Israel Putnam was in overall command of the area. From Bayard's Hill fort along the line of lower Manhattan forts, Hamilton sounded the alarm. Down from Harlem Heights at the north end of the island galloped Washington. He was met by the militiamen fleeing in panic from Kip's Bay. He tried furiously to rally them to stand and fight, but they kept on running away. Seeing from "this dastardly conduct" that nothing more could be expected of these panicky recruits, he commanded all units to consolidate all defenses up at Harlem Heights. From the lower end of the island, General Israel Putnam sent reinforcements to Kip's Bay, but they were too late. To avoid being cut off, they joined the other brigades in the general retreat streaming northward up the spine of the island. According to Hercules Mulligan, Hamilton and his Provincial artillery held fast at Bayard's Hill fort, ready to defend it to the last man. Suddenly Colonel Henry Knox came running in to take cover, mistakenly supposing that all roads of escape to the north had now been cut off. He and Hamilton set to work and aimed their cannon northward for a last ditch defense of a besieged bastion cut off behind enemy lines. Remembering them, General Putnam, who had joined his other brigades in flight to the north, sent his aide Major Aaron Burr back to Bayard's Hill fort "to call off the pickets and guards" and bring them up with the main body. Burr passed the order along to Colonel Knox and Captain Hamilton, pointed out to them that the road north, up the west side of the island, was still open, and offered to lead the way. Some say that this rescue of Hamilton by Aaron Burr was the first time the two men had ever met. Both had been prominent young army officers in New York for months, and Hamilton knew the way to Harlem Heights as well as Burr. Whether or not it was the first meeting of the two men, in drama it would be surpassed only by the last—and one other encounter in between.

If the British, as they broke out of their beachhead at Kip's Bay, had moved swiftly west to the Hudson across the waist of the island, they could have bagged Hamilton, Knox, Putnam, and Burr and all the other defenders to the southward. They could have cut Washington's already depleted army in two and chopped up the pieces at leisure. Instead they wheeled their columns north, while Burr led Hamilton and the other defenders out of the southerly line of forts and up the still open west side of the island along Broadway. In columns moving parallel to Burr's, the British streamed north up the East Side in pursuit of Washington.

As they dragged their cannons and ammunition, it took Hamilton and his New York Provincial artillery till after nightfall to rout-march the nine miles to Harlem Heights, where the main force of the army already encamped there opened ranks to let them pass through. They finally halted near what is now about 147 Street and Broadway, close to where Hamilton later built his Grange.

Weary as they were, their captain had drilled his men well. Before quitting to fling themselves down for some exhausted sleep, they got out their shovels, dug emplacements, and threw up earthworks around their guns in defilade positions formed by Harlem ridge. Then they set up a watch on the perimeters for the night.

Earlier that day at Kip's Bay, General Washington had furiously tried to rally his beaten militia. From astride his horse, he had laid his riding crop smartly across the men's backs to check their flight and lash them into a stand, with no success. The contrast between those fleeing militiamen and the discipline of Hamilton's artillerymen digging in for the night behind earthworks, their cannons aimed for the next day's firing, caught the commander's eye. Egbert Benson, a longtime friend of both Hamilton and Washington, wrote that it was here that night that Washington asked someone the name of the captain of the New York Provincial artillery. Told that his name was Alexander Hamilton, Washington invited him to join him in the general's marquee, the large tent he used for field headquarters. According to Hamilton's son John Church Hamilton, Washington inspected "the works which he was engaged in throwing up, entered into conversation with him, and formed a high estimate of his military capacity."

Thus began Hamilton's close, intense, complex, stormy relationship with the man he would describe as "an aegis very essential to me." From this night's encampment in Harlem Heights, Hamilton would go on to become Washington's junior partner in the business of creating the United States.

Next morning, before dawn, Washington's orders of the day called for one of his finest officers, the courteous, elegant, affable Lieutenant Colonel Thomas Knowlton, the idol of all soldiers in his command, to lead an attack on the British pursuers with his 100 Connecticut Rangers. Knowlton's men ran into British light infantry moving north up the slope of the ridge, formed a skirmish line, held firm, and exchanged fire with the enemy. A sudden skirl of bagpipes meant that strong units of the Black Watch were moving up to reinforce the light infantry. Knowlton's Rangers broke off in good order and beat a disciplined retreat.

The British then launched a general attack on the ridge. Washington ordered larger American forces to counterattack. He committed to action the reorganized militiamen who had so cravenly fled in panic the day before at Kip's Bay. Now he saw them stand and fight almost toe-to-toe against the same British regulars who had chased them off Long Island and smashed through them at Kip's Bay. From well dug-in emplacements on the Heights, Hamilton's cannoneers kept up a steady morale-stiffening blanket of covering fire on the enemy lines.

Suddenly the British regulars began to retreat! Back through a field of buckwheat near what is now the site of Barnard College, falling back through an orchard that bordered the field, the bright red coats and blue green kilts and tall black bearskins of the fabled British and Scottish battalions, whose very names were the terror of the world, fell back before New Englanders and Marylanders and Virginians in hot pursuit. Through fringes of smoke farther south in the distance Hamilton could see British and Hessian reserve units being hustled forward at double time to reinforce the front lines falling back. Knowlton's armed reconnaissance had developed into a general engagement against superior British numbers. It was too much of a risk for Washington. Wisely and coolly he ordered his troops to pull back. Young Tench Tilghman of Pennsylvania wrote that the troops greeted this order derisively, for "the pursuit of a flying enemy was so new a scene that it was with difficulty that our men could be brought to retire . . . they gave a Hurra! and left the field in good order."

Here was a remarkable achievement. Troops from different provinces thrown into the battle for New York had finally demonstrated that when it came to courage, there was little to choose between them. Washington's army had been transformed from the beaten mob of Kip's Bay the day before into a fighting army. On Harlem Heights that day every man knew it.

Some 130 Americans fell in this fierce little fire fight, but the British suffered twice as many casualties. Among the Americans lost was the gallant Lieutenant Colonel Knowlton.

The Battle of Harlem Heights was the first of the war in which Americans from many different states advanced on British regulars and forced them to give ground. It was not lost on Hamilton that the victory had been a national one, a truly American victory. Sensing the larger meaning of the small battle, Joseph Reed, an aide who would later fall out with Washington, wrote: "You can hardly conceive the change it has made. . . . The men . . . feel a confidence which before they had quite lost."

On October 9, British frigates broke through underwater obstructions in the Hudson River channel and sailed up the river, flanking Washington's position on the west. Three days later Howe's troops landed in force on Throg's Neck and Pell's Point, flanking him to the east. Between them the Americans on the ridge at Harlem Heights were threatened with being cut off.

Something had to be done before Howe, as Washington realized, should "enclose us . . . by taking post in our rear," By moving across Westchester, Howe could pin Washington against the Hudson and cut him and his army off from the rest of the country. From this tactical cul-de-sac, the commander in chief wrote home to his cousin Lund Washington: "Such is my situation that if I were to wish the bitterest curse to an enemy on this side of the grave, I should put him in my stead with my feelings." Washington clung to the position on Harlem Heights, too weak to break out in force, but also too weak to withdraw in safety.

It seems likely that having already come to Washington's favorable notice, Hamilton, as one of the ranking artillery officers under Knox, looked in on some of the commander in chief's long conferences at the headquarters in the magnificent Georgian frame and shingle manse that is now known as the Jumel Mansion, at the highest point in Manhattan on the bluffs above the Hudson. In attendance at conferences of high ranking officers there would be also Lord Stirling who, like General John Sullivan, had been taken prisoner on Long Island and then exchanged. Returned from the south, General Charles Lee now echoed the earlier advice of Nathanael Greene to abandon Manhattan and move up into Westchester County. The idea of giving up New York City died hard.

By October 16, evacuation was decided upon, with one foolish politically motivated reservation: Even though all supply and communication from the Jersey shore would be interdicted by British cruisers in the Hudson, a toehold at Fort Washington, on the rocky ledge near what is now West 180 Street, was to be held by a large garrison of 2,800.

The army's main force withdrew north to White Plains. Supply trains of shaky carts and hungry horses had to be relayed in short hauls. Men outmarched rations and ammunition. Many deserted; others lost their way. General Howe followed in pursuit. At White Plains, on October 28, his army attacked an outpost of Washington's army at Chatterton's Hill, a detached ridge lying to the southwest of the main American lines.

Hamilton's son and others ascribed to his father a valiant role at the Battle of White Plains, but no records have been found to show exactly what he did or where his cannons were that day.[8] This is not surprising, especially in a defeat. If the infantrymen who must protect the gun emplacements break and flee, the artillery's gun positions are overrun. Enemy cannoneers are often marked for vengeful slaughter when the victors reach them. The sweating, smoke-choked, powder-burned, all-but-deafened artillerymen who must stay with their precious guns and provide covering fire for the infantry become the ultimate objective of a charging enemy's attacks.

In command at Chatterton's Hill was Hamilton's old friend General Alexander McDougall of New York, many of whose 1,600 militia were still recovering from the shocks of Long Island and Kip's Bay. Howe threw his main attack toward McDougall's weak and exposed position. Under their own covering fire and up steep slopes, Hessians charged across the Bronx River. The British cannonade threw the American militia into confused retreat. Continental troops put up a brief defense, but the saber-swinging 17th Dragoons Cavalry galloped down and crushed them. Fifteen minutes gave the British and Hessians possession of the field. The Americans "moved off the hill in a . . . body, neither running nor observing the best order," as one apologist said.

The first full-dress cavalry charge of the war had a devastating impact on the raw American militiamen. Hamilton's son reports only that at the scene of this disaster his father's conduct was favorably marked.

Winter was coming on, and the enlistments of 2,000 of Washington's men expired December 1; most of the rest expired a month later.

Moving on from his victory at White Plains, Sir William Howe prepared to invade New Jersey. At the same time, he sent a force south to storm isolated Fort Washington. Like Fort Lee on the New Jersey Palisades nearly opposite, Fort Washington now was useless. Washington was downcast by his defeat at White Plains, distracted and confused by the formal counsel of his officers, by General Greene's misplaced confidence, and by the political demands of Congress that the forts be held, that the river be kept blocked, and that a toehold in New York City be maintained.

Timely evacuation of Fort Washington would have saved 2,800 troops, many cannon, and arms and supplies and, equally important, the spirits of the patriot army and of the country. The enemy moved freely on all sides of both forts by land and water. The American forces surrendered unconditionally on November 16. The calamity was blamed on Washington's hesitation to give positive orders for evacuation until, standing on the ground, he saw that he had delayed too long. Its fall was the final event of the war on Manhattan Island until the commander in chief entered the city in triumph seven years later.

Hamilton's son reported that "The fall of that fortress which sealed the fate of the city of New York, and cut off so large a portion of the army, awakened all the soldier's spirit in his [father's] breast; and, after a careful observation of the post, he volunteered to General Washington to storm it; saying that if he would confide to him an adequate number of men, one half under the command of Major Ebenezer Stevens, the residue of himself, he would promise him success."

At this dark hour, nothing would have warmed Washington's heart more than to recapture the fort bearing his name. It would mean at least symbolically that he had not entirely lost New York. Hamilton's proposal offered a ray of hope at a time that must have seemed to Washington the very nadir of his country's fortunes. All the "summer soldiers" were heading back to their farms and firesides. The more foolhardiness the commander in chief saw in the proposal, the more he had to admire the courage and zeal of its young maker.

Deeper nadirs than this one were to come.

Hamilton's company retreated from White Plains with Lord Stirling's brigade, crossed the Hudson to Haverstraw on November 9, 1776, and then hurried south to Hackensack through the gap in the Palisades known as the Clove. Washington and the main army followed the same route. Up the Hudson at

North Castle General Charles Lee, with 10,000 men on the roster if not on duty, remained positioned to shield New England against an enemy move to the north. After the fall of Fort Washington, Lee wrote to the Philadelphia physician-congressman Benjamin Rush, complaining that Washington had disregarded his advice to "draw off" the garrison from Fort Washington "or all will be lost." Lee suggested that if he were the commander in chief instead of Washington, he could do far better. "A total want of sense pervades all your councils," he said. "Had I the powers, I could do you much good." A little later Lee wrote to the Massachusetts Assembly that "There are times when we must commit treason . . . for the salvation of the state. The present crisis demands this brave, virtuous kind of treason."

Cold weather came on, and the men's enlistments neared expiration. They were thinly clad and often shoeless. Sometimes a regiment would shrink to the size of a single company, and a company to the size of a platoon. None of this created incentives to reenlist.

By the time he reached Hackensack, Washington had with him "not above 3,000 men and they much broken and dispirited." On November 19, Cornwallis landed 3,000 troops at Alpine, New Jersey, opposite Yonkers, and next morning they clambered up the Palisades and captured Fort Lee. General Nathanael Greene pulled out in such haste that his men abandoned all weapons and stores: 146 cannons, 12,000 rounds of shell, 1,000 barrels of flour, 2,800 muskets, 400,000 cartridges, and all tents, blankets, and entrenching tools. Joining Washington at Hackensack, General Greene's demoralized regiments brought his total to about 5,400 poorly supplied troops. Hackensack was "a dead flat" and useless for defense. Now the British were pressing west to trap the dispirited Americans between the Hackensack and Passaic rivers. Hamilton's company kept marching. It deployed and redeployed its guns to provide cover for Stirling's brigade of 1,200 when it crossed the Passaic and moved on down to Newark. Washington followed behind with the main body of the men. Enemy columns pursued them to Hackensack, and an American rear guard had to destroy the bridge to delay their pursuit. Still in the van with Lord Stirling, Captain Hamilton's company marched 20 miles westward, dragging their guns and ammunition to the Raritan River and across the wooden bridge there into New Brunswick, while Washington rested five more days at Newark with what he called "the wretched remains of a broken army." At New Brunswick, Hamilton sited his cannons high on the west bank of the Raritan, a few hundred yards from the river, on what is now the main campus of Rutgers University to protect the river crossing. Washington and the remnants of his retreating army straggled across the wooden bridge with Cornwallis close behind pressing his pursuit. The last of the rear guard barely made it across the wooden bridge ahead of the pursuers. Hamilton's guns laid down and returned a "smart cannonade." Washington described his narrow escape, writing Congress: "The enemy appeared in several parties on the heights opposite Brunswick and were advancing in a large body towards the crossing place. We had a smart cannonade while we were parading our men, but without any or but little loss on either side." Washington was in despair, but indomitable: "It being impossible to oppose them with our present force . . . we shall retreat to the west side of Delaware." That meant somewhere far to the south, near Philadelphia or beyond.

Hamilton's New York Provincial company continued firing until Washington's army, or what was left of it by then, could escape safely on its way west again. Long afterward, G. W. P. Custis, George Washington's stepgrandson, wrote that the commander in chief was "charmed by the brilliant courage and admirable skill" of Hamilton in that desperate scrape and "marked him for his own."

During the two-day halt at New Brunswick, Washington wrote a letter to Congress, informing it that the enemy had twice his numbers and more than twice his strength. It had reached nearby Bonumtown and was closer all the time. The letter finished, Washington added a postscript the same afternoon: "the enemy are fast advancing, some of them are now in sight." The same afternoon Washington resumed his flight west to Princeton.

As Hamilton and his artillerymen covered the retreat of Washington and his remnants of an oft-beaten army, a veteran artillery officer observing him wrote that he "noticed a youth, a mere stripling, small, slender, almost delicate in frame, marching . . . with a cocked hat pulled down over his eyes, apparently lost in thought, with his hand resting on a cannon, and every now and then patting it, as if it were a favorite horse or a pet plaything."

He watched Hamilton march on into the college town: "The day Hamilton's company marched into Princeton, it was a model of discipline. At their head was a boy, and I wondered at his youth; but what was my surprise when . . . he was pointed out to me as that Hamilton of whom we had already heard so much."

The Americans retreated toward a helpless capital, which they would be too weak to defend. Loss of Forts Washington and Lee had stripped the army in New Jersey of the supplies and ordnance it needed to survive a victorious enemy in hot pursuit across flat country with few natural defensive barriers. Soldiers who had not already deserted would disappear when enlistments expired. To make Washington's peril worse, his only reserves, the army under General Charles Lee at North Castle, failed to join him. Lee ignored Washington's orders until every excuse was exhausted and then moved southwest at a leisurely pace—so leisurely, in fact, that he was captured by the British after being routed out of a prostitute's blankets in a tavern at Baskenridge, New Jersey. The name of the place was changed to Basking Ridge.

Bedding down in the retreat with his bedraggled matrosses and ammunition bearers under tattered blankets in frostbitten woods, Hamilton was bound to have little sympathy for the self-inflicted misfortune of a malingerer like Lee.

Death and desertion dogged the ranks of the stumbling Continentals. A British officer was shocked to see that "many of the Rebels who were killed . . . were without shoes or Stockings, & Several were observed to have only linen drawers . . . without any proper shirt or Waistcoat . . . also in great want of blankets . . . they must suffer extremely."

Washington appealed through Governor Livingston for help from the people of New Jersey, but they could see for themselves that things were going badly for the Americans. Many refused to take up arms in their own defense and instead sought the protection and favor of General Howe. Instead of rallying to help the desperate remnants of the patriot army, many signed oaths of British allegiance. Still Washington remained indomitable. He asked Adjutant General Joseph Reed of Philadelphia whether, if he were driven to retreat "to the back parts of Pennsylvania," the inhabitants there would support him. Reed's answer gave no comfort. If the enemy overran the eastern counties, and they gave up, he said, "the back counties will do the same." In that case, Washington retorted, he would take refuge in mountainous Western Virginia. If the British pushed him from there too, he would move further west across the Alleghenies and fight on from there, at the head of whatever band of revolutionaries might remain with him then.

At a later stage in the war, a British comment was that "any other general in the world other than General Howe would have beaten General Washington; and any other general in the world than General Washington would have beaten General Howe."

In Washington's errors in the early battles may be discerned the qualities that led to ultimate victory. For all his retreats, he was a more aggressive fighter than most generals are. Congress's and his army's weaknesses laid upon him the tactical necessity of avoiding a major engagement. Nothing could be more galling. But he was beginning to see that the way to win was to survive and keep the army intact until the enemy wearied of a war it could win only by a quick, dramatic, crushing victory. He wrote to Congress in September 1776, "On our side the war should be defensive."

At this desperate hour of the American Revolution, nothing really remained of it but the courage and resolve of George Washington and the little band of officers and men like Hamilton and his company who remained faithful through the long bitter marches, retreating with him. Cornwallis and his army could cover a good 20 miles in a single day. In pursuit, the miles are shorter than in retreat. When the Americans flung themselves down to rest at night after fleeing only the same distance that Cornwallis had pursued them, the Continental Army was twice as weary and spent.

By December 8 Washington had completed his first, little-remembered crossing of the Delaware to take refuge in retreat on its west side. Cornwallis's troops, still in close pursuit, had entered Trenton on its east side. If the Delaware River froze over and made it possible for them to cross, an enemy drive to take Philadelphia was still possible. To keep up what remained of patriot morale, Congress at first promised not to leave Philadelphia, a political decision that was as militarily foolish as its insistence on holding Fort Washington had been. Washington warned Robert Morris, chief of the Committee of Congress on the War, "I will give you the earliest information in my power of immediate danger; in the meantime, I advise . . . that you detain no papers you can possibly do without, for I am satisfied the enemy waits for two events only to begin their operations upon Philadelphia, ice for a passage, and the dissolution of the poor remains of our debilitated army." On December 13, Congress scuttled south to the safety of Baltimore.

A few days before Christmas, Adjutant General Joseph Reed wrote a plea to Washington to make some kind of an attack on Cornwallis. If nothing else, it would be good for the morale of the colonies, he thought: "We are all of opinion that something must be attempted to revive the aspiring credit, give our cause some degree of reputation and prevent total depreciation of the continental money . . . even a failure cannot be more fatal than to remain in our present situation."

It would be a political attack. Reed suggested a bold move: "In short, some enterprise must be undertaken . . . or we must give up the cause. Will it not be possible . . . to make a diversion or something more at or about Trenton . . . Our affairs are hastening fast to ruin if we do not retrieve them by some happy event."

The capital was defenseless. What passed for the Continental government had fled. All that seemed to be left of the gloriously proclaimed Revolution were Washington and Hamilton and their "wretched remains of a broken army."

With Christmas the end of most enlistments drew near. Under Washington's command, scattered along the west bank of the Delaware in bivouacs on either side of McKonkey's Ferry, were about 6,000 men, some of them, by Washington's own grim account, "entirely naked and most so thinly clad as to be unfit for service." In a private letter he confessed that unless he found many more men, "the game will be pretty well up."

Christmas arrived with the Delaware in full flood, jammed with massive sheets of ice that any experienced soldier of either army could see at a glance made it completely impassable.

Once again the commander in chief called for the specialized skills of John Glover's Marbleheaders, the same amphibious corps that had rescued his army from the trap on Brooklyn Heights after the defeat on Long Island.

On the night of December 25, Hamilton's and other New Yorkers, New Hampshiremen, Virginians, Pennsylvanians—men from all the provinces in revolt—bending forward against the gale-driven sleet, slogged toward the river and the waiting Durham boats. Their paths through the snow were "tinged here and there with blood from the feet of men who wore broken shoes"—or no shoes. "It will be a terrible night for the soldiers," wrote one officer, "but I have not heard a man complain."

Hamilton's boat and the others shoved out into the ice-choked flood, low in the water with the weight of guns, horses, and shivering men in remnants of blue and buff uniforms. If river-soaked muskets should become useless, Washington ordered, "Tell General Sullivan to use the bayonet. I am resolved to take Trenton."

Comfortably billeted in Trenton, contemptuous of the ragtag Americans bivouacked in the snow nine miles away on the other side of the ice-flooded river, Colonel Johann Gottlieb Rall and his Hessians had celebrated Christmas with wassail and grog as only lonely Teutons can. Rall sent a small patrol to keep watch on the river at McKonkey's Ferry and posted a few pickets a half mile out of town, but they failed to detect the American river crossing and approach march. American battle orders called for landing on the Jersey shore by midnight, but the crossing was so slow that it was not until four in the morning that Hamilton and his company assembled there to begin the nine-mile march to Trenton. A snowstorm, which from time to time turned to driving sleet, slowed their march still further, but kept them well hidden from Rall's patrol and pickets when dawn broke. On the march the infantry from time to time broke into its fast-paced "long trot." Hamilton's artillerymen, weighted down with guns and ammunition, struggled, panting to keep pace.

Hamilton positioned his company's cannon at the edge of the town to fire into it from the head of King Street. The assault of the American infantry caught the Hessian garrison completely by surprise and badly hung over. Hessian Lieutenant Andreas Wiederhold saw movement, heard shouts, then raised the alarm. "Der Feind! Der Feind!" he screamed. "Heraus! Heraus!" (The enemy. The enemy. All out. All out.)

It was too late. Hamilton's fieldpieces thumped out their cannonballs over the heads of advancing infantry. Mercer's men charged in attacking columns with bayonets fixed. Farther south, John Glover's amphibious command, after their backbreaking night work on the Delaware, brought up more reinforcements across the Assunpink.

Scanning the scene from high ground near what is now Princeton Avenue, Washington sent Lord Stirling's brigade into action, spearheaded by George Weedon's Third Virginia Regiment. More Americans under Captain William Washington and Lieutenant James Monroe (later to assume higher rank) shot down and bayoneted the gunners and loaders who manned two Hessian artillery pieces. Arthur St. Clair's brigade joined the charge. Leading its right wing, John Stark "dealt death wherever he found resistance and broke down all opposition before him."

Muskets and pistols were drying out. Infantrymen took aim, and small arms fire began to rattle and flash and pop all along the line. Rall, the garrison commander, still groggy from holiday celebrations, rambled up and down King and Queen streets, bravely trying to rally his men. A shot found him; he fell, mortally wounded. General Sullivan wheeled his whole command up from the river to meet St. Clair's moving down from the north. In a snow-covered apple orchard, after a battle of less than three-quarters of an hour, the beaten remains of the British garrison of Trenton stacked their arms and surrendered.

Washington counted 918 enemy prisoners, including 30 officers, as many muskets as men, six brass cannon, and four of the prized Hessian battle standards. Thirty Hessians had been killed and three times as many wounded. No American had been killed and only four slightly wounded.

The snowstorm was getting worse. Weary from battle after the long night's march, the Americans retraced the nine miles to McKonkey's Ferry and Glover's Durham boats and were back in their bivouacs in Pennsylvania 48 hours after Operation Christmas present had begun.

The brilliant stroke lifted the despair of the colonies. New recruits found their way to Washington's camp; others, whose enlistments were expiring, agreed to stay on. General James Grant, the British commander at New Brunswick in overall command of the Hessians' Trenton outpost, commiserated with their commander, von Donop, on "a most unfortunate business." He added, "I did not think that all the rebels in America would have taken that brigade prisoners."

By December 30, Washington was able to write to Congress that "I have the pleasure to acquaint you that the Continental Regiments from the Eastern Governments have, to a man, agreed to stay six weeks beyond their term of enlistment. . . . ."

So, with a little more battle time left in his newly inspirited army, Washington ordered a corps across the Delaware again on the night of December 30–31 to make another armed reconnaissance, this time all the way to Princeton. He was pressing his luck into a British trap.

After the British debacle at Trenton, a home leave General Cornwallis had been scheduled to enjoy had been abruptly canceled. He had nearly 8,000 well-clothed, well-equipped men under his command, and he now rushed them from Princeton toward Trenton. Here was a chance to take reprisal against the American force of only 5,000, now isolated on Cornwallis's side of the river. Undaunted, Washington resolved to press on to "beat up the rest of the [enemy's] quarters bordering on and near the river. . . ." For the Continentals tragedy loomed. Washington's force was exhausted from lack of sleep and food. Ice in the Delaware was too thin for safe crossing on foot, but too thick for swift passage by Glover's boats; the roads were mire. The king's men under proud, energetic Cornwallis were determined to punish the Americans for Trenton and cancelled home leave.

As Cornwallis advanced, the Americans retreated back to the south of Assunpink Creek, near Trenton. Interdicting artillery fire from Hamilton's company held off Cornwallis for a few critical hours while Washington made plans for escape. Cornwallis's army was billeted in the town, with Washington's army trapped in low ground between the creek and the river. Cornwallis boasted jubilantly that he had caught "the old fox" and would "bag him in the morning." Sir William Erskine, who was with Cornwallis, said, "If Washington is the general I take him to be, he will not be found there in the morning." At Washington's council of war that night, one of the officers made the bold suggestion that there be no retreat back across the Delaware. Instead, the whole force should slip out by night past the British left and plunge deeper into New Jersey toward Princeton.

A rear guard flung on more logs to build up blazing campfires and kept up a noisy clatter with entrenching tools to deceive the British pickets. Washington's main army, with Captain Hamilton in the "great train of artillery," hitched up their horses, wrapped the wheels of the gun carriages with sacking to silence them on the frozen road, and marched northward out of the trap toward Princeton. Hamilton's cannoneers held the trace chains with gloved hands to silence the slightest clank. The ruse succeeded better with Cornwallis than it had with Howe on Long Island.

In the wintry night men stumbled against tree stumps in the rutted road. Horses bruised their shanks against them and reared up neighing. "We moved slow," wrote one man in the column, "on account of the artillery, frequently coming to a halt . . . when ordered forward again, one, two or three men in each platoon would stand, with their arms supported, fast asleep; a platoon next in rear advancing on them, they, in walking . . . would strike a stub [stump] and fall."

When British regimentals moving unconcernedly out of Princeton by the old road, toward what is now Lawrenceville, saw American General Hugh Mercer's column advancing on them in broad daylight, British Colonel Charles Mawhood was as surprised "as if an army had dropped perpendicularly upon them." He wheeled his columns, marched them back over the Stony Brook bridge, and hastily formed them in a defensive line in an orchard there. "Follow me" cried Hugh Mercer, urging his men forward in a bloody charge toward Mawhood's line. A hail of British grapeshot and musket balls hit them. At the line, thrusting British bayonets slashed American bodies. The gallant Mercer, who had led the charge, fell, many times wounded. His men and Cadwalader's, who had come up to support them, fled in disorderly retreat. An eyewitness reported that "But two pieces of artillery stood their ground and were served with great skill and bravery." Panicky American troops swirled around Hamilton's exposed artillery position to provide what protection they could for their artillery cover. Washington moved up with a relief column and rallied what remained of Mercer's and Cadwalader's brigades. These drove back toward the British line and through it, routed them from the field, and drove on into the college town, waving Knox's and Hamilton's artillerymen forward with the van. Units of the British South Lancashire Regiment rallied to form a new line of defense around the college buildings, but fell back again and finally took refuge in Nassau Hall.

Washington pressed the attack. Hamilton deployed and laid his gun sights on Nassau Hall. A well-aimed round crashed through a window and smashed through a portrait of King George II. It is a soldier's tale hallowed by countless retellings that can be neither proved nor disproved. In any event, Hamilton was there.

Hamilton's famous cannonball also nearly finished off James Wilkinson, who sarcastically wrote in his memoirs:

> There was but one gun fired at the college, and this from a six pounder, by an officer who was not advised the enemy had abandoned it; the ball recoiled, and very nearly killed my horse as I passed in the rear of the building.

Besides aiming it well, Hamilton must have set off this famous cannonball with a singularly heavy powder charge.

Unfortunately, the witness to this memorable story of Hamilton's skill as an artillerist, Colonel James Wilkinson, was one of the most duplicitous marplots and unreliable reporters that Hamilton would ever meet in his life.

The number of enemy troops who surrendered at Princeton also has the vagueness of legends, being variously reported as somewhere between 60 and 200. The casualties on both sides are also uncertain, with perhaps 40 Americans and twice as many of Cornwallis's troops killed or wounded.

If accounts of Hamilton's remarkable aim at the battle of Princeton are true, he has the distinction of being America's first student revolutionist known to have fired a cannonball into the hall of the college that turned down his admission application, during what in less turbulent times would have been the Christmas vacation of his sophomore year.

New Brunswick was the enemy's command headquarters for all of New Jersey. Riding the momentum of his attack on Princeton, Washington had hoped to press on to another surprise attack there. But his men were exhausted from days of continuous river crossings, forced marches, holding actions, and lucky escapes. Cornwallis, in the meantime, had turned his army back from Trenton to bring its full weight to bear on Washington at Princeton. With his commander, Henry Knox, Hamilton could chuckle over the arrival of Cornwallis and his men at Princeton, too late to catch Washington, who had moved on. Cornwallis was "in a most infernal sweat—running, puffing and blowing and swearing at being so outwitted."

Cornwallis now suspected that Washington and his army were indeed marching eastward to attack New Brunswick; so he hastily marched his own troops back to that valuable depot to trap Washington there. Washington told Congress that "with six or seven hundred fresh troops, upon a forced march," reaching New Brunswick before Cornwallis returned, he could have "destroyed all their stores, and magazines, taken . . . their military chest, containing 70,000 pounds, and put an end to the war." But for want of these men, he could not. So he wheeled his columns north, passed them by route march through Kingston, Rocky Hill, Somerset Court House, and Pluckemin to winter quarters on the Morristown plateau with Thimble Mountain rising behind it. Twenty-five miles due west of New York City, almost equally distant from the main British strongholds at New York, Amboy, Newark, and New Brunswick, Morristown was protected on all these approaches from attack by any large body of enemy by heavy forests and inaccessible heights. Various defiles to the west, leading to fertile and sympathetically peopled countryside, provided secure avenues for last-ditch retreat to the rear.

Arriving at Morristown winter quarters, Captain Hamilton's New York Provincial Artillery Company positioned its guns to cover the easterly approaches with flat fields of grazing fire. The men dug gun emplacements, threw up earthworks, camouflaged them with branches, set out sentries in a perimeter defense, and pitched their tents. Those who were not on the roster of the first watch fell to the ground for some exhausted sleep until their time came to be shaken awake for the second watch.

Unlike the artillery of modern battlefields—105 and 255 mm howitzers and huge mortars, which lob heavy shells aimed by surveys or forward observers into high trajectories from well-hidden positions a mile or more back of the front lines—crude six-pound cannon like Hamilton's had to be positioned almost shoulder to shoulder with the front line infantry. They fired their shot and ball in a flat trajectory aimed over open sights at enemy troops the cannoneers could usually see. Enemy troops could see the cannoneers and fire at them or stab them with bayonets if they got close enough.

Artillerymen could manhandle their heavy clumsy cannon only slowly and for short distances from fixed emplacements in the thick of a battle. Infantrymen could move quickly and for much greater distances, either to counterattack an advancing enemy or to take cover from an enemy threat. The infantry was also supposed to protect the artillery's positions. Because of the characteristics of their roles and moves, the infantry came to be known as the Queen of Battles; the artillery was the King. As in chess, loss of the King's position meant loss of the battle on the field. Infantrymen, like the Queen, could break and run and keep their muskets to fight another day, but not artillerymen. Their cannon were all but irreplaceable even if the men were not. If gun crews ran away and abandoned them, it clinched the enemy's victory. The balance of firepower for the next engagement shifted with the number of guns lost by one side to the other. So artillerymen had to stay with their guns until their positions were overrun. At the climactic moment of a losing battle, this usually meant bloody slaughter for the gun crews.

Memoirs of battles by high-ranking field grade officers—generals and colonels—are common; memoirs by company grade combat officers like Hamilton and the enlisted men of their combat commands are rarer. For a typical general or field grade officer pulling his cloak around him on an observation post out of musket range and pointing at the infantry in the distance for respectful aides to follow with their binoculars, the direction of men on a battlefield from a distance was an enthralling game like chess. There was no immediate necessity either to kill or be killed by a particular redcoated private advancing with musket aimed or bayonet fixed.

For the company grade combat officer and enlisted man, on the other hand, a battle was an experience of random terror, nothing like a chess game. Comrades fell or survived, were quickly killed or agonizingly wounded to die later, or escaped unscathed as part of a random process of arbitrary selection decreed as much by luck as by skill or bravery or cowardice. For one who survives it, a single day of battle in the line may contain more moments of fright, cowardice, despair, pain, gallantry, terror, luck, irony, heroism, and grandeur than all the other days of a long lifetime.

In 1776, Hamilton spent four months of such days at places with such deceptively peaceful sounding names as Brooklyn, Long Island, Manhattan, Harlem, White Plains, Hackensack, New Brunswick, Trenton, Princeton, and Morristown.

With the exception of Washington himself, most of the men who would be

Hamilton's friends and associates for the rest of his life were high-ranking officers who saw most of the war from command and observation posts or on very occasional forays onto the field. Few but Hamilton had been through the entire company officer's course of recruiting, training, and slogging along with his own men and guns; dragging and patting his cannon; petitioning for equal pay and better uniforms for forgotten men; reporting their sicknesses, desertions, and deaths; writing them up for citations when he needed sleep himself; sentencing a brawler to 39 lashes; or promoting an enlisted man from the ranks only to see him killed redemonstrating why he had been promoted.

In private, most generals respectfully yield their admiration to company grade officers like Hamilton who survive the generals' chess moves under fire on the field. Few generals but Washington, with his early years in the French and Indian War, overmatched Hamilton's record for intense combat experience with a line company. It is not surprising that he and Washington would see much else alike. The combat service of Hamilton with his company is of no historical importance in itself. But the imprint it left on Hamilton and all who knew him for the rest of his life and theirs is all-important for an understanding of him and them.

Thirteen years later, looking down from the lectern of St. Paul's Chapel on some of his comrades in arms, delivering his "Eulogium on General Nathanael Greene," he looked back on these as the days of "this little band of patriots . . . rallying the scattered energies of the country . . . and changing the whole tide and fortune of the war."

Hamilton kept meticulous records of his men's pay and other important matters of company management while busy fleeing and retreating and deploying and covering. He also jotted down in his *Pay Book* some maxims for the management of men that in the years that followed he also used in the management of the nation. One such jotting was the following extract from Demosthenes' *First Philippic:*

> As a general marches at the head of his troops, so ought wise politicians, if I dare use the expression, to march at the head of affairs; insomuch that they ought not to wait *the event*, to know what measures to take; but the measures which they have taken ought to produce the *event*.

United States Secretary of State Henry Kissinger has also said much the same thing: "Statesmen know the future, feel it in their bones, but are incapable of proving the truth of their insights." Nations as a whole, he added, "learn only by experience; they 'know' only when it is too late to act."

War was a terrible thing, of course, as the conventional wisdom held. But there was an important further point about it that Demosthenes had observed and described in the *First Philippic*, as recorded in Hamilton's Pay Book:

> Where attack him it will be said? Ah, Athenians, war, war itself will discover to you his weak sides, if you seek them.

To Demosthenes' observation, Hamilton appended his own assent: "Sublimely simple."

Being Hamilton, he was not content with his own untested assent to Demosthenes' proposition. He tested it to see whether other wise men agreed. Racking his recollection, he recalled another scholar who supported the thesis and added this citation to the entry in his *Pay Book:*

Vide Long: Ch. 16.

By this he meant that the passage he admired so much in Demosthenes was also cited in Dionysius Longinus' tract *On the Sublime*. Scholars have pounced upon the fact that Hamilton's *Pay Book* citation of Longinus quoting the admired passage from Demosthenes is in error. It is not in Longinus, Chapter XVI, as Hamilton recalled, but in Chapter XVIII. It is somewhat reassuring to an ordinary reader that Hamilton, the combat artilleryman recalling and jotting down classical cross-references in his company's pay book—shepardizing them mentally, as a lawyer might say—while on the march, was human enough to make a mistake.

Diversionary sniping by scholars from their armchairs does not obscure the point made by Demosthenes, Dionysius Longinus, and Alexander Hamilton about a man at war: "War itself will discover to you his weak sides, if you seek them." Higher-ranking comrades in arms discovering no weak sides in Hamilton at war would later unhesitatingly follow him wherever he led in peace. After a shared experience of such intensity, no weak sides that peace might discover could matter at all.

6

HEADQUARTERS INTELLIGENCER

TO HAVE THE MIND ALWAYS UPON THE STRETCH, SCARCE EVER UNBENT, AND NO HOURS FOR RECREATION MAKES A MATERIAL ODDS.
—*George Washington, distinguishing his aides-de-camp from other kinds of officers.*

AMIDST MY AMOROUS TRANSPORTS, LET ME NOT FORGET THAT I AM ALSO TO PERFORM THE PART OF A POLITICIAN AND INTELLIGENCER.
—*To Catharine Livingston, April 11, 1777.*

The honor of being the officer chosen to carry the four Hessian battle standards captured at Trenton to Philadelphia and proudly present them to the Second Continental Congress had fallen to Lieutenant Colonel George Baylor, who was Washington's "first [that is, principal] Aid de Camp." As in classical times, Congress rewarded the bearer of good news. It voted Baylor a commission to command a line cavalry regiment. He had not returned to Washington's staff at Morristown winter quarters. He was less of a loss to Washington than might have been expected because Baylor was "not in the smallest degree a penman." Another of the senior aides, Robert Hanson Harrison, was ill and unready for duty. On January 20, 1777, Washington wrote Harrison in his own hand, asking that Harrison "forward the enclosed to Captain Hamilton." It was probably Washington's personal invitation to Hamilton to join his staff as an aide-de-camp.[1]

John Church Hamilton and Egbert Benson fixed the time that Hamilton first came to Washington's favorable attention as the night before the Battle of Harlem Heights. Other accounts involve other persons, times, and places. Most contribute elements of partial truth; all tend to confirm the fact of the strong lifelong bond between the two officers, one 45 years old and the other barely 20.

General Nathanael Greene is another who is said to have recommended Hamilton to Washington. His biographer wrote that in the summer of 1776, on a visit to Washington's New York headquarters, Greene passed by The Fields and was impressed by the close order drill of a company of artillerists and the skill and bearing of their commander. He sent his compliments to Captain Hamilton and invited him to dinner, thus beginning their lifelong friendship. Elias Boudinot recommended Hamilton for a place on the staff of his friend and brother-in-law William Alexander, Lord Stirling. When Hamilton declined that appointment, Boudinot may have put in a good word for Hamilton for a place on a still higher staff. Or Lord Stirling himself, a loyal old crony of Washington's, may have done so. Or, with Hamilton's exploits at the Raritan, Trenton, and Princeton fresh in mind, Henry Knox may have done so, although a general who has a competent and hard-to-replace officer under his own command is often tight-lipped about praising him to an outsider who might want him for his own. In an army as small and for the most part as poorly disciplined as Washington's, it would be surprising if through four months of combat the captain of the crack artillery company, who had covered his retreats as well as his attacks, could have failed to attract General Washington's direct favorable notice. Such notice would not be hostage to anyone else's recommendation.

Washington set high standards of excellence for his aides. "Aides de camp are persons in whom entire confidence must be placed," Washington explained, "and it requires men of abilities to execute the duties with propriety and dispatch." He added plaintively: "I give in to no kind of amusement myself, and consequently those about me can have none, but are confined from morning to eve, hearing and answering the applications and letters." His standards were strikingly similar to those set for acolytes of Wall Street law firms: "If these gentlemen had the same relaxation from duty as other officers have in their common routine, there would not be so much in it. But, to have the mind always upon the stretch, scarce ever unbent, and no hours for recreation makes a material odds."

The "old secretary," Robert Hanson Harrison, for example, who brought Hamilton his invitation from Washington, was a fine man, but he did not quite measure up to Washington's standards. Ten years older than Hamilton and senior in service to most of the other aides; he had been Washington's neighbor and occasional lawyer in Alexandria before the war. Washington wrote of Harrison in a 1775 letter that although "clever, and perfectly confidential," Harrison "has never yet moved upon so large a scale as to comprehend at one view the diversity of matter, which comes before me, so as to afford the ready assistance which every man in my situation must stand more or less in need of." But Harrison was intensely loyal, and he kept him on. Of his fellow aide's writing style, Hamilton wrote that it was "perhaps too diffuse, and somewhat hurried."

It was Harrison who nicknamed the new aide, who soon displaced him, "The Little Lion." Hamilton's son says that Harrison always treated his father "with parental kindness" and that his epithet was "a term of endearment by which he was familiarly known among his bosom friends to the close of his life."

Washington did not really expect to find in a single aide one who would "comprehend at one view the diversity" of his command problems. It was enough if the aide should have education, sense, and a good temper, but "As to military knowledge, I do not expect to find gentlemen much skilled in it," Washington sighed. "If they can write a good letter, write quick, are methodical and diligent, it is all I expect to find in my aides."

Being a young officer who was all this, who was also cheerful and prepossessing and a former line unit commander as he himself had once been, would have served as recommendation enough for Hamilton. Besides, the staff of aides was shorthanded just now.

Hamilton's formal appointment as Washington's aide came on March 1, 1777; on the same day he received a promotion to the rank of lieutenant colonel. Skipping entirely over the rank of major, he thus skipped majority of rank almost a year before attaining majority of status. The excitement of a double promotion did not make him forget to look out for his war-worn New York Provincial Artillery Company. Only 25 weary veterans had made it through the campaign to winter quarters. Sickness, expiring enlistments, wounds, desertions, and deaths made his own company an unforgettable example of what was continuously happening to all companies throughout the Continental Army all during the war. On March 6 he wrote to the New York Provincial Convention, the Provincial Congress sitting as a legislative body and draftsmen of a new state constitution, outlining the problems of his unit, which were representative of all others like his.

Captain Lieutenant James Moore, a promising officer, "who did credit to the state he belonged to," had died on Christmas after "a short but excruciating fit of illness"; the useful Mr. Johnson's enlistment had expired at the end of the year. That left only two officers, Lieutenants Bean and Thompson, available to succeed Hamilton as unit commander. Bean had a drinking problem. Hamilton had first written that "he is so incurably addicted to a certain failing that I cannot, in justice, give my opinion in favour of his preferment." But to spare Bean's feelings, he softened his first draft to say in the final version merely that, "Mr. Bean though a brave man, h(as) *a failing* that disqualifies him for any farther preferment." So he recommended Lieutenant Thomas Thompson for the captain lieutenancy instead. Hamilton characteristically anticipated another problem: now that it seemed to be permanently attached to the Continental Army, Hamilton's Provincial Company would be of no further use to New York. "As the rest [of] the Company can hardly answer any special good purposes to the s[tate I] imagine you will resolve to resign it." To make certain that his men were properly taken care of, he proposed a practical solution: "There will be no (difficulty) in having it transferred to the Continental establishment." He also apologized for his delay in writing. It had been caused by his own "long and

severe fit of sickness" after the hard campaign across the Jerseys. Such hard-
ships had been severe enough to bring on many kinds of disorders both physical
and mental; speculation as to their exact nature would be useless. Hamilton
would suffer many recurrences of such illness through his lifetime.

The New York Convention approved his recommendations. He had seen to
it that his old artillery company, like its former captain, would move up to a
higher and more secure status. The New York Convention deputed Gouverneur
Morris to inform its ex-commander of the welcome news.

During the army's first winter at Morristown in 1776–1777, Washington's
headquarters was the Arnold Tavern on the west side of the village green. In
later winter encampments at Morristown, Washington's headquarters would be
the Jacob Ford mansion, which now stands restored to its original condition in
the Morristown National Historical Park. Mrs. Ford and her children continued
to occupy the rooms to the right upon entering the house; Washington took over
the front room to the left as his office. In and out of it passed streams of visitors
and the orders and correspondence that could not be diverted or delegated to his
aides. In other small rooms to the rear of Washington's the aides worked at their
desks. All the aides slept together in one small room on the second floor, across
the hallway from George and Martha's bedroom. At every hour of the day and
night Washington's aides had to be within instant call across the hall. Whether
headquarters was in the Arnold Tavern or the Ford House or somewhere else,
the one necessary constant was that there be a room for the aides near enough
to Washington's that he could communicate with them easily and quickly at all
hours of the day and night.[2]

Washington complained of being bogged down in paper work: "At present
my time is so taken up at my desk, that I am obliged to neglect many other
essential parts of my duties; it is absolutely necessary . . . for me to have persons
that can think for me, as well as execute orders." He carefully explained that
his letters from his headquarters were "first drawn by his secretary and . . . aide
de camp."

Tench Tilghman of Maryland had volunteered early to be an aide, had
refused pay and rank, and would become one of Hamilton's closest friends. His
was a style like Hamilton's and one that Hamilton greatly admired, saying that
it "partook of the character of his sprightly temper. His sentences were brief
and simple, giving results rather than the processes by which they were
reached." To Hamilton, they often seemed "to have been written on the drum-
head, but still always breathing throughout a general air of elegance." Tilghman
wrote to his friend Robert Morris that "winter quarters [brings] an increase in
business in the way of paper, pens and ink." He assured his father, "You need
be under no apprehensions of my [losing my health] on the score of excess in
living. Vice is banished from the general's family. We never sup but go early to
bed and are early up." Of the commander in chief's work load, Tilghman wrote,
"The weight of the whole war may be said to lay upon his shoulders."

In the course of the whole war, Washington had 32 aides in all, but generally only five or six were with him at any one time. Besides Harrison and Tilghman there were also now Richard Kidder "Dick" Meade, who was Washington's choice for riding assignments more often than writing assignments. After his marriage, Meade followed the general's advice and example and became a Virginia planter. John Walker of Virginia served as an extra aide in the Morristown camp in a civilian capacity. Others who were on the staff for different periods and later played prominent roles in public life were Thomas Mifflin, James McHenry, and David Humphreys. Hamilton's closest friend among all the aides was the one who displayed the greatest personal devotion to Washington: John Laurens. When General Charles Lee spoke disparagingly of Washington's generalship after the Battle of Monmouth and John Laurens challenged Lee to a duel to vindicate Washington's honor, Hamilton served as Laurens's second.

Before Hamilton had arrived on the staff, Aaron Burr served for a few weeks as an aide, but he soon departed under the cloud of a dispute with Washington, the exact nature of which remains a mystery. Afterward Washington always evinced suspicions of Burr which he never explained; when Burr's name would come up, Washington was content to misprize him by calling him an "intriguer."

Recovering from his illness after the fall campaign, Lieutenant Colonel Hamilton, with leonine vigor restored, quickly assumed first place among his peers of equal rank and more seniority. G. W. P. Custis recorded that in 1777 and 1778, "the habit at . . . headquarters was for the General to dismiss his officers at a very late hour of the night to catch a little repose, while he, . . . drawing his cloak around him, and trimming his lamp, would throw himself upon a hard couch, not to sleep, but to think." Close by, in a blanket but "all accoutred," snored the short but active Billy, his body servant. If an express arrived, the "dispatches being . . . read, there would be heard in the calm deep tones of that voice, so well remembered . . . , the command of the chief to his now watchful attendant, 'Call Colonel Hamilton.' "

Of Hamilton's contribution as the most important of the aides to Washington's dispatches from headquarters, Hamilton's lifelong friend Adjutant General Timothy Pickering wrote, "I have every reason to believe that not only the composition, the clothing of the ideas, but the ideas themselves, originated generally with the writers . . . Hamilton and Harrison in particular, were scarcely in any degree his amanuenses."

During the next four hectic years Hamilton would usually be daily, almost hourly, in Washington's company—at Morristown headquarters, at Valley Forge, and at other encampments and on most of the marches, journeys, and battlefields of the Revolution. Washington's headquarters was a political as well as a military headquarters. All intelligence came to him there, and all major orders and correspondence with public authorities issued from it. He was the de facto chief executive of a nation that had no de jure chief. Every question had to be dealt with in the context of the Continental Congress's executive as well as legislative supervision of the war. The whole ideological point of the war was representation of the people through Congress in their struggle to throw off the yoke of a dictatorial king. It was obvious that George Washington could not prosecute the war as a chief executive himself, but only as the servant and agent of an often refractory and divided Congress. Money was short; inflation was rampant; terms of troop enlistment were continually expiring. Each state treated units of its own provincial or state forces as its own. Continental generals could not deploy them without weighing the geographical and political effect that such deployments, and the resulting casualties and costs, would have on the states from which they came. From time to time troops mutinied because their pay was in arrears. All the while, the British, with larger and better trained forces and with naval control of the entire seaboard held the principal city at the central notch of the associated states.

Besides matters of politics and military grand strategy there were small problems that were hardly less intractable: promotions, jealousy of one general toward another, applications of enthusiastic but untrained Frenchmen for instant lofty rank.

As general and aide, Washington and Hamilton worked together as a team in as many different ways as the situations and people they were dealing with required. Sometimes Washington dictated a memorandum of what was to be said and Hamilton then transcribed it. Other times, Washington stated the general idea and let his aide-de-camp compose the text and send it out over the aide's signature. Sometimes Washington signed what Hamilton had written. At other times Washington copied in his own hand without change what Hamilton had written out and sent it as his own. In collected writings of the two men, Hamilton's drafts that received Washington's signature are identified as to date and subject but credited to Washington, whereas only letters that Hamilton signed are credited to him. Many documents that Hamilton drafted for Washington, but that Washington signed or copied in his own hand, are in a style that is distinctly Hamiltonian in purpose, content, and form. Yet such documents are not reproduced in the Hamilton Papers and are not credited by scholars to Hamilton. They are credited entirely to Washington's authorship. Some documents drafted by Hamilton, or another aide, for Washington to sign or copy out in his own hand probably contain ideas and forms of expression that do not represent the aide's own idea or his characteristic style, but only the aide's idea of what Washington would wish to do or say. Some documents written entirely by the aide probably do not reflect the aide's own views but Washington's. There were thousands of documentary collaborations between Washington and Hamilton. In these it is impossible to be certain, or even fairly sure, how much content, form, and style are Washington's and how much are Hamilton's, or even which of the two men originated the idea of creating the document in the first place.

Anyone who has ever worked as a clerk to a judge or as a junior lawyer for a senior partner or as a staff writer for a busy executive knows that the general public would be astonished if it knew how few changes the judge, senior partner, or executive to whom authorship of the finished product is ascribed makes in a draft document submitted by a competent aide. Usually, the time of the chief is simply too much taken up with other aspects of being chief: presiding at a trial, examining witnesses or arguing an appeal, or executing the duties of an executive that are the essence of what is required of the chief. The creation of documents, which seems so important to history-minded scholars, is not necessarily first among a chief's functions.

For Washington, creating documents by longhand was slow and exasperating work. As the only chief executive America possessed during these critical years, Washington had to rely on aides to produce documents for him so that he could carry on the myriad other kinds of state business he was called upon to perform. Washington's ability to draw from his aides a huge volume of useful, necessary, elegantly styled documentary material that brought the authority of his signature, pen, and office effectively to bear on so many areas of command and leadership, is further proof, if any were needed, of his greatness.

Hamilton did not write a system of shorthand. Washington's days did not contain enough hours to have allowed him to spend them dictating the lengthy documents that went out over his signature at a speed slow enough for Hamilton to transcribe in the neat, firm longhand in which Hamilton's drafts appear. In short, the conclusion is irresistible that Hamilton wrote out first on his own not only the documents in his handwriting or signed by him, but also the documents drafted by him that Washington signed or copied out in his own hand. Like all such valued aides, Hamilton did not boast about the largeness of his own contribution to such collaborations. In later years, all those who had worked closely with both of them tended to credit without question advice and orders from Hamilton as if they came from Washington. There was never any doubt that both men's thoughts were grooved to run along the same lines.

Harrison, Tilghman, and McHenry were all practiced writers, who demonstrated literary taste, animation, and humor in varying degrees. Hamilton's writing possessed these qualities and, in addition, a force of expression that surpassed that of the others. Putting thoughts into words seemed to come naturally to him. When he wished to say something, he said it easily, in words of pith and moment. First drafts usually differed little from the final product. He made revisions of verbal content to avoid needless offense; additions, frequently extensive, amplified the early thought. He rarely rearranged, showing that he had outlined or thought through the argument to its end before presenting it. He never paused for want of figures and dates, but left blanks open to be filled in later.

The subject matter of some of his dispatches illustrates how he dealt with the large and little of "the weight of the whole war" that lay upon Washington's shoulders.

For the commander in chief, Hamilton writes to reassure Lieutenant Colonel Archibald Campbell that he will not be treated unduly severely as a prisoner; he orders General Horatio Gates to investigate fraudulent recruiting and to arrange for inoculations for two Virginia regiments. He accepts the resignation of General Artemus Ward in Cambridge, thanks him for his zeal and service, and orders Major General William Heath to replace him. He admonishes Major General Joseph Spencer to make a proposed attack on the enemy in Rhode Island "only if success is certain." He reminds Gates not to forget the inoculation of his men. His efforts to work out a prisoner exchange for the return of General Lee, a man he regarded as arbitrary, eccentric, indiscreet, impetuous, and irregular, moved slowly and, not surprisingly, failed. According to Hamilton's son, the temperate tone of his correspondence on prisoner exchanges "increased the esteem in which the American character was held in Europe." Friends of America there "proudly referred to it" as more evidence that Americans "were not less accomplished with the pen than with the sword."

The Continental Congress had advanced five brigadiers junior to Benedict Arnold in service—Stirling, Mifflin, St. Clair, Adam Stephen, and Benjamin Lincoln—to major general, without promoting Benedict Arnold as well. Who could have foreseen that the polite, bland letter Hamilton wrote to Arnold, entreating him not to be too hasty in angry reaction, would only rekindle the smoldering resentment that would lead to treason?

Enemy prisoners and deserters from the army were often hauled into headquarters, as well as people accused of being Tories or at least of being disloyal to state or congressional governments. Among Hamilton's duties was the job of questioning them. Judgment and knowledge of human nature were brought to bear to sift truth from lies in their stories. Some cases had to be set down for military punishment; others, assigned to civil authorities; still others, quashed —demands on Hamilton's time, discretion, and patience were almost unlimited. His view was that it would be a prudent rule "to meddle with none but those whose crimes are supported by very sufficient evidence, and are of a pretty deep die." The best policy was "either to pardon offenders entirely or to inflict capital and severe punishments."

As usual, Hamilton buttressed his view with classical citation:

> The advice given by a certain general to his son, when the latter had the Roman army in his power, was certainly very politic. He advised him either to destroy them utterly or dismiss them with every mark of honor and respect. By the first method says he, you disable the Romans from being your enemies, by the last you make them your friends.

However gratifying or politic it might be to yield to public clamor, nothing justified false or baseless accusations:

> The apprehending innocent persons, or those whose offenses are of so slender a nature as to make it prudent to dismiss them, furnishes an occasion of triumph, and the foundation for a species of animadversion, which is very injurious to the public cause. Persons so apprehended generally return home worse than they were; and by expatiating on their sufferings first excite pity toward themselves and afterwards abhorrence toward their persecutors.

Hamilton was extremely wary and suspicious of the excuse that the exigencies of total war, even a revolution, justified any abridgement of laws intended to protect the freedom and civil liberties of people who were poor and helpless.

When some officious commissary officers took a hardworking farmer's hardworking oxen, Hamilton wrote to newly promoted Major General Adam Stephen at Chatham, New Jersey, in May 1777 to right the wrong. Due attention must be paid to the farmer's greivances:

> Mr. Carter, who I am told is a friend of the cause, has been here to complain that some persons under the commissary's orders, insist on taking from him two laboring oxen, which he cannot possibly spare from the business of his farm.

Officious rear echelon officers often aroused the ire of line officers like Hamilton and Washington in any event. Hamilton tactfully argued the issue on the lofty plane of general protection of husbandry in order to engage General Stephen's sympathetic attention, but his annoyance was not far beneath the surface:

> As agriculture is as necessary to go on as anything else, the General wishes not unreasonably to distress the inhabitants. Those who are charged with business of this kind are [often] incapable of weighing matters as they ought, and in some instances may act wantonly and oppressively, you will be pleased to pay some attention to this complaint, and if reasonable remove the cause.

Intelligence from the revolutionary army's headquarters was peculiarly important to leaders in New York. It lay between the northeastern and southern ranges of the thirteen states. The enemy's chief American base occupied its most important and strategic city, and through its river valley corridors lay the invasion routes from Canada.

The New York Provincial Convention had appointed a Committee of Correspondence to keep it advised of all developments in Washington's camp and named Gouverneur Morris to be chief correspondent.[3] Hamilton took over from Tench Tilghman the duty of keeping the committee informed, responding to Morris that "With cheerfulness, I embrace the proposal of corresponding with your convention, through you, and shall from time to time as far as my leisure will permit, and my duty warrant, communicate such transactions as shall happen, such pieces of intelligence as shall be received and such comments upon them as shall appear necessary to convey a true idea of what is going on in the military line."

Because so many letters of command, injunction, and reproof that issued in Washington's name were the product of the closest collaboration between both men, Hamilton had to go out of his way to dispel any idea the committee might have that he spoke for the general or was improperly disclosing official secrets. He cautioned the New York Committee of Correspondence "that whatever opinions I shall give, in the course of our correspondence, are to be considered merely as my private sentiment; and are never to be interpreted as an echo of those of the *General . . .*"

He was being discreet, protecting both himself and his commander in a situation where the temptation might have been great for many a young man to do otherwise: to inflate his own self-importance and the authority of his views by issuing them with nothing more than a general disclaimer like the passage quoted above. Hamilton went further, adding that the opinions he gave "will not really be" an echo of those of the general. "A construction of the kind may lead into errors and be productive of inconveniences."

On March 22, 1777, Hamilton again protested that "Wherever I give opinions, they are merely my own and will probably, so far from being a transcript of those of the General, differ widely from them in many respects."

Hamilton not only kept the committee posted on events at headquarters but he also gave them the benefit of his own prescriptions for improving the political health of his home state.

When New York proclaimed a new state constitution on April 20, 1777, Hamilton voiced his concern to Gouverneur Morris that the rights of the people might not have been well enough secured. The arrangements were too "aristocratical," Hamilton wrote. He criticized a requirement that senators have a freehold worth £100 and members of the lower house £20 as too restrictive a property qualification.

"The evil I mean is," he argued, "that in time, your Senate, from the very name and from the mere circumstance of its being a separate member of the legislature, will be liable to degenerate into a body purely aristocratical." A simple, single-house legislature might be preferable. The danger of an abuse of power would not be great, he thought, "in a government where the equality and fullness of popular representation is so wisely provided for as in yours."

The important thing, whether there were two houses or one, was a broad base of popular representation in the legislature. Hamilton distinguished sharply between what he considered true representative government, on the one hand, and mob rule on the other:

> When the deliberative or judicial powers are vested wholly or partly in the collective body of the people, you must expect error, confusion and instability. But a representative democracy, where the right of election is well secured and regulated and the exercise of the legislative, executive and judicial authorities, is vested in select persons, chosen *really* and not *nominally* by the people, will in my opinion be most likely to be happy, regular and durable.

There was no question that representative democracy was the most stable kind of government. He recognized that "unstable democracy, is an epithet frequently in the mouths of politicians." He believed that criticism on this count was disputable and wrong.

The New York Provincial Convention had adopted a resolution empowering courts-martial to try persons who came from the enemy as spies. This power extended to all persons taken going off privately to the enemy.

Hamilton perfunctorily approved the resolution, but he warned that, on the basis of his own experience, in dealing with the kinds of people who came in to headquarters, "In dispensing punishments, the utmost care and caution ought to be used. The power of doing it, or even of bringing the guilty to trial, should be placed in hands that know well how to use it."

When he knew his correspondent had a sense of humor, as Gouverneur Morris did, he was never too busy for a wager or a joke. He followed the complimentary close of one letter to Morris with the postscript: "Relying on your punctuality and favoring me with any important intelligence your way, I am likely to lose a beaver hat, which was staked against the truth of the report of the stores at St. John's being destroyed. If you forget me in the future, I will certainly excommunicate you."

At St. John's, on the Richelieu River, 20 miles southeast of Montreal, was a British fort which had stopped Richard Montgomery's incursion of 1775. On May 24, 1777, Gouverneur Morris replied from Kingston, New York, that there had been no destruction of stores at St. John's. Hamilton won his bet, kept his beaver hat, and spared Gouverneur Morris his "excommunication."

Diplomatic exigencies and fear of British reprisals required the French government to maintain a posture of official neutrality. But under cover, it backed a secret lend-lease program under the direction of a many-talented Gallic counterpart of Hamilton, Pierre Augustin Caron, the self-styled Comte de Beaumarchais. His drab, ostensibly workaday export-import firm of Hortalez et Cie. was carrying out a vast, secret program of aid to the colonies. News came from Portsmouth, New Hampshire, that the brig *Mercury*, out of Nantes, had docked there with 364 cases of arms, bales of "Cloath," caps, stockings, shoes, "Necloathes," and, most important, 11,000 gunflints and 1,000 barrels of Lavoisier's excellent gunpowder. The *Mercury* also brought word that no fewer than 34 more ships, similarly laden, would soon be clearing French ports for America. The army was in desperately short supply of all such French cargoes of munitions, whereas at the same time a mounting surplus of French gentlemen was arriving in camp to serve the revolutionary cause without the discomfort of serving in the ranks or on the barricades, demanding generals' rank and pay. Extreme tact was called for in dealing with the situation. Hamilton's own supply was running low when he wrote to his friend William Duer, the New York merchant, financier, speculator, and delegate to the Continental Congress about one M. Malmedi, a French gentleman of learning. At the recommendation of General Charles Lee, M. Malmedi had been made a brigadier general by the state of Rhode Island and now sought a commission from the Continental Congress at the same rank. Hamilton wrote Duer that "in this he will no doubt be mistaken as there are many insuperable objections. It would tend to raise the expectations of Frenchmen in general, already too high, to a pitch, which would be impossible to gratify or endure."

The human side of Hamilton wanted to "keep him in good humour, as he is a man of sense and merit," but the former line artillery captain thought high rank was a thing to be won in the line in New Jersey—not born to in France.

The problem was to some extent historical, Hamilton felt. "Congress in the beginning went upon a very injudicious plan with respect to Frenchmen. To every adventurer that came, without even the shadow of credentials, they gave the rank of field officers. This carried the expectations of those who had really any pretensions to the character of officers to a length that exceeded all bounds of moderation." So Congress had begun to retrench its excessive liberality, and "the consequence has been universal disgust and discontent."

Hamilton had many warm personal friends and admirers among prominent Frenchmen. His close friendship with the Marquis de Lafayette was one of many examples. But his cool, evenhanded analysis of the "French surplus" illustrates the sensibility and tact that made many Frenchmen think of him—as he spoke to them in his beguiling Creole patois from the West Indies—almost as one of themselves.

The problem remained, Hamilton said, that "we shall never be able to satisfy them, and they can be of no use to us, at least for some time. Their ignorance of our language, of the disposition of the people, the resources and deficiencies of the country, their own habits and tempers—all these are disqualifications that put it out of their power to be of any real use or service to us."

But they must be dealt with politely. "As the French are much addicted to national punctilio," he noted, "it would be bad to run into the opposite extreme to that first embraced," and "create a general clamour." He added, "Policy suggests the propriety of discriminating in favor of a few of the most deserving." Slyly he went further. This is best done by keeping "them in temper even by gratifying them beyond what they can reasonably pretend to." It is not possible to paraphrase his reasoning process without loss: "This will enable us to shake off the despicable part with safety, and to turn a deaf ear to the exorbitant demands of many." He then forecast the good practical effects of this policy in France.

> It will be easily believed in France that their want of merit occasioned their want of success, from the extraordinary marks of favor that have been conferred on others; whereas the united voice of complaint from the whole, might make ill impressions in their own country, which it is not our interest should exist.
>
> We are already greatly embarrassed with the Frenchmen among us, and from the genius of the people shall continue to do so.

Here, finally, is what should be done as a practical matter: "Our agents in France, instead of courting them to come out," should be "instructed to give no encouragement but where they could not help it"—where applications are made "by persons countenanced and supported by great men, whom it would be impolitic to disoblige."

Congress cast a cold eye that summer on the wide-eyed enthusiasm of Marie Joseph Paul Yves Roch Gilbert du Motier, the Marquis de Lafayette, who was making his stately way from South Carolina to Philadelphia. When he reached there, it warmed to him a little when he said he would serve without pay and did not even insist on troop command. All he wanted, he said, was the rank of major general and the chance to be "near the person of General Washington till such time as he may think proper to entrust me with a division of the army." Congress's blanket policy against "too many Frenchmen," yielded to Hamilton's policy of discrimination in Lafayette's favor in accordance with merit. Hamilton was charmed by the tall, redheaded Frenchman almost exactly his own age, and they became lifelong friends. Both became closer friends of Washington than any other men; their troop commands joined in the victorious assault at Yorktown; Hamilton interceded with Washington later in behalf of Lafayette's son and helped Lafayette make good his escape from later imprisonment by revolutionary France. For all the hard work at headquarters and no hours for recreation, there remained the reward of learning almost all that was important to know about the army, the states, all the men who played the leading parts in them, and all the strengths and weaknesses of the Continental Congress itself. From his vantage point at Washington's side, Hamilton came to know most of the men who would dominate the states and the new union that they comprised during the next three decades and more of its life.

Hamilton had a genius for friendship. He never forgot a comrade-in-arms, a mentor, or a sweetheart, and he kept the friendships in good repair by writing his friends often, even during the rush of the army's business. On February 14, still suffering from his postcampaign illness, he wrote Hugh Knox a letter that his old mentor in St. Croix found "very circumstantial and satisfactory." In March, from the bustle of headquarters, he wrote another that Knox described as "the fine, impartial, laconic and highly descriptive account you favour'd me with of your last year's campaign."

It is an incalculable loss that this account has not been found. From St. Croix many weeks away, Knox wrote in April 1777:

> We rejoice in your *Good Character and Advancement* which is indeed only the just reward of merit. . . . May you still live . . . to justify the choice and merit the approbation of the Great and Good General Washington, a name which will Shine with distinguished Lustre in the Annals of History—A name dear to the friends of the Liberties of mankind!

A reader joins Hugh Knox in regretting that the headquarters intelligencer, did not follow his old mentor's prescript and prepare to write a history of the war:

> You must be the Annalist & Biographer, as well as the Aid de Camp, of General Washington, & the Historiographer of the American

War! . . . take Minutes & Keep a Journal! . . . If you Survive the present troubles, I Aver few men Will be as well qualified to Write the History of the present Glorious Struggle. . . .

I Congratulate you on your recovery from A Long & dangerous illness. . . . With the tender of Every kind & friendly wish, My Dear Sir Your Affectionate Servt.

When Martha Washington arrived at the Morristown winter camp, it was the signal for the wives of the other ranking officers to join their husbands. Some of them brought their daughters. At least while Sir William Howe led the British, war, except for minor alarms and excursions, could be a seasonal business. When there were reviews and parades for visiting diplomats, Hamilton, John Laurens, Tench Tilghman, and the other young aides turned out in their best dress uniforms of blue and buff with yellow lining and piping, flat double gilt buttons, corded dimity waistcoats and breeches, gold epaulets, white gloves, hair powdered and kept in place with pomatum and a comb, and silver spurs on their boots.

Brother officers were invited to join Washington's table, and Hamilton became friendly with many of them. Alexander Graydon wrote of Hamilton during this first winter at Morristown: "He presided at the General's table, where we dined; and in a large company in which there were several ladies, among whom I recollect one or two of the Miss Livingstons and a Miss Brown, he acquitted him with an ease, propriety, and vivacity which gave me the most favorable impression of his talents and accomplishments. . . ." In the evening Graydon would go with Hamilton and Tilghman to take tea with ladies who lived in the village or with the visitors with whom they had dined at the headquarters table.[4]

Hamilton was noted for elegance, sparkle, and grace and spirited conversation. His friends remarked that he never seemed to take himself seriously. He usually expressed himself in society in a casual and facetious manner. Martha Dangerfield (Mrs. Theodorick) Bland wrote to her sister-in-law from Morristown that Washington is

> Our noble & agreeable commander (for he commands both sexes) . . . we visit [the Washingtons] twice or three times a week by particular invitation . . . He is generally busy in the forenoon—but from dinner till night he is free for all company; his worthy lady seems to be in perfect felicity while she is by the side of her *old man* as she calls him.

When spring came on, Martha Bland wrote, "We often make parties on horseback, the general, his lady, Miss Livingston & his aide de camps . . . at which time General Washington throws off the Hero and takes on the chatty agreeable companion—he can be downright impudent sometimes. . . ." Colonel Hamilton who is in "our riding party generally" is a "sensible, genteel, polite young fellow, a West Indian." She recalled the "pretty, airy look" of the surrounding villages:

"They present us with just such scenes as the poets paint Arcadia: purling rills, mossy beds, etc., but not crying swains or lovely nymphs."

The lack of swains and nymphs seemed at first surprising to Mrs. Bland because "there are some exceeding pretty girls." The problem was that "they appear to have souls formed for the distaff rather than the tender passions."

Cantering on ahead of the other aides in the party up the path alone with the adorable Kitty Livingston, Hamilton would never agree with Mrs. Bland's bleak conclusion. He would test out for himself whether Kitty's soul was not formed for warmer playthings than her distaff. After she had returned home to Elizabethtown, he wrote her on April 11. Spring was very much in the air, and his mind far from the serious business of the war.

"Amidst my amorous transports, let me not forget that I am also to perform the part of a politician and intelligencer. I challenge you to meet me in whatever path you dare," he added dreamily. "We will even sometimes make excursions in the flowery walks, and roseate bowers of Cupid. You know, I am renowned for gallantry."

Notwithstanding such occasional interruptions by spring side trips down flowery walks into roseate bowers of Cupid to provide a better plaything for a Kitty Livingston than her distaff, there could be no doubt that of all the general's aides Hamilton surpassed all the others in his "power of statement," a power Washington would remember two decades later when he called upon Hamilton to draft his "Farewell Address." General Philip Schuyler, the father of another pretty visitor to Morristown, Elizabeth Schuyler, looked over all of Washington's aides and concluded that the young man who had earlier manhandled heavy guns across the state of New Jersey outshone them all. Not knowing that the young man he described would become his closest confidant, political ally, dearest friend, and son-in-law besides, General Schuyler, appraising all the aides-de-camp, "discovered in all, an attention to the duties of their station; in some, a considerable degree of ability, but [in Hamilton] only I found those qualifications so essentially necessary to the man who is to aid and counsel a commanding general, environed with difficulties of every kind, and . . . whose correspondence must . . . be . . . frequently so delicate as to require much judgment and address."

Later Schuyler remarked on Hamilton's expertness in dealing with the French officers. He was proud that "men of genius, observation and judgment" confirmed his estimate.

It was an age of style, when style in writing counted for as much, or almost as much, as style in fighting. Hamilton's schoolmate and lifelong friend Robert Troup neatly straddled the profound question of which man was primarily responsible for the conspicuous elegance of Washington's and Hamilton's joint products. Troup wrote, "The pen for our army was held by Hamilton; and for dignity of manner, pith of matter, and elegance of style, General Washington's letters are unrivalled in military annals."

Long afterward, in 1798, during John Adams's administration, a dying Washington was now the figurehead commander in chief of a provisional army being raised for the expected war with France, and Hamilton was his handpicked second in command. After all the storms these two veterans of faithful service to the union had weathered during the two intervening decades, Washington could have been thinking of no one but Hamilton when he wrote:

> The variegated, and important, duties of the aides of a commander-in-chief, or, the commander of a separate army require experienced officers, men of judgment, and men of business, ready pens to execute them properly, and with dispatch. A great deal more is required of them than attending him at a parade, or delivering verbal orders here and there; or copying a written one. They ought, if I may be allowed to use the expression, to possess the soul of the general; and from a single idea given to them, to convey his meaning in the clearest and fullest manner.

Washington never forgot his and Hamilton's common bond of having seen combat service in the line of battle in their earliest years:

> This, young men unacquainted with the service and diffident, would not do; be their abilities what they may.

No matter what other abilities an aide might display in the peaceable office of headquarters intelligencer, in the end only a man acquainted with the service, not "diffident," and with "military knowledge" like Hamilton's, gained at firsthand in the field, would bring enough steel to the style of his pen "to possess the soul of the general."

7

THE IDOL OF AMERICA
GOVERNED BY ONE
OF HIS AIDES

PROMPT OBEDIENCE TO THE ORDERS CONVEYED BY HAMILTON, ON
THE PARTS OF GATES AND PUTNAM WOULD HAVE CUT OFF THE
COMMUNICATION BETWEEN THE BRITISH ARMY AND FLEET, AND
FULFILLING WASHINGTON'S PROPHECY, HOWE WOULD HAVE BEEN
REDUCED TO THE SITUATION OF BURGOYNE, THUS PROBABLY TER-
MINATING THE WAR IN THE SECOND YEAR OF OUR INDEPENDENCE.
—*John Church Hamilton, 1834*

The year 1777 opened propitiously. Prisoner exchanges brought missing
comrades back to the Morristown plateau. The main American army burgeoned
with spring, taking on shape and size in a way that seemed miraculous to
veterans like Hamilton, who remembered the ragged starving remnants of the
beaten army who had straggled south to the Delaware in 1776. It still had critical
weaknesses, of course—officers whose experience was limited to garrison service, men who were clumsy executing the manual of arms, shortages of muskets
and ammunition—but seemingly little was lacking that money, hard drilling, and
enthusiasm could not overcome. But beyond the horizons around the plateau

events were conspiring to confront the army with a harrowing campaign that would destroy illusions that victory would come any time soon.

To encompass the military grand strategy of 1777, the situation maps kept up by the headquarters intelligencer at Morristown army headquarters had to take in the whole eastern half of the continent of North America, from Montreal and Quebec to below Charleston and from the British forts on the upper Mississippi and the Great Lakes to the British fleets and squadrons prowling the ports of the Atlantic coast and holding sway over the trackless reaches of the continental shelf and all seven seas beyond.

To encompass the continental politics of 1777 and coordinate them with the military grand strategy, other larger scale headquarters situation maps had to show the reaches of upper New York State with the west to east Lake Ontario-Mohawk River Valley corridor intersecting the north to south Lake Champlain-Hudson River corridor, the latter cutting off the four New England states from the lower nine. Still larger scale tactical situation maps should have focused on every road, river crossing, valley, rill, and ridge of the central theater of the war that fanned out from Morristown around the compass from the northeast at West Point, swinging east toward New Brunswick and New York City, east by south to the Amboys, and around to Wilmington and Brandywine Creek below Philadelphia to the southwest.

Fort Ticonderoga was the supposedly invincible bastion guarding the northern approaches to New York but it always seemed to be falling to one side or the other. On July 6, 1777, not knowing of the disaster that was breaking there that day, Hamilton wrote Gouverneur Morris a cool appraisal of British grand strategy: "I am loth to risk a conjecture about Mr. Howe . . . If he acted like a man of sense, he would wait quietly on Staten Island, and there concenter all his forces. He would draw around all the men that could be spared from Canada and all that are now at Rhode Island."

But instead of doing what Hamilton expected of a sensible enemy commander, Sir William Howe had just embarked thousands of the best British and Hessian troops from New York and headed out into the Atlantic hazes with a great flotilla that could have had any number of important objectives. Hamilton thought that, instead of putting to sea, Howe should have made "a point of forcing us by some means or other to an action." Howe's only hope lay in defeating Washington's army. "But let him go to the northward or to the southward, every new post he takes weakens his main body. . . . Any object short of our army is a bad one, and that plan is the worse, where by a division of his forces he runs the hazard, in case of an accident either way, of having his whole scheme overturned."

Hamilton confided in a letter to Hugh Knox on July 5 that "Appearances lead us to suppose that Howe is fool enough to meditate a southern expedition." Loftily ignoring the conventional strategy that would call for holding the principle cities, Hamilton would willingly write off the capital, Philadelphia, if this would serve the larger purposes of the war. Should Howe "be satisfied with the splendour of his acquisition, and shut himself up in Philadelphia, we can ruin him by confinement." Hamilton knew there would be problems, of course, the worst of which would be political and economic. Loss of Philadelphia, he wrote Hugh Knox, would bring dangers of worse inflation:

> ... the foremost [disagreeable consequence] is the *depreciation of our currency*, which, from the importance in which Philadelphia is held, cannot fail to ensue.

Despite Hamilton's scorn of it, Howe's plan for an attack on Philadelphia had much to recommend it to armchair strategists. From Philadelphia, the largest city in America and the capital and seat of the Continental Congress, he could dominate the middle colonies. Worsening inflation would contribute to destroying the fragile continental economy; unpaid soldiers would desert. Then, to save his capital of troops and money, Washington would "have to risk a battle." Thereafter the fall of Charleston would open the door to the South. The fate of the colonies would be sealed.

Chafing under enemy occupation, the patriots of New York City demanded army action. They criticized Washington for seeming to do nothing but malinger out in the hills at Morristown. Hamilton knew how they felt and sympathized with the criticism. He assured the New York Committee of Correspondence he would do his utmost to keep Washington from remaining idle:

> Many people who have the management of affairs are of so lethargic a complexion, that they are to be kept in action only by the fear of immediate danger; and should they get it into their heads that the enemy would remain idle for six weeks, would think they had a right to doze away 40 days at least.

Robert R. Livingston, a member of the New York Committee of Correspondence and scion of the great old Livingston dynasty, was even more critical than Hamilton of the army's lack of aggressiveness. To spur Hamilton, he thought that the army should make a feint toward New York by sending two or three thousand men at a time on bold commando-style sorties. If nothing else, vigorous action by the Continental Army would have a good effect on wavering Tories.

The New York Convention had prescribed an oath of allegiance to the American cause. If they took it, Tories were "discharged" from taint. Livingston wrote that "Some very conscientious persons have declared (when they took the oath) that they held themselves absolved from all allegiance to a power that was no longer able to protect them. Though I do not think such conversions greatly to be relied on, yet they are of use in stopping the progress of disaffection and giving an appearance of strength and unanimity to our government on which more depends than is generally imagined."

The practical politics of the situation thus mandated army action even though grand strategy did not. Hamilton wrote up what was really a near debacle to sound like a victory for the benefit of Livingston and New York. His telegraphic description of a now largely forgotten skirmish of the long war—typical of many—skillfully satisfied Livingston's and New York's immediate political demands. It also illustrates Hamilton's grasp of the complex interrelationship of politics, local tactics, and grand strategy and the necessity for quick reversals of original misconceptions that were basic ingredients of success at the highest levels of Washington's command.

"The enemy has been trying a second experiment to tempt us to an engagement, on equal terms of ground," Hamilton wrote. Washington and Hamilton at first mistakenly believed that the enemy intended to evacuate the Jerseys. So "in order to keep up the idea of a pursuit, and to be in a posture to take advantage of any critical moment that might present itself to give them a blow," Washington marched the chief part of the army down to Quibbletown, pursuing the British as they retreated from New Brunswick. Howe welcomed this because far from retreating, at least at the moment, he was baiting a trap. "Finding this disposition taking place and expecting that, elated by what had passed, we might be willing to venture upon a general engagement, which is Howe's only hope, he came out with his whole army from Amboy early on Thursday morning and made a forced march towards our left, with design, if possible, to cut off some of our detachments, particularly one under Lord Stirling; and probably, if we were not expeditious in regaining the heights, to get there before us, by rapidly entering the passes on our left." This would cut the Americans off from their base at Morristown.

A disastrous climax loomed: "Lord Stirling's party was near being surrounded." But he extricated his men in the nick of time. "After a smart skirmish with the enemy's main body," they made their retreat good to Westfield and ascended the pass of the mountains back of Scotch Plains. "The other parties after skirmishing on their flanks came off to join the main body, and to take possession of the heights."

By retreat the Continentals had snatched something that could be written up to sound like a victory from an almost certain disaster. "The enemy marched towards Westfield while our army returned to the mountains lest it be their intention to get into them and force the continental army to fight on their terms." Hamilton adds, "Their loss we cannot ascertain; our own, in men, is inconsiderable. . . ."

From this inconclusive but dangerous series of feints and counterfeints and from another retreat from the battlefield to refuge on the plateau at Morristown, Hamilton, with assurance worthy of a Clausewitz, drew a lesson of grand strategy:

> I know the comments that some people will make in our Fabian conduct. It will be imputed either to cowardice or to weakness; but the more discerning, I trust, will not find it difficult to conceive that it proceeds from the truest policy, and is an argument neither of the one nor the other.

A profound strategic judgment rumbled forth in organ tones: "The liberties of America are an infinite stake. We should not play a desperate game for it or put it upon the issue of a single cast of the die." There were two reasons for patience and caution: "The loss of one general engagement may effectually ruin us, and it would certainly be folly to hazard it, unless our resources for keeping up an army were at an end, and some decisive blow was absolutely necessary; or unless our strength was so great as to give certainty of success. Neither is the case."

The winter and spring of retreats and defeats and pseudovictories had dispelled Hamilton's optimism about the easy victory in a few months that had breathed from his Vindicator and the Refuter of the Westchester Farmer, but it had confirmed his realistic faith in the basic strength of America:

> America can in all probability maintain its army for years. Our numbers though such as would give a reasonable hope of success are not such as should make us entirely sanguine.

A third disadvantage that time might bring was remote:

> A third consideration did it exist might make it expedient to risk such an event—the prospect of very great reinforcements to the enemy; but every appearance contradicts this, and affords all reason to believe, they will get very inconsiderable accessions of strength this campaign.

Hamilton was correctly prophesying that time would bring "accessions of strength" from Europe to America, not Britain.

From secret correspondence as headquarters intelligencer, Hamilton knew as well as any man that "We are continually strengthening our political springs in Europe, and may every day look for more effectual aid than we have yet received . . . Their affairs will be growing worse—ours better;—so that delay will ruin them. . . . Our business then is to avoid a general engagement and waste the enemy away by constantly goading their sides, in a desultory teasing way."

A long drawn-out war had another favorable aspect: "All the European maritime powers are interested for the defeat of the British arms in America, and will never assist them." Time is on America's side: "It is therefore Howe's business to make the most of his present strength, and as he is not numerous enough to conquer and garrison as he goes, his only hope lies in fighting us and giving a general defeat at one blow."

Hamilton could not ignore the human, and political problems such a militarily sound grand strategy created for the "little man" who experiences every war as a personal disaster and a potential tragedy. Hamilton's heartfelt sympathy went out to all such people:

> In the meantime it is painful to leave a part of the inhabitants a prey to their depredation; and it is wounding to the feelings of the

soldier, to see an enemy parading before him and daring him to a fight which he is obliged to decline. But a part must be sacrificed to the whole, and passion must give way to reason. . . .

In another letter Hamilton reminded Gouverneur Morris that Washington's Fabian tactics had been working well so far: "Their flourishes in the Jerseys, I believe, cannot have cost them less than six or seven hundred men. We have not lost above a hundred. This is the best way to ruin them, without risking anything." He added a hint of better battle reports to come:

> Perhaps your next favor will find me at Bound Brook. Headquarters will soon be moved there. Our family seems desirous of cultivating a closer acquaintance with the enemy than we have had the pleasure of, for sometime past.

Now depleted to man the flotilla moving out to sea, Howe's strength to the eastward at New York and New Brunswick no longer seemed to be a serious threat. Washington moved his army down off the heights of Morristown westward into Bucks County, Pennsylvania. There the Marquis de Lafayette, his petition granted by Congress, joined the army as an unsalaried major general at the camp near Neshaminy Ridge. Howe's moves baffled Washington and Hamilton. Who could be expected to understand why a commander whose front line was only 60 miles away from Philadelphia at New Brunswick should make a 400-mile sea voyage in order to be 70 miles away from the same objective at the end of it? For a time they both believed that the objective of Howe's flotilla had to be Charleston.

News of Washington's army's moving west made nervous New Yorkers and New Englanders feel all the more defenseless. With "Gentleman Johnny" Burgoyne now moving south from Canada, the American high command had to keep looking apprehensively over their shoulders northward to the Champlain Valley and Fort Ticonderoga. From the northwest British Colonel Barry St. Leger and his bloodthirsty Indian allies were driving east from Oswego along the Mohawk toward Oriskany. Sir Henry Clinton with some of the force that Howe had left behind was threatening to move north up the Hudson from New York City. The lines of march of all three British expeditionary forces converged on Albany.

If Burgoyne from the north, St. Leger from the west, and Sir Henry Clinton from the south should drive on to a link up at Albany, while Howe kept Washington's main army drawn off by what might turn out to be only a feint at Philadelphia, the Empire State would be dismembered north to south and east to west along its river valleys and lakes all the way north to Quebec and west to Lake Ontario. The possibility of a contiguous continental nation of thirteen states would be dismembered. The anger of New England and New York, now stripped of the protection of their own troops who were with Washington to the southward, would dismember the possibility emotionally and politically. On General Philip Schuyler, based at Albany, with the northern outpost of his command under Arthur St. Clair at Fort Ticonderoga, rested the awesome responsibility for thwarting Britain's grand strategy in the northern theater.

The peril to New York and New England engaged Hamilton's quick personal sympathy. He had the "warmest regard" for the people of the state, which he considered "in a great measure, as my political parent." But he coolly sifted and balanced and passed on to Gouverneur Morris and Robert R. Livingston reports and reassurances that testify to the effectiveness of his intelligence service and his coolness in the crisis. He judged, and Washington agreed with him, that Burgoyne could not advance below the New Hampshire Grants (Vermont) "with more than between five and six thousand men," exclusive of some Canadians and Indians. He seconded Morris's accurate sketch of the obstacles that Burgoyne would encounter in the form of rutted roads and lack of transport, provisions, and forage in a penetration of hostile country. General Schuyler would have 5,000 Continentals to stop the invader's progress. New England, roused to the danger, would, he hoped, supply up to twice as many militia. Two regiments from Peekskill and Daniel Morgan's picked corps were also on the march north to reinforce Schuyler. They were "well-used to rifles and to woodfights." They would help to dissipate the people's "panic dread" of Burgoyne's Indians. Hamilton had been urging that these sharpshooters be sent northward for some time. In popular reports their number, about 500, and their effectiveness could be exaggerated to boost the public's morale. Hamilton's confidence in their bold expertness was borne out in the event at Saratoga. Much else in his hopeful forecast turned out disastrously wrong. If Schuyler failed to check Burgoyne, Washington's army would have to move back toward New York, leaving Philadelphia entirely uncovered.

The undefended peak of Mount Defiance overlooked the star-shaped redoubts of Fort Ticonderoga. Early in July, John Burgoyne's second in command, Major General William Phillips, secretly hauled up to the summit and emplaced there a hidden battery of artillery. He aimed their muzzles to fire pointblank down into the inner works of the fortress. Looking up, discovering the guns, and realizing that the artillery on the mountain crest placed the defenders of Fort Ticonderoga under a hopeless checkmate, General Arthur St. Clair evacuated the fort and its entire garrison and fled southward. Burgoyne's men and their Indian cohorts fell upon the panicked and fleeing Americans. When the Americans tried to make a stand at Hubbardton, they were overrun. They were overrun again at Bemis Heights. Burgoyne moved on. He seized General Schuyler's own country house at Old Saratoga and turned it into his headquarters for what he planned as the final victorious push to Albany, only about 40 miles downriver.[1]

Once again events had proved Hamilton's optimistic reassurances to be nothing but idle hopes or empty public relations or both. A shocked and angry Robert R. Livingston wrote Hamilton in alarm. Hamilton tactfully wrote back, trying to mollify him a little by reluctantly concurring in Livingston's scathing criticism of General Philip Schuyler, Hamilton's future father-in-law:

> I have been always a very partial Judge of General Schuylers Conduct, and Vindicated it frequently from the Charges brought

against it, but I am at last forced to suppose him inadequate to the Important Command with which he has been Intrusted. There seems to be a want of firmness in all his Actions, and this last Instance in my Opinion is too unequivocal to be doubted. The Reason assigned for his last retreat is the panic among the army, which he seems to say is beyond anything that was ever known.

Out of his own combat experience with panicky troops, Hamilton drew an important distinction for Livingston's benefit. "Soldiers Commonly look up to those that Command them & take their Complection from their Armies. Under the best, Leaders may be seized with a sudden panic that may precipitate them into the most cowardly behaviour for the Moment, but a settled durable panic is generally a Reflection upon the Leader." A momentary panic of raw troops cannot be helped and should not be held against the commander, but he could not be exonerated from blame for "a settled durable panic." St. Clair, not Schuyler, had been the leader responsible. The panic had been momentary, not "a settled durable panic." The army had fought its retreat; it was still in being. Hamilton's attempt to mollify Livingston by blaming Schuyler for the debacle on the basis of inaccurate reports did not keep Hamilton's and Livingston's exchanges from becoming more and more disputatious. Still, both men preferred Schuyler to Major General Horatio Gates. Gates now was a favorite of Congress and New Yorkers and New Englanders generally, largely for no better reasons than that he was neither a retreating Schuyler nor a distant Washington, but those were reasons enough.

Political pressure forced Washington to recall Schuyler and St. Clair to his headquarters command and put General Horatio Gates in overall command of the north. Of Schuyler, Hamilton wrote Livingston, "I wish among other things he had not rendered himself odious to your state . . . but his appointment to this command could not be avoided."

The mystery of what had happened to Howe and his flotilla continued to keep Washington's army headquarters and Congress off balance. Washington called a council of war to decide between making a quick attack on New York or a move up the Hudson against Sir Henry Clinton. This produced a recommendation in favor of the latter and an order despatching Hamilton to Congress on August 21 to explain the reasons for it against his own better judgment. Congress's response to an army move away from Philadelphia was lukewarm. But before an irrevocable commitment could be made to one or the other of the two wrong horns of this dilemma, out of the cloud of rumors about where Howe's flotilla had gone finally emerged hard news on August 22. John Adams wrote his wife, Abigail, "It is now no longer a secret where Mr. Howe's fleet is . . . it is arrived at the head of Chesapeake Bay. . . ."

"His march by land to Philadelphia may be about sixty or seventy miles."

On August 29, Hamilton wrote to Gates for Washington that "his intentions against Philadelphia" were now "reduced to a certainty."

Hamilton's letters to the Committee of Correspondence in July and August of 1777 had served better to prepare the public's mind for the loss of Philadelphia than for the loss of Fort Ticonderoga. Loss of Philadelphia would not spell utter defeat though it would, as Washington said, putting the matter with excruciating mildness, "Strike . . . a damp" to the American cause.

Wars are as often won by popular impressions held far from the battlefield or by illusions about what has happened there as by what actually happens. Hamilton could not easily explain away the consequences of losing both Fort Ticonderoga and the capital. Now he cheerfully assured private correspondents that the loss of Philadelphia could have only the danger of pulling down public confidence, pushing up prices, and injuring the economic and political credit of the colonies with allies and friends abroad, as if this meant less than it did. He reserved his true forecast of the grand strategy of the situation for Hugh Knox, to whom he had written weeks earlier, "it may be asked, if to avoid a general engagement we give up objects of the first importance, what is to prevent the enemy from carrying every important point, and ruining us? My answer is, that our hopes are not placed in any particular city or spot of ground, but in the preserving of a good army, furnished with proper necessaries, to take advantage of favorable opportunities, and waste and defeat the enemy by piecemeal."

Still working his way north up the Hudson, Howe's second in command, Sir Henry Clinton, second guessed his chief's Philadelphia strategy. He urged Howe to strike directly at Washington and the army, not at the cities. As his columns moved north away from Washington's army, Clinton was not as aggressive in practice as in theory. He and Howe seemed congenitally opposed, and each tended to frustrate the other's plans. Clinton confessed in July 1777 that "By some cursed fatality, we could never draw together." His Hudson Valley expedition was to stumble onward but never close a similar gap between his army and Burgoyne's.

Howe had given Washington ample time. His armada had sailed out of New York harbor in late July and did not disembark at Head of Elk on Chesapeake Bay, near the present Elkton, until a month later. This gave Washington just time enough to move the American army through Philadelphia to the heights of Wilmington to position itself once again, as it had been before Howe's long voyage, between the British and the City of Brotherly Love.

August 24 brought fine weather. Large numbers of Philadelphia patriots turned out along Front and Chestnut Streets to see George Washington lead the American army, wearing the best uniforms they could patch together for parade, on their march through the city on the way to meet Howe and Cornwallis on the other side. First came a small advance guard, then the commander in chief carefully turned out in blue and buff. He was escorted and flanked by stout Henry Knox, Tench Tilghman, Alexander Hamilton, and the tall Marquis de Lafayette. On their first dress parade marching through the cobbled streets of the capital, the main army of the United States began to create an impression of a genuine fighting army. Two days later more troops marched through the red brick city and mildly impressed an American officer watching their passage.

"Though indifferently dressed," he wrote, they "held well burnished arms and carried them like soldiers, and looked . . . as if they might have faced an equal number with a reasonable prospect of success."

Howe outnumbered Washington by about 15,000 to 11,000, but Washington had chosen his own ground and could fight a defensive battle. The American army dug in to prepared positions a few miles southeast of Philadelphia near Wilmington, where Brandywine Creek, meandering in front of the entrenchments, provided an additional protective barrier. The Brandywine could be forded at several points, but it formed a useful natural obstacle, especially on the American left, where Washington positioned the poorly trained Pennsylvania militia.

Howe's troops were weak and sick from the long weeks below decks on a broiling summer sea when they landed at Head of Elk. He had to rest and refit his men and scour the country for transport and cavalry horses. Hamilton reported that most of Howe's horses had died on the time-wasting voyage. Howe gathered his British, Hessian, and Tory forces and began moving north toward the defenses Washington had set up in his way.

From Washington's headquarters on the heights of Wilmington, Hamilton wrote to Gouverneur Morris on September 1, "The enemy will have Philadelphia if they dare make a bold push for it, unless we fight them a pretty general action. I opine we ought to do it, and that we shall beat them soundly if we do. The militia seem pretty generally stirring: our army is in high health & spirits." On the relative numbers of men Hamilton was wildly wrong: "We shall I hope have twice the enemy's numbers." This miscalculation led to a serious misjudgment. "I would not only fight them, but I would attack them; for I hold it an established maxim, that there is three to one in favor of the party attacking." With so much in its favor, the American army would have to be extremely inept to lose. They were and did.

On the morning of September 11, four young girls "were walking in the road . . . close by Polly Buckwalter's Lane." They saw horsemen on the road to Kennett Square, riding through the fields under tall elms. It was a patrol sent out by British General "Scotch Willie" Maxwell and his Jerseymen. The girls kept on with their walk, and a horseman called, "Girls, you'd better go home!" "Why?" asked one of them. "Because the British regiments are coming up the road." One of the girls, Elizabeth Coates, remembered looking down the road and seeing them "in great numbers," and then scurrying home just ahead of the first waves of the British attack at the Battle of Brandywine Creek.

Howe's battle plan was the same one he had used with success against Washington at Brooklyn: a feint against the American center while the main thrust was delivered on a flank—this time the American right flank. Howe's inconclusive attacks on the American center under the command of Nathanael Greene covered a long sweep around the right flank by Cornwallis, whose 10,000 men caught Sullivan unprepared at the upstream or western end of the line and crumpled it back. Washington tried to make the best of a bad situation by moving most of his remaining troops under Greene to form a second line behind Sullivan's crumbling flank. Fighting stubbornly, Greene held the new line till dark; but the center, its troops gone to support Sullivan's flank, collapsed under Howe's pressure. As the firing died down at dusk, weary Americans beaten back in disarray left nearly a thousand of their comrades dead and wounded on the field held by the enemy.

Once again the psychological poison of panicky retreat gripped the Continental Army. Total disintegration threatened its ranks. The commander in chief retreated with Greene's division still holding, despite its killing, double-time march to back up Sullivan. A fleeing mass of fugitives swirled around the commander in chief and his aides.

As Hamilton had written two months earlier, "Soldiers Commonly look up to those that Command them" and "Under the best, Leaders may be seized with a sudden panic" that precipitates the men into cowardly behavior for the moment. "But a settled durable panic is generally a Reflection upon the Leader." It fell to the lot of Washington and his aides on the field to help spread the "complection" of courage among the fleeing troops that day to keep the contagion of panic to the dimensions of a "sudden panic." They did not allow it to swell into "a settled durable panic."

Scattered squads slowed to seek out and find their proper platoons; platoons, their proper companies. Captain Enoch Anderson of the brave Delawares remembered that night with grim pride:[2] "I saw not a despairing look, nor did I hear a despairing word. We had solacing words always ready for each other —'Come, boys, we shall do better another time.'—Had a man suggested, or merely hinted the idea of giving up—he would have been knocked down, and if killed, it would have been no murder."

Little by little order was regained. The army, beaten but still in being, trailed over the bridge at Chester Creek and beyond the village of Chester. Close to midnight a spent and weary Washington sternly reminded himself that he was a servant of the United States and responsible for Congress's army. He was too fatigued to write the bad news to them himself. Harrison was too "distressed." Finally, Timothy Pickering wrote the bitter communiqué from the once more defeated commander in chief: "I am sorry to inform you that in this day's engagement we have been obliged to leave the enemy masters of the field." He put the best face he could on the casualties and concluded on a note of hope, "Notwithstanding the misfortune of the day, I am happy to find the troops in good spirits." He added, "I hope another time we shall compensate for the losses now sustained."

The Marquis de Lafayette had gone ahead with Greene and Washington, plunging in among Sullivan's breaking troops in his own effort to show them the complexion of courage. A British bullet caught him in the thigh and put him out of action. Next day he wrote his wife, "Dear Heart," that *"Messieurs les anglais* . . . wounded me slightly in the leg, but it is nothing . . . for the ball did not touch bone or nerve."

Washington sent Dr. Benjamin Rush, the Philadelphia physician-politician, through the lines to treat wounded American prisoners that the losers had abandoned to the British on the field. When Dr. Rush returned, he compared the beaten, dispirited patriot army to the disciplined British regulars he had just been with.

He was, in general, scornful of the American commanders and compassionate toward the sufferings of the troops. The contrast he drew between the British and the Americans necessarily "gave offense" to his American countrymen. In his notebook, under the heading, "The state and disorders of the American army," he jotted down his diagnosis, as he might have done for any of his other wounded, sick, disturbed, or distressed patients:

> 1. The Commander in Chief, at this time the idol of America, governed by General Greene, General Knox, and Colonel Hamilton, one of his aides, a young man of twenty-one years of age.
> 2. Four major generals, Greene, Sullivan, Stirling and Stevens [*sic*]. The first a sycophant to the General, speculative, without enterprise, The second weak, vain, without dignity, fond of scribbling, in the field a madman. The third a proud, vain, lazy, ignorant drunkard. The fourth a sordid, boasting cowardly sot. The troops undisciplined and ragged, guns fired a hundred a day, pickets left five days and sentries twenty-four hours without relief; bad bread, no order, universal disgust.

Dr. Rush had seen both armies and ministered to the physical and mental "disorders" of men of all ranks after the trauma of Brandywine Creek. Hamilton, the only nongeneral and by far the youngest member of Dr. Rush's "enemies list" of officers who "governed" Washington, is the only one who emerges unscathed from his critique. Hamilton is the only one whose influence on the "idol of America" is not in Rush's words prima facie a malignant one.

Hamilton lacked the major general's rank that would have required his views to be heard and considered ipso facto. He possessed an extremity of youth that would almost seem to require them to be ignored. The intellectual and emotional bond between him and Washington must have indeed been strong, and public demonstrations of it on the field of the lost battle must have been many to have produced from the prominent healer the diagnosis that, insofar as Washington was not under other malignant influences, the idol of America was governed by this one of his aides.

Few Americans had been taken prisoner, largely because most had run away too fast. By next morning they were regrouping in their old units. Although the Americans had not yet been able to win a battle from the British by winning the field, they had showed that they at least had the resiliency of guerrillas to retreat with steadiness gained by much experience with retreats and regroup in time to stave off total disaster. The British had suffered more than 500 casualties. Howe, as usual, failed to follow up his victory by pursuing Washington's army. Instead he plodded on toward Philadelphia. Congress sat nervously watching his unimpeded progress toward the capital, wondering why

Washington's army could do nothing to stop him and save themselves and it.

A delicate message had to be written, and a dangerous mission carried out.

From Yellow Springs on September 17, Hamilton wrote Washington's dispatch describing the situation to the Continental Congress and warning it of the danger. It raised Congress's panicky fears for its own safety, but Congress did not act.

In the path of Howe's march from the Schuylkill to the capital were some mills at Daverser's Ferry near Valley Forge, where flour intended for the use of the American army was stored. The day after his dispatch to Congress, Washington directed Hamilton to take a troop of horsemen under Captain Henry Lee to destroy the flour at the mills and reconnoiter to find the exact location of the enemy forces.

On the summit of the hill above Daverser's Ferry, which overlooked the long descent to the bridge over the mill race, Hamilton posted two lookouts. Down below he took possession of a flat-bottomed boat, in case of need for a hasty retreat.

Just as his and Lee's horse troop had finished destroying the stores at the mill, a British force attacked their party. The lookouts at the top of the rise shouted a warning down to Hamilton and Lee below by firing on the van of the British troops as they first came into view. Then, as Hamilton's son tells the story, "The enemy's horse came clattering down the hill," close behind the fleeing lookouts. The British volleys killed one of the dragoons, wounded another and one of the boatmen, and knocked down Hamilton's horse. Hamilton and four of his dragoons sprang into the flat-bottomed boat and pushed off. Lee dashed back toward the bridge and momentarily drew some of the British fire toward himself. Describing this desperate moment later, "Light-Horse" Harry Lee noted that Hamilton's sagacity in posting the lookouts at the top of the rise and mooring the flat-bottomed boat below had saved both of them that day.

But at the desperate moment of the British attack, neither Lee nor Hamilton knew whether the other had escaped safely. Each feared the other might have been cut off or captured or killed.

Lee's dash for the bridge delayed the attack upon Hamilton's boat for a few minutes and gave Hamilton a better chance of escape, "although the enemy's front section emptied their carbines and pistols at the distance of ten or twelve paces." Although from point-blank range, their volleys miraculously missed him, "Hamilton was committed to the flood, struggling against a violent current, increased by the recent rains." Lee and his detachment galloped off out of danger.

But Lee's fears for Hamilton's safety continued to grow as he heard "volleys of carbines discharged upon the boat, which were returned by guns singly and occasionally." Safely out of reach of pursuit, Lee sent off a horseman to the commander in chief, "describing with feelings of anxiety what had passed, and his sad presage" that Hamilton had fallen.

When Washington received Lee's foreboding letter that evening, he blanched. Just about then, Hamilton himself staggered into headquarters, obviously somewhat the worse for wear, but alive. As Washington caught sight of him, the letter containing Lee's account of his loss may have fluttered from Washington's hand to the ground. Hamilton may have told Washington in alarm that Lee was lost, because, as he reported, "instantly after he turned for the bridge, the British horse reached the mill, and commenced their operations upon the boat." Washington may have embraced him as he reassured Hamilton that Lee, too, had survived.

With such convincing evidence of enemy presence in armed force en route to Philadelphia from the west, Hamilton wrote a second warning to John Hancock in Congress. The main body of the enemy was only four miles from Swedes' Ford, he pointed out. They were at a point on the Schuylkill on the site of what is now Norristown, and they could use boats of the same kind he had used for his escape to ferry fifty men at a time, "in a few hours perhaps sufficient to overmatch the militia who may be between them and the city. This renders the situation of Congress extremely precarious. . . . My apprehensions for them are great. . . ."

At Hamilton's second warning, Congress took alarm. An entry for September 18, 1777, in the *Journals of the Continental Congress 1774–1779*, cited Hamilton's letter as the authority for "the necessity of Congress removing immediately from Philadelphia" to Lancaster. One fast departing Congressman, John Adams of Massachusetts, lamented bravely to his diary as he fled, the "timorous, defensive part, which has involved us in so many disasters." He prayed, "O, Heavens! grant us one great soul! One leading mind would extricate the best cause from . . . ruin which seems to await it."[3]

He harshly criticized Hamilton for the "false alarm which occasioned our flight from Philadelphia," adding, "Not a soldier of Howe's has crossed the Schuylkill." Contrary to his defiant scouting of Hamilton's report of British presence to the west, Adams's actions showed he believed Hamilton's warning. He leapt to his horse and galloped due east to Trenton, then north many miles to Bethlehem, then circled west and southward along a great circle route to the safety of Lancaster.

Howe reached and crossed the Schuylkill. One of his foraging parties blundered into a little-known spot called Valley Forge, where the guards were not as watchful as Hamilton's had been at Daverser's Ferry. There the British seized a depot that held "3800 Barrels of Flour, Soap and Candles, 25 Barrels of Horse Shoes, several thousand tomahawks and Kettles and Intrenching Tools and 20 Hogsheads of Resin." Not far away the usually alert Anthony Wayne left his command without posting a proper watch. The men were trapped in their bivouac near Paoli and overrun by a British force that swept down on their camp in total silence, using only bayonets. They killed the Americans by stabbing them as they roused themselves from sleep in disorganized horror. Americans rightly feared and hated the bayonet. Those who survived fled the field screaming cries of "Massacre!"

Chilly and despondent from failure in the field as the summer that had begun so full of promise ended and fall came on, Hamilton on September 21 wrote an order to himself from Washington. Go to Philadelphia to requisition supplies from the inhabitants "in proportion to the ability of each." It was a "melancholy truth" that the situation of the army was "distressed" and "deplorable."

He left for the city that night, and from there next day he wrote John Hancock, trying to put the best possible face on the recent Valley Forge and Paoli debacles: "The loss 'tis said was not great. . . ." Once again, the watch was at fault: "This seems to have been a bad lookout," he explained.

No job was more vital and at the same time held out less hope of credit or glory than the tough, gritty business of extracting supplies for the army from the city it had failed to protect and that was about to be invested by the victors.[4] Washington wrote Hamilton, "The business you are upon I know is disagreeable, and perhaps in the execution you may meet with more obstacles than were at first apprehended . . . call in such a number of militia as you think necessary." The strictest discipline must be observed, however, "to prevent every species of rapine and disorder." He would give certificates promising future payment for the supplies. Of course, the Philadelphians knew that if they waited a few days till the British came in, they would be paid solid British sterling, not worthless continental paper. Most craftily hid what they had, so Hamilton found little to bring back to the army's hungry, ragged, and half-shod troops.

After Paoli, Washington encamped to nurse the army's wounds at Pennypacker's Mill (today's Schwenksville) on Perkiomen Creek, a confluent of the Schuylkill. On September 26, Lord Cornwallis triumphantly led the British and Hessian grenadiers into Philadelphia. Thanks to Hamilton's "false alarm," the Continental Congress had escaped capture by eight days. The deliberation with which Hamilton's warning had enabled it to depart even left it with much of its dignity intact, especially as members like Adams who had taken easterly routes to the west caught up with it. Moving on west from Lancaster, Congress sequestered itself still more safely in the little town of York, which now became the new capital of the United States. Like Washington's beaten army still encamped between it and the enemy, Congress, though not very effective, remained in existence as a force in being to keep the flame of independence alive through another winter.

Cornwallis's troops marched into Philadelphia "amidst the acclamations of some thousands of inhabitants." There is little reason to doubt that the huzzahs were no less enthusiastic than those for Washington's army passing through a few weeks earlier. The rest of the victorious Anglo-German force took up forward posts at Germantown.

Washington had now demonstrated that he could not defend New York, the most strategic city, or Philadelphia, the capital, or Congress, the only national executive and legislative body, from Cornwallis and Sir William Howe. Was the Washington who had lost so many battles and cities really the right man to continue in command of the army? In York there were serious doubts. John Adams was not alone among patriots in beseeching heaven for "one great soul" to save the cause from the "ruin which seems to await it."

Even some men closest to Washington began to doubt him. Adjutant General Timothy Pickering said to General Nathanael Greene, "Before I came to the army, I entertained an exalted opinion of General Washington's military talents, but I have since seen nothing to enhance it." General Greene, who had urged Washington to hold Fort Washington, seen it fall, and then abandoned Fort Lee with all its supplies intact, agreed. "Why," he said, "the General does want decision." No such doubts were heard from Hamilton, who was with Washington helping him plan a full-dress attack. On October 3, Hamilton wrote out the General Orders to the Army for the attack on Germantown. He wrote out in French Washington's order to Count Casimir Pulaski to assemble his cavalrymen as soon as possible. Washington endorsed the text in Hamilton's hand, "Order of March and Battle Germantown 4th Oct. 1777." It was an aggressive battle plan. Four columns would attack the heart of the British advance positions at dawn after a long night march of more than 20 miles.

Seven P.M. on October 3, 1777, saw Washington's four columns on the march toward the village of small houses and stone mansions strung along the main highway leading to Philadelphia. By 3:00 A.M. Washington and Hamilton, with Sullivan's column, were inside the British picket lines. As dawn approached, an autumn mist rose with the sun, wrapping the whole sloping countryside in a thick, ghostly fog. Other columns that followed roads on the extreme right and left delayed and strayed and failed to reach the scene of the main battle at all. Seeing the American advance guard, British sentries at Mt. Airy put up a noisy resistance that alerted the main British force a mile to the rear. The American columns charged past the outposts. Inside Benjamin Chew's stone mansion, Colonel Musgrave and his men barricaded the doors and fired down on the attacking Americans from second-floor windows.

Hamilton and Timothy Pickering, who had just escaped one of Musgrave's men's bullets, urged Washington and Sullivan to drive on ahead, bypassing this bastion, to keep up the momentum of the attack. Washington should leave behind only enough troops to surround the Chew house and keep Colonel Musgrave's men bottled up there.

But Henry Knox opposed Hamilton's advice. According to Pickering, the former Boston bookseller rummaged through his well-read mind and came up with a perfectly proper military maxim that was fatally wrong for this situation: "It would be unmilitary to leave a castle in our rear," Knox opined.

In rebuttal to Knox, Hamilton and Pickering pleaded that the time it would take to reduce the house would sacrifice the momentum of the advance toward the main force battle ahead. If Knox's counsel were followed and if the whole attack focused on the Chew mansion, a call for surrender might be ignored by Musgrave's men or mistaken in the fog of the battle. Any American who advanced with the flag might be killed. But "the idol of America" was not governed by his aide in his final decision. Knox's military aphorism won the battle of words on the battlefield, overcoming Hamilton's and Pickering's tactical realism. It would lose the Americans yet another day. The result would remind Washington that in future he might better be governed by his aides' advice than his general's.

Brigadier Knox brought up all his sixpounders and blasted away at the stone fortress with no more effect than to leave some cannonball scars on it that are visible on the old stones to this day. Worse still, General Adam Stephen, hearing Knox's cannonade through the mist and thinking that the sound marked the scene of the main battle, turned his own column aside from its assigned route to the front to add his artillery to the useless clatter of Knox's on the stones of the Chew house.

Timothy Pickering's aide, Lieutenant William Smith, volunteered to advance toward the house with a summons for the enemy to surrender, did so, and was mortally wounded. Hamilton's closest friend among all the aides, Lieutenant Colonel John Laurens, leading a patrol with a young French engineer, the Chevalier de Mauduit du Plessis, circled around to the stable behind the house to gather straw. They began to set fires to scorch the British out of it, but Laurens, the young firebrand ready for the burning was shot through the shoulder.

Meanwhile, in the meadows to the southward, other American columns under Greene, Sullivan, and Anthony Wayne, drove through the main British line, seized some of their artillery, and crashed in among their tents. But with the main American column wasting more than an hour battering at the Chew house, the British were given a chance to rally their troops.

American ammunition was beginning to run low. Militia units often fired on each other in the persistent fog. Each then turned and fled blindly from the other. Self-activated panic spread to other units. Some commands fell back to draw more ammunition, found an irresistible charm in movement to the rear, and began to break and run out of impulse and old habit. A 17-year-old Massachusetts veteran, Private Joseph Martin, noted a stiffening of British resistance at the same time. He shrewdly attributed it to the enemy's hearing Americans calling to each other that they were out of ammunition, giving them a good excuse to move rearward.

Greene's columns, spent by their long march into action, were attacked by fresh British troops. Fighting blind in smoke and mist, Greene lost some guns and then fell back in reasonably good order, covered by Count Casimir Pulaski's raw cavalrymen, whom Hamilton rallied just in time.

Off to the west, John Sullivan's command were pulling back from the field they had come so close to winning. "The enemy kept a civil distance behind, sending now and then a shot after us and receiving the same from us," as soldier-pamphleteer Thomas Paine drily wrote sometime later.

Washington and Hamilton and other aides sought to rally the fleeing men once again, as they had by now so often done before, but this time their complexion of courage was not enough to stem the "settled durable panic" of the day. The rout did not end until sheer exhaustion set in way back at Perkiomen, 24 miles north of Germantown.

Even the Delaware Continentals, a rugged lot of men, admitted it had been a tough tour. Captain Enoch Anderson wrote that when they reached the Perkiomen mill, "Here we old soldiers had marched forty miles," fighting a two-hour battle with British regulars at the halfway mark of the march, and all the while "We eat nothing and drank nothing but water on the tour."

Anthony Wayne had learned from the British bayonets at Paoli to order his men to keep theirs fixed the next time. Wayne wrote in angry frustration that when "the Enemy were broke, Dispersed & flying on all Quarters . . . a *Wind Mill* attack was made on a House into which Six Light Companies had thrown themselves to Avoid our Bayonets. —this gave time to the Enemy to Rally. Our Troops . . . fell back to Assist in what they deemed a Serious matter—" Defeat was snatched from the jaws of victory, "the Enemy finding themselves no further pursued and believing it to be a Retreat followed—Confusion ensued, and we ran away from the Arms of Victory ready Open to receive us."

Looking far back on that day at Germantown, Hamilton's friend Light-Horse Harry Lee agreed that more was wrong than loss of precious time at Chew's, more than fog and the too long and complicated plan of approach that Hamilton had written out for the commander. The troops were worn down in body and mind and lacked the discipline that could substitute for refreshment, and, worst of all, they were led by eager but inexperienced, even stupid, generals.

Hamilton wearily drafted Washington's report to Congress, which attributed retreat "at the instant when Victory was declaring herself in our favor" to "the extreme haziness of the weather." Blaming still another crushing defeat, with American casualties of about 1,000, on the same hazy weather in which the British won did nothing to still the ominous tide of criticism of Washington's generalship that continued to rise among members of the Continental Congress at York and spread throughout the country.

But the army was still in being in the field, and war and politics went on. On October 6, Hamilton wrote a letter for Washington to Sir William Howe, returning a lost dog belonging to the British commander. On the seventh he wrote to Congress recommending Brigadier General Alexander McDougall, the old friend who had sponsored his speech in The Fields and who had recommended his own promotion to captain, for a promotion to major general.

Below Philadelphia, on the banks of the Delaware on either side, the Americans still held Fort Mercer and Fort Mifflin, which Howe had bypassed. These forts prevented supplies from moving up the river to Howe's troops. Noting this, Benjamin Franklin had commented shrewdly that he could not tell whether Howe had taken Philadelphia, or Philadelphia had taken Howe. Howe's army in Philadelphia was indeed cut off from supplies and naval support until the British could penetrate the fortifications of Fort Mifflin on the Pennsylvania side and Fort Mercer on the New Jersey side of the river. In the channel between the two forts had been strung a chevaux-de-frise—a protective barrier of timbers and projecting spikes—stretching across the river covered by American gunboats lying upriver, as well as by the guns of the two forts. The British knew that to escape from the trap they had fought their way into in Philadelphia, they would have to seize these two forts.

To protect this exposed but strategic position, Washington needed more troops than he had. But the only source of more troops was the northern army

under General Horatio Gates. Washington knew that if he did not find reinforcements soon, the two forts would fall, and Howe would be released from the
Philadelphia trap, which was all his victories at the Brandywine and Germantown had won him so far.

A letter Hamilton wrote for Washington's signature on October 15, 1777,
to Colonel Christopher Greene, whose First Rhode Island Regiment was helping
to defend these two forts, provides a good example of the trust that Washington
now placed in his aide's military and tactical judgment: "The British attempt will
probably be sudden and violent as they are hardly in a situation to delay a matter
so essential to them as that of removing the river obstructions." He went on, "It
is of infinite importance . . . their keeping or evacuating Philadelphia materially
depends" on their taking Forts Mercer and Mifflin. "Keep fully in mind the
prodigious importance of not suffering the enemy to get entire possession of the
Delaware. . . . spare no pains or activity to frustrate their efforts." The draft of
this letter is written in the third person, for Hamilton's signature, whereas the
original, the receiver's copy, is written in the first person for Washington's
signature. But the receiver's copy contains the following postscript: "The above
letter was written by his Excellency's orders; but as he went to bed before it was
finished, it will be handed you without his signature."

Hamilton had written it and had been so certain that Washington would
approve he had not bothered to awaken the general to read or sign it. Following
this urgent advice, Colonel Christopher Greene, ably seconded at Fort Mercer
by the Chevalier de Mauduit du Plessis, smashed a powerful Hessian attack.
Over in flimsy Fort Mifflin, Colonel Samuel Smith and Major Simeon Thayer of
Rhode Island and their men held out under terrific British bombardments from
ship and shore. But if fresh troops could not soon be found to raise the siege,
still another disaster loomed close to home for Congress to chew over in York
and blame on their perpetual loser of a commander in chief.

General Charles Lee, who was now intriguing widely against Washington,
did not let his and Horatio Gates's supporters in Congress forget Washington's
deficiencies as a military leader. To Horatio Gates himself, Lee wrote, *"Entre
nous,* a certain great man is most damnably deficient."

As Washington's star sank low into the Delaware and Hamilton's with it,
that of Major General Horatio Gates, up on the Hudson at Saratoga, as rapidly
rose with Congress back at York. Medium in build, shortsighted and bespecta-
cled, with thin graying hair, Gates looked more like a chief clerk than a commander in chief; but the physical contrast to Washington, who always towered over
the men around him, seemed to emphasize Gates's superiority in martial shrewdness and perspicacity. Even without overtly joining a cabal or adding his voice
to the rising rumble of dissatisfaction with Washington's performance as commander in chief, Gates's existence as an alternative at this low point in Washington's fortunes called for no action on his part to maintain himself and rise as a
formidable threat.

In Congress, General Thomas Conway, who had been in Washington's own command, and John Adams and others, who feared "ruin" under Washington's generalship, all helped build up Gates's importance by heaping praise on him to Washington's detriment.

Congress bent an eager ear to Conway's lavish praise of Gates. Word of Washington's defeats at the Brandywine and Germantown and the imminent loss of Forts Mercer and Mifflin, coupled with news of Gates's victory at Saratoga reaching York at about the same time, reinforced Congress's and Gates's impression of the contrast between Washington's hapless generalship and Gates's stunning skill.[5] All in Congress, and especially the delegates from New York and the New England states, recognized the importance of the Hudson River valley stretching from Manhattan Island northward past Fort Ticonderoga up Lake Champlain to Canada as the most strategic and most vulnerable artery anywhere in the whole length of the Continental Association. It was the obvious seam along which America could be split in two by application of the classic British military strategy of "divide and conquer."

The geography of the concept as it applied to the American colonies in revolt had not been lost on Major General John Burgoyne. In fact, he was the leading expert on the subject. When a new wagering book was opened at ultrafashionable Brooks's Club in London, other members crowded about to watch a handsome, florid, gregarious man record the first bet. His entry read, "John Burgoyne wagers Charles [James] Fox one pony [fifty guineas] that he will be home victorious from America by Christmas Day, 1777." Not long before, a military treatise of his authorship entitled with characteristic flamboyance "Thoughts for Conducting the War from the Side of Canada" had been approved in the highest echelons of command. The high command now entrusted the application of these "Thoughts" in the field to their confident thinker.

The year before, in June 1776, Sir Guy Carleton and Burgoyne had beaten back a second American invasion of Canada led by unlucky General John Sullivan at Trois Rivières. Carleton's counter incursion down Lake Champlain in October had been thwarted by Benedict Arnold's delaying action at Valcour Island, and the year's campaigning had ended as it began with the Americans back at Fort Ticonderoga.

Burgoyne's plan to sweep down Lake Champlain, capture Fort Ticonderoga, and drive a wedge through the Hudson Valley to Albany struck terror into hearts of all New Englanders. General Philip Schuyler, the American commander of the northern theater, had become the focus of their hopes and fears.

To New Englanders, Schuyler's military sins included more than the failure of ill-fated expeditions to Canada. He had rejected the claims of the Green Mountain Boys to the New Hampshire Grants, which, largely through Hamilton's efforts, would later become the state of Vermont. He was a patroonish holder of spreading lands in the Dutch tradition and influential with the Indians who supplied the rich fur trade. This made him an automatic object of jealous suspicion by the small yeomen farmers east of the Hudson. He was the friend of Washington, who at the beginning of the war had withdrawn from Boston, which he held, for New York, which he lost. When Schuyler refused to be drawn north with his main army to meet Burgoyne's new 1777 thrust above Saratoga, the antagonism of the mighty Adams family turned against him. Schuyler, on his part, had an aristocratic way of not turning the other cheek. He abrasively returned as good as he got to his critics. From his post as headquarters intelligencer, Hamilton, of course, knew all about this dangerous schism.

As Burgoyne's advance pressed southward toward Saratoga, where Schuyler's own lands and large country house stood directly in his path, Schuyler, who knew the terrain better than anyone else, had combed the Hudson Valley for woodsmen, found tools for them, and sent them north to add obstacles to Burgoyne's days and miles. Schuyler's men set to felling trees across trails, adding to existing deadfalls, damming up brooks, and creating viscous swamps where before sure footing had been. He had carefully laid out fortified positions for a final line of defense beside the Hudson at Old Saratoga.

But at the end of July, Congress clamored for an investigation into the latest fall of Fort Ticonderoga, remanded Schuyler to headquarters and directed Washington to name another area commander to replace him. In the name of all New England, delegates like Samuel Adams demanded Horatio Gates. Washington demurred, reminding Congress that as they had taken separate responsibility for the northern department, the portentous choice of a substitute general should be theirs. They promptly appointed Gates.

After seizing Fort Ticonderoga in July, Burgoyne's advance had become slow and painful. St. Leger's eastward invasion along the Mohawk was beaten back by Marinus Willett at Fort Stanwix and by Nicholas Herkimer's Tryon County men at Oriskany. But gambler that he was, Burgoyne pressed on, recklessly hoping that he could still win his bet with Fox on the books at Brooks's by Christmas. Well dug into the fortifications General Schuyler had laid out blocking the route down the Hudson, the northern army, now under General Horatio Gates, brought Burgoyne to a halt at Saratoga. In September and again in early October, Burgoyne's men attacked in vain to break through. Sir Henry Clinton in New York City, concerned at the possibility of disaster northward, moved some columns up the Hudson. By the middle of October he had reached Esopus, now Kingston, leaving a gap of only 80 miles between him and Burgoyne's army. On October 16, Clinton set fire to the town. More important, the next day at Saratoga, Burgoyne surrendered to Gates with all 5,700 men he had left in his army.

Saratoga is said by many to be one of the ten decisive battles of world history. It was quickly saluted around the world as a sensational defeat for British arms and as notable a victory for Americans. Gates had not only beaten Burgoyne, but he had even bested his own severest critic, Benedict Arnold, who had angrily criticized Gates for not following up his success in the early engagement there at Freeman's Farm. James Lovell, a Massachusetts member of Congress, after picturing a Washington powerless to halt an enemy rampaging unopposed around Philadelphia on the Delaware, confided that "Your army & the eastern militia are now strongly contrasted with those in the Middle State(s). . . . It is said Howe would not have passed more than 70 Miles, from the Ships which landed him, in his whole Skin in Y neighbourhood, or among Yankee Stone walls. . . . Our hope springs all from the Northward, and about all our Confidence."

Some leaders of Washington's own army hustled to congratulate Gates effusively on a success that so spectacularly highlighted Washington's failures. Joseph Reed, one of Washington's former aides, after a salute to Gates, regretted that "this Army, . . . notwithstanding the Labours . . . of our amiable Chief [,] has yet gathered no Laurels." Anthony Wayne too was disgruntled: ". . . whether I shall remain longer in the service than this Campaign depends on Circumstances—there are Certain Generals—as *Lee—Gates—Mifflin* & c. who will point out by their Conduct the line which I shall follow . . ." Gates's success "Must eventually save this [Otherwise] *Devoted* Country." Brigadier General Conway would send to Gates his plan for instruction of the whole army. To his letter he added a slur on Washington's command that would soon cause a sensation. To Washington, all such congratulatory letters to Gates from civilian correspondents, some in official posts, seemed gratingly extravagant in praise.

Congress thanked Gates in the name of the thirteen United States for defeating an army of 10,000 men and securing the surrender of 6,000. It voted to strike a gold medal and presented it to him. It called on the people for a day of thanksgiving that God "hath been pleased . . . to crown our arms with most signal success."

Washington theoretically was in overall command, even in the northern theater; but when Gates officially announced his victory to Congress, Gates sent the message directly to it by his adjutant, Colonel James Wilkinson, bypassing his nominal commander in chief. Far from rebuking Gates for the slight to Washington, Congress complied with a request of Gates's by promoting his messenger, Wilkinson, the bearer of glad tidings, from colonel to brigadier general.

As usual, troop enlistments were expiring, and by Christmas the men would be leaving for home in droves. Under siege without relief, the fate of Forts Mercer and Mifflin still hung in the balance. There was also speculation that Howe was mustering his forces to attack and overwhelm the Continental Army before winter and put an end to the campaign. Washington's prestige was at its lowest ebb. The fate of the Revolution, or at least Washington's own fate as commanding general, seemed to depend on finding a large number of fresh troops capable of standing up to the victorious Howe or, at least, of raising the siege and saving the river forts.

At this dark hour of his fortunes, ten days after receiving the officially glorious, but inwardly galling news of Burgoyne's surrender to Gates, Washington called a council of war of five major generals and ten brigadiers at his temporary camp at Whitpain on October 29, 1777. He assigned his unwaveringly loyal aide with the ready pen, Alexander Hamilton, to keep the minutes, as well as to see and be seen by the innermost circle of his generals. Howe had 10,000 men; Washington, 11,000. But expiration of enlistments would soon reduce

Washington's men to 9,000. Before Washington could successfully attack Howe, the generals agreed, 20 regiments must be drawn down from the northern theater to the main army, in addition to Daniel Morgan's riflemen, who were already on their way. To pry the reinforcements loose from Gates's command, Washington must dispatch one of his aides northward.

Hamilton wrote a cautious letter to Congress for Washington, assuring it that this would not "frustrate any important plans" that Gates "may have formed," but that nothing was more important now than "the destruction of the enemy in this quarter."

From Washington's point of view this was one of the most delicate missions of the war and of his own career, if not the most delicate of all. His position as the commander in chief, as well as the fate of the continental effort in the most critical theater of the war, and indeed the safety of the Continental Congress itself were all at stake. For this critical mission Washington chose the youngest of his aides. He wrote Hamilton on October 30, 1777, from his headquarters at Philadelphia:

> Dear sir—It having been judged expedient by the members of a Council of War held yesterday, that one of the Gentlemen of my family should be sent to General Gates in order to lay before him the state of this army; I thought it proper to appoint you that duty, and desire that you will immediately set out for Albany, at which place you will find General Gates.
>
> You are so fully acquainted with the two principal points on which you are sent, namely the state of our army and the situation of the enemy, that I shall not enlarge on those heads.

The problem with Gates was going to be to get him to release some of his troops voluntarily without bringing the matter to a test of wills or a test vote in Congress. There New England's backing of Gates and the Middle States' and Southern disillusionment with Washington might well result in Washington's downfall, a fatal split in colonial unity, and Washington's own replacement by Gates. Many, like Benjamin Rush, were saying that Gates's army was like "a well regulated family" while Washington's "imitation of an army was like an unformed mob." Now, because Congress, not Washington, at Washington's insistence, had replaced Schuyler in the northern command, Gates was "more peculiarly under . . . direction of Congress" than Washington. So Hamilton's mission was one of diplomacy and persuasion, not just to deliver a command. There was no certainty that Washington any longer even had the authority to give a command to Gates or, if he did in theory, that Gates would obey it. Or that it would stick with Congress if Gates should defy it.

As Washington explained it, "What you are chiefly to attend to, is to point out in the clearest and fullest manner to General Gates the absolute necessity that there is for his detaching a very considerable part of the army at present under his command to the reinforcement of this."

Washington was still counting on being able to save Forts Mercer and Mifflin, starve out Howe, and gain the one great victory that had eluded him so far. With additional troops from Gates, Washington hoped "in all probability" to "reduce General Howe to the same situation in which General Burgoyne now is, should he attempt to remain in Philadelphia without being able to remove the obstructions in Delaware, and opening a free communication with his shipping."

Washington also wrote a separate letter to Gates, congratulating him coolly on his victory, but in reproof regretting that Gates had bypassed him sending back news of it. He introduced Hamilton, explained that his aide was sent "by the advice of my Gen. Officers," and added that "he is well informed . . . and will deliver my sentiments upon the plan of operations now necessary." He forbore to go into more detail because he was not "well advised how matters are circumstanced on the North River"—another pointed reproof to Gates for not reporting to him more fully. Washington's letter revealed full understanding of the hostility Hamilton could expect to meet when he arrived at Gates's headquarters.

The key passage of Washington's instructions to Hamilton entrusted to him complete discretion in final judgment: "If . . . you should find that [General Gates] intends, in consequence of his Success, to employ the troops under his command upon some expeditions, by the prosecution of which the common cause will be more benefited than by their being sent down to reinforce this army, it is not my wish to give interruption to the plan."

This left Hamilton with the broadest possible discretion—and responsibility. If Hamilton found virtue in Gates's independent intentions, he was to approve them and disregard the decision of the war council at Washington's headquarters. This meant no less than that Hamilton was to decide, in the light of Gates's designs, whether the war was to be prosecuted during the next months in the north, for example, by Gates against Sir Henry Clinton, who was still burning down houses and mills around Kingston, or by Washington around Philadelphia against Sir William Howe.

By Hamilton's route, Albany was 254 miles from Washington's camp. If Washington's emissary had lacked discretion to settle matters with Gates, a round trip and a return message to Albany would have been necessary, which, even if performed by express riders, would have taken ten days or more. This was too long if the forts were to be saved. With the reinforcements and without such delays, it might still be possible to raise the siege. But if reinforcements should reach Howe from New York City before Washington's reached him, it would be too late. Every day, every hour was vital if the lonely forts' gallant garrisons were to be saved.

As bidden on October 30, Hamilton had set out on his horse for Albany, covering 60 to 75 miles a day. As he passed Daniel Morgan's and other corps moving south, he stopped long enough to hurry them on their way and send reports back to Washington.

He reached New Windsor, at a distance of 150 miles, late on November 1, spent some time at Fishkill on November 2 in conversation with General Israel Putnam and other commanders, and from there wrote Washington of some extra help he had found and rushed on its way: "I have directed General Putnam, in your name, to send forward with all dispatch to join you, the two continental brigades and Warner's militia brigade. . . ." even though their enlistments were expiring at the end of the month. "Your instructions did not comprehend any militia; but . . . I concluded you would not disapprove of a measure calculated to strengthen you, though but for a small time." Even a few weeks more might be enough to save the forts; they had been just enough to make possible the victory at Princeton. Hamilton followed up on earlier detachments: "Neither Lee's or Jackson's regiments, nor the detachments belonging to General Mac-Dougall's division, have yet marched. I have pressed their being sent, and an order has been dispatched for their instantly proceeding."

Deferentially, but unmistakably, he counseled Washington on certain faulty troop dispositions. "Will your Excellency permit me to observe, that I have some doubts . . . of the propriety of leaving the regiments proposed to be left in this quarter? But if my doubts on this subject were stronger than they are, I am forbid by the sense of council from interfering in the matter."

The zealous, fast-riding emissary added an aggressive postscript: "So strongly am I impressed with the importance of endeavoring to crush Mr. Howe, that I am apt to think it would be advisable to draw off all the regulars—'the Continental troops'. Had this been determined on, General Warner's 1600 militia might have been left here."

There was no question in Hamilton's mind that the main effort was "to crush Mr. Howe," regardless of what, if anything, Gates might plan to do to pursue Sir Henry Clinton. Recrossing to the west side of the Hudson after bypassing Sir Henry Clinton's forces, having ridden hard through rough, cold, desolate country for six days, snatching brief hours of sleep when he could, he arrived in Albany around noon November 5, weary and probably half sick as well. There he "waited upon General Gates immediately on the business of my mission." Gates received Hamilton in the company of several of his subordinate officers. To all the reasons for hostility that Hamilton and Washington had foreseen was no doubt added the chagrin that the touchy Gates must have felt at first sight of the extreme youth of Washington's emissary.

From Hamilton's letter of the same date to Gates and his report to Washington the following day, are taken their points of difference, which are incorporated in the following imaginary approximation of their tense dialogue. It was to have fateful consequences for all three men and for the future conduct of the war.

HAMILTON: The commander in chief wants you to send three brigades from here to White Marsh to join him.

GATES: I cannot spare any more troops from this command.

HAMILTON: You promised Washington that when you disposed of Burgoyne's threat, you would send him reinforcements.

GATES: I have already sent him Learned's and Poor's and Warner's brigades from here.

HAMILTON: He is already counting on those, but they are under-strength and not enough. If Washington receives more troops soon, he may be able to raise the siege of the Delaware forts and bottle up Howe in Philadelphia; if not, they will fall to Howe.

GATES: Are the forts really so important?

HAMILTON: Of course. They command the Delaware and keep reinforcements and supplies from New York from reaching Howe before winter.

GATES: I am inflexible in the opinion that two brigades at least of Continental troops should remain in and near this place.

HAMILTON: When you wanted reinforcements, you were quick enough to send for them last summer to Artemas Ward, to Benedict Arnold, and to Benjamin Lincoln. Why can't you comply with Washington's urgent request for troops now?

GATES: Only last month Sir Henry Clinton took Forts Montgomery and Clinton on the Hudson, and we had to destroy Fort Constitution ourselves. The enemy is still to the south of us and threatening.

HAMILTON: How do you know?

GATES: We found this out when we unscrewed a hollow bullet swallowed by a spy we captured and found an enemy message inside.

HAMILTON: I do not think Sir Henry Clinton still intends coming on this way.

GATES: The intelligence of Sir Henry Clinton's having given up the idea of joining Burgoyne is not sufficiently authenticated to put it out of doubt. There is still a possibility of his returning up the river. This would expose the finest arsenal in America here in Albany to destruction should this place be left bare of troops, as you propose.

HAMILTON: Captain Caleb Gibbs, my aide, and I have just ridden up the other side of the river from where Clinton's men are supposed to be. We saw very little trace of an enemy. Besides, your troops can bring the contents of the arsenal south with them.

GATES: It would be impossible to remove the artillery and stores for a considerable time. The roads are too difficult.

HAMILTON: Not so. We have just ridden over them to reach here.

GATES: Besides, the New England states would be left open to the ravages of the enemy.

HAMILTON: You do not need to leave more than one brigade here to assure the safety of the New England states.

GATES: Leaving only one brigade here would put it out of my power to enterprise anything against Fort Ticonderoga.

HAMILTON: You do not really mean you intend to attack it?

GATES: I think it might be done in winter.

HAMILTON: There would be surprise, certainly, at the folly of it.

GATES: I think it would be important to undertake it.

HAMILTON: The British more likely will evacuate it without an attack.

And so it went on. Gates remained unyielding to Hamilton's strongest arguments. He would promise only one brigade to Washington, and that one would be Paterson's. Judging from Hamilton's later angry reaction, he was induced to acquiesce in this half a loaf or, really, third of a loaf by representations of Gates that Hamilton later considered to have been false.

Robert Troup, Hamilton's King's College classmate, was now serving in Albany as an aide-de-camp to Gates. After Hamilton's long, lonely ride with Captain Caleb Gibbs and the hostile, inflexible reception of the best of his reasoning, argument, importunings, and wit by Gates, his mission seemed to be a failure. Hamilton was happy to find a trusted old friend that night to share his fatigue and his sense of futility and from whom to seek useful inside information. Somehow Hamilton found out, perhaps from Troup, that Gates still had three brigades left under his command, of which Brigadier General John Paterson's was much the weakest. Of General Nixon's brigade, all 854 were regulars; Glover's had 1,362 men, of whom 918 were regulars and 444 militia; Paterson's had only 732 regulars and 330 militia. Paterson's was the weakest in numbers of regulars. Gates may have told Hamilton the total of 1,070 for Paterson's brigade, without disclosing that it included so many militia. Hamilton was acutely conscious of the problem of militia whose terms were always expiring: they did not count as effectives.

Hamilton could find in Gates's trick a personal grievance to add still more force to his official demands. Hamilton wasted no time. He followed up his interview with a peremptory letter to Gates the same day: "Sir, by inquiry I have learned that General Paterson's brigade, which is the one you proposed to send, is, by far, the weakest of the three now here and does not consist of more than about 600 rank and file fit for duty. . . . It is true there is a militia regiment with it of about 200 but the term of service for which this regiment is engaged is so near expiring, that it would be past by the time the men could arrive at the place of their destination, and to send them would be to fatigue the men to no purpose." Hamilton was human enough not to want to fatigue them needlessly just as they were about to rejoin their wives and sweethearts for Christmas. Now he did not consider himself bound by his earlier acceptance of Paterson's brigade only: "I cannot consider it either as compatible with the good of the service or my instructions from his Excellency General Washington, to consent, that [Paterson's] brigade be selected from the three, but . . . I am under the necessity of requiring, by virtue of my orders from him, that one of the others be substituted . . . either General Nixon's or General Glover's, and that you will be pleased to give immediate orders for its embarkation."

Hamilton admitted that he had accepted Gates's first offer too easily, but did not forbear to brandish new arguments based on the highest command judgments: "I am not myself sensible of the expediency of keeping more than one here, in conjunction with the detached regiments in the neighborhood of this place; . . . my ideas coincide with those gentlemen, whom I have consulted on the occasion, whose judgment I have more reliance upon than my own and who must be supposed to have a thorough knowledge of the circumstances. . . . Their opinion is, that one brigade with the regiments before mentioned would amply answer the purposes of this post."

Nothing is more characteristic of Hamilton than his refusal to quit after an initial reverse or even after two or three; time after time by a second effort or a new tack he would eke out an unexpectable change that would open to an astonishing success. He was not ready to give up on Gates: "Knowing that General Washington wished me to pay great deference to your judgment, I ventured too far to deviate, from the instructions he gave me, as to consent, in compliance with your opinion that two brigades should remain here instead of one."

Unknown to Hamilton, the night of November 8, his last in Albany, was the very night that Washington in camp at White Marsh was reading the report of a mysterious letter from Thomas Conway to Gates, which had been intercepted. In it Conway had written the slur: "Heaven has been determined to save your country, or a weak General and Bad Counselors would have ruined it."

Reacting angrily to this slur on himself and counselors like Hamilton, Washington seized his pen to scratch out a two-sentence note to Conway. Washington would have applauded any undercover efforts his aide was making in Albany to gather all possible intelligence from his old college friend, who was also the adjutant of his enemy, as well as all the troops he could pry loose.

The day after his first meeting with Gates, crushed by the sense that his mission had been a failure, Hamilton wrote Washington with no excuses. He explained the problem to Washington in terms of the whole delicate national political and military situation. The danger, indeed, seemed more political than military. Also, Hamilton had just found out something else that was so sinister he did not dare put it in writing in a letter that might be intercepted by one of Gates's spies. Troup or someone else, perhaps General Schuyler, may have warned Hamilton of the strength and power that the Conway cabal had already drawn to itself among Gates's innermost circle.

Writing Washington, Hamilton found the pros and cons of whether or not to put more pressure on Gates in delicate balance. He laid out the options carefully for his chief to reflect on: "I found myself infinitely embarrassed, and was at a loss how to act. I felt the importance of strengthening you as much as possible, but . . . I found insuperable inconveniences in acting diametrically opposite to the opinion of a gentleman whose successes have raised him to the highest importance. General Gates has won the entire confidence of the Eastern States; if disposed to do it, by addressing himself to the prejudices of the people he would find no difficulty to render a measure odious which it might be said was calculated to expose them to unnecessary danger."

Then Hamilton gave a hint of a secret cabal of which it would be too dangerous to write more: "Gates has influence in Congress to discredit the measure. It appears dangerous to insist. These considerations and others which I shall be more explicit in when I have the pleasure of seeing you determined me not to insist upon sending either of the other brigades remaining here."

Hamilton could not know that by the time Washington received this letter, having read Conway's intercepted letter to Gates, he would understand exactly what Hamilton meant but did not write.

We catch the young aide in a rare but human confession that none of what he could prudently put down on paper would excuse apparent failure:

> I am afraid what I have done may not meet with your approbation as not being perhaps fully warranted by your instructions; but I ventured to do what I thought right, hoping that at least the goodness of my intention will excuse the error of my judgment.
>
> I was induced to this relaxation the more readily, as I had directed to be sent on 2,000 militia, which were not expected by you, and a thousand continental troops out of those proposed to be left with General Putnam . . .
>
> [But] I cannot forbear being uneasy, lest my conduct should prove displeasing to you . . .

After his talks with Robert Troup, Hamilton must have followed up his November 5 letter to Gates with yet another meeting, or perhaps he delivered his November 5 letter to Gates in person. In any event, he hammered away at Gates with his old arguments and some new ones from Troup. Surprisingly, or not so, being Hamilton, he won a reversal on appeal. After repeating all the reasons why he disagreed with the idea of doing so, Gates reluctantly agreed to send Washington two brigades instead of one. He added Glover's brigade to Paterson's.

A passage that Gates wrote into the first draft of his letter to Washington giving his reluctant consent shows how much he resented the personal pressure Hamilton had brought to bear on him. Gates had written, "Although it is Customary & even Absolutely necessary to direct Implicit Obedience to be paid to the Verbal Orders of Aids de Camp in Action, or while upon the Spot—yet I believe it is never practiced to Delegate that Dictatorial power, to One Aid de Camp sent to an Army 300 Miles distant."

Gates's second draft omitted the above passage and stated only his formal compliance: "Upon mature Consideration of all Circumstances, I have, nevertheless, ordered General Glover's Brigade to be added to General Paterson's, in Reinforcement to your Army, and they will march, immediately. . . ."

In the course of their later meetings, Gates must have talked with Hamilton at large and gained enough trust in his discretion and capacity, despite his youth, to add that, "Col. Hamilton . . . will report everything that I wish to have you acquainted with, as well with Respect to the present State, as the future Operations this Way."

Gates's subsequent actions showed that the ostensible reasons he had advanced against sending troops to Washington were a bluff, if not a part of the larger design of Conway's cabal. He forthwith reduced danger to the Albany arsenal by sending 30 brass cannon and 3,000 stand of arms inland; he wrote to Congress that a splendid aftereffect of his great victory was that the enemy had "evacuated every post on this side," would probably evacuate Fort Ticonderoga within the month, and must surely have done so had Washington left him with troops to threaten it.

By November 16, two weeks later, Gates was able to tell Congress proudly that the enemy had indeed evacuated Ticonderoga and the mountain that looked down into it as well and had retired all the way north to St. John's and Ile aux Noir. Southward, Sir Henry Clinton had abandoned the Hudson River posts all the way back to Kingsbridge at the north end of Manhattan. Gates's freeing of the entire Hudson Valley from the enemy would stand in proud contrast to Washington's imminent loss of the Delaware forts to Howe.

On November 10 from New Windsor near Newburgh, about a hundred miles south of Albany, where he had arrived the night before, Hamilton reported to Washington the good news from Gates laconically, with some pride but no preening, and no time for resting on laurels: "Having given General Gates a little time to recollect himself, I renewed my remonstrances on the necessity and propriety of sending you more than one brigade . . . and finally prevailed upon him . . . for Glover's addition to Patterson's. . . ."

Hamilton followed up to make sure these brigades actually got on their way and by transport that was hard to turn back. As an expert on administration, as well as command, Hamilton knew that a strong follow-up was at least as important as a good order: "It was thought conducive to expedition to send the troops by water, as far as it could be done. I procured all the vessels that could be had at Albany fit for the purpose; but could not get more than sufficient to take in Paterson's brigade. . . ." It was the less reliable one, and with more militia, whose enlistments were expiring, they could more easily wander off toward home if left on land.

He had marched off Glover's brigade, with more regulars, down the east side of the river, the roads there, as he knew from having just pounded up them, "being much better than on this side." He kept an eye on their progress, too. There was a contrary wind, but "our sloop with a part of Paterson's is arrived and the others are in sight."

Hamilton also checked to see whether the orders he had left with General Putnam, who was, like Gates a hero in New England eyes, had been carried out and found they had not been. The general, who had been in overall command of Hamilton's Provincial artillery at the Bayard's Hill Fort the year before, had paid no attention to commands from a former junior officer. There was a big new problem with Putnam. Hamilton told Washington, "Everything has been neglected and deranged by General Putnam." Poor's and Learned's brigades had not moved. No attention had been paid to his earlier order for a detachment of 1,000 men from the troops stationed there. "Everything is sacrificed to [General Putnam's] whim of taking New York." It was a "hobby horse" with Putnam that excused him from releasing troops.

Not distracted by Putnam's "hobby horse," Hamilton wrote out a "positive order" to old "General Putt," telling him that by his delay "the cause of America is put to the utmost conceivable hazard." Hamilton reminded him that he had given the order to him not once but twice, the second time in writing.

He then brandished command authority to the limit of its force, something he had refrained from doing with Gates: "I now sir, in the most explicit terms, by his Excellency's authority, give it as a positive order from him, that all the Continental troops under your command may be immediately marched to Kings Ferry, there to cross the river and hasten to reinforce the army under him."

Poor's and Learned's brigades mutinied, and refused to move for lack of food and money. Hamilton reported that "several of the regiments having received no pay for six or eight months passed. . . . A captain killed a man and was shot himself by his comrade." These were only some of the "difficulties for want of proper management" that "stopped the troops from proceeding."

Hamilton found a way to solve the mutiny and murder problem, but did not boast much about his part in the solution, giving the credit to Governor George Clinton, from whom he had raised the money: "Governor Clinton has been the only man, who has done anything toward removing the difficulties, but he failed 'for want of General Putnam's cooperation.' "

Hamilton adds briskly, "On coming here, I immediately sent for Colonel Bailey who now commands Learned's brigade, and have gotten him to engage for carrying the brigade on to headquarters, as fast as possible, . . . by means of five or six thousand dollars which Governor Clinton was kind enough to borrow for me. The money, Colonel Bailey thinks, will keep the men in good humor till they join you." Hamilton did not rest upon high hopes and happy assurances. He waited and saw that "They marched this morning toward Goshen."

When an old plan was no longer practical, Hamilton could drop it and improvise a new one to accomplish the objective, as he now explained to Washington: "The plan I before laid having been totally deranged, a new one has become necessary." It was too late to send Warner's militia because their terms of enlistment would be out by the time they arrived. Instead, he "sent an order in the most emphatical terms to General Putnam, immediately to dispatch all the Continental troops under him to your assistance; and to detain the militia instead of them."

As for Putnam's pet project of catching up with Gates in glory by retaking New York, grand strategy came first:

> Tis only wasting time and misapplying men, to employ them in a farcical parade against New York; . . . New York is no object if it could be taken; and to take it would require more men than could be spared for more substantial purposes.
>
> I wish General Putnam was recalled from the command of this post, and Governor Clinton would accept it. The blunders and caprices of the former are endless.

Although neither Hamilton nor Major General Israel Putnam was aware of it, on November 5, 1777, five days before Hamilton's letter, Congress had, in fact, relieved Putnam of his command and ordered him to join the main army under Washington at White Marsh.

Hamilton now fell into one of the acute illnesses that were to recur throughout his life. On November 12, 1777, he wrote plaintively to Washington from New Windsor: "Dear sir, I have been detained here these two days by a fever and violent rheumatic pains throughout my body. This has prevented my being active in person . . . but I have taken every other method in my power, in which Governor Clinton has obligingly given me all the aid he could." He had pressed the troops to march immediately, but they were also unwell: "I was told they were under an operation for the itch, which made it impossible to proceed till the effects of it were over."

Having scoured the whole north for troops for his beleaguered general, Hamilton was racked with a "fever and violent rheumatic pain." Imagining that he was over it and anxious to be "attending to the march of the troops," he left New Windsor and crossed by the ferry to Fishkill "in order to fall in with General Glover's brigade, which was on its march from Poughkeepsie." But at Dennis Kennedy's house near Peekskill, Hamilton had a relapse and could march no further. Governor Clinton, alarmed by his condition a week later, sent to Bellemont for Dr. John Jones to attend him. The physician himself was ill and could only send back a messenger with a prescription for Hamilton's treatment. This did no good, and two days later Hamilton "seemed to be drawing nigh his last." After two more days, "the coldness came on again, and increased (he was then cold as high as his knees)," so that when Dr. Jones got well himself and came to him, he "thought he could not survive . . ." But four hours later the fever abated, and Hamilton was soon pronounced to be on the mend.

His illness and frustrations, compounded with his youth, helped cause Hamilton's normally civil and genial personal manner to grate on older local commanders. Colonel Hugh Hughes, a partisan of Gates, remarked that "Colonel Hamilton, who has been very ill of a nervous disorder, at Peekskill, is out of danger, unless it be from his own sweet temper." It is significant that observers of Hamilton's frequent illnesses, including Hamilton himself, often associated them with a "nervous disorder."

Apparently recovered once again, Hamilton kept harrying the reluctant troops southward on their wintry march. "Glover's may be expected at Fish Kill tonight, hence they will be pushed forward as fast as I can have any influence to make them go," he wrote, but he did not manage to infect them all with his own fierce enthusiasm. He was sympathetic with their human limitations, too, if not willing to ease up on himself. He reported to Washington, "I am sorry to say, the disposition for marching in the officers and men in general . . . does not keep pace with my wishes or the exigency of the occasion. They have unfortunately imbibed an idea that they have done their part of the business of the campaign and are now entitled to repose. This and the want of pay makes them averse to a long march at this advanced season." He admitted to Washington that, "I am very unwell; but I shall not spare myself to get things immediately in a proper train, and for that purpose intend, unless I receive other orders from you, to continue with the troops in the progress of their march."

Washington was pleased with Hamilton's reports. From headquarters at White Marsh, Pennsylvania, November 15, 1777, Washington wrote, by Tench Tilghman's hand, "Dear sir, I have duly received your several favors from the time you left me to that of the 12 inst. I approve entirely of all the steps you have taken, and have only to wish that the exertions of those you have had to deal with had kept pace with your zeal and good intentions." Better than anyone else, he appreciated the importance of Hamilton's pushing the troops on by his physical presence and example, even, or especially, when he was in poor health himself: "I hope your health will before this have permitted you to push on the rear of the whole reinforcement beyond New Windsor."

But there were ominous forebodings of yet another humiliating loss that compounded Washington's danger and the enemy's military, and Gates's political, strength. Washington added, "The enemy have lately damaged Fort Mifflin considerably." He passed along the sad personal news that although "our loss in men has been but small," one of Hamilton's fellow artillerymen, Captain Samuel Treat, of the Second Continental Artillery, "is unfortunately among the killed." He closed, "I wish you a safe return, and am, Dear Sir, your most obedient servant, George Washington."

Hamilton made one last effort with Gates that he was sure was doomed to fail because of a "design" whose hidden shape he remained too prudent to commit to a dispatch. An intercepted dispatch of General Putnam's saying that "the enemy have stripped New York very bare," and that "the people there—that is, the Tories—are in a very great fright," seemed to mean that Sir Henry Clinton had gone off with more reinforcements to Howe in Philadelphia, making Washington's peril there still greater, and Gates's correspondingly less.

Hamilton wrote Washington that "I have written to General Gates . . . to try if this will not extort" further reinforcements from him.

Hamilton's unsaid reasons for trying to "extort" the troops, without issuing a "positive" order remained. ". . . Perhaps you will think me blamable in not having exercised the powers you gave me, and given a positive order . . . but deliberately weighing all circumstances, I did not and do not think it advisable to do it." Contrasting the blundering foolishness of "Old Putt" with the artfully contrived objections of Gates, Hamilton ruefully added, "the *ignorance* of some and the *design* of others have been almost insuperable obstacles."

Lacking timely reinforcements, Fort Mifflin fell November 15; and Fort Mercer, on the twentieth. As Hamilton and his son John Church saw it, if only Gates and Putnam had promptly obeyed the orders Hamilton had given them, the forts could have been saved, the British army would have been cut off from the navy, and Sir Henry Clinton's reinforcements and all logistical support would have been cut off from the hostile countryside. Washington's prophecy to Hamilton of October 30 would have been fulfilled: "Howe would have been reduced to the situation of Burgoyne, thus probably terminating the war in the second year of our independence."

But the bitter reality was that on November 22 British naval vessels sailed unchecked into Philadelphia harbor bringing supplies and ammunition for Howe's army. More important, they demonstrated by their presence that Howe's lines of communication and reinforcement were now secure and that Washington had lost everything possible he could have lost, except his army command. Now his failure to save the forts and the burgeoning strength of Conway's cabal on Gates's behalf were working toward losing him that.

Congress called Gates down from the northern theater and appointed him president of the newly created Board of War, an office something like a cabinet secretary of war. None of the five members of the Board of War was a member of Congress, and Gates could keep his military rank and return to field command any time he chose. The president of Congress wrote Gates November 28 of its high regard for his fitness to fill the office on which "the safety and interest of the United States eminently depend."

Gates was nominated with the "warm Sollicitude" of Major General Thomas Mifflin "from a Conviction that his Military Skill would suggest Reformations in the different Departments of the Army essential to good Discipline, Order and Oeconomy, and that his Character and Popularity in the Army would facilitate the execution of such Reformations when adopted by Congress." The back-handed slap at hapless Washington was not to be missed.

In full uniform and rank, yet also with semicivilian status as president of the Continental Congress's own Board of War, Gates was in more than titular control of all military operations. Although Hamilton had helped pry troops away from Gates's command for Washington's, Congress in a confusing way had now leapfrogged Gates back over both his own and Washington's old commands. Nothing could have been more of a threat to Washington's status as commander in chief.

Loyalty to Washington persisted even in the minds of leaders who thought he lacked force as a commander and skill as a tactician. His enemies like Gates, Thomas Conway, Charles Lee, and Thomas Mifflin saw that the safest and surest way to rid him of his command would not be to oust him, but to force him to resign in anger or discouragement. Under the leadership of Mifflin, Gates's new Board of War created the office of inspector general with broad powers to reorganize the army and report directly to it without going through Washington. To this office it appointed Thomas Conway, the man Washington had forced to resign as head of the commissary department in October, the man who had written Gates that "Heaven has determined to save your country, or a weak General and Bad Councillors would have ruined it." It promoted Conway to major general at the same time. To a furious Washington, such promotion of the man he hated most in the army was "extraordinary" and would outrage all the brigadiers in the army.

To Conway, the youngest and lowest ranking of the "bad counselors" around the "weak general" was Lieutenant Colonel Alexander Hamilton. But while the army was moving into winter encampment at Valley Forge after the failures at Forts Mifflin and Mercer, the youngest aide, who "governed" the "idol of America," according to Dr. Benjamin Rush, was delayed at New Windsor and Fishkill by recurring "violent rheumatic pains," near fatal chills, and nervous disorders. He was not able to rejoin the "weak general" with the army at Valley Forge until about January 20, 1778.

Unfortunately, Washington lacked the benefit of the secret information Hamilton had learned in Albany about the cabal that he had not dared to put in a letter.

On November 9, without the benefit of Hamilton's information, Washington reacted angrily to Conway's insulting letter to Gates, which, among other things, had also charged that the Battle of Germantown would have been an American victory if Washington had kept his head. The insulting charges were bad enough, but the fact of the letter itself, demonstrating as it seemed to do the close confidential and conspiratorial relationship between Conway and Gates to bring down Washington, angered him still more.

His short note to Conway of November 9 puts much unspoken rage into two sentences:

> Sir: A letter which I received last night contained the following para-graph.
> In a letter from General Conway to General Gates he says: "Heaven has been determined to save your country; or a weak general and bad counselors would have ruined it."
> I am, sir, your humble servant, George Washington.

For all Conway would know when he received Washington's letter, Washington had a spy network as extensive and effective as Gates's or a headquarters intelligencer somewhere who was able to supply him with the innermost secrets of the cabal that he, Lee, Gates, and Mifflin were hatching. Nowhere did Washington's bullet of a letter disclose how he had learned the contents of Conway's letter to Gates. Hamilton had just been with Gates. Conway would easily jump to the conclusion that Hamilton was the spy who had stolen his letter.

Within a day or two of Washington's note to Conway, Gates learned not from Conway, but from an entirely different source, Thomas Mifflin, that a letter of Conway's to him had been leaked to Washington. Mifflin told Gates that it was his aide Wilkinson, now newly promoted to brigadier general, who had blabbed, and that Gates was in trouble, thanks to his adjutant's loose tongue. Mifflin added, "An extract from General Conway's letter to you has been procured and sent to headquarters." The sentiment was "such as should not have been en-trusted to any of your Family." "My dear General," Mifflin begged Gates, "take Care of your Generosity & Frank Disposition; they . . . may injure some of your best friends."

Gates realized that a storm was about to break about his head. But he studiedly ignored Mifflin's warning that it was his precious adjutant Wilkinson who had been the "leak." Gates wrote to Conway in panic at what Mifflin had just told him: "I intreat you . . . to let me know which of the letters was copied off. It is of the greatest importance, that I should detect the person who has been guilty of that act of infidelity: I cannot trace him out, unless I have your assistance." Without it Gates would have trouble constructing a holeproof cover story to protect Wilkinson and pin blame for the leak on someone in the opposite camp.

That was it! Hamilton, Washington's aide, not his own aide, was responsible. When Hamilton had been at the interview with him in Albany, he had stolen Conway's letter to him out of a closet in his room and copied it!

According to Wilkinson, who had a lifelong record of extreme unreliability as a reporter, the very moment he returned to Albany, Gates had called him in and announced angrily, "I have had a spy in my camp since you left me!"

"I do not comprehend your allusion," Wilkinson replied cautiously, somewhat relieved but still nervous. Gates had put the whole blame on Hamilton: "Colonel Hamilton had been sent up to him by General Washington; and would you believe it, he purloined the copy of a letter out of that closet." Gates pointed an accusing finger at the closet door.

"I conceive that impossible," Wilkinson claims he said.

"I insist," Gates retorted. "When the family was called out on business . . . Colonel Hamilton was left alone an hour in this room. During that time, he took Conway's letter out of that closet and copied it, and furnished the copy to Washington."

Wilkinson knew but did not mention that it was more likely that leak of the letter had come from himself and reached Washington before Hamilton had even left Albany. Here was a good chance to spatter suspicion on a rival aide of Gates. Wilkinson argued that Gates's aide Robert Troup was a close friend of Hamilton's; he must have been the one who told Hamilton what was in Conway's letter; they had seen each other when Hamilton was at Albany.

Gates insisted that Hamilton was the leak, and Hamilton alone.

Wilkinson feared that if Gates pursued this line, it would lead to Hamilton's airtight alibi and turn back to some drunken maunderings of his own at the Reading tavern and thence to Washington. He explained to Gates obliquely that he himself had not really considered Conway's letter confidential because Gates had read it *publicly* in Wilkinson's presence. Wilkinson had taken it merely "as a matter of information from the grand army." He turned blame gently back to Gates, "so therefore I did not dream of the foul imputations it was destined to draw upon me."

What had really happened was that, as Wilkinson later shamefacedly admitted, during a drunken carouse with William McWilliams and others of Lord Stirling's staff at a tavern in Reading, at which that "drunken sot" Stirling himself had also hoisted a few, the conversation "became general, unreserved and copious." Stirling and others became so drunk that they did not know what they were saying. Wilkinson could not recall details, but would "acknowledge it possible in the warmth of social intercourse, when the mind is relaxed and the tongue is unguarded, that observations may have elapsed which have not since occurred to us." They were all so drunk that, as Wilkinson put it, "the nature of our situation made it confidential."

This was all evasive double-talk. Wilkinson himself had been carrying the letter from Conway to Gates. He had read some of its choicest passages to his no doubt raucously laughing listeners at the Reading tavern. Earthy officers like that "sot" Stirling could join in drunken laughter at the lofty Washington's expense and then loyally pass the message on to Washington.

Gates insisted on bringing his accusation against Hamilton to Hamilton's chief. He immediately wrote Washington, ". . . I conjure your Excellency, to give me all the assistance you can, in tracing out the author of the infidelity which put extracts from General Conway's letters to me into your hands. Those letters have been *stealingly copied* . . . It is . . . *in your* . . . *power* to do me and the United States a very important service, by detecting a wretch who may betray me, and capitally injure the *very operations under your immediate direction.*" Gates added that he was sending a copy of this letter to the president of Congress. Perhaps they could come up with some clues.

Hamilton had an airtight alibi. He had refused to write Washington what he knew. Washington demolished Gates's elaborate falsification with crushing candor. He ignored Gates's charge against Hamilton. He recalled that Stirling "from motives of friendship" had passed on the story Wilkinson had blurted out at the Reading tavern. Washington closed with a stinging rebuke to Gates's pretended efforts to prove that Hamilton was a "wretch who may betray me." Washington wrote that until now he supposed Gates had meant to forewarn him against that "dangerous incendiary," General Conway. But, he added, "in this, as in other matters of late, I have found myself mistaken."

With Congress at York, now at the pinnacle of power as president of the Board of War, Gates backed away from his charge and took a new tack. Yes, he said now, it was Wilkinson, not Hamilton, who was the guilty culprit and ought to be punished. This was a remarkable reversal of the encomiums Gates had showered on Wilkinson to take with him to Congress three months earlier: "from the beginning of the Contest I have not met with a more promising military genius than Col. Wilkinson . . . whose services have been of the last importance to this army."

In the same letter to Washington, Gates took another entirely inconsistent tack. The paragraph that Stirling had quoted to Washington was "spurious . . . a wicked forgery." Conway's genuine letter had mentioned neither a "weak general" nor "bad councillors."

Hamilton drafted the reply to this for Washington's hand. He acidly demolished the evasions and deceptions of his traducer. He coldly pointed out the inconsistency of Gates's first accepting the authenticity of the charge by blaming Hamilton, or Wilkinson, for disclosing it, and then denying its existence. If Conway's genuine letters did not contain the charge, why had Gates not produced them? By his silence under Washington's indictment, Gates tacitly admitted genuineness of the letter. By taking Gates's disclaimers at face value, Washington was willing to bury the correspondence in silence "and as far as future events will permit, oblivion."

Writing long afterward, Robert Troup confirmed much of his part in this infamous uproar by explaining that Hamilton, "though then very young, had, by his extraordinary talents . . . acquired a standing at Head Quarters that kindled the jealousy of some officers who were inclined to think unfavorably of General Washington."

Henry Laurens, president of Congress, and father of Hamilton's dearest friend and fellow aide, John Laurens, said of the congressmen who lent themselves to the Conway cabal that there were men involved who respected Washington, but lacked "the honor to defend" him publicly. The majority would go whichever way a few active and powerful ringleaders pushed them. Laurens added that "in all such juntas there are prompters, and actors, accommodators, candle snuffers, shifters of scenes, and mutes."

Washington knew as well as Hamilton that both of them had powerful scheming enemies. "My Enemies take an ungenerous advantage of me," he charged; "they know the delicacy of my situation, and that motives of policy deprive me of the defence I might otherwise make against their insiduous [*sic*] attacks." He complained of "a malignant faction . . . for sometime forming to my prejudice." He told Patrick Henry that "General Gates was to be exalted, on the ruin of my reputation and influence."

Lafayette, who had come as close as any man to standing as a "son" in Washington's eyes, was convinced that the conspiracy to displace Washington with Gates was genuine. Gates was flattered and receptive, but it was Conway who "was a principal mischievous intriguer." Lafayette thought that in the event the cabal should succeed in dislodging Washington, the chief command would probably not devolve on Gates, who would remain with the Board of War, but on Major General Charles Lee, the next most senior general in the army.

Washington and others closest to him were also certain that the conspiracy was real. Hamilton at first had only thought that there was an opposing faction, or party, not a real cabal, or conspiracy, but changed his mind. He wrote George Clinton February 13, 1778, that he had "discovered such convincing traits of the monster that I cannot doubt its reality in the most extensive sense." Only Wilkinson's premature blabbing at the Reading tavern had forestalled its success. "I believe it unmasked its batteries too soon," the young old artilleryman wrote, "but will only change the storm to a sap." That is, instead of an open attack on Washington, the cabal would go underground and try to destroy him with a "sap," a hidden explosive charge placed against the base of his power. Hamilton cautioned Clinton that "all the true and sensible friends to their country, and of course to a certain great man, ought to be on the watch to counterplot the secret machinations of his enemies," just as they should be on guard against "Tories and other enemies of the state."

The false charges of theft and leaks against Hamilton that the Conway cabal had sought to shape into a charge that would undermine both the "idol of America" and the aide they called his governor, backfired against its inventors —with some comic opera curlicues.

Wilkinson's fellow officers turned against him and forced him to resign his ill-deserved brigadier's commission and post as secretary of the Board of War.

Returning from Albany to Pennsylvania, he learned that Gates had denounced him "in the grossest language." Blathering on about his innocence and of all he had done for Gates, Wilkinson challenged Gates to meet him in a duel behind the English Church and shoot it out. Gates accepted, but then at the last minute sent Wilkinson a request for an explanation. As they walked up and down the back streets of Philadelphia, Gates burst into tears. Wilkinson's dubious honor was saved for later scrapes, as were two scarce powder charges.

Stating Washington's own basic opinion, adding un-Washingtonian embellishments, Hamilton called Thomas Conway a "villainous, calumniatory incendiary." He was "one of the vermin bred in the entrails of the chimera dire." And that was putting it mildly. Conway was wounded in a duel, resigned as inspector general of the army on April 28, and slunk back to France whence he had come.

By comparison with what he said about Conway and his caballers, Hamilton was more guarded but no less devastating in what he wrote about Gates. "I shall not hesitate to say, I doubt whether you would have had a man from the northern army, if the whole could have been kept at Albany with any decency."

With Hamilton's return to camp, Washington seemed to recover some of his old political sway over Congress. When Gates attempted to patch up the quarrel by protesting that he had had no thought of displacing Washington, he was rebuffed in a way that showed Washington's suspicions had not been laid to rest. Gates soon stepped down as president of the Board of War and was assigned to defend Fort Ticonderoga, a reward that had been a disastrous dead end for all of its defenders.

Hamilton came close to identifying loyalty to his commander in chief with loyalty to the Revolution itself. So did his commander in chief.

In the end Congress came to agree with Hamilton. Some of its members now switched so far as to say that anyone who displeased the commander in chief should forthwith be removed from the army. Of all the many ways there are to weave a bond between two men, one a chief executive and the other an aide, none creates a stronger and longer lasting link than for the junior of the two to be, and to be seen as, the enemy of the enemies of the senior. Viewed in this light, the failure of Hamilton's mission to Gates, though it meant the fall of Forts Mifflin and Mercer, was probably a more important event in Hamilton's rise than its success could possibly have been.

8

VALLEY FORGE

I ACKNOWLEDGE THE UNITED STATES OF AMERICA TO BE FREE,
INDEPENDENT AND SOVERIGN STATES . . . OWE NO ALLEGIANCE OR
OBEDIENCE TO GEORGE III, KING OF GREAT BRITAIN, . . . RE-
NOUNCE, REFUSE AND ABJURE ANY ALLEGIANCE OR OBEDIENCE
TO HIM, . . . I DO SWEAR THAT I WILL TO THE UTMOST OF MY POWER,
SUPPORT, MAINTAIN AND DEFEND THE UNITED STATES AGAINST
THE SAID KING GEORGE III, HIS HEIRS AND SUCCESSORS AND HIS
OR THEIR ABETTORS, ASSISTANTS AND ADHERENTS.
  —Oath sworn by Lieutenant Colonel Alexander
  Hamilton before William Alexander, Lord Stirling,
  May 12, 1778, at Valley Forge

As Washington's deputy, Hamilton had done everything humanly possible
to get troops moving toward his army. His sickness lingered. Still Hamilton went
out of his way to assert his deputed authority to protect some upstate farmers
from high-handed and lawless behavior of men in uniform.

"Thank God!" he had written George Clinton of the New York Committee
of Correspondence from Peekskill on December 22, "I am now so far recovered
that I promise myself, if the weather is good, to begin my journey to headquarters tomorrow." He was grateful to Clinton "for the interest you took in the
restoration of my health, and in the safety of my person during my illness."

But the money and medical aid that Governor Clinton had supplied him on his mission were not enough to make Hamilton forbear demanding that Clinton redress a wrong inflicted on a citizen in the name of privilege: "At the time of some incursion of the enemy this way, a great number of cattle belonging to the inhabitants were driven off—sold at a kind of mock auction by order of a general officer—sent into Connecticut, and no kind of account rendered as to proceeds." The general in question was "high in command in this quarter," but his "seizing the property of the inhabitants of this state, and converting it to (his) own use, without any compensation either to the right owners, or to the states" is "unjust, disgraceful to the army, and injurious to the common cause."

There was extra iron of noblesse oblige in Hamilton's insistence on fair treatment of poor people. He was not trying to pass the buck by pressing Clinton about the problem: "I determined to make a careful scrutiny into the matter, in order to furnish myself with proper materials to lay before General Washington . . . But my slow recovery and my impatience to get home will not allow me leisure nor opportunity to pursue my intention."

Clinton crustily agreed with Hamilton that "little good can be expected of an army whose interest it is to suffer a country to be abandoned to the enemy thereby to justify plundering the inhabitants . . . it is this trade that makes people so very fond of little expeditions." Clinton would help Hamilton make amends.

At the darkest hour of the war, a time when Congress still seemed almost ready to replace Washington with Gates, Hamilton received a letter from his old mentor Hugh Knox, whose prescripts fortelling the future had helped teach Hamilton his own remarkable habit of foresight.

"The very minutiae of that incomparable man," Knox wrote, "will be read with assiduity by posterity." Knox disparaged his own gift of prophecy as mere "superstition," yet he felt himself, at times, "under a strong impulse, to *prophecy* that *Washington* was born for the deliverance of America; that providence who has raised and trained him up for that very purpose will watch over his *sacred* life with a paternal and solicitous care, will shield his head in every day of battle, *will guide* him to see America *free, flourishing and happy*, and *will* adorn his fame, among latest posterity, with a garland of laurel more verdant, blooming and enviable, than ever adorned the brow of a Marlborough."

Back at Washington's army, still near White Marsh, blankets were scarce and shoes still scarcer; tattered uniforms were patched, and patched again on the patches. Hard money was scarce too. The commander in chief offered a reward of ten dollars in coin for a "substitute for shoes, made of raw hides." Governor Patrick Henry of Virginia sent a load of clothing, not for general distribution to any soldier according to need, but for Virginia troops alone. Other states were just as selfish or sent nothing at all. Lieutenant Colonel Henry Dearborn wrote resignedly: "This is Thanksgiving Day . . . but God knows we have very little to keep it with, this being the third day we have been without flour or bread." No, there was one thing: "Upon the whole I think all we have to be thankful for is that we . . . are not in the grave with many of our friends."

An officer with Washington wrote to General Gates: "We are ill cloathed, the Winter is on, to Hutt near the Enemy will be as arduous as dangerous, to retire back for Quarters & thereby leave the Country Open appears to be intolerable . . . Our troops express their wishes for another tryal and must be greatly animated by the arrival of yours." General Arthur St. Clair saw no hope except in help from Gates. "It is certain our Discipline and . . . Numbers . . . are inferior to theirs, but when your victorious Troops arrive, they will make our Scale preponderate."

It was particularly galling for Washington to see the British comfortably billeted in Philadelphia, whereas the settlements outside the city were crowded with refugees he felt he could not displace to commandeer ready-made accommodations for his defeated soldiers. Unlike the refugee civilians, his army would have to survive out in the winter weather until it could construct its own encampment. With a nonvictorious army he could not justify "plundering the inhabitants" as Clinton had put it. The politics of Washington's situation would permit only "little expeditions."

Too weak to mount an attack, too wise to count on Howe's lethargy, Washington decided to move out of reach of any sudden Anglo-Hessian attempt at a *coup de grace* to his army. Twenty-odd miles to the west and a little north of Philadelphia, where the placid Schuylkill is joined on its eastward course by Valley Creek flowing up from the south, the ground east of the creek rises abruptly to a 250-foot crest, then flattens out into a rolling two-mile plateau. There was little to mark this terrain on a map—just a ford across the Schuylkill known as Fatland, or Fatlands—and an old forge on the ravinelike creek that travelers called the Valley Forge.

It was only thirteen miles from White Marsh to Valley Forge, but it took the army more than a week to get there. Baggage wagons went astray; the air sharpened; powdery snow sifted through oak and pine boughs; the snow thickened, became stinging sleet, and softened into pelting rain. Mud roads stiffened into knifelike ruts that slashed at rag-bound feet. Washington said "you might have tracked the army . . . to Valley Forge by the blood of their feet."

When the main columns reached the plateau the afternoon of December 19, chilled, exhausted men lurched to their campsites and lighted fires. Short of tools and nails, weakened by hunger, they stumbled into the woods, felled trees, split out boards, kneaded clay to plug into wall chinks, and laboriously, over weeks, built a crude hut city on the plateau. Beside the campfires, broken boots dried out too quickly, stiffened, cracked, and split. Foot wrappings charred and fell away from bleeding feet. Surgeon Albigence Waldo of the 1st Connecticut, who had been in the field since '75, described one poor soldier whose bare toes protruded through worn-out shoes. "His breeches not sufficient to cover his nakedness . . . his whole appearance pictures a person forsaken & discouraged. He . . . crys . . . I am Sick, my feet lame, my legs are sore, my body covered with this tormenting Itch."

There was a shortage of water on the plateau. Officers mounted guard in old padded dressing gowns. One guard was seen at his post properly presenting arms while standing on his hat to keep his bare feet out of the snow. The story of Valley Forge may have been told over and over again, but as historian Christopher Ward said, "not once too often."

Upon his return to the army at Valley Forge about January 20, Hamilton reported immediately to Washington all he had learned about the Conway cabal from Troup and others, but had not been able to write. It fitted in with much the commander in chief already knew. Hamilton then briskly submitted a detailed expense account for himself and Captain Caleb Gibbs from October 30, 1777, through January 20, 1778. Written up in detail by Gibbs, it shows the complete itinerary of Hamilton's mission to Gates and Putnam and their expenses at each stop along the way, including such items as paying various ferry men, hiring a guide, a dinner at Tobias' Tavern at Claverack, payments to Hamilton's doctor, and food for their horses. The only gap is the four-day period they were at Albany. This tends to show that they must have enjoyed the hospitality of Troup there or of someone else. Perhaps they stayed with General Philip Schuyler at the Pastures.

In totaling the expense account, Gibbs made an extraordinary error of expense voucher padding of a kind that goes on in all armies and is not unheard of in civilian life. The two-page total of £115.9.9 should in fact have been only £65.11.9. Gibbs totaled the first page and carried that sum (£49.18.0) over to the second page and there added the carry-over twice, once as a carry-over from the first page and a second time as one of the items on the second page. If the future secretary of the treasury checked over Gibbs's addition, he failed to catch a familiar kind of "accidentally on purpose" error in favor of the expense account traveler.

Time and again Washington's letters implored Congress to redress the army's grievances lest they "starve, dissolve, or disperse." After his return January 20, Hamilton knew and shared the trials of the winter camp. He, too, blamed most of the troubles on the fecklessness of Congress. The Vindicator of Congress of 1774 wrote to Governor Clinton February 13 from Valley Forge that individual members were able, but "Folly, caprice, a want of foresight, comprehension and dignity" described the body as a whole. Hamilton would always afterwards insist that this was true of committees generally, regardless of how capable their individual members were. Valley Forge showed him that Congress's conduct, "with respect to the army . . . is feeble, indecisive, and improvident—insomuch that we are reduced to a more terrible situation than you can conceive . . ." The food situation had not improved three months after Lieutenant Colonel Henry Dearborn had described their flourless and breadless Thanksgiving. "At this very day," Hamilton told Clinton "there are complaints from the whole line of having been three or four days without provisions."

Not far away, in the snug little town of York, if members of Congress had been kept waiting half an hour for their dinners, they would probably have roused themselves to more effective action than was provoked by reports of the sufferings of the thousands on that "cold bleak hill . . . under frost and snow" at the Valley Forge.

Valley Forge was not entirely Congress's fault. It muddled along in the backwoods with often as few as 20 members or even fewer in dispirited attendance, not so different from Washington and his army; it held sessions and dreamed dreams. It was never quite sure what its powers were. It was perpetually frustrated by the cantankerousness with which, at one time or another, every one of the thirteen states resisted its efforts and ignored the decrees of its own representatives deputed to it.

There had never been a definition of just what the "new nation" really was. Was it merely a loose league of individual states or a single firmly federated state? In the early summer of '76, Richard Henry Lee of Virginia had boldly asked that question. State-minded men from each of the thirteen had exploded in hot anger. Even to consider such a question was to stray beyond delegated powers. Lee had stood firm and moved that "a plan of confederation be prepared and transmitted to the respective Colonies for their consideration and approbation." Against heavy opposition, Farmer John Dickinson and others were named to a committee to prepare "Articles of Confederation and Perpetual Union."

On November 15, 1777, a day on which Major Thayer was wearily planning his withdrawal from the mudbanks of Fort Mifflin and Hamilton was berating Israel Putnam for holding back reinforcements, the Articles of Confederation were finally adopted and sent on to the various states for "consideration and approbation," a process that was to drag on until spring of 1781. The Articles were makeshift and sought to paper over the most divisive issues, leaving the Congress of the United States of America almost entirely dependent on the collective willingness of the states to do what had to be done, if anything was to be done at all. Congress could call on the states for whatever was thought necessary, but the states, collectively and individually, were empowered to refuse if they saw fit. Yet the concept of "Perpetual Union," if not the reality, was definitely stated in the Articles; and from them, weak and unworkable as they were, Hamilton and the other Framers would, a decade later, forge the ultimate political instrument of freedom and unity of the states: The Constitution of the United States. In the meantime, a mediocre Congress busied itself with politics as usual.

Hamilton wrote an angry letter to Governor Clinton: "The great men who composed our first council; are they dead, have they deserted the cause, or what has become of them?" "Economy" is the watchword, "even if it leads to famine, nakedness and mutiny among the soldiers." There was favoritism in promotions: "Let a foreigner come before them, no matter how rascally, and he is promptly given rank over competent Americans who have fought since the beginning." Lafayette, von Steuben, Kosciuszko, Pulaski, and de Kalb were only exceptions that would prove the rule.

No! Hamilton answered himself. The great men are not dead, nor have they deserted the cause. But the spirit of a common nationalism was weak. The best men had seen fit to quit Congress for the battlefield or the civil offices of their respective states. They preferred to serve their own state governments instead of a Congress whose authority was limited and depended entirely on the good will of the states. Some of the largest states sent no representatives to Congress, and sessions often adjourned for lack of a quorum. Hamilton concluded, "The only remedy then is to take them out of these employments and return them to the place where their presence is infinitely more important. . . . It is time that men of weight and understanding should take the alarm, and excite each other to a proper remedy."

Governor Clinton agreed with Hamilton about Congress. He replied sympathetically, "I wish the Defects of a certain great Body were less apparent. Even their Want of Wisdom but too Evident in most of their Measures would in that Case be less Injurious. . . . Could our Soldiery subsist on Resolves, they would never want Food or Cloathing."

The committee of congressional oversight of the army, critical of Washington's leadership, as indeed the whole Congress had shown itself to be by elevating Gates to presidency of the Board of War, came to camp from time to time to find out what was going wrong with Washington's army. It was scheduled for another tour of inspection on January 29, 1778. Late in October of 1777, Washington had requested his general officers, and at least one of his lieutenant colonels, Alexander Hamilton, to give him their ideas about a whole new system of regulations for the army.

No one doubted that the troops lacked discipline and suffered for the lack in battle. They were recruited, tardily, by the states separately, on one-year enlistments. Except for the few who chose to reenlist, a new force had to be collected for every campaign. Americans had been trained in Indian warfare, in which it was each man for himself. Marches were in single file, which prevented massing of troops to make or meet a powerful attack. The idea of unified large scale action under coordinated commands seemed uncongenial to the habit of the country. Methods of drill, where any were practiced, followed different forms— English, French, or German. Few American officers knew the manual of arms or close order drill, let alone how to conduct field maneuvers. Or how to dress a line when the poor recruits in it were half clad or how to carry out precision movements when they craved food.

Hamilton addressed to Washington a catalog of improvements for the service. "There are still existing in the army so many abuses," he declared, "absolutely contrary to the military constitution, that, without a speedy stop . . . it will be impossible . . . to establish any order or discipline among the troops." He laid down penalties for officers overstaying their leaves, taking too many soldiers as servants, or demanding standing guards. Officers must remain with their men. Arms and ammunition should not be issued to noncombatants. Remembering how he had saved himself and Congress from capture by proper precautions at Daverser's Ferry and the disasters that had befallen others like Anthony Wayne at Paoli, he gave detailed directions for sentries to protect advanced posts against surprise. He suggested that each regiment be held accountable for the arms and accoutrements in its possession. Absences due to sickness, whether the men were in the hospital or in private houses in the country, should be reported regularly. Men on furlough or away from camp on special duty should be recalled within a reasonable time. All such rules have a familiar ring to twentieth-century soldiers.

At Washington's request, Hamilton worked up all the replies, both the generals' and his own, into a single long report in Hamilton's handwriting, which Washington signed and gave to the congressional Committee of Conference on its January 29 visit. This document also contained the basis for the modern manual of military courts-martial. Every officer or soldier who acted contrary to regulations for the order and discipline of the army established by Congress should be tried and punished. Arms were to be taken away from men who failed to use them in time of action.

The report also called for a settled plan of half pay or other pension on retirement for all the men, an annual draft of troops with a small bounty for reenlistment only, expansion of the cavalry, a provost marshal, and a consolidation and reduction of the number of weak regiments. This review of the situation of the army ended with the solemn admonition to Congress that unless remedies for suffering and discontents in the army were applied at once, "the most alarming . . . consequences" would follow.

As the reader who has just skimmed the preceding has no need to be told, few things make duller reading than old army regulations. Without the right drillmaster to personify the rules, to bring them to life by pounding them into the heads of the soldiers by Prussian pedagogy, Hamilton well knew that his fine regulations would make even less of an impression on troops in the field than they do on a reader in his armchair.

Washington had raised the question of the appointment of a permanent inspector general in his questions to his generals in October. Hamilton's January report repeated a short paragraph on the subject, but totally without enthusiasm, as if he thought the idea was a mistake. It is probable that he did because if the office were made permanent, the most likely congressional choice for appointment to it was Brigadier General Thomas Conway, the man who presently held it on an interim basis. The Board of War had appointed him inspector general on December 13, 1777. Now, far from approving Hamilton's and Washington's detailed plans for reorganizing the army, the Board of War rejected theirs and approved Thomas Conway's plan instead.

No matter what his other qualifications, Hamilton and Washington would have welcomed with open arms that winter any reasonably well-qualified candidate for the position of inspector general of the army whose name was not Thomas Conway. Baron Friederich Wilhelm Ludolf Gerhard Augustin von Steuben, late of the armies of Frederick the Great of Prussia, brought more than a different name to the job—although some of the qualifications he claimed were more bogus than Conway's. Von Steuben's hair was carefully dressed; he wore a blazing decoration over his heart; and he carried his pistols in enormous holsters over the pommel of his saddle.

Knowing very little English, von Steuben could read only with difficulty the extravagant letters of praise that Benjamin Franklin had put in his dossier. As far as he could, he acquiesced in the praise. Von Steuben's "fondness for . . . importance" as Hamilton put it later to his friend William Duer, a member of Congress, prompted the baron's complicity in the amiable deception that he had been "a lieutenant general in foreign service." In fact, he had been a half-pay captain, out of work for fourteen years, when Benjamin Franklin met him in Paris, helped him assemble his dossier, and packed him off to America. His title of baron had been honestly conferred by the prince of Hohenzollern-Hechingen; he was a knight of the Order of Fidelity by the intercession of Princess Frederica of Wurttemberg; and on his chest he always wore the jeweled star of her order. He offset small deceptions by serving at first as a volunteer, as Lafayette had begun, but without any particular rank or command. This was always the way to start off on the right foot with Washington and Hamilton.

Von Steuben arrived at Valley Forge at the end of February 1778, and from the time of his first meeting with Hamilton, an affectionate, lifelong friendship grew up between the two men. The differences between them seemed to matter little—Hamilton was 21; von Steuben 48; Hamilton was as careful in handling money as Baron von Steuben was careless, although both were openhanded. Their affinities were major devotion to the common cause, eagerness to introduce system into military organization, a strong wish to combine field action with staff duty, and a knowledge of French, although Hamilton's was superior to the baron's. His English was even worse than his French. Hamilton solicited no special favors for him and was entirely candid about the limitations of his dear old soldier friend. In his letter to William Duer, Hamilton made two points about von Steuben that Washington could not openly put to Congress. He dispatched the letter to Duer by von Steuben himself, which says how much Hamilton trusted either him or his lack of command of English. Able and well-intentioned, according to Hamilton, von Steuben was nonetheless apt to seek too large a sphere. He should by no means be given disciplinary powers that belonged to the commanders and ultimately to Washington. Also, Washington should be kept in full charge, subject to later ratification by Congress, and the inspector general should in no event be given the same kind of practical independence of the commander in chief that calumniator Conway had been given.

Von Steuben saw the problems that Washington's and Hamilton's reports to Congress had sought to remedy. Casualties, desertions, illness, and furloughs and no new recruits coming on had reduced the army to impotence. Von Steuben noted that ". . . the officers who had coats, had them of every color and make" and as for "military discipline, I may safely say no such thing existed." Hamilton saw in von Steuben not only a kindly, able, and militarily knowledgeable friend, but the walking personification of the abstract ideals of discipline and order he had written into the plans for army reorganization he had presented to the congressional committee of oversight in January.

On the parade ground, von Steuben's aura of Prussian authority would flesh out and put muscle on the dry bones of Hamilton's and Washington's army regulations. They had found the model pedagogue to build a weak, sick, discouraged rabble into a professional army full of skill, pride, and courage. John

Laurens and Hamilton would take turns translating von Steuben's German to French and then to English. Then by some nonverbal magic of his own, von Steuben managed to establish an immediate personal entente cordial with the hungry, ragged men who reported for drill. Beginning with small groups, the indefatigable baron toiled from sunrise to sunset and later. When his first control group learned to drill with precision that suited him, he would send them back to their own commands to spread his teachings there and begin again on another demonstration group.

In spite of his tough disciplinary duties, his gruff Teutonic accent, and his awesome displays of rage and profanity punctuated by explosive curses in German and French, salted down with a few words of mangled English, nearly everyone in camp liked the baron. He inspired great personal loyalty in men close to him like Hamilton and his own aides Major Benjamin Walker and Colonel William North. His colorful persona made him much more effective as a man to create an army from a rabble than the now departed Conway had been.

Von Steuben noted that in the rabble in arms he had taken over, ". . . the words, company, regiment, brigade, and division . . . did not convey any idea upon which to form a calculation. . . . They were so unequal in their numbers that it would have been impossible to execute any maneuvers." Sometimes a regiment was stronger than a brigade. He was appalled that "I have a regiment consisting of 30 men and a company of one corporal."

What difference did this really make, as long as the same number of men were available for duty? Hamilton knew what von Steuben meant and explained it carefully to William Duer in Congress on June 18: "The composition is good or bad, not only according to the quality of the men, but in proportion to the completeness or incompleteness of a corps in respect to numbers. A Regiment for instance with a full complement of officers but only fifty or sixty men, is not half so good as a company with the same number of men."

Why was that? Not simply because it failed to conform to an abstract diagram on the wall in a commander's office, but because of the psychological effect on the men involved: the human factors: "A Colonel will look upon such a command as unworthy [of] his ambition and will neglect and despise it. A captain would pride himself in it and take all the pains in his power to bring it to perfection. In one case we shall see a total relaxation of discipline, and a negligence of every thing that constitutes military excellence; in the other, there will be attention energy and every thing that can be wished."

"Energy" was a favorite word with Hamilton. To him the presence of "attention" and "energy" was a *sine qua non* of a successful human organization or system of any kind. Life, to him, was a perpetual energy crisis. He drew a general lesson from von Steuben's point about numbers of men in units: "Opinion, whether well or ill founded, is the governing principle of human affairs. A corps much below its establishment comparing what it is with what it ought to be, loses all confidence in itself, and the whole army loses that confidence and emulation which are essential to success."

Washington added a hundred picked men to the commander in chief's guard to form a model corps, "to be instructed in the maneuvers necessary to be introduced in the Army. . . ." Soon von Steuben had trained it to parade with stunning effect throughout the camp. He progressed from squad to platoon to company to regiment, and then on to whole brigades and divisions, until the largest units could maneuver smoothly and in unison upon command. A real American army was being hammered out by von Steuben on the Valley Forge.

Washington formally appointed von Steuben inspector general, with Hamilton's friends, Lieutenant Colonels William Davis of Virginia, John Brooks of Massachusetts, Jean Baptiste Ternant, and Francis Barber, Hamilton's old schoolmaster from Elizabethtown, as subinspector generals. By May Congress had ratified von Steuben's appointment to the rank of major general.

With Hamilton's help, von Steuben prepared written instructions for the troops that later became the standard army training manual, *Rules for the Order and Discipline of the Troops*. Congress approved, and the *Blue Book*, as it was familiarly called from its cover, remained the official army manual until the War of 1812. In transmuted form, it remains in effect to this day. The secret of the success of von Steuben's rules and of their author lay in his understanding of Americans, which was revealed in his observation to a European officer: "the genius of this nation is not in the least to be compared to that of the Prussians, Austrians or French. You say to your soldier, 'Do this, and he doeth it'; but I am abliged to say, 'This is the reason why you ought to do that: and then he does it.' "

Von Steuben's comment took note of a fact that from his time to ours has been noted among American junior grade officers—second and first lieutenants and captains—of line infantry companies: "the American makes a wonderful soldier, he'll go anywhere at all, except in front of you."

Although he brought all his Prussian background to bear on them to try to teach them to respond to commands like automatons, even von Steuben was not able to train American enlisted men to move out ahead of their officers into an attack ordered by their officers from the rear. It has always been the proud tradition of American infantry that the company grade officers must go first. The "command" the line unit commander issues is "Follow me." To signal an attack, he raises his right arm straight up over his head, moves out, and brings his arm down to the horizontal, pointing ahead and shouting, "Follow me."

Thanks to von Steuben's infantry basic training, for the rest of the war when a line officer, including Hamilton, would cry out, "Follow me," the enlisted men were more likely to follow than before. This by no means meant that American soldiers' habits of panicky flight were a thing of the past. It would mean only that they might be counted on to respond reasonably well to the command of a good officer to "follow me" a good part of the time.

After Valley Forge, as Hamilton saw from Monmouth, soon to be fought, to Yorktown, five long years in the future, the outcome of future battles would rest squarely on the shoulders of the officers of the line, whose duty it was to cry, "Follow me" to the men behind, as they rose from cover to draw the heaviest enemy fire on themselves in the van leading the troops behind the way to go.

Hamilton's remarkable ability to inspire unfading friendships brought in some invaluable political intelligence from Ned Stevens, his St. Croix boyhood friend. Stevens had prepared the way for his own futurity by getting his doctorate of medicine at Edinburgh. When he wrote Hamilton from the enemy's home islands on December 23, 1777, he sorely missed word from his dear old friend: "Why have you not written me a single line since our separation? . . . Have you forgotten those vows of eternal friendship, which we have so often mutually exchanged?" Spontaneously he gave Hamilton trustworthy political intelligence that the enemy's will to fight seemed to be flagging: ". . . The inhabitants of Great Britain begin to despond and if the provincial forces are but strenuous in their opposition, they have nothing now to fear. The time is approaching, when I hope to see America one of the most flourishing republics in the world." He closed with, "Excuse this hasty, wild scrawl. . . . Believe me to be my dear Ham, yours inviolably."

Ned Stevens in Edinburgh sensed the impression that Washington's improving army was making on the people of Britain, and the same lesson was not lost on the chancelleries of Europe. In London Lord North began to arrange another peace commission. Britain was prepared to offer amnesty to the revolutionaries, but not yet prepared to recognize full independence of the colonies.

Congress countered that no parley was possible while King George's armed forces remained in America and the country's independence unacknowledged. British Captain Richard FitzPatrick, an intimate friend of Charles James Fox and an influential Whig, being about to return home, sought the views of the Marquis de Lafayette. The marquis invited his friend Hamilton to accompany him "to a friendly dinner at Germantown [lying] between the two armies." There "much political discourse took place between them [sic] three where Captain FitzPatrick was assured that the mission of the Commissioners from Great Britain would prove fruitless and that nothing short of Independency could be accepted by the United States." Ignoring this rebuff, the British deputed William Tryon, the former royal governor of New York, a man not apt to conciliate patriot opinion, to bypass American leaders and broach the amnesty proposal directly to the men in the American forces.

Washington branded Tryon's request to circulate the acts of Parliament in the American army "extraordinary and impertinent." Hamilton prevailed on Washington to answer Tryon with a politer form of disdain. With Hamilton-style diplomacy, Washington replied that the British proposals had been freely circulated to the army because Washington was confident that his men were loyal to the independent United States; his men had rejected them. He demanded that Tryon now circulate among loyalists a reciprocal proposal of Congress: all loyalists who had fled to British-held Philadelphia and New York could have amnesty if they would return to their home states.

Prisoners were an endlessly vexing problem for Washington's headquarters intelligencer. Major General Charles Lee remained in British hands, and so did

Lieutenant Colonel Ethan Allen of the Green Mountain Boys, who had been captured at Montreal in September 1775. These high-ranking officers were exceptions because most American prisoners in British hands were untrained militiamen, easy to replace, not easy to find use for in any event. On the other hand, the captive British in American hands were mostly well-trained regulars whom the British would find hard to replace at a distance of 3,000 miles.

Washington appointed an American commission consisting of Hamilton, Harrison, and Elias Boudinot to negotiate with the British for exchanges. The Congressional committee appointed to watch over the army and Washington, much as French political commissioners later kept an eye on suspect generals, was slyly opposed to the idea of a broad and general exchange of prisoners because they thought it would work to the disadvantage of the States: let the British keep the militiamen and Lee prisoners.

The congressional committee proposed a hypocritical scheme to Hamilton and his fellow commissioners: Let the cartel for exchange offered to the British be a mere pretense; maneuver so that the negotiations break down, but do it skillfully so that the blame for the break will fall on the British. Congress would then explain to the army and the people that maximum effort had been made to get Americans back, but it had failed. Congress would keep the British regulars prisoners, let the American militia rot in British hands, and get political credit for efforts, at least, to free the Americans. Congress knew that open espousal of any such policy would provoke rage in the army and among the relatives and friends of American prisoners. The politics of prisoner-of-war exchanges has always been full of pious humbug.

Hamilton disagreed with Congress. He pointed out that it was wrong for Congress to treat Americans, even unreliable militiamen, as ciphers to be traded off and left in enemy hands. The commissioners rejected Congress's plan. With Washington's approval, they arranged a plan for bringing back more Americans, even though it might mean also bringing back Major General Charles Lee, that "sap" which a Conway's cabal might still make use of to undermine Washington. Hamilton reported his outrage at Congress's duplicity to Clinton on March 12, 1778: "The general notions of justice and humanity are implanted in almost every human breast; and ought not to be too freely shocked." But "I would ask, whether in a republican state and a republican army; such a cruel policy of exposing those men who are foremost in defence of their country to the misery of hopeless captivity, can succeed?"

In fact, Hamilton thought that Congress showed a lack of honesty, small respect for the national character, and bad faith. "For my own part," he added, "I have so much of the milk of humanity in me, that I abhor such Neronian Maxims; and I look upon the old proverb, that honesty is the best policy to be so generally true, that I can never expect any good from a systematical deviation from it; and I never can adopt the reasonings of some American politicians deducible from their practice, that no regard is to be paid to national character, or the rules of good faith."

When the commissioners rejected Congress's scheme, Congress, in anger, retaliated by assailing Washington for having appointed Hamilton and the other commissioners "to settle the Cartel, whom he knew held principles adversary to the true interests of America." Hamilton, even more than Washington himself was a favorite target of Washington's enemies in Congress. Washington, at least, would appreciate that he also served as a lightning rod.

The three commissioners offered to resign, but, reported Boudinot, Washington sternly "ordered us to the . . . Duty, and told us to make the best treaty in our power, and he would ratify it, and take the risk upon himself."

They did. They made the exchanges their way, not Congress's way and brought back the poor, more or less useless militiamen, as well as Major General Charles Lee to the American camps.

As the highest-ranking American officer in British captivity, General Lee had been quite comfortable in confinement and may have been almost unpleasantly surprised, if not altogether discomfited, to find himself back on the duty roster in Washington's camp. While he had been a prisoner of the British, Lee had sent a proposal to Congress that they send commissioners to Sir William Howe to sue for peace, but Congress had rejected his plan. It was not at all clear whether Lee was more dangerous in British hands, or in American. In the American camp, at least, Washington and Hamilton could keep an eye on him, but his high rank kept him in a position where he could do their cause unimagined damage.

Congress later came around to Hamilton's views of the prisoner exchange question. When Boudinot went to Congress as a delegate, fellow members told him that "Congress was so ashamed of the measure that was run upon them by the Committee from the Army, that in two or three days after, they had expunged the whole from their minutes."

Hamilton could be a hard bargainer even while claiming to be moved by "the milk of humanity." When American commissioners met the British at Perth Amboy on December 11, 1778, they had added Colonel William Grayson to the original three, for a very important reason of state, not involving milk. Boudinot wrote that the negotiators "agreed to Dine together—we were very sociable— We had previously obtained the Characters of our opponents and were convinced that they depended much on out drinking us, we knew Coll Grayson was a match for any of them, and therefore left all that part of the business with him—They soon found themselves foiled."

But the negotiations were broken off because the British team were without plenary powers to settle matters. By refusing to send ambassadors with plenary powers, as they would have done to a sovereign foreign country, the British made it appear that they were dealing with a dependency. Field officers had rank enough to deal with rebellious colonials. In the negotiations the Americans insisted that officers be exchanged for officers and privates for privates, whereas the British sought to regain their well-trained privates first and allow their officers to wait a while longer in American jails.

Hamilton and Harrison drafted a formal protest against the British position:

"We join with you in lamenting that the purpose of our meeting has been frustrated, and we assure you, that it is to us matter of equal concern and surprise to find, that there should be a difference in our respective constructions of the Resolve, to which you refer." In Hamilton's logical style, the protest reviewed the history of the negotiations and placed the onus for the breakdown on the British for their technical refusal to grant plenary diplomatic powers to their commissioners.

The commissioners themselves parted on cordial personal terms. Colonel O'Hara, on whom the British had counted to drink William Grayson under the table, shook hands and is supposed to have said, "If I am ever taken prisoner, I shall call on Colonels Hamilton, Harrison and Boudinot to come to my aid and take care of me."

So it happened years later at the surrender ceremony at Yorktown, where O'Hara was second in command to Lord Cornwallis. When his turn came to surrender his sword, he called out for Alexander Hamilton. "Now, sir," cried O'Hara, "perform your promise, though when you made it, I little thought that I should ever have an opportunity of requiring your performance of it." Hamilton, fresh from storming the last redoubt, took personal custody of his old enemy. The first round would be on him and probably not milk.

A number of exchanges of prisoners took place before and after these abortive attempts at a general cartel, occasionally a few individuals at a time, oftener prisoners in batches; but such exchanges were always by special arrangement and on a case-by-case basis. No mutually accepted system for extensive exchanges to be automatically applied was in force at any time during the war. As in recent wars and peaces, prisoner exchanges and amnesties and the like remain national political issues in which the prisoners and those who receive amnesty remain pathetic pawns of power politics.

Late that winter the severity of life at Valley Forge was mollified when Martha Washington, always a gallant campaigner, came up from Mount Vernon. She brought a warm smile to the sick and wounded in the dank hospitals and cranked up some social life among her general's official family. In her ambience the under officers flocked to a small salon in a flimsy addition to the crowded Potts house. Here the Baron de Kalb might be seen bowing beside John Sullivan and Anthony Wayne, and there the flamboyant Casimir Pulaski beside Thaddeus Kosciuszko would wait for a chance to speak after Alexander Hamilton had left off his bantering with the first lady or with one of her young lady friends. At first, Elias Boudinot thought the first lady of the army was "almost in a mope for want of a female companion." He wrote Mrs. Boudinot to come at once. Later Lady Stirling appeared and then Lucy Knox and Catherine Littlefield "Kitty" Greene. The last became a magnet for lonely foreign officers as she recycled a respectable stock of textbook French into passable conversations. Years later some favors Hamilton tried to arrange to ease the poverty of Nathanael Greene's gracious widow after his death would become a strand of a web of scandal in which lifelong loyalty to old friends of army years would entangle Hamilton's fame.

As Washington's chief correspondent, Hamilton was well aware of the secret negotiations Benjamin Franklin and Silas Deane and others had been conducting on America's behalf in Paris, but Hamilton could not help voicing concern that Congress might frustrate their best efforts. He wrote Clinton from Valley Forge February 13, 1778: "Realize to yourself the consequences of having a Congress despised at home and abroad. How can the common force be exerted, if the power of collecting it is put in weak, foolish and unsteady hands." Appearances counted in diplomacy: "How can we hope for success in our European negotiations, if the nations of Europe have no confidence in the wisdom and vigor, of the great continental government?"

Now after the news of Saratoga and the display of increasing strength and morale at Valley Forge, France would do more—not on the basis of sentiment, though they admired the courage of the states and the firmness of Washington, the commander in chief, but on a hardheaded estimate of America's chances, just as Hamilton had foretold in *A Full Vindication* and *The Farmer Refuted*. Helping America would weaken France's enemy, Britain. Power politics, not ideology, would bring a despotic monarchy to the aid of a struggling republic.

At the end of February 1778, Congress received a message from Franklin announcing that "the most Christian King agrees to make a common cause with the United States . . . [and] guarantees their liberty, sovereignty, and independence, absolute and unlimited."

Years afterward, Hamilton's friend Nicholas Fish claimed that this boon had originated with Hamilton: ". . . for some considerable time previous to the arrival of the French army . . . Hamilton had conceived the idea," and had weighed it in his own mind before suggesting to Lafayette the effect a small cooperating French force would have, especially if under the Marquis' command. Lafayette took to it with zeal and promptitude, addressed the French government, and used the influence of his family to obtain action. Fish was exaggerating the importance of his friend Hamilton's role, but, without doubt, Hamilton was one of many who foresaw and urged this turn of events, actively sought it, and belonged to the small number who were in a position to help bring it about.

Washington heard of the treaty in April and wrote Congress that "no event was ever received with more heartfelt joy." By midsummer France would be officially at war with England. Spain would declare war on England a year later, though not going as far as France in recognizing the United States as a separate nation.

On May 5, 1778, the General Orders at camp reflected the official ratification of the treaty; "It having pleased the Almighty Ruler of the Universe propitiously to defend the cause of the United States of America finally by raising us up a powerful friend among the Princes of the Earth . . ."

French funds and supplies no longer needed the secret cover of Beaumarchais' lend-lease firm of Hortalez et Cie. Washington would have the wholehearted cooperation of the French army and navy. The momentous news touched off a joyous celebration.

Nathanael Greene, the quartermaster general, asked Washington if military preparations could be relaxed with such powerful outside help in sight. While the whole camp was celebrating on May 5, 1778, Hamilton wrote for Washington a sober reply, which was plainly intended for a wider audience than the quartermaster general. The favor of France could not "justify the least relaxation in . . . the provisions you . . . are making in your department . . ." These must "be continued in their fullest vigor and extent." Britain, confronted by a fresh enemy, could muster further resources. Besides, the enemy army was formidable. It would not be withdrawn without a furthur push, "if . . . only to make the way for a negotiation." Our failure to prepare against British victories "might be fatal" to home sentiment and growing friendships abroad. We might need to take the offensive, which would call for our amplest strength at all points. In any event, salvation lay only in unremitting effort. The letter examined all contingencies and showed how each demanded "a powerful army, well furnished with every apparatus of war." No writing could be more typical of Hamilton's own unremitting effort or expository technique.

Reasons of state kept out of Washington's and Hamilton's letter other reasons why the treaty with France might not be an unmixed blessing. France might try to reestablish her lost North American empire stretching from the Arctic to the Gulf of Mexico. Bigots cursed any alliance with a Catholic power. Old soldiers remembered French officers leading bloody Indian raids against frontier posts in wars of other years. Few grasped the fact that entry of France into the struggle would turn a limited internal clash between Britain and her thirteen fractious colonies into a world war as widespread as and coextensive with the spread of Western civilization up to that time. But for all the problems it brought with it, French aid, as Hamilton had foreseen, would in the long run insure the ultimate success of the American Revolution. In the very long run all are dead; so the great question remained of just how long the long run would be. The long run was to be much farther in the future from the day of that glorious Valley Forge celebration of May 5, 1778, than anyone then could imagine.

A congressional resolution of February 3, 1778, had required all officers of the army to swear to an oath of allegiance before the commander in chief or any major general or brigadier general. Hamilton got around to complying on May 12 before William Alexander, Lord Stirling. By its text he acknowledged "the United States of America, to be free, independent, and sovereign states." He declared that "the people thereof owe no allegiance or obedience to George III, King of Great Britain." He renounced, refused, and abjured any allegiance or obedience to him. He swore that he would "to the utmost of my power, support, maintain and defend the United States, against the said King George III, his heirs and successors and his or their abettors, assistants and adherents." He also swore to "serve the United States in the office of aide de camp which I now hold, with fidelity according to the best of my skill and understanding."

Things had been moving in this direction since July 4, 1776, and before, but the date of the congressional resolution of February 3, 1778, may well be said to be the operative date when the United States finally and officially severed the last link to the Crown and became totally independent of Great Britain.

All the rest of his life and afterward, charges of being a "monarchist" or a "monocrat" and of secret subservience to the British Crown would be brought again and again against Hamilton. In evaluating the substance of such charges and the motives of the makers, one finds it useful to note the specificity of the text of the congressional oath; to mark the date when Hamilton swore it, May 12, 1778; and to recall that the venue where he and the army had spent most of that winter and spring, was Valley Forge. As a rule, Hamilton did not set much store by loyalty oaths. In the case of this one, however, the name of the place and the date affirmed more than the jurat itself.

9

MISBEHAVIOR AT MONMOUTH

Q (TO COLONEL HAMILTON): DID YOU CONCEIVE GENERAL WASH-
INGTON'S ORDERS, OR THE SPIRIT OF THEM, TO GENERAL LEE,
WERE TO ATTACK THE ENEMY AT ALL EVENTS?

A: I DO NOT. I CAN'T CONCEIVE THAT GENERAL WASHINGTON
COULD MEAN TO GIVE ORDERS SO EXTREMELY POSITIVE, BUT
THAT CIRCUMSTANCES, WHICH HAD BEEN UNFORSEEN, MIGHT
ARISE, TO LEAVE THE OFFICER, WHO HAD THE EXECUTION OF
THEM, LIBERTY TO DEVIATE.
    —*Cross-examination of Alexander Hamilton at
    Court-martial of Major General Charles Lee, July 4,
    1778*

Thomas Conway, Thomas Mifflin, and Horatio Gates were gone. The only high-ranking officers left at Valley Forge still openly showing disgruntlement toward the commander in chief were Major Generals Benedict Arnold and Charles Lee.

Arnold was still a semi-invalid from both physical and psychic wounds—a leg badly cut up fighting Burgoyne at Saratoga and a spirit rankling with ire at the army's failure to accord him the glory he considered his due for his heroics at Quebec, Bemis Heights, and Freeman's Saratoga Farm. Although the troops at Valley Forge still suffered from an acute lack of food and clothing, he defiantly attempted to stage a lavish banquet drawn from army stores for a select guest list of 20. He had drawn a terse rebuke from Washington instead. He then found himself an heiress, young, vivacious, beauteous, extravagant Peggy Shippen of Philadelphia, and soon drew her into marrying him.

However, the man who remained a more likely candidate than Arnold to replace Washington as commander in chief if things should continue to go badly was gaunt, hard-favored Charles Lee. Recently returned through a prisoner exchange after capture far from his troops at Basking Ridge, Lee remained unchastened. He disparaged everything he saw at camp and made light of the results of all von Steuben's winter troop training. He produced a set of his own plans for "the Formation of the American Army," since "I understand it better than almost any man living." He claimed, too, that he ought to stand "well with General Washington" because "I am persuaded . . . that he cannot do without me." On top of this he broached the outrageous theory that American troops could never defeat British troops of the kind he had just been with, no matter what the circumstances. Writing to Elias Boudinot, he confided that Washington was not fit to command a sergeant's guard.

After an enthusiastic send-off at an elegant farewell ball in Philadelphia given by his officers in his honor, Sir William Howe, the conqueror of the city, had left for England, and reassignment. Sir Henry Clinton replaced him as commander of all British forces in North America and came down from New York to take command of the British main army. The French-American alliance would slowly help turn the tide of war in North America. But it also meant that North America now was only one of many theaters of the worldwide war between the two great powers.

Almost as soon as he had installed himself in Philadelphia, orders from London directed Clinton to detach 5,000 men to the West Indies for an immediate attack on the French-held island of St. Lucia. Statesmen in London thought that West Indies sugar islands were more important objectives than North American colonies because their produce, especially sugar, was so important to the English economy, particularly at teatime. Another 3,000 men were dispatched to St. Augustine in Florida to deal with French and Spanish threats there. A hundred British ships soon disappeared down the Delaware for parts unknown. Clinton was ordered to move his Philadelphia troops back to New York. From the point of view of the high command in the war office at Whitehall, North America, for the time being, was a minor theater.

At three in the morning of June 18, 1778, Clinton and his army began to cross the Delaware, leaving Philadelphia. In seven hours his command was on Jersey soil, ready for its long, exposed march overland across New Jersey to Sandy Hook, where it could take ship to carry it back to New York. For Clinton this would be a dangerous march because it would present the flank of his long columns, encumbered by heavy wagons and artillery trains, to any American attack sweeping down on it from the north and west.

Washington's 10,000 effective troops newly retrained by von Steuben now slightly outnumbered the British. As soon as he had word that Clinton was on the march, Washington sent a small detachment under Benedict Arnold into the city—enough to occupy it, but not enough for much of a triumphant entry celebration. Washington led the main army straightaway across the Delaware into New Jersey to follow and parallel the British line of march to the north of it as a blocking force to remain between it and the roads northward to New York City.

Here was another chance to bring the war to a quick end. If Washington could cut off, trap, and destroy Clinton's grand army before it wheeled north or keep it from reaching the ships that had sailed to pick it up off Sandy Hook and carry it back to its sanctuary on Manhattan, the war would be over and won. The losses of Forts Mercer and Mifflin, not to mention Brandywine and Germantown, would be retrieved at one stroke.

Hamilton rode out of Valley Forge with Washington on the pursuit march soon after sunrise June 19. On the march he busied himself assisting Washington and Lafayette with gathering intelligence of enemy movements and organizing obstructions by militia and detached parties. The march commenced agreeably enough. James McHenry, a close friend and fellow aide, frequently included Hamilton in jocular asides to his diary. He described the pleasant scene at the first camp near Doylestown: "A raining evening, the Company . . . within Doors included a pretty, Fullfaced, Youthfull, playfull Lass, & a Family of Quakers meek & unsuspicious. Hamilton thou shalt not tread on this ground, I mark it for my own."

The next day, Saturday the twentieth, was "A Rapid Mornings March" in spite of weather so "excessive hot" that "some of the soldiers die suddenly," a forewarning of the day at Monmouth when the mercury would stand at 96 degrees. On Sunday the twenty-first, at Holcombe's house: "Here are some charming Girls," recorded McHenry, "but one of the Drums of the General's Guard more a favorite than Hamilton."

At Hopewell Township, near Princeton, about 25 miles northwest of Howe's column, Washington asked his general officers for advice at a meeting for which Hamilton acted as secretary and amanuensis. Should he risk a general attack on the British grand army? If so, what should the tactics be?

General Charles Lee was full of inhibitions, delivered with his usual air of authority. Let Clinton cross New Jersey unhampered; the French alliance was America's promise of victory; equal numbers of Americans could not battle successfully with trained European soldiers. Lee's assurance carried a four to three vote of the generals in favor of this timid tactic. Others of bolder purpose so far yielded as to accept the compromise of at least sending forward a skirmishing party. Those who wanted to attack in force—Lafayette, Wayne, and Greene—wrote to Washington urging that he disregard Lee's timid advice.

"Fight, Sir," said Anthony Wayne.

Hamilton wrote out the final compromise decision, and it was signed by all but Wayne, who insisted on a decisive battle. Like Wayne, Hamilton urged a bolder attack. The others, outwardly at least, were content with the compromise plan: to advance 1,500 men to worry the enemy's left flank and rear, while the main body remained close behind to be governed by events. This result of the council, "unluckily called," said Hamilton, "would have done honor to the most honorable society of midwives, and to them only. The purport was, that we should keep at a comfortable distance from the enemy, and keep up a vain parade of annoying them by detachment."

Hamilton's son John Church Hamilton reported a story he had heard at his father's knee. After the council of war broke up, Hamilton urged Greene to go with him to beg Washington to give battle. As they approached him, Washington drew himself up to his full, towering height and said, "Gentlemen, I anticipate the object of your visit—you wish me to fight." Hamilton and Greene repeated all the good reasons for a full-scale attack that the aggressive minority had advanced in the council. Washington agreed, and thus "an attack was decided upon." A score of years later, in his "Eulogium" in Greene's memory, Hamilton denounced the fainthearted cautions that others had urged on Washington before Monmouth in terms that must have been similar, with discreet modifications, to those he used in his meeting with Washington. Hamilton condemned "those important councils, which, by a formal vote, had decreed an undisturbed passage to an enemy . . . dispirited by desertion, broken by fatigue, retiring through woods, defiles, morasses . . . in the face of an army superior in numbers, elated by pursuit, and ardent to signalize their courage." He and the courageous Greene had "left nothing unessayed . . . to frustrate so degrading a resolution."

Under their influence, Washington began to overrule the older generals. By an order delivered by Hamilton, he sent Brigadier General Charles Scott forward with about 1,500 good troops to cooperate with smaller detachments "to gall the enemys left flank and rear." Morgan was to gain the right flank, while small bands of foot under General Cadwalader and of horse under Colonel White were pressing forward.

By now Washington could see that Clinton's column was taking the shortest route to the sea, by way of Monmouth Court House to Shrewsbury, and would shortly escape him. Lafayette and Wayne were spirited leaders ready for aggressive action, but Washington felt obliged, before giving full command responsibility to the marquis, to obtain Lee's consent to yield his claim as senior major general to lead the attack. This Lee did, with the disdainful remark that the assignment was "a more proper business of a young volunteering general, than of the second in command of the army."

After his first day's testimony at Lee's subsequent court martial, Hamilton described Lee's farcical indecision to Elias Boudinot: "General Lee's conduct . . . was truly childish. According to the incorrect notions of our army, his seniority . . . entitled him to the command of the advanced corps; but he in the first instance declined it in favor of the marquis. Some of his friends blamed him for doing it." Besides, there was a new rival: "Lord Stirling interposed his claim. So then General Lee . . . inconsistently reasserted his pretensions."

Hamilton continued: "Washington accommodated him [Lee] a second time. Then General Lee and Lord Stirling again agreed to let the marquis command. General Lee, a little time after, recanted again and became very importunate.

The general [Washington], who had all along observed the greatest candor in the matter, grew tired of such fickle behavior, and ordered the marquis to proceed.

"This was still not the end of the farce. When Lee saw that a third of the army was to be turned over to the Frenchman, he reversed himself once more and demanded the honor, his third or fourth chance at the command."

The indecisive Lee was confidently playing on the indecision that he knew was also his superior's failing at times—a failing Lee had previously condemned. Washington finally put Lee, with additional brigades, in command of the whole forward body, but with the reservation that Lee was to aid any design that Lafayette adopted. The Marquis, who was for attacking the enemy forthwith and forgetting internal quarrels, wearily accepted this technically absurd but practical compromise, which, of course, dangerously split command responsibility.

Hamilton spent the days leading up to the battle riding between Washington's headquarters and the commanders of the scattered units of his army, gathering information of their troop dispositions and of the enemy's whereabouts, bringing it back to the commander, and riding off again. In an eighteenth-century army without sophisticated telephone, wireless, and radar communications and intelligence systems, aides like Hamilton served as their chiefs' radar on horseback.

When Hamilton rode into Cranbury on the night of June 25, he found Lafayette's advance detachment in disarray. They had lost contact with the British and also with Lafayette. When Hamilton found Lafayette, Lafayette asked Hamilton to seek out his missing detachments for him and bring him back word of where they, and the British, were.

Though Hamilton had already ridden long and hard that night, he remounted his horse and galloped on to Hightstown and Allentown, where Lafayette's advance scouts were supposed to be operating. He found that each was operating on his own. No patrol was near the enemy or would be heard from before morning. Hamilton issued crisp orders to the scout detachments to send out new patrols at once. It was vital to keep in constant contact with the enemy. But by this time it was dawn, and the British were on the march again. A chance to cut them off during the night had been lost! Hamilton dashed off a note to Washington, saying he was still in favor of a swift, hard blow at the retreating foe.

Lafayette's pursuit was now brought to a stop by hunger. Worse, Hamilton continued, "We are entirely at a loss where the [main American] army is . . . If the army is wholly out of supporting distance, we risk the total loss of the detachment in making an attack." Lafayette now learned from somewhere else that the enemy were in motion, their rear seven or eight miles ahead. He was going after them and might attack in the morning if they did not elude him in the night, "which I much fear, as our intelligence are not the best ones." He would be more confident in striking a blow if Washington's reserves were nearer to him.

Washington stressed prudence in his prompt replies that day to the eager

Lafayette, stimulated by the energetic Hamilton. The troops should not be pushed too hard in the heat. Food was on the way, but his own army, too, was halted for the want of it.

Hamilton replied the night of the twenty-sixth, giving important information and reassuring the commander in chief that he and Lafayette would be prudent. The enemy was encamped with the van of the column slightly east of Monmouth Court House. But to attack them without support of the whole army would be "folly in the extreme." They had rearranged their march to put the baggage in front and close the rear with their best light troops. There was a rear guard of a thousand men a quarter of a mile back of the main body to fend off the pursuing Americans. Hamilton then outlined a plan for attacking them if Washington would come up soon with the main force.

Washington ordered Lafayette to march to Englishtown, where the main army could both support an attack or cover a retreat, and be prepared to assail the enemy's rear. Hamilton dashed off an order to Brigadier General Charles Scott: "This part of the troops marches instantly—if you can find Morgan. Keep close to the enemy and attack when we attack.—We are to join in the Monmouth road one mile this side of Taylor's tavern." Now came Lafayette's turn to back away from the prospect of an attack, and Lee became his excuse. He had now deferred the project of attacking. He would join Lee, marching at two the next morning. He could not resist expressing his disappointment at not being allowed to act independently of Lee, adding, "I do not believe General Lee intends to make any attack tomorrow, for then I would have been directed to fall immediately upon them without making eleven miles entirely out of the way. I am here as near as I would be at Englishtown."

As Lee's aides Mercer and Edwards testified later at Lee's court martial, the light horseman brought Hamilton's attack order to Lee shortly after one in the morning of June 28. It probably was worded much like the order Hamilton had dashed off to Brigadier General Scott, but no copy of it has ever been found. Lee had his large detachment of 5,000 men up and on the march from Englishtown eastward toward Monmouth Court House by five the same morning. Washington followed by two or three miles with the reserve units of the army. Sometime before eight Lafayette's advance guard caught up with Sir Henry Clinton's main rear guard, with Lee's men close behind. Everything now depended on Hamilton's order to Lee and Lee's judgment in transmitting it to the troops arrayed before him. Lee's brigades deployed to form a main battle line facing the British rear, stretching northeastward from Monmouth Court House, with Lafayette on the right flank nearest the Court House, Wayne northward to his left, and Scott on the extreme left flank to the northeast of Wayne.

Underestimating the number of men ahead of him, Lee told Wayne to take 600 Pennsylvanians and two fieldpieces and strike the British rear. That message was the last coherent command that anyone heard from Lee that day. Anthony Wayne, bold, handsome, and eager, drove ahead, smashed through some British outposts, hit unexpected strength, wisely took up a holding position at the edge of a long, swampy ravine, and sent back to Lee for support.

Charles Lee, self-acknowledged master of the art of war, had scattered his command widely over broken terrain as though scattering torn paper from a sack and then apparently forgotten the dispositions he had made. Clinton increased the pressure of his counterattacks against Wayne. But no further orders from Lee reached the firing line or the reserves. Behind Wayne, other regiments and brigades marched and countermarched aimlessly, undirected. Lafayette, still cheerfully in action though having again lost touch with his troops, urged a general advance all along the line and received Lee's chilling reply: "Sir, you do not know British soldiers. We cannot stand against them."

When Hamilton rode up to Lee at a point some distance back of Monmouth Court House, Lee's troops were in confusion. Hamilton ordered Lee to attack and ordered Lafayette to attack the British left flank. He then galloped back to Washington to report. Washington, advancing at the head of the main army, had reached Tennent Church, about three miles west of where the American and British front lines were strung out northeastward from the court house. Lee would soon engage the British, Hamilton told Washington. He recommended, with reasons "which were thought good," that the right wing, under Greene, should be thrown to the south "and . . . follow with the left wing (under Stirling) directly in General Lee's rear to support him."

While Washington was issuing orders to carry out the troop dispositions that Hamilton had recommended, a farmer rode up with a fifer in uniform behind him. "Our people are retreating," the farmer cried, pointing to the fifer. "That man told me so."

Robert H. Harrison, one of the aides in his chief's party that day, recalled the awful moment. ". . . We met a fifer, who appeared to be a good deal frightened. The General asked him whether he was a soldier belonging to the army. He answered that he was a soldier, and that the Continental troops who had been advanced were retreating."

The General was thunderstruck. "And," Harrison added, "rather more exasperated, appearing to discredit the account." He "threatened the man, if he mentioned a thing of this sort, he would have him whipped. He then moved on a few paces . . . (perhaps about fifty yards) where we met two or three persons more on that road." One was a soldier who gave news "that all the troops that had been advanced, the whole of them, were retreating." His excellency appeared to discredit the account, "having not heard any firing except a few cannon a considerable time before." However, as the report came from different persons, it could not be disregarded.

Up front, out at the swampy ravine, Wayne's men, now backed by Scott's Virginians, fought on doggedly, awaiting the reinforcements Wayne had called back to Lee to send up. Out of the smoke in front of them, the Queen's Rangers pounded down on them in a wild charge, followed by cavalrymen of the 16th Dragoons. In 1776 at Chatterton's Hill, near White Plains, a cavalry charge had stampeded American troops, but not now, not after Valley Forge. Now the von Steuben-trained men under Wayne and Richard Butler and Scott stood firm, fired steady volleys into the phalanx of armored horsemen as they came at them, and then slashed at the horses' bellies and girths with their bayonets as the dragoons overrode their shallow entrenchments. The dragoons' charge failed, and the American lines held. Sir Henry Clinton wrote later that his horsemen had "to retreat with precipitation upon our infantry."

But there was no supporting infantry now on Wayne's right or left or behind coming up. Lee, without notifying any save the units nearest him, had ordered a general retreat, leaving Wayne and Scott and the others at the spearhead of the attack isolated and cut off. Wayne, too, had to join the American retreat. Both forces, Clinton's and Wayne's, broke contact. Both turned and headed toward their own rear. Clinton's troops reformed, and returned to the attack, while Wayne and Lafayette fell back to the west, where Stirling's and Greene's reserves had dug in in defensive positions.

At Washington's command post, an officer of William Grayson's regiment told him that streams of men were retreating. Another did not know why they retreated, "that they had lost but one man." Colonel Ogden, farther back in the line, exclaimed, "By God! They are flying from a shadow." No officer seemed to know the cause of the sudden panic, but after a short time "the enemy's light infantry and grenadiers came pouring out of the woods, pressing very hard upon us" at a few hundred yards' distance. The American lines had crumbled. Yet there was no sound of fighting ahead. In the steaming heat the troops had thrown down their blanket rolls and stripped off their shirts. Men of two Continental regiments appeared "in some disorder." The men were so hot and fatigued that "They could hardly stand." Hamilton heard Washington exclaim that he was "exceedingly alarmed" to find the advanced corps falling back on the main body. Lee's entire force was in disorderly retreat.

An aide galloped up and shouted, frantically to Washington that the advancing enemy would be upon him, Hamilton, and the rest of the command party in fifteen minutes. Just then, from the direction of the front lines, there came a familiar, scarecrow-like figure cantering toward Washington's command party, his pack of pet hounds capering around his horse's hooves. Lee was shouting unintelligibly. Washington spurred his huge horse forward, reined up, confronted Lee, and shouted, "What's the meaning of this?" Lee looked up in confusion and cried, "Sir? Sir?"

Washington thundered, "What is all this confusion for and retreat?"

Reports of what was said from this point on conflict sharply. Some hold that Washington erupted like a volcano and cursed out Lee with a string of sulfurous oaths.

Lee later testified at his court-martial that "I confess I was disconcerted, astonished and confounded by the words and the manner in which His Excellency accosted me . . . ," a manner "So novel and unexpected from a man whose discretion, humanity and decorum" he had always admired. However, James T. Flexner, in his biography, *George Washington*, says that "It is highly improbable that Washington could, even if he had let himself go, have sworn with the stunning eloquence legend has attributed to him." Lee was, no doubt, especially "disconcerted" by the fact that, as he testified, he had been "flattering myself" that he would receive "congratulations and applause" for rescuing the army from what he had perceived to be terrible danger instead of Washington's abuse.

Hamilton and the others present could not fail to sense that the moment was the supreme turning point of the American Revolution. The cream of King George III's army,—chasseurs, grenadiers, light infantry—was pounding down on them all. The fate of both grand armies was poised in delicate balance. The scales in motion seemingly now were unbalancing in favor of the British side.

Lee's advance corps of the army was fleeing past them in panic. Their "contagion" of "settled durable panic" might well spread to the other half of the army, past whom they rushed by in headlong, *sauve qui peut* flight. George Washington and his indomitable little command group, including Hamilton and the other aides, stood firm like a rock amid the torrent of panicky troops streaming westward around them in the heat and haze.

Hamilton described the terrifying moment there in the fierce heat of that June morning facing Monmouth when Washington reversed Lee's retreat: ". . . The General rode forward and found the troops retiring in the greatest disorder and the enemy pressing upon their rear. I never saw the general to so much advantage. His coolness and firmness were admirable. He instantly took measures for checking the enemy's advance, and giving time for the army, which was very near, to form and make a proper disposition."

Wayne's men fell back westward, and Wayne joined Washington's command party. After the last of the retreaters had straggled past, some throwing away their muskets, Washington and Wayne thought the ground where they stood—behind a ravine southeast of Freehold Meetinghouse—"appeared to be an advantageous spot to give the enemy the first check." To the panicky troops, the giant in his sweat-stained blue and buff uniform on the huge white horse loomed up untouched by panic out of the dusty haze. Lafayette never forgot the sight: "Washington's presence stopped the retreat . . . his calm courage . . . gave him the air best calculated to excite enthusiasm." He rode "all along the lines amid the shouts of the soldiers, cheering them by his voice and example."

Hamilton was almost as spellbound by Washington's performance as Lafayette, but noticed some other important practical points: "He had the troops formed on a very advantageous piece of ground . . . in other transactions of the day General Greene & Lord Stirling rendered very essential service, and did themselves great honor." But most of the credit belonged to the commander in chief: "The sequel is, we beat the enemy and killed and wounded at least a thousand of their best troops. America owes a great deal to General Washington for this day's work; a general rout, dismay, and disgrace would have attended the whole army in any other hands but his. By his own good sense and fortitude he turned the fate of the day. Other officers have great merit in performing their parts well, but he directed the whole with the skill of a Master workman . . . he brought order out of confusion, animated his troops and led them to success."

Had Washington not saved that day, another Conway cabal or something like it, touched off by Congress's anger at his once again snatching defeat from the jaws of certain victory, might have exploded to displace him with General

Charles Lee or Gates. Such an outcome was not far from the top of Hamilton's mind as he acidly compared the day thus saved with what might have happened under Gates: "He did not hug himself at a distance and leave an Arnold to win laurels for him, but by his own presence he brought order out of confusion, animated his troops, and led them to success." The attempt of Gates's friends to remove Washington from command had already been much weakened, said Lafayette, "but from that day [Monmouth] it totally vanished away."

Washington dispatched Hamilton to order Lieutenant Colonel William Livingston Smith to proceed at once to the support of some exposed artillery. From there Hamilton galloped over to a remnant of James Varnum's brigade, whose commander, Lieutenant Colonel Jeremiah Olney, was vainly trying to make his men stop retreating and take a stand. Hamilton rallied the fleeing men, and together the two officers succeeded in forming them behind a fence line just as the British troops attacked. The British were met with a well-aimed fusillade of rifle fire. As Hamilton rallied the Americans to meet the charge, a musketball wounded his horse. The animal stumbled and fell and threw him headlong to the ground. The British charge was beaten back, and he was rescued. But he was badly bruised, and the pain of his hurts, coupled with the fierce heat of the day and the fatigue from days and nights of riding as his general's radar, forced him from the field, where he had seemed to many to be everywhere at once.

The Battle of Monmouth brought Hamilton wide recognition as a hero. Everyone but Major General Lee hailed his courageous exploits. James McHenry, most recent member of Washington's official family, wrote of him to Boudinot: "I am happy to have it in my power to mention the merit of your friend Hammy. He was incessant in his endeavours during the whole day—in reconnoitering the enemy, and in rallying and charging. But whether he or Col. Laurens deserves most of our commendation, is somewhat doubtful—both had their horses shot under them, and both exhibited singular proofs of bravery. They seemed to court death under our doubtful circumstances, and triumphed over it as the face of war changed in our favor."

Washington's personal assumption of front line command had converted an impending debacle into a technical victory. The British withdrew at nightfall and left the Americans in possession of the battlefield. But their army was still intact and still safely on its way to New York. Washington's last best chance to attack it and smash it and end the war at Monmouth had been lost by Major General Charles Lee's unnecessary and disorderly retreat.

Still it might have been much worse. If it had not been for von Steuben's training of the troops at Valley Forge to follow when well led by their officers, and if Washington and Hamilton had not been at the right places at the right times on the field, Wayne's men and Varnum's might not have held as well as they did. Lee's sudden panicky retreat might have infected all with a "settled durable panic." The whole army so painfully stitched together at Valley Forge might have been unraveled and routed, and with it who knows what hopes in the long run for eventual victory over the British? In the short run, after such a rout, Washington would have been hard put to weather another crisis of congressional confidence in his leadership. After all, he had made his reputation by saving the army through timely retreats of just the sort Lee had claimed he was leading that day.

That night Washington and Lafayette slept on the ground under the same mantle "talking over the conduct of General Lee." Hamilton, no doubt, added his comments to theirs as "night set in and we failing in our attempt to turn the enemy's flank, composed ourselves to sleep behind the line of battle under a large tree." Of the British army there were 294 killed, wounded, or dead of heat and 64 missing; for the American, 62 killed, 161 wounded, and 132 missing. The following day was spent burying the dead and trying to relieve the sufferings of the wounded.

After the battle, Lee smoldered under the lash of Washington's battlefield reprimand. By his lights he had accomplished a masterful retreat. According to Lee, Washington had "sent me out of the field when victory was assured," leaving Washington "scarcely anymore to do in it than to strip the dead." It was Lee who had saved the whole army, and it was to him that "the success of the day was entirely owing." He wrote a letter to Washington saying as much and demanding "reparation" for the "very singular expression" Washington had used on him at the critical moment. He had noticed Hamilton and other aides nearby. Surely what Washington had said had been "instigated by some of those dirty earwigs who will forever insinuate themselves near persons in high office." Lee followed up with a second letter, hoping that the "temporary power" and "tinsel dignity" of Washington's office would not objurgate the truth. He suggested that he be vindicated by a court-martial. Washington briskly complied, "I have sent Colonel Scammell to put you in arrest, who will deliver you a copy of the charges. . . ."

The court-martial of Major General Charles Lee convened on July 4, 1778, the second anniversary of the celebration of Independence Day, at Ross Hall, a large handsome house in the Dutch style fronting on the Raritan near New Brunswick. Less than two years earlier a cannonade laid down by Hamilton's New York Provincial Company of Artillery on Cornwallis's troops in hot pursuit had smartly covered Washington's retreat across the wooden bridge not far away.

Washington appointed the officers who acted as the judges at Lee's court-martial. Lord Stirling was president judge. The charges against Lee were three: (1) disobedience of orders in not attacking the enemy pursuant to repeated instructions, (2) misbehavior before the enemy "by making an unnecessary, disorderly and shameful retreat," and (3) disrespect to the commander in chief in two letters written after the battle.[1]

The man who would become one of the greatest American lawyers of his time received his first trial experience in the uncomfortable role of key witness for the prosecution. He had to testify from memory about a missing document that would never be found. Lieutenant Colonel Alexander Hamilton being sworn, the judge advocate general led off the questioning:

Q: Did you deliver General Lee any orders from General Washington
    the 27th or 28th of June, respecting his attacking the enemy?

A (by Lieutenant Colonel Hamilton): I wrote out an order, and delivered
    it to Lee by a light horseman.

Q: Do you have a copy of the order?

A: No, I do not.

Q: When did you write this order?

A: I wrote General Lee a letter the evening of the 27th of June, by
    General Washington's order.

Hamilton had written out the crucial order for the whole battle the night
before the battle, but Washington had never seen it. No copy of it has ever been
discovered; yet it remains the pivot on which turns the whole mystery of the
glorious victory, as most contemporary Americans saw it, or the miserable lost
opportunity, as many later historians saw it, or the more or less disappointingly
drawn battle that it was. Surprisingly enough, at the court-martial trial of
General Lee, no one, not even Lee himself, discredited the text of the written
order as Hamilton recollected it and recited it orally from the witness stand. Nor
did anyone question the fact that when Hamilton wrote out an order and put
Washington's name to it, it was Washington's order even though Washington
had never seen it. On the other hand, it is not so surprising if the reader accepts,
as General Lee and the court-martial did, that what the aide wrote in Washington's name or in his own name in anything that was Washington's responsibility
incorporated or became Washington's essential thought. It seemed not to matter
which man's name was used or whether Washington had read it first or not.

Q: What was the occasion of this order?

A: It was occasioned by an apprehension (as declared to me by General
    Washington) that the enemy might move off either at night or very
    early in the morning, and get out of our reach, so that the purpose
    of an attack might be frustrated.

Q: What were the contents of the order?

A: The order was conceived in the spirit, as I understood, of former
    orders that had been given by Washington to General Lee.

Q: State what the order said, if you recall.

A: The order directed that General Lee detach a party of 6 or 800 men
    to lie very near the enemy, as a party of observation, in case of their
    moving off, to give the earliest intelligence of it, and to skirmish with
    them so as to produce some delay, and give time for the rest of the
    troops to come up.

Q: Was there anything else?

A: Yes, the order also directed Lee to order Colonel Morgan to make
    an attack on them.

Q: How was that attack to be conducted?

A: It was to be in such a manner as might also tend to produce delay, and yet not so as to endanger a general rout of his party, and disqualify them from acting in concert with the other troops, when a serious attack should be made.

Q: Was there to be a "serious attack" at all?

A: Yes, there was.

Q: How do you know?

A: This, I understood from General Washington, was in pursuance of his intention to have the enemy attacked, and conformable to the spirit of previous orders he had given General Lee for that purpose.

Later close questioning of Hamilton would bring out that the order to attack was by no means as clear and positive as this first answer of Hamilton's on direct examination tended to indicate.

The accused, Major General Charles Lee, now grimly took over the cross-examination of his accuser. General Lee's question: What hour was the letter sent off to me?

A: It was rather late in the evening. I went to bed soon after.

As yet, no one had even proved that Lee actually received Hamilton's order. For this, Captain John Francis Mercer, of Virginia, General Lee's aide, was sworn.

Q: What hour was the letter received from Colonel Hamilton by General Lee?

A: To the best of my recollection, it was past one o'clock in the morning of the 28th of June.

Captain Evan Edwards, another of Lee's aides, being sworn, corroborated:

Q: What hour was the letter received from Colonel Hamilton by General Lee?

A: When the express came I got up and looked at the watch, and think it was near two o'clock by the watch.

Q: What did you do then?

A: I then immediately wrote to Colonel Morgan, General Dickinson, and Colonel Grayson, to comply with the contents of the letter that General Lee received from Colonel Hamilton, and sent off the light-horsemen to them.

Q (to Colonel Hamilton): Did you conceive General Washington's orders, or the spirit of them, to General Lee, were to attack the enemy at all events?

A: I do not. I can't conceive that General Washington could mean to give orders so extremely positive, but that circumstances, which had been unforseen, might arise, to leave the officer, who had the execution of them, liberty to deviate.

The commanding general had given no firm order to attack to anyone at all! He had given Hamilton the same sort of unlimited discretion that he had given him for dealing with Gates. But at Monmouth no such intervening distance or pressure of time made such discretionary latitude an absolute necessity. Hamilton was to order Lee to attack unless "unforseen circumstances," which could mean anything, including a British force to the front, should make it seem advisable to "deviate." This was broad enough even to encompass a retreat instead of an attack.

It all boiled down to how Hamilton, not Washington, had appraised the situation on the spot, what he had decided, and how he had expressed his decision in words in the order he had issued in Washington's name. And it was now missing from the record.

Hamilton's answer could not have entirely pleased Washington. By it Hamilton, in effect, seemed to knock out the first charge against Lee: If obedience to his order encompassed Lee's "liberty to deviate" from the attack, then Lee had not necessarily been disobedient to the order. The question now became narrower and much more difficult for the prosecution to prove: whether Lee had exercised good or bad judgment, or acted in good or bad faith. It was ambiguous at best whether "liberty to deviate" did not include liberty to order a tactical retreat.

Q: Would you explain what it means to give the officer "liberty to deviate" Sir?

A: From everything I knew of the affair, General Washington's intention was fully to have the enemy attacked on their march, and that the circumstances must be very extraordinary and unforseen, which, consistent with his wish, could justify the not doing it.

But still, were there no circumstances of any kind when a retreat such as Lee's would be encompassed within the scope of the order?

Lee took over again and pressed Hamilton sharply:

Q: Did you either by letter to me, or in conversation with me, communicate this idea of General Washington's intention as fully and clearly as you have done it to the Court?

Hamilton gave ground.

A: I do not recollect that I ever did.

Lee pressed his advantage with skill:

Q: Was your idea of General Washington's intention that I should attack the enemy, had I found them in the situation which General Dickinson's intelligence assured me they were; that is, the whole arranged in order of battle, at or near [the] Courthouse?

Hamilton was forced to agree with the thrust of Lee's well-framed leading question:

A: I knew nothing of General Dickinson's intelligence. But if the enemy's whole army were drawn up in order of battle near the Courthouse, I do not conceive it was General Washington's intention to have them attacked by your detachment.

Lee could not have failed to pause, raise his eyebrows, look up at the silent, unsmiling judges, then across at the glum prosecutor, and then revolve his stare around the courtroom in Ross Hall while a crooked smile of triumph slowly spread across his features.

"No more questions," he would say.

The last answer that Hamilton, the prosecution's chief witness, had given under cross-examination seemed to have all but discredited the prosecution's own case on the first count.

Much as he disliked Lee; much as he would like to have served Washington by bringing down the "sap" of the Conway cabal, the man who constantly disparaged him; embarrassing to himself as it might be to change his own earlier testimony that he had given a clear order to attack, Hamilton would not shade his testimony about the content and meaning of the order the relatively slight amount which would have been necessary to permit the first of the three charges against Lee to stand.

On Hamilton's testimony, at least, the first charge, that Lee had disobeyed the order, had to fall.

The court-martial adjourned, and Hamilton was excused until nine days later when the court would reconvene.

As Hamilton had written his friend William Duer on June 18, "Opinion, whether well or ill founded, is the governing principle of human affairs." Hamilton's testimony at Lee's court-martial and the unsworn opinions he circulated during the days before the trial reconvened, contrasting Washington's conduct at the great battle with Lee's, contributed as much as anyone else's to history's confused view of the whole affair ever since.

The day after his first testimony, Hamilton wrote to his old friend and fellow member of the commission for prisoner exchanges, Elias Boudinot. He told his friend the story of the battle and noted that "American arms gained very signal advantages." But he added, "I can hardly persuade myself to be in good humour with success so far inferior to what we, in all probability, should have had, had not the finest opportunity America ever possessed been fooled away by a man, in whom she has placed a large share of the most ill judged confidence. You will . . . know that I mean General Lee. This man is either a driveler in the business of soldiership or something much worse." He realized that his testimony had been weak. "Whatever a court martial may decide, I shall continue to believe and say his conduct was monstrous and unpardonable." Hamilton unmistakably suspected Lee of "something much worse," something that went deeper than being merely the sap of the cabal. He could not prove treason, and he would not give shaded testimony that would contribute to a legally questionable verdict against Lee.

The second charge was that Lee's retreat had been "unnecessary", "shameful," and "disorderly." Obviously, whether it had been "unnecessary" and "shameful" were subjective questions. In the heat and haze of the day and the shock and smoke of battle, the way things looked to Lee from where he stood on the battlefield were matters of judgment, and who was to say that his judgment had been entirely wrong? Was there at least a "scintilla of evidence" that Lee's retreat had not been "shameful" or "unnecessary?" But whether it had been "disorderly" (as distinguished from "unnecessary" and "shameful") was different. That was an objective matter. Hamilton and many other witnesses could testify to what they had seen. To most of them, including Hamilton, Lee's misbehavior before the enemy and his troops' retreat were indeed "disorderly," and worse. Hamilton was certain that if Lee had carried out the true intent of the order he had given with the energy that should mark all good leadership, the events that followed that day might well have brought the American Revolution to a glorious close then and there.

The court-martial moved with the army to Paramus and reconvened on July 13. On the issue of whether Lee's retreat had been "disorderly," Hamilton resumed his testimony, and on direct examination, all went smoothly. He averred that he "saw nothing like a general plan or combined disposition for a retreat . . ."

There had been a retreat, and the vice of it was that Lee had failed to make proper preparation for it.

Q: Were the troops, when you fell in with them the second time retreating in order or disorder, and in what particular manner?

A: The corps that I saw were in themselves in tolerable good order, but seemed to be marching without system or design, as chance should direct . . . I saw nothing like a general plan, or combined disposition for a retreat.

Q: Was there any body drawn up in their rear to cover their retreat that you saw?

A: I saw no such thing.

Q: Were the orders that you heard General Lee give that day, given distinct and clear?

A: I recollect to have heard General Lee give two orders, at both times he seemed to be under a hurry of mind.

Q: Did General Lee to your knowledge advise General Washington of his retreat?

A: He did not to my knowledge.

On cross-examination, Hamilton was pressed, and not a little embarrassed. Lee sought to rebut Hamilton's testimony with a thrust at the aide's own excited, extravagant behavior at the supreme moment. Lee asserted that Hamilton's testimony about Lee's "hurry of mind" "has hurt me the more, as it comes from a man of esteemed sense, and whose valor I was myself a witness of." But Hamilton's valor, said Lee, should have been under much better control.

Hamilton described Washington's encounter with Lee to the court, but nowhere said that Washington had cursed Lee. According to Lee, Washington had met Lee retreating, accosted him with "the most disgraceful reproach," and demanded, "I desire to know, Sir, what is the reason—whence arises this disorder and confusion, and retreat." Lee had offered no coherent explanation and seemed to equivocate. Lee claimed he had finally said, "I myself will be one of the last men off the field." No one else had heard him say this. Washington ordered Lee to the rear. Lee said he had answered, "I undoubtedly would go."

Years later when asked again what Washington had said, Hamilton was circumspect: "Washington was modest. He was careful of his words. He had no time to curse. He had to retrieve the day." This does not in so many words deny that Washington cursed Lee out roundly. If he had not, Hamilton could have defended him with a single word instead of four sentences.

Then Lee described the moment when Hamilton had delivered his battlefield order to Lee. It must have embarrassed Hamilton no little. In the hushed courtroom, Lee went on, ". . . Colonel Hamilton flourishing his sword, immediately exclaimed: That's right, my dear General, and I will stay, and we will all die here on this spot." Lee added, "I could but be surprised at his expression, but observing him much flustered and in a sort of frenzy of valor, I calmly requested him to observe me well and to tell me if I did not appear tranquil and master of my faculties; his answer was, that he must own that I was entirely possessed of myself; well, then (said I), you must allow me to be a proper judge of what I ought to do." Lee had then made a retreat, as he thought the British regulars in front of him held the higher ground.

The day after giving his testimony, Hamilton found it necessary to write to Lord Stirling, the chief judge, to explain what he had meant by his rather inconclusive statement about Lee's behavior, or misbehavior.

Yes, it was true that on the battlefield Lee had asked him, "Do I appear to you to have lost my senses, do I not possess myself?" Hamilton admitted that his own "answer to these questions was a favourable one." But "So singular and unexpected a question was not a little embarrassing; and it is possible, I may have replied in terms of less reserve and caution, than I should have done at a moment of greater tranquility and cooler reflection." In other words, he probably had cursed Lee out roundly, too, filling in any curses Washington had left out. Yes, Lee's answers to what was said to him "were pertinent." Yes "his behaviour had not the least appearance of concern on the score of personal security. He could not be said to have lost his senses," Hamilton conceded. "But," Hamilton went on, and this was the vital distinction, "he certainly did not appear to me to be in that collected state of mind or to have that kind of self-possession, which is an essential requisite of *the General*, and which alone can enable him, in critical emergencies, to take his measures with the promptitude and decision they require. A certain indecision improvidence and hurry of spirits were apparent."

As Hamilton had said before, Lee's was not a complexion to radiate courage to his men; their "settled durable panic" was the reflection of his poor generalship.

The testimony of John Laurens and Richard Kidder Meade was more pointed than Hamilton's. Laurens swore that Lee gave no orders to attack, except a direction to General David Forman to cut off some of the enemy who were retreating. Laurens had brought a message from Washington saying that the commander in chief was ready to support Lee with his whole army and had asked Laurens for Lee's reply. Lee "answered that he really did not know what to say." When part of Lee's detachment fell back and the enemy, 150 or 200 at most, pursued, Lee "ordered the whole of our troops to retreat." Lee's directions were given indistinctly. Laurens attributed Lee's embarrassment "to want of presence of mind." This stung Lee into anger that made him go too far. Lee disparagingly asked Laurens one further question on cross-examination. Laurens's answer helped save the case for the prosecution that Hamilton's testimony had almost lost: "Were you ever in the action before?" Veteran of many a battle, shot through the shoulder trying to set fire to the Chew house at Germantown, John Laurens, the South Carolina aristocrat, drawled a crushing reply: "I have been in several actions; I did not call that an action, as there was no action previous to the retreat."

The officer-judges found Lee guilty on all three charges, except that the word "shameful" was deleted from the second charge, so that his "misbehaviour" in ordering the retreat, though not necessarily shameful, remained "unnecessary" and "disorderly." He was sentenced to be suspended from any command in the armies of the United States for the term of twelve months. This confirmed Hamilton's judgment that he was not fit to be a general, but was otherwise remarkably mild. There had been no proof of treason, and most of the evidence for the prosecution except Laurens's, and including Hamilton's, had been rather equivocal.

The court-martial's verdict was referred to Congress for approval, but approval was slow in coming. While Congress carefully reviewed the correctness of the verdict against its former favorite, Lee reacted to the verdict in a way that would remove doubts of the rightness of Hamilton's judgment that his "hurry of mind" made him unfit for command, even of his own case. Lee published a "vindication" of his generalship. It attacked the court-martial itself as an "inquisition." It accused Washington of being a military incompetent who was jealous of any men around himself like Lee and Thomas Conway, who had real skill. Lee imputed cowardice to von Steuben, who had also testified against him at the trial, by writing that at the battle von Steuben had been only a "very distant spectator." Lee discounted and discredited the testimony of Hamilton, John Laurens, and the other "earwigs" around Washington. These were nothing but "an idolatrous set of Toad Eaters who gave perjured testimony."

As if by such a "vindication" Lee had not done enough harm to his appeal to Congress, he went down to Philadelphia himself, as one observer reported, "damning Washington . . . and the Congress, and threatening to resign, *aye, God damn them, that he would,* and frowning and dancing like a Caledonian stung by a Tarantula."

Lee's former aide, Major John S. Eustace, charged loudly in the presence of many officers that he *"thought Colonel Hamilton was perjured at the trial."* Later Eustace reported to Lee: "I met Hambleton [sic] the other day in company with the favourite Green [General Nathanael Greene] the *Drunkard* Stirling, and their several classes of attendants—He advanced towards me . . . with presented hand—I took no notice of his polite intention, but sat down, without bowing to him or any of the clan . . . he then asked me if I was come from Camp —I say'd, *shortly, no,* without the usual application of SIR, rose from my chair —left *the room* and him *standing before the chair.* I cou'd not treat him much more rudely—I've repeated my *suspicions* of his *veracity on the tryall* so often that I expect the son of a bitch will challenge me when he comes." There is no record that Hamilton challenged the man who responded to his outstretched hand by calling him a son of a bitch to an interview with pistols.

If Washington's position confined him to smoldering in silence in the face of such calumny, it did not prevent him from unleashing all his loyal "earwigs" like a a pack of hounds in full cry on the trail of Lee.

Being witnesses for the prosecution of Charles Lee endeared the "earwigs" to Washington. Earwigs who were willing to hunt Lee down to the kill for Washington were doubly dear. Hamilton urged others on to slash at Lee from several quarters in a way he himself could not do as a witness for the prosecution.

Von Steuben's Prussian rage exploded at being called a "very distant spectator." Von Steuben's aide, Captain Benjamin Walker, brought Lee the irate baron's challenge to a duel. Lee backed down, saying he had not questioned von Steuben's courage, but only his "forwardness" in testifying for the prosecution. He would make this statement publicly, but "If you found that I have not dealt honestly, I am ready to satisfy you in the manner you desire." Von Steuben accepted this as sufficient explanation.

Von Steuben was hypersensitive to Lee's sarcasm because, as inspector general, he had, in fact, been denied a command in the line. Hamilton, who was beginning to feel sensitive himself about his own "groveling condition" as a staff member, had helped the baron write his challenge to Lee and wrote the baron sympathetically: "I have read your letter to Lee, with pleasure—it was conceived in terms, which the offense merited . . . Considering the pointedness and severity of your expressions, his answer was certainly a very modest one and proved that he had not a violent appetite, for so close a *tête à tête* as you seemed disposed to insist upon. His evasions, if known to the world, would do him very little honor."

John Laurens, Hamilton's closest friend among the "earwigs," heard "that General Lee had spoken of General Washington in the grossest and most opprobrious terms of personal abuse." He, too, challenged Lee to a duel. As Hamilton saw it, full of sympathy, Laurens "thought himself bound to resent" the slur "as well on account of the relation he bore to General Washington, as from motives of personal friendship, and respect for his character." Laurens chose Hamilton for his second.

Lee accepted, but pleaded that his appeal still pending with Congress had delayed him. "I will do myself the Honour of meeting you attended by a Friend with a brace of pistols tomorrow (Dec. 22, 1778) 1/2 past 3. P.M." If they should be unsuccessful at killing each other with pistols, Lee would bring along swords for a backup, to make sure they would not fail to produce a fatality, but his legs and gout were a problem. "I would willingly bring a small sword at the same time, but from the effects of my fall and the quantity of Physick I have taken to baffle a fit of the Gout . . . I do not think myself sufficiently strong on my legs." He named "a very convenient piece of wood . . . on the point no point road, to the left hand a little on the Philad. side of the four mile stone." There, "unless it should rain" he would present himself. If all went well, one or the other would wind up either as a cadaver (by pistol) or as mincemeat (by sword).

Lee arrived promptly with his aide Major Evan Edwards as his second, but they had to wait there a while for Laurens and Hamilton to appear. As agreed, the combatants, provided with two pistols apiece, advanced toward each other, firing when they chose. At five or six paces they blazed away almost simultaneously. As Laurens was cocking his second pistol for another try, Lee cried out that he was wounded. Laurens and the two seconds rushed to help him, but he protested that his wound was a trifling one and that he, too, wanted another shot at his opponent. Both Hamilton and Edwards insisted that all requirements of honor had been fully satisfied and that the encounter must end without more ado. While the seconds conferred, Laurens insisted that he was not satisfied. Lee admitted that he had given an opinion of Washington's military character to his close friends and might do so again, but that the things he had said were not as bad as some claimed. He esteemed him as a man. This was enough for Laurens.

Hamilton and Edwards as the seconds published the usual report of the event, pronouncing that after the two gentlemen met, "their conduct was strongly marked by all the politeness, generosity, coolness, and firmness, that ought to characterize a transaction of this nature." Lee is reported to have said later of Laurens, "I could have hugged the noble boy, he pleased me so."

Major Samuel Shaw commented acidly to John Laurens's father, Henry Laurens, the president of Congress, that his son's challenge in defense of Washington's honor had been issued in accordance with the ancient knightly custom of *pro vidua,* by which "monks, old women, and widows [like Washington?] were allowed a champion like Henry Laurens's son John. John had written his father privately of suspicions of Lee's treachery that he shared with Hamilton: "Mr. Clinton's whole flying army would have fallen into our hands" but for Lee's "defect of good will." Henry Laurens gave voice to his son John's and Hamilton's suspicions of treason on the floor of Congress; a supporter of Lee challenged Henry Laurens to a duel; they exchanged shots; but both men missed.

Of the father's duel, Shaw observed that in Philadelphia, "duels are now exceedingly in vogue, though fortunately seldom attended with fatal consequences.''

Among other things this almost farcical record of near fatal fallout from the court-martial of Major General Charles Lee shows that any eighteenth-century gentleman like Hamilton lived easily with the deadly etiquette of dueling. Hamilton had learned from lifelong experience as well as any man could that there were innumerable ways that a challenge to a duel could be finessed or a duel once begun be broken off, without fatality, yet with honor intact, if either one of the parties to the challenge had a desire to avoid a fatal issue. Five months after the court-martial's verdict, Congress finally confirmed it in December by a somewhat equivocal vote of eight states to two.

Many years after these events, there came to light a plan of military campaign that Lee had drawn up for Sir William Howe while he had been a prisoner of the British before Hamilton had helped arrange for his exchange. By his plan Lee had showed Howe the way to restore the colonies to the empire. Lee's most sympathetic biographer was of the opinion that ''Had this plan fallen into American hands when he could be brought before a military court, it is not unlikely that he would have been found guilty of treachery and sentenced to death.'' The finding confirmed all the black suspicions of something much worse that incompetence, which Hamilton had expressed to Boudinot to account for Lee's weird behaviour at the Battle of Monmouth and before. No less penetrating than his ability to forsee future events and act on what he saw were Hamilton's insight deep into motives hidden in dark recesses of other men's minds and his confidence despite lack of other proof to act on the truth of what it told him.

Lee was dismissed from the army in 1780 and died in 1782 in disgrace with all but a few. His will directed that his body not be buried within a mile of any Presbyterian or Baptist meetinghouse. ''I have kept so much bad company while living,'' he explained, ''that I do not choose to continue it while dead.''

One of the few who had a good word to say about Lee was Sir Henry Clinton. He complimented Lee on his skill by pointing out that Lee's retreat before Clinton's attacking force was excellent generalship because ''the quality of all my corps far exceeded anything he had to oppose them.'' To Hamilton and Laurens this paralleled so closely what Lee had always said—what they conceived to be Lee's cover story for his treasonable retreat—that it went far to confirm their suspicions of treason. This was the ''something much worse'' than ''misbehavior'' at Monmouth.

10

EMANCIPATION— OR A GOLDEN CHAIN?

THE CONTEMPT WE HAVE BEEN TAUGHT TO ENTERTAIN FOR THE
BLACKS, MAKES US FANCY MANY THINGS THAT ARE FOUNDED NEI-
THER IN REASON NOR EXPERIENCE . . . THEIR NATURAL FACULTIES
ARE AS GOOD AS OURS . . .
AN UNWILLINGNESS TO PART WITH PROPERTY OF SO VALUABLE A
KIND WILL FURNISH A THOUSAND ARGUMENTS TO SHOW THE IM-
PRACTICABILITY OR PERNICIOUS TENDENCY OF A SCHEME WHICH
REQUIRES A SACRIFICE . . . BY OPENING A DOOR TO THEIR EMANCI-
PATION
> —*To John Jay March 14, 1779*

THERE IS NO VIRTUE IN AMERICA—THAT COMMERCE WHICH PRESIDED
OVER THE BIRTH AND EDUCATION OF THESE STATES HAS FITTED THEIR
INHABITANTS FOR THE CHAIN, AND THE ONLY CONDITION THEY SIN-
CERELY DESIRE IS THAT IT MAY BE A GOLDEN ONE.
> —*To John Laurens September 11, 1779*

Sir Henry Clinton's army trundled eastward from the battlefield of Monmouth toward Sandy Hook. There ships of Lord Richard Howe's fleet that had
sailed down the Delaware from Philadelphia around Cape May and up the Jersey

coast took them aboard and ferried them back to their old positions on Staten Island, Manhattan, and Long Island. It was a smooth, well-coordinated, large-scale amphibious operation. Washington made no further attempt to give chase. Instead, he gave his men two days at the battlefield in which "to breath themselves," care for the wounded, and bury their dead. Congratulations from the rest of the country and Congress poured in to Washington and the army for the unusual accomplishment of holding the field where the battle had been fought after the battle was over instead of turning up as usual somewhere well to the rear of it.

With the main British forces holed up again in key ports like New York and Newport and weakened by detachments sent to the West Indies, Americans complacently turned back to their customary commercial pursuits in Philadelphia, Boston, Baltimore, and elsewhere. Vigorous pursuit of independence wound down. The American war effort fell back to its customary posture of being a little less than a match for the weakened British and badly needing foreign aid from France to bring the scales into balance. As for independence, the American public's attitude seemed to be "Let George do it" or "Let France do it."

Lethargy and complacency on the national scene and war profiteering in high places were not too far beyond the army's encampments to engage Hamilton's quick ire. Besides, he was coming more and more to feel as his friend von Steuben did that the groveling condition of an aide on the staff without a field command too narrowly constricted his talent. War to Hamilton was too important a matter to leave to the generals. It had to be fought and won on political and economic battlefields far from Monmouth Court House. To Hamilton, Congress was a battlefield on which the national interest was constantly in a retreat as disorderly as General Lee's. Two and a half months after Monmouth, he took up his pen under the pseudonym of *Publius* to do battle. In Holt's *New York Journal and General Advertiser*, published in Poughkeepsie, where Holt had continued to issue his New York City paper just beyond the periphery of British military outposts around the city, Publius published three broadsides beginning October 16, 1778. Publius' broadsides singled out Samuel Chase, a member of Congress from Maryland, as the special target of his attack, but it was clear that Chase merely personified the general attitudes of complacency and greed that were widely represented in Congress and in Congress's constituencies throughout the nation. "There are abuses in the state, which demand an immediate remedy," Publius cried. "When avarice takes the lead in a state, it is commonly the forerunner of its fall. How shocking it is to discover among ourselves, even at this early period, the strongest symptoms of this fatal disease?"

The events that provoked Publius' fierce protest against the prevailing climate of public and private greed had begun with the good news of the arrival of the French fleet. Twelve ships of the line, including six frigates and two xebecs, sailed up Delaware Bay on July 8, 1778, under the command of Charles Henri Hector, the Comte d'Estaing, vice admiral of the French fleet. This was the first tangible and powerful reinforcement resulting from the new French

Alliance. Unfortunately, d'Estaing was just a month too late to intercept Howe's smaller fleet of transports as they had sailed out of Philadelphia around Cape May to rescue Clinton.

Had he not unnecessarily delayed his Atlantic crossing, Comte d'Estaing might have destroyed Howe's fleet in the Delaware or off the Jersey coast and left Clinton's army stranded ashore somewhere near Sandy Hook, where Washington might have finished him off at his leisure. Leisure was what Washington's army now picnicking at Passaic to the northward would have needed. But finding Clinton's troops and Howe's fleet inside the snug harbor of New York, d'Estaing merely followed and demonstrated in force outside of Sandy Hook, daring the British to come out and fight, but doing them no damage except psychological.

Washington had urged d'Estaing to sail into the harbor at once and attack the British fleet at their anchorage. But French "sixty-fours" drew 27 feet of water, and their British counterparts drew only 22. Comte d'Estaing was fearful of grounding his ships on sandbars their bottoms could not clear. Meanwhile, with all these fruitless pursuits and parades, d'Estaing's sailors worked up healthy appetites and had to be kept fed by the American commissary.

When news that d'Estaing's fleet was on its way had reached Congress, amid high hopes for letting France provide the further effort necessary to win independence for the states, Congress secretly planned to purchase large quantities of grain supplies for the French fleet in the open market. This set the stage for an early foreign grain sale scandal. As a member of Congress, Samuel Chase had received the earliest inside information of Congress' grain purchase plans. Thus assured of a future grain shortage, he alertly sent out agents to buy up all available grain they could find.

Jeremiah Wadsworth, the commissary general of purchases, offered a plan to Congress that would have made it possible to requisition the necessary grain for public use without driving up the price, but Chase engineered things so that the congressional committee in charge bottled up its report in committee until Chase's agents had had enough time to buy up all the grain they needed. By the time Congress was able to act, the price had more than doubled, and Chase had doubled his money.

Having served as a secret scourge for Washington to slash back at General Charles Lee through John Laurens, von Steuben, and Henry Laurens, Hamilton now lengthened his lash to flay Congress and the country at large. Publius struck out at all those who, like Congress's most newly rich member, Chase, were of "that tribe who, taking advantage of the times, have carried the spirit of monopoly and extortion to an excess which scarcely admits of a parallel." Any member of Congress who turns "the knowledge or secrets, to which his office gave him access, to the purposes of private profit . . . ought to feel the utmost rigor of public resentment, and be detested as a traitor of the worst and most dangerous kind."

Henry Laurens had already accused Congress of "venality, peculation and fraud." His son John Laurens knew that no pen was deadlier than Hamilton's when it came to serving as a scourge. On December 5, urging Hamilton to take up pen against General Lee, John Laurens had written Hamilton that "The pen of Junius is in your hand . . . you will . . . expose such a tissue of falsehood and inconsistency as will satisfy the world."

Junius, of course, was the pseudonymous penman whose letters to the London *Public Advertiser* from 1769 to 1772 attacking the ministry, Lord Mansfield, and King George III himself had created a sensation by their vigor, elegance, and white hot malignity. To John Laurens, Hamilton, and their contemporaries, Junius was the paradigm of polemical style without a peer. In the British Ministry and King George III, Hamilton, like Junius, had already found targets in the same slavemasters.

But Hamilton saw himself and his own role a little differently from the way Laurens did. The small difference tells much that Hamilton would never allow himself to reveal about how he saw himself. One of several prominent figures of classical times named Publius was Publius, or Publilius Syrus, a Latin writer of the first century B.C., a native of remote Syria, who had been brought as a slave to Rome, where, by his wit and talent, he won the favor of his master, who educated him and then freed him. The earlier Publius had enjoyed great success not as a writer of polemics, like Junius, but as a writer of mimes. He had enjoyed even greater success as an actor of mimes that he had written for himself and still greater success as an improvisatore, who composed mimes and poems extemporaneously as he performed them. In one mime contest Publius had vanquished all his competitors, including the celebrated Decimus Laberius, and won a coveted prize from the hand of Caesar himself.

The Vindicator of Congress and the Refuter of the Westchester Farmer had rallied New Yorkers from slavery under the *Asia*'s guns to fight for independence from British Ministry and king. Now these first three papers of Publius sought to rally Congress and the whole new nation against enslavement to vices within themselves. It is significant that nine years after these first three *Publius* papers appeared, after writing many other public papers under many other pseudonyms, Hamilton returned to Publius as his pen name for the greatest of all of his essays in public persuasion, *The Federalist Papers*. Not only would he revive the mime Publius for the most important of his public papers—there are about 18,500 documents in the collected Hamilton Papers—he would persuade two other great men, James Madison and John Jay, to step into supporting roles under the name of the same mime.

The question may be asked, Can a penniless, illegitimate orphan boy from a remote dependency who comes of age at the headquarters of an emerging empire in a prominent role visible to the commander in chief ever be entirely without an inward sense of performing a mime he writes as he goes along—in competition for some unannounced grand prize to be awarded at an unspecified future date? In the case of a Publius, none but a negative answer seems possible. His formal curriculum completed, he was now assured of the favor of his master by having disposed of both Major Generals Charles Lee and Horatio Gates. As Publius I, II, and III, Hamilton felt free to move into competition on the national stage beyond the confines of the army and his own dependent status as a general's aide.

In a leisurely way, still in theory keeping Sir Henry Clinton's army covered as the two armies moved at right angles away from each other, Washington marched his army northward to Brunswick, where Hamilton testified at the first hearings of Lee's trial. From there by easy stages Washington moved on to Paramus on the New Jersey Palisades opposite Fort Washington, where Hamilton continued his testimony. From Paramus the army moved on up the Hudson to Peekskill and Haverstraw below West Point. There the great fortress intended to block the Hudson River valley from future invasions like Burgoyne's and Sir Henry Clinton's was still under hasty construction.

On the way to Paramus, Washington and Hamilton and the command party stopped for a picnic lunch on the ledge opposite the Great Falls, where the Passaic River flows over a cliff into a deep gorge in a veil of spray. It is a natural wonder, where every minute tons of falling water crash unharnessed into a cleft in the rock and slowly unwind down the river's canyon to the sea. A dozen years later Hamilton and some associates would select this for the site of the first planned industrial complex in America, the Society for Establishing Useful Manufactures, or SUM. That shortly thereafter, under the close personal supervision of Hamilton, it would fail did not prevent its later success under other management. The factories and mills of the SUM changed the veil of spray that was snow white the day Hamilton and Washington picnicked beside it in 1778 into the greenish brown miasma of industrial pollution that a visitor to the decaying park there sees rising above the gorge today.

With the army encamped around Haverstraw blocking the Hudson Valley, outpost troops astride all other land and river approaches, and with d'Estaing's fleet blockading New York by sea, Washington worked up a new tactical plan to pressure the British out of their principal base by means of a pincers movement. The plan required close coordination between the French fleet and the American army.

A strike at New York would be a strike at the British in the heart of their strength. But if it should fail, an alternative use for d'Estaing's powerful fleet, more profitable than continuing the vain parade in the ocean outside the Narrows, would be to send it up Long Island Sound to attack the British base at Newport in a combined attack with General John Sullivan's American troops. D'Estaing's orders from Paris strictly limited the time he could stay on the North American coast before returning to the West Indies, where his mission was to guard French islands like St. Lucia from British coups in that theater. Now there was only time enough for one swift blow.

For a third time, Washington entrusted Hamilton with a battle plan that left to Hamilton's judgment the ultimate decision between opposite strategic alternatives, depending on how Hamilton should appraise the situation. As with Hamilton's decision's on whether or not to order Gates to send reinforcements or to order Lee to attack or withdraw, Hamilton's decision on whether to attack New York or Newport could possibly have ended the war that summer either way for either side or merely serve to prolong it. Whichever way Hamilton should decide, the French naval and American ground forces involved would make it one of the largest-scale, most ambitious allied amphibious assaults known to warfare before the twentieth century.

"I am sending you Colonel Hamilton," Washington wrote d'Estaing, whom he had never met, "in whom I place entire confidence. He will be able to make you perfectly acquainted with my sentiments, and to satisfy any inquiries you may think proper to propose; and I would wish you to consider the information he delivers as coming from myself."

After arranging to find d'Estaing a sea pilot for his fleet, one Patrick Dennis, who knew the local coasts and harbors, Hamilton galloped down from Haverstraw with Washington's letter on July 18 to meet d'Estaing at a rendezvous on the New Jersey coast at Black Point. D'Estaing's fleet outweighed the British fleet in numbers of ships and guns, but his concern for the delicacy of his ships' deep bottoms in New York's deep harbor was profound. D'Estaing made no mention of fear of enemy shore batteries.

Hamilton reported back to Washington on the twentieth that d'Estaing "has had the River sounded and finds he cannot enter." Some use had to be got out of the French fleet; so realism dictated the decision to make an amphibious assault on Newport instead. Hamilton ordered the French fleet on its way and reported to Washington that "He will sail for Rhode Island tomorrow evening; in the meantime he is making demonstrations to deceive the enemy and beget an opinion that he intends to operate in this quarter." To keep in touch with General Sullivan and coordinate their land-sea assault on Newport, "We have agreed, that five cannon fired briskly shall be a signal of his arrival by day, and the same number, with five sky rockets a signal by night. In communicating this to General Sullivan, the Count wishes not a moment may be lost." D'Estaing also wanted to "have persons stationed on the Coast and intermediate expresses to facilitate the Communication between them." Hamilton enclosed a letter from d'Estaing to Washington, which he translated from the French for Washington's comprehension.

The French admiral weighed anchor and proceeded to Rhode Island for the joint operation with General Sullivan and his nearly ten thousand men. D'Estaing's single strategic interview with Hamilton to plan the assault on Newport and abandon the idea of taking New York made such a profound impression on d'Estaing that later, after months of dealings with Lafayette, Sullivan, du Portail, and others, forwarding a confidential letter to Washington, d'Estaing would add a postscript: "I entreat you not to confide the secret to any person, except Colonel Hamilton. His talents and his personal qualities have secured to him for ever my esteem, my confidence, and my friendship."

After completing his mission to d'Estaing, Hamilton fell sick again, partly perhaps from rough equestrian passages and partly perhaps from the tension of not having been able to tilt the momentous strategic decision toward the decisive theater of operations, the British base on his own Manhattan Island. Besides, it was summer, and he habitually had spells of sickness then.

D'Estaing having sailed east to Newport and there being no immediate emergency at headquarters, Hamilton apologized to Washington for delaying his return for a short while, which "no more than a moderate attention to my frail constitution may make not improper." His health continued poor all the rest of the summer. His friend, James McHenry, who had given up his medical practice to join Washington's staff, wrote Hamilton a prescription: "In order to get rid of your present accumulations," he said, "you will be pleased to take the pills agreeable to the directions; and to prevent further accumulations observe the following table of diet." He added, "This will also have a tendency to correct your wit."

Dr. McHenry was leery of milk, saying, "I forbid the free use of milk until your stomach recovers its natural powers. At present you would feel less uneasiness in digesting a pound of beef than a pint of milk."

"Water is the most general solvent," McHenry advised, "the kindliest dilutent, and the best assister in the process of digestion. I would, therefore, advise it for your table drink. When you indulge in wine let (it) be sparingly—never go beyond three glasses—but by no means every day."

Having no doubt whatsoever of the rightness of his prescription, McHenry noted,

> Should this table be strictly observed, it will soon become of little use, because you will have recovered that degree of health, which is compatible with the nature of your constitution. You will then be your own councellor in diet, for the man who has had ten years experience in eating and its consequences is a fool if he does not know how to choose his dishes better than his doctor.

But McHenry knew he could not count on strict obedience from his sick army friend; so he gave him some hangover pills: "In case you should fall into a debauch, you must next day have recourse to the pills. I hope however that you will not have recourse to them often. The great Paracelsus trusted to his pill to destroy the effects of intemperance, but he died (if I forget not) about the age of 30 notwithstanding his pill." On the other hand, Luigi Coronaro, the Venetian nobleman who ate only one egg a day after forty "was wiser. He trusted to an egg, and I think he lived to above 90."

It was a large and daring amphibious operation that Hamilton had planned and ordered when he met with d'Estaing at Black Point in July. There was time enough to bring it off only if all went smoothly. It did not. After a promising start in the last days of July, the French fleet closed in on Newport. General John Sullivan, Hamilton's friend who had everything a good general needed except good luck, marched a large command of more than 10,000 men bolstered by additional Continental regiments and New England militia south out of Providence to the Tiverton Ferry and the Sakonnet Passage. Then the whole grandiose operation began to fall apart.

A reinforced British fleet under Admiral Richard Howe hove into view up the sound before D'Estaing had fully disembarked his troops. Unready for action D'Estaing in haste reloaded his troops on their transports and put out to sea. A storm of hurricane proportions then struck both fleets. Fair weather found their ships widely scattered and badly damaged. Howe put back for New York, and d'Estaing sailed north to Boston to refit.

Now abandoned by d'Estaing, Sullivan's army found itself pinned down on the northern part of Newport Island by strong British units. A new American disaster loomed. "Should the expedition fail, thru' the abandonment of the French fleet," Washington wrote in Hamilton's prescient words, "the officers . . . will be apt to complain loudly. But prudence dictates that we should put the best face upon the matter and, to the world, attribute the removal to Boston to necessity" caused by the storm, not French timorousness. It was politic to avoid an open rupture with the great ally.

But in a fine Irish fury, Sullivan in general orders blasted the French: "the event will prove America able to procure by her own arms, which her allies refuse her in obtaining." Once more, John Glover's Marbleheaders shuttled expertly handled craft of all sorts across the water to salvage another beaten American command. Sullivan slunk back to the Sakonnet beaches. Newport's high Tory tone remained intact.

Lafayette, who with Greene was in command under Sullivan, took Sullivan's side against d'Estaing. Recriminations poured in on Washington. When d'Estaing's ships were finally repaired, the ration of his precious time reserved for the continent had run out, and he sailed for the West Indies.

Washington asked Hamilton to help patch things up by writing a delicately worded reproof to Sullivan: "The disagreement between the army under your command and the fleet," it ran, "has given me . . . singular uneasiness. The continent at large is concerned in our cordiality . . . In our conduct towards [the French] we should remember that they are a people old in war, very strict in military etiquette and apt to take fire where others scarcely seem warmed. Permit me to recommend in the most particular manner, the cultivation of harmony and good agreement." Hamilton helped write a similar soothing letter from Washington to d'Estaing.

Hamilton then wrote a semipublic letter of his own to Boudinot in Congress on September 8, 1778, that explained his own reading of the problem. He condemned Sullivan's tactless criticism of the French as "the summit of folly" and an "absurdity without parallel." He praised the courage of a French major, Louis Tousard, who had lost an arm in a solo charge against a British fieldpiece. Because this letter to the congressman issued from American headquarters, though it was not signed by the commander in chief, it diplomatically helped to calm the French, "a people old in war" and etiquette. Hamilton knew that Congress, if left its own head, far from reprimanding Sullivan for his indiscretion, would more likely applaud his skill at saving the situation, blame all on the French, and sympathize with his complaints at being left in the lurch by an easily frightened foreign ally. Hamilton's letter to Boudinot and his fulsome praise of the unfortunate Tousard resulted in Congress's avoiding all negatives. It first officially thanked Sullivan and his army and at the same time declared the French admiral and his officers "fully entitled to the regards of the friends of America."

With Hamilton's diplomatic retrieval of the alliance from military defeat by the British and denunciation by Sullivan's Irish, the first joint effort petered out. Hamilton continued to write documents for Washington—to Sullivan, to d'Estaing, and to officers seeking promotions—and to give orders for patrols. He wrote to Charles Pettit "to prevent any wood from being cut on Mr. Jay's farm." He wrote to an unnamed Westchester gentleman who owned a bearskin rug that was coveted by d'Estaing's aide, Andre Michel Victor, M. the marquis de Chouin, "the French Gentleman who lives at Head Quarters," that he had informed M. Chouin tactfully that "I thought it very improbable that you (the Westchester gentleman) should have any but what you wanted for your own use." This letter both forewarned Chouin and forearmed the Westchester gentleman by giving him a written defense against any high-handed official attempt of M. Chouin's to claim the bearskin rug as a trophy of war for his own.

With the failure of Sullivan's and d'Estaing's allied amphibious attack on Newport, the war quieted down again in the fall of 1778. The season for winter quarters for the army once more came round. As usual, Congress neglected to provide adequate supplies for the troops. With Christmas holidays ahead and their terms of enlistment, as usual, expiring, Washington decided that if the whole army were not huddled together in one encampment, as they had been at Valley Forge the winter before, but instead were scattered across the countryside in smaller units, they would be better able to supply themselves from local sources and would not be so dependent on supplies that had to be requisitioned for them by Congress and then hauled to them over long distances by almost nonexistent wagon transport. So he deployed the army for the winter in a series of encampments along a sort of zigzag arc that stretched from Danbury in Connecticut westward and southwesterly about 75 miles to Middlebrook and Elizabethtown in New Jersey west of Staten Island. If Congress refused or neglected to send supplies to units so widely scattered in the field and with such tenuous lines of communication to headquarters, local unit commanders could let their men help themselves to local produce. This is what poorly organized armies have always done since men became civilized enough to organize armies. The local unit commanders tell their troops, "Don't get caught looting."

This proved to be a much easier and healthier winter for the troops than the previous one at Valley Forge. Isolated outposts provisioned themselves well under such orders, but discipline and morale went slack. What made life so much pleasanter for the men in the army spoiled them for effective service to the country. The rigorous von Steuben regime the previous winter at Valley Forge had been worse for the men, but made for more effective service to the country.

Washington's encircling camps at least served to block Sir Henry Clinton's principal routes for armed sorties both northeastward into New England and westward across New Jersey to Pennsylvania and the south. The most vulnerable route of all, the one most inviting to attack, remained as always straight north up the broad Hudson River valley to Albany, Lake Champlain, and Canada to split the states in two. Astride it, Washington's cork in the bottle was the looming citadel 50 miles upriver at West Point. The largest part of the dwindling army was encamped just south of West Point at Fort Montgomery and about ten miles south at Stony Point and around Haverstraw Bay. From there troops could quickly move by river sloop or forced march to reinforce the West Point citadel or any other post in the defensive arc around New York City, which Sir Henry Clinton might choose to probe by an attack to test whether military force or will to fight still remained to back up the vociferous bleats and blasts that continued to issue against King George III and his ministers from the rebellious colonies.

Savage and bloody guerrillalike warfare went on in the areas that neither of the two organized armies controlled. Small craft of each side launched raids around Long Island Sound. In Great South Bay "the Whaleboat War" found small parties sculling back and forth to pounce on supplies they found desirable or people whom they found objectionable. Westchester County became a no-man's-land with roving bands raiding any objective weak enough to promise success and rich enough to hold loot. Off in western New York State, Joseph Brant and Walter Butler made murderous raids in which honors for savagery were about evenly shared between Indians and Tories. In these areas far from the main armies, the issue was not the sharply focused one of American colonists disputing the British imperialists' right of taxation without representation. Here the prevalence of a war elsewhere permitted the populace to dispute more traditional, age-old issues by cheaper, quicker, and more forceful methods than the limited remedies provided by the law courts in time of peace: large landholder versus small farmer, Indian versus settler, young versus old, and haves versus have-nots.

Putting away the sword for the winter, Washington kept up the illusion that his army's widely scattered encampments remained a powerful revolutionary force in being, the hammer of a united people's will, and so forth, mainly through a steady flow of communications from the ready, agile mind and pen of aides like Hamilton. He asked Major General Alexander McDougall for his opinion on the kind and number of ships necessary to destroy the enemy's naval force on Lake Ontario. He warmly congratulated Major General Philip Schuyler on his acquittal of charges arising out of the loss of Fort Ticonderoga and stated that a winter campaign was now impossible. He agreed that reduction of Niagara was important and had made plans for it.[1] He wrote Baron von Steuben, complimenting him on his letter challenging Major General Charles Lee to their duel.

Though being called the "earwig" of the general by Lee had enraged him, Hamilton was known by all to have Washington's ear. A stream of applicants plagued Hamilton with all manner of appeals. He turned few down flatly and usually managed to produce some kind of practical help. He also managed to infuse his letters with a touch of humorous bawdry or flippant cynicism or a note of compassionate understanding. No one was too unimportant for his intense, careful attention. He knew well how to rivet the interest of the recipient of his appeal on its purpose. No applicant was too humble or recipient too important for Hamilton to refrain from asking a favor for fear of "wasting a favor." The letter he wrote on behalf of an elderly parson to General "Mad Anthony" Wayne, the crusty old hero of Monmouth whose brave stand there had saved the day, is typical:

> Doctor W. Mendy is one of those characters that for its honesty, simplicity, and helplessness interests my humanity.
>
> He is exceedingly anxious to be in the Service, and, I believe, has been forced out of it not altogether by fair play. He is just what I should like for a military parson, except that he does not whore or drink. He will fight, and he will not insist upon your going to heaven whether you will or not. He tells me there is a vacancy in your Brigade. I should be really happy if, through your influence, he can fill it.

How could the crustiest old warrior resist what Hamilton asked then: "Pray take care of this good old man."

For an importunate old woman, he wrote an introduction to Governor Clinton:

> The bearer of this is an old woman, and, of course, the most troublesome animal in the world. She wants to go to New York. It was in vain we told her no inhabitant could be permitted by us to go within the enemy's lines without permission from the civil power. Old and decriped [sic] as she is, she made the tour of the family, and tried her blandishments upon each. . . . As she showed a disposition to remain with us till she carried her point with true female perserverance—as we are rather straightened in our quarters, and not one of the gentlemen of the family would agree to share his bed with her, and as you must at all events have the favor of a visit from her, I at last promised her a letter to you —the direct and sole end of which is to get rid of her.

Then the comradely flippancy ends with a sudden flash of human compassion for a person in trouble, even a troublesome person. There is an irresistible appeal in Hamilton's sweetly simple final sentence: "She seems to be in distress, and to have a claim upon our compassion."

Catharine Livingston's younger sister Susannah, or Suki, another daughter of the William Livingstons of Elizabethtown, with whom Hamilton had spent the winter six years before, wanted passes so that some cousins of hers in New York could pass back and forth through the lines to visit them in New Jersey, where her father was the governor. Only a year or so older than Hamilton, Suki had grown up to be another beauty like her older sister "Lady Kitty." Suki was not in distress like the poor old woman. She had strong claims on Hamilton and Washington for favor, but not on their compassion. Her appeal to Hamilton played on their old friendship:

Sir—The fond desire we all feel to be indulged with a sight of those who are dear to us, after a long detachment from them, has led my cousins Miss Van Horne Miss Clarkson, and Miss Browne to sollicit an interview with their Friends in Jersey. . . . I might urge many reasons to induce you to this, but your own humanity will tell you that the anxious solicitude of sisters to see their brothers after a tedious absence who have passed through various perils in our service, is of itself a sufficient one.

Susannah closed by wishing that after the war she and her friend Hamilton "may participate in the same social intercourses."

On March 18, 1779, with flippant, sweetly affectionate warmth from nearby Middlebrook, sister Suki's old friend Hamilton told her "No." He wrote:

I can hardly forgive an application to my *humanity*, to induce me to exert my influence in an affair, in which ladies are concerned; and especially when you are of the party. Had you appealed to my friendship or to my gallantry, it would have been irresistible. I should have thought myself bound to have set prudence and policy at defiance, and even to have attacked *windmills* in your Ladyship's service. I am not sure, but my imagination would have gone so far, as to have fancied New York an *inchanted castle*—the three ladies, so many fair damsels, ravished from their friends and held in captivity, by the *spells* of some wicked magician—General Clinton a huge giant placed as keeper of the gates, and myself a valorous knight, destined to be their champion and deliverer.

But when instead of availing yourself of so much better titles, you appealed to the cold general principle of humanity . . . I resolved to show you, that all the eloquence of your fine pen could not tempt our Fabius to do wrong . . . I put your letter into his hands and let it speak for itself. I knew indeed, this would expose his resolution to a severer trial than it could experience, in any other way. . . .

Washington had told Hamilton to tell her "No." But politely. Hamilton was not one to bore a smart girl like Susannah with such "stuff" as the kind of conventional polite expressions as might be used by the older generation. This called for a jibe at Washington's stuffiness:

This he desired me to tell you, though to be sure it was done in a different manner; interlarded with many assurances of his great desire to oblige you and of his regret that he could not do it in the present case, with a deal of stuff of the same kind; which I have too good an opinion of your understanding to repeat.

Hamilton added that there was no rule against her cousins' coming out to New Jersey and staying, instead of passing back through the lines, because "they will be an acquisition," provided that "the ladies on our side" are not made jealous and also providing, because New York City was infamous as a hotbed of Toryism, that Susannah's darling cousins "are not found guilty of treason."

As the commander in chief moved, taking with him in train the command headquarters of the war, Hamilton wrote for him every imaginable kind of order to generals, report to Congress, letter, requisition, and reproof. The datelines of his letters mark the place of the headquarters to be at White Plains in late summer of 1778, then up the Hudson at Fishkill, then Fredericksburg and Haverstraw, then, as autumn wears on, southeastward to Middlebrook and Elizabethtown, New Jersey, and finally, in time for Christmas and New Year, to Philadelphia and a month or more of appearances, both official and unofficial, before Congress and the committee on the army. There Washington and Hamilton pressed appeals for everything that the defense establishment absolutely had to have and, of course, a little more—to allow Congress political leeway to slash the usual "fat" from the defense budget to leave only the usual "muscle."

When Washington's headquarters reached Philadelphia that winter, Washington and Hamilton and the other members of the general's staff were swept into a round of lavish entertainments. Peggy Shippen and Benedict Arnold and Robert Morris and his wife led most of their revels. The beautiful Peggy Shippen was one suspect Tory who had not removed from Philadelphia to New York with Sir Henry Clinton's baggage trains as so many others had. She remained behind and now reigned over colonial and congressional society much as she had held sway over the British the winter before. Now her partner on the social rounds was the commanding general of the new occupying army, Major General Benedict Arnold, still stumping about on the short left leg he had almost lost first at Quebec in 1775 and again at Bemis Heights at Saratoga in 1777.

Arnold raged and stormed at Congress when it questioned his use of army funds for his private pleasures and went on enjoying life with Peggy as far as his wrath and his physical and psychic wounds permitted him to. He also began sending letters signed "Gustavus" through devious channels to Major John André, adjutant to Sir Henry Clinton, hinting strongly that a highly placed but unnamed American officer might offer "his services to the commander in chief of the British forces in any way that would most effectually restore the former government and destroy the then usurped authority of Congress, either by immediately joining the British army or cooperating on some concealed plan with Sir Henry Clinton."

The 38-year old Arnold recopied a love letter he had sent without success to another young beauty five months earlier and resent it to 18-year-old Peggy, saying that her "heavenly image is too deeply impressed ever to be effaced." He begged her to let her "heavenly bosom . . . expand with a sensation more soft, more tender than friendship." This time it worked. Peggy Shippen and Benedict Arnold were married April 8, 1779, and with large levees and displays of fine china and plate they began to entertain ever more lavishly. This caused many proper Philadelphia eyebrows to rise, because Arnold had always been hard up for money. Peggy and her general now seemed to seek out as intimates the wealthy Tories who had not evacuated with Clinton.

As he saw the great coaches and carriages and randoms of the rich rolling by and their polished dining tables stacked high with many times more succulent viands than bloated guests could down, Hamilton must often have thought of the empty stomachs, bleeding feet, and unrewarded bravery of the soldiers in the camps with whom he had been campaigning for so long. Like the lavish life style of the Benedict Arnolds, that of the Robert Morrises prompted Washington to rumble, "speculation, peculation, and an insatiable thirst for riches seem to have gotten the better of every other consideration, and almost of every order of men." By all outward tests, both Benedict Arnold and Robert Morris were in the first rank of the first order of such men, but there was a secret inward difference between the two. Unlike Arnold, Robert Morris did not offer his talents for sale to the British. Instead, he diverted his talent for speculation and thirst for riches to patriotic purposes.

Hamilton was, no doubt, quickly and often drawn into conversations with Robert Morris at one or another of the great houses in Philadelphia that winter. Nicholas Cruger's former countinghouse keeper and the great Philadelphia merchant prince would find in common much to talk about.

A large part of Hamilton's headquarters correspondence had consisted of letters to Congress begging for supplies and for money with which to pay the soldiers. The purchasing power of the currency fell lower and lower as he read the helpless replies of the congressional financiers. Raising money to fight a war had proved beyond the capabilities of the Continental Congress. The gentlemen from the sovereign states who were deputed to Congress had no power to levy taxes—all they could do was request the several states to furnish funds when needed. Congress resorted to a series of loans and—what amounted to the same thing—printing paper money. Congressmen were "struck by the charm of converting a piece of paper not worth a farthing into a 30 dollar bill."

But paper money without specie—gold or other reserves of intrinsic value —to back it up sooner or later declines in the value of what it will buy. The currency printed by the Continental Congress was no exception to this ancient rule and continuously fell. A paper dollar at the end of 1779 was worth two cents in real coin. Prices rose to astronomical figures; printing presses turned out more paper; prices soared higher; more paper was issued. "It's not worth a Continental!" still denotes worthlessness. If France had not made substantial loans to her impecunious ally, the American Revolution might have been the first to fail merely because it was financially bankrupt.

The states followed the example of Congress, and from the Merrimack to the Savannah local printing presses spilled out valueless paper money that, at first, most people accepted willingly enough. But as times grew darker, laws had to be passed to force acceptance. Where people refused it, boycotts, imprisonment, and riots of city and town mobs spread. The value of such paper money varied widely from state to state. Rhode Island notes might be worthless in Massachusetts while passing at a deep discount in Pennsylvania or Maryland. Prices of basic commodities jumped alarmingly, and people began to hoard against the next skyrocket jump in the average of consumer prices. Urban and rural interests clashed. Farmers withheld their produce to win higher prices from city consumers. Mechanics and laborers suffered too. Their pay scales rose, but their cost of living always jumped well ahead of each pay increase. Abigail Adams wrote husband, John: "The merchant scowls, the farmer growls and everyone seems wroth that he cannot grind his neighbor."

Speculators like Samuel Chase cornered supplies of shoes, clothes, and vital food supplies and sold out at huge profits while Washington's troops wrapped rags about their feet or wound quilts around their bodies in place of unobtainable breeches. Paper fortunes were made and lost and made again. Privateers swarmed out of every port and returned low in the water with decks and holds piled high with captured goods and chests of prize money. But such windfalls were of little benefit to the people of the country as a whole because Congress had no way of channeling captured specie into the national treasury. Hard money remained so scarce that a bonus of only ten dollars, paid in coin not paper money, had induced hundreds, perhaps thousands of men to stay beyond their enlistment terms in the winter of 1776–1777.

Always alert to the economic and political debility that sapped military strength, Hamilton, writing for Washington in May of 1779, rejected an ambitious plan of Congressman Gouverneur Morris for the coming campaign. "The rapid decay of our currency," Hamilton reminded Morris, "the extinction of public spirit, the increasing rapacity of the times, the want of harmony in our councils, the declining zeal of the people, the . . . distresses of the officers of the army . . . are symptoms . . . of a most alarming nature." At a time like this, a patriotic statesman like Gouverneur Morris could best aid the skeleton army by helping "to pacify party differences, to give fresh vigor to the springs of government, to inspire the people with confidence, and above all, to restore the credit of our currency."[2] Somehow a way must be found to harness the wealth, talents, energy, influence, and avarice of men like Robert Morris and Gouverneur Morris in the service of the revolutionary cause by a strong chain, one of specie, not paper; one might call it a golden chain.

Broadly speaking, military plans for 1779 called for keeping up a show of military activity but not exposing the cause to the risk of a crushing defeat by Clinton's main British army. But in order to keep the colonies from being split in two, it remained important above all else to keep the citadel up at West Point secure at all times. For the Americans it remained the most strategic position of all. So when the British seized the fort at Stony Point south of West Point on the same side of the Hudson and also the fort at Verplanck's on the east side of the river opposite Stony Point, the threat to West Point itself and Washington's whole continental strategy appeared to be grave.

For Washington, Hamilton wrote to Anthony Wayne, "the importance of Verplanck's and Stony Points to the enemy is too obvious to need explanation." An assault should be made "by . . . surprise in the night," on "the south flank of the works." This plan should be carried out by a stealthy bayonet attack. "Mad

Anthony" Wayne stormed and seized the fortress and its garrison the night of July 15–16, 1779. It was an exploit of derring-do that Hamilton envied and would like to have commanded himself. Hamilton's French friend, François Louis T. Fleury, the Marquis de Fleury, was the one who had struck the British flag. Hamilton wrote a commendation of his bravery to Congress.

Hamilton also prepared general orders for the parallel attack on Verplanck's Point, but this failed. Washington would soon abandon Stony Point, but in the meantime Congress and the public were furnished the thrill of the tale of "Mad Anthony" Wayne's brilliant stroke of American arms. Like Henry Lee's raid on the British outpost at Paulus Hook, now Jersey City, that same summer, the public relations impact far outweighed the military importance. The public's opinion that important victories had been won made the real, underlying Fabian policy of doing nothing politically possible. As Hamilton often said, what the public thought was happening was often more important than what actually happened.

It was important that the public receive good news. The British war office in London had decided to make the South the main theater of war that summer, hoping to find more Tory support there and at last begin to "fight Americans with Americans."

Down in Georgia, Sunbury, Augusta, and then Savannah fell to the British. An effort to retake Savannah on October 9, 1779, by an allied force of French troops from the French fleet under Comte d'Estaing and American troops under General Benjamin Lincoln and Count Casimir Pulaski failed miserably, with losses of over 800 men out of a total American strength of about 5,000. The British under General Augustine Prevost and Lieutenant Colonel Archibald Campbell held the old city with losses of only about 100. The following spring Charleston would fall, and the British would string a chain of forts all the way across the state to lop the two southernmost states from the former thirteen. Things were looking up for the enemy. Southern Tories who had been lying low began to heed the calls to join the British cause.

Washington expected that after his attack on Savannah, Comte d'Estaing would sail northward to join in another joint amphibious operation of French and American forces that would succeed where the one at Newport the year before had failed so miserably. As before, he sent Hamilton to meet d'Estaing and give him the orders for the joint operation. With Hamilton went Brigadier General Louis Le Beque du Portail, commandant of the Corps of Engineers, to help with planning.

By Washington's order of October 7, 1779, Hamilton was to "explain to you fully my ideas of the proposed cooperation; the means we shall be able to employ; the obstacles we shall have to encounter on our side; the plans which it may be proper to pursue and the measures which we are taking and may be taken by the enemy to counteract them. This will enable your Excellency to determine what you can with propriety undertake."

Once again, under the broad general outline contained in Washington's letter, discretionary authority was left entirely to Hamilton and his friend du Portail, the engineer, to work out directly with another commander in chief all of the tactics and troop dispositions and the thousand and one logistical details of what was to be the biggest joint allied amphibious operation of the war—and another one that could be decisive for either side. Hamilton's authority would permit him to divert the amphibious assault to Newport if he should wish to do so.

Concluding the letter of authorization, which Hamilton was bringing to d'Estaing, the man who could not tell a lie told a whopper: he would be bringing 25,000 effective men into the field! Never before had he had more than about 10,000 effective troops directly under his command in the field, and Congress was showing no signs of adding more men to the numbers it had given him before. A simpler explanation is that Washington often did not read, or glanced over only hastily, important papers that Hamilton wrote out for him to sign, and that Hamilton was improving the occasion.

Washington closed:

> I shall only add that if your Excellency will engage to cooperate with your whole naval and land force against the enemy's fleet and army at New York 'till the winter is so far advanced that the ice will make it impracticable to remain with yr. fleet any longer in the port, I will bring Twenty five thousand effective men into the field and will exert all the resources of the country in a vigorous and decided cooperation.

All military planning for a climactic joint allied amphibious operation against New York City twice as big as anything ever before attempted in the war was entrusted to Hamilton. Washington's prized personal reputation for veracity was laid on the line. All was lodged in the 22-year-old Hamilton's wisdom, judgment, tact, discretion—and ability to bluff—in dealing with the Comte d'Estaing.

Hamilton and du Portail set out in October to flag down d'Estaing's fleet from whatever out-of-the-way landfall along the coast their sails might first heave into view above the horizon, coming up from their misadventures at Savannah. The pair passed through Philadelphia and moved down to Lewes, Delaware, where they waited anxiously for a month. They then moved up to Great Egg Harbor, New Jersey, a few miles north of Cape May, but the sails of no great French men-of-war ever hove into their ken. James Duane, a New York delegate to Congress with whom Hamilton had struck up a friendship, had written him on September 16 that "Count d'Estaing appears to have the ball at his feet . . . I have, however, some distrust of the count's *planet*. His former ill luck on our coast has led me to think that he is no Felix." Duane read the stars aright. After the debacle at Savannah, d'Estaing had reembarked his ground troops and hauled anchor from the poorly sheltered harbors there. Casting a lingering, guilty glance northward over his shoulder toward chilly New York, Comte d'Estaing gave orders to his scurvy-racked helmsmen and crews to swing their helms and set sail on a southerly course to sunny Martinique, before another hurricane season and winter on its traces should again rack them up at sea. No one knows whether Washington's 1779 plan to attack New York with 25,000 men and d'Estaing's fleet and seaborne troops was to have been the supreme effort of the war to date, in which case it had aborted; or whether Hamilton and du Portail, by their wanderings along the coast looking for d'Estaing's fleet, had helped pin Clinton's troops down in New York all summer in lieu of 24,998 nonexistent troops. In the latter case, it had been Washington's most masterful feint of the war to date. At the end of 1779 the British evacuated Newport and moved their entire garrison back to New York.

While peering from time to time toward the horizon from Lewes, Delaware, and Great Egg Harbor, New Jersey, for d'Estaing's fleet, which never came, Hamilton had much time left on his hands to reflect on the shortcomings of Congress, the weakness of the economic underpinnings of the war effort, and the conversations he had carried on concerning these matters with Robert Morris and Gouverneur Morris and the other moneyed men in Philadelphia. When he returned to the winter encampment of the army at Morristown on December 1, 1779, he wrote a long and masterful letter to an influential public official, probably Robert Morris, recommending and explaining with easy assurance a number of solutions for the nation's economic problems. The letter contains in outline many of the later important measures of Hamilton's program as secretary of the treasury.

From the command center of a war that had dwindled into a war of attrition, Hamilton saw that sound financing was more important than victory in the field and just as elusive as d'Estaing. Congress had failed the country. The commander in chief of the army had eschewed the role of chief executive in the battle of the budget. Hamilton had no doubt of his own ability to take on this role when he wrote his remarkable letter. He did not sign his own name to it, but if the addressee wanted further explanations or further thoughts or a personal conference, "a letter directed to James Montague Esqr. lodged in the Post Office at Morristown will be a safe channel of any communication . . . and an immediate answer will be given." The finance minister of a nation can understand Hamilton's reasons for such secrecy better than an ordinary reader: public discussion of the subject of weakness in finances "adds false terrors to well founded apprehensions" by "exposing our weak sides to the popular eye."

Hamilton in this fine performance deploys all his mature powers. Facts are correct and impressively marshaled; reasoning, cogent; logic, sober. On the strength of it Hamilton qualifies as a close student of theories of government, an expert on political economy, and a practical executive capable of managing the most multifarious and complex enterprises.

The principal concern of the country, he begins, is the state of the currency: "In my opinion, all our speculations on this head have been founded in error." To fight a war requires money, and a money revenue is usually derived from taxation. But Congress has no power to tax, only the power to make requisitions upon sovereign states, which have it in their own discretion to comply or not. And even if Congress had such a power, the amounts that could be raised would be insufficient. The wealthiest nations of Europe, with the fullest recourse to taxes, always float foreign loans in time of war. The United States should adopt the same method.

"Taxes are limited," he goes on, "not only by the quantity of wealth in a state, but by the temper, habits, and genius of the people; all of which, in America, conspire to render them moderate. As to loans, men will not be prevailed upon to lend money to the public when there is a scarcity, and they can find a more profitable way of employing it otherwise. Hamilton has no illusions that the patriotism of the moneyed man involves self-sacrifice or the risk of loss of his stake.

Because income from taxes was not sufficient and because native men of wealth were too intent on profits to make risky loans to the state in response to appeals to patriotism, the only remedy was to borrow abroad at favorable interest rates. There was another argument in favor of foreign loans. The sums borrowed could be used to buy merchandise brought to this country for sale by the government at a profit. Such profits, in turn, would tend to support the currency.

From foreign loans Hamilton turns his attention to the problem of the farmers. They are largely self-sufficient and purchase few goods on which taxes are levied. They, therefore, contribute hardly at all to the support of the government. Yet they insist on and obtain high prices for their products. Farmers were no more public-spirited than "moneyed men" when money and profit were involved. High farm prices led to inflation and further diminution of the currency. To compel farmers to pay a fair share of taxes and at the same time keep food prices down, Hamilton advocated a tax on farmers in kind—a government levy of a percentage of the annual crops—a kind of gross income tax.

But even these two remedies, he realizes, cannot alone restore the currency to a sound level. "The only plan that can preserve the currency," he admitted, "is one that will make it the *immediate* interest of the moneyed men to cooperate with government in its support."

A government could be strong and its finances stable—only if moneyed men were given a financial stake in its durability. In other words, the private capital of the country must be induced to come to the support of the currency.

Some who have written about Hamilton have snatched the above passage, in which he calls for enlisting the "moneyed men" to "cooperate with government," out of its rather technical economic context and misread it as a sort of vague and general piece of social commentary. Such a misreading is made to serve as the foundation for woolly-headed generalizing to the effect that Hamilton favored the rich against the poor, was against "the people" and for "vested interests," and favored "haves" against "have-nots."

None of this is justified by this passage, which applies with equal force to merchant princes like Robert Morris, rich plantation owners like Jefferson and Schuyler, and small farmers who consume or barter their produce instead of selling it for taxable, inflatable cash.

To enlist the immediate cooperation of these "moneyed men," Hamilton proposed that a national bank be chartered for a test period of ten years. Once it was begun, he did not "suppose it will ever be discontinued." Part of its stock was to be paid for by a foreign loan of two million pounds; part, by a domestic subscription of two hundred million in Continental currency. Repayment of the investment at the end of the charter period was to be guaranteed by the government in Spanish dollars in the ratio of twenty to one. A Spanish dollar on November 17, 1779, about the time of his proposal, was worth thirty-eight and one-half Continental dollars. Hamilton's scheme would mean a profit to "the moneyed men" of about 100 percent on their original investment after ten years, without taking the effect of inflation into account. Moneyed men today, of course, seek a significantly higher return than this for putting their money at risk in an undeveloped country. On such an investment, the usual return to payout is considered to be three or four years.

From this bank Congress would be permitted to borrow two million annually at four percent; private borrowers would pay six percent. Certificates of bank stock would be negotiable and would circulate as additional currency. Half the stock and half the profits were to go to the government; the other half, to the private subscribers. The actual management of the bank was to be placed in a private board of trustees, chosen by the private owners, though it would be subject to inspection by a governmental board.

Hamilton concluded his proposal with an expression of confidence in its feasibility, because, he said, it "stands on the firm footing of public and private faith . . . it links the interest of the State in an intimate connection with those of the rich individuals belonging to it . . . it turns the wealth and influence of both into a commercial channel, for mutual benefit, which must afford advantages not to be estimated."

This was the first time that a bank with governmental assistance and, in part, for governmental purposes had been proposed in America though the idea itself was not original with Hamilton. He was modeling his institution on the existing Bank of England. Though he was, at present, busily prosecuting a war against the country where his model flourished, he made no secret of his admiration for the practical model of working governmental institutions for free men that he saw in operation there.

The fortunate result of Hamilton's insistence on, and eventual practical success in, bringing "moneyed men" to the support of the newly emerging, undeveloped country's economy was intensive capital investment and the rapid emergence of the strongest, economically soundest country with the highest general standard of living for all its people that had ever been seen anywhere on the face of the globe. Hamilton's letter to Robert Morris explained exactly how this could be brought about. He devoted much of the rest of his life to proving the truth of the insights contained in this letter.

This letter shows that Hamilton's basic economic ideas were fully developed by the time he was twenty-two. Ten years later, in 1790, and 20 years later, in 1800, his basic philosophy would remain remarkably consistent with the points he made in this letter of 1779. The national bank he put into effect when he became secretary of the treasury bore a marked resemblance to the one he had outlined here to Robert Morris. Later experience and state papers refined and ripened these concepts, but made few basic changes.

The importance to the United States of having had a Hamilton with the prescience to work to create an economic framework that would yoke the self-interest of the moneyed men to the development of the country can hardly be overemphasized. Countries rich in mineral resources, land, and people—Brazil, Argentina, Peru, and Indonesia are examples—whose economic prospects at the time of gaining political independence have appeared to be as bright or brighter than those of the thirteen American states appeared to be in 1779, have miserably failed to realize on early promise as rapidly, or to come close to matching America's fulfillment of economic potentialities, lacking a Hamilton at their beginnings.

It would have been and was easy enough for the moneyed men of Hamilton's time to invest their wealth securely abroad in Britain, Holland, Switzerland, or France, much as the few moneyed men of most developing countries do today. Hamilton's policies, not rhetoric of patriotism, served to induce many of the moneyed men of the states to invest their capital productively at home. If the economic strength of the American economy that grew out of Hamilton's proposals has seemed to weaken in recent years, it has weakened relatively less than the economies of most other free developed countries. When modern remedies for economic weaknesses like inflation are sought, many of them—the "old-time religion" for example—are little different from those that might have been recommended by Hamilton. A rueful wish that is often expressed by officials wise in matters of national economic management begins with the words, "If Hamilton were only here today—."

Of course, in 1779 Hamilton's proposal for a national bank was an impossible dream. The states were jealous of any centralized monetary institutions and would not consider accepting a bank that would deprive them of control of their own money. But if he had not started the process of education in 1779, his economic programs of a decade and more later would have had to start the process of public education that much later.

The only proposal in Hamilton's letter that Congress actually adopted was the one that called for requisitions in kind from the farmers, and it did not work. Farmers resisted it fiercely and hid their crops when the tax collectors came to requisition, and the yield proved small. Farming has always been a pursuit full of tax shelter possibilities.

John Laurens, Hamilton's closest friend among the aides, like Hamilton himself and von Steuben too, had grown restless in the servitude of aideship to an inactive Fabius Cunctator. He sought a command of troops in the line and at the end of 1778 had returned to his native South Carolina to see action in what would soon become the war's most active theater of combat.

Hamilton would have loved to go south with his friend and see some more combat with a line command too, but Washington would not hear of it. No line officerships were available because the troop levies of the southern states were exhausted, and there was no more enlisted manpower there left to be commanded. Laurens had the novel notion of raising battalions of slaves to hurl upon the British. No one would be better trained to do as they were ordered by their commanders in the cause of freedom than former Negro slaves. They would be promised freedom if they survived their soldiering in freedom's cause.

Another young Southerner who also wanted to see action was the studious, gawky James Monroe, who had just resigned his commission. On May 22, Hamilton furnished Monroe with a humorous introduction to John Laurens, writing Laurens that "Monroe is just setting out from Head Quarters and proposes to go in quest of adventures to the Southward. He seems to be as much of a knight errant as your worship; but as he is an honest fellow, I shall be glad he may find some employment, that will enable him to get knocked in the head in an honorable way. . . . He will relish your black scheme. . . . You know him to be a man of honor a sensible man and a soldier."

Hamilton added defensively, but mysteriously, "Business is plenty. I cannot enlarge. I wish ardently to hear of your success. Affectionately yours."

Later Hamilton would have violently disagreed with his own friendly sentiments expressed to Laurens that spring about James Monroe. From his early appraisal of the man he later came to suspect of exposing to the public his role in the Reynolds affair, Hamilton would withdraw the words "honor" and "honest" and strip all jesting from the jocular wish that "he get knocked in the head."

After the failure of unlucky General John Sullivan's expedition against the Indians in western New York State during the summer of 1779 and a mutiny of New Jersey troops in a protest against the possibility of being brutally massacred in what would be another essentially cosmetic attack to rally public opinion, Hamilton wrote for Washington a politic letter to the New Jersey officers, chiding mutiny as this "hasty and imprudent step." To Congress he wrote an explanation that his rebuke of the officers "had to be mild, when our situation is considered. The causes of discontent are too great and too general and the ties that bind the officers to the service too feeble to admit of rigor." Of this troop mutiny and all the other distressing events of this year, Hamilton poured out his deepest feelings in his affectionate letters to John Laurens. On September 9 his thoughts returned:

> I think your black scheme would be the best resource the situation of your country will admit. I wish its success, but my hopes are very feeble.

Like his friend Hamilton, Laurens despised the selfish arguments with which the institution of slavery was supported by the rich planters they knew in Virginia, South Carolina, and the West Indies. ". . . We have sunk the African[s] and their descendants below the standard of humanity," he lamented to his father Henry Laurens, "and almost render'd them incapable of that blessing which equal Heaven bestow'd upon us all." He conceded that slaves probably should be brought to freedom gradually, by "shades and degrees," and enrollment in the revolutionary army, with the promise of liberty to those who survived the service, would be a long step toward emancipation. After he joined Washington's staff, Laurens urged this proposal on his father not only in his capacity as president of Congress but as an individual slaveholder. John Laurens would even take his own family patrimony in the form of Negroes and contribute them to a black battalion in defense of South Carolina. The elder Laurens approved manumission in principle, but pointed out practical obstacles to his son's scheme. He even feared that, if precipitately put to the test, the proposal might "soil [his] excellent character with a charge of . . . Caprice." He "would not have heard the last jeer till the end of [his] life."

Hamilton was not a man to worry about jeers or charges of caprice, nor was he the man to let a good idea like Laurens's die for lack of pressure for adoption. His discouragement in September arose out of having labored earlier to bring it to fruition without success. In March he had written John Jay, who was then the president of Congress, the most powerful friend he knew who was in a position to do something useful about it. Hamilton was not simply expressing laudable sentiments; he sought the formal sanction of Congress for Laurens's plan and money to back it up: This was a plan to take two, three, or four battalions of slaves into Continental pay. He did not write to Jay out of a fatuous romantic conception of Negroes as corrupted noble savages, nor treat them as persons happy with their servile lot if given a kindly, smiling benign master whose overseers were chary with the whips. Growing up among slaves as a poor white boy in an aristocratic, white, slave-owning society, he knew the truth about slavery. His blunt realism is refreshingly free from the hypocrisy, cant, and self-serving piety that infects much writing of whites about blacks.

To Jay he wrote on March 14, 1779:

> I have not the least doubt that the negroes will make very excellent soldiers, with proper management. It is a maxim with some great military judges, that, with sensible officers, soldiers can hardly be too stupid. . . . I mention this because I have frequently heard it objected to the scheme of embodying negroes, that they are too stupid to make soldiers. This is so far from appearing to me a valid objection, that I think their want of cultivation (for their natural faculties are as good as ours), joined to that habit of subordination which they acquire from a life of servitude, will enable them sooner to become soldiers than our white inhabitants. Let officers be men of sense and sentiment; and the nearer the soldiers approach to machines, perhaps the better.

Hamilton, in his usual realistic way, recognized that the problem was not any intrinsic inferiority of Negroes themselves as a "race" or "class," but the conventional wisdom of the times and the wrongs to which white masters had subjected blacks. From his boyhood days on Nevis, St. Kitts, and St. Croix, Hamilton knew that Negroes shared common humanity with whites and that the conventional wisdom to the contrary was wrong. In their conversations, he had given Laurens the benefit of the same insight he expressed in the following paragraph of his remarkable letter to John Jay:

> I foresee that this project will have to combat much opposition from prejudice and self-interest. The contempt we have been taught to entertain for the blacks, makes us fancy many things that are founded neither in reason nor experience; and an unwillingness to part with property of so valuable a kind will furnish a thousand arguments to show the impracticability or pernicious tendency of a scheme which requires such a sacrifice. . . . An essential part of the plan is to give them their freedom with their muskets. This will secure their fidelity, animate their courage, and I believe will have a good influence upon those who remain, by opening a door to their emancipation. This circumstance, I confess, has no small weight in inducing me to wish the success of the project; for the dictates of humanity and true policy equally interest me in favor of this unfortunate class of men.

Hamilton's good offices with Jay helped produce not jeers, but an early success in Congress for Laurens's plan. Congress recommended that South Carolina and Georgia raise 3,000 Negro troops under white officers. The Continental Congress would recompense the masters for slaves thus serving and freed at the end of the war. After these forceful and effective efforts toward emancipation of slaves in March, by September Hamilton was explaining sadly to Laurens how difficult it was to bring Americans to see that emancipation of the slaves was clearly the right policy, regardless of economic consequences.

In his letter to Jay, Hamilton had said as forcefully as words can that Negroes are equal to whites, that no sound distinction between blacks and whites can be based on skin color, and that a principal reason why slaves have been kept in servitude, or said to be inferior to whites, was the greed of moneyed men, many of whom were large slave owners. Men of good will like Washington and Jefferson and Laurens's own father, who were owners of many slaves, did not favor his plan. "Prejudice and private interest will be antagonists too powerful for public spirit and public good," Hamilton wrote gloomily. Of Laurens's scheme, Hamilton added:

> The favourable events in Europe will probably be a casting weight against you. Your sanguine politicians, will think the war at the end and imagine we have nothing to do, but to sit down quietly and see the destruction of British power. Even the animated and persuasive eloquence of my young Demosthenes will not be able to rouse his countrymen from the lethargy of voluptuous indolence, or dissolve the fascinating character of self interest, to inspire them with the wisdom of legislators and with the natural enthusiasm of republicans!

Hamilton concluded with a remarkable prescript for Abraham Lincoln's comment on the kind of slavery into which the institution of chattel slavery chained slaves and master alike, by the golden chain of greed:

> Every hope of this kind my friend is an idle dream; every reflection will convince you that there is no virtue (in) America. That commerce which presided over the birth and education of these states has fitted their inhabitants for the chain, and that the only condition they sincerely desire is that it may be a golden one.

This passage is sometimes cited by anti-Hamilton writers to argue that Hamilton had no faith in America. Its real meaning is that Hamilton had high hopes for America, but that the lack of virtue of Americans, to wit, the greed that fitted them only for commerce and chained them to their slaves by a golden chain, would prevent their emancipation and keep America from fulfilling his highest hopes for it.

Hamilton was not the dupe or tool of the moneyed men. To him economic wealth gave them no special right to continue the institution of chattel slavery. It was a human wrong. Hamilton recognized the usefulness of yoking the moneyed men into his plans for accomplishing his overriding purpose of building an economically strong American union by appealing, if necessary, to their greed for profit, but he was no admirer of their greed and self-interest for its own sake, or of moneyed men for the sake of their money. Far from it. Few men of his time were more articulate critics of the materialism that is the defect of the useful virtues of moneyed men and a basic defect of the capitalist system, if not of human nature in general under all political and economic systems.

The prejudice and self-interest that Hamilton had foretold killed his and Laurens's plan in the South Carolina legislature. The lily white army remained too weak to keep the British from occupying the whole state in 1780. Southern whites had no intention of placing army muskets in the hands of blacks even to save their state. Laurens gave up his visionary plan and rejoined the all-white ranks of the Southern army. Too weak to defend their countrymen against the British, they remained strong enough to defend themselves and their slaves against emancipation from the golden chain of chattel slavery from which Hamilton and Laurens had hoped to free them eighty-five years before Lincoln.

11

ELIZABETH SCHUYLER COMES TO MORRISTOWN

BELIEVE ME, I AM LOVER IN EARNEST, THOUGH I DO NOT SPEAK OF
THE PERFECTIONS OF MY MISTRESS IN THE ENTHUSIASM OF CHIV-
ALRY.

—*To John Laurens, June 30, 1780*

The second summer of the grand alliance had produced nothing but another
French leave by the French fleet and a fib from Fabius. Hamilton and du Portail
rode back from where they had watched and waited at Great Egg Harbor to the
army regathering again on the Morristown plateau for another winter.

Colonel John Mitchell, the deputy quartermaster general at Philadelphia,
added a disappointing personal postscript to a letter to Hamilton. "Your Cloths
are not yet finished," he was sorry to say. "The Taylor has disappointed me but
promises to have them done in a day or two, when they shall be sent to you."
The wardrobe of a twenty-two-year-old lieutenant colonel of Washington's staff
needed replenishing for winter campaigning at headquarters. The ladies of Philadelphia and feminine visitors to camp under Martha Washington's chaperonage
would not waive their high standards of male fashion just because a war was
still supposed to be going on.

Besides Martha Washington, a remarkable omnium-gatherum of other la-dies and gentlemen found their way to the winter headquarters encampments —wives, daughters, sisters, journalists, French travelers, tourists, curiosity seekers, and prostitutes. Bored young officers were only too happy to arrange balls and dances, whisper sweet nothings to charming visitors like Susannah Livingston and her cousins in firelit parlors or the shadows of the huts or on cold, moonlit promenades. Young Hamilton outdistanced most of the officers in these endeavors, and his reputation as a gallant spread beyond the confines of camp.

A Tory newspaper wove his amatory repute and the proposed new American flag into a single snicker. "Mrs. Washington," it reported, "has a mottled tom-cat (which she calls, in a complimentary way, 'Hamilton') with thirteen yellow rings around its tail," and "His flaunting his tail suggested to the Congress the adop-tion of the same number of stripes for the rebel flag."

Conspiracies and rumors of conspiracies against the commander in chief had not ended with James Wilkinson's drunken mutterings in the Reading tavern that prematurely exposed the Conway cabal. Plotters now realized that it was not enough to win coconspirators in Congress and among discontented army officers; it was necessary to destroy Washington's standing with the common people, who clung to their trust in him through year after year of inaction, defeat, and growing congressional disillusionment with the fruits of the policy of "Let France do it" and "Let George do it."

Smythe's Journal charged Hamilton with doing what his old friend Hugh Knox's letters had taxed him with failing to do: writing a history of the American Revolution: "It is said little Hamilton, the poet and composer to the Lord Protec-tor Mr. Washington, is engaged upon a literary work which is intended to give posterity a true estimate of the present rebellion and its supporters."

The Tory journal was contemptuous of a nonexistent work in progress by a man it saw as no more than a frivolous pip-squeak, Martha's ring-tailed tomcat, and George's little lion. A literary reputation for dalliance with love letters and amorous pastorals would hardly make him an instrument equal to setting down what would have been one of the most precious historical documents in the entire American heritage, if it existed.

Hamilton was the target of new accusations aimed at discrediting Washing-ton through identification with his confidential aide. According to the rumors, Washington was secretly plotting to make himself a military dictator. Congress was to be done away with—jailed; perhaps murdered. All civil authority would end. How was this known? Through a statement of Alexander Hamilton. Ru-mors had it that while carousing in a Philadelphia tavern on his way back through the capital from the fruitless search for d'Estaing, the hotheaded aide had said, "it was high time for the people to rise, join General Washington, and turn congress out of doors."

The story spread like wildfire. People heard it, nodded gravely, and added other damning details. The idol of America was governed by his aide. Word of the scandalous remarks came back to Washington. An astute commander in chief would probably not be particularly upset by the attribution of such well-directed zeal to one of his young aides. Hamilton was merely performing one of the valuable functions of an aide, that of a lightning rod to draw off fire really aimed at the chief. Washington remained circuited out of the direct line of hostile charges made by dissident leftovers of Conway's cabal, partisans of Gates and Lee, other detractors, self-seekers, and ordinary people who were just plain disappointed with how badly everything was going up and down the line. But Hamilton could not see such calumny against his name in the same serene light as his chief, who, of course, could not publicly defend his indiscreet aide.

Hamilton set about running down the author of the calumny to challenge him to prove his words with pistols. He wrote sharp notes to two men who had been heard repeating the tale—William Dana and Colonel John Brooks of Massachusetts. Dana admitted his guilt in spreading the report, but offered in defense that he had had it from Brooks, who, in turn, had received it from the Reverend Dr. William Gordon. Dana added that, because Hamilton denied making the incriminating remarks, he would believe him. One more point won without going to the interview was added to Hamilton's life score as a grand master of the game of duels.

Hamilton wrote to the Reverend Dr. William Gordon, demanding to know from whom he had heard the story. Dr. Gordon had been born in England, leaned to the Tory side, and was just then engaged in writing his own history of the American Revolution with a strong Tory tilt and scant regard for truth. The reverend doctor would not divulge the name of his informer unless Hamilton agreed in advance not to give or accept a challenge to a duel.

Writing the Reverend Dr. Gordon from West Point September 5, 1779, Hamilton expressed some characteristic views on zeal, the reverend's understanding, duty, dueling, and fate: "It often happens, that our zeal is at variance with our understanding. Had it not been for this, you might have recollected, that we do not now live in the days of chivalry; and you would have judged your precautions, on the subject of duelling, at least, useless. The good sense of the present times has happily found out, that to prove your own innocence, or the malice of an accuser, the worst method, you can take, is to run him through the body, or shoot him through the head."

In his mordant way, Hamilton did not forbear to lay on the reverend the benefit of a religious insight: " 'Tis a good old maxim, to which we may safely adhere in most cases, that we ought to do our duty, and leave the rest to the care of heaven."

Hamilton, of course, could privately laugh at himself for sounding as fierce as all this sounds. He jokingly described what had happened in a postscript to his long letter of September 11, 1779, to John Laurens:

> Don't you think *The Cabal* have reported that I declared in a public house in Philadelphia that 'it was high time for the people to rise, join General Washington and turn Congress out of Doors.' I am running the rogues pretty hard. . . .
> You will remember the old Jesuit; he made us a visit at Fredericks-

From Mr. Daniels and the Grange *by Eric Sloane and Anthony Edward.*
Copyright © Funk & Wagnalls Publishing Company, Inc., 1968.

Following the presidential election of 1800, Hamilton withdrew from active political life to concentrate on personal matters, including the building and furnishing of a country residence set on 30 acres of land in upper Manhattan, called the Grange. The drawing shows the house and a commemorative statue of Hamilton that stands before it as they appear today in Harlem.

I

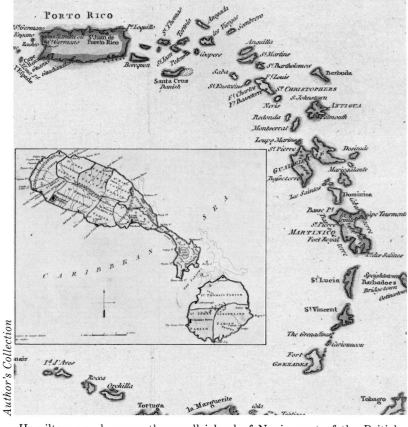

Hamilton was born on the small island of Nevis, part of the British Virgin Islands in the Leeward group of West Indies Islands. The large map is dated June 30, 1781; the inset is c. 1812.

The young Hamilton's first employer was a New York merchant, Nicholas Cruger, who ran a trading business in St. Croix.

Universitetsbiblioteket, Copenhagen

Universitetsbiblioteket, Copenhagen

By H.G. Beenfeldt: Rigsarkivet, Copenhagen

Cruger's shop was located at the lower end of the colonnaded building on King Street, at the center of the port of Christiansted (seen in the watercolor). As the newspaper advertisements suggest, Cruger's enterprise sold a variety of goods.

IV

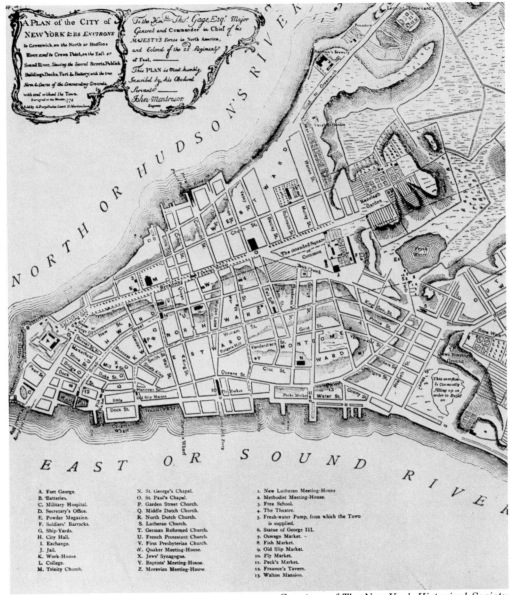

Courtesy of The New-York Historical Society

This map, executed in 1775, shows the City of New York and its environs when Hamilton arrived from St. Croix in 1773.

V

The smooth passage of Hamilton's early career was immeasurably aided by the friendship and support of the four men shown on these two pages (clockwise from left): Elias Boudinot, William Livingston, Myles Cooper, and Alexander McDougall.

Comte d'Estaing (right), Admiral of the French fleet, failed to provide expected naval support for Washington's troops in battles in Rhode Island and Georgia. As a newly elected member of the New York State Assembly in 1787, Hamilton found that his federalist philosophy brought him into conflict with the state's popular governor, George Clinton (above).

Attributed to Charles Shirreff:
Courtesy of the R.W. Norton
Art Gallery, Shreveport, La.

X

Pictorial Field-Book of the Revolution

While stationed at Washington's headquarters in Morristown, New Jersey, during the winter of 1779–80, Hamilton (miniature c. 1790) met and courted Elizabeth Schuyler. Their first meeting took place at a "dancing assembly" held at the Morristown home of General Schuyler (below).

Pictorial Field-Book of the Revolution

Attributed to Thomas McIleworth: Courtesy of The New-York Historical Society

General Philip Schuyler (right) and his wife, Catherine van Renssalaer (above), met with Hamilton in the spring of 1780 and accepted his proposal to marry their daughter Elizabeth.

By John Trumbull: Courtesy of The New-York Historical Society

A strong bond of friendship and affection developed between Hamilton and members of the Schuyler family. Elizabeth's two attractive and popular sisters, Angelica (left) and Cornelia (below), are shown in two charming portraits.

Century Magazine: Photo Frick Art Reference Library

By John Trumbull: Yale University Art Gallery

XIII

The Schuyler summer home, near Saratoga, New York, is seen in the drawing.

Hamilton returned to his military duties in New Windsor, New York, shortly after his marriage. A reception was given there in honor of the newlyweds (seen beneath the chandelier) by General and Mrs. Washington.

XIV

The climactic events in Benedict Arnold's (portrait top) plot to transfer military secrets to the British began with the landing of John André, the British agent, and Joshua Hett Smith, Arnold's representative, on the shore of the Hudson River near Haverstraw, New York. The pen-and-ink sketch of this scene (shown directly above) was drawn by André on the day before his execution.

XV

Miſs Margaret Shippen
daughter of Chief Justice Shippen

In the days between his arrest and execution Hamilton became well acquainted with Major André, whom he found to be a sympathetic and honorable figure caught in a desperate situation. In 1778 André sketched the portrait (top) of another person involved in the tragedy, Margaret Shippen, who a year later married Benedict Arnold. André drew the self-portrait (shown directly above) the day before his death.

XVI

burg and is writing the history of America. The proverb is verified—
There never was any mischief, but had a *priest* or woman at the bottom.
I doubt not subornation and every species of villainy will be made use
of to cover the villainy of the attack. I have written to Gordon and what
do you think is his answer?—he will give up his author if I will pledge
my honor 'neither to give nor accept a challenge, to cause it to be given
or accepted, nor to engage in any encounter that may produce a duel.'
Pleasant terms enough. I am first to be calumniated, and then, if my
calumniator takes it into his head, I am to bear a cudgelling from him
with christian patience and forbearance. . . . I have ridiculed the proposal, and insisted on the author, on the principle of *unconditional
submission.* What the Doctor's impudence will answer, I know not.

Hamilton in this letter to Laurens follows these good-natured mock heroics
with a quick reversal. His self-mockery is unexpected and full of quicksilver
charm, "On revising my work I find several strokes of the true School-boy
sublime. Pray let them pass and admire them, if you can." Publius the mime
extempore par excellence has just caught himself acting out a public pose in a
private letter to his most intimate friend. He knows that John Laurens is not
taken in by the public posturing.

Dr. Gordon's reply had evasively tried to cast suspicion on a third party in
demanding advance exculpation from a challenge. Hamilton accused Dr. Gordon
himself not some mysterious third party he was making a pretense of covering,
of being the real author of the slander—as indeed he was. Hamilton had broken
off his letter to Gordon saying, "I only lament that respect to myself obliges me
to confine the expression of my contempt to words."

Thereupon the reverend, the sanctity of his calling having forestalled Hamilton's challenge, took his accusation directly to Washington. The general replied
curtly that he had turned Dr. Gordon's complaint over to his lightning rod,
Hamilton. If Gordon had any charges to make "cognizable by a military tribunal,
you have only to signify your wish and the time you will be able to procure your
witnesses, and I shall proceed in it accordingly."

It cannot be said that nothing more was heard of the charge. Failure of
substantiation does not cancel out a false news story. Denial or discredit of the
charge never catches up with the charge itself. Dr. Gordon's accusations remain
a source often cited by critics as tending to prove that Hamilton was anti-
Congress, against the people, and a malignant influence on poor old Washington
who pushed him in the same misguided direction. That Hamilton often in his own
person and also as Publius made many harsher but well-justified charges against
Congress both in Philadelphia and elsewhere should be cited in his defense
against such oft repeated but insubstantial derogation.

During its second winter encampment at Morristown that winter of 1779–
1780, the army endured more suffering than any other winter of the war. For
cold and hunger it was worse than Valley Forge, at least for the enlisted men.

Amid the snows and sleets of what such sketchy records as exist permit to be
called the worst New Jersey winter of the eighteenth century, the soldiers toiled
at felling hardwood trees to hut themselves and to reconstruct Fort Nonsense
—so called because its site on Thimble Mountain above the town made it obvious
to all that it served no useful military purpose—except to give the men hard
work to do to keep their bodies warm. Of one brigade von Steuben said the men
"exhibited the most shocking picture of misery I have ever seen, scarce a man
having wherewithal to cover his nakedness, and a great number very bad with
the itch." Some had no blanket; as usual, shoes were all but unprocurable.
Nathanael Greene, the quartermaster general, declared, "there never was a
darker hour in American prospects than this. . . . Our treasury is dry and
magazines empty; how are we to support the war is beyond my conception.
Shillings cannot be had where pounds are wanting." Washington warned a
neglectful Congress that the army was on the point of breaking up, unburdening
himself on May 31, 1780, by Hamilton's hand to President Joseph Reed of
Pennsylvania: "All our . . . operations are at a stand and unless a system very
different . . . be immediately adopted throughout the states our affairs must soon
become desperate beyond the possibility of recovery. . . . Indeed I have almost
ceased to hope."

For the headquarters officers billeted in the Jacob Ford mansion or in nearby
houses, life was nothing like as rugged as it was for the enlisted men in their
self-constructed huts. The officers' quarters were comfortable, food was fairly
abundant, and visitors came and went. Martha Washington brought a touch of
domesticity with her from Virginia. Married officers' wives came for compassionate visits during the dull winter months and brought their daughters. Young
ladies busied themselves about the camp, dutifully doing good deeds for sick
enlisted men. In off duty hours they brightened the lives of young officers who
were perfectly healthy but who loved gazing into the lively eyes of these pretty
young angels of mercy. The horrors of war took time out for tender gallantries,
witty badinage, formal dinners, and agreeable balls.

Hamilton played a leading part on the headquarters scene. The cloth for his
new coat finally arrived from his tailor in Philadelphia. As well as any man, he
knew how to make the most of a girl with a well-turned ankle and a bright smile.
From helping Washington tell Joseph Reed all about the mess the national
economy and the budget of the defense department were in, he could shift with
easy grace—as only the really young really can—to brittle repartee and airy
nonsense without missing a beat, whether a drumbeat, a hoofbeat, or a heart-
beat.

Among other subjects of mastery, he was a master of toasts. The Chevalier
François de Chastellux, afterward marquis, came down from French headquarters in Rhode Island to look over American headquarters at Morristown. At
General Washington's midday table, he wrote, "*the toast* is but a kind of refrain
to the conversation." But "at dinner the toasts were more ceremonious: some
were for etiquette others were suggested by the General and named by whichever aide-de-camp was doing the honors. Every day one of them sits at the end

of the table beside the General in order to help serve all the dishes and dole out the bottles." Chastellux vividly remembered the easy informality with which Hamilton had called the toasts when his turn came: "that night the toasts were called by Colonel Hamilton and he gave them just as they occurred to him, haphazard and informally."

There was another charming custom. Chastellux reported that: "At the end of supper the guests were always asked to give a *sentiment*, that is, any woman to whom they may be attached by some sentiment, either love, friendship, or simple preference. This supper or conversation lasts from nine to eleven at night, always easy and agreeable." In the course of such distended dulias the names of the three lovely daughters of General Philip Schuyler, like three graces on parole from an enchanted castle up the Hudson, cannot have gone unmentioned.

By a letter of the previous April, Hamilton professed platonic love for his dearest friend John Laurens, now absent in South Carolina: "Cold in my profession, warm in my friendships, I wish, my dear Laurens, it might be in my power, by action rather than words, to convince you that I love you." With this letter he had enclosed to Laurens a letter smuggled out of New York from the mother of Martha Manning, the young bride Laurens had left in England with their infant daughter, neither of whom Laurens was ever to see again. The bearer of his letter, Hamilton adds, "speaks of a daughter of yours, well when she left England." Hamilton's own thoughts then concenter on other matters matrimonial.

"And now my Dear, as we are upon the subject of wife," he writes, "I empower and command you to get me one in Carolina. Such a wife as I want will, I know, be difficult to be found, but if you succeed, it will be the stronger proof of your zeal and dexterity. Take her description—she must be young, handsome (I lay most stress upon a good shape), sensible (a little learning will do), well-bred (but she must have an aversion to the word *ton*), chaste, and tender (I am an enthusiast in my notions of fidelity and fondness), of some good nature, a great deal of generosity (she must neither love money nor scolding, for I dislike equally a termagant and an economist). In politics I am indifferent what side she may be of. I think I have arguments that will easily convert her to mine. As to religion a moderate stock will satisfy me. She must believe in God and hate a saint."

Hamilton has never managed to live down the charge that he married the daughter of General Philip Schuyler of The Pastures in Albany and Catharine van Rensselaer Schuyler of Rensselaerwyck without loving her but to gain money, status, and power through the Schuyler connection. The indictment begins with the following two sentences with which Hamilton humorously polished off the above paragraph to his absent confidant: "But as to fortune, the larger stock of that the better. You know my temper and circumstances and will, therefore, pay special attention to this article in the treaty."

It is not easy to identify any Founding Father or Framer of the Constitution who married young who married a woman who failed to bring him a respectable stock of fortune of her own: Martha Custis Washington, Martha Wayles Jefferson, and Sarah Livingston Jay are ready examples. It is harder still to identify any Founder or Framer whose young wife brought with her to him as many qualifications that Hamilton placed ahead of her stock of fortune, as Elizabeth Schuyler would bring to him. It perhaps reveals more about the devil theory of American historical scholarship than it does about Hamilton that he seems to be the only one among the Founders and Framers of whom the fact of his marrying a popular beauty is framed as an indictment of his hunger for the money, status, and power she brought him too. Hamilton's humorous reference to a dream wife with a fortune in his letter to his friend hardly justifies the charge that he was a fortune hunter. No eighteenth-century man as candid and articulate as a Hamilton would omit from a lighthearted scheduling of an ideal South Carolina wife's endowments the advantages of fortune. Rather curiously, no mention at all is made in Hamilton's letter of the qualifications of his ideal wife's family, an item few eighteenth-century Southern gentlemen would omit from such a schedule.

For a man like Hamilton so often charged with vanity, as well as fortune hunting, it is remarkable how seldom in the vast outpouring of his writings Hamilton ever wrote about himself. To Laurens he unburdened himself as he never did to any other man or woman, and when he is on the subject of women and money with Laurens, his innermost yet still objectified thoughts are worth intercepting to read.

"Though I run no risk of going to Purgatory for my avarice," he adds, "yet as money is an essential ingredient to happiness in this world—as I have not much of my own and as I am very little calculated to get more either by my address or industry; it must needs be, that my wife, if I get one, bring at least a sufficiency to administer to her own extravagancies."

One other point, a rather technical one. Hamilton would have no invincible aversion to an inexperienced virgin who had to be taught. He thought of himself as a master quite willing to take some trouble to initiate an otherwise good wifely prospect into the arts of love:

> NB You will be pleased to recollect in your negotiations that I have no invincible antipathy to the *maidenly beauties* & that I am willing to take the *trouble* of them upon myself.

Hamilton was not the man to charge Laurens with finding him a wife and then leave the assignment simply dangling in the air. Laurens must follow through with practical steps to carry out the assignment. Hamilton suggests some in the following humorous fantastification:

> If you should not readily meet with a lady that you think answers my description you can only advertise in the public papers and doubtless you will hear of many competitors for most of the qualifications required, who will be glad to become candidates for such a prize as I am. To excite their emulation, it will be necessary for you to give an account

of the lover—his *size*, make, quality of mind and *body*, achievements, expectations, fortune, &c.

It is necessary to explain that Hamilton's usage of the word *make* did not then have the humorous denotation of a brand name (my make of car is Chevrolet) that two centuries have added to it. As he used the word, it meant "form" or "shape" or "build."

Forced into drawing a word picture of himself, Hamilton breaks off in boredom at a point just beyond the length of his nose. "In drawing my picture, you will no doubt be civil to your friend; mind you do justice to the length of my nose and don't forget, that I (———)."

The above sallies and what is broken off left unsaid catch Hamilton as close as he is ever found in the sudden lunges of thought, reconsidered reversals, tentative probes, and backtrackings of an unguarded moment of talking "off the top of his head." He lets his stream of consciousness ripple carelessly back across the features of his subject—the all but inexhaustible subject of wife:

> After reviewing what I have written, [he runs on] I am ready to ask myself what could have put it into my head to hazard this Jeu *de follie*. Do I want a wife? No—I have plagues enough without desiring to add to the number that *greatest of all;* and if I were silly enough to do it, I should take care how I employ a proxy. Did I mean to show my wit? If I did, I am sure I have missed my aim. Did I only intend to (frisk)? In this I have succeeded, but I have done more. I have gratified my feelings, by lengthening out the only kind of intercourse now in my power with my friend. Adieu.
> Yours.
>
> A. Hamilton

To intimates like Susannah Livingston and Laurens, Hamilton was mindful that well-meant but formal expressions of politeness used by Washington and other members of the older generation sounded like so much "stuff." He finished his letter off, "but not in the stile of ceremony":

> All the family send their love. In this join the General & Mrs. Washington & what is best, tis not in the stile of ceremony but sincerity.

By and large, she met his specifications. Except that in some eyes she might not have been quite as beautiful as he had specified, and her piety was deeper than he required. But so far as anyone knows, it was not so deep as ever to cause her to be a nuisance or fail to hate a saint.

The second daughter of Philip and Catharine van Renssalaer Schuyler, Elizabeth was born on August 9, 1757. She was therefore only seven months younger than Hamilton, a Lioness well starred for his Capricorn. Although not as much of a belle as her sister Angelica, who was one year older, or her sister Margarita, who was one year younger, she had a luster of her own that had been warm enough to attract the admiring attention of a gay young blade like Tench Tilghman four years earlier, when she had just turned 18.

Describing his first introduction to "Miss Betsy Schuyler, the General's 2d daughter," to his journal on August 22, 1775, Tilghman had commented: "I was prepossessed in favr of this young Lady the moment I saw her. A brunette with the most good-natured lively dark eyes that I ever saw, which threw a beam of good temper and benevolence over her whole Countenance. Mr. Livingston informed me that I was not mistaken in my Conjecture for that she was the finest tempered Girl in the World."

With Tilghman on a picnic trip to Cohoes Falls she had shrugged off his proferred hand and clambered unaided over rough rocky ground. She laughed at the other helpless girls who had to lean on strong male arms.

To Hamilton she brought with her to boot things he had not even thought of asking of the ideal wife he had requisitioned from Laurens. Politically, socially, militarily, and financially, there was no better family than hers to be found in the state of New York. Only three others might lay claim to equal distinction —the Van Rensselaers, of whom her mother was one; the Van Cortlandts, and the Livingstons. Philip Schuyler was of the fourth generation of Dutch patroons with vast holdings along the Mohawk River and in the region surrounding Albany. On his estates he dwelt like a feudal baron. His word was the law, and his will was supreme. From his fertile valleys came flax, and from his forests, prime lumber. He built his own ships and floated them down the Hudson for trade with England and the West Indies.

With the coming of the Revolution, unlike many men of his class and status, he chose the side of the colonies and rose rapidly to the rank of major general. He had commanded the northern forces in the first Canadian campaign. His proud air and aristocratic style, not to mention his military reverses, had made him many enemies, particularly among the small holders of New England. When Fort Ticonderoga fell to Burgoyne's sweep down Lake Champlain, they were quick to accuse him of incompetence and even disloyalty and caused him to be replaced by General Gates. In court-martial proceedings brought against him for the loss of Ticonderoga, he had been acquitted, but not without scars.

The time and place where Elizabeth Schuyler and Alexander Hamilton first met remain, like the dates of most of his rites of passage—his birth, his arrivals in Boston and New York, and his first meeting with Washington—the subjects of intense disagreement among authorities of various qualifications.

Alice Curtis Desmond, author of the novel *Alexander Hamilton's Wife, A Romance of the Hudson* (1953), whose credentials are weakest, places the date earliest, as far back as the spring of 1774; her guess is too charming to fail to record and, if read as a guess, will do no damage to history. Elizabeth was walking one day with her sisters, Angelica and Margarita, or Peggy, along Batteau Street in Manhattan near The Fields, when they passed a group of students from King's College. One of them was "a short slender youth with auburn hair and the rosy cheeks of a girl." He "stalked along, lost in thought, muttering to himself, such phrases as 'unjust tax on tea,' and 'tyranny of George the Third.' " Having herself grown up among Indians, Elizabeth had called him by an Indian name, "The Boy Who Talks to Himself."

Others have thought the two must have met, appropriately enough, at Elizabethtown, when she was visiting the William Livingstons there with her parents. In those days he would probably have had eyes only for her cousins Kitty Livingston and sister Suki.

It is quite possible, as still others have speculated, that Hamilton first met Elizabeth in early November of 1777 during the course of his delicate mission from Washington to obtain troops from General Gates to save Forts Mifflin and Mercer. Hamilton's most thorough recent biographer, Broadus Mitchell, thinks not, largely on the strength of a letter Hamilton wrote to his future mother-in-law in April 1780, in which he regrets that "I have not the happiness of a personal acquaintance with you. . . ." Professor Mitchell's thesis presupposes that if Hamilton had paid a call at The Pastures, the Schuyler mansion in Albany, in November of 1777, he would have had no occasion in 1780 to express regrets for lack of personal acquaintance. But if Hamilton had paid a visit to The Pastures that November, perhaps on the evening of the very day he had, according to Gates, purloined Thomas Conway's letter from Gates's office drawer, both Hamilton and Schuyler might well have been too preoccupied with secrecy to wish to involve Mrs. Schuyler in their meeting.

Of Philip Schuyler, Daniel Webster would later say, "He was second only to Washington in the service he rendered the American colonies." General Schuyler was one of Washington's closest friends, a comrade-in-arms from the French and Indian war, the former commander of the Northern Department. He had carefully planned the deadfalls in the forests and the elaborate fortifications at Old Saratoga that had done much to secure the victory there for which Gates took all the credit. Not only had he been ignominiously shorn of top command by pressure from New England, but just before the final battle, Burgoyne's soldiers had burned to the ground his country house or "plantation" at Old Saratoga (now Schuylerville) near the battlefield, forcing Schuyler and his family to move 40 miles back down river to their Albany mansion.

At the surrender ceremony held at the burned-out site of his Old Saratoga plantation, where only a small outbuilding and sawmill still standing had escaped Burgoyne's torch, "Gentleman Johnny" apologized to Schuyler. Schuyler had smilingly outgentlemanned Johnny by replying, "It did not much matter, for in war, it could not be otherwise." A few weeks later Philip Schuyler, gentleman that he was, took it upon himself to entertain "Gentleman Johnny" and about 20 of his staff officers as his guests in Albany at The Pastures in the days before Gates marched the lot of them off as prisoners to Boston.

As the man in Albany closest to Washington and with as good reason as Washington to be an enemy of Gates, General Schuyler was a friend on the scene well qualified to report to Hamilton on the progress of the Conway cabal at Gates's headquarters. It would have been unlike Hamilton if he had not improved his trip to Albany by making a secret visit to the Schuyler house. The nights he spent there are the only four nights of his mission for which he listed no out-of-pocket expenses for night lodgings on the expense account he and Captain Caleb Gibbs turned in after the trip.

Even if no reasons of state had brought Hamilton to The Pastures, his friend Robert Troup, knowing Hamilton, would know where to take his old college roommate to find not one, but three of the most beautiful girls in Albany, without necessarily troubling their mother with an unwelcome secret like knowledge of the local rendezvous of two of Gates's most notable enemies.

Of the Schuyler's eleven children, five daughters and three sons survived infancy. The youngest of the five beauteous sisters, Catharine van Rensselaer Schuyler, 21 years younger than Elizabeth, had no doubt about where and when Elizabeth and Alexander Hamilton first met. In her book *"A God-Child of Washington"*,—she was the godchild—she recalls as fact that in the afternoon of a pleasant fall day "shortly after the surrender of Burgoyne a young officer wearing the uniform of a member of Washington's military family, accompanied by an orderly, left the ferryboat," which then landed at a point in the river a little north of the present Arch Street. The young soldier and his orderly immediately mounted their horses and rode westward across Albany's communal pastures, where the British troops had often encamped, toward the Schuyler mansion. She remembered that his bearing "exhibited a natural, yet unassuming superiority; his features gave evidence of thought, intellectual strength and a determined mind." His "high expansive forehead, a nose of the Grecian mold, a dark bright eye, and the lines of a mouth expressing decision and courage completed the contour of a face never to be forgotten." She even had kind words for her future brother-in-law's horse: "The elegant horse he rode seemed conscious that he bore the weight of no common rider, and his proud step was the curbed motion of a blooded charger." The young hero "sat in the saddle with grace and ease, showing that he was master of himself and his horse. His figure of the middling height strongly framed and muscular, gave the appearance of strength and activity." He soon arrived at The Pastures. It was a foursquare, rose red, brick structure with two chimneys and a white wooden balustrade around dormer windows on the third floor with white shutters and trim and a center hall design typical of important Hudson Valley houses of the 1760s.[1] He dismounted, gave his horse's reins to his orderly and his card to a Schuyler servant who appeared at the door, and "in a few moments was welcomed by the General himself, to a mansion destined ever after to be linked with his future destiny." Gertrude Atherton, who studied the facts of Hamilton's life as carefully as anyone else, and the fancies as well, wrote a novel about him, *The Conqueror,* instead of a biography, in order to move beyond missing facts to psychological truths. She agreed with Washington's godchild that Elizabeth and Hamilton had first met that day at The Pastures three years before Elizabeth Schuyler came to Morristown in 1780. In their opinions this writer joins the ladies.

In 1777 Hamilton may have spoken only briefly with Elizabeth in the night, passing by her in the entrance hall to take counsel with her father and sparing little time to her and her older sister Angelica for his characteristic round of gallantries. Had they not first met on the occasion of such a tense, dramatic secret visit, it seems likely one or the other of them would have mentioned the date and circumstances of their first meeting at some later time in their romance. If they had met and broken the ice three years before Morristown, they could thus the more easily there reach the intimacy they did.

Having won acquittal at his trial for the loss of Fort Ticonderoga, Philip Schuyler had been elected to the Continental Congress. He progressed to Philadelphia with his wife and daughters and took his seat there. From Philadelphia, Elizabeth came up to Morristown to visit her aunt, Mrs. John Cochran, the wife of the surgeon general of the Middle Department. The Cochrans lived in a two-story frame house, which still stands about a quarter mile toward the village from the Jacob Ford mansion that served as Washington's headquarters.

Elizabeth and her sister Angelica helped out with volunteer work among the sick enlisted men in the wards near their encampment at Jockey Hollow. Soon their father was appointed to the congressional committee to oversee the army, and when the Schuylers came up from Philadelphia to oversee things—the army and their daughters as well—they stayed at the Cochrans' too. The Cochran house has been restored as a memorial to the Schuylers, and a portrait of Betsy graces the living room, which was the scene of her and Alexander's winter courtship.

Elizabeth and Angelica had brought with them a letter of introduction from their father to Baron von Steuben, "one of the most gallant men in camp." But the baron was away on an inspection tour when they arrived; so his dashing but diffident young aide, Captain Benjamin Walker, passed the letter along, sending regrets to the two young beauties that his own shabby coat and hat disqualified him from filling the office in place of the gruff old baron.

Even without such a formal introduction the Stirlings, the Mortons, the Boudinots, and others had houses in the neighborhood where two radiant young stars like Alexander and Elizabeth could hardly fail to swing into each other's orbits. All winter long there were private and public parties, subscription dances at the commissary storehouse, and sleigh rides between headquarters and all the country estates.

Elizabeth recalled that it was the Jacob Fords' young son Timothy who had brought her and her mother their first invitation to Washington's headquarters. The very first time she met Martha Washington, Elizabeth remembered, "she received us so kindly, kissing us both, for the general and papa were very warm friends." Still handsome at nearly fifty, Martha was quite short, "a plump little woman with dark brown eyes, her hair a little frosty and very plainly dressed for such a grand lady as I considered her. She wore a plain brown gown of homespun stuff, a large white neckerchief, a neat cap and her plain gold wedding ring which she had worn for more than twenty years. Her graces and cheerful manner delighted us." According to Elizabeth, Martha Washington's thoughts were then much on the poor soldiers who had suffered such hardship during the dreadful winter. She expressed her joy at the approach of a milder springtime.

From life models are made the best reproductions. It tells much about Elizabeth Schuyler Hamilton that in 1849 at the age of 92, seventy years after that first Morristown meeting with Martha Washington, she would still recall and write down the above account of the scene and then add of her hostess that "She was always my ideal of a true woman."

Elizabeth referred matter-of-factly to "Mr. Hamilton" as Washington's secretary at the time. She made no special remark of having first met him on her first visit to headquarters.

Early in his courtship of Betsy, in February 1780, Hamilton wrote to her sister Margarita, or Peggy, as she was called, who was one year younger, "I venture to tell you in confidence," probably confident that she would tell her sister instantly, "that by some odd contrivance or other your sister has found out the secret of interesting me in everything that concerns her; and though I have not the happiness of a personal acquaintance with you, I have had the good fortune to see several very pretty pictures of your person and mind which have inspired me with a more than common partiality for both. Among others, your sister carries a beautiful copy constantly about her drawn by herself, of which she has two or three times favored me with a sight."

For the most part, Hamilton's letter is the familiar one of a literate man in love burning to tell someone else of his love who will tell his love. But there is also an overtone that seems to go beyond merely ingratiating himself with a future sister-in-law.

The pictures of Margarita that Betsy had drawn for him, of her person in pencil and of her mind in words, had excited Hamilton's interest in her too, thus testifying to Margarita's beauty; Betsy's ability to sketch vividly with both pencil and language; and Hamilton's sensitivity to art and beauty, women in general, and Schuyler daughters in particular.

To Margarita he continued, "You will no doubt admit it as a full proof of my frankness and good opinion of you, that I with so little ceremony introduce myself to your acquaintance and at the first step make you my confidante. But I hope I run no risk of its being thought an impeachment of my discretion. Phlegmatists may say I take too great a license at first setting out, and witlings may sneer and wonder how a man the least acquainted with the world should show so great facility in his confidences—to a lady. But the idea I have formed of your character places it in my estimation above the insipid maxims of the former, and the ill-natured jibes of the latter."

More by the thrust of his words than by direct affirmation, he flatters her by seeming to disagree with the conventional view that a woman cannot keep a secret. Though he is a man of the world, he thinks those who hold the conventional view are "phlegmatists and witlings." He addresses Peggy with mature respect yet with enough ardor not to let her forget that even though they are future in-laws, there remains an interesting difference between their sexes.

Hamilton goes on to describe his feelings for Betsy: "I have already confessed the influence your sister has over me—yet notwithstanding this, I have some things of a very very serious and heinous nature to lay to her charge. — She is most unmercifully handsome"—She thus satisfies one of his stipulations to Laurens—"And so perverse that she has none of those pretty affectations which are the prerogatives of beauty." The conviction that he thinks of her, for all practical purposes at least, as a beauty could hardly be better affirmed. Hamilton would not have thought he could fool her sister on the matter, nor wish to be thought a fool by Peggy by so strongly affirming a fact that was plainly otherwise. If an authority of Hamilton's standing thought she was a beauty and said so, it seems rather silly that a number of later writers have made much of the claim that she was not. He goes on: "Her good sense is destitute of that happy mixture of vanity and ostentation which would make it conspicuous to the whole tribe of fools and foplings as well as to men of understanding so that as the matter now stands it is little known beyond the circle of these. She has good nature, affability and vivacity unembellished with that charming frivolousness which is justly deemed one of the principal accomplishments of a *belle*. . . ."

Peggy's own reputation as *belle* full of the charming frivolousness that Betsy lacked was not unknown to Hamilton.

"In short she is so strange a creature," he writes, "that she possesses all the beauties, virtues and graces of her sex without any of these amiable defects, which from their general prevalence are esteemed by connoisseurs necessary shades in the character of a fine woman. The most determined adversaries of Hymen can find in her no pretext for their hostility, and there are several of my friends, philosophers who railed at love as a weakness, men of the world who laughed at it as a phantasie whom she has presumptuously and daringly compelled to acknowledge its power and surrender at discretion. I can the better assert the truth of this, as I am myself of the number." Like a true benedict, Hamilton has tried to resist, but it is no use.

"She has had the address to overset all the wise resolutions I had been framing for more than four years past, and from a rational sort of being and a professed condemner of Cupid has in a trice metamorphosed me into the veriest inamorato. . . ." The scoffing benedict has fallen in love with her.

Thinking of his friend Tench Tilghman, who had, after all, known and admired Betsy first, Hamilton wrote, "I should never have done, were I to attempt to give you a catalogue of the whole—of all the hearts she has vanquished—of all the heads she has turned—of all the philosophers she has unmade, or of all the standards she has fixed to the great prejudice of the general service of the female world."

Notwithstanding his fixation on her sister, Hamilton was also opening wide his arms in welcome to a charmingly frivolous belle like Peggy. To the Schuyler sister theme that he already knew and loved so well she would add some exciting new variations:

It is essential to the safety of the state, and to the tranquility of the army—that one of two things take place, either that she be immediately removed from our neighborhood, or that some other nymph qualified to maintain an equal sway come into it. By dividing her empire it will be weakened and she will be much less dangerous when she has a rival equal in charms to dispute the prize with her. I solicit your aid.

Peggy must come to Morristown too.

Nothing in his letter rules out, and much invites, an affair with a belle of a Schuyler sister like Peggy whenever she might arrive. It was only a question of time before he would fall under the still more powerful spell of the third variation on the Schuyler sister theme, Betsy's sister Angelica, who was one year older than Betsy.

Another's description that seemed to fit Betsy well was contained in a poem written for Hamilton by his friend Colonel Samuel Blatchley Webb in honor of his latest romance:

> Within the circle of her eye;
> A thousand sweet delusions lye;
> Within the oval of her face
> Love's wily charms and winning grace,
> Besides in all she does or says
> An air that even Stoics praise.
> . . . .
> 'Tis true her eye is well enough,
> But why of such superior stuff;
> Why call it better than her neighbors,
> Because more hearts may crown its labors.
> Talk as you please, of grace and wiles
> Of lips and looks and winning smiles,
> She's but,—Sweet Sir, nay do not fret,
> She's but—a beautiful brunette.

That Sweet Sir, the fickle Hamilton, whom Webb apostrophizes, is obviously now far gone on his favorite type, a beautiful oval-faced brunette, never to stray again, or "bow to another shrine,"

> What, bend the stubborn knee at last,
> Confess the days of wisdom past,
> He that could bow to every shrine,
> And swear the last the most divine.

Before, the Sweet Sir had but to whistle and many would bow, but now he has finally settled on one—

> Like Hudibras, all subjects bend,
> Has Ovid at his finger's end;
> Could whistle ev'ry tune of love,

(You'd think him Ovid's self or Jove)
Now feels the inexorable dart
And Yields Cornelia all his heart!

Cornelia? In January of 1780? What about Betsy?

Is Webb merely using the name of Cornelia in a classical manner as a figurative stand in for Betsy and to avoid premature identification? One might wish so, but such is not the case. Hamilton seems to have been dividing his time between Betsy and a real Cornelia, the latter perhaps as a stand in for a second or third Schuyler sister.

On the last page of the manuscript of his poem, Colonel Webb writes, "To Lt. Col. Hamilton on his being attentive to C. Lott, Jany 1780." Cornelia Lott was the daughter of Abraham Lott of Beverwyck, near Morristown, a house that Washington had used briefly as a headquarters in 1777. She was apparently a long time recovering from the memory of Ovid's fingers and Jove's whistle. It was seven years before she got over her "Sweet Sir" and finally married Comfort Sands and settled down, perhaps with "an air that even Stoics praise."

One wintry evening Hamilton was not sure whether it would be he or Tench Tilghman who would be called on to work late into the night with Washington, planning future campaigns, or on some other campaign, amourous or military. Without thought of irony at the balls and dances that winter, over and over again the fiddlers would play the most popular tune of the year, *A Successful Campaign.* This could hardly allude to army actions of the recent past. Hamilton had received an invitation for the same evening to come to a party bringing both Elizabeth Schuyler and Kitty Livingston. It held out bright promise for sweet future passages of arms. So he wrote to both of them a joint, simultaneous declination and acceptance, offered them Tench Tilghman as a consolation prize, a gallant classical allusion that would flatter their brains, and kept all possible options open for himself, in the following masterpiece of amorous ambiguity that he sent to them in January 1780:[2]

Col. Hamilton's compliments to Miss Livingston and Miss Schuyler. He is sorry to inform them that his zeal for their service make him forget that he is so bad a Charioteer as hardly to dare to trust himself with so precious a charge; though if he were only to consult his own wishes like Phaeton he would assemble the chariot of the sun, if he were sure of experiencing the same fate. Col Tilghman offers himself a volunteer. Col Hamilton is unwilling to lose the pleasure of the party; but one or the other will have the honor to attend the ladies.

For aught that appears in this letter, it covered the fact that Cornelia Lott had lighted a candle in the window at Beverwyck, waiting for him to keep a late date with her that same night.

Hamilton had discarded another mistress, one Polly, whose surname is concealed from history. Tench Tilghman realized that he had lost out with Betsy to Hamilton, and not only that; Polly, Hamilton's former mistress, was too young for him to take over as a consolation prize.

"Alas poor polly!" Tilghman writes his brother William. "Hamilton is a gone man, and I am too old for his substitute—She [Polly] had better look out for herself and not put her trust in Man. She need not be jealous of the little Saint —[Betsy] She [Polly] is gone to Pennsylvania and has no other impressions than those of regard for a very pretty good-tempered girl, the daughter of one of my most valuable acquaintances." Apparently Polly's passion for Hamilton had been intense, and his new love for Betsy had been a secret well kept from her, or Tilghman would not have been so much concerned at the shock to her hopes when news of Hamilton's and Betsy's engagement leaked out.

James McHenry is more likely than Tilghman to have given the toast or the "sentiment" at the general's table when word of the engagement became official. On March 18 he wrote Hamilton, who was away in Perth Amboy working on prisoner exchanges:

> The family since your departure have given hourly proofs of a growing weakness. Example [such as Hamilton's] is infectious. For such a predominance is beauty establishing over their hearts, that should things continue to wear as sweet an aspect as they are now beheld in, I shall be the only person left, of the whole household to support the dignity of human nature.

Raillery aside, McHenry adds, "God bless both you, and your weakness, and preserve me your sincere friend."

Hamilton pursued his lovemaking with the same intensity that he pursued everything else. His addresses to Betsy and her parents occupied vast commitments of time, paper, ink, and blotting sand. His letters to her vary greatly in their nature—some are ardent and full of extravagant language and graceful romantic conceits characteristic of the late eighteenth century; others tell her of the momentous historical events of the times as they swirl past his eyes at the side of his chief at command headquarters. He does not write to her as if he thought of her as a self-centered doll incapable of joining him in his excitement at seeing these great events unfold, even though it might a good deal divert him from thinking of her.

Early in March 1780, still in Amboy on one of the endless prisoner exchange missions, Hamilton found that the proceedings, as before, depended more on the quantity of wine downed than the merits of the case. The three Schuyler sisters, Betsy, Angelica, and Peggy, as he wrote Betsy on Thursday afternoon, March 17, were "the daily toasts at our table, and for this *honor* you are chiefly indebted to the British gentlemen; though, as I am always thinking of you, this naturally brings Peggy to my mind, who is generally my toast."

Hamilton was not impressed with the personal qualities of his British counterparts:

I have learned a secret by coming down here. Our interview is attended with a good deal of sociability and good humor, but I begin, notwithstanding, to be tired of our British friends. They do their best to be agreeable and are particularly civil to me, but, after all, they are a compound of grimace and jargon and, out of a certain fashionable routine, are as dull and empty as any gentlemen need to be. One of their principal excellencies consist in swallowing a large quantity of wine every day, and in this I am so unfortunate that I shall make no sort of figure with them.

The short absence from Eliza in Perth Amboy with the "grimace and jargon" of his British friends spurred Hamilton's ardor. Back in Morristown, writing her when she is away, he is less wittily impersonal, more intense and ardent:

I should regret the time already lost in inactivity if it did not bring us nearer to that sweet reunion for which we so ardently wish. I never look forward to that period without sensations I cannot describe.

I love you more and more every hour. The sweet softness and delicacy of your mind and manners, the elevation of your sentiments, the real goodness of your heart—its tenderness to me—the beauties of your face and person—your unpretending good sense and that innocent simplicity and frankness which pervade your actions, all these appear to be with increasing amiableness, and place you in my estimation above all the rest of your sex.

He proposed formally to her, was accepted, and sought an interview with General Schuyler. The general welcomed him, knowing him well as Washington's emissary to their common enemy General Gates and as Washington's articulate young headquarters intelligencer from the days when Schuyler was a member of the New York Provincial Congress and received the reports Hamilton sent to it as army correspondent.

A generation apart in ages, both men had a similar cast of mind. Both favored a strong, forceful government and the maintenance of Washington's command against the machinations of the Gates faction in Congress; both shared a common general disapproval of the slackness of the times. Both were military men, veterans of warfare in the line, and knew how to manhandle big guns across rough country; they had known staff responsibilities as well. In Congress, Schuyler was one of the best-informed members on fiscal matters. He was the author of a 1779 pamphlet entitled *Causes of Depreciation of the Continental Currency*. He had written, "I wish I could say that there was one member of Congress adequate to the important business of Finance," and informally appointed himself to fill the vacancy. He would have read and discussed with pleasure the proposals Hamilton had made in his masterful letter of December 1779 written to Robert Morris over the pseudonym of James Montague, Esq.

From the most strategic part of the most strategically situated of all the thirteen states, with his wealth and connections, Schuyler was an important figure in state and national politics. An alliance with him through the close ties of marriage could be of inestimable benefit to an ambitious young man. A patrician patroon like Schuyler would easily sniff out an arriviste adventurer when he saw one. But the proud, old, aristocratic father not only raised no objections to his beloved daughter's marriage to a moneyless Creole bastard from somewhere down in the Lesser Antilles, he even extended him his warmest paternal blessings. Only when the ardent swain asked for an immediate wedding did the general put down his gouty foot. Mrs. Schuyler had returned to Albany, and he must write to her for her approval.

On April 8 General Schuyler reported to Hamilton that "yesterday I had the pleasure to receive a line from Mrs. Schuyler in answer to mine on the subject of the one you delivered me at Morristown. She consents to comply with your and her daughter's wishes." But this related only to their engagement. As for Hamilton's insistence on an immediate marriage, "you will see the Impropriety of taking the *dernier pas* where you are. Mrs. Schuyler did not see her Eldest daughter married. That also gave me pain, and we wish not to Experience it a second time."

Angelica, the eldest and most brilliant of the Schuyler daughters, had just eloped with an unknown Englishman who had suddenly appeared in the colonies under the name of John Carter, reportedly fleeing from a scandal in England caused by killing a man in a duel.

Philip Schuyler had been furious. "Carter and my eldest daughter ran off and were married on the twenty-third of July," 1779, he growled to William Duer. "Unacquainted with his family connections and situation in life the matter was exceeding disagreeable and I signified it to them."

John Carter was, in fact, John Barker Church, and when word eventually came after the war that the man he had supposedly killed in the duel remained alive and well, he resumed his own name. With the charming, nay irresistible Angelica as his wife, and Schuyler's belated blessing, he would become commissary supplier to Admiral Rochambeau and General Jeremiah Wadsworth; accumulate a large fortune; later return to England, accompanied by his wife; win election to the British Parliament; and live abroad off American war profiteering and other profitable enterprises in the most lavish imaginable style.

Hamilton bowed to the insistence of Betsy's parents on a longer engagement, and the wedding was postponed until December, when it could be solemnized in fitting style at a lavish ceremony at The Pastures.

Hamilton thanks Catharine Schuyler for her consent to their marriage by his letter of April 14, 1780:

> I leave it to my conduct rather than expressions to testify the sincerity of my affection for her, the respect I have for her parents, the desire I shall always feel to justify their confidence and merit their friendship.
>
> May I hope Madam, you will not consider it as mere profession, when I add, that though I have not the happiness of a personal acquaint-

ance with you, I am no stranger to the qualities which distinguish your character. . . ."

Despite his own "family connections" that could hardly have been more suspect, Hamilton was welcomed into the proud old family.

Hamilton's friend the Marquis de Fleury, a hero of Stony Point second only to "Mad Anthony" Wayne, congratulated Hamilton on making a fine match with sure Gallic understanding of the meaning of such an alliance:

Mrs. Carter [Angelica] told me you was soon to be married to her sister, Miss Betsy Schuyler. I congratulate you hearty on that conquest, for many Reasons: the first that you will get all that family's interest, and that a man of your abilities wants a Little influence to do good to his country. The second that you, will be in a very easy situation, and happiness is not to be found without a large Estate. The third (this one is not very certain) that we shall be or connected or neighbors. For you must know, that I am an admirer of Miss Peggy, your sister-in-law; and that if she will not have me; Mr. Duane may be coax'd into the measure of giving me his daughter; this little jest is between you and I. It would be very improper for anybody else.

When word of their engagement reached Kitty Livingston, whom both Betsy and Alexander had known so well, Kitty wrote Betsy on June 20 from Lebanon full of long lingering thoughts about her cousin's fiancé, whom she had known for so much longer:

If you should see the Col. present my compliments and tell him I hope to see him on the banks of Hudson near Clermont where Flora shall mix his Laurels with Flowers and Pomona heap him with fruit.

As the long year of their engagement wore on, Hamilton wrote Betsy on July 6, 1780, from Colonel Dey's house in Bergen County, New Jersey: "Here we are in a house of great hospitality—in a county of plenty." There is "a buxom girl under the same roof—pleasing expectations of a successful campaign—and everything to make a soldier happy, who is not in love and absent from his mistress."

In the fact that he writes her so openly of the "buxom girl under the same roof" is the strongest proof of his openness with and fidelity to Betsy now as his only lover and mistress.

A rich coquette who insists on waiting until after the solemn rites before becoming her fiancé's lover is not likely to receive letters from him describing with such disarming candor buxom girls so conveniently positioned.

Naturally, Hamilton cannot tell Betsy that he is happy though so far away from her, but his sufferings through her absence are not of the most serious order: "I cannot be happy; but it is a maxim of my life to enjoy the present good with the highest relish. . . ."

There is, after all, that buxom girl under the same roof.

He will do his best when he is with her next ". . . to soften the present evil by a hope of future good. I alleviate the pain of absence by looking forward to that delightful period which gives us to each other forever; and my imagination serves up such a feast of pleasure as almost makes me forget the deprivation I now experience."

He continues: ". . . Assure yourself my love that you are seldom a moment absent from my mind, that I think of you constantly." Indeed "I am never happier than when I can engage Meade in some solitary walk to join me in reciprocating the praises of his widow and my Betsy."

Being apart from her now is the more painful because when they are together, he has become her "lover in earnest." He writes:

> I have told you, and I told you truly, that I love you too much. You engross my thoughts too entirely to allow me to think of anything else. You not only employ my mind all day, but you intrude on my sleep. I meet you in every dream, and when I wake I cannot close my eyes for ruminating on your sweetness.

His "nut-brown maid" has changed, or worn down, a hardy soldier to a "puny lover" from loving:

> 'Tis a pretty story indeed that I am to be thus monopolized by a little *nut-brown maid* like you, and from a soldier metamorphosed into a puny lover. I believe in my soul you are an enchantress. I have tried in vain, if not to break, at least to weaken the charm, but you maintain your empire. In spite of all my efforts, my heart clings to you with increased attachment. To drop figures, my lovely girl, you become dearer to me every moment. I am more and more unhappy and impatient under the hard necessity that keeps me from you.

The love affair of the twenty-three-year-olds was full of warmth, humor, and trust; confiding and passionate. It probably began nearer the beginning than the end of their long year's engagement.

At the end of a letter to John Laurens written from Ramapo, New Jersey, on June 30, 1780, following long paragraphs commenting upon the surrender of Charleston to the British, at which Laurens had been captured; on an enemy "incursion" into the Jerseys and excursion out of it; on countrymen who "have all the folly of the ass and all the passiveness of sheep in their compositions," Hamilton offhandedly lets drop the really sensational news: he has managed to find for himself the wife he had a year earlier charged Laurens to find for him. With soldierly bluffness, just before the close, where the shock effect will be greatest, Hamilton drops the bombshell:

> Have you not heard that I am in the point of becoming a benedict? I confess my sins. I am guilty. Next fall completes my doom. I give up my liberty to Miss Schuyler. She is a goodhearted girl who I am sure will never play the termagent; though not a genius she has good sense enough to be agreeable, and though not a beauty she has fine black eyes —is rather handsome and has every other requisite of the exterior to make a lover happy.

Here, to Laurens, he revises the earlier chivalrous raptures he had sent to Peggy. He gives Laurens a more objective assessment of his fiancée; not a genius, but good sense, fine eyes, and handsome, yes, and a popular belle, too, but not a "beauty" in the more conventional sense that her sisters were.

These were merely her "requisites of the exterior" to "make a lover happy." As for her interior, the part that counted, it was hardly necessary to admit to his friend that

> believe me, I am lover in earnest, though I do not speak of the perfections of my Mistress in the enthusiasm of chivalry.

Her sister Angelica had attended a fashionable ladies' seminary in New Rochelle while Betsy remained at home at The Pastures and at Old Saratoga to learn the domestic arts that every Dutch patroon's housewife ought to know under the supervision of her mother, a paragon of proper patroonship. So when they were apart, Hamilton occupied his time trying to polish and perfect his absent lover and mistress by correspondence school. She should add to her "amiable" qualities some "splendid" ones:

> I entreat you, my charmer, not to neglect the charges I gave you, particularly that of taking care of yourself and that of employing all your leisure in reading. Nature has been very kind to you, do not neglect to cultivate her gifts and to enable yourself to make the distinguished figure in all respects to which you are entitled to aspire. You excel most of your sex in all the amiable qualities, endeavor to excel them equally in the splendid ones. You can do it if you please, and I shall take pride in it. —It will be a fund too to diversify our enjoyment and amusements and fill all our moments to advantage.

After Hamilton and Betsy's marriage at The Pastures the following winter, Schuyler hastened to congratulate his new son-in-law: "You cannot my Dear Sir be more happy at the connection you have made with my family than I am. Until a child has made a judicious choice the heart of a parent is continually in anxiety, but this anxiety vanished in the moment I discovered where you and she had placed your affections."

By this time Hamilton was well and favorably known throughout the army

and among men of substance and influence. His talents were widely acknowledged, and it was predicted that he would go far. His manners were polished;
his bearing, dignified; and his ideas, sound. The only real rub lay in his notably
suspect "family connections."

It was known that he had come from the West Indies while still a boy; but
very little else of his antecedents was known. Hamilton must have disclosed the
bar sinister to General Schuyler before soliciting his final consent: "I am pleased
with every instance of delicacy in those who are dear to me," Schuyler wrote
Hamilton after the ceremony, "and I think I read your soul on that occasion you
mention." In a letter he wrote to Betsy after their marriage, Hamilton found no
need to explain to her why his late brother, Peter Lavien, had a different surname
from his own.

Schuyler yielded to his son-in-law's spell and became one of his most ardent
admirers and followers. For Schuyler, set off against Hamilton's vivid personal
charm and political genius, his lack of family connections mattered not at all. For
Hamilton, one Schuyler family connection was all he needed to paper over the
lack of a birth certificate that might have troubled some among whom he moved
in Federalist society. Republicans like Jefferson would not fail to take note
nonetheless.

There is no doubt that Hamilton sincerely loved Elizabeth Schuyler though
from time to time he would love others as well, once or twice with perhaps a
touch more intensity. Betsy's enduring qualities probably appealed to his good
sense more than her transient handsomeness stormed his emotions. There is no
doubt that Betsy was deeply in love with the glamorous young aide and remained
unswervingly loyal to him through the tumultuous quarter century and eight
children of their life together. For the span of another half century by which she
survived the duel she was indomitably faithful to his memory and repute.

We have no letters from Betsy to Hamilton, although there are many tanta-
lizing acknowledgments in his letters of those she sent to him. All of hers to him
she destroyed. Although she did not outshine her husband or her sisters Angelica and Peggy when out in society, she left an impression of being a woman
of grace, charm, and beauty with all who met her as the years went by.

Her highest talents were, no doubt, of the interior more than the exterior
order. She was full of gaiety and courage and fond of domestic affairs. As her
mother's chief assistant in managing the houses at Albany and Old Saratoga,
she was accustomed to the sight of soldiers' weapons and the dangers of living
on a colonial frontier that lurking Indians sometimes terrorized. General Schuyler's military career was table talk, and the Schuylers had kept open house at
Albany during the entire revolutionary period. English, French, and American
visitors alike had all come away with vivid impressions of Betsy's intelligence,
charm, and "bright dark eyes."

In the twenty-five years that were all she and Hamilton had left, she wore
herself out carrying, bearing, nursing, weaning, and rearing their eight children.
She would also regularly manage to entertain their many friends and clients at
one of New York's most brilliant tables. Her special contribution to Hamilton's

life was to furnish him with undeviating devotion—even when she had reason to believe, or rather, no doubt at all, that he was unfaithful to her. Unfaithful though he might be from time to time, Hamilton always returned to her, secure in her love. There is extant no record of reproach from her to him.

When Elizabeth Schuyler Hamilton died in 1854 at the age of 97, having survived by half a century the death of her husband and firstborn son in duels, there was found in a tiny bag which hung from around her neck, which she had evidently worn there all her adult life, a piece of frayed and yellowed paper, the torn fragments of which at some time or other had been sewn together with a piece of ordinary thread. Sometime or other during the spring of the first rapturous year of their love of 75 years before, Hamilton, recalling a lyric of Sir John Suckling, had written out for her in that neat hand that would elsewhere indite a federal empire, the following little love poem:

ANSWER TO THE INQUIRY WHY I SIGHED

Before no mortal ever knew
A love like mine so tender—true—
Completely wretched—you away—
And but half blessed e'en while you stay.

If present love [illegible] face
Deny you to my fond embrace
No joy unmissed my bosom warms
But when my angel's in my arms.

12

TREASON!

MY REMEDIES WERE GOOD . . . YOU CAN HARDLY CONCEIVE IN HOW
DREADFUL A SITUATION WE ARE . . . THE WORST OF EVILS SEEMS
TO BE COMING UPON US . . . A LOSS OF OUR VIRTUE.
—*To John Laurens, September 12, 1780.*

From the headquarters of the French army's American expeditionary force
at Newport Hamilton's friend the Marquis de Fleury on September 7, 1780 sent
him a warning framed in the language of a favorite sport: "I do not like your
situation at Lee's Fort. You throw the glove to Clinton, he will take it, and we
are not near enough to be your seconds." The French were suffering from a local
malaise: "Ours sicks increase not much, but they increase." By his fractured
Franglais Fleury reminded Hamilton that his fellow Americans had caught a
creeping malaise that was nationwide, not just local, and psychological, not
physical, and that no physician knew a nostrum to cure it.

In his letter of June 30 to John Laurens, just before slyly letting drop the
news that he was about to become a benedict, Hamilton had been telling his
dearest old friend, the newly captured prisoner of war, about the sloth of "our
countrymen" who "have all the folly of the ass and the passiveness of sheep."
These qualities, he felt, were well mirrored by their elected representatives in
the Continental Congress: "They are determined not to be free," Hamilton
railed. "They can neither be frightened, discouraged nor persuaded to change
their resolution. If we are saved, France and Spain must save us. I have the most

pygmy-feelings at the idea, and I almost wish to hide my disgrace in universal ruin. Don't think I rave," he raved, "for the conduct of the states is enough most pitiful that can be imagined."

A recent horrible example was the armed "excursion" of British forces under Baron von Knyphausen. He had invaded New Jersey in June of 1780 and then retreated after fierce skirmishes with American militia.

"Would you believe it" Hamilton wrote, "a German baron at the head of five thousand men, in the month of June insulted and defied the main American army with the commander in chief at their head with impunity, and made them tremble for the security of their magazines forty miles in the country."

Bands of robbers roamed southern New Jersey. There was a plot afoot to kidnap Susannah's father, Governor William Livingston. According to information "given by a female in the tory interest," there was even a plot to seize George Washington himself. Livingston indignantly wrote to Sir Henry Clinton that he had uncovered plans that a general in Clinton's command had drawn up for his assassination.

Someone on Washington's staff thought of a counterplot: Why not snatch Sir Henry Clinton out of his own house in New York at the tip of the island, only a few yards from the Hudson River, hustle him into a waiting whaleboat, and row him back to American lines?

Washington went so far as to appoint Lieutenant Colonel David Humphrey, one of his aides, as leader of the undercover kidnap attempt, but Hamilton raised an objection.

"There could be little doubt of its success," said Hamilton, "but, sir, have you examined the consequences of it?"

"In what respect?" Washington asked.

"Why," replied Hamilton, "we shall rather lose than gain, by removing Sir Henry Clinton from the command of the British army. We perfectly understand his character. By taking him off we only make way for some other, perhaps an abler officer, whose character and dispositions we will have to learn."

Washington countermanded his orders to Humphrey and canceled the counterkidnapping of his counterpart. Things were falling apart. The center could not hold. There was no center.

While the army occupied itself with guerrillalike diversions, Congress bumbled through one of its own most serious crises. Inflation made Continental currency more worthless than ever, if possible. The army, too feeble to fend off von Knyphausen's raid, was disintegrating for lack of supplies and pay. The states ignored the feeble requests of the so-called national government for funds, having enough trouble raising funds of their own. To many thinking men the Revolution was fast approaching its end; many lost interest in it and turned back to patch up their private affairs.

James Duane, a deputy from New York to the Continental Congress, with whom Hamilton, as New York's headquarters intelligencer, had been keeping up correspondence, came up to Morristown from Philadelphia to take a look at the army's deteriorating situation at first hand. Duane was a man of property and rather conservative in his social and economic views, although he staunchly supported revolution against English rule.

Ever since the Great Meeting in the Fields, Duane, and the Livingstons and John Jay and an ever-growing group of important New Yorkers in temporary exile from their enemy-occupied city had been receiving the youthful aide's reports and opinions with growing respect. In their correspondence with him they discussed problems of local political governance that during the summer of 1780 seemed to be all but insoluble, not just military matters.

On his congressional visit to camp, Duane sought Hamilton out and asked for his views. Hamilton thought things were going from bad to worse; unlike others Duane interrogated, Hamilton knew what to do about the spreading malaise. Duane asked Hamilton to write down what he had told him and send it to him in Philadelphia.

"I will," said Hamilton, "agreeably to your request and my promise." He added with crisp assurance, "Apply it and the country can be saved."

So from headquarters encampment at a place called Liberty Pole in northern New Jersey, west of Fort Lee, close enough to British lines to throw "the glove to Clinton," Hamilton wrote Duane a remarkable letter.

The opening sentence of Hamilton's letter to Duane of September 3, 1780, drove straight to the heart of the national malaise: "The fundamental defect is a want of power in Congress." The magnitude of the problem was no occasion for false modesty on Hamilton's part: "I sit down to give you my ideas of the defects of our present system, and the changes necessary to save us from ruin." The want of power in Congress was largely due to the timidity of Congress itself. Hamilton brushed aside the arguments of those who said that Congress had no authority to act because the Articles of Confederation granted no definite powers to it, that it could only recommend, but not command. "Nonsense," said Hamilton. "They have done many of the highest acts of sovereignty . . . the declaration of independence, the declaration of war, the levying an army, creating a navy, emitting money, making alliances with foreign powers, appointing a dictator, etc., etc."

Buttressed with historical analogies, informed with knowledge of political economy and philosophy, Hamilton's letter contained a practical plan for reorganization of the national government if the government was to continue to exist. When he was writing to Duane, Hamilton had no need to adopt the tone of polemical political pamphleteer. It was unnecessary and was absent; the mime of Junius was put aside; Hamilton the statesman emerged upon the stage.

He quickly passed beyond criticisms of defects of the present system. His political plan was the second chapter of his ongoing treatise on the subject of how to create a United States. The first had been his Morris plan—his comprehensive plan for an economic union of the states set forth in the earlier letter he had sent to Robert Morris over the pseudonym of James Montague, Esq.

A bold Congress, Hamilton explained, would have assumed the necessary powers: "The public good required that they should have considered themselves as vested with full power to preserve the republic from harm." Here was the seed of the great constitutional doctrine of implied powers.

Nevertheless, it was true that Congress was not entirely to blame: "The Confederation itself is defective, and requires to be altered. It is neither fit for war nor peace." As long as each state had complete sovereignty in internal affairs, there could be no proper union. What was the essential precondition for a strong and vigorous nation? Centralized power with independent control of its own funds: "Without certain revenue, a government can have no power. That power which holds the purse-strings absolutely, must rule."

But under the confederation the states held the purse strings. That was intolerable to Hamilton. Let perpetual sources of revenue be placed at the sole disposition of Congress. For this Hamilton recommended a poll tax, a general tax on land, and imposts on commerce.

The problem of finances disposed of, Hamilton turned to an attack upon the Congress whose powers he had earlier defended. "Congress," he declared, "have kept the power too much in their own hands, and have meddled too much with details of every sort. Congress is, properly, a deliberative corps, and it forgets itself when it attempts to play the executive."

Hamilton's remedy was to let Congress immediately invest itself with those powers that were inherent in its original appointment. If the delegates were too timid to do so, then let it call a convention of all the states with full authority to form a general confederation. This confederation should grant to Congress complete and unhampered sovereignty over war and peace, foreign affairs, trade, finance, coinage, banks, and treaties. To the states should be left matters relating "to the rights of property and life among individuals." Here is the earliest call for a constitutional convention.

Such a Congress should appoint a series of executives. Each would be responsible for the administration of each great department. There should be "A secretary for foreign affairs—a President of war—a President of marine—a Financier—a President of trade." Or instead of this last, "a Board of Trade may be preferable as the regulations of trade are slow and gradual and require prudence and experience (more than other qualities), for which boards are very well adapted." Hamilton went so far as to tell Congress whom to appoint: Schuyler, his prospective father-in-law, for president of war; Alexander McDougall for the marine; and Robert Morris for finance.

Let the war be fought with a regular army enlisted for at least three years or for the duration, Hamilton advised. The state militia troops like those who had failed to stop von Knyphausen were all but worthless. If an army could not be raised by voluntary enlistment, introduce conscription according to the Swedish plan. Then pay and supply the army from funds raised by Congress. Where would the money come from? Borrow from France, raise taxes, and, above all, create a national bank. "Free countries have ever paid the heaviest taxes," Hamilton pointed out. "The obedience of a free people to general laws however hard they bear is ever more perfect than that of slaves to the arbitrary will of a prince."

A national bank was a centerpiece of Hamilton's program. He had advocated it strongly in his earlier Morris plan; now he again urged it on Duane. He repeated all the old arguments and added some new ones. Paper credit was of no value unless founded "on a joint basis of public and private credit." Public credit alone was not enough. John Law had tried such a scheme in France, and results had been disastrous. Similar attempts in America had proved no more successful. New emissions of paper money were depreciating as rapidly as the old. Why? Because—and here Hamilton hammered home another of his fundamental theses—"The moneyed men have not an immediate interest to uphold its credit. They may even, in many ways, find it their interest to undermine it."

Hamilton the realist wasted no time on politically easy but practically useless criticism of the lack of patriotism and public spirit on the part of "moneyed men." It was simply a fact of economics and of human nature, to be accepted as such and dealt with. Greed was no more a part of the human nature of moneyed men than it was of small farmers, but no less. All men by their natures have some but not all of the characteristics of economic man; though neither rich men nor poor are solely economic men and nothing else.

To establish permanent paper credit, a bank was needed in which people who bought shares would be granted a pro rata share and control plus "the whole or a part of the profits." Such shares had to be made a sound investment, or money would not find its way into them. It would, of course, find its way elsewhere; perhaps to England or France.

Hamilton drew analogies to the bankers of Venice and the Bank of England: "The Bank of England underwrites public authority and faith with private credit; and hence we see what a vast fabric of paper credit is raised on *a visionary basis*. Had it not been for this, England would never have found sufficient funds to carry on her wars." He drove home the point: "with the help of this she has done, and is doing wonders."

Never in blind awe of "moneyed men" nor blindly tied to British precedents, Hamilton was simply pointing out the only way of getting a big job done. "It is sure," Hamilton knew, that "individuals in America are not very rich, but this would not prevent their instituting a bank."

Hamilton reenunciated a basic rule. "Men are governed by opinion," he concluded. "This opinion is as much influenced by appearances as by realities. If a government appears to be confident of its own powers, it is the surest way to inspire the same confidence in others."

Statesmanship and a vision of the future course of the government of the United States are spelled out by Hamilton in this letter. At a time when centrifugal political tendencies of the separate states were pulling them apart, Hamilton was calling boldly for a centralized, unified national government. At a time when Congress was showing itself to be weak, slothful, incompetent, and corrupt, he demanded more power be given it. With cold calculation he exposed the folly of what Congress was doing—issuing paper money backed by nothing but government fiat that was not worth a continental.

He scouted reliance on the idealism of rulers as a way to govern. He enunciated the principle of linking the public benefit of rich and poor to private capital.

Nowhere has the theory of private capitalism in America been stated with more concision, power, and realism.

James Duane perceived the soundness of Hamilton's plan, but as a practical politician, he also realized that it would be more popular with congressmen who represented national and mercantile constituencies than with those from primarily rural areas. One of Hamilton's proposals bore immediate fruit: Duane himself sponsored the plan for creation of an executive department. The rest would unfold slowly with the years.

To many, late that summer of 1780, it seemed that time was running out. In the main theater of war, now shifted to the south, things were even worse than in the north. French fleets had been beaten off by strong British squadrons. Almost all of South Carolina was in enemy hands. General Horatio Gates, the hero of Saratoga, dispatched south to stem the tide, had met Cornwallis at Camden, South Carolina, on August 16, 1780, and the result had been one of the most crushing American defeats of the entire war. At the first onslaught the militia had fled in yet another now customary "settled, durable panic." Gates, according to all accounts, had outrun even his own militia. A thousand Americans were killed or wounded; another thousand were taken prisoner; the brave Baron de Kalb died in a vain attempt to rally panic-stricken troops. Gates turned up safe at Hillsborough, 180 miles away!

Word of Gates's debacle reached Hamilton as he was sending off his great political plan to Duane. He wrote Duane a second letter three days later, "What think you of the conduct of this great man? I am his enemy personally, for unjust and unprovoked attacks upon my character, therefore what I say of him ought to be received as from an enemy, and have no more weight than is consistent with fact and common sense."

Having forewarned Duane that his critique might be colored by personal animosity, Hamilton changed roles from constitutional architect to military tactician to tell Duane what went wrong: "Did anyone ever hear of such a disposition for a fight? His best troops placed on the side strongest by nature, his worst, on that weakest by nature, and his attack made with these. . . . His left ran away and left his right uncovered. His right wing turned on the left and has in all probability been cut off." He added, "Though in truth the General seems to have known very little what became of the army."

The architect of American economic capitalism for the far distant future then explained in detail the tactical plan that Gates should have followed. For his long-range plans to have a chance, it was first necessary to win the war:

> Had he placed his militia on his right supported by the Morass and his Continental troops on his left, where it seems he was most vulnerable, his right would have been more secure, and his left would have opposed the enemy; and instead of going backward when he ordered to attack would have gone forward. The reverse of what has happened might have happened.

He had not quite finished with Gates: "Was there ever an instance of a general running away as Gates has done from his whole army? . . . and was there ever so precipitous a flight? One hundred eighty miles in three days and a half. It does admirable credit to the activity of a man at his time of life. But it disgraces the General and the soldiers."

General Schuyler, no less Gates's enemy than Hamilton, foresaw that good might come from Gates's rout: his adherents in Congress would no longer have it "in their power to play him off against the General." But as an immediate result of his rout at Camden, all four southern states—Georgia, the Carolinas, and Virginia—now lay wide open and defenseless before Lord Cornwallis and his seasoned British regulars, secure in the pride of a string of recent victories at Savannah, Charleston, and Camden.

Remembering Cornwallis's hot pursuit of Washington's beaten retreat across New Jersey in 1776, Hamilton knew that the most effective and aggressive of all British commanders in America would follow up a victory like Camden by pressing north to Virginia.

Hamilton also had the practical solution to this seemingly insoluble problem. Congress could save the situation. Problems of war were simpler than problems of peace. In fact, Hamilton's plan to win the war in the south consisted of only two words. "Send Greene," he told Duane. "You know my opinion of him. I stake my reputation on the events, give him but fair play."

Hamilton recommended, Congress decreed, and Washington acted. On October 14, 1780, Washington appointed Major General Nathanael Greene to replace Gates as commander of what was left of the shattered Southern army.

Confiding his innermost thoughts about Gates's debacle to Betsy, Hamilton wrote that "this misfortune affects me less than others . . . because I think our safety depends on a total change of system, and this change of system will only be produced by misfortune."

Out of this black mood, he speculated about flight and the consequences of disgrace in phrases that would recur in his private writings throughout his life: "Pardon me my love for talking politics to you. What have we to do with anything but love? Go the world as it will, in each other's arms we cannot but be happy. . . .

But lurking beneath the surface of his love for her was his sense of personal responsibility for American liberty, no matter how hard he tried to dissemble it: "If America were lost we should be happy in some other clime more favourable to human rights. What think you of Geneva as a retreat? 'Tis a charming place; where nature and society are in their greatest perfection. I was once determined to let my existence and American liberty end together. My Betsy has given me a motive to outlive my pride, I had almost said my honor; but America must not be witness to my disgrace."

These few sentences of this curious love letter contain a peculiarly complex mixture of thought. He is not saying anything as simple as give me liberty or give me death. But he may be saying that if America does not turn out to be a country as "favourable to human rights" as he thinks it should be, he would consider suicide. Flight with Betsy to Geneva would permit him to outlive his "pride," but not even Betsy could make him "outlive my honor." This identification of his sense of personal honor with the cause of American liberty regardless of all other consequences is the essence of the inner Hamilton.

Gates's defeat had brought on one of the earliest of the moods of severe depression that would recur throughout his life: "As it is always well to be prepared for the worst, I talk to you in this strain; not that I think it probable we shall fail in the contest . . . I think the chances are without comparison in our favour."

He closed with classic fatalism: If the worst does not happen, "my Aquileia and I will plant our turnips in her native land."

Hamilton seemed in despair because his plans for creating the nation he had taken it upon his own shoulders to create would remain only a vision. It was extravagant language, but Hamilton still saw the situation in similar terms, writing Laurens on September 12:

> You told me, my remedies were good, but you were afraid would not go down at the time. I tell you necessity must force them down; and if they are not speedily taken the patient will die . . . You can hardly conceive in how dreadful a situation we are. The army, in the course of the present month, has received only four or five days' rations of meal.
>
> This distress at such a stage of the campaign sours the soldiery. 'Tis in vain you make apologies to them.

This September's pathological depression brought with it uncanny foresight. Hamilton made an oracular comment that soon would explode into the tragedy of treason at West Point: "The officers are out of humour, and the *worst of evils seems to be coming upon us—a loss of our virtue.*"

Hamilton went on angrily: " 'Tis in vain you attempt to appease; you are almost detested as an accomplice with the administration. I am losing character, my friend, because I am not overcomplaisant to the spirit of clamour—so that I am in a fair way to be out with everybody. With one set I am considered as a friend to military pretensions however exorbitant, with another as a man, who secured by my situation from sharing the distress of the army, am inclined to treat it lightly." The groveling condition of enjoying the privileged status of an aide while less privileged line soldiers suffered grated on the nerves of the former line commander.

Just at the point where his mind seemed all but unbalanced by the burden of his and the nation's troubles, he supplied his own self-psychoanalysis: "The truth is I am an unlucky honest man, that speak my sentiments to all and with emphasis."

But the moment of sudden self-insight failed to end his terrible sense of unease. He wound up his tirade to Laurens spraying unaimed fire on all targets of opportunity: "I hate Congress—I hate the army—I hate the world—I hate myself. The whole is a mass of fools and knaves."

Closing with another mercurial shift of mood and a flash of wit and grace, he added a reassurance, "I could almost except you and Meade. Adieu." And as a postscript: "My ravings are for your own bosom. The General and family send you their love."

Things were not as bad as Hamilton said; they were really much worse. On the secure defense of the looming citadel at West Point hinged all American grand strategy, north and south. The commander in chief at West Point was Major General Benedict Arnold.

Hamilton had written angrily to Laurens of "officers out of humour," the "worst of evils," and "a loss of our virtue." There is no evidence that at the time of Hamilton's writing Laurens he or Washington had received hard intelligence that Arnold had accepted a secret British offer to pay him and his pretty, young second wife, Peggy, good hard British silver and gold in a sum that would escalate: the more American troops and positions he was able to betray, the larger the payment would be. Another kind of American was in thrall to another kind of golden chain.

Hamilton's subconscious mind was foretelling him that the shocking news of Arnold's treason would have political repercussions as damaging as the treason itself. Public support for the cause of American independence was waning and such proof of disaffection at the highest levels of command could dissolve it altogether.

According to William Smith, the royal chief justice of the province of New York, Sir Henry Clinton boasted that if Major John André had not been "catched with his papers which forced Arnold to come off before the design was accomplished," Clinton by means of Arnold's treason would have succeeded in winning "an instantaneous termination of the war."

Smith claimed that if all had gone according to plan, Clinton would have taken both Washington and Rochambeau prisoners. At the time public opinion among Americans agreed with Smith that Arnold, the arch traitor, working with Clinton, the arch enemy, had fully expected to be able to capture Washington, Lafayette, Hamilton, Knox, and Rochambeau at the same time they seized the most important military position in the states.

On the scene at the moment of unfolding of the plot, Hamilton saw how close the arch traitor and the arch enemy came to bringing it off. No special display of American brilliance or skill kept the plot from succeeding. Two or three lucky mischances—Washington's habit of doing everything "by the book," the aggressiveness of the artillery battery that fired on the British sloop of war *Vulture*, and three sturdy Westchester countrymen whose names were Williams, Paulding, and Van Wort—came together to save the day.

Major General Benedict Arnold had long considered himself unjustly treated by Congress. By his lights, his brilliant gifts had been overlooked and less able officers promoted over his head. He was in debt, not only as a result of his own expenditures but also from the extravagances and demands of his captivating young wife, the former Peggy Shippen. He shared the spreading conviction that the states were losing the war and could never win.

As far back as 1779, Sir Henry Clinton's handsome, elegant, young adjutant, Major John André, had been receiving mysterious letters in code through secret channels from a general officer of the Continental Army who signed himself "Gustavus," hinting that he might offer "his services to the commander in chief of the British forces in any way that would most effectually restore the former government and destroy the authority Congress had usurped, either by immediately joining the British army or cooperating on some concealed plan with Sir Henry Clinton."

By June of 1780 Benedict Arnold was issuing concrete proposals. He would obtain command—and here André's breath must have quickened—of the fortress at West Point! This was exactly what Sir Henry Clinton wanted. He had André write at once to Arnold of his interest, adding that there would be an "ample stipend."

West Point! As Sir Henry Clinton knew, the fortress of West Point, 50 miles up the Hudson from New York, was the only true strongpoint created by the Continental Army anywhere in the colonies during the whole course of the war. Colonels Thaddeus Kosciuszko and Louis du Portail, volunteer engineers from abroad, had designed it; soldiers had spent three years of hard labor and millions of inflated Continental dollars hard won from Congress to erect its towering ramparts pierced with cannon ports. Above the precipitous West Shore of the Hudson the main redoubts clung to a sheer crag like a monstrous crab. It was linked by secret passages to three separate supportive fortresses crowning nearby peaks. Although some of the mazelike, interweaving walls of logs, turf, and stone were still incomplete, guns in the emplacements could support each other by hidden fields of covering fire. To learn their layout was worth much to Sir Henry Clinton. Just south of the fort, where the Hudson narrows into a sharp bend, a swift current would slow any vessel that dared venture within range of the main batteries. Below the dark waters, at the place on which cannons were aimed, there stretched from bank to bank a huge iron chain, whose massive links were intended to entrap the keel of an enemy vessel slowed by the current until the artillerymen on the crags could zero in on the target.

As dickering dragged on, Arnold began to turn his possessions into cash and bank the proceeds of sale in British-held New York through various obliging agents.

Recalling Arnold's earlier clamor for a field command, Washington assigned him the American left wing. His Excellency must have misunderstood, said Arnold. What he really wanted was to command at West Point, not to lead troops in the field. Washington wearily had the orders changed and sent Benedict Arnold up the Hudson to take command of West Point on August 3, 1780. There were very few "ifs" left in the bargaining, and Arnold and Clinton now came to terms on the treason.

The French allies were stationary in Newport, vainly awaiting the arrival of a second division, which the British had blockaded in Brest. There was no news of Admiral de Guichen, whose fleet was far away somewhere at sea in the West Indies. General David Forman, from his lookout on the Jersey shore, reported that British Admiral Rodney had arrived at Sandy Hook with a dozen ships of the line and four frigates to add to British naval superiority. In the Carolinas, where Cornwallis was now the master of Gates's beaten army, the British seemed poised to complete their conquest and move north to invest Virginia. Hamilton wrote Elizabeth on September 6, "Peoples imaginations have already given up North Carolina and Virginia"; but he disagreed with the conventional wisdom: "I do not believe either of them will fall."

With General Nathanael Greene sent south and no longer quartermaster general, transport had broken down. Local farmers refused to accept worthless Continental currency in payment for food. The terms of enlistment for a large part of the army would run out, as usual, in December. Washington had to turn away new recruits he could not feed. For Washington, Hamilton wrote a letter to Congress that "if something satisfactory be not done, the army must either cease to exist at the end of the Campaign, or it will exhibit an example of more virtue, fortitude, self-denial, and perseverance than has . . . ever yet been paralleled in the history of human enthusiasm."

Much to Philip Schuyler's alarm, conventions of delegates from the New England states were being held in Boston and Hartford for "appointing a Dictator with a vice dictator in each state, invested with all the powers conferred formerly by the roman people on theirs; I made great Interest to be left out of the delegation and obtained It altho not with out much difficulty. Gen. McDougall is appointed in my stead."

Hamilton, not yet giving up, wrote out for Washington a detailed set of plans for an attack on New York City, calling for deployment of 20,000 men all around Manhattan, or as he called it then, York Island: "Fire ships and fire rafts should be preparing to burn the enemy's ships in the sound. . . ." But West Point must be held secure at all events: "When the garrison of West Point will permit, another corps may come to this side." Hamilton prepared a long position paper for Washington for the proposed conference at Hartford with the Comte Jean B. D. de Rochambeau, commander of the French expeditionary forces, and Charles Louis d'Arsac, the Chevalier de Ternay, who commanded the French naval squadron. The attack on New York was to be coordinated with a French feint at Charleston to draw Rodney's British fleet back to the south. If the New York plan failed, Hamilton proposed another winter expedition into Canada.

Hamilton carried these plans with him when he took horse on September 17 from army headquarters at New Bridge, New Jersey, with the small headquarters party—Washington, Knox, Lafayette, McHenry, and a few others—to meet with General Rochambeau and Admiral de Ternay at Hartford to plan joint strategy for salvaging something creditable from 1780's military activities before winter froze another lost year to a standstill. They would pass by West Point on their way from New Jersey to Hartford, and on the return trip they would pause for an inspection of the defenses there.

For success against the British, all agreed that constant naval superiority was necessary and that "of all the enterprises which may be undertaken, the most important and decisive is the reduction of New York, which is the center and focus of all the British forces." West Point remained the key to New York; and its commander, Benedict Arnold, the key to West Point.

En route to Hartford, the night of the seventeenth, Washington and Hamilton and the rest of the party lodged at the house of Joshua Hett Smith, the brother of Sir Henry Clinton's friend, William Smith, the royal chief justice. About ten miles south of West Point on the west side of the Hudson near Stony Point, it came to be known as the "treason house." General Benedict Arnold was one of the guests at Smith's for dinner that night, and he boldly sought to ensnare Washington in his cover story for the first stage of his plot.

As Arnold slyly explained it to Washington at dinner that night at Smith's, he had just received a letter from Colonel Beverly Robinson, written from on board the British sloop of war *Vulture*, anchored offshore in the river, enclosing a letter addressed to General Israel Putnam. Robinson said he wished to interview Putnam on a private matter, adding that if Arnold could not reach Putnam, Arnold should come to see Robinson aboard the *Vulture* himself.

Colonel Beverly Robinson was a well-known New York Tory, the colonel of a Tory regiment. Robinson's house, directly across the river from the West Point citadel itself, had been commandeered by Arnold for his own headquarters establishment. Washington's party was to lodge there on the return trip from Hartford when he made his tour of inspection. Arnold purported to consult Washington about Robinson's request, assuming that Washington would make no objection to a routine communication across enemy lines between officers and gentlemen from opposite sides. Arnold implied that it might have something to do with their use of Robinson's house. Had Washington approved Arnold's seemingly innocuous request, Arnold and Robinson could have worked out the remaining details of the plot under the cover of a "flag" of truce. They would make it easy to bag Washington and his entire headquarters party on their return passage.[1]

But Washington turned down Arnold's request. He observed that because it seemed to relate to Robinson's private affairs, Robinson should be referred to the civil authorities. Arnold could not carry out the meeting under a flag of truce. Long habit of deferring to Congress ingrained in Washington now saved him from Arnold's trap.

Hamilton later wrote Laurens that Washington's high principled, or brilliant, or sagacious, or lucky decision was made "with his usual caution, though not the least surmise of the design." He added, "This . . . fortunately deranged the plan and was the first link in the chain of events that led to the detection. The interview could no longer take place in the form of a flag, but was obliged to be managed in a secret manner."

The next day, Washington and Hamilton rode on to Hartford, where the meeting with the French commanders focused on Hamilton's two lengthy position papers. But the planned attacks turned on the availability of French naval aid. The chief point was "That of all the enterprises which may be undertaken, the most . . . decisive is the reduction of New York. . . ."

With Washington's party gone for a few days, the British ship *Vulture* moved in a little closer to the Haverstraw and the treason house to hover in wait for its prey.

On the night of September 21, while Hamilton and Washington were still in Hartford, Joshua Hett Smith, at the direction of Benedict Arnold, was rowed out to the *Vulture* by the Cahoon (or Colquhoun) brothers with a letter. Smith later testified that he believed the letter was for Colonel Beverly Robinson and that Robinson was the man Arnold wanted him to bring back to shore from the *Vulture* in his skiff. But the man whom Smith picked up from the *Vulture* that night was not Robinson. He was wrapped up in a cloak that hid his face and did not even pretend to answer to the name of Colonel Beverly Robinson. Who he was and what uniform he wore under the cloak were wrapped in mystery. When Smith's boat grated onto shore just below Havershaw, the hooded man clambered up the bank and there was met by a shadowy figure who emerged from among the trees. His stiff limp gave him away as General Benedict Arnold himself. The two men talked for awhile, and then the hooded man came back to Smith's boat. But the suspicious Cahoon brothers refused to row him back to the *Vulture*—Smith said he was sick with the ague. So Arnold and the hooded man —and Smith—went back through sentry lines to Smith's own house, the treason house. There Arnold gave the man who had come ashore from the *Vulture* a packet containing a plan of the fortifications of West Point, an engineer's report on methods of attack and defense of the citadel, and a duty return of the garrison, ordnance, and stores showing the numbers of men that manned the mazy ramparts and the level of their supplies. There were a copy of the minutes of a council of war held by Washington three weeks before and a pass for one "John Anderson," written out in Arnold's hand.

Later Hamilton suspected that all this was still not everything that Arnold had given André and that the contents of the packet were but part of Arnold's larger plan for betraying Washington, Hamilton, and their whole party into the hands of the British. The *Vulture*'s earlier move in closer toward the shore batteries had signaled this most threatening part of the treasonous plan.

The next morning, the twenty-second, a second lucky event occurred to derange the plot. As Hamilton later wrote admiringly of an alert fellow artilleryman, Colonel James Livingston, the commanding officer at Kings Ferry across from Stony Point, with no orders from Arnold, had moved a couple of cannon to a point opposite where the *Vulture* lay, fired on her, and "obliged her to take a more remote station" about 10 miles down the river near Ossining.

The mysterious cloaked figure Smith had rowed ashore was, in fact, none other than Major John André, adjutant general of the British army of occupation at New York City. André was Clinton's close confidant, being in about the same close relationship to Clinton as Hamilton to Washington.

According to Hamilton, it was the *Vulture*'s move downriver and the extra rowing distance that had caused Smith's oarsmen to refuse to row André, alias John Anderson, back to the *Vulture* after his nocturnal rendezvous with Arnold, not Smith's ague. According to Hamilton, "This event, at a time of lurking distrust, made the boatman refuse to convey the two passengers [André and

Smith] back." An even more important consequence of the *Vulture*'s move was the psychological derangement that it caused Arnold. It forced him into the miscalculation that was to prove fatal to the plan and to Major André. This "disconcerted Arnold so much," Hamilton wrote, "that by one of those strokes of infatuation, which often confound the schemes of men conscious of guilt, he insisted on André's exchanging his uniform for a disguise, and returning in a mode different from that in which he came." Though "André remonstrated warmly against this new and dangerous expedient," André's protests were unavailing, according to Hamilton. A high-ranking British officer, wearing his British uniform under his cloak, if captured could expect to be treated as a military prisoner, not as a spy. "But Arnold persisting in declaring it impossible for [André] to return as he came, he at length reluctantly yielded to his direction." So instead of being able to return André to the safety of the *Vulture* in uniform as he had come ashore, Smith was obliged to escort André two days later, with Arnold's pass, across Kings Ferry to Verplanck's point, to make his uncertain way south through West Chester toward New York City by land, wearing the disguise of a merchant. West Chester was a no-mans land in which roving bands waged guerilla war. André had fifteen miles to go to reach the nearest British outpost at White Plains.

Just north of Tarrytown near what is now Patriot's Park, three American militiamen challenged him. The pass he carried, signed by General Arnold, did not impress them. In a panic, merchant "John Anderson" confessed to them that he was a British officer. He was taken into the bushes, stripped, and searched, and they found in the feet of his stockings the packet containing all the plans of the fortifications and the other secrets of the fortress. They hauled André before Dragoon Lieutenant Colonel John Jameson, who was puzzled after seeing the treasonable documents, because André carried a signed pass from Major General Benedict Arnold. So Jameson compromised by forwarding the packet of captured plans directly to Washington and returning André himself to Arnold under guard, sending a letter of explanation ahead to Arnold.

With the commander in chief's party passing back and forth to meet the French high command in Hartford, military security had been tight in the whole district. Washington's intelligence officer, Major Benjamin Tallmadge, was alarmed at the action taken by Jameson in sending the prisoner directly back to Arnold; so he sent out a patrol to recall André. Jameson's letter describing André's capture and forwarding the packet containing the West Point plans continued on its way directly to Washington. The separate letter from Jameson to Arnold, which also described André's capture, continued on its way to the traitor. Depending on one's point of view, this was a brilliant, lucky, or negligent oversight or trick of Tallmadge. It caused the whole plot to blow up in the face of its instigator, but it also tipped off Arnold to his only chance to escape.

Meanwhile, Washington and Hamilton, journeying back by easy stages toward West Point, arrived at Fishkill, where the Chevalier de la Luzerne had invited them to spend the night at his lodgings and await the morning before continuing their journey to the Robinson house.

Washington sent two other aides, Majors Samuel Shaw and James McHenry, on ahead to the Robinson house, and they notified Arnold that the general would breakfast with him that morning, September 25, before making the tour of inspection. But fifteen minutes earlier that same morning a messenger brought Arnold the letter that Jameson had sent and Tallmadge had allowed to go forward unrecalled, telling of André's capture. Arnold rushed upstairs to his wife, Peggy. Moments later another messenger arrived, announcing that Washington and his party were at hand. Arnold's aide, Major David Franks, rushed up to Peggy's room after Arnold to inform him that the commanding general had arrived.

According to Franks, Arnold "came down in great confusion, and, ordering a horse to be saddled, mounted him and told me to inform His Excellency that he was gone over to West Point. . . ." McHenry, who had already arrived at the Robinson house, "observed an embarrassment (in Arnold) which I could not at that time account for."

When Washington and Hamilton reached the front door of the Robinson house, they met a disappointing reception. Neither Arnold nor his pretty young Peggy were there to greet them with open arms. Instead, Arnold's aides, Franks and Lieutenant Colonel Richard Varick, told them that Arnold had been called across the river to the fortress and would return within the hour. Peggy remained in seclusion in her bedroom upstairs.

After their brisk morning's ride, Washington and Hamilton and the other members of the party took a leisurely breakfast, still unsuspecting. Arnold meanwhile was fleeing down the river toward the *Vulture*, its hopes for scavenging bigger game already dashed by Arnold's panic. After breakfast Washington left with his command party for the barge to cross the river for his inspection of the fortifications and, of course to join the still absent commander. Hamilton was left behind to receive dispatches, alone in the house with Arnold's aides and beauteous young Peggy upstairs.

Suddenly Peggy's cries "called us all to her assistance." Hamilton later wrote Elizabeth that "I paid her a visit and endeavoured to soothe her by every method in my power . . . It was the most affecting scene I was ever witness to."

Pretending to a composure she did not feel, Peggy first inquired after Varick's health. Then she burst into "hysterics and utter frenzy." She was "raving distracted" and screamed of hot irons on her head, Hamilton recalled. She screamed that Varick had ordered her baby to be murdered. She rolled out of her bed on to her knees to entreat him to spare the child's life. He sought to assure her that all were her friends and that Arnold would soon return, but she cried, "General Arnold will never return. He is gone. He is gone forever, *there, there, there:* the spirits have carried him up there." She pointed at the ceiling. "They have put hot irons in his head."

According to Varick, Peggy was "raving mad to see Washington." Her hair was "disheveled and flowing about her neck." She was clad only in "her morning gown with few other clothes remaining on her—too few to be seen even by a gentleman of the family." Hamilton's emotions were always profoundly affected by feminine beauty, and distress. He was positive she was innocent. It is not known how far his eager efforts to console her had carried him toward her arms by the time Washington returned to the Robinson house from West Point that afternoon. He had not found Arnold; West Point's defenses were in disarray.

In Washington's absence, Jameson's courier, Captain Jeronimus Hoogland, had already delivered the packet addressed to Washington to Hamilton. Whether or not he had opened it, Hamilton by now had many reasons to suspect Arnold of treason: his unaccountable absence at Washington's arrival and reports of Arnold's barge being seen going down river and "of a spy . . . being detected nigh our lines." Peggy's ravings confirmed Arnold's guilt.

Washington dismounted and strode to the door, enraged at Arnold's unexplained absence. Hamilton met him in the doorway and handed him the packet from Jameson. There was also a letter from André to Washington, which had been enclosed with Jameson's. Washington quickly scanned Jameson's letter, leafed through the papers that had been taken from André, and read André's letter. In it André identified himself as adjutant general of the British army, ashore from the *Vulture* seeking military intelligence. He had been forced against his will, he said, to come within American lines and put on civilian clothing as a disguise. By his letter he wanted to rescue himself "from an imputation of having asserted a mean character for treacherous purposes. . . ." He was not a spy, he insisted. He did not name Arnold as the person with whom he had negotiated, but the pass in Arnold's handwriting, Arnold's inexplicable absence, and the other contents of Jameson's letter could have left little doubt in Washington's mind by now that Arnold had betrayed him.

Hamilton called out to Lafayette to come instantly. Lafayette rushed down the hall to Washington's room and found both men there shaking with extreme emotion. Washington pulled shut the door behind Lafayette and Hamilton. Holding the dispatches in a trembling hand, Washington said in the hush to his two closest confidants: "Arnold has betrayed us. Whom can we trust now?"

It was a moment of the war as critical as the rout at Kip's Bay or the headlong retreat at Monmouth.

Washington then ordered Hamilton to summon McHenry and ride to Verplanck's Point, some eight miles downriver, where there was an American post from which Arnold might be intercepted if he had not already reached the *Vulture*. The two aides leaped to their saddles and galloped south as fast as their horses could carry them. But when they reined in their steaming, foam-flecked animals and looked out from the shore of the Verplanck's Point, they saw no barge. The *Vulture* was under sail and moving swiftly down the tide toward New York City with Arnold aboard.

How wide did Arnold's plot spread? Hamilton scribbled a note back to Washington telling him that Arnold had outrun their pursuit. Hamilton was taking command steps on his own responsibility to meet the emergency. They might prove to be unnecessary, but grave risk remained. It was better to take the trouble to be prepared for it than run it. "You will see by the enclosed that we are too late," Hamilton reported. "Arnold went by water to the *Vulture*. I shall write to General Greene, advising him, without making a bustle, to be in readiness to march, and even to detach a brigade this way; for, though I do not believe the project will go on, yet it is possible Arnold has made such dispositions with the garrison as may tempt the enemy, in its present weakness, *to make the stroke this night,* and it seems prudent to be providing against it."

West Point was no position to leave at risk if Arnold's packet to André was only one part of a coordinated plan of Sir Henry Clinton to pull tight the drawstring and bag the whole American high command now that Arnold had put the defenses of its citadel in disarray.

With speed and force, Hamilton issued commands for the emergency deployments: "I shall endeavor to find Meigs, and request him to march to the garrison, and shall make some arrangements here. I hope your Excellency will approve these steps, as there may be no time to be lost. The *Vulture* is gone down to New York."

Hamilton's letter to General Greene (who had not yet departed for the south to take over Gates's command) reported the terrible story to him and warned that the British might yet strike: "There has just been unfolded at this place a scene of the blackest treason; Arnold has fled to the enemy. André the British Adjt. Genl is in our possession as a spy. This capture unravelled the mystery. West Point was to have been the Sacrifice, all the dispositions have been made for the purpose and 'tis possible, tho' not probable tonight may still see the execution. The wind is fair, I came here in pursuit of Arnold but was too late. I advise your putting the army under marching orders, and detaching a brigade immediately this way."

The Americans received one more lucky break. After Hamilton wrote Greene, the wind shifted from fair to foul for Clinton. His sloops would make but slow headway tacking upstream against it. Clinton's chances to move in force and bag the entire American high command was gone. Hamilton's letter must have impressed Washington again that in Hamilton he had an aide who could act wisely with speed and decision in any emergency.

Hamilton's letter to Washington from Verplanck's Point enclosed an extraordinary letter written the same day by Arnold on board the *Vulture.* Addressed to Washington, Arnold had left it under a flag of truce at Verplanck's. It began . . . "The Heart which is Conscious of its own rectitude, cannot attempt to palliate a step, which the world may censure as wrong. . . ." The world, as Arnold saw it, was out of step with the traitor: "I have ever acted from a Principle of Love to my Country, since the Commencement of the present unhappy Contest between Great Britain and the Colonies, the same principle of Love to my Country Actuates my present Conduct, however it may appear Inconsistent to the World: who very Seldom Judge right of any Mans Actions." Arnold will ask for no favor, he tells Washington. Then he proceeds to ask a favor: "I have no favor to ask for myself. I have too often experienced the Ingratitude of my Country to Attempt it: But from the known humanity of your Excellence I am induced to ask your protection" for Peggy "from every insult and injury that the mistaken vengeance of my country may expose her to. It ought to fall only on me. She is as good, and as innocent as an angel, and is incapable of doing wrong. . . ." He added some personal flattery: "From your Excellency I have no fears on her account, but she may suffer from the mistaken fury of her country."

He then asked two more favors—that he and Peggy be permitted to exchange letters, that his "clothes and baggage," which "are of little consequence" be sent to him and that, "If required their value shall be paid in money." First to last money was the thing most on his mind.

At the Robinson house late that afternoon, after his private outburst to Hamilton and Lafayette, Washington kept his own counsel, as if nothing were amiss. Varick and Franks and Peggy were nervous and apprehensive, uncertain of how deeply Washington would implicate them in Arnold's treason.

Washington paid a visit to the bedside of the "Poor . . . frantic and miserable lady." Then all sat down to dinner. There, as Varick put it with excruciating blandness, considering the tense circumstances, "Dull appetites surrounded a plentiful table."

Having done all he could to safeguard West Point in the emergency, Hamilton galloped back to Robinson's. Peggy Arnold had gone into another fit of hysterics. Hamilton was deeply touched. Here was beauty in distress, a lovely woman deserted by a traitor husband and crying out in anguish. Of her innocence he still had no doubt at all.

That night he wrote Eliza about her pathetic condition: "An amiable woman, frantic with distress for the loss of a husband she tenderly loved; a traitor to his country and to his fame . . . it was the most affecting scene I ever was witness to. She, for a considerable time, entirely lost herself. The General went up to see her, and she upbraided him with being in a plot to murder her child. One moment she raved, another she melted into tears. . . . All the sweetness of beauty, all the loveliness of innocence, all the tenderness of a wife, and all the fondness of a mother showed themselves in her appearance and conduct."

Hamilton added, rather naïvely, "We have every reason to believe that she was entirely unacquainted with the plan, and had her first knowledge of it when Arnold went to tell her he must banish himself from his country and from her forever. She instantly fell into a convulsion and he left her in that situation."

Writing his fiancée, Hamilton seemed to betray disquieting passion for Peggy in her disheveled distress: "This morning she is more composed. I paid her a visit and endeavoured to sooth her by every method in my power, though you may imagine she is not easily to be consoled . . . her sufferings were so eloquent that I wished myself her brother, to have a right to become her defender. As it is, I have entreated her to enable me to give her proof of my friendship."

Elizabeth Schuyler's love for Alexander Hamilton must have been strong and constant indeed, and he supremely confident of her love, if she could keep on reading his insistent effusions about pretty Peggy without annoyance, and he not expect her to be annoyed.

"Could I forgive Arnold for sacrificing her honor, reputation and duty," he went on, "I could not forgive him for acting a part that must have forfeited the esteem of so fine a woman. At present she almost forgets his crime in his misfortune, and her horror at the guilt of the traitor is lost in her love of the man. . . ."

Her crazy act fooled them all. Washington allowed Peggy go home to Philadelphia. Some, like Aaron Burr, shrewdly insisted all along that she had helped her husband with his treason. Indeed, her extravagances may have pushed him into it in the first place. Burr had known her as a belle in Philadelphia at least as well as Hamilton had. History has shown that Burr was right and that Hamilton could hardly have been more wrong.

In Arnold's own letter to Washington protesting Peggy's "innocence," he had first written that she was "ignorant" of doing wrong and then crossed out the word *ignorant*, and substituted the word *incapable*. Much later, when Sir Henry Clinton's private papers came to light, they revealed that she had been the inspiration and accomplice, if not the instigator, of Arnold's treason. Indeed, part of Arnold's correspondence with the British had passed through her hands.

Arnold was paid the impressive sum of £6,315 sterling, a pension of £500 per annum for Peggy, and pensions of £100 per annum for each of his children by her. No American troops had surrendered with him; so he received no extra increments under the "per head" escalation clause of his deal. He was commissioned brigadier general in the British army. He had been a major general in the American army; so he actually lost one grade in rank. Still, the demotion was worth it. It would not be lost on Hamilton that, as a major general of the disheartened American army looking to a hapless Congress to keep him paid in all but worthless Continental currency, ten loyal lifetimes could never have earned Brigadier General Benedict Arnold a tenth as much hard money as the British paid him for one night of treason.

13

RECONCILED TO HIS BEING SHOT, BUT NOT TO HIS BEING HANGED

THE AUTHORIZED MAXIMS AND PRACTICES OF WAR ARE THE
SATIRES OF HUMAN NATURE.
              —*To John Laurens, October 11, 1780*

Back at Beverly Robinson's house, after Hamilton's and McHenry's furious but futile hot pursuit of the traitor that terrible night of September 25,
there was no time to rest or to moon any more over poor little Peggy. Writing
at night now, in Washington's name, Hamilton confirmed the orders he had
given earlier from Verplanck's and issued new ones. Greene should put the
left division in motion to Kings Ferry. André must be brought to West Point,
and Joshua Hett Smith, that hospitable go-between, must be searched out
and captured.

Arnold had added a postscript to his letter to Washington, declaring that
Smith (like Peggy and Varick and Franks) was ignorant of his treason. To
Washington and Hamilton Arnold's postscript only seemed to point the finger
of guilt more emphatically in Smith's direction.

On the twenty-sixth, Smith was captured and brought to headquarters un-

der guard, protesting furiously. He was, after all, a property holder of substance.

At Robinson's house, in the presence of Knox, Lafayette, Harrison, and
Hamilton, Washington himself, still in high temper, conducted the preliminary
questioning. As Hamilton later put it gently, Washington "expressed himself
with some warmth." Smith was wary in his answers, perhaps on the advice of
his brother William, the royal chief justice. Joshua's story was that he had only
been an innocent go-between. Arnold had deceived him like everyone else by
telling him that the hooded man in the red coat who had been the uninvited guest
at his house was one "John Anderson," an American spy. Smith said he had
believed him.

No stenographic transcript of Washington's angry early morning interrogation of Smith was kept. Later testimony conflicted sharply about what had
actually been said. But after the questioning, Washington was more certain than
ever that Smith "had a considerable share in this business." He insisted that
Smith had even "confessed facts sufficient to establish his guilt." But others, less
emotionally committed to a guilty verdict than Washington, denied that Smith's
testimony had implicated him.

Once again, it fell to Hamilton and other aides to back up the commander
in chief's finding of misbehavior to explain a setback that cried to high heaven
for a scapegoat, as they had done at the court-martial of General Charles Lee
after Monmouth. Smith was brought to trial before a general court-martial in
Tappan, New York, about 25 miles downriver from West Point, four days later,
on charges of going aboard the enemy ship *Vulture;* of hiding André in his
house, furnishing him with civilian clothes, and passing him through the sentry
posts at Stony Point and Verplanck's in disguise, under a false name, and carrying secret intelligence to the enemy; for conspiring with Arnold and the enemy
to "take, kill and seize . . . loyal citizens and soldiers . . . in garrison at West Point
and its dependencies"; and for acting as a spy.

To help corroborate his chief, Hamilton began his testimony on October 2
by confirming that he had heard Smith's "confession" under Washington's interrogation the morning of his capture. Hamilton said that Smith had "asserted his
innocence" of the transactions between General Arnold and Mr. Anderson "with
very solemn protestations and appeals to heaven."[1]

Washington had pressed Smith to tell how he could possibly have failed to
know that his mission to the *Vulture* "must necessarily have been with the
privity of Sir Henry Clinton" and for promoting the interests of the enemy.
Hamilton testified that "Mr. Smith appeared at first a good deal embarrassed"
but that he "finally replied that he acted from the perfect confidence he had in
General Arnold." Hamilton went on: "Mr. Smith, on being questioned if the
person he brought on shore was dressed in a uniform, answered, that he could
not perfectly distinguish whether he wore a uniform or not, but that he had on
a red coat, with a blue surtout."

As Hamilton related it, Smith's testimony was made to appear evasive and
incredible: if it were not too dark for Smith to see that the coat Anderson was

wearing was red, how was it too dark for him to distinguish whether or not it was a British redcoat's uniform?

Smith later charged that while Hamilton's "evidence was perfectly correct," yet he "artfully threw in a chain of reasoning, tending to prove my being in full knowledge of Arnold's intentions." From the fact that "Arnold was very anxious to ascertain from Smith the precise day of his return" and that "the enemy's movements seem to have corresponded to this point. . . ." with Smith's, Hamilton built the implication, as Washington had asserted, that Smith was a knowing party to the plot, not an innocent "tool" of it.

Cross-examination of Hamilton, Smith's accuser by proxy for Washington, was conducted by Smith himself. From the uncomfortable perch of the hot seat of the witness chair under Smith's questioning Hamilton was able to add more links to the artful "chain of reasoning." By his spur-of-the-moment answers to each hostile question of Smith, Hamilton succeeded in turning Smith's own questions against him:

Q: (by Mr. Smith to Lieutenant Colonel Hamilton): Do you mean that I declared my ignorance as to General Arnold's designs, as they were then discovered, or of General Arnold's intentions in sending me on board the vessel?

A: You declared your ignorance of any criminal intention whatsoever in General Arnold.

This neither answered Smith's question nor exonerated Smith.

Q (by Mr. Smith): Don't you recollect my saying that General Arnold, when he applied to me for a coat for Anderson, said he was only a merchant, and from pride had borrowed a coat from an officer in New York?

A: I do not.

Q (by Mr. Smith): Don't you recollect my appealing to you . . . at the time of the examination, with respect to my political character as far as you know it?

A: I recollect you appealed to me respecting your political character; and that my answer was, that in the early part of this contest, you had exhibited appearances of an intemperate zeal for the cause of America.

Q (by Mr. Smith): What do you mean by an intemperate zeal?

A: An excessive warmth.

Q (by Mr. Smith): Was not my character in New York always esteemed as a warm friend to the cause of America, before we quit the city, as far as came to your knowledge?

A: Many persons esteemed you as a zealot on the popular side; though intimations of doubt have been made to me of the sincerity of your pretensions, I believe from a suspicion of your family.

By his answers upon this extraordinary cross-examination, the witness, Hamilton, was managing to call into question not only Smith's truthfulness but also his credibility as an American patriot—on the grounds that his overzealousness aroused suspicion.

In answer to a later question of Smith, Hamilton testified that Smith had been asked to give an account of everything he knew of General Arnold's transactions:

> Q (by Smith): Was it in consequence of threats from General Washington that I gave that account?

Smith's imputation by the word *threats* was that Washington had been guilty of browbeating the witness. Hamilton could not let that stand. He answered Smith evenly:

> A: . . . The General expressed himself with some warmth.
> Q (by Smith): Don't you recollect that General Washington mentioned to me that this man, whom I brought on shore by the name of John Anderson, was the Adjutant-General of the British army?
> A: I think I do.

Hamilton's "I think I do" is the weakest possible form in which a hostile witness, forced to give an affirmative answer on cross-examination (or else lie), can put his affirmation.

> Q (by Smith): Did I not appear very much surprised at hearing it?
> A: I do not exactly recollect your appearance at this time.

Hamilton's answer left Smith with nothing at all to show for this line of questioning.

Finally, Smith asked Hamilton, "Don't you recollect that when I said that I had brought one Anderson on shore, that I said I understood that Anderson was to negotiate Robinson's business with General Arnold?"

Hamilton's answer consisted of five well-chosen and ordered words. It is impossible to think of five words that are more "perfectly correct," as Smith had to admit, yet that convey a more profound sense of disbelief of the proposition they ostensibly affirm than the following five, with which Hamilton drily ended his testimony:

> A: You did profess that supposition.

Smith's interrogation of Hamilton provides an excellent model of the kind of leading questions a cross-examiner should never propound to a well-prepared, hostile witness.

On October 26, the court-martial acquitted Smith for lack of proof that he knew that Robinson and Arnold had been up to treason. This did not mean he had not known in fact, nor did it convince Washington or Hamilton that he was innocent. It meant only that guilt of a high crime that turned on guilty knowledge, or scienter, had failed of proof beyond a reasonable doubt. Smith was handed over to New York civil authorities for a new trial, escaped from a Goshen jail, and fled to safety behind the British lines, thus corroborating Hamilton's suspicions.

Joshua Hett Smith's acquittal for failure of proof was a keen disappointment to Washington, but he could not help appreciating all the help Hamilton had tried to give with his artful testimony as a star witness for the prosecution. Washington's disappointment at Smith's acquittal was much less keen than it would have been if the furious public clamor for a scapegoat, aroused by Arnold's treason, had not been largely satisfied by the bigger and better scapegoat who by now had already been hanged.

As Hamilton explained it crisply in a letter to John Laurens of October 11, 1780: "André was without loss of time conducted to the Head Quarters of the army, where he was immediately brought before a board of General Officers, to prevent all possibility of misrepresentation or cavil on the part of the army. The Board reported, that he ought to be considered as a spy and according to the laws and usage of nations to suffer death; which was executed two days after."

Major John André's trial at a closed hearing in the Old Dutch church at Tappan two days after his capture before a board of generals, who summarily issued an unappealable report of guilty, produced a sentence of death by hanging. Some might call André's trial a Star Chamber proceeding. For a big scapegoat like André military justice was more than twice as swift as for a small one like Smith.

To his chief, Sir Henry Clinton, Adjutant General John André was as much a favorite as Lafayette or Hamilton was to Washington. André's defense and the British position, as Sir Henry Clinton later argued it to General Nathanael Greene, were that "under no Description [can] Major André be considered as a spy; nor by any usage of nations at war, or the Custom of Armies." This was because André had gone to West Point at the request of its commanding officer, Arnold, under "a flag of truce . . . with which he went on shore . . . acting under [Clinton's] immediate orders, as a military Man. What happened after was from the entire Direction and positive Orders of major General Arnold, your Officer commanding. . . . Major André can merely be considered as a messenger and not a spy."

There had been no military campaigns in 1780 to produce anything that might be called a victory. Financial support from the French alliance seemed as impalpable as the French fleet was elusive.

There had been crushing defeats at Camden and almost everywhere else. It became known to the public that Arnold had been keeping British intelligence informed of all of Washington's movements near West Point. Starved for even a crumb of good news, the exposure of the plot, the preservation of West Point, and the narrow escape of Washington and Rochambeau and the rest of the top command from Clinton's bag were received by the public with as much emotional release as if a major victory had been won. In reality, it was no more than a lucky deliverance from disaster. The hanging of a redcoat scapegoat like André would add mightily to the momentary elation of popular opinion. Before the hanging, Hamilton eloquently urged objections on Washington, but the general could not allow Hamilton's scruples to stand against a cyclone of popular feeling. Washington's policy would help revive flagging support for the army's cause by going along with and gratifying popular clamor.

On this difference with Washington, Hamilton commented with bitterness that "some people are only sensible to motives of policy, and . . . from a narrow disposition, mistake it." His phrase "some people" rather pointedly included his chief, who alone had the power of final decision.

British apologists depicted Washington's insistence on having André hanged as arising not so much from a "narrow disposition . . . sensible only to motives of policy" as from his overreaching ambition to bring the colonies under a government with power in the hands of a single man, who would be none other than himself. By Washington's enemies, Hamilton was publicly implicated in this dark scheme, even though Hamilton privately opposed Washington's policy and remonstrated with his chief against carrying out the sentence.

Rivington's *Royal Gazette*, published in New York at the end of October, ran a long account of André's hanging under the heading "Case of Major John André . . . put to death by Rebels."[2] It claimed that Washington could not have been motivated by personal resentment or a desire to take out his personal anger at Arnold on André, but that André was "the victim of policy." Rivington argued that the "object of this 'political stroke,' this 'dark scheme' " was made clear by a certain letter Hamilton had written on October 12, 1780, to Isaac Sears, a copy of which had been intercepted. This letter was supposed to show that Hamilton sought to make Washington a dictator. The accusation ran that Hamilton had approvingly noted Sears's comment that "the same spirit of indifference to public affairs prevails" in Boston as elsewhere. Hamilton had then gone on to offer his usual recommendations: to aid a contest that could not "be much longer supported on the present footing, we must have a Government with more power . . . We must have an administration distinct from Congress, and in the hands of single men under their orders."

Rivington's *Royal Gazette* expanded this into an all-out attack on Hamilton. Five years after Hamilton had defended the freedom of Rivington's press to print stories Hamilton opposed from destruction by Sears's Sons of Liberty, Rivington's *Gazette* said that Hamilton's letter to Sears, written by "General Washington's confidential friend . . . ," contained "the General's sentiments." Therefore, Rivington charged, Hamilton was thrusting Washington forward in the crisis as a protector or king or dictator. Nothing was better adapted to serve Hamilton's purpose "than the putting of Major André, Adjutant General of the British army to death."

Their acquaintance of less than a week between André's capture and his death brought him and Hamilton into a friendship of the most intense and instantaneous kind. It is likely that during their several conferences in his prison cell, André confided to Hamilton the story of his affair with the beautiful Honora Sneyd, whose parents had refused her permission to marry him. She had married one R. L. Edgeworth, but she and André had remained lovers. When André was taken prisoner at the capture of St. John's in 1775, he had been "stripped of everything except the picture of Honora, which I concealed in my mouth." He proudly proclaimed that "Preserving this I yet think myself fortunate." During the British occupation of Philadelphia in 1777–1778, André courted Mrs. Benedict Arnold who was still the belle Peggy Shippen. He may have shown Hamilton his exquisite pencil drawing of her in costume for a fancy dress ball that he had designed for her.

Writing to Elizabeth on October 2 of his intense admiration for André, Hamilton says, "I wished myself possessed of André's accomplishments for your sake; for I would wish to charm you in every sense . . . In your eyes I should wish to be the first, the most amiable, the most accomplished of my sex; but I will make up all I want in love."

Describing André, the eldest son of Huguenot emigrés to England, Hamilton expresses his own idea of the masculine beau ideal. It is an ideal that includes proficiencies Hamilton himself never displayed—skill in poetry and painting, for example. In a long letter to John Laurens, Hamilton wrote, "There was something singularly interesting in the character and fortunes of Andre. To an excellent understanding, well improved by education and travel, he united a peculiar elegance of mind and manners, and the advantage of a pleasing person. 'Tis said he possessed a pretty taste for the fine arts, and had himself attained some proficiency in poetry, music and painting."

André also had a peculiar modesty of style that appealed to Hamilton, suggesting emulation: "His knowledge appeared without ostentation, and embellished by a diffidence that rarely accompanies so many talents and accomplishments; which left you to suppose more than appeared. His sentiments were elevated, and inspired esteem: they had a softness that conciliated affection. His elocution was handsome; his address easy, polite, and insinuating."

To Hamilton, André's inadvertent self-entrapment in Peggy and Benedict Arnold's get-rich-quick scheme contained elements of high tragedy: "By his merit he had acquired the unlimited confidence of his general, and was making a rapid progress in military rank and reputation. But in the height of his career, flushed with new hopes from the execution of a project, the most beneficial to his party that could be devised, he was at once precipitated from the summit of prosperity, and saw all the expectations of his ambition blasted, and himself ruined."

The remarkable thing was that André did not seem concerned about himself, but only that his death might cause Sir Henry Clinton some self-reproach. On one of the visits Hamilton made to his cell, André "begged me to be the bearer of a request to the General, for permission to send an open letter to Sir Henry

Clinton. 'I forsee my fate,' said he, 'and though I pretend not to play the hero, or to be indifferent about life, yet I am reconciled to whatever may happen, conscious that misfortune, not guilt, has brought it upon me.' " *In extremis*, one thing that disturbed André's tranquility was Sir Henry Clinton: "He has been too good to me; he has been lavish of his kindness. I am bound to him by too many obligations, and love him too well, to bear the thought that he should reproach himself, or that others should reproach him, on the supposition of my having conceived myself obliged, by his instructions, to run the risk I did. I would not for the world leave a string in his mind that should embitter his future days."

Deeply touched by such selfless sentiments, Hamilton added that André "could scarce finish the sentence, bursting into tears in spite of his efforts to suppress them. With difficulty André collected himself enough afterwards to add, 'I wish to be permitted to assure him I did not act under this impression, but submitted to a necessity imposed upon me, as contrary to my own inclination as to his orders.' "

Rather like a schoolmaster showing off a bright pupil, Hamilton enclosed a copy of André's letter for Laurens to see, adding the comment that Laurens would be as much pleased with it as he was "both for the diction and the sentiment." Hamilton assured Laurens that he had complied with André's next-to-last wish.

When the sentence of the general court-martial was announced to André, he remarked that since it was his lot to die, there was still a choice in the mode, which would make a material difference in his feelings. He would be happy, if possible, to be indulged with a professional death, like a soldier before a firing squad, not by hanging like a spy. He made a second application by letter in concise but persuasive terms. With memories of Nathan Hale's famous martyrdom and his own characteristic preoccupation with niceties in the manner of dying in mind, Hamilton urged André's wishes on Washington, but without success. He strongly disapproved of Washington's insistence that André be hanged like a spy instead of being shot like a soldier. Hamilton avoided direct criticism of Washington, but made clear to Laurens his exquisite distaste for Washington's insistence on going ahead with the hanging: "It was thought this indulgence, being incompatible with the customs of war, could not be granted, and it was therefore determined, in both cases, to evade an answer, to spare him the sensations which a certain knowledge of the intended mode would inflict."

On October 2, the day of André's hanging, Hamilton wrote Betsy, "I urged a compliance with André's request to be shot and I do not think it would have had an ill effect; but some people are only sensible to motives of policy, and sometimes from a narrow disposition mistake it. When André's tale comes to be told, and present resentment is over, the refusing him the privilege of choosing [the] manner of his own death will be branded with too much obduracy." Only a minority of the opinion of the time agreed with Hamilton. In later times a majority has come over to Hamilton's side of this sad argument with his inflexible chief.

A spy like André made a bigger and better scapegoat than a go-between like Smith. But a traitor like Arnold was still bigger game than an involuntary spy like André. The argument could be made that Arnold was a traitor to the British as well as the Americans because he had arranged his meetings with André in such a way that, if discovered, Arnold could place all blame on André and sacrifice André to his own safety. In the event he had done so. All sympathy was on André's side; yet the rules of war made the exchange of a mere spy like him for a traitor like Arnold unthinkable. The British would, of course, agree. No one knew better than Hamilton the force of the rules of war.

Although such an exchange was contrary to international law and military honor, from the American side it had an almost irresistible popular appeal. Washington came down on the popular side; Hamilton, on the unpopular side. And on this rock of honor they would split.

There is not much doubt that Washington badly wanted to exchange André for Arnold, gave orders that would have had the practical effect of making the exchange possible, and took steps to have his proposal made known to Sir Henry Clinton. Because André was a favorite of Clinton, it was possible that the British commander would be willing to waive the niceties of honor to retrieve him by a trade to save his life. Washington, no doubt, understood as well as Hamilton the legal and moral difficulties involved in hanging André as a spy. And Washington could sense better than Hamilton Clinton's vulnerability to the threat of death for his young aide. But he would allow none of these sentiments to stand in the way of the chance to shore up popular support for the prosecution of the war at this dark hour.

Washington did not want his own name and person to be associated with a proposal that he knew Hamilton and a like-minded minority would find dishonorable, but he did not scruple to lend the talents of his aide to it. An irony of history has branded Hamilton with whatever dishonor may attach to having communicated the proposal to exchange André for Arnold to Sir Henry Clinton.

Hamilton confided his side of this strange episode to Elizabeth: "It was proposed to me to suggest to him [André] the idea of an exchange for Arnold." Such a proposal could have come from no one but Washington. Hamilton turned down his chief: "I knew I should have forfeited André's esteem by doing it, and therefore declined to do it. As a man of honor he could not but reject it and I would not for the world have proposed to him such a thing, which must have placed me in the unamiable light of supposing him capable of a meanness, or of not feeling myself the impropriety of the measure."

From Washington's headquarters quickly came a second attempt to play upon Clinton's vulnerable personal affection for André, whose sexual identity seemed ambiguously defined.

The key document in this second approach is a mysterious letter in a disguised hand dated September 30, 1780, addressed to Sir Henry Clinton, signed AB (or AH). Many historians have attributed it to Hamilton's authorship. Others, perhaps misguidedly zealous to defend him, have denied he had a hand in it. Still others claim that it was *by* his hand though not *in* his hand.[3]

According to Lieutenant Colonel John Graves Simcoe, commander of the Queen's Rangers, "amongst some letters which American Captain Aaron Ogden passed [from American to British headquarters] a paper was slid in without signature, but in the handwriting of Hamilton, Washington's secretary, saying that the only way to save André was to give up Arnold."

The text of the "AH" letter in the disguised handwriting read:

> Major André . . . was captured in such a way as will according to the laws of war justly affect his life. Though an enemy, his virtues and his accomplishments are much admired. Perhaps he might be released for General Arnold, delivered up without restriction or condition . . . Arnold appears to have been the guilty author of the mischief, and ought more properly to be the victim, as there is great reason to believe he meditated a double treachery, and had arranged the interview in such a manner, that if discovered in the first instance, he might have it in his power to sacrifice Major André to his own safety . . .
>
> I have the honor to be etc.
> AH

No time is to be lost.

How did this document find its way to Clinton? On the morning of September 30, 1780, Washington met Captain Aaron Ogden all alone at the door of his headquarters in the old DeWint house at Tappan and, giving him a packet of letters addressed to Sir Henry Clinton, ordered Ogden to take it, with a powerful escort of 25 dragoons, to Lafayette for special instructions. Thereafter the packet should be delivered under a flag of truce to the enemy post at Paulus Hook (Jersey City). The "AH" letter was later found "slid in" among the letters in this packet. Ogden's "special instructions" from Lafayette were to arrive so late in the evening that it would be necessary to spend the night. Lafayette also told Ogden that he should let it come out to the British commanding officer that if Clinton would allow Arnold somehow to get within Washington's power (for example, by allowing Arnold to be "accidentally" captured by Ogden's dragoons), André would at once be released.

When Ogden arrived at Paulus Hook, he told the British post commander that he had an important message for Clinton. But after being gone more than two hours, the post commander returned from British headquarters with the curt message "that a deserter was never given up" and that Captain Ogden's horse would be ready in the morning. The message that the British post commander passed back to Ogden seemed to come from the highest authority—Clinton himself. It responded directly to the oral message Ogden had delivered. But it did not respond directly to the letter signed "AH." Perhaps Clinton had not yet noticed it, or perhaps the "AH" letter had not yet been "slid in" to the packet of letters from Washington that Ogden delivered.

On October 1, 1780, the day after Ogden and his dragoons had delivered

Lafayette's message and Washington's packet of letters, Clinton posted three commissioners aboard the *Greyhound* to sail up the river to Dobbs Ferry to make a plea to Washington to rescind André's death sentence. When the vessel anchored at Dobbs Ferry, the British commissioners were informed that General Nathanael Greene would receive only Lieutenant General James Robertson and his aide, but that the other British commissioners, Chief Justice William Smith, Joshua's brother, and Lieutenant Governor Andrew Elliot, should not even land.

An eyewitness reported that "Murray, the aide of General Robertson, walked elsewhere with Hamilton, Washington's aide-de-camp, and two other Rebel officers." To Greene, Robertson reiterated Clinton's arguments that André was not a spy while Murray and Hamilton talked. In his response to Robertson, Greene echoed Hamilton, saying that "The time, manner, object of the interview, change of dress, and other circumstances" all pointed to spying. There was only one way André could be saved. In the course of the conference, Greene managed to convey Washington's proposal for an exchange to Robertson as a mere suggestion, without appearing to do so on Washington's responsibility or even on Washington's initiative.

Upon returning to the *Greyhound*, General Robertson wrote to Clinton, "He [Greene] said that there was no treaty about spies. I said no military Casuist in Europe would call André a spy, and I would suffer death itself if Monsieur Rochambeau or General Knyphausen would call him by that name." Greene replied coolly that "the army must be satisfied by seeing spies executed—but there was one thing that would satisfy them—they expected if André was set free, Arnold should be given up."

Robertson professed to be appalled and shocked at Greene's proposal, seeming as it did to come from Washington through Greene, as it had. Robertson was not fooled by Greene's offhand manner. Robertson wrote, "This I answered with a look only, which threw Greene into confusion."

Perhaps recalling the campfires Washington had left burning in Brooklyn Heights and at Trenton while his troops escaped traps in the darkness, Robertson thought Washington was bluffing again and that Clinton would think so too. His misreading of Washington's intentions sealed André's fate. He wrote Clinton: "I am persuaded André will not be hurt."

Washington was not bluffing.

André was hanged the next day as a spy.

At some unknown time or other after the hanging, the "AH" letter in the disguised handwriting "slid in" to Washington's packet was endorsed by Clinton in a sketchy fashion: "Hamilton was [or possibly "W's," meaning Washington's] aide de camp received after A's [André's] death."

The "AH" letter differs from Hamilton's usual handwriting in being written in a backhand slant. Some capitals are structurally different from his. The bottom lines run uphill, but the same thing is often true of Hamilton's own manuscripts. The initials AB might just as easily be read AH. There is no reason to suppose that Simcoe or Clinton would have known Hamilton's regular handwriting well enough to recognize the disguised hand as his unless Hamilton himself had passed word to them through Robertson's aide Murray at the parley the previous day to be on the lookout for the important note he had written. Hamilton's written note, coupled with the wide knowledge that he was the aide closer to Washington than any other, would prove to Clinton that Greene's seemingly casual suggestion to the outraged Robertson was backed up by written evidence of the authority of the American commander in chief himself.

This writer's conclusion is that the penmanship was Hamilton's, but the proposal was Washington's alone. Hamilton put down on paper against his own will and over the objections of his conscience words dictated by his chief. Hamilton's crude dissembling of his handwriting and signature was his only way of protesting. The use to which he was being put in writing it was a painful reminder of the groveling condition of an aide.

The argument against Hamilton's having written the note rests on the same clear record of Hamilton's disapproval of the exchange proposal. The "Gentleman" (for which read *Washington*) had suggested that André might propose such an exchange to Clinton, and André had declined to do so, to Hamilton's intense satisfaction. As Hamilton wrote, "The moment he had been guilty of so much frailty, I should have ceased to esteem him." When asked to suggest the exchange proposal to André, Hamilton had refused to offend André's honor or stain his own with "the impropriety of the measure." Much against his will, scruples, and principles of honor, Hamilton wrote the letter at Washington's command and made sure that it was "slid in" to Ogden's packet, probably at the time when Ogden received his orders from Lafayette. The next day at the parley, Hamilton passed along the word that Clinton should look for it there and note from whom it came.

There was no logical reason for Clinton to append to the "AH" letter the curious footnote that he did ("received after A's death") unless he had, in fact, received it before André's death. His notation would be a necessary, if self-serving, exoneration of himself to history and the memory of André. Even his self-serving rewrite of history could never exonerate Clinton's conscience from the inward shame of having failed to act, particularly when a response to Hamilton's letter might well have saved his beloved aide's neck from the noose.

A single step by Washington, or Clinton, was all that would have been needed to preserve André's life, but Clinton made no move from his side, nor Washington from his.

On October 2, André's execution day, Hamilton wrote Betsy, "Poor André suffers to-day. Everything that is amiable in virtue, in fortitude, in delicate sentiment, and accomplished manners, pleads for him; but hard hearted policy calls for a sacrifice. He must die . . ."

From behind the British lines a dispatch came in from Benedict Arnold. He threatened that if André were executed, he, personally, would "think myself bound by every tie of duty and honor to retaliate on such unhappy persons of your army as may fall within my power . . . I call heaven and earth to witness . . . the torrent of blood that may be spilt in consequence!"

Enemies of Hamilton and Washington, like Joseph Reed and other Pennsylvania radicals, tried to put blame on Washington and Philip Schuyler. The commander had shown gross and suspicious favoritism to the traitor Arnold by having placed him in command at West Point in the first place, they said.

On André's execution day, the macabre procession from cell to gallows passed close by Washington's headquarters. Seeing the gibbet at last, André would suffer a sudden shock, struck for the first time to learn of the denial of his dying request. Closed windows would not have shut out the sound of the muffled drums of the death march from the ears of the commander in chief as the procession passed. There would be the awful moment after reaching the place for the hanging when handsome young André's eyes swung round, expecting to see a firing squad, and fell instead on the empty noose dangling from the gibbet. Would granting the condemned man's dying wish have been too serious a deviation from principle and accepted procedure? Was popular clamor so insistent on this? Washington in deep gloom sat alone in his room. The hanging of Clinton's favorite, his adjutant general, a charming young man so like one of his own beloved aides, had already reduced many in camp to tears. Washington ordered that none of his own aides be witness to the hanging itself.

In a letter to John Laurens afterward, Hamilton described André's last moments with economy and not without emotion:

"In going to the place of execution, he bowed familiarly as he went along, to all those with whom he had been acquainted in his confinement. A smile of complacency expressed the serene fortitude of mind. Arrived at the fatal spot, he asked with some emotion, 'Must I die in this manner?' " He was astonished to be told so late of the denial of his request to be shot, not hanged. All, including Hamilton, had kept from him this last awful secret. Hanging was unavoidable, he was told. "I am reconciled to my fate," said he, "but not to the mode." Soon, however, recollecting himself, he added: "It will be but a momentary pang." Springing upon the cart, he performed the last offices to himself, with a composure that excited the admiration and melted the hearts of the beholders. Upon being told that the final moment was at hand and asked if he had anything to say, he answered: "Nothing but to request you will witness to the world that I die like a brave man." Hamilton gave a benediction: "Among the extraordinary circumstances that attended him, in the midst of his enemies, he died universally esteemed and universally regretted." Hamilton's account of the affair was published in many newspapers, and the public's opinion of what had happened came to a large extent to be formed by what Hamilton wrote.

Of Arnold, Hamilton wrote, "This man is in every sense, despicable. Added to the scene of knavery and prostitution during his command in Philadelphia, which the late seizure of his papers has unfolded, the history of his command at West Point is a history of little, as well as great villainies. He practised every dirty act of peculation, and even stooped to connections with the sutlers of the garrison to defraud the public."

The exemplary conduct of André's captors formed a striking contrast to

Arnold's dirty acts of peculation. André had attempted to bribe the three good patriots who had arrested him, Isaac Van Wart, John Paulding, and David Williams, with offers of his watch, his horse, and any sum of money they should name. These heroes of the common people "rejected his offers with indignation, and the gold that could seduce a man high in the esteem and confidence of his country, who had the remembrance of past exploits, the motives of present reputation and future glory, to prop his integrity, had no charms for three simple peasants, leaning only on their virtue and an honest sense of their duty." Out of the whole tragic episode, the real heroes were these Westchester members of the silent majority. "While Arnold is handed down with execration to future times, posterity will repeat with reverence the names of Van Wart, Paulding, and Williams," Hamilton concluded.

Though the names of Van Wart, Paulding, and Williams never managed to join the pantheon of American heroes as household words, Hamilton's clear, vivid, and moving account convinced the public that the plot against West Point had been the work of only one man. He showed that the plot had been promptly and skillfully exposed and thwarted by Washington and his aides and that there would be no widespread repercussions from it during the autumn when American fortunes lay so low. Hamilton's account brought a feeling of relief, even exultation, that Washington and the other leaders had safely escaped the traitor's net.

Washington's own summing up for the media added to Hamilton's account a reminder of whose side God was still on: "Never has the interposition of Providence appeared more conspicuous than in the rescue of the post and garrison of West Point from Arnold's villainous perfidy."

As a result of the upswing in popular gratitude for Washington's deliverance, Joseph Reed and the Pennsylvania radicals gave up their efforts to tar Washington, Schuyler, and Hamilton with guilt-by-association with Arnold's treason. They contented themselves merely with banishing Peggy from her father's house in Philadelphia and forcing her to join her connubial conspirator behind the British lines in New York. To Hamilton, or, indeed, almost anyone but a Philadelphian, such a switch of cities, if not the mildest of all possible punishments, would look more like a reward.

For public consumption, Hamilton would pass off an event that had moved him so deeply in private by saying rather neatly, "Never . . . did a man suffer death with more justice, or deserve it less." More complex and revealing of the inward Hamilton was his private opinion. It was not that of a colonial or a partisan or a narrowly legalistic lawyer or a popularity seeker, but that of a 23-year-old man of the world. Far from welling up out of undifferentiated sentiment, kindliness, or benevolence toward André, his view was based on reasoning from a peculiarly Hamiltonian premise, which he carefully and consciously identified with honor.

"I speak not of André's conduct in this affair as a philosopher," he wrote Laurens, "but as a man of the world. The authorized maxims and practices of war are the satires of human nature. They countenance almost every species of seduction as well as violence; and the general that can make most traitors in the army of his adversary is frequently most applauded.

"On this scale we acquit André; while we could not but condemn him, if we were to examine his conduct by the sober rules of philosophy and moral rectitude. It is, however, a blemish on his fame, that he once intended to prostitute a flag; about this, a man of nice honor ought to have had a scruple; but the temptation was great: let his misfortunes cast a veil over his error." Thus, like André himself, Hamilton had reconciled himself to what Washington had insisted be done, "but not to the mode."

The question of what to do about André confronted Washington and Hamilton as his chief aide with an agonizing set of conflicts between the chief executive's need to maintain popular backing for his own leadership on the one hand, the need to conform to objective standards of law and justice on another hand, and the need to temper justice and rigorous policy with mercy in a particular person's case on still another hand. To most chief executives, the perfect aide is one whose loyalty to his chief is such that the aide's personal views are never pressed where they differ from the chief's. For all his energy, experience, skill, discretion, and power of statement, by such standards, Hamilton in André's case had proved himself to be something less than the perfect model of an aide. And something more.

14

I AM NO LONGER A MEMBER OF THE GENERAL'S FAMILY

—TO PHILIP SCHUYLER FROM HEADQUARTERS, NEW WINDSOR, NEW YORK, FEBRUARY 18, 1781

The double promotion to lieutenant colonel that Hamilton had won after six months as captain of a line artillery company on becoming Washington's chief aide was almost four years behind him. Others who had served no longer had won promotions to higher rank. As the year 1780 drew to a close, Hamilton grew more and more restless in the groveling condition of an aide. When he had written Neddy Stevens, "I wish there was a war," Hamilton had thought of it as emancipating him from such a condition, not chaining him to it.

It was exactly this length of service in the same rank and staff position that now made him seem irreplaceable to Washington. Hamilton shared with Washington a unique fund of experience and knowledge of revolutionary men and events gained both as a headquarters intelligencer and a former line commander during the most intense period of combat the army had seen. Washington could not help feeling that Hamilton was infinitely more valuable to him and the nation continuing as he had been than he could possibly be doing anything else. Hamilton disputed this.

Much of Hamilton's frustration with his own position came from his own inescapable perception of the logic of Washington's position. If there were to be any change, it would have to come, and it could only come, from the aide's side.

In July, Hamilton had obliged a comrade on the staff, James McHenry, with a note to Congressman Duane, requesting Duane to use his influence to obtain an appointment in the line for McHenry. "He [McHenry] wishes to quit a station which among foreigners is not viewed in a very reputable light—and to get into one more military," Hamilton wrote. He was seeking for his good friend what he would have liked for himself.

In October the aborted exchange of André for Arnold and André's hanging added to Hamilton's frustration emotional resentment against Washington himself. It would have been impossible in any event for two such strong characters to remain so long in constant contact without abrasions. Hamilton would have liked a transfer to a line regiment, but he knew Washington would never assent.

A second possibility was a position in the diplomatic service, for which Washington's consent would not be necessary: the post of secretary to the Ministry to France was open. Hidden wires began to be pulled. Philip Schuyler, his future father-in-law, wrote from Congress as a piece of fresh news that "you have been mentioned in private conversation to go as Secretary to the Embassy at the Court of Versailles; there is but one obstacle which prevents me from making up my mind on the subject; that you will know when I have the pleasure of seeing you. In the meantime revolve the matter in yours."

To Schuyler the "one obstacle" was, of course, Hamilton's long-planned marriage to Elizabeth, which would either have to be postponed indefinitely or else hurried up if he obtained the appointment.

Hamilton would have been well suited for the mission. The most pressing purpose of the Ministry to France was to obtain a loan. Hamilton had urged such a loan upon Congress as one of the most important steps America could take to stabilize her finances. He had studied the subject thoroughly, he knew the arguments that would appeal to the French mind, he had many French connections through his intimacy with French comrades-in-arms, and he spoke their language with a West Indies flavor that even Parisians found beguiling.

On December 9 the names of Hamilton and John Laurens, along with several others, were placed before Congress in nomination for the post.

On December 11 a vote was taken in Congress to decide between Hamilton and the son of Henry Laurens, the former president of Congress, who was now held as a political prisoner by the British in the Tower of London. On the first ballot, Hamilton and Laurens tied. On succeeding ballots votes shifted from some of the lesser candidates to Laurens, whereas Hamilton received no additional support. Laurens was elected unanimously.

Laurens had not even known he was being considered for the mission and felt that the vote in his favor was really a vote for his father. Besides, he did not wish to block his own best friend, Hamilton. When he received the news of his selection, he promptly declined and suggested Hamilton in his place as being much better qualified.

Congress ignored his suggestion and on December 17 nominated James

Lovell, who also declined in favor of Hamilton. After more inconclusive balloting, they tendered the mission again to Laurens, who now saw no alternative but
to accept. But he wrote to George Washington that he still considered Hamilton
the better choice:

> Your Excellency will not be a little surprised to learn, that Con-
> gress have determined to send me to France, for the special purpose of
> representing the present state of our affairs and soliciting the neces-
> sary succours. I was in great hopes, that Congress would have availed
> themselves of the abilities of Colonel Hamilton for these important
> objects, and that I should have been suffered to persevere in a line of
> duty, to which I feel myself more adequate. But, unfortunately for
> America, Colonel Hamilton was not sufficiently known to Congress to
> unite their suffrages in his favor.

Congress's true reasons for refusing Hamilton can not be gleaned from the
dry husks of the proceedings recorded in the *Secret Journals*. The suspicion that
Philip Schuyler may have had a hand in Hamilton's losing out (in order to keep
Hamilton at home in the midst of the wedding plans) is out of keeping with
everything else known about the kind of man Philip Schuyler was. On the other
hand, Washington had far better reasons for seeing that Congress did not send
his aide away and the influence to translate his reasons into votes.

Far from envying Laurens his appointment to the Ministry, Hamilton was
happy for Laurens and the country, believing that only he himself could serve
it better as minister than his friend. Never envious rivals, the two men were
more like fond brothers. Hamilton happily agreed with Washington's recommendation and did all he could to prosper Laurens's mission to France. Hamilton
prepared a letter for Washington's signature for Laurens to take with him that
is not so much a set of instructions to the American envoy as it is a plea to the
French Ministry for all possible aid. The letter is a remarkable prescript of things
that Hamilton would write in support of public credit a decade later as secretary
of the treasury.

In carrying on the war, he wrote, America had exceeded its natural abilities.
Decay of public credit was due primarily to lack of wealth or of funds for the
redemption of paper. Efforts to support the army by collections of food and
forage had proved unworkable. Domestic loans could yield little, for the few
monied men could and would invest more profitably and safely elsewhere.

France must not conclude that, if no outside help were supplied, America's
desire for independence or resources to secure success would flag. Borrowings
could be repaid: "Our debts are hitherto small. The vast . . . tracts of unallocated
lands, the variety and fertility of soils; the advantages . . . we possess for
commerce, insure to this country a rapid advancement in population and prosperity and a certainty, its independence being established, of redeeming in a short
term of years, the comparatively inconsiderable debts it may . . . contract."

As Laurens's intelligencer-by-proxy for the French mission denied to him in person, Hamilton was one of the first to compose a plea on behalf of a typical underdeveloped nation coming tin cup in hand to an affluent one for a foreign aid handout. Hamilton had made the same kind of appeal for foreign aid to Jean Baptiste Donatien de Vimeur, the Comte de Rochambeau, commander of the French forces in America, at the allies' summit meeting at Hartford that September. Afterward Rochambeau had written to Vergennes, the French foreign minister, compressing Hamilton's action recommendations, but not his hopes for America, into a nutshell: "Send us troops, ships, and money, but do not depend upon these people [the Americans] or upon their means"; they have neither money nor credit; their resources for resistance are "only momentary."

Simply to resign as aide for private reasons (with a war on and a vital role to play in it) was unthinkable to a man with Hamilton's high hopes for the country he saw as a personal client and with his own highly personal concept of public honor. He also wanted glory in battle to raise himself "above mediocrity." He proposed to Washington that he be given a battalion command in Lafayette's expedition against the British on Staten Island. Washington refused. Line unit commanders were constantly being lost in action and had to be replaced all the time.

He saw Washington every day in person, but he made another request by letter on November 22:

> Some time last fall, when I spoke to your Excellency about going to the southward, I explained to you candidly my feelings with respect to military reputation, and how much it was my object to act a conspicuous part in some enterprise that might perhaps raise my character as a soldier above mediocrity. You were so good as to say you would be glad to furnish me with an occasion.

Yet when such an occasion had arisen at Staten Island, Washington had turned him down. Now an attack was contemplated on Bayard's Hill on Manhattan, where he had seen his first combat of the Revolution. If given command of a corps of two hundred men, Hamilton would storm and capture the hill. No doubt appalled by the recklessness and danger of the plan, Washington turned him down again.

Colonel Alexander Scammell, the former adjutant general, had just been promoted to the rank of brigadier general; the post of adjutant general was vacant; and Hamilton set to work on two of his warmest friends in the army, the Marquis de Lafayette, then at the height of his popularity, and General Nathanael Greene, who had just gone south to take command to try to reclaim Gates's losses. These two influential men, both favorites of Washington, now tried to obtain the vacant post for Hamilton.

Lafayette wrote to Washington:

> If . . . you were to cast your eye on a man, who, I think, would suit better than any other in the world, Hamilton is, I confess, the officer

whom I should like to see in that station. . . . His knowledge of your opinions and intentions on military arrangements, his love of discipline, the superiority he would have over all the others, principally when both armies shall operate together, and his uncommon abilities, are calculated to render him perfectly agreeable to you . . . On every public or private account, my dear general, I would advise you to take him.

Greene wrote a similarly strong letter of recommendation.

Following up Hamilton's formal letter of November 22, which had also sought a field command, these letters gave Washington much difficulty.[1] Hamilton had been seeing him every day, consulting him on every imaginable army matter, handling his correspondence. Washington could not brush requests from Lafayette and Greene aside as easily as he could requests from the aide himself. Between commander and aide there was no longer much spirit of warmth or trust. It was almost as if Washington were keeping Hamilton a prisoner on his staff.

Much troubled, Washington replied stiffly to Greene: "Without knowing that Colo. Hamilton ever had an Eye to the office of Adj. General, I did . . . recommend Genl. Hand for reasons which may occur to you." These reasons were chiefly that the adjutant general was "the Second officer in that line. It would have been disagreeable, therefore, to the present Sub-Inspectors, some of whom are full Colonels, to have a Lt. Colonel put over them."

He put off Lafayette in much the same way, adding that in any event it was too late because he had already dispatched his recommendation of Hand to Congress by messenger on horseback. Lafayette, in his eagerness to help Hamilton, offered to send an express to intercept Washington's messenger, but Washington pointed out that to do so would be highly irregular. Lafayette, like Greene, appreciated the irony of the fact that Hamilton's peculiar usefulness to the general stood squarely in the way of his being transferred to any other post in the army. When he recommended Hamilton as the replacement for Scammell, Lafayette's strongest argument had been that this would not really take Hamilton away from Washington: "An adjutant general ought always to be with the commander in chief. Hamilton should, therefore, remain in your family." His industry would allow him to fill both functions. Doing his best to break the bad news to Hamilton gently, Lafayette assured him: "I know the General's friendship and gratitude for you . . . both . . . greater than you perhaps imagine. I am sure that he needs only to be told that something will suit you, and when he thinks he can do it he certainly will. Before this campaign, I was your . . . very intimate friend. . . . Since my second voyage, my sentiment has increased to such a point the world knows nothing about."

Secure enough in the love of friends like Laurens, Greene, and Lafayette, Hamilton was all too secure in Washington's high but stony regard for his indispensability.

He was also secure in the heart of his mistress, who was also his fiancée, though she was far away in Albany, while he was still stuck in New Jersey.

When he thought about her, he made a pretense of believing that she would repent her foolish choice and renounce him, but he was not really worried: "Well, my love, here is the middle of October; a few weeks more and you are mine; a sweet reflection to me; is it so to my charmer? Do you find yourself more or less anxious for the moment to arrive as it approaches? This is a good criterion to determine the degree of your affection by. You have had an age for consideration, time enough for even a woman to know her mind in. Do you begin to repent or not? Remember you are going to do a very serious thing."

In modern times of the late eighteenth century—he wrote—you, Betsy, have been given a good deal of liberation. Men no longer have the power they once did, but they still have a little left: "Our sex have generously given up a part of its prerogatives, and husbands have no longer the power of life and death, as the wiser husbands of former days had, yet we still retain the power of happiness and misery."

He put her love for him to the test: "I give you warning; don't blame me if you make an injudicious choice; and if you should be disposed to retract, don't give me the trouble of a journey to Albany, and then do as did a certain lady I have mentioned to you, find out the day before we are to be married that you 'can't like the man'; but of all things I pray you don't make the discovery afterwards, for this would be worse than all."

But the case of the "certain lady" was no precedent for them. They already knew each other in the deepest sense, as compatible lover and mistress: "I do not apprehend its being the case. I think we know each other well enough to understand each other's feelings, and to be sure our affection will not only last but be progressive."

He was jocularly defensive about writing his love too often: "I would not have you imagine Miss that I write to you so often either to gratify your wishes or to please your vanity." The reason is "to indulge myself and to comply with that restless propensity of my mind, which will not allow me to be happy when I am not doing something in which you are concerned." This is not as silly as it sounds because "I can plead illustrious examples in my justification. Achilles had like to have sacrificed Greece and his glory to his passion for a female captive; and Antony lost the world for a woman."

Unfortunately, he regrets, passions to match those of antiquity are lacking in the humdrum, modern eighteenth-century world: "I am sorry the times are so changed as to oblige me to summon antiquity for my apology, but I confess, to the disgrace of the present age, that I have not been able to find many who are as far gone as myself in such laudable zeal for the fair sex."

They shared a lovers' secret. "I suspect, however, if others knew the charms of my sweetheart as well as I do, I should have a great number of competitors. I wish I could give you an idea of her; you have no conception how sweet a girl she is; it is only in my heart that her image is truly drawn. She has a lovely form, and a mind still more lovely; she is all goodness, the gentlest, the dearest, the tenderest of her sex—ah, Betsy, how I love her!"

Hamilton, even in such transports as a lover, would no more dash off a love letter and post it without reading it over than he would send off a state paper written for Washington to send by Laurens to France to save America without first rereading it. Not only did he reread his love letter to Betsy, but he also followed rereading by self-analysis of a heart full of tenderness, touched by sadness: "I stopped to read over my letter; it is a motley mixture of fond extravagance and sprightly dullness; the truth is I am too much in love to be either reasonable or witty; I feel in the extreme; and when I attempt to speak of my feelings I rave. I have remarked to you before that real tenderness has always a tincture of sadness, and when I affect the lively my melting heart rebels. It is separated from you."

What is love then? "Love is a sort of insanity and everything I write savors strongly of it; that you return it is the best proof of your madness also."

And he closes: "I tell you, my Betsy, you are negligent; you do not write me often enough. Take more care of my happiness, for there is nothing your Hamilton would not do to promote yours."

As their wedding day approached, problems that lay in the future and in the grain of his character put love's insanity into momentary partial eclipse. The future secretary of the treasury, the founder of the Bank of New York and of the Society for Useful Manufactures, the archprophet of American capitalism, with his usual foresight, knew in his bones that he would never be a rich man. The glamour of his position as the closest aide to the commanding general would fade with peace, if not sooner. "Tell me," he asked her in September, "Do you soberly relish the pleasure of being a poor man's wife? Have you learned to think a home spun preferable to a brocade and the rumble of a wagon wheel to the musical rattling of a coach and six? Will you be able to see . . . your old acquaintances flaunting it in gay life—tripping along in elegance and splendor —while you hold a humble station and have no other enjoyments than the sober comforts of a good wife? . . . If you cannot my Dear we are playing a comedy of all in the wrong, and you should correct the mistake before we begin to act the tragedy of the unhappy couple."

Charges of fiscal improprieties, kickbacks, graft, bribes, adultery and other embarrassments would beset their future life together. With unerring fore- knowledge he forewarned her: he was putting these questions to her "with an air of levity," but "they merit a very serious consideration, I have not concealed my circumstances from my Betsey—they are far from splendid . . . An indiffer- ence to property enters into my character too much and what affects me now as my Betsey is concerned in it, I should have laughed at or not thought of at all a year ago. But I have thoroughly examined my own heart. Beloved by you, I can struggle with every embarrassment of fortune with patience and firmness[.]"

He added: "Your future rank in life is a perfect lottery—you may move in an exalted, you may move in a very humble sphere—the last is most probable; examine well your heart."

But, above all, he was still her lover: "So far My Dear Betsy as the tenderest affection can compensate . . . in making your estimate, you cannot give too large a credit for the article. My heart overflows with every thing for you that admiration, esteem and love can inspire. *I would this moment give the world to be near you and only to kiss your sweet hand.*"

As the date approached, it was necessary to be meticulous about details: "You will laugh at me for consulting you about such a trifle, but I want to know whether you would prefer my receiving the nuptial benediction in my uniform or in a different habit. It will be just as you please, so consult your whim and what you think most consistent with propriety . . ."

It salted sex with savor to stir in some filial flirtation: "Tell my Peggy I will shortly open a correspondence with her. I am composing a piece, of which, from the opinion I have of her qualifications, I shall endeavour to prevail upon her to act the principal character. The title is 'The way to get him, for the benefit of all single ladies who desire to be married.' "

His lesson for Betsy was much more difficult, made so partly by her sisters: "For your own part, your business is now to study the way to keep him, which is said to be much the more difficult task of the two, though in your case I thoroughly believe it will be an easy one and that to succeed effectually you will only have to wish it sincerely. May I only be as successful in pleasing you, and may you be as happy as I shall ever wish to make you."

Into this atmosphere of marital transport came a report from Lafayette of the failure of his martial transfer. Lafayette apologized for "interrupting your Amorous occupations" in Albany, but "I have been Angry with you for not permitting my speaking immediately to the General on your Affair—this Curs'd way of a letter you have insisted upon has been the cause of my miscarrying, as the General had innocently put it out of his own power to oblige you."

The former penniless orphan immigrant from the Lesser Antilles hid his bar sinister under his immaculate blue and buff lieutenant colonel's uniform. With him to Albany he brought a troop of dashing young army friends who added a gallant military ambience to the wedding party. The British had recently been making threatening forays down Lake Champlain toward Fort Ticonderoga and had raided to within five miles of The Pastures, but these customary perils of a northern outpost did not prevent family, friends, and relations from responding to Catharine van Rensselaer and Philip Schuylers' request for the pleasure of their company at the great wedding reception to be held in the family mansion on December 14, 1780.

Throwing a cloak over his uniform against the upstate chill, surrounded by his galaxy of friends, the aide easily slipped unobserved through high patroon class lines. For three nights before the ceremony, in the wide upper hall of the Pastures, decorated with holly and lighted by dozens of wax candles, the young people danced until the early hours of the morning. The details of the event do not matter much to history, only the fact. There is no documented eyewitness account of it. On the basis of reconstruction by writers who have looked into the matter, it is safe to say that the bride wore white, which provided a striking contrast to her nut-brown complexion and sparkling dark eyes. Her shining black hair was hidden beneath a towering white wig, from which hung a lace veil that had belonged to her grandmother, Angelica Livingston Van Rensselaer. As his bride had requested, at the ceremony itself, Colonel Hamilton did not wear his uniform. Instead he wore a black velvet coat, white satin knee breeches, white silk stockings, and rhinestone shoe buckles, which he had received as a wedding present from Lafayette. In accordance with the dictates of a current fashion, which he disliked, his reddish hair was covered by a white wig with a long queue behind.

"As they have given and pledged their troth, each to the other," Dominie Westerlo of the First Reformed Church of Albany intoned solemnly, "I pronounce that they are man and wife." He raised his hand and gave the benediction. Afterward, back at The Pastures, standing before the carved mantel in the blue drawing room opening off the great hall to the right, past the curving balustrade that soon would be deeply scarred by the tomahawk blade of an Indian raider, beside Betsy's father and mother, Philip and Catharine Schuyler, Alexander and Betsy Hamilton received their guests. In a long line they moved slowly past to wish the young couple happiness. Most gave the usual assurances that it had been the most beautiful wedding and handsomest couple that anyone in those parts could remember. In truth, a finer looking pair had not often been seen. The groom of twenty-three, rosy and fair as a Scot, exuded self-assurance and energy. The bride, three inches shorter and seven months younger, known best to her family for most of her girlhood as a spirited, tomboyish gypsy, on the day of her wedding at least was not outshone by her brilliant, blonde younger sister Margarita, or Peggy. On that day at least, Peggy would hardly waste a glance of her sparkling eye on the much younger man who clung adoringly by her side—the patroon Stephen van Rensselaer, with whom she would eventually dwindle into marriage herself. Nor, on that day at least, would anyone admit that Betsy could be outshone by her sister Angelica Carter Church, who was one year older.

But no matter what they might politely say to Betsy and Alexander, no guest present could fail to be dazzled by Angelica. Her powdered and bejeweled hair was piled high into a tower that stood taller than that of any other woman's in the hall. She was the Schuyler sister with the swelling bosom drawn tightly down by the curve of a seductive corset into the smallest waist of any woman there. At other times, Angelica Church would be acknowledged, not only in Albany, not only in Philadelphia and New York, but in London and Paris as well, as one of the most beautiful women and greatest belles of the age. The ardent attention of the groom to the bride did not keep him too preoccupied to fail to ply his comely sisters-in-law with smiling gallantries.

Hamilton's close friend, groomsman, and physician, James McHenry, wrote a 72-line poem entitled simply "Epithalamium" in celebration of Alexander and Betsy's wedding night.

From what McHenry called his muse's "exhaustless store," his "choicest fancies" described three exciting climaxes in the upstairs bedchamber.

> Last night I sought her dear retreat
> And laid me at the fair one's feet.
> She knew my errand, sway'd her wand,
> Then pointed to a rising stand.

Things began to happen fast.

> (As thus ye lay the happiest pair,
> A rosy scent enriched the air
> While to a music softly sounding
> Breathing, panting, slow, rebounding)
> Love arose with pow'rful spell.

That was the first time; two more were yet to come.

> This is ground for holy feet
> Here the sports and pleasure meet.
> Chains of Priests or modes of art
> Weakly hold the human heart,
> Hence my Eloisa said
> "Give me those that love has made."
> Now his fluttering wings outspread
> Three times he bless'd the bridal bed,

Such good things can't keep coming forever, and there was this slowdown:

> Last Prudence came, in sober guise
> With Pilgrim's pace, and wisdom's eyes . . .

Then, with a few afterwords they fell asleep in each other's arms.

McHenry had seen Hamilton taking long hard looks at Peggy and still longer and harder looks at Angelica. He appended a warning specifically applicable to Hamilton:

> When love his choicest gifts has giv'n
> He flies to make another heav'n;

To take after Peggy or Angelica would be a mistake; so be sensible and stick to the fine Schuyler sister you've just had:

> But as he wheels his rapid flight
> Calm joys succeed and pure delight.
> Faith adds to all; for works we're told
> Is Love's alloy, and faith the gold.

Be prudent, too—get to work; make some money. Let a little moderation set
in according to the mode of Quintus Horatius Flaccus and the golden mean:

> Whilst Prudence all his succour lends
> To mark the point where pleasure ends.
> For, borne beyond a certain goal,
> The sweetest joys disgust the soul.

Dr. McHenry has already noted that his friend is inclined to neglect such
essential matters as looking out for his own (wealth) and health. Still, his life
expectancy is good, if he will only follow McHenry's prescriptions:

> What's more a blessing than the muse (wealth):
> For well he knows, deprived of this
> That toil and care is human bliss.
> All these attendants Ham are thine,
> Be't yours to treat them as divine;
> To cherish what keeps love alive;
> What makes us young at sixty-five.
> What lends the eye its earliest fires;
> What rightly managed still inspires.

Ham thanked his friend Mac for the nuptial song in honor of bride, groom,
and bedchamber. The one point of it all that seemed to catch Ham's mind's eye
most sharply was his line that "all ladies may be won."

Albany, December 16, 1780

I thank you Dear Mac for your poetry and your confidence. The
piece is a good one—your best. It has wit, which you know is a rare
thing. I see by perseverence all ladies may be won. The Muses begin to
be civil to you, in spite of Apollo and my prognosis.

You know I have often told you, you wrote prose well but had no
genius for poetry. I retract. Adieu.

A. Hamilton

The "Epithalamium" and Hamilton's reply were a one-sentence prescript of
the rest of his life. "In spite of Apollo," Dionysus, the god of orgiastic rites,
Apollo's eternal adversary in the competition for men's souls, would lead Hamilton to pursue "the sweetest joys" beyond "a certain goal" to the point where
they would, indeed, "disgust the soul."

On December 19, Hamilton wrote Washington: "Mrs. Hamilton presents her
respectful compliments to Mrs. Washington and yourself. After the holidays we
shall be at Headquarters." The first of the year found him back with Washington

at New Windsor. In her new status Betsy immediately established herself as one of the most popular members in the circle of official wives. Martha Washington came to know her well and welcomed her with kindness.

After much debate, plagued by a winter of mutinies in the army, Congress adopted some parts of the plan that Hamilton had long advocated for reforming the finances of the Revolution. It decided to replace the inept Committee on Finances with a single responsible financier. But who would be appointed financier?

General John Sullivan, a member of Congress, had heard of Hamilton's proposals for economic reform. James Duane, another member, was reminded of the brilliant essay on government and finance he had received from Hamilton. Even Isaac Sears of the New York Liberty Boys recalled the intercepted letter, dated October 12, 1780, from Hamilton that gave the gist of the other essays: "We must have a Government with more power. We must have a tax in kind. We must have a foreign loan. We must have a National Bank, on the true principles of a Bank. We must have an Administration distinct from Congress, and in the hands of single men under their orders. We must, above all things, have a regular army for the war, established on a sound basis that will keep good officers in the service."

On January 29, 1781, Washington received from Sullivan still another letter inquiring about his aide: "I wish your Excellency would be so obliging (when you have Leisure to favor me with another Letter) as to give me Yr. opinion with respect to Colo. Hamilton as a Financier."

Washington knew his aide as a many-sided young man who could be particularly useful when special knowledge was called for, such as composition of financial and economic sections of the letter John Laurens had taken with him to France. Washington had not made use of Hamilton as a financier, but he hoped no one else would take him away for that purpose. Here was the latest in a series of letters with a single purpose—to deprive him of the services of the aide who was a one-man cabinet in his own person. If he was annoyed or inconvenienced, Washington's generous reply showed little trace of it, but he put the narrowest possible construction on the word *financier*. He could not tell a lie: "How far Colo. Hamilton, of whom you ask my opinion as a financier, has turned his thoughts to that particular study, I am unable to ansr., because I never entered upon a discussion of this point with him. But this I can venture to advance, from a thorough knowledge of him, that there are few men to be found, of his age, who have a more general knowledge than he possesses; and none, whose soul is more firmly engaged in the cause, or who exceed him in probity and sterling virtue."

With this recommendation from Washington in hand, Sullivan put out some feelers among his fellow congressmen, but the results were discouraging. He reported to Washington: "I am happy to find your Excellency entertains the Same Sentiments of the virtues and abilities of Colo. Hamilton, as I have ever Done myself. After I wrote your Excellency I found The Eyes of Congress Turned on Robert Morris, of this City as Financier. I did not, therefore, nominate

Colo. Hamilton as I foresaw that it would be but a vain attempt. I shall this Day nominate him as Secretary of Foreign Affairs in which I think I shall meet the approbation of most of the State."

But the post of foreign affairs was likewise given to another. Not enough Congressmen yet were interested in this young man whose political fortunes the New York, and some of the New England, delegates were so anxious to advance.

Whether or not it was realistic of Hamilton to think that he had a serious chance to be appointed to any such posts, he suspected Washington of having a hand in all these failures. He saw his advancement blocked by a "narrow disposition" on Washington's part, "only sensible to motives of policy."

As Washington saw it, Hamilton was more valuable to him, to the war, and, indeed, to the country, performing services as his aide, which no one else he knew could perform so well, than he could possibly be as commander of a line unit, where there were many experienced men, any of whom was in constant danger of becoming a casualty. No doubt, Washington was aware of Hamilton's problem and his own and was content to wait to let fate work out the solution as chief executives in his position often do. Otherwise, Washington would not have tolerated the constant badgering he was receiving as a result of Hamilton's untiring efforts to break free of the office of aide. Betsy, at headquarters at the time, later noted that Washington "expressed himself as not having been treated, for some time, with proper respect."

As 1781 began, Hamilton's career was at a standstill, and the war was going badly. Troops of the Pennsylvania line mutinied on January 1; troops of the New Jersey line mutinied at Pompton, New Jersey, on January 20; General Schuyler wrote that troops in Albany were also threatening to mutiny unless they were better paid and supplied. Washington sent Major General Robert Howe to suppress the New Jersey mutiny. On January 27 he put it down and executed two of the mutineers by hanging. On February 4, Hamilton wrote John Laurens in disgust of word from Nathanael Greene about the "deplorable" situation of the southern army "destitute of everything," with Cornwallis about to recommence his offensive northward. Benedict Arnold had conducted an incursion into Virginia and seized Richmond. With "part of the Jersey troops having [emulated] the Pennsylvanians by mutinying," there was no interposition and, of course, "we uncivilly compelled them to an unconditional surrender and hanged their most incendiary leaders.

Hamilton's sarcasm was unmistakably directed against Washington's early slackness and late overreaction in taking cruel reprisals against the mutineers.

Washington was, no doubt, right in believing that Hamilton was doing the most important job for the country, and for Washington.

Hamilton was, no doubt, right in believing that it was absolutely necessary for Hamilton to do something else to become an autonomous man, not merely the dependent, appendage, apologist, and wire-puller of the idol of America. But Hamilton, realist that he was, no doubt understood Washington's point of view; Washington, realist that he was, no doubt understood Hamilton's. Any move to break the stalemate would have to be made by Hamilton. He made it.

Benedict Arnold's legion had triumphantly sacked Richmond and put to flight Virginia's unready governor, Thomas Jefferson, leaving the most important state defenseless in the path of Cornwallis, now marching north.

On the night of February 15, Washington and Hamilton worked late by smoky candlelight until "very early in the morning," writing dispatches to Rochambeau in Newport planning a joint land and sea venture to capture Arnold. After a night of such work, giving "the most positive directions concerning expedition," tempers were bound to be short the following day.

Hamilton was hurrying down the narrow stairs in the headquarters house with an order that had to be delivered immediately to the commissary department. Halfway down, he met Washington coming up.

The general paused. "I would like to speak to you, Colonel Hamilton," he said.

Hamilton nodded. "I will wait upon you immediately, sir." Then he continued down, as Washington continued up. On the lower floor Hamilton found Tench Tilghman and handed him the order. It was "of a pressing and interesting nature," and he gave instructions for delivery. He started back up the stairs to attend on Washington, but Lafayette stopped him. They spoke together briefly on a matter of business; then Hamilton excused himself rather abruptly and hastened on up the stairs.

Instead of being in his room, Washington was waiting for Hamilton on the top landing, his hand clenched on the balustrade and his face grim. Hamilton later said Washington had accosted him "in a very angry tone."

"Colonel Hamilton," Washington said, "you have kept me waiting at the head of the stairs these ten minutes. I must tell you, sir, you treat me with disrespect."

"I am not conscious of it, sir," Hamilton replied, "but since you have thought it necessary to tell me so, we part."

According to Hamilton, his reply was "without petulancy, but with decision."

Washington stared at him. "Very well, sir," he said, "if it be your choice."

They separated. General and aide departed each for his own room in anger.

Writing to General Schuyler two days later, Hamilton said, "I sincerely believe my absence which gave so much umbrage did not last two minutes." He said that he and Lafayette had conversed only about half a minute, and "he can testify how anxious I was to get back, and that I left him in a manner which but for our intimacy would have been more than abrupt."

Within the hour Washington sent Tilghman to Hamilton, "assuring me of his great confidence in my abilities, integrity, usefulness, etc., and of his desire, in a candid conversation, to heal a difference which could not have happened but in a moment of passion."

Hamilton gave Tilghman a message to take back to Washington that was the product of much careful thought. It was not something dashed off in a few minutes of pique and dispatched without rereading: it was in five well-planned parts. Hamilton's resolution was not to be revoked. He begged to be excused from an interview that would be mutually disagreeable. Out of the family, he would conduct himself toward the general as he had while in it. He would not embarrass Washington's business by quitting him until absent aides returned. Meanwhile, he proposed that they behave toward each other as if nothing had happened. By way of reply, Washington "consented to decline the conversation and thanked me for my offer of continuing my aid, in the manner I had mentioned."

For most of the rest of his life, Washington was to trust, rely on, promote, and back up Hamilton and remain closer to him in matters of great affairs of state than to any other man. Most historians and biographers of both men have struggled, without much success, to explain how the relationship between Washington and Hamilton could have remained so close for the rest of their lives after a personal break of this kind, in which the junior appears in such a bad light. Many add it to other evidence tending to prove that Washington was a supersaint in forbearance, and let it go at that.

The incident itself, considered separately from its aftermath, is unremarkable and indeed trivial. From what we know from other sources of Washington's short temper, we have no reason to doubt that he had accosted Hamilton "in a very angry tone."

We may permit ourselves to doubt whether Hamilton's reply was entirely "without petulancy, but with decision" and still leave ourselves plenty of room to believe that his reply was entirely civil, and not inappropriate despite their differences in rank and age. The two men had forged an intimate relationship as comrades-in-arms during the four dramatic years they had lived through together.

It seems clear that Hamilton made the trivial incident the conscious occasion for removing himself from his job as Washington's aide without exposing himself to the charge that he was leaving the position voluntarily when the cause of the Revolution needed him most. In rejecting Washington's overture for a "candid conversation," he no doubt believed he would be taxed with this defection. Logically, it was hard to square his leaving now with his exalted concept of honor, even though the break was, as he wrote his father-in-law, "the deliberate result of maxims I had long formed for the government of my own conduct."

Lafayette, distressed, knowing that Hamilton's half minute with him had caused the breach, "explained the delay" and "privately expressed to each of them his own feelings . . ." But he concluded, with a logical Gallic shrug at the neatness and balance of the thing, that "He found each disposed to believe that the other was not sorry for the separation."

The only eyewitness account of the incident is Hamilton's contained in the letter he wrote explaining it two days later to Philip Schuyler. When the first draft of this letter is compared with the final version, and all Hamilton's careful revisions are noted, more is revealed about the reasons for the break than by any summary, paraphrase, or extract.

It was uncharacteristic of Hamilton to do much rewriting. As printed in Volume II of the Hamilton Papers, this letter, with all its rewritings and deletions, is one of the most fascinating Hamilton papers of all.

As Hamilton purports to explain all on a mundane level, he creates new mysteries on a deeper level. Some of the most significant words of the letter are those that are crossed out and rewritten or those that are not written at all, but leap from between the lines.

Writing to his new father-in-law of two months, he begins, "I am no longer a member of the General's family." His story would surprise Schuyler, and "the manner of the change will surprise you more." Hamilton then tersely relates the trivial encounter on the stairway and its aftermath.

Of his personal relations with Washington, Hamilton writes, "I always disliked the relation of an Aide de Camp to his general as having in it a kind of personal dependence." Then he changes the word *relation* to *office* and crosses out the phrase "to his general." This change makes the sentence less revealing, less personal, more guarded. "I always disliked the office of an Aide de Camp, as having in it a kind of personal dependence."

He goes on to explain that early in the war he had refused invitations to serve in a similar capacity with two other generals, but "an idea of the General's character which experience taught me to be false overcame my scruples . . . and induced me to accept his invitation to enter into his family." Rewriting, he softens the harsh word *false* to *unfounded*. Because he knew Washington as well as any man, his private opinion of Washington would shock a public that has idolized him: "It was not long before I discovered he was neither remarkable for delicacy nor good temper, which revived my former aversion to the station . . . and it has been increasing ever since."

Here was an astonishing secret: "The place I held in the General's confidence and councils . . . will make it the more extraordinary to you to learn that for three years past I have felt no friendship for him and professed none. The truth is our own dispositions are the opposites of each other, and the pride of my temper . . . could not suffer me to profess what I did not feel."

Washington had an intense desire for affection from Hamilton's side. Vainly he sought admission to a circle of friendships like Hamilton's friendships with Laurens, Lafayette, and McHenry. The advances toward such a relationship all came from the lonely older man's side. Had the general's advances gone too far?

"When advances of this kind have been made to me by the General," Hamilton went on, "they were received in a manner that showed at least I had no inclination to court them, and that I wished to stand rather upon a footing of military confidence than of private attachment." Such brusque rebuffs from the junior would cruelly hurt the senior's self-esteem. But what was the difference in their "dispositions" that made Hamilton see Washington's as opposite to his own? He was, of course, the passionate young lover of Schuyler's daughter. Ordinarily, in an army command or other hierarchical organization, it is easy enough for seniors and juniors up and down the ladder to profess for each other personal liking they do not feel. What else made the difference between Hamilton and Washington so deep that the junior could not bring himself to profess friendship or even liking for the senior, who was the idol of America? With

André, Washington had demonstrated cold rigor. He had ridden on the crest of the tide of public clamor. André had engaged Hamilton's warm affection. Hamilton had never become reconciled to Washington's reasons of state for having him hanged.

Secret disliking for Washington did not prevent Hamilton from working with him successfully. He continued: "The General is a very honest man. His competitors have slender abilities, and less integrity. His popularity has often been essential to the safety of America, and is still of great importance to it. . . . I think it is necessary he should be supported."

Secrets about a chief that are hidden from all others—wife, friends, and, of course, biographers—are known to an aide of four years. What made Hamilton bristle with such personal hostility toward "a very honest man" who, he admitted, was essential to the safety of his country? The detailed specification of charges remains unwritten, except between these lines. It is not easy to argue with the judgment of a young man of the world who is shrewd enough to add, writing to his shocked father-in-law, "You are too good a judge of human nature not to be sensible how this conduct in me must have operated on the self love of a man to whom all the world is offering incense." Hamilton then crossed out the phrase "the self love of" and added, "I give you this as a key to the rest." Then he struck out the entire sentence and rewrote it to read "with this key you will easily unlock the present mystery. At the end of the war I may say many things to you concerning which I shall impose upon myself 'till then an inviolable silence." In basic political, economic, and military philosophy and outlook, Hamilton and Washington were much alike. But Hamilton knew that somehow his relationship of "dependence" to Washington must end. If anything, Washington was dependent on him.

The later relationships between the two men, which were so fruitful for the new nation, would have been different or impossible if Hamilton had been content to acquiesce in Washington's insistence on keeping him on as an aide instead of forcing the break. Once Hamilton had won his release, he and Washington were free to form a new relationship between themselves that would render better service to their client. The old relationship of master to servant or principal to agent changed to that of senior to junior partner, but partners nevertheless. Afterward Hamilton always acknowledged that Washington was "an aegis very essential to me."

Schuyler, though finding no personal impropriety in Hamilton's conduct toward Washington, was, as Hamilton had, of course, foreseen, "surprised" and "afflicted" by his wish to quit the general's staff. Schuyler hoped "that the unhappy breach should be closed, and a mutual confidence restored."

Immediately after Hamilton's final departure, Washington would commit a serious breach of etiquette in dealing with the French. Schuyler foresaw its happening. He also thought that the difference between commander and confidential aide, added to other divisions observed among the Americans, would have a bad effect, "especially with the French officers, with the French minister, and even with the French court." Washington would not have "one gentleman left sufficiently versed in the French to convey his ideas." A substitute would be "incapable of conducting business with any competent degree of address, propriety, or delicacy." Schuyler pointed out that Washington, by his overture for reconciliation, had acknowledged and repented his haste. Hamilton should remember that "It falls to the lot of few men to pass through life without one of those unguarded moments which wound the feelings of a friend." He should impute Washington's moment of angry passion to "the frailty of human nature, and with Sterne's recording angel, drop a tear and blot it out of the page of life." Schuyler added, "Your services are wanted . . . in that particular station which you have . . . filled so beneficially to the public, and with such extensive reputation."

Hamilton had refused to meet with Washington after the break to avoid hearing from him words of reproof like these from Schuyler. But the head of Hamilton's new family added some words he could not have expected to hear from the head of his old. No reproof was intended, Schuyler hastened to add. He well understood and approved of Hamilton's lofty concept of personal honor: "I am as incapable of wishing as you are of doing, anything injurious to those principles of honor, which . . . are the test of virtue." Schuyler had just received a letter from Washington and "he mentions not a syllable of this unhappy difference."

Hamilton's divorce from Washington's family to enter Schuyler's was "unalterable," but his decree did not immediately become final. Between the break on February 16 and his formal resignation on April 30, 1781, Hamilton for ten weeks continued to perform diligent services as Washington's aide, to all outward appearances as if nothing had happened. Tilghman was "just recovering from a fit of illness the consequence of too close application to business," as Hamilton wryly wrote McHenry, and Humphrey and Harrison were away. Hamilton worked harder than ever for Washington to fulfill his commitment to fill in as long as necessary.

"I do not wish to distress him or the public business, by quitting him before he could derive other assistance by the return of some of the Gentlemen who were absent," he said. On March first, as hostess at the New Windsor headquarters to Washington, Knox, and the headquarters aides when the special guest was Baron Jean von Closen, who had come with important letters from French headquarters at Newport, Betsy Hamilton "served . . . tea with much grace" as if nothing had happened at all.

The profound change in the inward personal relationship between two strong men caused not an outward surface ripple at headquarters. Nor did it cost either man any loss of esteem of any friends, acquaintances, admirers, confidants, or outsiders. Nor did it cause a pause in the public business. With Hamilton the "public business" and the growth of his own capacity to further the public business in a new and more significant role came ahead of private inclinations.

The breach has provided material for much scholarly argumentation, most of which assigns a heavy burden of blame and guilt to Hamilton. Men of the world often see and readily understand the kind of an inevitable, purposeful breach in one kind of relationship between two men that is soon replaced by another more productive one as time goes by. That is how men like Lafayette and Schuyler saw it. In modern law partnerships, for example, the smooth announcement to the public, with pleasure, that a former, longtime salaried associate has finally been admitted to the firm may conceal a better outside offer, a threat to quit, a traumatic confrontation, and belated appreciation by the seniors of the indispensability of their former clerk. Ranks close thereafter, and from then on, for mutual advantage, the former indispensable dependent is made a junior partner, and more or less the equal of his former master.

The law firm analogy is not a perfect fit. Washington was a senior of uncommon rigor who would not bend. On April 30, Hamilton said good-bye, quit the headquarters at New Windsor, and went home to his in-laws at Albany. Out of an enviable position as a member of the general's family, he faced a bleak spell of unemployment—just when his pregnant bride would be plumpening—without a better job offer in his pocket.

15

FIX BAYONETS! FOLLOW ME!!
TO THE LAST
YORKTOWN REDOUBT!!!

HOW CHEQUERED IS HUMAN LIFE!
I AM GOING TO DO MY DUTY. OUR
OPERATIONS WILL BE SO CONDUCTED,
AS TO ECONOMIZE THE LIVES OF MEN.
—*To Elizabeth Hamilton, September 15, 1781*

Hearing the news of the break with Washington, Hamilton's friends affirmed their deep affection for him. Colonel Robert Hanson Harrison, the "Old Secretary," himself resigning as an aide to assume the chief justiceship of Maryland, wrote Hamilton, "as for affection, mine for you will continue to my latest breath." Lafayette, marching south toward Virginia as a major general leading his first independent command, wrote from Head of Elk (now Elkton), Maryland, on April 10, 1781, that "had the French fleet come in Arnold was ours," but the archtraitor had escaped. Lafayette continued, "Owing to the tender sentiments of my friendship . . . public and private nature conspire in making me wish your woe be not accomplished. . . ."

Making ready to move south from French headquarters at Newport, the Marquis de Fleury wrote, "I have very Little time left, but enough to inquire after your happiness. Are you come back from Albany, with your sweet-heart; are you already, out of the general's family? What are you doing? What are you thinking? Let me know everything, which may be interesting to you; you know it is so to me." Fleury added, "We are making preparations, to Leave at Last; our inchanted iland." Enchantment is not automatically associated with the name of Rhode Island; perhaps a satisfying mistress had contributed to Fleury's there. He blamed the alarming news coming from Virginia on the debilitating effect of southerly climes on the character of the people: "I pity much our virginia friends. They want Constance and patriotics virtues which I believe, are scarce in those southern countrys."

In his charmingly fractured Franglais, the Marquis de Fleury seemed to be referring to the panicky flight of Governor Thomas Jefferson from the capital, and the disappearance of all semblance of civil government there at the time of the incursions or threatened invasions of Benedict Arnold, Cornwallis, and Banastre "Bloody" Tarleton.

Benedict Arnold had threatened that if André were executed, Washington would be "justly answerable for the torrent of blood that may be spilt in consequence." To unleash him to make good this threat and earn his bribe, Sir Henry Clinton had sent him to Portsmouth, Virginia, on the James River, with a permanent raiding force. Arnold asked a prisoner he was interrogating what his own fate would be if caught and was told, "They will cut off that left leg of yours, bury it with all the honors of war, and then hang the rest of you on a gibbet." To keep the traitor on a short leash, Clinton had sent along with him Colonel John Graves Simcoe, the officer who had identified Hamilton's hand in the prisoner exchange negotiations for André, and Colonel Thomas Dundas as officers "by whose advice [Arnold] was to be guided in every important measure." Without such chaperonage, who could completely trust an unleashed traitor to stay bought?

In January 1781 Arnold had landed some 1,200 men near Westover and by the fifth was at Richmond, pushing on to Westham, spreading havoc and destruction wherever he went, before falling back to Portsmouth and going into winter quarters. After taking over the dispirited remnants of Gates's broken army in December at Charlotte, North Carolina, General Nathanael Greene, with Francis Marion ("the Swamp Fox"), Henry Lee (the famous "Light-Horse Harry"), Daniel Morgan ("the Old Wagoner"), Edward Carrington, Andrew Pickens, Thomas Sumter, Wade Hampton, William Washington, John Eager Howard, and other heroes, had been winning back the Carolinas by losing small battles to well-led corps under Cornwallis and Tarleton. As Greene put it, "We fight, get beat, rise, and fight again."

In February 1781 and the following months, Hamilton was writing letters for Washington to congratulate Greene on battles technically lost that were guerrilla-style successes: Cowpens, Kings Mountain, and Guilford Court House. Greene had said that he was too weak to afford technical victories. Daniel Morgan helped teach Greene the tactics of winning while losing: "You have a great number of militia," Morgan wrote. "If they fight, you beat Cornwallis, if not, he will beat you. Put the . . . militia in the center with some picked troops in their rear to shoot the first man that runs." Hamilton wrote Washington shrewdly on April 9 of Guilford Court House that "General Greene thinks his little defeat will be of service to his affairs."

Tired of winning only Pyrrhic victories in the Carolinas, Cornwallis and Tarleton turned north and marched into Virginia in May as Benedict Arnold moved westward to threaten Richmond again. The governor, Thomas Jefferson, having failed to ready the state's defenses against these new incursions, fled his capital posthaste for the west. He fell off his horse Caractacus, hurt himself, and hid out incommunicado at a remote estate he owned at Poplar Forest in Bedford County. Debate raged over whether the state government had abandoned him or he had abandoned the government.

Miss Betsy Ambler, the daughter of Rebecca Burwell, wrote, "Governor, Council, everybody scampering." Others had fled, "But this is not more laughable," she said, "than the accounts we have of our illustrious Governor, who, they say, took neither rest nor food for man or horse till he reached C—r's mountain."

Sent to Virginia to train militia to fight, Hamilton's friend Baron von Steuben criticized Jefferson's unreadiness and defection. So did a resolution later introduced into the state legislature.

In fairness, it should also be recorded here that Jefferson's biographer Dumas Malone says that "This was not a precipitate flight but a dignified, if discouraged, retirement before a new alignment of superior forces." Civil government in Virginia completely broke down, faded away, and disappeared. So far as the governor was concerned, "it ceased to exist." This had not happened in New York or Pennsylvania or South Carolina when the British seized the state capital.

Tarleton's brigade, the "scourge of the South," occupied Monticello itself, and Jefferson later charged the British with wrongly freeing some slaves there.

With these new disasters overwhelming Washington's home state, the largest, richest and formerly most influential of all thirteen, Washington had sent Lafayette with a force of about 1,200 New Englanders and New Jerseymen marching south. Too little to fight off the redcoat tide, it seemed a little too large, conspicuous, and important to serve merely as bait for a trap for the bloody traitor Arnold.

From Head of Elk, where he had written his letter to Hamilton, Lafayette pushed on south as far as Richmond before realizing the strength of the enemy forces massing against him. He managed to add some Virginia militia and Continentals from von Steuben's training camps, but even with these he could count barely 3,000 men. On his first independent field command, operating in strange country, facing strong British forces, with no one to turn to for advice, the young marquis proudly wrote Hamilton, "Our forced march saved Richmond," but his troops were inexperienced and far outnumbered in veterans and cavalry. "The Government wants energy, and there is nothing to enforce the laws" in Virginia, he complained. When the governor fled Richmond, he had set up no effective government for the commonwealth anywhere else.

But Lafayette kept a clear head. In late May 1781 he wrote Washington, "Were I to fight a battle, I should be cut to pieces, the militia dispersed and the arms lost. Were I to decline fighting, the country would think itself given up. I am therefore determined to skirmish, but not to engage too far . . ." He was one degree worse off than Greene: "Were I always equal to the enemy, I should be extremely happy in my present command, but I am not strong enough even to get beaten."

Hamilton's last public business at headquarters after his break with Washington that spring of 1781 was the most important headquarters business of all: planning the summer and fall campaigns, and coordinating them with the French allies.

In March he traveled with Washington from New Windsor to Newport to meet with Rochambeau again and speed the departure of Admiral Destouches with his fleet for southern waters to help Lafayette and Greene. So far the French troops in their staging area had not had much else to do but parade; Washington and Hamilton reviewed them.

On his first visit to Newport, William Ellery Channing had been amazed to find that "The French Troops are a fine body of men . . . neither officers nor men are the effeminate Beings we were heretofore taught to believe them. They are as large and as likely men as can be produced by any nation."

In the glowing candlelight of evening in the high church, the town of Newport offered Washington an address of honor. Hamilton prepared Washington's acknowledgement of the welcome. It embraced, in graceful sentences, appropriate compliments and thanks to the large and virile French forces and nation, commiseration to Newport for injuries suffered at enemy hands, and promises of full restitution for British depredations.

Washington was rarely imprudent; Hamilton often was. But if Hamilton had still been active at headquarters immediately after the party's return from Newport, he might have saved the commander in chief the embarrassing slur against the French that the overworked Tench Tilghman allowed to slip by.

In a private letter of March 28 to his kinsman and Mount Vernon manager, Lund Washington, the commander in chief deplored the fact that the French fleet, which he had just seen sail at sunset from Newport, had not undertaken the expedition "when I first proposed it to them; the destruction of Arnold's Corps would then have been inevitable before the British fleet could have put to Sea. Instead the small squadron . . . was sent, and could not, as I foretold, do anything without a Land force at Portsmouth." This letter, with others from headquarters, was intercepted next day from the post rider at Smith's Clove, and promptly published in Rivington's *Gazette*. Lafayette, learning of this on his way to Virginia, sent Washington a feeling reproach: "A letter from you relating to the delays of the French makes a great noise at Philadelphia. Indeed it gives me pain on many political accounts."

Rochambeau, too, was pained, pointing out that the French had not been delinquent in obeying Washington's orders.

After Hamilton and Elizabeth moved out of the headquarters at New Windsor about the middle of April 1781 to the east side of the Hudson at de Peyster's Point near King's Bridge, Hamilton remained near enough to headquarters to keep in touch and in the way of any new opportunity for a command in the line that might open up. On April 30 Washington called Hamilton back to help patch up the diplomatic gaffe that had upset the French allies. He needed all the diplomatic talents of his most skillful headquarters intelligencer to write an apologetic yet dignified letter to Rochambeau.

The general made some revisions, but as an explanation it could not be a success. Beginning with the caution that the enemy, fond of damaging forgeries, may have changed some of his text, and with the mitigating circumstance that his letter was private and no such complaint against the French allies had been offered to a public body, Washington was obliged to admit "the general import to be true." He hoped his indiscretion would not disturb the harmony between them. No more could be said. Fortunately, Rochambeau's habitual generosity canceled a slip of Washington's that Hamilton would probably have prevented. Hamilton, at Washington's request, had done his best to retrieve it. The break of February 16 had not lessened, and, if anything, it had heightened, Washington's realization of his dependence upon the talents of his former chief headquarters intelligencer.

In his letter to Schuyler describing the break with Washington, Hamilton had written that he would like to go back into the artillery, but that unfortunately he would be obliged to come in as the youngest colonel instead of as the oldest. Things might be less mortifying in a different branch of the service: "If a handsome command for the campaign in the light infantry should offer itself, I shall balance between this and the artillery." Calculating that the war might end sooner than anyone thought, he realized that a situation in the artillery would be "more solid and permanent," but that "as I hope the war will not last long enough to make it progressive this consideration has less force." He did not seek more soldiering for the sake of more rank or a peacetime military career.

Still working in his son-in-law's behalf, Philip Schuyler felt that Hamilton would be safer in the moribund Congress; combat infantrymen are not immortal. On May 30 he wrote from Albany that he was down with the quinsy, "but I propose to attend the [New York] Legislature the latter end of next week, when I shall have the pleasure of seeing you at Fishkill [where the Legislature met] on the Sunday following. I believe you may prepare yourself to go to Philadelphia, as there is little doubt but you will be appointed [to Congress]."

But Hamilton was not yet ready to enter politics if any chance remained of winning military glory in the field. It would be ironic if the success of his efforts in helping to plan the coming campaign on paper should bring the war to a successful close while he remained shut out of the real war he had always wished for in the field.

He turned down Schuyler's well-meant offer, though the rumor of his impending election as delegate to Congress had already reached his friend John Laurens.

"I am indebted to you, my dear Hamilton [wrote John Laurens], for two letters; the first from Albany, as masterly a piece of cynicism as ever was penned; the other from Philadelphia, dated the second March; in both you mention a design of retiring, which makes me exceedingly unhappy. I would not wish to have you, for a moment, withdraw from the public service: at the same time, my friendship for you, and the knowledge of your value to the United States, makes me most ardently desire, that you should fill only the first offices of the Republic. . . ."

Laurens, too, wanted Hamilton in Congress, if only as a stepping stone to "the first offices of the Republic." He added, "I must confess to you, that, at the present stage of the war, I should prefer your going into Congress, and from thence becoming a minister plenipotentiary for peace, to your remaining in the army, where the dull system of seniority, and the tableau, would prevent you from having the important commands to which you are entitled; but at any rate I will not have you renounce your rank in the army, unless you entered the career above mentioned. Your private affairs cannot require such immediate and close attention. You speak like a paterfamilias surrounded with a numerous progeny."

From Richmond, Lafayette wrote his friend on May 23 in similar vein: "Come here, my dear friend, and command our artillery in Virginia. I want your advice and your exertions."

But Washington, the one man who could place Hamilton in military command, remained silent. So Hamilton remained in wait across the river, or in Albany, silent, too, except for the scratching of his pen. He had turned to writing a series of great state papers that would soon begin appearing in the press under the overall title of "The Continentalist."

While doing so, Hamilton almost in desperation, appealed directly to Washington: "It has become necessary to me to apply to your Excellency to know in what manner you foresee you will be able to employ me in the ensuing campaign. I am ready to enter into activity whenever you think proper, though I am not anxious to do it till the army takes the field, as before that period I perceive no object."

Washington replied with the excuse that regular officers of the line were resentful at being pushed aside to make room for newcomers fresh from the staff, whose previous experience consisted only of chairborne pen-pushing. In three recent cases, in fact, he said, such superseding appointments had given rise not merely to loud complaints, but almost to mutiny. But Hamilton knew better than anyone else that these were transparent excuses, that they did not apply in his case, and that exceptions had and always could be made by a commander who had the will to make them.

Washington laboriously explained that he never deviated from the rules. Such an appointment would, "I am certain, involve me in a difficulty of a very disagreeable and delicate nature, and might perhaps lead to consequences more serious than it is easy to imagine." He ended by pleading with Hamilton not to think his refusal had been caused by their breach: "My principal concern arises from an apprehension, that you will impute my refusal of your request to other motives than those I have expressed." Hamilton did.

He replied to Washington with cool insistence that his case was "peculiar and dissimilar to all the former" that Washington had cited. As far as he was concerned, he wrote drily, he could see no "insuperable obstacles to a compliance." Washington continued to offer him nothing.

Still only a few miles away across the river, Hamilton could be made use of on headquarters assignments that required his special talents, such as delicate dealings with the French allies.

For a while, as he sought a new assignment, Hamilton shared General Lincoln's quarters at King's Bridge, some ten miles from the main camp. He was back at headquarters frequently and often saw his brother-in-law John Barker Church there. Church had come down from Newport, where he had been acting as a contractor for supplies for the French army. Hamilton kept alive his old friendships with the French officers and the other aides.

On July 28 Hamilton served as a member of a court-martial that tried Captain David Livermore of the First New Hampshire Regiment on charges of threatening and insulting Lieutenant Colonel John Barnard Murnan, his superior officer, "in a most outrageous manner." Not content with verbal abuse, Livermore was guilty of "striking him with his own Espontoon and after having broken that with striking him, with that of another officer." The sentence was dismissal from the service. Washington reviewed the sentence and approved. However, after thus being punished as an example to others, Livermore was reinstated in service the same month. Hot-blooded fighters, not panicky malingerers, were needed in the south to save Virginia.

Meanwhile, Sir Henry Clinton had depleted his northern forces that Washington's army had been covering to send 1,500 of his men south to support Cornwallis's army. Washington saw this as an opportunity and again proposed to the French his scheme for a joint assault by land and sea on New York City. Rochambeau favored a combined blow, but in the south, not at New York. But he gave in to Washington's hardy, perennial New York idea.

Hamilton cared little whether the battle was north or south as long as he held a command. Hearing of the proposed operation, he left Betsy in Albany and went south to Dobbs Ferry on July 8 to press Washington once again for a field command. Once again Washington brushed him off. Finding that "nothing was said on the subject of a command," Hamilton wrote a letter to Washington, resigning from the army. He enclosed with it his prized lieutenant colonel's commission. He staked all his hopes of finding the war again on one last desperate, irretrievable, dramatic gesture. The conventional wisdom of armies is that the attention of the liveliest minds is chiefly engaged in finding ways to get out of line combat duty into safe staff positions; few service records compare with Hamilton's for machinations to move the opposite way.

On July 13 Hamilton wrote Betsy from Dobbs Ferry out of one of his blackest moods. He had "no object of sufficient importance to occupy my attention." His "dissipations are a very imperfect suspension of my uneasiness." He was entirely absorbed in thoughts of her, but things were going downhill, more or less as a result. "Indeed Betsey, I am intirely changed—changed for the worse

I confess—lost to all the public and splendid passions and absorbed in you." This inadvertent put-down of her was not his usual gallant style at all. Was she to blame for his exclusion from momentous campaigns? "Amiable woman! nature has given you a right to be esteemed, to be cherished, to be beloved; but she has given you no right to monopolize a man, whom, to you I may say, she has endowed with qualities to be extensively useful to society." His own idleness, dissipation, and black thoughts raised questions in his mind about his usefulness to society at large: "Yes my Betsey, I will encourage my reason to dispute your empire and restrain it within proper bounds, to restore me to myself and to the community. Assist me in this; reproach me for an unmanly surrender of that to love and teach me that your esteem will be the price of my acting well my part as a member of society." He closed by telling her, "love me and let your happiness always consist in loving." He promised to send her some money, not now but soon. He also, curiously, directed her to deliver two separate letters he was enclosing to her sisters, one to Angelica, and one to Margarita. He did not give her permission to read his letters to them, nor did he tell her what he said in them; the only reassurance he provided to her suggests fatalistic brinkmanship: "Your sisters will show them to you." Or would they?

By sending in his commission, Hamilton had put all to risk. It was Washington who yielded. With his famous patience strained to heroic tension, Washington sent Tench Tilghman to Hamilton on another peace mission. As Hamilton later described it to Betsy, Washington "pressed me to retain my commission, with an assurance that he would endeavor, by all means, to give me a command, nearly such as I could have desired in the present circumstances of the army. Though I know my Betsy would be happy to hear had I rejected this proposal, it is a pleasure my reputation would not permit me to afford her. I consented to retain my commission and accept my command."

General orders of July 31, 1781, announced that the light companies of the First and Second New York Regiments, with two newly raised companies, "will form a battalion under command of Lieutenant Colonel Hamilton and Major Fish." When formed, Lieutenant Colonel Hamilton's battalion would join the advanced corps under Colonel Alexander Scammell. It added to Hamilton's satisfaction that his subordinate was Major Nicholas Fish, his King's College classmate.

Hamilton's concept of honor had not bent to yield Betsy anything ordinarily believed to be necessary for a wife's happiness or to her father's wishes or to John Laurens's urgings to other offices or to Washington's desire to patch up the break with a conference. Yet he had won the independence he had fought for all along. By the dramatic gesture of sending in his commission, he had taken the final step over the brink. Such an outcome of such confrontations provided Hamilton with reinforcement of the rightness of his course of insisting on following out his own special concept of honor. But such reinforcement is dangerous to the man who obtains it because it brings with it a *hubris* that many will fail to survive.

Hamilton set to work looking out for the needs of the men of his new command with his usual zeal, just as he had done for his artillerymen of five years before. No fear of wasting a favor from the highly placed would keep him from going straight to the top without going through channels.

From Quartermaster General Timothy Pickering, Hamilton required two wall tents for his officers, also an orderly book and stationery. As a copious correspondent, he needed to know exactly what the allowed quota of paper was, so that he could "regulate the consumption accordingly." Camp kettles and pails had been ordered but not delivered. He applied directly to Tench Tilghman for shoes for the two companies of levies. Tilghman refused on the ground that this was something the states had to pay. Hamilton recalled that in the last campaign a distinction had been made in favor of the advanced corps; Congress should pay. He cited Colonel Philip Van Cortlandt's regiment as an example. He carried the argument directly to Washington, pointing out that the service of an advanced corps, more active than that of others, and in rough country, made "the article of shoes . . . indispensable." The men had spent their bounty of 30 pounds each and could not purchase shoes for themselves; the state had sent them forward shoeless. Clothing might be refused, but shoes his men must have, and from Continental stores. Memories of Valley Forge and Morristown welled up. Washington agreed promptly, but enjoined strict accountability on Hamilton for the shoes.

From the Schuyler farm at Saratoga came two horses, one for riding, the other a "portmanteau horse." Schuyler reported that Hamilton's Old Gray Horse, after appearing to be in good health, had suddenly died, and "The black is thin and I believe too aged or too Infirm for future service." One of Hamilton's saddles had fallen apart, and no new one could be purchased. Would Pickering, the quartermaster, furnish a substitute or have the old one repaired? Hamilton added that he did not want a special favor from his friend Pickering if the same thing were not done for other officers.

Conventional history is that until late July 1781 Washington was undecided whether to launch the main American attack on New York City or in Virginia. All early signs had pointed to an attack on New York. Washington had written to Lafayette and Greene that from every point of view an attack on New York was preferable to a southern operation "as we had not command of the water." Sent out by regular post, this plausible plan of campaign was intercepted, not very surprisingly, by the British on June 3. But when Washington learned that Sir Henry Clinton had found out these secret plans, he made light of it, telling Rochambeau that "The enemy can gain no material information from my letters." This led Clinton to suspect a ruse. At headquarters, Hamilton allowed an American spy, found to be a double agent in British pay, to see a map marked for a land and naval attack on New York. The spy asked Hamilton the destination of the army. Hamilton replied, "We are going to Virginia."

Whether Washington's indecision was real or feigned and whether Hamilton was wittingly or unwittingly being used by Washington as part of the ruse, all such conflicting disclosures served splendidly to confuse the enemy.

Clinton thought he knew very well how close Hamilton was to his chief. He remembered his own and Robertson's misjudgment that Washington's threat to hang André was a bluff. His general familiarity with disguised handwriting and other dirty tricks of headquarters intelligencers led Clinton to deduce astutely that New York was indeed Washington's real objective.

Seven years later, when Noah Webster asked him just when he had resolved on the "southern strategy," Washington replied, "It was determined by me nearly twelve months beforehand." Thereafter, he would "give out and cause it to be believed by the highest military as well as civil officers that New York was the destined place of attack." His purpose was "to spur the Eastern and Middle states to greater exertions in furnishing specific supplies and to render the enemy less prepared elsewhere."

If this solemn statement by the man who could not tell a lie to the great lexicographer is true, it bespeaks the greatest strategic subtlety. Washington's own private diary entry of May 22, 1781, notes that the plan of campaign fixed upon with Rochambeau gave preference to the capture of New York. Neither Hamilton nor Lafayette nor Greene nor Rochambeau nor Robert Morris were let in on any such long-standing firm resolve of Washington's to make the attack in Virginia—until the grand army he assembled to carry it out was on the march.

Washington eventually admitted that the French had conceived and planned the Yorktown campaign, whereas he had pressed for an attack on New York, but he never publicly stated that he had gone along unwillingly. Rochambeau, in his *Memoirs*, depicted Washington as a military primitive so obsessed with attacking New York that he could see no other alternative. No wonder once again Sir Henry Clinton misread a Washington "bluff."

On August 14, 1781, news came to Washington that Comte François Joseph Paul de Grasse had cleared the French West Indies, sailing north with 28 ships of the line and a cloud of troop transports with them. New York had received reinforcements from England; any assault there would have to wait until later in the season and be much riskier.

Old plans were thrown away. Americans and French were to march over-land to join Lafayette and "Mad Anthony" Wayne in Virginia, where de Grasse would land three West Indies regiments. There were three disturbing "ifs." If de Grasse failed to keep control of the waters about Chesapeake Bay, Cornwallis could either be reinforced or whisked out of reach by the Royal Navy. If the allied troops failed to reach Virginia by the long overland marches in time, the whole effort would go for naught because de Grasse and Saint-Simon were under orders not to stay in North American waters after October 15, 1781. As Hamilton had learned well in previous summers going back to his boyhood, fragile battle fleets had to be safely moored in West Indian harbors before the onset of hurricane season and winter storms.

In the Continental Treasury there was no money for such a large scale expedition. It would be too late if the troops were to wait for Congress to act. Luckily, Rochambeau came generously to the rescue, offering Washington half of what was left of his own military appropriation as an advance for the financing of the offensive.

Hamilton wrote Betsy in Albany on August 22, trusting his beloved to keep the secret: "A part of the army, my dear girl, is going to Virginia, and I must, of necessity, be separated at a much greater distance from my beloved wife." He does his best to sound unhappy about marching off to the war he had always sought, but the more he tries to convince her of his unhappiness, the more he fails: he must go, alas. He writes, "I cannot announce the fatal necessity, without feeling every thing that a fond husband can feel." So far so good. But there is unintended humor in his further protestations, "I am unhappy my Betsy. I am unhappy beyond expression. I am unhappy because I am to be so remote from you; because I am to hear from you less frequently than I am accustomed to do. I am miserable because I know you will be so. I am wretched at the idea of flying so far from you, without a single hour's interview to tell you all my pains and all my love."

Hamilton cannot persuade himself to ask headquarters for the small favor of a leave to visit her. No matter how much he insists, the anguish he expresses does not go deep, nor is it likely that, knowing her husband as she does, Betsy is misled that it does. He concludes, "But I cannot ask permission to visit you. It might be thought improper to leave my corps at such a time and upon such an occasion. I must go without seeing you—I must go without embracing you; —Alas! I must go."

Resplendent in their crisp, white uniforms set off by vivid crimson or yellow or black facings and cuffs to denote the home provinces of the different regiments, the French expeditionary force passed in review one last time and marched off the parade ground at Newport and kept on marching.

The St. Onge and the Soissonais and the Bourbonnais and the blue-coated Royal Deux-Ponts swung onto ferry boats that carried them across Narragansett Bay. They marched off again and up to the high road near Westerly. Five thousand well-drilled regulars of the king of France were on the march at last to help the states fling off the yoke of the king of England. They marched westward through southern New England, lances and sabers glittering in the August sun; gaitered legs swinging in long, easy strides; varicolored pompoms slanting up from little cocked hats, rolling along the rutted high roads through little Connecticut villages and towns like Plainfield and Windham, Bolton and Hartford and Farmington, making windows rattle with the clank and rumble of d'Abouville's seemingly endless imperial artillery trains. Nothing like them had ever before been seen in rural America.

As His Catholic Majesty's columns approached chaste, white, clapboard Congregational meeting houses on village greens, steeple bells were drowned out by the rataplan of copper-sheathed dreams. Long cavalry trumpets, throbbing and blaring, struck up in full-throated chorus, as they passed in review before the town elders, "The Huron March." Or "Malbrouk S'en va-t-en guerre —Mironton, mironton, mirontaine!"

Marching on through Westchester, a small detachment turned aside briefly to help General Benjamin Lincoln crush a British outpost. The main army rolled over and past all resistance to Dobbs Ferry. There they caught a glimpse of

America's supreme monument, their own supreme allied commander, General George Washington.

General Cromot du Bourg reported that there the American commander welcomed Rochambeau "with the affability that is so natural to him." Washington was "a very fine looking man." The French agreed: "His bearing is noble in the highest degree . . ." His "dignified address . . . won every heart." Over the Hudson at King's Ferry, with no time to lose, the French boated troops, guns, wagons, horses, and bandsmen on an endless shuttle of barges and longboats and rafts. Here they fell into columns behind Alexander Hamilton's Connecticut and New York light infantry and John Laurens's mixed brigade of Massachusetts, Connecticut, and New Hampshire men. Henry Knox's guns rumbled along behind the troops of John Lamb of New York and Ebenezer Stevens of Massachusetts. The army's engineer train, under the Frenchman Chevalier Louis Le Beque du Portail, brought up the rear. All were off to rescue still another French countryman from the trap in Virginia for which he had been serving as the bait. Even past the Hudson, few in the marching columns knew that their ultimate objective was not York Island, New York City, but the other Yorktown far to the south in the Old Dominion. Observing the American allies who had fallen in with them on the long march, the French were struck by the lack of regulation uniforms and the great number of fringed hunting shirts. They could see that Americans, traveling light, were troops intended for action, not for show. They backpacked their "tents, where three or four men live," but even so, they carried "not over forty pounds of baggage." The Americans shambled and slouched along, arms unslung or trailed behind, but at an easy gait that could carry them far in a day's march. When passing through a town, they hardly bothered to form their columns or bring their muskets to shoulder arms, although sometimes they struck up a popular marching song. "The Drum" was one that was popular. But even when trying to look their sharpest as they moved through the little towns, they rarely managed to keep in step with their drum or with each other.

Reveille sounded at 3:00 A.M., and the troops were on the march by 4:00. Washington had ordered that on the march, light infantry battalions like Hamilton's "were . . . always to be fit for action and free from every incumbrance." They must dispense with nonessentials and rid themselves of "every article of baggage . . . including such of the women as are not able to undergo the fatigue of frequent marches."

In the van of the column and to protect the flanks of the expeditionary force, Hamilton's battalion marched from Haverstraw, New York, south to Paramus, New Jersey, and then on to Springfield, and on from Springfield to Chatham. There a large bread bakery oven had been built, and past it 30 flatboats mounted on carriages were ostentatiously hauled. British spies duly reported to Sir Henry Clinton that these portents meant that Washington and Rochambeau intended to attack Staten Island from the big base at Chatham by way of a float bridge across Kill Van Kull.

"The success of our enterprise depends on the celerity of our movements," Washington admonished General Benjamin Lincoln, and "delay, therefore may be ruinous to it." Washington did not order boats to be assembled for crossing the Delaware until most of the columns were well past Chatham, "because I wished to deceive the Enemy with regard to our real object as long as possible, our movements have been calculated for that purpose and I am still anxious the deception should be kept up a few days longer." Dr. James Thacher recorded that in the American army curiosity was "wrought to the highest pitch." Bets were taken on the destination of the march. To keep the buildup for crossing the Delaware as inconspicuous as possible, no boats were to be used for the animals. To speed progress, "every horse and Oxen should be Swam over the Delaware," Washington ordered, adding, "A few boats above and below the place they are made to enter the River, to give them a proper direction, will remove all difficulty and greatly facilitate the passage across."

As Hamilton marched at the head of his New York and Connecticut light infantry battalion, the names of the places he passed unreeled memories of earlier scenes of the war before his mind's eye like a diorama. Past Stony Point opposite Verplanck's Hamilton and McHenry had reined in their spent horses as they watched Arnold escape downriver aboard the *Vulture*. Paramus, Chatham, Springfield, New Brunswick, Princeton, and Trenton, the Delaware, Germantown, Valley Forge, Philadelphia, the Brandywine, the heights of Wilmington recalled Cornwallis's pursuit of four years earlier. Now Cornwallis was their quarry instead of their being his.

When they marched through Philadelphia in choking dust on September 1, the two allied armies furnished the crowds of well-wishers a notable contrast, which gave rise to much comment. The Americans in their nondescript outfits of every ragtag kind, were followed by the French "in complete uniform of white broadcloth, faced with green." By now even Sir Henry Clinton knew what was up, as did even the Philadelphia crowds. Clinton wrote a typical self-serving excuse in his diary. He could not, he said, when informed of Washington's march toward the Delaware, "have passed an army in time to have any impression on him before he crossed that river."

From Head of Elk, Maryland, on September 6, Hamilton wrote Betsy, five months pregnant with their first child, "Tomorrow we embark for Yorktown." He added words of affection and comfort: "I would give the world to be able to tell you all I feel and wish, but consult your own heart and you will know mine . . . you, who have the most female of female hearts."

His thoughts reverted to military matters: "Circumstances that have just come to my knowledge assure me that our operations will be expeditious, as well as our success certain."

Then he impulsively added, "Every day confirms me in the intention of renouncing public life and devoting myself wholly to you. Let others waste their time and their tranquility in a vain pursuit of power and glory; be it my object to be happy in a quiet retreat with my better angel."

This was fine for home consumption in Albany—after the long forced marches, Hamilton could bring to this kind of thing a conviction that would compel total belief in anyone who knew him less well than his wife.

The "circumstances" that had just come to Hamilton's knowledge that would make "success certain" were, no doubt, the sighting of de Grasse's 28 ships and four frigates within the Virginia capes, carrying 3,000 more ground troops to be debarked immediately at Jamestown to join the Americans under Lafayette already bivouacked there.

After setting sail from Head of Elk in a nondescript flotilla of little schooners, open barges, and derelict ferryboats before light and contrary winds, Hamilton's battalion took nearly a week to get to Annapolis, with three-quarters of the remaining distance still ahead.

Just at this time Hamilton received an unsettling letter from Philip Schuyler telling of fears that pregnant Betsy was about to have a miscarriage, but that now all was well: "My dear daughter is in good health but was so sensibly affected by your removal to the southward that I apprehended consequences; she is now at ease." Other family news was that beautiful Angelica had just given him a grandchild, a second Philip, and "a fine boy. I hope her sister will give me another."

From Annapolis about September 15, Hamilton dashed off a reassurance to Betsy. With its talk of economizing "the lives of men," it was anything but reassuring. If he were risking his life or anyone else's, it was not without awareness of the gravity of what he was doing. "How chequered is human life!" he philosophized. "How precarious is happiness! How easily do we often part with it for a shadow! These are the reflections that frequently intrude themselves upon me, with a painful application. I am going to do my duty. Our operations will be so conducted, as to economize the lives of men. Exert your fortitude and rely upon heaven."

Like Hamilton, Washington saw the coming engagement as the decisive battle of the war. He wrote, "Our progress from the opening of the trenches to the capitulation . . . of the British General . . . must necessarily go a great way towards terminating the war. . . ." Now, unfortunately, after the long forced marches at speed, the alarming delay at Annapolis meant that the time the French fleet could remain in northern waters was running out.

Also, de Grasse started to withdraw his fleet from blockading Chesapeake Bay to go cruising at sea in search of the British squadron. Washington's renowned patience again was tested. He begged de Grasse to stick to the allied plan and not go cruising at sea: "Our success . . . against York[town] under the protection of the . . . fleet is as certain as any military operation can be rendered by a . . . superiority of strength and means—it is in fact a matter of mere calculation."

De Grasse, claiming he had not received Washington's remonstrances, reported that his own officers had dissuaded him from the sea chase. As Washington desired, de Grasse agreed to staying within the capes. He anchored his main fleet in the York River, patrolled the James, and from then on acted "in concert for the good of our operation."

From Annapolis, Hamilton's light infantry sailed down Chesapeake Bay and up the James River and came ashore at College Landing, then called Archers

Hope, on the south side of the peninsula only a mile from Williamsburg and about ten miles from Yorktown itself.

With the Americans and French landing astride the penninsula of which Yorktown formed the tip, Cornwallis found himself in a trap about to snap shut. For this, his superior, Clinton, was largely at fault. Preparing for Washington's feigned attack on New York, unaware of reinforcements already on the way from England, Clinton had called on Cornwallis to send north every man he could possibly spare and assume a defensive position with the rest at Yorktown, where the British fleet's naval superiority could protect him with its guns and men.

Obeying, Cornwallis moved into the trap. Out at sea the covering British fleet, under Admirals Thomas Graves and Samuel Hood, was defeated by de Grasse in a five-day-long battle, leaving the British remnants fleeing toward New York and Cornwallis at Yorktown to fend for himself. Newly won French naval superiority permitted a convoy of French troops under Comte Louis de Barras to enter the Chesapeake and join the growing allied forces. With Hamilton's light infantry battalion and all the other reinforcements from the north reaching them on the peninsula, the numbers of the French and American forces under Lafayette and Wayne grew from 11,000 to 14,000 and finally to a peak of 16,500.

It was the largest force ever assembled under Washington's overall command. Cornwallis's army was about half its size, but Cornwallis was dug in behind a maze of fortifications well covered by heavy artillery. On September 28, 1781, at 5:00 in the morning, Hamilton's light infantry marched down from Williamsburg to join the rest of the army deployed in a semicircle facing Cornwallis in his Yorktown defenses. He was now completely surrounded. He held the town of Yorktown itself on the broad estuary of the York River. Other British forces held Gloucester Point across the water to the north, but the French fleet, instead of Cornwallis's own, was now in command of the straits between. His elaborate fortifications around the town faced the allied army's lines in a semicircle stretching from a point on the river bank northwest of the town south in an arc bending around the town itself to another point back on the river bank below the town a mile downstream. Looking from the allied trenches back toward Yorktown, the French held the left sector of the semicircle; and the Americans, the right. Of the three divisions holding the American sector, Hamilton's battalion and the other brigades of light infantry were in advance on the far right under the overall command of Lafayette. In the American center were brigades commanded by Anthony Wayne and Mordecai Gist, belonging to a division under the command of Baron von Steuben. On the American left was Lincoln's division: brigades under the command of General James Clinton and Colonel Elias Dayton. Covering these powerful forces of Continental regulars about 5,500 strong were medium and heavy batteries of artillery under the command of General Knox. There were detachments of sappers and miners and a 5,000-man force of militia, including a corps of Virginia mountain riflemen commanded by the brave new governor who had replaced Jefferson, General Thomas Nelson.

The well-disciplined French regiments of infantry, batteries of artillery, and troops of cavalry were about 7,200 strong, mustering about 1,700 more regulars than the Americans. They were under the overall command of Rochambeau, who reported to Washington. Particular friends of Hamilton among the French officers were Marquis François Louis de Fleury and the Vicomte Louis Marie de Noailles, who was a brother-in-law of Lafayette. Hamilton's own brother-in-law, John B. Church, was also with the French at Yorktown in his capacity as their commissary contractor.

Hamilton's battalion on the right flanking sector of the line quickly took cannon fire from the British redoubts opposite; one British cannon shot off the leg of one of Hamilton's men.

Hamilton took charge of preparations for a long siege. His men dug trenches and threw up earthworks in the sandy soil, then reinforced the protective mounds with gabions and saucissons (wicker cylinders filled with dirt) and fascines (bundles of sticks, staked down in front of the trenches). These served to protect the men in the trenches against any sudden assault from the British redoubts in the same way that later armies use barbed wire to trap and tangle charging infantrymen before they approach near enough to the trenches to kill the loaders and gunners of the covering guns.

As artillery and small arms fire opened up from the allied lines, the infantry pushed advance trenches and earthworks closer and closer toward British lines until Cornwallis was forced to abandon some of his outer works; he did not have enough troops to man them all.

On the night of September 29, as Cornwallis evacuated some of the outer fortifications and an allied patrol probed the remaining British defensive works, Colonel Alexander Scammell, Hamilton's immediate superior, was shot, wounded, and captured and after a few days was said to have died of his wounds. Many Americans suspected that Scammell had been shot to death after capture by Tarleton's dragoons, considered it murder, and threatened to kill any British officer who fell into their hands. Hamilton's good friend Lafayette now proposed to Washington that, with Scammell gone, Hamilton's battalion should be enlarged to equal Huntington's and that he should "put the eldest of the two lieutenant colonels [Hamilton] upon the right [that is, the leading position] of the brigade." Washington approved.

Cornwallis had collected many small boats just offshore of the town of Yorktown, keeping open the possibility of escaping by stealth across the water to Gloucester Point, even under the guns of the French fleet. He had received word from Clinton that a large rescue fleet and 5,000 men would be sailing from New York October 5 to reinforce him, and it was usually no more than an eight-day voyage. Only about two weeks' time remained in which de Grasse could keep his blocking fleet in position at the mouth of the Chesapeake in the face of such a formidable British naval threat. Washington feared that there would not be time to starve out Cornwallis. Yorktown had to be taken quickly and by storm, without necessarily trying to economize on infantrymen's lives, if it were to be taken at all.

On October 3 de Choisy pushed the French lines forward up closer to the

British works on the left. A sudden charge by Lauzun's brightly uniformed troopers badly mauled Banastre Tarleton and one of his columns. Tarleton himself narrowly missed death at the hands of Lauzun.

Extending outward from the town of Yorktown in front of Hamilton's sector, the British had constructed two advance redoubts from which deadly flanking cross fire could be poured upon any frontal attack on the town itself. If there were to be economizing of the lives of charging infantrymen, the best way was to destroy these two redoubts before making the main assault.

Under the fire of the British cannon, Hamilton and his men and the other American troops began laboriously digging siege approach trenches toward the fortified redoubts. By October 6 they had dug a "parallel" trench 3 1/2 feet deep and 7 feet wide, extending for more than a mile across the exposed flat level field in front of the British fortifications. The digging of the last few yards took place at night under orders for strict silence while French troops under Saint-Simon over on the far left of the semicircular line staged clamorous diversionary attacks.

By the morning of October 7, after the French attack, the left, or French, end of the first parallel trench was 600 yards from the British center; and the right, where Hamilton's troops were, was about 800 yards from the two advanced British redoubts, known as numbers 9 and 10.

The allies' preparatory bombardment began at 3:00 in the afternoon of October 9. The thunder of the twenty-four pounders was joined by the hollow thump of the mortars and the louder crash of the howitzers. It was a far more destructive barrage than the one the *Asia*'s guns had laid on New York.

The heaviest British artillery were only eighteen pounders; so the defenders of the fortified town were outgunned. As time went on, the weight of the allied barrage and success of the allied marksmanship gradually silenced the lighter British guns one by one. These artillery barrages were the heaviest ever fired up to that time in the western hemisphere.

Under a flag of truce, an uncle of Governor Thomas Nelson was sent out from Yorktown to report to Washington that the fortifications had been damaged and that the defenders were killing horses they could not feed, but that Cornwallis would not surrender because he expected Clinton's fleet to arrive with relief within a week. The allied pounding resumed.

Well-aimed shells from the French cannoneers on the allied left set fire to the British warship *Charon*, lying just offshore. The blaze, as she burned to the waterline through the night provided a spectacularly dispiriting sight to every defender. The blaze spread to Cornwallis's other smaller getaway vessels moored offshore. This emboldened de Grasse to dispatch some of his ships from the flotilla blocking the river mouth upriver past the guns of the town to cut off Cornwallis's retreat across the water.

While the bombardment was going on, Hamilton's troops kept pushing their siege trenches closer to British redoubts 9 and 10 until by October 11 they had extended a second parallel trench, working under heavy, close-range fire from the redoubts, to a point only about 350 yards away from them.

All the while, the allied guns returned the fire from the redoubts. Both redoubts, numbers 9 and 10, had earthen walls rising from deep ditches some 20 feet from bottom to top. Sharpened stakes driven in at an angle bristled from the walls. In front was a 25-yard-wide barricade of felled trees also bristling with tangled and sharpened sticks and branches. Veteran British troops, 120 strong, garrisoned redoubt number 9; about 45 defended redoubt number 10.

Sunday afternoon, October 14, Rochambeau assigned his chasseurs and grenadiers, under Baron de Viomenil, to assault redoubt number 9. American light infantry of Lafayette's division would make the final assault on redoubt number 10. Lafayette chose his former aide, Lieutenant Colonel John Joseph Gimat, to command the American forces in the van. According to the plan of battle, Gimat's battalion would lead. Hamilton's would follow. Laurens's would come up on the flank. Colonel Francis Barber's would follow as a supporting column. Hamilton was bitterly disappointed. He thought his supreme chance to lead the charge had slipped away. A following place in the final assault on the last redoubt at Yorktown was not what Hamilton had marched, ridden, sailed, and burrowed all the way from Dobbs Ferry to occupy.

Hamilton went to Lafayette and demanded that he be put in overall command. Lafayette pointed out that Gimat's battalion had been with Lafayette much longer and had wearily fought, pursued, and fled from Cornwallis all summer, whereas Hamilton's had "just come from the Northward." Hamilton was senior to Gimat, it was true. Precocious as he was said to be, his long service as an aide, after his line duties as an artilleryman, had left him "over age" in grade. Besides, for what it was worth, that particular Sunday happened to fall on Hamilton's regular turn as "officer of the day." Lafayette took Hamilton's demand directly to Washington. Hamilton came along to help argue his case, which seemed to be based largely on a technicality.

Hamilton burst out of Washington's tent and embraced Major Nicholas Fish. "We have it, we have it," cried the officer of the day.

Hamilton was to have command of the entire American assault team. The plan of attack worked out by Lafayette with Hamilton's aid placed Gimat in charge of the right column, reinforced by a detachment of sappers and miners under John Gililand to remove obstructions. Lieutenant Colonel John Laurens's column on the left would circle the redoubt "to take the enemy in reverse, and intercept their retreat." Major Fish, now commanding Hamilton's old battalion, was to bear to the left to enter the redoubt from that side. All troops would advance under cover of darkness, as silently as possible, rifles and muskets unloaded, but with bayonets fixed and at the ready. They would rely on surprise and terror to repeat the success that similar tactics learned from the enemy at Paoli had won for "Mad Anthony" Wayne at Stony Point.

Just before dark, Washington paid brief visits to both the French and American assault teams. By this time the whole army was expecting "something grand to be done by our infantry."

Soon after darkness, the general cannonade fell silent. Then six quick aerial shell bursts from a French battery signaled the beginning of the attack. On the far left flank, Saint-Simon's forces staged another noisy diversionary demonstration. Over across the water from Gloucester Point, de Choisy's troops began to fire, raising fears inside Yorktown of an attack from the water side. In the darkness over on the left, Hamilton could hear the muffled shuffle of boots and the clank of bayonets being affixed to muskets. The French light infantry were massing behind Comte Guillaume de Deux-Ponts in the trench at the line of departure for the attack. Hamilton's New York and Connecticut Continental light infantry assembled in the trench behind him.

Now was the time. The shuffle and clank fell silent. Shell bursts and muzzle flashes from the diversionary demonstrations and British counterfire in the distance glinted fitfully on bayonet blades jutting from rifles and muskets held by men crouching in the trenches at port arms, pointing toward Yorktown. Suddenly, Hamilton stood erect in the trench facing redoubt number 10, his upper body outlined against the night sky by the firing opposite. He extended his right arm straight up above his head, pointing his sword toward the sky.

"Fix bayonets!" he whispered loudly. He paused as his men tested the fit of the collar and slot one last time. Keeping his sword, wrist, and elbow straight and stiff as if all were a guidon's lance, he swung his arm downward in an arc until it and his sword paralleled the ground. As he did so he called back over his shoulder in a low voice, "Follow me!" He lunged forward, bending low, running ahead of the infantrymen of Mansfield's vanguard who were strung out behind him. Hamilton moved swiftly and silently through the first parallel trench to the end and on into the second and to the end of it and then up over the lip of the trench onto the exposed flat sandy plain. It was scarred with shell holes and treacherous puddles of water from the weeks of artillery cannonading. With a thrust of his sword, Hamilton waved his men on toward the last Yorktown redoubts. Three hundred yards across the flat, muddy, shell-pocked, open field at night, sporadically illuminated by signal flares and muzzle flashes from enemy guns in the darkness, would seem like three miles. Throats would constrict from exhaustion, lack of air, stress and pounding hearts! Over on the left flank, toward where the French were moving in on redoubt number 9, a Hessian guard gruffly challenged an advancing Gatinois of Colonel L'Estrade's battalion, "Wer da?"

The Gatinois returned no countersign or password. There was a moment of stillness. Then Hessian musket fire flashed and roared point-blank into the faces of the brave French attackers. The defenders' volley scorched and deafened Hamilton and his men. Hamilton pushed on into the sharpened ends of the branches of the first prickly abatis, mounted it, and skidded down the sloping wall of the counterscarp into the ditch and up palisades of stakes beyond it. Scattered firing of the aroused defenders flashed out at the terrified attackers all along the line. The firing in the French sector had alerted all the defenders. Hamilton was too short to climb over the heavy stakes of the palisade, but now there was no time to pause under fire for the engineers and sappers to clear an opening. Hamilton ordered one of the men coming up behind him to kneel. He climbed up on his shoulders, vaulted over the palings onto the scarp and up the parapet wall. More enemy muskets blazed along the line, but Hamilton's men did not fire a shot. Now on the top of the parapet wall, he thrust his sword forward again, looked back toward his men, and brought his arm down to the horizontal, softly calling, "Follow me!" He leaped down into the inner works of the redoubt.

The men behind him clambered and fell and picked themselves up and slashed and scrambled on through the barrier, across the ditch, and up the bristling embankments of the redoubt. Gasping for breath, they clambered up it, slipping between the stakes. Some pulled themselves up on the outthrust, sharpened ends.

Musket blasts now crashed at point-blank ranges, blinding their eyes, deafening their ears, and choking their lungs with the acrid smell of burned powder and smoke. Startled, plaintive cries suddenly spurted out as shot hit men. Screams erupted as sharp bayonet blades sliced and splashed through flesh and blood. Steel scraped on bone. The first American over the top and inside the works was Hamilton himself. Men of Gimat's battalion clambered down close behind him, their bayonets quivering at the ready and some already dripping blood or raggedly fringed with bloody flesh. Laurens's men crashed into the open rear of the redoubt. Major Patrick Campbell, the commander, his little fortress overwhelmed by the sudden superior force brought to bear with shock effect on all sides of it, surrendered his person to Laurens. At the same moment, Fish, leading Hamilton's old battalion, swarmed in from the left flank.

Colonel Gimat had been struck in the foot by a defender's musket ball, Captains Thomas Hunt and Stephen Betts of Laurens's company suffered bayonet wounds, and Lieutenant Captain Kilpatrick of the sappers and miners lay wounded in the ditch. One sergeant and eight privates were killed, and 25 privates were wounded. Of the British garrison of the redoubt, who, Hamilton later acknowledged, were "intitled to the acknowledgement of an honorable defence," eight were killed or wounded by the Americans' bayonets. Major Campbell, a captain, an ensign, and 17 others were taken prisoners. The rest escaped in the darkness back to the inner defenses of Yorktown. It was all over in less than ten minutes.

As Major Campbell surrendered, a New Hampshire captain lunged at him with his bayonet, shouting that he would take revenge upon him for the death of Colonel Scammell. He considered it murder. Hamilton threw himself between the New Hampshire captain and Major Campbell. He ordered the New Hampshire man to stand back. He would allow no reprisals and would see no man injured after resistance had ended. If Colonel Scammell had not died, it would have been he, not Hamilton, who led the charge.

De Viomenil's French had a harder fight for redoubt number 9, and it took them longer to invest it at a much higher cost in killed and wounded—15 killed and 77 wounded; the British defenders lost 18, and 50 were taken prisoner.

The French had borne the brunt and suffered the most. Hamilton had been more successful in economizing on the lives of his infantrymen. His silent, night, bayonet attack on redoubt number 10 created a great stir. The same day, October 15, Hamilton wrote a report of the attack to Lafayette, mentioning the gallantry of everyone in it but himself.

Anyone who has ever led troops in taking an enemy redoubt knows that the personal side of the experience is too intense for any but the most matter-of-fact and impersonal words: "The rapidity and immediate success of the assault are the best comment on the behaviour of the troops," Hamilton wrote. "As it would have been attended with delay and loss to wait for the removal of the abatis and palisades the ardor of the troops was indulged in passing over them."

Good planning had produced an effective coordination of movement in the attack: "The redoubt was in the same moment envelloped and carried on every part." Mindful of the strong suspicions that Colonel Scammell had been shot after being taken prisoner, Hamilton wrote that his men, "incapable of imitating examples of barbarity, and forgetting recent provocations, the soldiery spared every man, who ceased to resist."

Lafayette forwarded Hamilton's report to Washington, filling in the gap that the intensity of Hamilton's own personal involvement had left, writing:

> I beg leave to refer our excellency to the report I have received from Colonel Hamilton, whose well known talents and gallantry were on this occasion most conspicuous and serviceable. Our obligation to him, to Colonel Gimat, to Colonel Laurens, and to each and all the officers and men, are above all expression.

Washington's own praise of the attack must have given Hamilton special satisfaction: "The bravery . . . was emulous . . . Few cases have exhibited stronger proofs of Intrepidity, coolness and firmness than were shown upon this occasion." The success in capturing the redoubts on the enemy's left flank, Washington wrote to Greene, "will prove of almost infinite importance in our Approaches . . ."

The allied forces at once extended their second set of parallel trenches to take in the two captured redoubts. They hauled Knox's cannon forward and emplaced them to fire out of the open backs of the redoubts directly down upon Cornwallis's inner works in the town, now only about 200 yards away.

From under the new threat of the close-range allied cannonade, Cornwallis wrote to Sir Henry Clinton on October 15:

> My situation now becomes very critical; we dare not show a gun to their batteries, and I expect that their new ones will open tomorrow morning. Our fresh earthen works do not resist their powerful artillery. We shall soon be exposed to an assault in ruining works, in a bad position, and with weakened numbers. The safety of the place is, therefore, so precarious, that I cannot recommend that the fleet and army should run any great risk in endeavoring to save us.

The capture of the two redoubts broke effective British resistance. On the sixteenth, the British made a desperate predawn sortie, entered the Americans' second parallel trench, and spiked six of Knox's cannon before being driven off, leaving casualties on both sides.

After the sortie, the allied bombardment rose to a crescendo, while return fire from the enemy guns diminished. On the night of the sixteenth, Cornwallis attempted to ferry his main force across the river to Gloucester Point, but the overloaded little fleet of 16 boats was dispersed by a violent rainstorm and returned to Yorktown.

Cornwallis wrote, "We . . . could not fire a single gun . . . only one eight inch and little more than a hundred cohorn shells remained . . . Our numbers had been diminished by the evening's fire, but particularly by sickness."

With all going well against the British, the French suddenly became a problem again. Comte de Grasse announced that his fleet had to depart within 48 hours. Washington remonstrated that he had too few men of his own to assault the fortified town and would be compelled to raise the siege on the brink of victory. De Grasse refused to change his mind.

Washington was not above allowing a trusted subordinate to try a secret strategem across the lines of a kind that no commander could countenance in his own name. Hamilton's friend Elias Boudinot later revealed the curious episode. Hamilton and some other officers moved toward the British lines under a flag of truce. During a brief conversation with some of the British—their amicable sortie was supposedly a private venture—they made it known to the British that an American assault in force was, in fact, in the making; that everyone was "so exasperated at the Conduct of the British to the Southward, that they could not answer for the Consequences, as they did not think they could be restrained by authority and Discipline." Hamilton reinforced this by telling the story of having barely saved Major Campbell's life from reprisal in the redoubt.

However, Hamilton added, they knew Washington's "humane Temper." If the British would surrender now, before the final all-out attack got under way, Washington would certainly grant more favorable terms and heavy casualties would be spared. It should be recorded that there is little corroboration for this story of Boudinot, but it serves to explain the otherwise inexplicable promptness of Cornwallis's surrender.

On the morning of the seventeenth, a red-coated drummer mounted the parapet of the nearest British fortification and "beat a parley." An officer waved a white handkerchief. Washington ordered his guns into silence. Out of the ruined British fortifications a messenger brought to him one of the most momentous documents of American history. It read:

> Sir, I propose a cessation of hostilities for twenty-four hours, and that two officers may be appointed by each side, to meet at Mr. Moore's house, to settle the terms for the surrender of the posts at York and Gloucester.
>
> I have the honor to be, etc.
> Cornwallis.

Well aware that reinforcements from Clinton might arrive at any moment or that de Grasse might sail away, Washington agreed to suspend the artillery barrage for two hours, but not twenty-four. Lieutenant Colonel John Laurens and Vicomte Louis Marie de Noailles from the allies met with Lieutenant Colonel Alexander Dundas and Major Alexander Ross from the British army to negotiate the detailed surrender terms.

Washington earlier had ordered that American deserters fighting with the British army be hanged. Formal surrender terms did not permit them to be exchanged as prisoners of war. For Cornwallis to have included them in the surrender by sending them back to American lines would have been to sign their death warrants. So it was agreed that Cornwallis would be permitted to send the armed sloop *Bonetta* to New York with dispatches for Sir Henry Clinton "without examination." This meant that the allies could not examine the vessel, although they were aware that this would permit Cornwallis to ship out some 250 deserters. Washington's liking for stern measures being known, it was also provided that captured British officers would not be subjected to retaliatory hangings. This was a detail that would later save Washington from committing a barbarity Hamilton had warned him against. Recaptured slaves who had run away to join the British army to gain their freedom would be returned to their former owners. This brought two of Washington's slaves, who had escaped from Mount Vernon to freedom with the British, back to their former condition of servitude with him. Washington, Rochambeau, and Barras put their signatures to the surrender document in the same redoubt Hamilton had stormed.

There is scholarly dispute as to whether or not Hamilton's turn as officer of the day had really come round again on October 19, only four days after the assault on redoubt number 10, thereby putting him center stage at a second historic occasion. It would, of course, have been out of character for Hamilton to shirk any possible chance to direct the ceremony as well as the charge.

The ceremony took place on the Yorktown siege ground at one in the afternoon of October 19, 1781. Lord Cornwallis did not appear, pleading sickness, and no wonder. In his place he sent Brigadier General Charles O'Hara, his second in command. O'Hara marched up to Rochambeau, mistaking him for Washington, and presented his credentials. Rochambeau corrected him. O'Hara then marched up to where Washington stood with Hamilton at his side. Washington ignored him. A deputy should treat with a deputy, not the chief, Hamilton told him. He sent O'Hara on down the line to General Benjamin Lincoln, Washington's second-in-command.

Eighteenth-century warfare set great store by the right of the vanquished to salute the victor by playing one of the victor's tunes. This was supposed to show that even in surrender, the vanquished had not given over their pride. But the British had not allowed the Americans to play a British tune when the British had captured Charleston and John Laurens with it; so as part of the Yorktown surrender ceremony, John Laurens stipulated that the British play one of their own tunes, not an American one.

British commissioned color bearers objected to handing over their regimental colors to American sergeants—noncommissioned officers—in accordance with the original plans. Hamilton interceded and directed that an ensign, the youngest commissioned officer in the American army, but an officer nevertheless, accept the colors from the British guidons and then turn them over to a sergeant. After this display of American generosity, the British and Hessian troops, their unit colors cased, marched through the ranks of American and French troops drawn up in parade formation. Hamilton would remember the beaten retreat across New Jersey of five years earlier while the British army bands played the British air, "The World Turned Upside Down."

Hamilton's friend the Marquis de Fleury wrote James Duane about the victory. Cornwallis and Colonel O'Hara had suffered another setback: Fleury wrote, "we shall I hope by this last blow, get the better, of the british obstinacy, to enslave america . . ." In postscript he added, "I Din'd yesterday with Lord Cornwallys & o'hara. I was so bold as to inquire of the last, why they took so many nigros. by god, said he, we had no other allieds Left in this Country." Fleury had the last word, " 'You forget,' did I answer, 'your faithfull friends the Indians.' "

Victory at Yorktown after a spectacular charge against a heavily fortified enemy position demonstrated to Americans that their troops were as good as any others. They did not need to fight from the protection of elaborate fortifications as they had done at Saratoga. They did not always have to get beaten and hit and run as Greene did in the Carolinas. Victory at Yorktown showed Americans that they could win a set piece battle. Working together and with the French, they could end the war as a nation, and they were already far along the road toward doing so.

Newspapers in Philadelphia and elsewhere carried prominently the story of how Hamilton had led the American charge that overwhelmed the defenders of redoubt number 10.

The Frenchmen who were heroes of redoubt number 9 soon sailed away for home. Hamilton's close friends John Laurens and Francis Barber, the other two heroes who had crashed into redoubt number 10 at almost the same glorious moment he had, would be killed in meaningless skirmishes before the war was finally over. This left Hamilton's image more or less alone in the public's imagination, silhouetted by an occasional rocket's red glare, standing atop the parapet of redoubt number 10 the night of October 15, thrusting his sword up and then down, whispering to his men with fixed bayonets below: "Follow me!"

Risk taking is not in itself heroic. The heroism of mythology and classical antiquity is the exceptional readiness of the singular individual to dare greatly for the sake of the welfare of someone else or many other people because no one else steps forward.

No great civilization has been able to last long without that sort of man, though his type is out of fashion and he seems rare today in the United States. Despite keen awareness of personal risk, Hamilton was readier than most, indeed eager, to step forward at Yorktown. In a perceptive and generally rational man like Hamilton, the mystery of the complex combination of thoughts of personal honor, military glory, future usefulness to the nation, and escape from the condition of an aide that made him insist on rising to seize the risk is as deep as any in his story.

He had found the war he wished for. He had proved that the nation he had envisioned could win freedom at least partly on its own. He had won an unforgettable place in the hearts of his countrymen for the rest of his life and, indeed, for the rest of its history. More important, he had earned the right to regard himself with self-respect. He had sought and passed a self-imposed test that would permit him to erase from his mind the ambiguities of his "hurry of mind" the day he had encountered Major General Charles Lee retreating from the field of Monmouth. His testimony for the prosecution at Lee's court-martial had projected his own "hurry of mind" on to Lee to help Washington obtain Lee's conviction. No one had reproached him for his hurry of mind at Monmouth but Lee—and himself. Only his own inward ideal of honor had required that the stain of that hot summer's day at Monmouth be scraped away on the parapet of the last redoubt at Yorktown.

16

AFTER THE BATTLE
COMES THE LAWGIVER

I WISH TO SEE A CONVENTION OF ALL THE STATES, WITH FULL
POWER TO ALTER AND AMEND, FINALLY AND IRREVOCABLY, THE
PRESENT FUTILE AND SENSELESS CONFEDERATION.
                            —*To Robert Morris, April 30, 1781*

From "camp before Yorktown," on October 12, two days before the successful storming of redoubt number 10, Hamilton had written Betsy: "Five days more the enemy must capitulate or abandon their present position . . . and then I fly to you. Prepare to receive me in your bosom . . . receive me decked in all your beauty, fondness and goodness. Adieu my darling wife, my beloved angel adieu."

His five-day forecast was accurate. His own action did much to make it so. His successful storm was the night of the fourteenth to fifteenth, he arranged the surrender informally on the seventeenth, the white flag showed and the drummer boy beat the parley on the eighteenth, and the formal surrender ceremony was the nineteenth. In his letter of the twelfth he had first written "four days more." This would have been off by one day. Then he had crossed out the word *four* and written in the correct forecast, *five.*

On October 16 Hamilton wrote Elizabeth again: "Two nights ago, my Eliza, my duty and my honor obliged me to take a step in which your happiness was too much risked." But he had risked it for the following reason: "I commanded an attack on one of the enemy's redoubts; we carried it in an instant and with little loss. You will see the particulars in the Philadelphia papers . . ."

The Philadelphia newspapers had given him rave reviews on his performance. It was not the kind of performance that needed to be repeated. He assured her "There will be, certainly, nothing more of this kind . . . If there should be another occasion, it will not fall to my turn to execute it." He would make sure of that by leaving the army forthwith.

Two days later, he wrote Elizabeth his last letter from Yorktown:

> My uneasiness at not hearing from you is abated by the sweet prospect of soon taking you in my arms . . . In two days after I shall . . . set out for Albany, and I hope to embrace you in three weeks from this time . . . Conceive my love from your own feelings, how delightful this prospect is to me. Only in your heart and in my own can any image be found of my happiness . . . Adieu my charming beloved wife, I kiss you a thousand times, adieu, my love.
>
> A. Hamilton.

Easy retirement from active military service at an officer's own discretion without risk of disgrace for being absent without leave was a casual matter in 1781. Hamilton's quick and easy retirement provides an amusing contrast to the long, arduous campaign he had waged to obtain his brief command.

From Morristown headquarters in May of 1777 he had written Catharine Livingston that "I do not wonder at your antipathy to [war]. Every finer feeling of a delicate mind revolts from the idea of shedding human blood and multiplying the common evils of life by the artificial methods incident to that state. Were it not for the evident necessity; and in defence of all that is valuable in society, I could never be reconciled to a military character; and shall rejoice when the restoration of peace on the basis of freedom and independence shall put it [in] my power to renounce it."

To Hamilton war as such was an idea that was repellent. It was a thing that "multiplied the common evils of life." No one would disagree with that sentiment, but it was not that simple. More must be said. Sometimes war became a necessary evil for "defence of all that is valuable in society." Freedom and independence, for example, were two such values. There are times when such precious values can be preserved in no other way than by fighting for them.

The image of Hamilton as a militarist who loved war for its own sake is one that has often been put forward by doctoral dissertaters and other detractors. It is a false image, a simpleminded cartoon drawn by hard-line armchair pacifists.

Nothing Hamilton had seen during the four years of war since he had written Catharine Livingston had changed his conviction that he could "never be reconciled to a military character." All he had seen had only reinforced this conviction.

Renouncing his "military character," he would write to Washington that he wished to preserve his rank in the peacetime army but "without involvements and unattached to any corps as an honorary reward for the time I have devoted to the public service." Thinking no doubt of future public usefulness in dealing with foreigners, he added, "As I may hereafter travel abroad I may find it an agreeable circumstance to appear in the character I have supported in the revolution." Rank-conscious French friends of the war years, for example, might not recognize him in mufti.

With more than 500 miles to ride from Yorktown to The Pastures at Albany, but riding alone without command responsibility for columns of infantry rambling slowly along beside him under billowing clouds of dust, Hamilton anxiously spurred his horse northward over the newly rutted roads as fast as the horse's shanks and lungs could keep him a-going.

". . . he thought of nothing but reaching [his wife] the soonest possible," Philip Schuyler later reported from Albany, "and Indeed he tyred his horses to accomplish it, and was obliged to hire others to come on from Red Hook."

He rose early and rode fast and continued late. A three-week ride through the cool and frosty late October and November woods would powerfully concentrate his mind. He had found the war he wished for to raise himself from the condition of an aide, but he was not primarily a military man. He was a political man, a practical revolutionist. He had found the war to be necessary as a means to pursue political goals by other than political means. Without the war, the political objectives for which the Revolution was fought might not have been won for decades or even a century or more. Without the political shock of the war and events of its aftermath—like the army's mutiny against Congress—the form of national constitutional government constructed on strong economic foundations that Hamilton helped to build would have taken an entirely different form. He hated the bloodshed and other evils of war, but sometimes such evils were justified in "defence of all that is valuable in society."

As he spurred his horse north his mind rescanned the plans he had been broadcasting beyond the army encampments to foster "all that is valuable in society" by non warlike means. He was not abandoning the war except in the narrowest sense. He was redeploying his efforts from the war in the field to the wider war of politics that had to be waged with words throughout the thirteen states.

After the triumph at Yorktown, Robert Morris had said, "What remains of the war is only a war of finance." In many letters and dispatches and broadsides, in his long letter to Robert Morris signed "James Montague," and in his letter to James Duane from Liberty Pole, Hamilton had been saying much the same thing in many different ways—but less succinctly—from almost the beginning of the war. Hamilton's characteristic method was to build general plans on the ratchets of specific problems. In July 1780 the Marquis François de Barbé-Marbois, secretary of the French legation in Philadelphia, had written Hamilton that the new bank of Pennsylvania was issuing bank notes to volunteer ladies' groups there so that they could buy linen to run up shirts for the soldiers. In February 1781 Hamilton had cautioned him, "Paper credit cannot be supported without pecuniary funds." He forecast the failure of the French assignats, a scheme adopted in France a short time later that provided for backing the franc by liens on the nation's land:

> Back lands are very good resources in reserve, but I suspect they will not have so much present efficacy as is imagined. I only regard the acquisition of territory to Congress as useful, so far as it enables them to procure credit.

The local problem of financing volunteer ladies' groups sewing soldiers' shirts had led him on to the national problem of sewing up the war. He added, to Barbé-Marbois, "God send that the negotiation abroad for money may succeed; for it is only this that can give success to our interior efforts."

The appeal to France that Hamilton had written for Washington and that John Laurens had taken with him to France as envoy had helped bring much success in exterior efforts. On April 9, 1781, Laurens had written Congress from Versailles that he had secured a loan of 10 million livres to be opened in Holland with French guarantee, 4 million to be appropriated to cover bills drawn by Congress on Franklin, and 6 million for military supplies. Laurens had also obtained the firm promise of the indispensable French naval blockade that had just made the army's triumph at Yorktown possible.

On April 30, 1781, the day his resignation as Washington's first aide became final, Hamilton had sealed and placed in the mail a second long essay addressed to Robert Morris, setting forth another comprehensive plan for putting the disordered finances of the country on a sound and durable basis. It was the third such plan he had written within the space of a year and a half, and it contained much of the best from the two earlier efforts.

Congress had appointed Robert Morris, the Philadelphia merchant banker, to be financier of the Office of the Finance, the highest ranking fiscal officer of the Confederation. Robert Morris chose as his assistant Gouverneur Morris, Hamilton's friend from New York and one of Catharine Livingston's suitors from Elizabethtown days. The two Morrises were not related by blood, but both thought alike. Like Hamilton, they felt that a sound economic foundation and sound money were the indispensable foundation for all interior efforts to achieve enduring political freedom and independence. At the same time, Robert Morris was also the guiding spirit of the firm of Willing, Morris and Co., a spectacularly successful private banking conglomerate that was active in shipping, privateering, and brokerage—buying or selling anything that could be bought or sold on a large scale. Morris profiteered, but only patriotically. He would buy and hold goods, waiting for a jump in price, and then sell them to the army. The phrase "conflict of interest" as a pejorative one was not much heard in eighteenth-century commerce. Morris employed the inside knowledge that his governmental positions afforded him to further his own private ends, which also, fortunately, usually coincided with the success of the revolutionary cause. Morris's unflagging readiness to pledge his ever-swelling wealth to Congress and to make loans out of his own private capital stood in sharp contrast to many other men, nearly as wealthy. They were fearful of taking the same risks he did and of losing their stake if the revolutionary cause should fail.

Robert and Gouverneur Morris commanded the highest respect and confidence of the moneyed men. Hamilton himself had urged Robert Morris's appointment. As well as anyone else, Hamilton understood the practical difficulties that confronted the new financier.

Costs of the war were enormous; there was very little hard coin in circulation; the paper money issued by Congress had depreciated over forty to one; but the chief trouble was that the Articles of Confederation failed to give Congress the power to levy taxes.

The program Hamilton urged on the financier was that "by introducing order into our finances—by restoring public credit—not by gaining battles, we are finally to gain our object." Hamilton opposed use of committees where action was necessary on such complex and difficult matters. Hamilton urged that "An Administration by single men and conspicuous for probity, abilities and fortune, is essential to proper management of the affairs of this country." Committees were useful primarily to excuse nonaction, to create the appearance of action where the reality was inaction, to muddle through to a consensus that would reflect the lowest common denominator, or to whitewash wrongdoing.

The national government was still dependent on requisitions from the states for its own support and for support of the war. But the states, jealous of each other, reluctant to burden their own citizens, complaining that their particular allotments were unfair, had failed to supply the sums that were requisitioned. Had it not been for loans and outright gifts from France, the war would have long since gone bankrupt. Now France, pressed to the limit, was resisting further demands for loans. Yet it was still essential to obtain hard money at once to support the war.

Hamilton's paper told Morris how to overcome these seemingly insuperable problems. Like the plans he had urged on Morris and Duane earlier, it had as its central idea a national central bank. Hamilton offered the draft of a charter for one, relying on examples of past experience by the Bank of England. He added modifications of his own to adapt it to American conditions.

The first step, he told Morris, was to estimate the country's capacity for revenue, which Hamilton thought did not amount to more than $6,000,000 annually. Because the cost of government and the war ran to $10,000,000, there would be an annual deficit of $4,000,000, "which deficiency must of course be supplied by credit, foreign or domestic, or both."

There was little chance of borrowing this sum abroad. France and Spain and Holland, the most likely foreign sources of credit, had done all that could be expected and had troubles of their own. Nor was it easy to borrow from domestic sources because there was "the want of confidence of a sufficient number of men with sufficient moneyed capitals to lend the sums required, and the want of confidence in those who are able to lend make them unwilling to part with their money."

Some commentators angrily impute lack of patriotism to moneyed merchants because they tended to deploy their money on the basis of their appraisal of risk, return, reward, and other economic factors, whose answers lay shrouded in the unknown future, instead of deploying it on the basis of predominantly patriotic motives. Such commentators betray simple ignorance of men, money, and economics and their own double standard. No similar criticism is imputed by them to moneyed men who were self-proclaimed patriots and lovers of the common man who refused to free their valuable slaves on patriotic and humanitarian grounds as men like Laurens and Hamilton had urged.

Hamilton was not the man to wring his hands over the alleged lack of patriotism of moneyed men. He was the realist who acidly but calmly observed that "They can employ it to greater advantage in traffic rather than by merely lending it on interest."

A primary interest of rich men with capital was to obtain the highest possible rate of return. Hamilton was for soaking the rich, not the poor. He stressed the equality of fortune in America, as compared with Britain, France, and Holland, as a favorable circumstance. This "puts it in the power of Government to raise an equal proportion of revenue without burthening the lower Classes of the people in the same degree as in Europe." As a fortunate result of this general equality of fortunes in America, "The men in this country may be made to contribute in a much juster proportion to their property."

Hamilton was not a social reformer, nor a die-hard conservative who insisted on preserving and increasing the advantages held by the moneyed men. He was a realist. The new nation needed money. The best source of money was the moneyed men of the new country, modest as their resources might be when compared with those of the moneyed men of Europe. He knew that the result he desired for America would not be accomplished by deploring wealth or calling for a social revolution or by a forced leveling of all social classes, but by doing what was necessary to induce the men with capital to use it in ways that would support the new country and its finances. Far from being an admirer of the moneyed men, Hamilton might more accurately be described as their foremost coolheaded critic.

The timidity of capital was part of the natural order of things. It was necessary to bring it out of hiding by the prospect of attractive profits and safety.

Only a national bank could do this. Under both public and private auspices, it would

erect a mass of credit that will supply the defect of moneyed capital, and answer all the purposes of cash; a plan which will offer adventurers immediate advantages, analogous to those they receive by employing their money in trade, and eventually greater advantages; a plan which will give them the greatest security the nature of the case will admit for what they lend; and which will not only advance their own interest and secure the independence of their country, but, in its progress, have the most beneficial influence upon its future commerce, and be a source of national wealth and strength.

Here is the essence of Hamilton's philosophy of governmental finance. To yoke together all the separate, private interests and energies of individual men pursuing their private goals—an important one of which is the pursuit of profit —to draw all in the general direction of a single, unified national government for the separate states. On a national scale the sum of all of these separate efforts would add up to Adam Smith's "invisible hand" guiding all men and women in the general direction of the common good.

The bank Hamilton proposed was in most respects similar to the ones he had suggested before to Morris and Duane, but now to Morris he developed it in greater detail. Of its capital stock of £3,000,000, no more than half might be subscribed by the United States government and foreign citizens, for "it is of primary importance that the moneyed men among ourselves should be deeply interested in the plan."

The bank would have the power to issue "sight notes" that bore interest at four percent so that it would be profitable to use them in place of specie. These notes would be legal tender for taxes and customs duties, but not for private debts. The bank would be obligated to lend £1,200,000 to Congress at 8 percent, the loan to be amortized over 20 years from governmental revenues. No debt would be permanent. All would be paid off within a finite time on a realistic repayment schedule. For the duration of its charter—30 years—no other bank, public or private, might be chartered. Management was to be placed in a directorate of twelve—eight chosen by the private stockholders and four by Congress.

To many of his day, Hamilton's idea that the new government should burden itself with a debt this large seemed improvident. But Hamilton hailed a national debt as a positive good in itself. "A national debt," he asserted, "if it is not excessive, will be to us a national blessing. It will be a powerful cement of our Union. It will also create a necessity for keeping up taxation to a degree, which, without being oppressive, will be a spur to industry." No other plank in his program was to arouse as much opposition as this one. Hamilton understood as well as anyone else that no one likes to pay taxes. But taxes were the price of civilization, a necessary evil, like war, to be endured as the price of freedom and independence. He insisted that the burden of taxes should be equitably apportioned and criticized the inequity of the tax burden as it had developed in France, where the rich might escape taxes by what we now, more emotionally, would call "tax loopholes." For example, it was inequitable that they could take advantage of "tax exempt bonds" and "foreign tax havens."

"In France, the rich have gained so entire an ascendant that there is a constant sacrifice of the ease and happiness of the people to their avarice and luxury," Hamilton commented. He noted that "their burthens are in no proportion to those of the middle order and still less to those of the poor." In England

and Holland, Hamilton added, "The case is in a great measure the same."

Having given Morris the solution to the financial problems of the new country, Hamilton turned to his second lifelong theme—the need for a strong, central government with sovereignty independent of, and superior to, that of the several states. The Articles of Confederation were worse than useless, he insisted, and unless immediately revised, must lead to dissolution. He had a plan to fix them. "It has ever been my opinion," he told Morris, "that Congress ought to have complete sovereignty in all but the mere municipal law of each state; I wish to see a convention of all the States, with full power to alter and amend, finally and irrevocably, the present futile and senseless Confederation."

This short sentence contains large thoughts. It points straight to Hamilton's call at Annapolis for the Constitutional Convention, to *The Federalist Papers*, and to the ultimate adoption of the Constitution of 1787.

At nineteen, Hamilton had expressed many of the same basic ideas of this letter as he now did at twenty-four. Although he would continue to elaborate and refine them, he would not change them in their essentials for the rest of his life.

Morris's reply contained a generous acknowledgment of Hamilton's "genius." "My office is new," he wrote back, "and I am young in the execution of it." Generously, he added, "Communications from men of genius and abilities will always be acceptable; and yours will always command the attention of Robert Morris."

Morris submitted his own plan for a bank to Congress a few days after receiving Hamilton's letter, but his bank was on a more modest scale, calling for subscriptions of a mere 400 shares of $400 each. On the same day of Morris's reply to Hamilton, Congress set its seal of approval on his scheme. The Bank of North America was duly incorporated and ready for business by the last day of the year. It incorporated most of the basic principles Hamilton had laid down in his three letters on public finance of 1780 and 1781. It was a quasi-public bank, for which the government provided most of the capital and the right of inspection. Management control was in the hands of private stockholders. The bank loaned money to the government in anticipation of revenue.

But subscriptions to capital proved few because the terms of the bank's charter were less attractive for private investors than those Hamilton had proposed. Only $70,000 was subscribed out of an authorized $160,000. Congress was compelled to deposit $200,000 with the bank that had been received as a loan from France to capitalize it. The bank helped a little with financing the Revolution, but it would fall into popular disfavor soon after the end of the war.

Morris's modest bank plan was politically practical, but its failure would tend to confirm the superior economic wisdom of Hamilton's bolder one. Hamilton's plan was too far ahead of the politics of its time. But like many of his plans, it pointed the way toward the future for those who would eventually, at some later time, be looking in that direction. His new, bold, and sophisticated institutional solution for the country's economic, political, and social problems contributed much to the laborious but necessary process of educating the people to understand, favor, and finally accept his views.

After submitting his plan to Morris and resigning as Washington's chief aide in April 1781 and before moving over from de Peyster's Point to Dobbs Ferry in July, Hamilton had occupied the time that he described to Betsy as being wasted in idleness and "dissipation" by writing a masterful series of six essays, which he called "The Continentalist." He had sent the first of the series off to Samuel Loudon, editor of the *New York Packet* and the *American Advertiser*, published at Fishkill, on July 12, 1781, with an introductory note, which boldly proclaimed, "I send you the first number of a series of papers which I intend to publish on matters of the greatest importance to these States." They should be "read with as much candour and attention as the object of them deserve." "No conclusions will be drawn till these are fully developed," he added.

While Hamilton was marching south to Yorktown, the publication of the first four numbers of this great series, on July 12 and 19, August 9 and 30, 1781, was making a powerful impression on the minds of thinking men and women in the North.

"The Continentalist" hammered away at a single theme and proposed a single solution: the theme was—Continental nationalism; the solution was—more power to Congress! The arguments he had used the year before in his letter to James Duane were now honed and polished.

The fatal defect in the Articles of Confederation, he still insisted, was a "want of power in Congress." Those who were fearful of increasing centralized power and saw despotism as the end failed to see that, "as too much power leads to despotism, too little leads to anarchy, and both, eventually, to the ruin of the people." It was ridiculous to believe that the federal system of the United States could ever lend itself to despotism. The danger was in the other direction—"that the members will be an overmatch for the common head."

People were wont to blame Congress for all their troubles. "That body," he acknowledged, "is no doubt chargeable with mistakes, but perhaps its greatest has been too much readiness to make concessions of the powers implied in its original trust."

Since Congress was perhaps justifiably fearful of asserting these implied powers, there should be an express grant to it of such powers. Hamilton set forth a minimum program: Congress should be ceded the right to regulate trade and impose import duties, to appoint its own officers, to levy land and poll taxes, and to become the custodian of the Western territories.

He examined in detail the question of regulation of trade by Congress. He had read and digested Adam Smith, but he followed a cautious middle course between the old mercantilism and the heady new spirit of free enterprise: "to preserve the balance of trade in its favor ought to be the leading aim of a nation's policy." New opportunities for trade beyond the resources of private capital, "may require no small assistance, as well from the revenue, as from the authority of the state." Yet, he added quickly, he was utterly opposed to any governmental interference with prices or to any restrictions on private enterprise.

With this remarkable linking of what seemed to be polar opposites, Hamilton laid the foundations for that combination of benevolent assistance to business and laissez-faire as to the administration of business that has become a familiar feature of the American scene and the platforms of both political parties.

As he made his way north toward home, he mentally outlined the two last articles of the series, which would be published on April 18 and July 4, 1782. In these he would prove to both the landed interests and "the laboring poor" that both ought to favor federal control of external commerce. Otherwise, he argued, each state, fearful of imposing import duties lest commerce be diverted to others and to freer ports, would be compelled to rely on heavy land taxes for revenue. This, in turn, would raise the prices of food and other necessities, and the poor would suffer both from the higher cost of living and from unemployment because of foreign competition.

On the small farms he passed and in the villages where he put up for the night, farmers and laborers he saw and spoke with sharpened his concern to see that federal regulation must not look primarily to the interests of the trading and mercantile classes. National supervision, Hamilton maintained, should insure that "the laboring poor" would not be thrown out of work and the labor that remained employed would not command too high a price. "To reduce which, and not increase it, ought to be a capital object of our policy," he maintained. Hamilton's perception of the problem anticipated the paradoxical complex reality observable 200 years later of wages that do not fall even when unemployment remains high. The peroration of the sixth and final paper of "The Continentalist" series, to be published on the sixth anniversary of the Declaration of Independence, would offer a stirring vision and a characteristic warning:

> There is something noble and magnificent in the prospect of a great Federal Republic, closely linked in the pursuit of a common interest, tranquil and prosperous at home; respectable abroad; but there is something proportionably diminutive and contemptible in the prospect of a number of petty states, with the appearance only of union, jarring, jealous, and perverse, without any determined direction, fluctuating and unhappy at home, weak and insignificant by their dissensions in the eyes of other nations.

Hamilton's exploit leading the American light infantry over the ramparts of redoubt number 10 had been reported not only in the Philadelphia papers but elsewhere in the new country. After so many years of military defeats and lost opportunities, it lost nothing in the telling and retelling from people's hunger to personify their elation in adulation of a new hero.

When realization that the hero of the last redoubt at Yorktown, the financial genius who was advising Robert Morris, and the writer of "the Continentalist" who was providing a noble and magnificent vision of a future federal republic were all one and the same man, the name of Alexander Hamilton crossed the threshold of the American public's consciousness like a thunderclap.

He was not just the young man who had been a shrewd, articulate aide-de-camp to the father of his country nor just the brave officer who had led the final assault in the conclusive battle of the war and not just the pamphleteer of "The Continentalist" in powerful command of the most sophisticated economic and political ideas of his age. Nor was he merely a scholar with a seemingly inexhaustible stock of knowledge of irrefutable analogy for argument nor merely a prose stylist who wrote with direct thrust that struck to the heart of public issues with the power of an Addison or dissolved an opponent with the acidulousness of a Junius. It was much that he was General Philip Schuyler's son-in-law. But Hamilton was all of these remarkable young men rolled into one. At twenty-four he stood at the threshold of a public career that seemed to have no limits to the direction or distance it could go.

When the young lieutenant colonel dismounted wearily at The Pastures in November three weeks after leaving Yorktown and handed his reins to one of the Schuyler grooms, he would be one of the most famous young men in America. He looked forward to being overwhelmed by adoring embraces and kisses and shouts and cries of joy and love from his own seven months' pregnant Betsy; her sisters Angelica and Peggy; their mother, Catharine; their father, General Philip; and the three strapping Schuyler sons. Angelica's little Philip, and her mother Catharine's newborn baby Kitty, the godchild of the George Washingtons, might also join the welcome. Their precious Hamilton was home a hero from the wars. He knew that they would have almost as much to tell him as he would them.

Much to everyone's surprise, Betsy's mother, Catharine Van Rensselaer Schuyler, in the winter of 1780, at the age of 47, had given birth to a fifth daughter and named her after herself. On March 4, 1781, on the way to Newport with Hamilton, General and Martha Washington had stopped at The Pastures to be godparents at little Kitty's christening. They signed the parish register of the Reformed Dutch church in Albany as witnesses to Catharine's baptism by the same Reverend Eilardus Westerlo who had married Hamilton and Betsy. Catharine and Betsy's sister Peggy had signed along with the Washingtons.

That January, Betsy had written Peggy telling her that "I am the happiest of woman; my dear Hamilton is fonder of me every day; get married, I charge you."

Hamilton, after only a month and a half of marriage to Betsy, wrote to Peggy in a slightly different vein. He was still a self-confessed "fanatic in love." Or else, he added mysteriously, "a good dissembler." This left ample room in his love for Peggy as well as Betsy. The realist in him qualified Betsy's charge to "get married" with some cautionary advice about suitors and men in general: "Get a man of sense, not ugly enough to be pointed at—"

He hoped that Peggy would heed his charge "Because your sister has the talent of growing more amiable every day, or because I am a fanatic in love, or both—or if you prefer another interpretation, because I have address enough to be a good dissembler, she fancies herself the happiest woman in the world, and would need persuade all her friends to embark with her in the matrimonial voyage."

Matrimony in and of itself was not quite the same thing as a love affair, Hamilton explained to Peggy: "Do not let her advice make you matrimony-mad." A love affair without marriage could be managed nicely with a little dissembling: "Tis a very good thing when their stars unite two people who are fit for each other, who have souls capable of relishing the sweets of friendship and sensibilities." Marriage was not necessary, he was about to add, but he checked himself and wrote instead, "The conclusion of the sentence would carry me too far; I trust the rest to your fancy." But then he (or his son or another later editor) thought he had already gone too far. He struck out the words *would carry me too far* and *the rest*, changing the passage to read tamely and lamely: "The conclusion of the sentence I trust to your fancy." Hamilton concludes with the practical message that "it's a dog of life when two dissonant tempers meet, and 'tis ten to one but this is the case. I join her in advising you to marry, but I add the cautions in the choice. Get a man of sense, not ugly enough to be pointed at —with some good-nature—a few grains of feeling—a little taste—a little imagination—and above all a good deal of decision to keep you in order; for that I foresee will be no easy task. If you can find one with all these qualities, willing to marry you, marry him as soon as you please."

In all of this there is no question of his deep affection for Betsy. The only question raised is whether he would carry his extramarital love for his wife's sister "too far." He ends his letter to her with the simple and endearing, yet not unambiguous, understatement, "I must tell you in confidence that I think I have been very fortunate," whichever sister he meant.

Recent letters from Albany had reassured Hamilton that all was well there, but he could not help being desperately anxious to see for himself that no harm had come to any of his loving relatives from the terrifying Tory and Indian raid on The Pastures the night of August 7. In the darkness that night, John Waltemeyer, a notorious Tory and a gang of his followers, some renegade Canadians and "their faithful friends the Indians," as Fleury called them, had smashed into the house, overwhelmed three guards, and raged through the downstairs and upstairs rooms, threatening to seize and kidnap Philip Schuyler and his family and carry them off to Canada for ransom.

The night of the attack Angelica and her new baby Philip, Betsy four months pregnant, Catharine Schuyler, and the rest of the family had fled up a secret back stairway and hidden in the attic.

According to a well-remembered and often retold but undocumented story, the frightened women, huddled in hiding in the attic as the terrorists thudded and slammed about the floors below, suddenly realized that little Kitty, the godchild of George Washington, had been forgotten in the panic of their flight and left sleeping in her crib below. Terror-stricken, trembling Peggy fought back a cry of dismay.

Suddenly past the startled Indians, seemingly from out of nowhere, a ghostly apparition with a deathly pale face, long, golden hair streaming over her white nightgown, slipped down the stairs past the raiders, snatched the baby from her cradle, and disappeared up the stairs out of sight again into hiding. Recovering from his surprise, one Indian flung his tomahawk after Peggy's white-clad figure fleeing up the stairs with precious little Kitty in her arms. The aim of the tomahawk's axhead was low. It struck behind girl and baby and wedged quivering in the banister, where the scar it left, about three inches long and an inch deep, may be seen to this day on the banister rail of the main staircase of The Pastures—on the outward edge near the foot where it curves toward the newel-post.

Looking out an upstairs window and seeing his house surrounded, Philip Schuyler fired his pistol out into the night air to summon the night watch and neighbors to the family's rescue.

Neighbors and guards came running. The Schuylers escaped harm, but the raiders kidnapped two men of the watch they had surprised and overpowered. The Schuylers' silver plate and other valuables the raiders stole were never recovered. The Schuylers paid ransom to obtain release of the captured watchmen.

Philip Schuyler had written Hamilton guardedly but alarmingly of the near miscarriage Betsy's fright had brought on. She had been in danger, Schuyler said, but was now recovered. But things that Hamilton's beloved and her father might have spared him in their letters had made him spur his mount all the harder through the crisp autumn days to speed him back to his new family and home.

After a hero's homecoming to The Pastures no less warm and tumultuous than he had imagined it would be, Hamilton collapsed in a serious spell of illness that had him "in and out of bed" past the end of December. So he probably did not begin intensive study to become a lawyer until well into January of 1782. New York had formerly required a five-year clerkship before admission to the bar. But by the time Hamilton reached Albany in November, a three-year clerkship before admission was the new rule, even for holders of an A.B. degree. In January 1782 the three-year rule was suspended for "young gentlemen who had directed their studies to the profession of the law, but upon the breaking out of the present war had entered into the defence of their country." Unfortunately, this exception could be availed of only until the end of the April term of court. This would leave Hamilton less than five months to prepare for bar exams that formerly would have called for five years or at least three years of preparation.

Evidence that Hamilton had directed his studies toward the law at King's before the war is scant. However, he applied for admission to the bar under the veteran's exemption provision anyway. But, as he admitted, "being unprepared for an examination" as early as the April term, he prayed "that . . . the rule . . . may be further suspended until October term next."

Even Hamilton did not think his extraordinary powers of concentration could compress a successful course of law study into five months, particularly because he was sick in bed part of the time.

But he threw himself into cramming for his bar exams with the same fierce energy he brought to bear on everything else he did. He jotted down salient points from treatises and reports of cases and worked them up into an outline in order to fix them more firmly in his memory.

In the eighteenth-century state of the law in America, Blackstone's *Commentaries* alone was a sufficient text for most purposes. Hamilton had read Blackstone, Coke's *Reports*, Beawe's *Lex Mercatoria*, and works on principles of feudal tenures. His political pamphlets demonstrated that somewhere or other he had learned the law of nations well from the treatises of Berlamaqui, Grotius, Locke, Vattel, Montesquieu, and Pufendorf. There can be no doubt that Hamilton had come to be profoundly read in general principles of substantive law that had wide application throughout the western world.

On the other hand, he knew almost nothing of matters of practice and procedure, the bread and butter part of most lawyers' work. So he quickly made himself into the leading New York authority on the subject. Until Hamilton went to work, matters of New York practice and procedure were not generally committed to writing, but would persist as usage among judges, clerks, and the more experienced members of the bar. It was preeminently a "memory jurisprudence." In the hundred years between the publication in 1687 of William Penn's gleanings from Lord Coke and the issuance of Buller's *Nisi Prius* and Gilbert's *Evidence* in 1788, not a single book that could be called a treatise for the use of practicing lawyers was published in the British American colonies and American states. Hamilton partly filled a large gap with his 177-page practice manual known as *Practical Proceedings in the Supreme Court of the State of New York*. Written at a time when New York's first state constitution was but five years old and the British army still occupied New York City, it is the earliest treatise on practice and procedure in the courts of the independent state of New York. It remained in use among members of the profession until 1794, when large portions of it were incorporated in Wyche's *Practice Manual*. It remained in use by many attorneys into the early 1800s, until after the time of Hamilton's death in 1804. This handbook of practice rules whose forty or so sections treated of such esoteric legal matters as process, venue, release, covenant, judgment, execution, scire facias, habeas corpus, joint partners, trespass in ejectment, and so forth, that Hamilton wrote and compiled while studying for his bar exams that spring is the direct lineal ancestor of all the innumerable volumes of *New York Civil Practice Acts, Laws,* and *Rules* that have been published since then. In his time and only a little less so at all times since, such a work is the single most important book in the library of a lawyer's lawyer.

Hamilton's *Practical Proceedings* is written in a scholar's tone of resignation and dry humor. It is a tone that sets a style that continues to serve after two centuries as the appropriate one for the best of learned legal writing. Hamilton says, for example, "The court . . . lately acquired . . . some faint idea that the end of suits of law is to investigate the merits of the cause, and not to entangle in the nets of technical terms." Like talk of constant change in the law, as elsewhere, some things never change. Hamilton notes that inconsistent pleading is "among the absurdities with which the law abounds." He speaks for all generations of law students since his time when he recognizes with appropriate disdain that the action of trespass and ejectment "is a creature of Westminster Hall and subsists chiefly upon fiction."

As a comparative legal study, Hamilton's treatise carefully calls attention to the points on which the authorities in his own jurisdiction diverge from the comparable English rule. Speaking of jury process, Hamilton notes that New York's procedure differs from England's and then continues acidly, "Some say it [the English writ of Distringas] is still proper to be used where there is a jury of View, but there seems to be no reason for this." The reason for the difference, according to Hamilton, was that colonial lawyers had simplified their own jury processes whereas in England a fourteenth-century procedure, which had been made unnecessary by changes of fifty years earlier, continued to be blindly followed because of English lawyers' ignorance of the change. The rule had persisted after the reason for the rule had disappeared.

Besides being in and out of a sick bed while cramming for bar exams that January, Hamilton had another distraction. Betsy's labor pains came. The family doctor, Dr. Samuel Bard, was summoned.

Thinking of the child who was about to be their firstborn while in camp before Yorktown on October 12, Hamilton had written Betsy that "My heart disposed to gayety is at once melted into tenderness. I embrace the mother and embrace her child a thousand times. I can scarce refrain from shedding tears of joy."

With his customary confident foresight, he had no doubt what the sex of the unborn child would be: "You shall engage shortly to present me with *a boy*. You will ask me if a girl will not answer the purpose. By no means. I fear, with all the mothers charms, she may inherit the caprices of her father and then she will enslave, tantalize and plague one half [the] sex." In the certainty of his own firstborn's being a boy, he added, of Angelica, who had just had her Phil, "Tell Mrs. Carter I partake in the joy she has made a present of to the world." He hoped his and Betsy's boy "may have as many good qualities" as her Phil; "but I protest against his being too much a rival."

As Hamilton had ordained, on January 22, 1782, Betsy gave birth to a boy, the first of their eight children born alive. According to Schuyler custom, the healthy, vigorous firstborn was named Philip for his grandfather just as Angelica's had been.

When Hamilton's April term deadline for admission to the bar as a veteran came round, the Supreme Court of Judicature granted him an extension to October that it apparently had granted to no one else. As it turned out, this was three months longer than he actually needed.

Alexander and Betsy and their little Philip moved out of The Pastures into a small, shabby house of their own on the Albany waterfront. In April, Robert Troup, Hamilton's old King's College friend who was already working as a lawyer, agreed to move in and make his home temporarily with the Hamiltons and help Hamilton with his preparations. Troup recalled that Hamilton reread his Blackstone and committed much of it to memory "while walking to and fro" during the cramming sessions. Hamilton made much use of the extensive library at The Pastures, where he would often meet another young veteran who was also cramming for the bar exams, Aaron Burr.

Burr, after dropping out of the army, had begun studying law a year earlier with Judge William Paterson in New Jersey, where a three-year requirement was still in effect. But when Burr heard that New York had waived the three-year rule for veterans, he hastened to Albany to seek a place in New York's more nearly instant aristocracy of lawyers. He came armed with a letter of introduction that Hamilton's early backer General Alexander McDougall had given him, addressed to General Schuyler.

Schuyler was pleased to show Colonel Burr "every attention" and urged him to visit The Pastures and make use of all his books.

Only a year older than Hamilton and almost as handsome in a darker way when he came to make use of the library, Burr may have found the Schuyler sisters a beguiling distraction. But there is no evidence that any of them were numbered among the almost innumerable casual conquests with which Burr's life was punctuated. There would be more than enough other differences between Hamilton and him as long as both lived without his having had a clandestine affair with a precious Schuyler sister for one of them.

Mr. Chief Justice Morris objected to granting Burr the veteran's waiver of the three-year clause because Burr had, after all, dropped out of service almost three years earlier. Burr figuratively wrapped a recently neglected American flag around himself and with Chesterfieldian *suaviter in modo* argued, "surely, no rule could be intended . . . to injure one whose only misfortune is having sacrificed his time, his constitution and his fortune to his country." The flag-waving was three years out of date, but it won Burr his argument, and he passed the examination.

Not too much need be made of the rigor of the bar examinations Hamilton and Burr and Troup passed. They were as much tests of whom one knew as what one knew. Writing about the state of the law when he was first appointed to the Supreme Court of Judicature, Chancellor James Kent remarked, "We had no law of our own and nobody knew what it was." He recalled that "at this time a lawyer's library could all be put on his mantelpiece." Until 1785, as another contemporary said, "there was not a solitary volume of reports in any court in this country." Even in his later years, after Kent had published his own *Rules of Practice*, favoritism was not unknown when the question of admitting candidates to the bar arose. Levi Beardsley, a prominent upstate attorney, related how he had won his own admission when he had applied to Chancellor Kent:

"What books on chancery had I read?" Kent asked.

"Not any, but I have today bought your new rules and am going to read them."

"Well," ruled the Chancellor, "I knew your brother Sam . . . Your father and I were born in the same neighborhood. . . . I will admit you."

On April 19, 1782, beating Hamilton to admission to the bar by three months, Burr became a counselor-at-law. On July 2 he also became the husband of Mrs. Theodosia Prevost. The groom and older bride saved expenses by being joined in a double wedding, the other bride being her much prettier, younger sister, Catherine de Visme, and her groom one Joseph Brown.

Theodosia Prevost was ten years Burr's senior, the widow and sister of officers of the British army. Bearing five children had done her figure no good. A scar on her forehead left her a face with slight claim to beauty. At no other time of his life is it likely that Aaron Burr would have looked twice at Theodosia. The economy of their double wedding contrasted sharply with the future extravagance in which they would live at Richmond Hill in Manhattan: at the beginning "The fates," wrote Theodosia to Sally Reeve, "led Burr on in his old coat. It was proper my gown should be of suitable gauze."

The extension Hamilton had obtained until October was more time than he needed. He was "admitted as attorney" in July 1782 and was able to pass the examination and be admitted to the "degree of counsellor" by October 26. "Counsellor" was a rank, like that of an English barrister, which privileged him to argue cases in court, even though his courtroom experience, up to that time, had been limited to being a witness for the prosecution at trials like those of General Charles Lee and Joshua Hett Smith. Robert Troup, who had been admitted as an attorney before Hamilton, did not qualify for the more restricted rank of counselor until April 1783, six months after Hamilton. In winning quick permission to be trial lawyers, Hamilton, Troup, and Burr came in just under the wire. Immediately afterward the court ordered that no one could be admitted as a counselor who had not been in active practice for more than two years.

What made these three and so many other bright young men suddenly decide to become lawyers? Why should Hamilton not have become a merchant like his early mentor Nicholas Cruger or a banker like his brother-in-law Church or a well-to-do farmer and businessman, like his father-in-law, Philip Schuyler?

In his Preface to the twelfth edition of *Democracy in America*, Alexis de Tocqueville wrote, "After the battle comes the lawgiver." His analysis of the workings of American democracy pay generous tribute to Hamilton's part in its creation—helping to draft the Constitution and explaining it to the people as Publius in *The Federalist Papers*. Speaking to his own countrymen, de Tocqueville then went on: "According as we establish either democratic liberty or democratic tyranny, the fate of the world will be different."

De Tocqueville equated the word *democracy* with democratic tyranny, not democratic liberty. In his chapter explaining to his countrymen the secret of what, in America, tempers the tyranny of the majority over the minority, he added, "The more one reflects on what happens in the United States the more one feels convinced that the legal body forms the most powerful and, so today, the only counterbalance to democracy in that country." When the American people might otherwise permit themselves to become intoxicated and violent in their revolutionary passions, it is the lawyers who apply an invisible brake that slows them down.

Lawyers' "aristocratic inclinations," according to de Tocqueville, are secretly opposed to "the instincts of democracy. Their superstitious respect for all that is old to its love of novelty, their narrow views to its grandiose designs, their taste for formalities to its scorn of regulations, and their habit of advancing slowly to its impetuosity." Democratic forms of government favor the political power of lawyers, de Tocqueville explains, because "when the rich, the noble, and the prince are excluded from the government, the lawyers then step into their full rights, for they are then the only men both enlightened and skillful, but not of the people, whom the people can choose."

De Tocqueville concludes, "If you ask me where the American aristocracy is found, I have no hesitation in answering that it is not among the rich, who have no common link uniting them. It is at the bar or bench that the American aristocracy is found."

If such high grounds for becoming lawyers as de Tocqueville's were not sufficient reason for bright young ex-veterans to turn to the law, there were more mundane reasons. The patriots of New York had passed a law that required all lawyers to take a strict loyalty oath to the revolutionary cause. This automatically disbarred not only lawyers who were avowed Tories, but those of lukewarm revolutionary faith as well. Able young lawyers with impeccable revolutionary credentials like Hamilton's were few. Nothing was more natural than for veterans like Hamilton and Burr to become lawyers.

By gaining admission to the bar and joining the legal profession, Hamilton and Troup and Burr stepped onto center stage as members of a new American aristocracy. They were a new class. But they were nothing like the nobles, the princes, and the landed and moneyed rich of European aristocracy. Yet as members of the bar, they were no longer entirely "of the people." They were aristocrats "whom the people can choose." The people could and would elect large numbers of them to public office. The difference was that they could also turn them out again. Lawyer aristocrats enjoyed no tenure based on birth, wealth, or the arbitrary favor of a prince. They prospered only as they performed useful service for people. They could be hired and fired by clients and constituents in much the way that household servants were. In this sense, Hamilton, as an aristocrat of the bar, became, as de Tocqueville put it, a servant of the people "whom the people can choose."

17

A FEW MONTHS MORE
IN PUBLIC LIFE

YOU ARE CONDEMNED TO RUN THE RACE OF AMBITION ALL YOUR
LIFE. A GOOD *pater familias* I AM ALREADY TIRED OF THE CAREER
AND DARE TO LEAVE IT. I SET OUT FOR PHILADELPHIA IN A FEW
DAYS.
　　　　　—*To the Marquis de Lafayette, November 3, 1782*

For people with a cast of mind like Hamilton's it is easier to explain an entire
body of learning, as he had the entire body of New York civil practice in his
Practical Proceedings, than to practice the day-to-day proceedings once they
have been explained. In day-to-day law practice, patience and attention to the
detail of significant variations in each repetition is more often called for than
extraordinary breadth, scope, and quickness.

Most of the prickly problems that clients bring to be solved through legal
processes involve small but significant variations on well-worn precedents found
in books like *Practical Proceedings*, but fall far short of having revolutionary,
continental, or constitutional ramifications. Quite often a client's cause falls
short of having much merit. Yet skillful attention to causes with small merit can
provide a practicing lawyer large fees or at least a comfortable livelihood.

Hamilton was now faced with the gritty, down-to-earth routine of learning the legal ropes he had elucidated—of gaining a practical understanding of the workings and refinements of the rules he had laid out with such Olympian omniscience. Cases with revolutionary, continental and constitutional ramifications quite often come in with a client who can pay no fee. Hamilton's immediate problem was to earn fees to support his family.

In March 1782 he explained to his old friend Colonel Richard Kidder Meade, a former comrade as an aide, that he was determined to shun public affairs. Private life and the company of his wife and infant son were all that mattered to him now. "You cannot imagine how entirely domestic I am growing," he wrote in March 1782. "I lose all taste for the pursuits of ambition. I sigh for nothing but the company of my wife and my baby. The ties of duty alone, or imagined duty, keep me from renouncing public life altogether. It is, however, probable I may not any longer be engaged in it."

A month later, in the fifth essay of "The Continentalist" series appearing in *The Packet* at Fishkill, he was urging that all such minute details so characteristic of private practice of the sort he had explained in *Practical Proceedings* should be subordinated to "measures of evident utility," which would have a "general tendency" to create a great and happy American people:

> It is too much characteristic of our national temper to be ingenious in finding out and magnifying the minutest disadvantages, and to reject measures of evident utility even of necessity to avoid trivial and sometimes imaginary evils.
>
> In human society, there is scarcely any plan, however salutary to the whole and every part, by the share, each has in the common prosperity, but in one way, or another, and under particular circumstances, will operate more to the benefit of some parts, than of others. Unless we can overcome this narrow disposition and learn to estimate measures, by their general tendency, we shall never be a great or a happy people, if we remain a people at all.

Hamilton's own mind had the rare knack of being able to switch quickly from ingenious magnification of the minutest particulars, as in *Practical Proceedings,* to an Olympian god's eye view of the "general tendency" of measures of continental scope necessary to create "a happy people." In today's filmic terms, it might be said that he had a mind capable of fast cuts from microscopic close-ups to stratospheric aerial panoramas.

Hamilton also had the gift of being able to encompass by a very small gesture a long symbolic reach, much as a good actor crushing out a lighted cigarette can signify—with an extra tremor of wrist—the end of a lifelong love affair. Such gifts were only idling in amusement when Hamilton wrote Richard Kidder Meade from Albany again on August 27 about his and Betsy's son Philip, who, at the age of seven months, was remarkably different from the rather undifferentiated puddings that other seven-month-old babies were:

He is truly a very fine young gentleman, the most agreeable in his conversation and manners of any I ever knew—nor less remarkable for his intelligence and sweetness of temper. It is agreed on all hands that he is handsome, his features are good; his eye is not only sprightly and expressive but it is full of benignity.

His attitude, in sitting, is, by connoisseurs, esteemed graceful; and he has a method of waving his hand that announces the future orator. He stands however rather awkwardly and his legs have not all the delicate slimness of his father's. It is feared he may never excel as much in dancing, which is probably the only accomplishment in which he will not be a model. If he has any fault in manners, he laughs too much.

Little Phil, the Hamilton paragon, had been less than two months old when Hamilton wrote Meade in March that "Betsy proposes to form a match between his Boy & your girl provided you will engage to make the latter as amiable as her mother."

Indeed, so genial is Hamilton's mood, thinking of Meade and Meade's own amiable bride, the former Mary Fitzhugh Grimes Randolph, that he writes, "if fortune had not cast our lots at such a distance" the four of them—Mary, Dick, Betsy, and Alexander—"would make a most affectionate and most happy *partie quarré*."

Hamilton's forecast for little Phil was more accurate than Betsy's, unfortunately. When Phil became 21, old enough to make a match and dance attendance on the Meades' daughter, his power of impetuous oratory entangled him in a dispute with a political enemy of his father. He was shot to death in the duel that followed, before the match could be made.

Congress had acknowledged the value of Hamilton's wartime services by adopting a report citing his "superior abilities and knowledge of his profession." It included his name in the select list of officers who were permitted to retain their wartime rank in peacetime.

The war was still on, though not actively, when Hamilton wrote Washington March 1, 1782, noting that while "it is the duty of a good citizen to devote his services to the public, when it has occasion for them," there did not seem to be much occasion for them now. He could not "with propriety . . . obtrude them." He takes a surprisingly peremptory tone with Washington. After alluding to "the difficulties I experienced last campaign in obtaining a command," he said, "I am unwilling to put it out of my power to renew my exertions in the common cause, in the line, in which I have hitherto acted." He was not asking a favor. Indeed, he seemed to be giving an order to his former chief: "I shall accordingly retain my rank." He added, "[I] shall be at all times ready to obey the call of the public, in any capacity, civil, or military (consistent with what I owe to myself) in which there may be a prospect of my contributing to the final attainment of the object for which I embarked in the service."

On October 24, 1781, when Tench Tilghman had reached Congress in Philadelphia with Washington's official announcement of the surrender of Cornwallis, Elias Boudinot reported an unfortunate circumstance that foreshadowed peacetime battles Hamilton would fight for the next two decades: "When the Messenger brought the News of this Capitulation . . . it was necessary to furnish him with hard money for his expenses. There was not a sufficiency in the Treasury to do it, and the Members of Congress, of which I was one, each paid a Dollar to accomplish it."

In the cloud of national euphoria that followed Yorktown, many of the best men left Congress and the army to return to their home states and their private affairs without further thoughts of remaining ready, like Hamilton, "to obey the call of the public in any capacity." Congress returned to the states responsibility for maintaining the army and creating state currencies. But the states refused to levy and turn over to Congress the taxes that were required of them. If this continued, interest on the national debt and foreign loans would fall into default. The army's soldiers would be left without supplies and food. Robert Morris complained that "those who trusted us in the hour of distress are defrauded." The Articles of Confederation, Morris observed acidly, gave Congress "the privilege of asking everything," but gave the states "the prerogative of granting nothing."

Morris had persuaded Congress to ask the states to cede to the general government the right to raise funds to support the national government by collecting a tax of five percent on foreign commodities imported into the United States. The amount thus collected by this "impost" would not be enough even to pay the interest on the foreign debt, not to mention back pay of soldiers and claims of other creditors, but at least it would be an entering wedge for other federal taxes and federal measures. Robert Morris scoffed at the impost as hardly more than "a Tub for the whale." Nevertheless, if adopted, it would represent a revolutionary shift of power from the states to the central government.

But to make the "impost" mandatory, an amendment of the Articles of Confederation was necessary. This required unanimous consent of all thirteen states.

In the fifth and sixth papers of "The Continentalist", published in April and July of 1782, Hamilton joined Morris's campaign to urge the states to vote Congress the power to collect the "impost." Hamilton offhandedly explained that these numbers of "The Continentalist" "were written last fall, but accidentally got out of the possession of the writer. He has lately recovered them, and he gives them to the public more to finish the development of his plan, than from any hope that the temper of the times will adopt his ideas."

Moderate duties on commerce, he explained, were "one of the most eligible species of taxation." They were best administered by the central government. He conceded that the duties raised in each state should be credited against that state's quota of contribution, which was otherwise based on land. The gain or loss of a particular state in trade with its neighbors would depend in the end on its own industry and frugality. He also conceded the multiple practical exceptions to "nice and abstract distinctions," but insisted that national benefit must supersede local advantage.

Without import duties, taxes on land would be burdensome, would make labor dear, would raise costs of necessaries of life, and would induce migration from old settlements to new frontiers. He repudiated the physiocratic contention that because all taxes ultimately rested on land, they were most economically collected at the source, on land itself. Agriculture and commerce were mutually dependent; if one were penalized, the other would suffer too.

In the meantime, Congress had set New York's quota of Continental taxes at $375,598. Robert Morris, as the superintendent of finance, knew that Congress would be unlikely to collect even a fraction of this sum, but if anyone could do so, Hamilton was the man. (Cruger's clerk had written long ago, "I dun as hard as is proper.") On May 2 Robert Morris offered Hamilton the job of receiver of Continental taxes for New York. As compensation, Hamilton would be entitled to keep "one fourth of the monies you receive." Morris added, "I make to you no professions of my confidence and esteem because I hope [they] are unnecessary . . . my wish that you would accept the offer I make is the strongest evidence I can give of them."

That the 59-year-old "financier of the Revolution," whose office was the nearest thing to a civilian chief executive the new nation yet had, should write thus to the 25-year-old ex-officer and financial correspondent in offering him the chief financial post in one of the wealthiest states demonstrated that Hamilton had won the highest respect of the leading men of the nation. Hamilton's initial rejection of the post only served to enhance their respect.

He was immersed in his legal studies, the position was politically unpopular, the pay was small compared with the labor required, and Hamilton was under the time pressure that the imminent expiration of the veterans' bar admission waiver imposed, he told Morris. But his reply to Morris of May 18 betrayed the strain of a deeper, more generalized, less tractable pressure than any of these: the job was not big enough for him. "Time is so precious to me," he said, "that I could not put myself in the way of any interruptions unless for an object of consequence to the public or myself. The present is not of this nature."

Morris was insistent. A man with Hamilton's talent could easily handle the job as a part-time affair, he explained. He increased the pay. Hamilton's salary would be based on New York's full quota, whether or not he actually succeeded in collecting all of it, and would come to about $940 a year. Hamilton accepted.

In appointing Hamilton, Morris was passing over another man, one who had been strongly recommended by Governor George Clinton, a man who had better formal qualifications for the job than Hamilton's: Abraham Yates, Jr., of Schenectady, who was already the Continental loan officer of the state.

Yates protested publicly that he, instead of Hamilton, should have been appointed Continental receiver. He had served diligently as loan officer for deferred pay. He was "Dayly obliged to shift for the necessarys of life," while Hamilton now was preferred with a "generous and Immediate salary." Yates demanded that James Duane, the New York delegate who was chairman of the

Congressional Committee of Oversight, institute an investigation of the superintendent of finance, find out the cause of this shabby treatment, and say how Yates could "obtain redress." Duane gave a soft answer to Yates's pride, but backed Hamilton notwithstanding his lack of qualifications as far as the public knew. To Yates, Duane repeated Morris's reasons for naming receivers who were not loan officers. Hamilton passed along to Morris his private opinion of Yates: "The people have been a long time in the habit of choosing him in different offices," because he was "preacher to their taste." Yates "assures them, they are too poor to pay taxes." A man so fearful of unpopularity would not make an effective tax extractor. Hamilton added a gratuitous insult: he "deserves to be pensioned by the English Ministry." His "ignorance and perverseness are only surpassed by his pertinacity and conceit." Besides, according to Hamilton, Yates "hates all high-flyers." This was the biting phrase the brilliant young Hamilton used to describe the way he knew he himself appeared to Governor George Clinton and his time-serving henchmen like Yates. Morris put down Yates sharply but firmly and backed Hamilton, but Morris could not ignore the political cost to himself for doing so. This early clash between Hamilton on one side and Yates and Clinton on the other was not very important in itself, but it foreshadowed the kind of political opposition that would array itself against him in New York politics in growing ranks the rest of his life.

Sending on to Hamilton the letter enclosing his commission, Morris wrote:

> I must request you to exert your talents in forwarding with your legislature the views of Congress. Your former situation in the army, the present situation of that very army, your connections in the state, your perfect knowledge of men and measures, and the abilities which heaven has blessed you with, will give you a fine opportunity to forward the public service, by convincing the legislature of the necessity of copious supplies, and by convincing all who have claims on the justice of Congress, that those claims exist only by that hard necessity which arises from the negligence of the States.

Alluding to Yates's and Clinton's objections, Morris added that to the extent Hamilton should succeed, "then the utility of your office, and of the Officer [will] be as manifest to others as at present to me."

Congress fixed the quota amounts, but the mechanism for collection of the quotas was obscure and entirely within the discretion of the state legislatures. Like Yates, most local state collectors were halfhearted in their efforts; citizens interposed every obstacle that taxpayers' ingenuity could suggest; receipts suffered further shrinkage through ill-defined deductions by local collectors before the residue was ultimately turned over to the state's Continental receiver.

For New York these problems were compounded by the fact that the governor was George Clinton. Stubborn, provincial in character, agrarian in outlook, he proudly represented the small yeoman farmer and artisan. A wealthy landowner himself, he posed as the Populist champion of small farmers against the large landed proprietors and the seaboard merchants. He was deeply suspicious of any congressional encroachment on sovereign powers enjoyed by his or any other state. One of the first of the so-called democrats, he fought the steady drive toward centralization of Continental government; Hamilton symbolized the drive toward union. Clinton did as much as any man to delay final consummation of the union Hamilton personified. He and Hamilton had worked together during the war, and he had staked Hamilton to money and medical aid on Hamilton's mission to Gates, but now the partisan lines of cleavage that would make them bitter political enemies were being drawn for life. They were drawn along the line of whether the state or the national government would control imposts and other revenues.

The state legislature, under the skillful leadership of Philip Schuyler and other like-minded men in the state senate, was more tractable than Clinton. Late in 1781, the legislature had passed a bill granting to Congress the import duties at the port of New York, to be levied and collected "under such penalties and regulations, and by such officers, as Congress should from time to time make, order and appoint." This cost no votes, with Sir Henry Clinton and 13,000 British troops still occupying the city. It was of no immediate use, except to serve Hamilton as a precedent for the future. Even this grant of nothing had been passed over Clinton's opposition. It was also contingent on similar grants by all the other states. Clinton saw clearly enough that congressional control over tax collections would ultimately render Congress independent of the states. He notified Congress that "they entertain very slender Hopes of their Ability in the present exhausted Condition of the State to comply with any of the requisitions of Congress." Other states also refused to grant similar powers to collect import duties to Congress. New York was the only state that could pass such a law, secure in the knowledge that British occupation would keep it a dead letter.

On July 14 Hamilton sailed downriver from Albany to Poughkeepsie, where the legislature was in session, to ply the art of persuasion as Morris's lobbyist. "I will endeavor by every step in my power to second your views," he informed Morris, "though, I am sorry to add, without any sanguine expectations," because "Mountains of prejudice and particular interest are to be levelled." It was a useful rehearsal for his effort six years later to overcome the New York Constitutional Convention's similar opposition to the new Constitution. On the 16th he forwarded his commission to Governor Clinton and requested that a conference be arranged for him with a committee representing both houses of the legislature. Appearing before the joint committee, he repeated the arguments for a solid financial system he had made as the Continentalist. The committee agreed with him that the existing system was unsatisfactory, but refused to consent to the solution he proposed: that Congress be given the power to levy and collect import duties within the state without making it contingent on a similar grant by the other states.

Hamilton's arguments failed of total success, but as often happened throughout his career, they won him more than half a loaf. The joint committee immediately laid before the legislature and caused to be passed certain significant bills, one of which was a tax to raise $18,000. But, Hamilton reported to the financier on July 22, "I cannot hope that it would produce in the treasury above half the sum, such are the vices of our present mode of collection."

The second measure was far more important: "Both Houses have unanimously passed a set of resolutions, to be transmitted to Congress and the several States, proposing a convention of the States, to enlarge the powers of Congress and vest them with funds. I think this is a very eligible step, though I doubt of the concurrence of the other States; but I am certain without it they will never be brought to co-operate in any reasonable or effectual plan." What was the reason for opposition? Hamilton explained: "Urge reforms or exertion and the answer constantly is what avails it for one state to make them without the concert of the others? It is in vain to expose the futility of this reasoning; it is founded on all those passions which have the strongest influence on the human mind." Although he did not say so, it is most probable that it was he who had ghostwritten these 1782 resolutions for Philip Schuyler to introduce that pointed the way to 1787 and the Constitutional Convention. As the first official call issued by any state for a convention to alter the Articles of Confederation, they marked the beginning of the movement that culminated in the Constitution.

Schuyler was leader of the senate and had supporters in the assembly, but there they were a minority outvoted by Clinton's party. A majority of the combined houses and Governor Clinton were firmly opposed to any further centralization of authority in a national government. Yet the law student lobbyist pleaded his case so effectively that these remarkable resolutions ceding great powers to Congress managed to pass without a dissenting vote. Clintonians, at least, would realize the long-range significance of such victories only much later.

Hamilton knew the mechanics working of his way through thickets of political difficulties by practical tactics to win long-run victories for Continental ends. Hamilton argued that the call for a constitutional convention did not bind New York to any particular course of action at the convention; once there, it might either favor or oppose. He also argued that the proposed powers to Congress were left unspecified and that, in any event, there was small likelihood that any other state would follow suit. Hamilton used the very fact that most of his tax plan had been voted down as the key to successful passage of this resolution. From Clinton's point of view, adoption of the resolution would be a gesture that showed New York's good will and harmed no one. Nothing definite followed immediately; it was a precedent that would serve the longer future.

Under the spell of Hamilton's arguments, the legislature on the same day passed two other significant measures, of which Hamilton wrote to Morris concerning only one: "The Legislature have also appointed, at my instance, a committee to devise, in its recess, a more effectual system of taxation, and to communicate with me on this subject." He made no mention of the other action. It might not have been so agreeable to Morris. The legislature had elected Hamilton as a delegate to the Continental Congress. This would require his resignation as New York's Continental receiver of taxes only four months after taking office.

After approving Hamilton's resolves calling for a constitutional convention, the New York legislature had reelected all its other delegates to Congress and named Hamilton as its only new delegate. It was a rather surprising choice in view of Yates's and Clinton's control of the assembly, even though the senate had nominated its leader, Schuyler, and he had at once withdrawn in Hamilton's favor.

It was anything but a choice resulting from universal acclamation of Hamilton's merits. More likely, the assembly backed Hamilton to rid itself of a nuisance who sought more power for Congress and more rigorous tax collection measures contrary to their own Clintonian instincts. Sending him to Congress without voting it more taxing powers was their perverse way of giving Hamilton his wish: "more power to Congress."

Whatever the reason, election to Congress served as a ratchet to lift Hamilton out of the New York receivership with grace after only four months in office and into the national arena at Congress Hall in Philadelphia for a one-year term beginning in November 1782.

In August 1782 Hamilton notified Morris of his resignation, effective on October 30, and Morris was sorry to receive it, but understood the reason for it. He conceded that Hamilton might be able to do more in Congress than in New York to help solve the problems. He wrote: "Your description of the mode of collecting taxes, contains an epitome of the follies which prevail from one end of the continent to the other. . . . God grant you success in your views to amend it."

There was the question of Hamilton's successor. Yates continued to have strong political qualifications and Clinton's backing. Hamilton knew Morris would rather appoint someone like himself who thought in Continental terms. But, on the other hand, Morris would want to avoid more political criticism for passing over Yates a second time.

In solving this problem for Morris, Hamilton demonstrated his skills as an administrator. He handled it in a manner often used by the most successful of executives: he presented the opportunity to Yates in a way that would cause him to reject it.

Yates reported how the conversation went.

"About a month or better ago," Yates wrote, Hamilton "said that the People Blamed him supposing that he had got this office upon his own Sollicitation. I told him I Never Blamed him; that the world was open to him. Indeed I thought [it] hard that he should Possess an office by way of Sine Cure with Immediate pay Torn as it [were] from the Loan Office while I had served as Loan Officer Near three years and had R[eceive]d Nothing."

Staying with Yates on the tangential issue, Hamilton told Yates that he had not sought the office.

"In this Conversation," Yates said, "and from letters he showed me it appears that so far from being the Solicitor that he [Hamilton] had Reluctantly taken the office upon him. He then told me he intended to resign the office and would have no pay for what he had Done."

Hamilton went on to tell Yates, a leader of the states' rights party, "that it was Necessary the Receiver of Taxes should be able to Look Continentally. He should have Continental Eyes, should not be under governmental Regulation &c That the Loan Officer was in some Measure a Provincial officer, was under [state] governmental Influence and Regulations &c." Yates could deny none of this.

Having thus obtained Yates's assent to propositions he knew made the job he was about to offer unthinkable for a states' rights democrat, Hamilton proceeded to offer Yates the job. Yates wrote, "He then asked me whether if the Financier appointed me Receiver of Taxes I would promise on Every Occasion to promote the views of the Financier tho It should be against my opinion & should Even I conceive it to be against the Interest of the State." Hamilton had not misread his man. Yates blew up. He refused the job he had so much wanted. As Yates put it, "I got a little out of Temper." Consistency ruled him. "I told him I was an Honest Man and Acted agreable to the Dictates of my Conscience."

The appointment of Dr. Thomas Tillotson, whom both Hamilton and Morris preferred to Yates, smoothly ensued without political static.

Announcing his resignation from the office of receiver, Hamilton sent Robert Morris a long report on August 13, which told much about the chaotic and desperate economic condition of New York.

Unlike other states that were unoccupied by the enemy, New York had five of its fourteen counties, including New York City, its commercial hub, still in enemy hands. Two other counties and part of a third had revolted and gone over to the Tories; two were "desolated by the ravages of the enemy"; the remaining four had suffered partial injury from the same causes. For all practical purposes, "the strength and force of the state will consist in little more than four counties." Refugees swarmed into them from the combat areas; yet the constant drain of able-bodied men into the army had brought about a serious labor shortage. The state was exhausted, there was a universal scarcity of hard money, and foreign trade was practically nonexistent. Hamilton had good excuses for his failure to collect more money as receiver of taxes.

He had exhorted the county treasurers in the name of the public emergency, the public faith, and the reputation of the state. He had said, "I shall feel a sensible mortification in being obliged to continue publishing to the others, that this State pays nothing in support of the war, as I have been under the necessity of doing the last two months." This was exaggeration for effect. New York was low on the list of contributors, but some states had in fact paid nothing whatever into the Continental treasury during 1782.

Of the $8,000,000, that Congress had assessed the several states, only $422,161.63 had been collected. Of this sum, only $302,734.84 had actually found its way into the Treasury. Pennsylvania, Massachusetts, New Jersey, Rhode Island, and Connecticut had the best records—and they had paid only about ten percent of their quotas. Of New York's quota of $375,598, Hamilton had collected only $6,250—less than two percent!

Yet Virginia, with a quota of over a million, had paid nothing. Nor had New Hampshire, Delaware, and North Carolina. Georgia and South Carolina considered themselves absolved from all contributions because they had furnished unspecified supplies to the Southern army. Nothing shows better how badly the nation's financial system had broken down than this bald factual record. Abraham Yates's popularity and ability to win elections as a collector on the strength of his gentle approach to making tax extractions personified not only a statewide but also a national malaise.

Hamilton drew the large lesson for Morris. The government of New York exhibited "the general disease which infects all our constitutions—an excess of popularity. . . . The inquiry constantly is what will *please*, not what will *benefit* the people." Taxes were fixed not by property ownership, but by "the discretion of persons chosen by the people themselves to determine the ability of each citizen." The desire to overburden Tories had boomeranged and resulted in "total unequality" of assessment. Levy and collection were unproductive, and all attempts to amend the iniquity "without totally changing it are fruitless."

Confidence in Morris himself was high, but Hamilton had been obliged to busy himself counteracting resentment because Morris was held to have made slighting remarks about the feeble exertions of New York. Hamilton acknowledged that there was "an extreme and universal scarcity of money." Hamilton estimated that in New York a third of the people still wished, secretly, for British success and that "the remainder sigh for peace, murmur at taxes, clamor at their rulers, change one incapable man for another more incapable." If left to themselves, he feared, they would purchase peace at any price.

Hamilton then furnished the financier with his confidential characterizations of the leading public men in the state by way of informing him of what exertions could be expected from them toward furnishing revenue. His openness here shows how intimate his friendship with Morris had become.

There was no one man who had "a decided influence in" the state government. Governor Clinton had declined in popularity, partly from vigorous law enforcement that did him honor. "He is . . . a man of integrity and passes with his particular friends for a Statesman; . . . without being destitute of understanding, his passions are much warmer, than his judgement is enlightened." The secret of Clinton's amazing talent for political survival year after year was this: "The preservation of his place is an object to his private fortune as well as to his ambition; and we are not to be surprised, if instead of taking a lead in measures that contradict a prevailing prejudice, however he may be convinced of their utility, he either flatters it, or temporises, especially when a new election approaches." Hamilton's father-in-law, Philip Schuyler, had more weight in the legislature than the governor, but was frequently mortified to see his measures miscarry. Robert Lansing, who would later be Hamilton's opponent in the Philadelphia and Poughkeepsie constitutional conventions, "is a good young fellow and a good practitioner of the Law; but his friends mistook his talents when they made him a statesman. . . ." Among public men the ability to characterize a colleague with precision, objectivity, color, boldness, and wit is an art that has declined to little more than expletives on the order of a tired S.O.B. since Hamilton's time. He took the trouble to etch some other unforgetable character squeezes, which tell much about himself. "Mr. [John Morin] Scot[t] . . . has his little objects and his little party. Nature gave him genius; but *habit* has impaired it. He never had judgment; he now has scarcely plausibility. . . ." Scott's coadjutor, William Malcolm, was resourceful and expert in business, but was a vain man. "He has it in his power to support or perplex measures as he may incline, and it will be politic to make it his interest to incline to what is right."

Morris thanked Hamilton with "warm approbation" on August 28 for "your accurate, clear and comprehensive descriptions of general and particular characters, sentiments and opinions." Morris added that Hamilton's ideas "do equal justice to your talents both for description and observation." They were, for the most part, "perfectly correspondent to my own."

A meeting of the unpaid public creditors of the government held in Philadelphia in June appointed a committee to draw up and circulate a report among all the states. It is all but certain that Hamilton prepared this widely circulated report. In New York the report was read at a follow-up meeting convened in Albany on September 25; Philip Schuyler served as chairman. In his report, Hamilton brushed aside the prevailing mode of assessments of taxes as inefficient and inequitable and proposed in its place a series of flat rate taxes—on land, dwellings, salt, tobacco, carriages, taverns, household servants, lawyers, and even the privilege of remaining a bachelor. There should be import duties on sundry specified articles. The revenue from land would support the state government, the tax on lawyers would support the judiciary, and the house tax would go to Congress "when the other states shall provide *similar* funds." The salt, tavern, and tobacco taxes were "to form, together with the interest on the late emission, a fund for a *loan office.*"

The public creditors, meeting at Philadelphia, had pleaded with Congress to resume the suspended interest payments on their loan office certificates. Hamilton in their committee's report sought to enlarge these grievances into a broader demand from all the states for a restoration of Continental credit that would help strengthen the central government. The ideas he urged in his address to the public creditors anticipate his later plans for assumption and funding of the national debt. Public creditors, he argued, whatever their degree of patriotism, have an equal claim upon the plighted faith of government. The government's violation of public engagements was due not to bad intent, but to bad management. Needs of the Treasury could not all be supplied from taxes, nor from further loans from the French government. Individuals could be induced to lend only by "the punctual payment of the interest, by substantial funds, permanently pledged for that purpose." Public securities, rendered valuable and negotiable, would increase the money supply and quicken commerce. Those unwilling to lend to the public must be solicitous for fair treatment of those who had done so, or else government, without other recourse, must lay swingeing taxes. The young republic must make good on all debt obligations, "especially on . . . first emerging into political existence."

Morris had emphasized heavier taxation; Hamilton was stressing more borrowing and credit. Hamilton's proposals were at once too comprehensive and too specific for political success. The committee of public creditors did not even propose them to the legislature, which adjourned "without doing anything decisive."

From the perspective of his own flourishing medical practice in Baltimore, James McHenry, a discerning friend who, knowing Hamilton more intimately than Robert Morris, did not have to be as polite. McHenry wrote on August 11, "I hear you are chosen a delegate to Congress . . . I would rather have heard you had not been chosen." The man who had written the knowing "Epithalamium" for Hamilton's and Betsy's wedding night at The Pastures warned his friend against public office with a powerful cautionary parable:

> Hamilton, there are two lawyers of this town, one of which has served the public in the General Assembly for three years with reputation, and to the neglect of his practice. The other has done nothing but attend to his profession, by which he has acquired a handsome competency. Now the people have taken it into their heads to displace the lawyer who has served them till he is become poor, in order to put in his stead the lawyer who has served himself and become rich.

The lesson was obvious:

> To be dependent on a father is irksome . . . the good things of this world are all to be purchased with money, and the man who has money may be whatever he pleases. . . . The moment you cease to be a candidate for public places, the people will lament your loss and wait with impatience till they can persuade a man of your abilities to serve them. In the mean time, you will be doing justice to your family.

Hamilton knew that his dearest friend of all, John Laurens, would disagree with McHenry. Laurens hailed Hamilton's decision to "put on the *toga*" and enter Congress. In July Laurens had written, "I would not wish to have you for a moment withdrawn from the public service . . . Knowledge of your value to the United States, makes me most ardently desire, that you should fill only the first offices of the Republic."

Laurens was making some, but not enough, headway in the South Carolina legislature with his plan to grant slaves their freedom if they would enlist. He had obtained twice as many votes for it as in an earlier session, but not enough. He was still opposed by landed slave owners, the "triple headed monster that shed the baneful influence of Avarice, prejudice, and pusillanimity in all our Assemblies." Hamilton in Congress could help his friend and the cause of black emancipation. Laurens reproached Hamilton for not telling him sooner of his election to Congress and entreated him not to withdraw "the *consolation* of your letters. You know the unalterable sentiments of your affectionate Laurens."

Hamilton ignored McHenry's advice and followed Laurens's urgings, which were, of course, his own true inclinations. Laurens had known he would. Taking last fond looks at little Phil and scenes of happy domesticity in Albany on the eve of setting out for Philadelphia, Hamilton on November 3 wrote to Lafayette, who had returned to France soon after the victory at Yorktown, "I have been employed for the last ten months in rocking the cradle and studying the art of *fleecing* my neighbors. I am now a grave counsellor-at-law, and shall soon be a grave member of Congress. . . ."

He wound up his affairs as receiver of taxes, collected his license as counsellor-at-law, and concluded his letter to Lafayette, "I am going to throw away a few months more in public life, and then retire a simple citizen and good *pater familias*. I set out for Philadelphia in a few days. You see the disposition I am in. You are condemned to run the race of ambition all your life. I am already tired of the career, and dare to leave it."

During the next two decades, the contrast of Lafayette's reverses and ultimate imprisonment at the hands of succeeding regimes in France set against Hamilton's rise to the peak of power in America would mock Hamilton's assertion. Hamilton was projecting on to his friend the self-realization that he, not Lafayette, was "condemned to run the race of ambition" all his life.

Throughout his life Hamilton often spoke and wrote yearningly of modest wishes to lead a quiet, private life; to cultivate his garden at The Grange; and to live in exile with Betsy in France or Geneva or Spain. And so forth. But his actions and the words he produced that incited others to action always placed him somewhere up near the parapet of the most advanced redoubt in war or at the cockpit of politics in peace in the heat at the center of the effort to create a constitutional republic under law. He never throughout his life willingly turned his back on this central purpose of it. More often than not, he went out of his way to seek to serve it.

Hamilton had described the ideal congressman nearly four years before he was scheduled to take his seat in Congress Hall in Philadelphia in terms so exalted that they seemed to fit no living member. Of that curious collection of generally prosperous but cantankerous and reluctant gentlemen with whom he would actually take his seat there, he had written in 1778, "The station of a member of Congress is the most illustrious and important of any I am able to conceive. He is to be regarded not only as a legislator, but as the founder of an empire. A man of virtue and ability, dignified with so precious a trust, would rejoice that fortune had given him birth at a time, and placed him in circumstances so favourable for promoting human happiness. He would . . . do good to mankind; from this commanding eminence, he would look down with contempt upon every mean or interested pursuit."

Such a paragon, "Anxious for the permanent power and prosperity of the State, would labour to perpetuate the union and harmony of the several parts. He would not meanly court a temporary importance, by patronising the narrow views of local interest." Moreover, "In Council, or debate, he would discover the candor of a statesman, zealous for truth, and the integrity of a patriot studious of the public welfare; not the cavilling petulance of an attorney, contending for the triumph of an opinion, nor the perverse duplicity of a partisan, devoted to the service of a cabal."

His description made a congressman sound more like the hero of a medieval morality play than a human being. Hamilton had, in fact, drawn this portrait of the ideal congressman writing under the pen name of *Publius* on November 16, 1778, in order to castigate a less than ideal one, Samuel Chase of Maryland. By cornering the supply of flour to be purchased for the French fleet, Chase had made profitable but dishonorable use of privileged congressional committee information. Such activities, said Hamilton, the winter at Valley Forge upper-most in his mind, were typical of many of Chase's sub-ideal fellow congressmen.

Of Chase, *Publius* had written: "Had you not struck out a new line of prostitution for yourself, you might still have remained unnoticed and contempti-ble." Seeking to give a "faithful description" of Chase's heart, Hamilton said, "It is hard to conceive, in theory, one of more finished depravity. There are some men, whose vices are blended with qualities that cast a lustre upon them, and force us to admire—while we detest!—yours are pure and unmixed, without a single solitary excellence, even to serve for contrast and variety."

Now it was Hamilton's turn to go to Philadelphia and do and be the ideal congressman that Chase had not been.

One indication that election to membership in the Philadelphia gallimaufry that Publius had both exalted and denigrated was not unwelcome to Hamilton was the elaborately offhand way he broke the news to his friend Richard Kidder Meade. At the very end of the long letter of August 27, otherwise devoted to the future graces of seven-month-old little Phil, Hamilton tossed in, "I had almost forgotten to tell you, that I have been pretty unanimously elected by the legisla-ture of this State, a member of Congress . . . I do not hope to reform the state although I shall do all the good I can."

Hamilton's bluff, soldierly dissembling to Meade is in amusing contrast to his warm, affectionate, outflowing candor to John Laurens. Theirs was a special, unique relationship. Of Laurens, Hamilton's son John C. Hamilton would write that he had "all the endearing and social affections, all the attractions of a noble nature, all the graces of a refined and cultivated intellect, and an address which possessed an irresistible, endless charm." He had the quality that brings weaker men more friendships than the strongest: "his intrepid spirit was coupled with a self-distrust, a confiding weakness of temper, which awakened in his friends surprise and love."

Hamilton was free, confiding, and open with Laurens in a way he was with no one else of whom we have any record. That Laurens was the closest friend Hamilton would ever have and that Hamilton was the closest friend Laurens would ever have tells much about both men. Hamilton's son said of Laurens that "while the world saw him graced with every virtue, he was still aspiring to some higher excellence—an ideal perfection, which is denied to our nature, and exists only in the warm conceptions of a mind deeply tinged with romance." Of Lau-rens's gentle reproach to Hamilton for not writing him at once of his election to

Congress, Hamilton's son wrote with an elegance worthy of his father that "nothing can more fully express this inward struggle for superior excellence, than his letter to Hamilton, and the latter's elegant rebuke: 'he refined on the refinements of sensibility.' "

Elegant rebukes were necessary incidents of a love affair between two young men of the eighteenth century with classical models like Damon and Pythias at the forefront of their minds. As Hamilton's son pointed out in 1834, Hamilton's and Laurens's intercourse approached "the tenderness of feminine attachment."

Hamilton had written to Laurens in April of 1779: "Cold in my professions, warm in [my] friendships, I wish, my Dear Laurens, it might be in my power, by action rather than words, [to] convince you that I love you. I shall only tell you that 'till you bade us Adieu, I hardly knew the value you had taught my heart to set upon you."

Now on his way to Congress, writing his loving soul mate on August 15, 1782, Hamilton was full of open, expansive enthusiasms that he knew Laurens would share:

> This State has pretty unanimously elected me to Congress . . . Peace made . . . a new scene opens. The object then will be to make our independence a blessing. To do this we must secure our Union on solid foundations—a herculean task,—and to effect which, mountains of prejudice must be levelled! It requires all the virtues and all the abilities of the country. Quit your sword . . . ; put on the toga. Come to Congress. We know each other's sentiments; our views are the same. We have fought side by side to make America free; let us hand in hand struggle to make her happy.

It is probable that Laurens never received his lover's letter.

John Laurens, "That sensible, gallant elegant fellow," the South Carolina idealist whose plan to free the slaves Hamilton had warmly seconded, the aide Hamilton had seconded on the dueling ground to defend Washington's honor against Charles Lee—John Laurens, the brave leader of Americans in battles at Savannah, Charleston, Rhode Island, Monmouth, Germantown, Brandywine, everywhere; the hero who had burst into the rear of the last redoubt at Yorktown moments after Hamilton had stormed the parapet at the front—twelve days after Hamilton sent off his letter, John Laurens was killed by the British in a fire fight.

At a party on a plantation near the Combahee River in South Carolina, he had been out late dancing and late to bed. There came an alarm and word of a British foraging party in the neighborhood. An hour or two after he had fallen asleep, he had roused himself, taken horse, gone to search it out and destroy it. With a score of companions and the war as a practical matter all but over, he had been ambushed and had fallen in a meaningless skirmish. Had his plan to make slaves free succeeded, a black man might have died in his place.

General Nathanael Greene wrote Hamilton, "Poor Laurens has fallen in a paltry little skirmish." It was an epitaph that might have served as Hamilton's as well if Washington had not so regularly refused his aide's demands for field command. "You knew his temper," Hamilton replied. "I predicted his fate. The love of military glory made him seek it upon occasions unworthy of his rank. This state will feel his loss."

Hamilton was heartbroken. He told Greene, "I feel the deepest affliction at the news we have just received of the loss of our dear and [inesti] mable friend Laurens. His career of virtue is at an end. How strangely are human affairs conducted, that so many excellent qualities could not ensure a more happy fate? The world will feel the loss of a man who has left few like him behind, and America of a citizen whose heart realized that patriotism of which others only talk." Hamilton added, "I feel the loss of a friend I truly and most tenderly loved, and one of a very small number." No evidence exists of Hamilton's having shared deeper intimacy with any other man. There would never be anyone else to whom he could say, "We have fought side by side to make America free; let us hand in hand struggle to make her happy."

18

FORFENDING MUTINEERS

LET NOT THE COMMANDER IN CHIEF CONSIDERED AS THE FIRST
AND MOST RESPECTABLE CHARACTER AMONG US COME FORWARD
IN PERSON AND BE THE AVOWED AUTHOR OF AN ACT AT WHICH
EVERY HUMANE FEELING REVOLTS.
—*To Henry Knox, June 7, 1782*

Hamilton's friend James McHenry had warned Hamilton of the personal financial reverses he would suffer by going to Congress to wrestle with the public fiscal problems of the nation. Hamilton would hear the same counsel from his brother-in-law John Barker Church, who had come to Philadelphia with his wife, Angelica, to look out for no one else's finances but his own. As Hamilton grew poorer, Church was growing rich. Formerly a commissary supplier for Rochambeau, he was now, in association with Jeremiah Wadsworth, a supplier of the Continental army. How he could do so well by himself by doing so poorly by the army is a question lacking a completely satisfactory answer. Having left Betsy back in Albany as an economy measure, Hamilton, when in Philadelphia, would often relax from the frustrations of Congress Hall in the Church's elegant drawing room.

Before Hamilton's arrival, McHenry had occasion to write news of his in-laws to the country's leading authority on Schuyler sisters: "I have been a second time on the point of gaining immortality by a fever. It seized me after the arrival of the French troops here, and has only permitted me to come abroad a few days since." But Angelica Church, one of the great belles of the age, and her sister Margarita brought much cheer to his recuperation: "Mrs. Church & Miss Peggy are with us. Of course you will think I have been often with them. I must tell you something of your relations. Mr. Church is the mere man of business; and, I am informed, has riches enough to make the longest life very comfortable. Mrs. Church is a fine woman. She charms in all companies. No one has seen her, of either sex, who has not been pleased with her."

But McHenry had reservations about Margarita. "Peggy, though perhaps a finer woman, is not generally thought so. Her own sex are apprehensive that she considers them poor things, as Swift's Vanessa did, and they, in return, do not scruple to be displeased. In short, Peggy, to be admired as she ought, has only to please the men less and the ladies more. Tell her so."

There was no doubt that despite her faults, or perhaps because of them, Peggy—"a young wild flirt from Albany, full of glee & apparently desirous of matrimony," as Harrison Gray Otis would later describe her still younger sister Catharine—had many a suitor in the capital. Through her mother, Catharine Shuyler, who was on a visit to Angelica in Philadelphia, Peggy had sent a letter to Colonel Dyer Wadsworth, begging him to remember that he "has many friends in this part of the world, *one in particular*. Don't forget your promise to send your picture. There is no *impropriety.*" Two years earlier, Hamilton had warned Peggy that "it's a dog of a life when two dissonant tempers meet." Peggy was now testing all tempers for consonance, apparently, and finding more harmony with Wadsworth than McHenry. There is no record of whether Hamilton, one of the men Peggy had always pleased most, followed McHenry's injunction to tell her to please the ladies more. Hamilton seems to have taken to heart one hint from McHenry, however. From this time on, the evenhandedness with which he had been accustomed to ladle out gallantry in matching grants to both Peggy and Angelica ended as far as Peggy was concerned. One night the following summer, in July 1783, Peggy climbed out of an upstairs window of The Pastures, down a ladder propped against the sill, and eloped with Stephen Van Rensselaer III, the boy patroon from next door, letting slip only a vagrant sigh for Dyer Wadsworth and other past Philadelphia improprieties. From now on, the gallantries Hamilton no longer lavished on Peggy became tumid attentions he would compound upon Angelica alone.

When Hamilton took his seat in the Continental Congress for the first time on November 25, 1782, he was angered but not surprised by the atmosphere of morbid stasis in which it met, confronted the nation's urgent problems, and, more often than not, did nothing decisive until time to adjourn. The army was unpaid and soldiers were clamoring for payment; so were other domestic and foreign creditors. The impost on imported commodities had been adopted by most of the states, but not by all. Under the Articles of Confederation, it could not become law without the unanimous approval of all thirteen.

Of New York's five delegates—Hamilton, James Duane, William Floyd, Ezra L'Hommedieu, and John Morin Scott—all but Hamilton were hold-overs from the previous session. On Hamilton's arrival, most of the others went home, leaving the state's delegation often short of the quorum of three that was necessary for formal action.

Once they had seen the futility of the situation of Congress, most busy men of affairs tired of the exercise of endlessly debating and adopting resolutions that would then be ignored by their states. Many went back to their own state legislatures, where authority was real. From some states no delegate was present. Some states' delegates who were in town found more worthwhile things than congressional sessions to occupy their time in Philadelphia: there were frequent balls, dinners, duels, and horse races, the latter being particularly well attended by Southern congressmen. Day after day, sessions adjourned for lack of a quorum.

In his maiden speech on the day of his arrival, Hamilton "warmly and cogently espoused ratification" of the exchange of Henry Laurens, John Laurens's father, who was held captive in the Tower of London, for Lord Cornwallis, captured at Yorktown. In debate, Hamilton made the point that John Laurens had once intimated to him that, prior to Cornwallis's capitulation, Washington had agreed with Cornwallis to such an exchange.

No man in the country could speak with more authority on the subject of prisoner exchanges, George Washington's views, or the confidences of John Laurens than Hamilton. His heart must have ached to think as he made his point that no exchange could bring his dead friend back to Congress to "put on the toga" there with him.

On December 3 Hamilton voted in favor of providing officers with subsistence money at the rate of four dollars per month in lieu of rations; he moved to oppose using money requisitioned from Pennsylvania by Congress to pay Pennsylvania creditors, a plan he thought was much too state-oriented. He won. The plan was dropped.

A committee composed of Hamilton, James Madison, and Samuel Osgood of Massachusetts "having high sense of the merit and services" of Captain John Paul Jones, granted permission to him to campaign with the Marquis de Vaudreuil, commander of a French fleet stationed at Boston. Hamilton opposed a motion of two French officers for arrears of pay because of "the present embarrassed state of the public finances." On December 5 he seconded a motion by Thomas Kean of Delaware that forbade New York from exercising authority over the territory of Vermont, a territory that had long been disputed among New Hampshire, Massachusetts, and New York. Hamilton's sponsorship of a national congressional solution against the territorial interests of his home state would, he thought, be a practical step that would "tend to cement the union."

With living expenses in crowded Philadelphia high, some states, including New York, were slow to pay their delegates' meager salaries. James Duane had written Clinton a letter to protest: "I hope your Excellency may be able to remit the supply for which I took the Liberty to write; otherwise I must hasten home. It is my wish to wait for Relief as I suppose Col. Hamilton and Col. Floyd will be here pretty early in the ensuing month—but propriety must yield to necessity."

With each state regulating its own money, exchange rate differentials existed between currency circulating in one state and currency circulating in another much as they existed between the different currencies of different sovereign nations. If the states were really one sovereign nation, Hamilton knew that flexible or "floating" exchange rates between one state and another must give way to a nationwide currency that circulated at the same fixed exchange rate in all states. The day after Hamilton arrived in Philadelphia, according to James Madison's notes of the congressional proceedings, it was moved that Congress renew the call on the states to redeem the Continental currency, which had been devalued to one-fortieth of face value, and leave it to the states to "level the money" by means of bilateral or multilateral negotiations among themselves. According to James Madison's notes of the proceedings, this leveling of the money "was Mr. Hamilton's idea," because, "it would multiply the advocates for federal funds for discharging the public debts, and tend to cement the union."

When Hamilton first took his seat in the meeting room in the State House, James Madison had already been a member of Congress for two years. He was now by far the best-informed man in the hall. Of a slighter physique than Hamilton and without Hamilton's erect military bearing, he dressed habitually in black. A graduate of the College of New Jersey at Princeton, where the president "had never known him to do or say an improper thing," he was on his way to outgrowing a priggish youth and would eventually marry Dolly Todd, who, like Angelica Church, was one of the most glamorous women of the age. It was an age of philosophers, in which such women paid their deepest homage to such men. Madison's skill in the thrust and parry of debate and his engaging and ingratiating manners made him Hamilton's match as a political man. Unlike Hamilton, he aroused neither hatreds nor hero worship. It was said of Madison that he united "The profound politician with the scholar." Later Jefferson would praise "the rich resources of his luminous and discriminating mind" while urging Madison to scourge Hamilton with anonymous attacks in the press. But now in Congress the Virginian and the New Yorker were quickly drawn to each other by an affinity of abilities, interests, and outlook. For the next five years until their split, both worked together in friendly harness for all measures that would "tend to cement the union."

It was a standard Hamilton never abandoned. But after five years of fruitful collaboration with Hamilton in its service, Madison came under the influence of his rising fellow Virginian, Thomas Jefferson, made an about-face, and marched off with those who championed the rights of states and the tendency of their policies to uncement the union.

Among their fellow delegates, for longer or shorter stays were a few other men of conspicuous talents—Oliver Ellsworth of Connecticut, James Wilson of Pennsylvania, John Rutledge of South Carolina, and Elias Boudinot, Hamilton's old friend of Elizabethtown days, who was president of Congress during the term Hamilton was a member. Others "high in the second order of ability" were McHenry; Oliver Wolcott of Connecticut; Daniel Carroll of Maryland; Nathaniel Gorham of Massachusetts; Thomas FitzSimons, Thomas Mifflin, and Richard

Peters of Pennsylvania; Ralph Izard of South Carolina; and Hugh Williamson of North Carolina. Attendance on any given day was rarely more than 20 delegates, and the same few men took the leading part in debate and committee work.

On the floor, Hamilton quickly became one of the leading figures, producing streams of motions and resolutions directed toward two purposes that were intertwined—sound finances and centralized national power. He was on innumerable committees—in many instances as chairman—and his quick pen was constantly drafting reports, memorials, and bills. Most of the members acted as if they considered themselves envoys from their own state governments, engaging in diplomatic negotiations and seeking a state and local advantage from every national measure. Hamilton and Madison were almost alone in their willingness to remonstrate against state legislatures and governors when their policies and actions ran counter to the best interest of the country as a whole.[1]

Beyond Philadelphia, the war had not ended with Yorktown. General Nathanael Greene had cleared most of the South, but with the British holding bases at Charleston and Wilmington, North Carolina, the army had to stand vigilant to keep clear what had been rewon. Once again the British had swept French naval control off the seas of the West Indies and from the coastal waters of the continent. They remained in secure possession of New York City at the hub of a defense system of surrounding outposts within a radius of 20 or 30 miles. From time to time they sent Benedict Arnold out on infuriating raids that terrorized towns around Long Island Sound. The threat from Canada to the Champlain-Hudson corridor always loomed. From his headquarters at the Hasbrouck House in Newburgh, 59 miles up the Hudson from New York City, and in the lonely troop encampments at nearby New Windsor, Washington and the Continental Army kept the vigilant watch that was the price of the nation's liberty.

Peace negotiations were going on in Paris, but news of progress came back slowly. Meanwhile, the army was still under arms, forlorn, poorly supplied, and idle, with its pay months in arrears. Promises for pensioning veterans at half pay were in default.

The problems of the army tended to converge with other problems in Congress and to require solutions that were mutually interdependent. Defects in methods of funding could give rise to army mutiny. To pay the army, Hamilton moved to impose a 5 percent tariff. He opposed a diversionary motion by Rhode Island that would permit the states individually to settle the debts to their own temporary troops and charge the amounts owing to Congress. This would, as a practical matter, still leave most of the troops unprovided for, particularly those from states that were in no immediate danger from the enemy.

Interest on the domestic debt was in default; requisitions of Congress upon the states were either evaded or ignored; the Confederation was bankrupt.

To make the 5 percent impost anything but a dead letter, unanimous consent of all states was required. Twelve had by now approved, but Rhode Island, the smallest and most individualistic of all objected and refused. Its legislature directed its congressional delegates to reject the impost.

Hamilton rose on the floor of Congress on December 6 and moved two resolutions. The first called on the states to fill their allotted quotas under the old requisition system, and the second proposed that a congressional deputation be sent to Rhode Island to persuade her legislature to approve the impost. Both his resolutions passed. Hamilton was made chairman of the committee, whose numbers included James Madison and Thomas FitzSimmons of Pennsylvania, to answer Rhode Island's objections. He wrote a powerful appeal: the manuscript is in his handwriting with few corrections and emendations by other committee members.

To the objection that the impost would bear hardest on a commercial state like Rhode Island, Hamilton countered "that every duty on imports is incorporated in the price of the commodity, and ultimately paid by the consumer, with a profit on the duty itself as compensation to the merchant for the advance of his money." This was a realistic economic analysis of the effect of the impost on profit. Earlier the same year, however, in "The Continentalist," he had made an argument that looked in the opposite direction: there he had insisted that the merchant, in order to meet competition, "must . . . content himself with smaller profits and lose the value of the duty, or at least part of it."

Both statements are, in fact, true enough, but neither gives the whole truth of the matter. Yet each statement seems true enough standing by itself so as not to be a misrepresentation of fact. Each is a good example of effective advocacy. The first argument was addressed to a small audience in Rhode Island; the second, to the unlimited audience of the whole continent. Hamilton here demonstrated his mastery of the art of advocacy by adjusting his argument carefully to fit the context. The art of framing issues is the trick that wins the hardest cases for the greatest lawyers.

Not only was the impost a hidden tax, Hamilton argued, but it would also fall hardest on the rich, those who were best able to pay: "The rich must be made to pay for their luxuries, which is the only proper way of taxing their superior wealth," he insisted. The impost would promote frugality by taxing extravagance. At the same time, by encouraging domestic manufactures, it would make the United States a more self-sufficient nation.

Hamilton brushed aside Rhode Island's objection—that Congress would send its own "unknown" collection officers into the state, unaccountable to the state—by noting acidly that Congress had already introduced its "unknown" post-office officials without any great harm.

A third objection, of course, was that if Congress could collect money without being accountable to the states for its expenditure, it would become independent of them altogether. Hamilton admitted the truth of the principle that the impost would tend to cement the union, but minimized the fear, arguing that its duration would be limited and only coextensive with the debts contracted during the war.

In the letter from the congressional committee to the governor of Rhode Island, Hamilton adopted a peremptory tone strikingly different from the usual deferential tone of communications from Congress to the chief executives of states. He warned that "The unceasing discontents of the army, the loud clamours of the public creditors, and the extreme disproportion between the current supplies and the demands of the public revenues were so many invincible arguments for the fund recommended by Congress." Introducing the concept that Congress had implied powers, he asked that congressional requisitions be considered compulsory. If Rhode Island continued to reject the impost, Hamilton predicted "calamities of a most menacing nature." Even Tom Paine, often a critic, joined Hamilton in an argument directed toward Rhode Island for "a more compact union." Paine was denounced in the state along with Hamilton as a subversive agent of Congress.

Rhode Island continued to reject the impost. Congress appointed a delegation to take up the matter directly with the state, but all such efforts came to nothing. At the end of December, the largest state switched and joined the smallest in opposition: Virginia announced that it had repealed its earlier approval of the impost. On behalf of the Confederation, it was appropriate to take a high peremptory tone with the sole, smallest, and only holdout, but such a tone was worse than useless with the largest. The impost was dead.

Hamilton had lost, but he had gained nationwide attention by his fight. The merchants, the hard-money men, the creditors, and the nationalists turned to him now as their spokesman and champion, even though one of his most telling arguments for the impost had been that it would tend to "soak the rich."

Philip Schuyler, in Philadelphia as an observer of the struggle, was so proud of his son-in-law that he wrote to Eliza, back in Albany with little Philip:

> Participate afresh in the satisfaction I experience from the connection you have made with my beloved Hamilton. He affords me satisfaction too exquisite for expression. I daily experience the pleasure of hearing encomiums of his virtues and abilities from those who are capable of distinguishing between real and pretended merit. He is considered, as he certainly is, the ornament of his country, and capable of rendering it the most essential services, if his advice and suggestions are attended to. In short, every true patriot rejoices that he is one of the great council of these States.

While toiling as "one of the great council" to cement the separate states into united states, Hamilton was suffering the fate of which his friend James McHenry had forewarned him. New York had failed to send him even the small allowance it was supposed to pay its delegates. On December 18 Hamilton wrote directly to Governor Clinton: "I shall very shortly be out of cash, and shall be much obliged to you to forward me the State allowance. It will answer as well in Mr. Morris' notes as specie, provided the notes have not more than a fortnight or so to run. It will be better if they are due. A disappointment in this will greatly embarrass me." Clinton sent a remittance on December 29, and Hamilton carried on.

Troop mutinies were a sadly familiar feature of the war years. The Pennsylvania line, under command of the once popular General Anthony Wayne, had mutinied in 1781. When the New Jersey line mutinied a short time later, Hamilton, on Washington's orders, instructed his old schoolmaster, Francis Barber, "to compel them to unconditional submission." Ringleaders had been executed. When unpaid Connecticut soldiers had marched away from their units to become privateers, officer ringleaders were shot or hanged. More trouble was brewing now as 1782 drew to a close.

As Washington's delegate from the army to Congress, with a longer and more distinguished war record than his peers there, no one was more sensitive than Hamilton to the fact that among idle men with poor leadership discontents could build up suddenly to the flash point of mutiny. The same general discontents—arrearage of pay, lack of supplies, poor food, shoddiness of weaponry—plagued all units. But only in a few particular units would matters that normally remained the subject of mere gripes erupt into open mutiny. As a former line unit commander, Hamilton knew that the question of whether or not troops would or would not mutiny depended more on local army unit leaders than it did on general conditions in Congress or elsewhere in the country. Officers and men of local units knew little and cared less about remote civilian politics. Hamilton knew that no matter how slow the pay, how short the rations, how dangerous or boring the duty itself, units whose officers kept them busy and well drilled and made it their duty to stay close to their men would never mutiny. The distant debilities of Congress had little or nothing to do with the matter. There was never a time when an alert soldier or officer could not find something to gripe about.

George Washington had written earlier to Secretary of War Benjamin Lincoln that "The patience and long sufferance of his army are almost exhausted. There never was so great a spirit of discontent as at this instant." In the past "The officers have stood between the lower order of soldiery and the public and, at the hazard of their lives, have quelled very dangerous mutinies." But now many officers had become almost as dissatisfied as the men. In December, Washington transmitted to Congress a petition presenting the officers' minimum demands: an advance of part of the pay due, security for the rest, and commutation of the previously promised half pay for life into either a lump sum or full pay for a number of years. Transmitting the petition, Washington noted to Congress that it was couched in "very respectful terms." But the high-ranking officers who brought it to Philadelphia did not agree with Washington's "respectful terms." They made it known that they intended to camp belligerently on Congress's doorstep until they got what they wanted. Hamilton's old friend General Alexander McDougall was the chairman of the officers' committee. When he met with Hamilton and other congressmen on the evening of January 13, 1783, he spoke in anything but "respectful terms." As Madison noted, McDougall described the officers' grievances "in very high colored expressions," declaring that the army was "verging on a state which will make a wise man mad." The fiery Colonel John Brooks threatened that "the temper of the army was such that a disappointment might throw them blindly into extremities." Hamilton was used to hearing this kind of tough talk from fellow officers in camp: it made a deeper impression on congressional civilians like Madison. On such minds, the impression could serve a useful purpose, Hamilton thought.

Hamilton described the situation calmly in a letter to Old Soldier George Clinton of January 12: "We have now here a deputation from the army, and feel a mortification of a total disability to comply with their just expectations." He added that "If, however, the matter is taken up in a proper manner, I think their application may be turned to a good account." As an old army general himself, Clinton would understand that the top brass had to rattle the saber with Congress from time to time to keep the military appropriations coming. All the officers were asking now was congressional appropriations to make good Congress's earlier promises of pay.

From high-ranking officers on the committee, Hamilton learned that Washington was becoming remote and distant from lower-ranking officers and the troops; he was too immersed in problems of his plantation at Mount Vernon, disheartened by the death of his cousin Jack Curtis, too concerned with his position of chief executive, too preoccupied with "crownmanship" to push the army's cause with Congress as forcefully as his top circle of officers thought he should.

The previous May Lewis Nicola had proposed in his infamous "crown" letter that Washington assume some such title as King George I of the United States. Hamilton knew better than anyone else how much serious thought Washington had given to the proposal before replying to Nicola that the scheme was "disagreeable" to him. What Hamilton was now hearing from McDougall and Brooks was that Washington's stiff inflexibility in playing the role of uncrowned, de facto chief executive of the Confederation was destroying his effectiveness in his de jure role as commander in chief of the army. Knowing Washington as he did, Hamilton understood better than anyone else how Washington's stiff remoteness could drive important and valuable under officers into serious breach with him. Madison noted that "Mr. Hamilton said that he knew General Washington intimately and perfectly. That his extreme reserve, mixed sometimes with a degree of asperity of temper, both of which were said to have increased of late, had contributed to the decline of his popularity."

There was no other man in the country who, like Hamilton, had dared provoke a breach with Washington and returned to his good graces on his own terms. Thus there was no one else in the country in or out of the army who had no fear of telling the sensitive, lonely man some hard and painful truths. Hamilton wrote Washington on February 13 in the firm, almost paternal tone of a fond but worried Dutch uncle. Washington should be more forceful in pushing the army's cause with Congress, Hamilton told him, in order to remain in control of a deteriorating situation:

I will not conceal from Your Excellency a truth which it is necessary you should know. An idea is propagated in the army that delicacy carried to an extreme prevents your espousing its interests with suffi-

cient warmth. The falsehood of this opinion no one can be better acquainted with than myself; but it is not less mischievous for being false.

If Washington's "delicacy" resulted in his losing control of his officers and
being displaced by a more violent and radical faction, Congress and the whole
country would be in grave danger. The tendency of Washington's "delicacy
carried to an extreme," Hamilton said, is "to impair that influence, which you
may exert with advantage, should any commotions unhappily ensue, to moderate
the pretensions of the army and make their conduct correspond with their duty."
Hamilton was better informed about the true state of morale and opinion among
Washington's own officers than Washington himself was. He did not hesitate to
bring Washington up-to-date on dangerous attitudes among Washington's own
officers that were being kept from him, but that he should have kept himself
informed about: "It appears to be a prevailing opinion in the army that the
disposition to recompence their services will cease with the necessity for them,
and that if they once lay down their arms, they will part with the means of
securing their rights." Hamilton in Philadelphia knew better than Washington
at Newburgh that "It is to be lamented that appearances afford too much ground
for their distrust."

What should Washington do about the situation? Money, of course, was a
problem, Hamilton readily acknowledged. The state "of our finances was perhaps never more critical." But Congress is a body "not governed by reason [or]
foresight but by circumstances." Hamilton pointed out realistically that "It is
probable we shall not take the proper measures." Washington simply must face
up to this ugly fact and prepare himself to meet the outrage among the officers
that would arise when truth dawned on them too.

Hamilton had no hesitation telling his erstwhile chief the middle course he
should steer, remembering always that his first duty was to remain effective as
commander in chief of the army: "The claims of the army urged with moderation,
but with firmness may operate on those weak minds which are governed by their
apprehensions more than their judgments, so as to produce a concurrence in the
measures which the exigencies of affairs demand. . . . So far a useful turn may
be given to them. But the difficulty will be to keep a complaining and suffering
army within bounds of moderation." Washington should make certain that his
officers knew he was working for them. A new vigorous campaign would keep
the "weak minds" of the more unstable under officers of the army with him and
under his control: "This Your Excellency's influence must effect. In order to [do]
it will be advisable not to discountenance their endeavours to procure redress,
but rather by the intervention of confidential and prudent persons, to take
direction to them."

On the other hand, Washington should remain sufficiently aloof so as to hold
the confidence of both the army and the country to "enable you in case of
extremity to guide the torrent, and bring order perhaps even good out of confusion."

During the previous summer, similar forceful advice from Hamilton to

Washington had helped Washington avoid a calamity that too much rigid aloofness would have caused. Hamilton tactfully reminded Washington of the Asgill affair now by way of a postscript: "General Knox has the confidence of the army and is a man of sense. I think he may be safely made use of." Hamilton had used Knox successfully to save Washington and the nation's honor from the blot it would have suffered if Washington had not relented in his insistence on hanging 17-year-old Captain Charles Asgill the previous May. Captain Charles Asgill of the Guards, the amiable, seventeen-year-old, only son of Sir Charles and Lady Asgill, one of the British officers surrendered by Cornwallis at Yorktown, was totally innocent of any wrongdoing beyond serving his country. His name had been chosen by lot to be hanged as a reprisal for the death of an American captain, Joshua Huddy, of the New Jersey State Artillery, who had been captured by a group of loyalists, taken to New York, accused of the murder of one Philip White, a refugee, and on April 12, 1782, hanged by a group commanded by Captain Richard Lippincott of the British Provincial Troops.

Huddy's hanging had stirred up violent popular feeling against the Tories, and Washington's plan to hang Asgill as a reprisal was hailed by a public clamoring for a scapegoat. From Albany, Hamilton had written to Henry Knox on June 7, 1782, scorning the public furor that Washington was bent on appeasing. Hamilton reviewed the situation with the calm of the Continentalist: "This appears to me clearly to be an ill-timed proceeding . . . derogatory to the national character . . . repugnant to the genius of the age we live in . . . without example in modern history nor can it fail to be considered in Europe as wanton and unnecessary." Hamilton minced no words about what Washington was about to do: "So solemn and deliberate a sacrifice of the innocent for the guilty must be condemned on the present received notions of humanity, and encourage an opinion that we are in a certain degree in a state of barbarism."

Washington's insistence on hanging André was not a precedent for hanging Asgill: "So violent a measure would want the plea of necessity. It would argue meanness in us that at this late stage of the war," in the midst of success we should suddenly "lose our collective tempers." Hamilton was still not reconciled to André's being hanged instead of shot: "The death of André could not have been dispensed with; but it must still be viewed at a distance as an act of *rigid justice;* if we wreak our resentment on an innocent person, it will be suspected that we are too fond of executions."

Popular anger against the Tories was deep-seated. There were widespread stories that as many as 20 or 30 thousand patriots had died in the hulking British prison ships in New York harbor. Nevertheless, Washington should not again yield to popular clamour: "I am persuaded it will have an influence peculiarly unfavourable to the General's character."

As usual, Hamilton offered a practical suggestion. A commander in chief could make effective use of an aide or underling as a lightning rod to avoid responsibility for inhumane, though currently popular, action. "Let under actors be employed," he said, recalling how he had been used as just such an under actor to transmit the exchange proposal for André to Sir Henry Clinton. "If it is seriously believed that in this advanced state of affairs retaliation is necessary let another mode be chose. Let under actors be employed and let the authority by which it is done be wrapt in obscurity and doubt. Let not the Commander in Chief considered as the first and most respectable character among us come forward in person and be the avowed author of an act at which every humane feeling revolts. Let us at least have as much address as the enemy, and, if we must have victims, appoint some obscure agents to perform the ceremony, and bear the odium which must always attend even justice itself when directed by extreme severity."

Nor should the fact that Washington had already committed himself publicly in favor of hanging Asgill be a bar to mercy: "But it is said the Commander in Chief has pledged himself for it and cannot recede. Inconsistency in this case would be better than consistency. But pretexts must be found and will be readily admitted in favour of humanity."

Let Washington permit the execution to be delayed and find reasons for satisfaction in the enemy response that would help calm down public clamor. Sir Guy Carleton, the new British commander in New York who had just replaced Clinton, "will in all probability do something like apology and concession. He will give assurances of preventing everything of the kind in the future. Let the General appear to be satisfied with these assurances. The steps Carleton is said to have taken to suppress the refugee incursions will give the better color to lenity."

Hamilton urged Knox to help bring Washington around to the humane view: "I address myself to you upon this occasion because I know your liberality and your influence with the General. If you are of my opinion I am sure you will employ it—if it should not be too late." A letter would not be enough; a personal remonstrance was required. "I would not think a letter necessary," as Hamilton put it tactfully.

Hamilton deplored what he saw as Washington's misguided willingness to bend to popular clamor for another hanging. This was the kind of thing an elective official might do:

> I know how apt men are to be actuated by the circumstances which immediately surround them and to be led into an approbation of measures which in another situation they would disapprove. Mrs. Hamilton joins me in compliments to Mrs. Knox; believe me to be very truly & Affecty Dr. Sir Yr. Obed ser
>
> A Hamilton

All turned out as Hamilton had urged.

Knox agreed with Hamilton and went to work on Washington with Hamilton's arguments. On July 24 Knox told Hamilton that a delay of Asgill's hanging was in prospect and that "after this possibly something may turn up to procrastinate the matter still further." He was more sympathetic to Washington's problem than Hamilton had been: "It will be difficult for the General circumstanced as he is with his own declarations, the resolution of congress on the subject and the expectations of the people, to find reasons to justify him to the publick for a total suspension of the matter."

As it turned out, Asgill was saved not by Washington's clemency, but by a legal technicality that Hamilton's remonstrances gave the British, Knox, and Washington the time and zeal to uncover. Someone recalled that by the express terms of Lord Cornwallis's surrender at Yorktown, the treatment prescribed for captured officers did not include retaliatory hanging, if innocent. Asgill was saved. He was released alive by an Act of Congress November 7, 1782. Washington was spared the embarrassment of having to reverse his public position in favor of no hanging on the humanitarian grounds that Hamilton had urged upon him.

Hamilton's letter of February 13 to Washington came to him as a shock, a rude awakening, and an occasion for gratitude toward Hamilton. Washington replied on March 4 that he might have been "on the brink of a precipice" without being aware of the danger. The commander in chief should be "let more into the political and pecuniary state of our affairs." He admitted that he had been out of touch. "So far was I from conceiving that our finances were in so deplorable a state *at this time* that I had imbibed ideas from some source or another that, with a loan from Holland we should be able to rub along." As for the army, he wrote back on March 14, "I shall pursue the same steady line of conduct, which has governed me hitherto." As Hamilton had advised him, he would be more visible to his officers in urging the claims of the army: "The just claims of the army ought, and it is hoped will have their weight with every sensible legislature in the United States, if Congress point to their demands."

Washington counted on receiving help from the states if Congress itself failed the army. But Hamilton knew better. Of their own free and sovereign will, the states would not respond as Washington wishfully hoped. He knew from his experience as Continental receiver for New York that Congress had been voting requisitions on the states and receiving no more than 10 or 5 or 2 percent or none of the amounts demanded and that every state was booked with a huge debt for unpaid balances. In Congress, Hamilton had moved on December 20 to reduce these enormous book debts. He pointed out "that the exorbitancy of the demands produced a despair of fulfilling them which benumbed the efforts for that purpose." But Congress preferred to continue to vote sums which they knew could never be collected, and "the motion meeting with little patronage was withdrawn."

Such a defeat drove home the point that although Congress could orate and pass resolutions, ultimate power rested only in thirteen particularistic state legislatures. On January 12, 1783, Hamilton wrote to Clinton, "Every day proves more and more the insufficiency of the Confederation. The proselytes to this opinion are increasing fast, and many of the most sensible men acknowledge the wisdom of the measures recommended by our legislature at their last sitting." He was reminding Clinton that he did not consider the call for the convention of the states, which he had written and Schuyler had pushed through over Clinton's opposition, a dead letter.

On January 27, 1783, James Wilson of Pennsylvania introduced a resolution calling for the establishment of general funds to be collected solely by Congress. Hamilton leaped to his feet to speak in favor of the resolution. Wilson's bill called for a system to raise permanent revenue, universal and uniform, throughout the United States, with Congress-appointed tax collectors in charge. Hamilton urged that Wilson's system replace the existing system of separate funds drawn at the will of each state from whatever sources it wished through its own collectors. Wilson's method, he argued, was simple, direct and invariable and required only a few officials. The other was complicated, uncertain, and peculiarly vicious in that the popularly elected state collectors, men like Abraham Yates, were interested in maintaining their vote-collecting popularity by not collecting the revenues. The speech was forceful, but the resolution failed.

Next day Hamilton rose again to answer to objections. He attacked the inefficiency of the state officers and, in the heat of the debate, let slip a remark that seemed to go too far: "As the energy of the federal Govt. was evidently short of the degree necessary for pervading and uniting the States it was expedient to introduce the influence of officers deriving their emoluments from and consequently interested in supporting the power of congress." He would send federal officers into the states.

As Hamilton framed it now, the issue was not just which of the two ways of collecting the revenues would be most effective. Hamilton was saying that the issue was the Continental one: which method would best serve the federal government in "pervading and uniting the States."

Madison, who usually agreed with Hamilton on the need for Continental measures, nevertheless thought he had made a terrible mistake in bluntly stating this as a reason for introducing into the states tax collectors who derived their emoluments from, and consequently supported, the power of Congress.

In his notes of the debates, Madison wrote: "This remark was imprudent & injurious to the cause w[hi]ch it was meant to serve." Madison added, "All the members of Congress who concurred, in any degree with the States in this jealousy smiled at the disclosure. Mr. B[land] & still more Mr. L[ee], who were of this number took notice in private conversation, that Mr. Hamilton had let out the secret."

Politicians operating in terms of short-range effects would never have introduced the issue of Continental collectors "pervading and uniting" the states into the debate. But the record of Hamilton's frank avowal of the purpose of "pervading and uniting the states" served his long-range purpose of tending to cement the union.

The legislative history of the debates that preceded the adoption of Wilson's plan would include Hamilton's argument that it would support the power of Congress to legislate nationally and that this was a desirable objective. Hamilton had staked out a vital principle at a point far beyond the limits of the issue of the particular debate.

Hamilton's frank avowal raised overwhelming opposition against Wilson's resolution. Madison offered a compromise amendment, omitting the objectionable phrase that the funds "were to be collected under the authority of congress," but this did not placate the opposition. They had further objections. Why should foreign and domestic creditors be paid equally in specie? Foreign creditors, yes; but the domestic debts arose chiefly from the loan of money to Congress in depreciated currency or from the sale of goods to the army at exorbitant prices; so it was neither necessary nor just to allow them to recoup in gold.

Hamilton rose the next day to protest this new issue. He denounced any plan "that made but partial provision for the public debts." To Hamilton, this was "an inconsistent and dishonorable departure" from the declarations made by Congress. Here was a dress rehearsal for later great debates on his assumption and funding measures.

Now he turned the opposition's snickers at his frank avowal of support for congressionally appointed tax collectors back upon the opposition. If distinctions between foreign and domestic creditors that worked against domestic creditors were made, domestic creditors would exert pressure on their local state legislatures to favor congressional revenue collection. The weight of their opinion, Hamilton argued, would force the opponents of this congressional revenue plan to accept the very plan they now opposed—and with it, Hamilton's hated plan for thereby "uniting the states."

A watered-down bill, including Madison's amendment and other changes, finally came up for a vote on February 12. It merely called for the establishment of permanent and adequate funds to operate generally throughout the United States, to be collected by Congress. It was too weak for Hamilton, and he voted "No." The only state beside New York that opposed was Pennsylvania, which considered it too strong. Each of the two states voted the same way for opposite reasons.

Neither Hamilton nor James Wilson was finished with the fight. On February 18 Hamilton proposed and Wilson seconded a resolution requiring that Congress make known to the public "the motives & views of their measures in all cases where the public safety w[oul]d admit." Therefore, when the subject of finances was under debate "the doors of cong[res]s s[houl]d be open."

Like most of the other delegates, James Madison was opposed to opening up the debates to the public. He sniffed suspiciously at Hamilton's motives. He wrote, "Perhaps the true reason was that, it was expected the presence of public creditors numerous & weighty in Pennsylvania, would have an influence & that it wd. be well for the public to come more fully to the knowledge of public finances."

Hamilton was arguing that the common people be let in to watch the innermost thoughts and proposals of their leaders. He and Wilson here were being more open and democratic than any of the other self-anointed spokesmen for the common man.

Nothing in Hamilton's proposal would have prevented members of the public who took Madison's side from flocking in to support him. Madison seemed to miss the point that whereas Hamilton and Wilson may have had special, and even selfish, reasons that served their cause for letting the public in on the particular occasion, the general principle was right. Hamilton sought a broader, more popularly based Congress. That all congressional and legislative sessions are open to the public today is a legacy from Hamilton for which he has received less credit than he deserves.

But Congress, reported Madison, "adjourned it being the usual hour & the motion being generally disrelished." When it came up for a vote, it suffered overwhelming defeat, with only Pennsylvania voting aye. Hamilton's colleague from New York, William Floyd, voted against Hamilton and with Madison and the majority against it. Hamilton's and New York's ballot was lost for both sides.

Hamilton did not give up. He continued working to reinstate the provisions of Wilson's original measure to permit Congress to collect import duties for the life of the public debt, instead of the compromise of being limited to 25 years. Congress should appoint the collectors. On March 11 he moved another compromise whereby the collectors would be nominated by Congress but appointed by the states. Hamilton and Wilson lost on this too, but now by only one vote.

When the final report on the funds was passed by a debate-weary Congress, Hamilton voted against the compromise package. There was no need for his vote as a moderate to carry the measure: every state but Rhode Island voted for it. New York was divided. The long-term interest of his cause was furthered by his holding out for something better than the compromise, and this was more important to him than the immediate satisfaction of voting on the winning side. To Jefferson, Madison critized Hamilton for this, writing that New York's "vote was lost by the rigid adherence of Mr. Hamilton to a plan which he supposed more perfect." It was a superficial criticism that Hamilton would have taken as an unwitting compliment. The compromise carried easily without his vote. Thus he kept alive for the long future the principle of congressional control of funding and collections; others were content to abandon it for the day's vote.

In the day-to-day debates, parlimentary maneuvers, and proposals of committees, Hamilton continued patiently to demonstrate leadership of the nationalist delegates by insistence on national power, sound money, the right of the public to be admitted to debates to learn about public finance, and the interrelationship of all three. Hamilton was also learning the hard way that no amount of patience, eloquence, arm twisting, or logrolling would ever succeed in making the feeble Confederation an effective political instrument for "pervading and uniting the states."

Beyond the walls of Congress's meeting room in the State House, the situation in the nation was swiftly changing for the worse. In February, Robert Morris threatened to resign as superintendent of finance unless Congress should immediately appropriate Continental funds to pay the army, saying, "I will never be the minister of injustice." By Hamilton's reckoning, this would not only have brought down the public credit, but Morris's own private credit as well by one single, fateful resignation. At an evening meeting at Thomas FitzSimons's house between congressmen and the army's angry deputation from Newburgh still camping on Congress's doorstep demanding their money, Hamilton affirmed that Washington would "never yield to any dishonorable or disloyal plans." There were others, however, who "foment and misguide their councils."

The headquarters of these other disloyal councils was that of none other than Hamilton's old enemy General Horatio Gates, second-in-command to Washington at Newburgh. One of Gates's aides, Major John Armstrong, wrote Gates that if Washington's troops had someone like "Mad Anthony [Wayne] at their head," instead of Washington, "I knew not where they [the troops] would stop. They feel like men and, could they be taught to think like politicians, they might do good." Armstrong's citation of "Mad Anthony" Wayne's leadership of troops would soon prove laughably wrong. Failing to follow the kind of advice that Hamilton had given Washington about keeping control of his command, Wayne would soon lose control of the troops under his command. In the end their mutiny, and not that of Washington's men, would prove to be the most serious threat to Congress and to civil order.

Armstrong and others, including Colonel Walter Stewart, another friend of Gates just up from Philadelphia, began to circulate inflammatory rumors in the Newburgh camp, which became known as the "Newburgh Addresses." One such was "that it was universally expected the army would not disband until they had obtained justice; that the public creditors looked up to them for redress of their own grievances; would afford them every aid, and even join them in the field, if necessary." Hamilton was tarred with the charge that "some members of Congress wished the measure might take effect, in order to compel the public, particularly the delinquent States, to do justice. . . ." There was talk of a coup d'état to establish a monarchy and to give Washington the crown. Washington viewed all such talk from Gates and his cohorts "with abhorrence" and reprehended it "with severity."

Washington claimed that there was "something very mysterious in this business" because the reports in Philadelphia of mutiny in the army came "at a time when there was not a syllable of the kind of agitation in camp." Every unit commander, even a Washington, tells this kind of fib to his superiors because existence of such "agitation" would reflect on the commander himself. If Washington really believed what he said, he was more dangerously out of touch with his under officers now than even Hamilton feared.[2]

Washington told Hamilton that the agitation—of which supposedly, "there was not a syllable" in camp—arose out of well-founded suspicion in camp that Congress intended using the army "as mere puppets to establish continental funds, and that rather than not succeed in this measure, or weaken their ground, they would make a sacrifice of the army and all its interests."

Hamilton knew that no such strained and artificial hypothesis could be the proximate cause or even a significant factor in bringing on a mutiny of well-led officers. Humanly enough, Washington was merely seeking to unshoulder from himself some of the blame for allowing the situation of which Hamilton had warned him to arise by asserting that "the scheme was not only planned but also digested and matured in Philadelphia . . . with great art." Still claiming that no agitation existed in camp, Washington nevertheless found it necessary to issue a general order "to arrest the officers on the spot." They had "stood wavering on a tremendous precipice." Arrest would "prevent the officers from being taken by surprise while the passions were all inflamed, and to rescue them from plunging themselves into a gulph of Civil Horror."

Washington now beseeched Hamilton to urge the delegates to do something for the army without delay, because their situation "is distressing beyond description." It was a stronger plea to Congress for military appropriations to avert a bloodbath. He added, "if any disastrous consequences should follow, by reason of [the delegates'] delinquency . . . they must be answerable to God and their country for the ineffable horrors which may be occasioned thereby." Washington needed help from his young friend in Congress to save his position from a second Gates's cabal. His threat was not veiled.

It has since been charged by some that Hamilton was trying to use Gates as a threat to frighten the states into granting plenary powers to Congress and funds for the benefit of the public creditors. Others charge the opposite, namely, that he was hatching a plan for the army to overthrow Congress and set up a military monarchy with Washington as its head.

In this writer's view, both charges are nonsense.

Hamilton coolly replied to Washington on March 14: "I do not wonder at the suspicions that have been infused; nor should I be surprised to hear, that I have been pointed out as one of the persons concerned in playing the game described." He explained that among his colleagues in Congress "there are dangerous prejudices in the particular states opposed to those measures which alone can give stability and prosperity to the union. There is a fatal opposition to Continental views. Necessity alone can work a reform."

He went on: "I have myself urged in Congress the propriety of uniting the influence of the public creditors, and the army as part of them, to prevail upon the states to enter into their views. I have expressed the same sentiments out-of-doors. Several other members of Congress have done the same."

The meaning of all this was simply that "Congress should adopt such a plan as would embrace the relief of all public creditors, including the army, in order that the personal influence of some, the connections of others, and a sense of justice to the army, as well as the apprehension of ill consequences, might form a mass of influence in each State in favor of the measures of Congress."

Hamilton was well aware of the dangers of threats of force or mutiny from any direction. Any such threat would work against the army's interests in Congress: "Any combination of *FORCE* would only be productive of the horrors of a civil war, might end in the ruin of the Country & would certainly end in the ruin of the army."

Anonymous pamphlets appeared in the Newburgh encampment calling for a great meeting of all officers on March 11 to demand forceful action instead of meek petitions. The army's deputation in Philadelphia "seem to have solicited in vain." A surly throng of disgruntled officers and men turned out in an angry mood. Alerted to the danger by Hamilton, Washington, forewarned and forearmed, acted with unusual force. He was ready to address the meeting with a speech that owed much, including its moderate tone, to the letters Hamilton had written to him to dispel his delusions about the situation in Congress and his own personal standing with his officers.

Washington came forward. He began with a moving plea for patience and trust in the good faith of Congress and the states. The mutinous officers continued to mutter in sullen silence, unmoved; they had heard pious promises often before. Washington came to his concluding words, among the loftiest he had ever delivered in public. He said haltingly:

> You will, by the dignity of your conduct, afford occasion for posterity to say, when speaking of the glorious example you have exhibited to mankind, had this day been wanting, the world had never seen the last stage of perfection to which human nature is capable of attaining.

After speaking these noble words, Washington paused and reached into his pocket for a letter he had brought with him from Joseph Jones, a member of Congress from Virginia, who had written of the "mountains" of prejudice (Hamilton had used the same word to Laurens) that delegates like Hamilton there had been trying to overcome in their efforts to help the army. When he looked down to try to read Jones's handwriting, Washington misread the words. He reached into his pocket again and pulled out and unfolded a new pair of spectacles. "Gentlemen," he said, fumbling with Jones's letter in one hand and his spectacles in the other, "You must pardon me. I have grown gray in your service, and now find myself growing blind."

One of the officers who was present wrote, "This little address, with the mode . . . of delivering it, drew tears from [many] of the officers."

Washington's spontaneous, moving self-reproach struck a chord that summoned up in the mutinous officers' memories of seven years of service in the common cause. It suddenly bridged the gulf that had opened up between the chief executive and his command. Tears welled up out of long-shared memories.

Though some of Gates's cohorts still wanted to replace Washington with Gates or another who would pursue more vigorously their demands on Congress, most of the officers agreed not to resort to violence or mutiny.

Recalling the ripple of the quiet laughter, the tears, and the solemn hush that had fallen as Washington finished his little speech and the mass meeting dispersed in silence, Samuel Shaw remembered, "What he says of the army may with equal justice be applied to his own character. 'Had this day been wanting, the world had never seen the last stage of perfection to which human nature is capable of attaining.' "

Congress, stirred by news of the dangerous imbroglio at Newburgh, hastily adopted a resolution introduced by Hamilton praising Washington for "his prudence and attachment to the welfare of the community" and the officers, not excluding the rebellious among them, for their patriotism. It voted to grant the officers five years' full pay in the form of interest-bearing securities.

Hamilton, realist that he was, knew that the army's grievances ran too deep for Washington's nostalgic gesture to put down mutinous anger for more than a short breathing spell. Madison recorded that Hamilton insisted on Washington's being "the conductor of the army in their plans for redress . . ." Although Gates in camp and some zealous army supporters in Philadelphia might want to displace Washington with another who would push the army's cause more forcefully than Washington, Hamilton argued in public and in private that Washington's "virtue, his patriotism and his firmness would . . . never yield to any dishonorable or disloyal plans . . ." Washington "would sooner suffer himself to be cut into pieces."

According to Madison, Robert Morris's letter of resignation as superintendent of finance in January 1783, to take effect the end of May, had "made a deep & solemn impression on Congress." It would be "ruinous . . . to domestic & foreign credit; & as producing a vacancy which no one knew how to fill, & which no fit man would venture to accept." Theodorick Bland and Richard Henry Lee disparaged Morris and threw oblique censure on his character, but "On the other side Mr. Wilson & Mr. Hamilton went into a copious defence & Panegyric of Mr. Morris" and the danger from his departure. Hamilton insisted to his fellow congressmen that "no man in this country but Morris could have kept the money machine a-going." Their supporters, fearing that a single financier might be supplanted by a board of treasury like the inefficient, if not corrupt, committee that Morris had replaced, kept Morris in office by referring his resignation to still another committee—of which Hamilton was a member.

With fiscal ruin or rescue hanging in the balance, Hamilton's committee sought to persuade the superintendent of finance to continue in office until at least an installment of pay could be raised to speed the soldiers, then on the point of dismissal, to homes and safe dispersal. Hamilton wrote the part of the committee report that explained Morris's difficulties, and Morris finally rescinded his resignation.

Beyond the reach of command leadership like Washington's, the uprising that had been suppressed at Newburgh soon blazed up again among troops of "Mad Anthony" Wayne's command in central Pennsylvania. Though soldiers and a proportionate number of officers were being furloughed home in anticipation of final peace by the signing of the Treaty of Paris, the states had failed to forward the taxes as Hamilton's earlier resolve had begged.

On June 7 Washington sent Congress a letter enclosing an angry complaint from officers who were to be turned out unpaid. Then, in mid-June, sergeants in command of new recruits in a barracks in Philadelphia itself remonstrated on Congress's doorstep against accepting their discharges until they were paid. Congress took no notice of this "mutinous memorial from the sergeants," as Madison's notes described it.

On Tuesday, June 17, 80 armed soldiers broke out of control of their officers in Lancaster and rampaged off to Philadelphia "to co-operate with those now in the city . . . to procure their pay (or perhaps to possess themselves of money at any rate)." They had thrown out hints that they might "rob the bank, the treasury, & c. & c." Their deposed commander, Colonel Richard Butler, explained to them in vain that they must remain at Lancaster to be paid and that furloughs were at their option. Butler unshouldered blame for his failure to keep control by the usual claim that the defection was the fault of Congress in Philadelphia "and that the flame is supported by inimical . . . people." He sent officers after the mutinous marchers to persuade them to return to Lancaster and their duty. He warned that if they kept on, they would be sent back empty-handed and that "your appearance at Philadelphia . . . will be justly construed into *menace*, rather than a proper mode of seeking justice."

The Executive Council of Pennsylvania had responsibility for keeping local law and order, including preserving the safety and security of Congress in Philadelphia. The council convened at the State House in Philadelphia in the room across the hall from where the Continental Congress met.

On June 19, two days after the Lancaster uprising, Colonel Butler's and William Henry's letters warning of the mutinous troops on the march reached President John Dickinson of the Executive Council. He "immediately transmitted" them to Congress. It named a committee of Hamilton, Oliver Ellsworth, and Richard Peters to forfend it from a real, not a hypothetical army mutiny.

On the same day that word was received, Hamilton and his committee hurried to Dickinson's Executive Council and demanded that they send out militia at once to intercept the mutineers before they could reach the city and join forces with the rebellious sergeants and other potentially mutinous local troops in Philadelphia. There must be a firm show of force at once. Hamilton reported back to Congress that the council turned down their request. The timorous Council was unwilling to act unless the mutinous troops actually committed some outrage—on the scale of physical violence to congressmens' persons. At the same time, Hamilton dispatched Major William Jackson, the assistant secretary of war, out on the road toward Lancaster to meet the marching mutineers and assure them of fair treatment if they returned to their officers in Lancaster. He would offer them extra provisions if they halted where they were. But the mutineers brushed off these proposals and kept on marching toward Philadelphia. The city erupted in panic. Alarming rumors spread: shops and homes would be looted; the banks, robbed; and congressmen, slaughtered in their slothful seats!

When the mutineers reached the city Friday morning, June 20, their ranks were swelled by several companies of veterans from Charleston barracks and 500 troops from the city barracks. Friday afternoon Congress adjourned for its weekend recess until Monday morning.

Hamilton, meanwhile, arranged with his friend Robert Morris, still superintendent of finance, for money to pay the unwelcome arrivals as promptly as possible, but only on condition that they turn around and march back to Lancaster to collect it there. General Arthur St. Clair, the commander of the Pennsylvania line, mobilized his veteran troops at the Charleston barracks for immediate action to disarm and arrest the mutineers. On Saturday the 21st President Boudinot of Congress learned to his horror that St. Clair's veteran troops, on whom he had been counting to remain loyal, had also joined the mutineers. This fearsome new force planned to break into the Bank of North America to collect their pay and any other money they could find. Boudinot summoned Congress into special session for one o'clock Saturday afternoon. By the time members had convened, the mutineers had posted sentinels at the State House doors. They surrounded the building with 300 or more soldiers, fifteen or twenty of them dangerously close to the south windows of the council chamber. Armed with guns and ammunition, some looted from the arsenals, surly and abusive and made aggressive with their success so far, the rebellious and disorderly troops now menaced all councilmen and congressmen alike with fixed bayonets. Some drunkenly threatened further outrages.

President John Dickinson of the Pennsylvania Executive Council rushed from the meeting room into Congress's chamber. He announced that the troops had demanded that the council immediately grant "authority to appoint commissioned officers to command us and redress our grievances . . ." Otherwise, the troops "shall instantly let in those injured soldiers upon you, and abide by the consequences. You have only twenty minutes to deliberate on this important matter."

Congress ordered General St. Clair to make an attempt to regain command of his regulars and order them back to their quarters. It dispatched a call to General Washington in Newburgh for a detachment of his troops to help. After sitting surrounded for nearly three hours, the members rose, put on brave faces, and walked through the cordon without being physically attacked. Though some of the mutineers were drunk and shouted imprecations, they did not break discipline or make good their loud threats to break into the State House or attack individual congressmen.

St. Clair managed to persuade some of the rebels to return to their barracks, promising that they might indeed designate their own officers to represent them in dealings with the Executive Council. The mutineers continued to hold the powder house, some other arsenals, and several artillery field pieces. Congress, fearing that the Executive Council would continue to fail to call out the state's militia or that, if called, the militia would fail to respond or defect to the mutineers, met again in the evening. Finding that the authority of the United States had been insulted, that the peace of the city was endangered, and that effectual counteracting measures must be taken at once, Congress directed Hamilton's committee to meet with the Executive Council, and if satisfactory assurances of protection were not obtained, to decide whether Congress should flee Philadelphia and hold its next session at either Trenton or Princeton the following Thursday, June 26.

Hamilton and Ellsworth took the resolutions to Dickinson immediately, read them to him and the council, and demanded action. The militia must be called out to end the danger. Congress would hold no more sessions in Philadelphia until it could be sure that members would receive adequate protection. The Pennsylvania Executive Council continued to stall.

On Monday, the council still felt that the militia could not be relied on "unless Congress suffered a greater outrage." Hamilton demanded that Dickinson put his refusal in writing for the record. Dickinson refused. Feeling that there was still danger, Hamilton argued that the state had failed to support public authority and that if the failure continued one more day, he would have to advise Congress to move to Trenton or Princeton.

Furious that Dickinson hugged the sovereignty of Pennsylvania with "an unbecoming stateliness" and "overwhelming nicety" in this crisis, Hamilton insisted that the safety and dignity of the national sovereignty symbolized by Congress was paramount to any state's rights. "Reserve" on the part of a state was "uncandid" and contrary to a working federal system.

Hamilton reported back that the Executive Council regretted the insult to Congress. But he scouted the sentiment because the members of the council "themselves had a principal share in it." Pennsylvania delegates in Congress rebuked Hamilton for this, offering a watered-down resolution not blaming the Executive Council and merely noting that it had shared in suffering insult from the mutineers.

The following day the mutineers were more bellicose and threatening than ever. The board of sergeants who led the mutineers turned the six officers chosen to negotiate for them with St. Clair and the council into hostages for their demands. The sergeants threatened them with death: "every effort in your power must be exerted to bring about the . . . most ample justice; . . . use compulsive measures should they be found necessary—. . . we will support you to . . . utmost of our power. Should you . . . not . . . do all in yours, Death is inevitably your fate."

To forfend death as Congress's fate, Hamilton's committee recommended on Tuesday, June 24, that Congress meet two days later at Princeton. President Boudinot, welcoming the prestige and prosperity that having the capital would bring to his state, immediately issued a proclamation citing the peril and officially ratifying removal. Aroused at last by the departure of Congress and finding the soldiers still "in a very tumultous disposition," the Executive Council bestirred itself to adopt the strong measures Hamilton had urged on it from the outset. It mustered 500 militiamen "as a measure indispensable and immediately necessary to secure government from insult, the State from disturbance, and the city from injury." Hamilton's measures worked. The mutineers, learning that a detachment from Washington's northern army was marching south and deserted by two of the officers who had been their instigators, put down their arms and capitulated. The Lancaster contingent marched home. The remaining four officers of the rebels' committee were arrested. Too late to prevent discredit, the Pennsylvania authorities exacted "dutyfull submission to the offended Majesty of the United States."

Abashed Philadelphia newspapers sought to minimize the danger, exculpate city and state authorities, and unshoulder blame on Congress and Hamilton as having been too alarmist. Benjamin Rush mocked: "If you remain one week longer at Princeton feeding one another with ideas of . . . wounded dignity . . . you may lose Pennsylvania forever from your plans of continental revenue."

Major John Armstrong sneered, "The grand Sanhedrin of the Nation, with all their solemnity & emptiness . . . have removed to Princeton, & left a State, where their wisdom has been long questioned, their virtue suspected, & their dignity a jest."

On the other hand, Hamilton's friend Elias Boudinot, the president of Congress, could not have been more pleased with the move to Princeton. He thought that New Jersey's hospitality "may fix Congress as to their permanent residence" in his home state. New Jersey authorities united in a chorus of welcome. Philadelphia papers soon began to beg Congress to return and to heap blame on Hamilton for having been so quick to order it out of the city of brotherly love. Some would recall that once before, in 1777, upon Hamilton's advice, Congress had fled the city to York, but not the state. Others hinted darkly that the move to Princeton was but a way-stop in Hamilton's grand design to obtain the capital for his own New York City once the British were gone. To unshoulder the blame of these attacks, Hamilton obtained a letter of October 16 from his new friend Madison, who testified that Hamilton "was opposed to the removal of Congress except in the last extremity . . . that when you finally yielded it appeared to be more in compliance with the peremptory expostulations of others than with any dispositions of your mind." Furthermore, said Madison, avowing his esteem for his congressional friend, "after the arrival of Congress at Princeton your conversation shewed that you received the removal rather with regret than with pleasure." To confirm the good faith of both his and Boudinot's actions, Hamilton wrote and seconded a resolution that John F. Mercer of New Jersey introduced on July 2, calling for Congress to move back to Philadelphia. Now Hamilton suddenly found himself caught in more political cross fire. In a self-serving report to the Philadelphia assembly, Dickinson twisted Hamilton's reluctance to order Congress out of Philadelphia into implied congressional approval of the way Dickinson and the council had handled the crisis. Dickinson alleged that Hamilton had "found great weight" in the council's deliberations and might have been willing to wait for reinforcements from Washington. Nonsense, said Hamilton. A complete falsehood. He hit back at Dickinson with a characteristically searing reply from a keen memory and copious notes, made contemporaneously. The committee of Congress never made "concessions in favor of the conduct of the Council," he said. They were so far from concurring that they "strongly urged the expedience and necessity of calling out the militia . . . against an unofficered and disorderly body of mutinous soldiers."

Once more, Madison forcefully backed up Hamilton, writing to John Dickinson that "This was not to be considered as the disorderly riot of an unarmed mob, but as the deliberate mutiny of an incensed soldiery, carried to the utmost point of outrage short of assassination."

News that loyal troops were marching down from Newburgh had much to do with putting down the mutiny. The formerly mutinous troops over whom Washington had regained control with Hamilton's timely advice and a lucky pair of new spectacles had saved Congress. Events proved to Hamilton that prompt mobilizing of overwhelming force—at the risk of public ridicule for overreaction

—to put down lawless breaches of civil peace would save casualties in the end by obviating the need to use any force at all. Seeing themselves outmanned by the forces of order, mutineers and lawless mobs would put down their arms without provoking a bloody fight.

Hamilton took the mutiny seriously but more coolly than Madison. In his customary long view, Congress's flight or its savaging by a mutinous army, with no citizens coming forward to defend the country's most important, indeed only republican institution, would have had far-reaching, indeed disastrous consequences: "I viewed the departure of Congress as a delicate measure," Hamilton said, with "consequences important to the national character abroad, and critical with respect to the State of Pennsylvania, and . . . the city of Philadelphia; . . . the triumph of a handful of mutinous soldiers, permitted in a place which is . . . the capital of America, to . . . imprison Congress, without the least effort on the part of the citizens to uphold their . . . authority, so as to oblige them to remove . . . would . . . be viewed at a distance as a general dissatisfaction of the citizens to the Federal Government." Such an unedifying spectacle would "discredit its negotiations [for peace], and affect the national interests . . ."

Hamilton and Mercer's motion to move back to Philadelphia was overwhelmingly defeated by angry resolutions of Massachusetts and South Carolina congressmen condemning Pennsylvania for its failure to provide them protection. Congress moved to Annapolis in November 1783, to Trenton a year later, and thence to New York City. It would not return to Philadelphia until seven years after the troop mutinies from which Hamilton had done so much to help forfend it, and then only as the end play of some more intricate moves of Hamilton.

Hamilton tended to make use of Philadelphia in its relationship with Congress in somewhat the same way a chess master uses his rook in the procedure known as "castling"—he sacrifices the rook's best interests to secure a better position for his king. As Hamilton's life went on, Philadelphia seemed to retaliate against him for such treatment by becoming a dangerous and unlucky city. It was all right for a visit, and it had its uses, and he would make the most of them. But as a place for a prolonged stay, it was not for him, especially when his wife was not with him.

19

JUDICIAL SUPREMACY

IT IS A RULE OF LAW THAT WHERE THERE ARE TWO LAWS, ONE NOT
REPEALING THE OTHER EXPRESSLY OR VIRTUALLY, THE JUDGES
MUST CONSTRUE THEM SO AS TO MAKE THEM STAND TOGETHER
... WHEN TWO OR MORE LAWS CLASH THAT WHICH RELATES TO THE
MOST IMPORTANT CONCERNS OUGHT TO PREVAIL.
—Brief No. 6. *Rutgers v. Waddington* (June 1784)

On July 22, 1783, Hamilton wrote Betsy from Philadelphia of the joyous new
vista that would soon be opening for them back in New York City, which was
to be evacuated "yesterday":

> I give you joy my angel of the happy conclusion of the important
> work. . . . Now in a very short time I hope we shall be happily settled
> in New York. My love to your father. Kiss my boy a thousand times.
> A thousand loves to yourself.

In his opening speech to the third session of the Fifteenth Parliament on
December 5, 1782, King George III had said, "I have pointed all my views and
measures, as well in Europe as in North America, to an entire and cordial
reconciliation with those colonies." But he had conditioned final settlement with
the colonies on a settlement with France.

When word of this reached North America, Hamilton congratulated George

Clinton on February 14, 1783, "on the strong prospect of peace which the speech of the British King affords." But with his usual foresight, Hamilton saw trouble ahead. A month before the Newburgh imbroglio, four months before he would face down the Philadelphia mutineers, he warned Clinton, "It is to be suspected the Army will not disband, till solid arrangements are made for doing it justice; and I fear these arrangements will not be made."

To forfend New York against trouble, Hamilton offered Clinton a practical solution for the problems the soldiers would bring home with them; "I wish the legislature would set apart a tract of territory, and make a liberal allowance to every officer and soldier of the Army at large who will become a citizen of the state . . . It is the first wish of my heart that the Union may last; but feeble as the links are, what prudent man would rely upon it?"

As usual, he was thinking in a practical way about the unthinkable: "Should a disunion take place, any person who will cast his eye upon the map will see how essential it is to our State to provide for its own security. I believe a large part of the Army would incline to set down among us, and then all we shall have to do will be to govern well."

He closed with a light, disarming shrug: "These are loose but important ideas."

The original 1778 treaty of alliance between France and the United States had stipulated that neither country could make peace without concurrence of the other. The peace commissioners had disregarded this and Congress's instructions as well and had kept their negotiations with the British secret from the French ministry until the provisional treaty had been signed on November 30, 1782. When Captain Joshua Barney arrived with the terms in March 1783, Congress professed to be shocked at what they had done.

On the whole, the terms of the Treaty of Paris were quite favorable to the Americans, but they included a secret clause setting a more generous boundary for West Florida if it should fall to Britain instead of Spain. This was, of course, prejudicial to the interests of Spain. To men of the world like Benjamin Franklin, signing the provisional treaty without telling France had made sense in order to nail down favorable terms from the British while they were available for the asking. Besides, there was the saving condition that it should not take effect until peace had been signed between Britain and France.

Some members of Congress denounced the commissioners for a breach of faith with France and Spain; others defended them, backing up Franklin on the grounds he gave. Hamilton rose to placate passions and take a middle position. He counseled coolness and circumspection on all sides. He had opposed the congressional resolution directing the commissioners to seek French advice before negotiating with the British from the beginning. But because the resolution had been passed, however unwisely, he said Franklin and his associates must be censured for signing the preliminary peace articles without first having disclosed them to France. He denounced the special secret clause setting the West Florida boundary. He criticized Britain for the "past cruelty and present duplicity of her councils . . . her watching every occasion and trying every project for dissolving the honorable ties which bind the United States to her ally, France." Obviously, American resentments ought to lie against Britain and American sympathies with France, and Hamilton now was outspoken in his support of France.

But congressional criticism of the secret article should not be made public, he advised. If it were, both internal and external dissensions would follow; in fact, the commissioners should be publicly commended, but the terms of the secret clause should immediately be communicated to the French. Hamilton's moderate position carried Congress with him, and it adopted and followed his advice. When he saw a useful purpose for moderation, Hamilton could be more forcefully moderate than anyone.

With peace about to break out, new battles in Congress loomed. The army still had to be demobilized and a peacetime army and fleet established; Hamilton was called upon to draft the plans. His report was a carefully elaborated scheme providing for a Continental standing army of six regiments, to be paid out of federal funds and augmented as occasion demanded by a universal militia of "all free male inhabitants in each State, from twenty years to fifty, except such as the laws of each State shall think it proper to exempt." Hamilton would have preferred a larger, federally controlled army, but he was well aware, as he told Washington, that "our prejudices will make us wish to keep up as few troops as possible."

He wrote Washington on March 25, 1783, that "Republican jealousy has in it a principle of hostility to an army whatever be their merits and claims to gratitude of the community." He added, "I see this temper, though smothered with great care, involuntarily breaking out upon too many occasions."

Within the militia itself, his plan set up a division conforming to ancient Greek and contemporary European practice consisting of those "who are willing to be at the expense of equipping themselves." They could join the cavalry and be classed as dragoons; those who could not afford the expense or were not horsemen would have to trudge along in the infantry. He also advocated the establishment of foundries and armament and powder factories. On grounds of expense, at this time, he disapproved of military academies for training professional officers. Later, he championed such academies and is entitled to credit as a foster father of West Point and Annapolis. This plan for a peacetime armed force would be a federal, not a state, plan because no single state should be allowed to "keep the keys of the United States." His splendid plan was read and commended, but civilian temper of hostility toward armies was unsmothered and inflamed by the mutineers. It was tabled without action. The time had come for Americans to turn back to warring with internal enemies among themselves.

A British agent in New York reported to his superiors that although Americans generally acknowledged that the peace terms "were much more liberal than they had any right to expect, at the same time they rediculed [sic] that Article which says that Congress should recommend to the different Assemblys the restoration of ye property of the Loyalists, well knowing that no attention would be paid to it by the Assembly's." Though he was foremost in stressing its importance, even Hamilton admitted that the clause was probably a dead letter: "Col. Hamilton, a member of Congress, acknowledged to me that he was of the same opinion."

Articles IV, V, and VI of the Treaty of Paris required that no legal obstacles be placed in the way of collection of prewar debts that Americans owed to British merchants and that all further confiscations of loyalist property be prohibited. In addition, Article V provided that Congress was to recommend to the states that any British or loyalist holdings that had already been confiscated should be restored to their former owners. This was only a recommendation. It remained optional for the states to observe it or not.

Well aware that these clauses were anathema to most of his countrymen, Hamilton decided that it was only right to enforce them. A matter of national good faith and honor threatened by popular clamor against loyalists was not an occasion that called for moderation on his part.

On May 30, 1783, he introduced a notably unpopular resolution: "that the several states be required to remove all obstructions which may interpose in the way of the entire and faithful execution of the fourth and sixth articles" of the peace treaty; and that the states "consider liberally the fifth recommendatory article relating to restitution."

Richard Peters of Pennsylvania was immediately on his feet to move for commitment of Hamilton's resolution. This would bury it without a record vote. Hamilton demanded that the delegates place themselves on record on Peters's motion, and they happily did so. The only vote against commitment was Hamilton's.

So strong was state sentiment and popular clamor against permitting loyalists to collect debts owed to them and restoring their property to them that Virginia ordered her delegates in Congress "neither to agree to any restitution of property confiscated by the State, nor submit that the laws made by any independent State of this union be subjected to the adjudication of any power or powers on earth." Virginia was insisting that her state law was superior to, and overrode, the terms of the treaty of peace.

Congress mildly reproved Virginia's parochial defiance of a national treaty with a statement that "the commissioners of these states cannot retract without a violation of the national faith." With such tepid affirmance of the letter of the treaty, Congress dropped the whole matter. The question of whether the treaty terms were binding on the states was to remain a blight on British-American relations for many years to come. It would be partially settled only by the Jay Treaty of 1794, in the creation of which Hamilton played a leading role.

Hamilton's stand on the high ground of national honor soon brought him many law clients. They would help him quickly establish a reputation as one of the leading lawyers of his newly liberated city.

With the mutineers still much on his mind, as a sort of swan song to Congress before moving on with Betsy to the joyous new life awaiting them in liberated New York, Hamilton informally introduced his favorite resolution of all; this was the one that, after reciting all the defects of the Articles of Confederation, called upon the states to appoint delegates to a convention "with full powers to revise the Confederation, and to adopt and propose such alterations as to them shall appear necessary; to be finally approved or rejected by the States respectively."

Hamilton included among the "essential points" in which the Confederation was "defective" his demand for broader implied powers for the national government; for separation of legislative, executive, and judicial powers into three separate and distinct branches of government; for vesting the national government with the powers of general taxation, borrowing, and lending; for providing interior and exterior defense by national land and naval forces; and for vesting the United States with "a general superintendence of trade." The national government should also be vested with all powers relating to treaties and intercourse with foreign governments. He called for a convention of all the states to overhaul the Confederation to repair these defects. In his manuscript he left blanks to be filled in that would state the time, place, and dates of the great national convention that sooner or later he knew, in 1783, would some day have to be called—as it finally was in 1787.

During Hamilton's seven months in Congress, he had worked feverishly on the floor and in numberless committees to overcome weaknesses to which his twelve-point program pointed as defects of the Confederation. The states remained strong sovereign entities; Congress dawdled along without power and with little respect. The results had been few, and his most important resolutions had been buried in committee, tabled, or overwhelmingly voted down. This early call of his for a constitutional convention, with its dozen "essential points" that form a sketch of a federal constitution, is endorsed by his hand on the manuscript: "Resolution intended to be submitted to Congress at Princeton in 1783; but abandoned for want of support."

His wife and baby were also beginning to feel abandoned for want of support. On May 14 he notified Governor Clinton: "I wish two other gentlemen of the delegation may appear as soon as possible, for it would be very injurious for me to remain much longer here. Having no future views in public life, I owe it to myself without delay to enter upon the care of my private concerns in earnest."

Of New York's five delegates, only William Floyd and Hamilton had thought it important enough to attend Congress regularly, and Floyd had long since retired from the scene, leaving Hamilton to stand alone.

Repeating his request on June 1, he told Clinton he wanted to go home, and soon. Much as Clinton disliked the idea of a national Congress, he considered it necessary for New York to be represented by someone, even Hamilton, if only to keep him informed of any overly nationalistic actions there. Writing sharply to the other delegates, who had gone home, Clinton said, "It is the business of the Delegates to make such arrangements among themselves as to prevent the State being unrepresented, as I can have no agency therein but barely that of informing You of what ought not to have taken place."

On July 16 James Duane finally arrived in Princeton. After bringing Duane up-to-date, Hamilton immediately set out for Albany, finished with the Continental Congress. At the time of his leaving, Congress was but the shadow of a shadow. Only six of the thirteen states had any delegates present at all; and of these six, not one was fully represented. Hamilton's fellow members viewed his leaving with regret. During his short term, he had made a deep impression on them. Both those who agreed with him and those who opposed him knew he was a force to be reckoned with in the future.

James McHenry, having advised Hamilton to shun politics as he would a plague, had caught the contagion of the toga himself. Now in Congress as a delegate from Maryland, he passed along to his friend some good things he had heard. "The homilies you delivered in Congress are still recollected with pleasure," he told Hamilton. "The impressions they made are in favor of your integrity; and no one but believes you a man of honor and republican principles." McHenry added the familiar caveat that a private fortune remained a necessity not only for a congressman, but for still higher office. "Were you ten years older and twenty thousand pounds richer, there is no doubt but that you might obtain the suffrages of Congress for the highest office in their gift."

Hamilton had been learning the hard way McHenry's lesson about the need for private as well as public credit. He vowed in a letter to his friend Nathanael Greene on June 10 that as soon as New York was evacuated, "I shall set down there seriously on the business of making my fortune."

Cleaning out his desk on July 25, 1783, after nine months as delegate, Hamilton wrote John Jay, one of the commissioners who had negotiated the peace treaty, "I have been making a short apprenticeship in Congress." Now he was about to take leave of public life "to enter into the practice of law."

He added:

> We have now happily concluded the great work of independence, but much remains to be done to reap the fruits of it. Every day proves the inefficiency of the present Confederation; yet the common danger being removed, we are receding instead of advancing in a disposition to amend its defects. The road to popularity in each State is to inspire jealousies of the power of Congress, though nothing can be more apparent than that they have no power; and that for the want of it, . . . we at this moment experience all the mischiefs of a . . . ruined credit. It is to be hoped that when prejudice and folly have run themselves out of breath, we may return to reason and correct our errors.

As he rode out of Philadelphia, Hamilton left this letter to Jay with John and Angelica Church to deliver for him in Europe. They were just off "making a jaunt to Europe" with Church's business partner, Jeremiah Wadsworth.

Even though Jay already knew John and Angelica Church well, Hamilton went out of his way to call for Jay's civilities to them in "the warmest manner," adding that "I anticipate the pleasure" which Sarah Livingston Jay and Angelica would enjoy in each others' society "possessed as they both are of every quality to please and endear."

News of the mutinous army and other troubles against which Hamilton had taken up civilian arms in Congress had weakened Jay's hand in concluding the final peace treaty, as Hamilton had foreseen they would. Jay replied to Hamilton on September 28, 1783: "American news papers for some months past contain advices which do us Harm. . . . The Complaints of the army—The Jealousies respecting Congress—the Circumstances which induced their leaving Philadelphia—and the too little appearance of a national Spirit pervading uniting and invigorating the Confederacy, are considered as omens which portend the Diminution of our Respectability, Power and Felicity."

Foolish financial policies disturbed Jay too: "Our reputation also suffers from the apparent Reluctance to [taxes] and the Ease with which we incur Debts without providing for their Payment."

Worst of all was the lack of good faith shown by the dishonorable reprisals being taken against Tories in violation of the terms of the peace treaty: "Violences and associations against the Tories pay an ill compliment to Government and impeach our good Faith in the opinions of some, and our magnanimity in the opinion of many." Not only was harsh treatment of Tories a breach of good faith and the treaty, but it also built up ill will against America abroad:

> The Tories are almost as much pitied in these Countries, as they are execrated in our's. An undue Degree of Severity towards them would therefore be impolitic as well as unjustifiable: They who incline to involve that whole Class of Men in indiscriminate Punishment and Ruin, certainly carry the Matter too far—it would be an Instance of unnecessary Rigour and unmanly Revenge without a parallel except in the annals of religious Rage in Times of Bigotry and Blindness.

To his friend Hamilton, Jay was but preaching to an already convinced, likeminded believer.

All through the war, New York City had stood as the strategic bastion from which the British held sway over the Middle Atlantic and New England states. Loyalist sympathizers who had remained in the city during the occupation had been a great help to them. Hamilton had written to Robert Morris August 13, 1782, that of "the people of New York, in the early period of the war, nearly half of them were avowedly more attached to Great Britain than to their liberty." Now "The state by different means has been purged of a large part of its malcontent; but there remains I daresay a third whose secret wishes are on the side of the enemy."

New York State had been the principal battleground of the war and had suffered the most damage from both British and Continental armies marching and countermarching and raiding and foraging and looting. Proximity to the occupying forces had helped to produce more Tory sympathizers in New York than anywhere else; the same causes had produced more fervent Tory haters in New York than anywhere else. So the postwar conflicts between loyalists and patriots were sharper and harsher and more violent in New York than in any other state.

Passing through the city on his way back to Albany in August 1783, Hamilton wrote James Duane in alarm at the mass exodus of frightened loyalists from the city:

> Some late indictments [under the Confiscation Act] in our state have given great alarm here. Many who have all along talked of staying now talk of going. We have already lost too large a number of valuable citizens.

According to the report of the British Commissary General, some 29,000 loyalist refugees sailed out of New York in 1783, a number the population of the city itself would not attain until 1789. This pitiful mass exodus of innocent people made homeless because of ineradicable imputed guilt of holding political opinions unpopular with the winning side, so untypical of eighteenth-century wars, foreshadowed the mass tragedies typical of those of the twentieth.

From Albany, Hamilton wrote to Robert R. Livingston, distressed that "characters of no political consequence, each of whom may carry away eight to ten thousand guineas Have I am told lately applied for shipping to convey them away. Our state will feel for twenty years at least, the effects of the popular phrenzy."

Chancellor Livingston answered Hamilton with equal consternation:

> I seriously lament with you the violent spirit of persecution which prevails here and dread its consequences upon the wealth, commerce & future tranquility of the state . . . In some few it is a blind spirit of revenge & resentment but in more it is the most sordid interest. One wishes to possess the house of some wretched Tory, another fears him as a rival in his trade or commerce; and a fourth wishes to get rid of his debts by shaking of his creditor or to reduce the price of living by depopulating the town . . .

One man's poison is another man's meat. For Hamilton the public's persecution of loyalists was both political poison and practical meat or, at least, the bread and butter of his early law practice. He brought Elizabeth and little Philip down from Albany in November 1783. He took a house at 57 Wall Street for their home and space for an office next door at 56. With so many loyalists leaving, rentals with good New York addresses were plentiful and cheap. Former loyalists who remained were desperately trying to salvage their property from patriot persecutions and confiscation. Loyalists with money were eager to pay for such legal protection as a bona fide, cockade-wearing young patriot veteran like Alexander Hamilton could supply.

As he set up his new establishment on Wall Street, Hamilton must have been pleased to receive word from Congress and a friendly note of November 6 from George Washington of his promotion to colonel by brevet, after almost seven years at the same rank of lieutenant colonel. This was a promotion of one grade that Congress automatically granted to officers who, like Hamilton, had been stuck in the same grade all those years since 1777 upon their leaving the service. Although in itself it was the least of all possible promotions he could have won, it served as the essential stepping stone from which he would vault fifteen years later over the heads of all the other generals in the army, including his old commander Henry Knox, to the rank of senior major general, and inspector general of the army—second only in rank to George Washington himself.

Not surprisingly, the cheering throng of happy patriots who welcomed George Washington and Governor George Clinton on their triumphant entry into the city on November 25, 1783, betrayed not a single loyalist scowl.

"Straight as a ramrod and noble as he could be," appeared the Conqueror to one viewer, as he rode his magnificent gray horse at the head of the triumphal procession, followed by Governor Clinton on a fine bay gelding, Colonel Alexander Hamilton, and a retinue of aides and civil and military officials, all escorted by the smartly caparisoned Westchester Light Dragoons. Most were wearing union cockades on their left breast and a sprig of laurel on their hats. As the procession moved along the rural lane called the Bowery, past Tea Water Pump in Chatham Street, among the charred remains of houses that the patriots had burned to save from the British, Hamilton could just make out the ruins of the Bayard's Hill fort.

"We had been accustomed for a long time," a woman spectator wrote, "to military display in all the finish and finery of garrison life; the troops just leaving with their scarlet uniforms and burnished arms made a brilliant display; the troops that marched in, on the contrary, were ill clad and weather beaten, and made a forlorn appearance; but then they were *our* troops and as I looked at them and thought upon all they had done and suffered for us, my heart and my eyes were full, and I admired and gloried in them the more, because they were weather beaten and forlorn."

Like the marchers, many in the patriot crowds also wore union cockades and sprigs of laurel in their hats. The union cockade was the badge of the patriots "in compliment to his Excellency and our great and good ally," King Louis XVI of France. The procession drew rein under the swinging sign of Cape's Tavern, and a committee of leading citizens presented Washington with a speech of welcome, to which he replied:

> May the tranquility of your city be perpetual—may the ruins soon be repaired, commerce flourish, science be fostered, and all civil and social virtues be cherished . . . may every species of felicity attend you, Gentlemen, and your worthy fellow citizens.

His benediction took note of the devastation that 2,000 days of British occupancy had left. Two great fires had leveled 800 houses. With news of the peace treaty, British military occupation had given way to near anarchy. Patriots whose goods had been confiscated by loyalists began a devil take the hindmost scramble for reconfiscation and revenge as many Tories emigrated to safer climes—Canada, Bermuda, and England. Those who delayed or remained behind felt the full weight of mobs unleashed—their houses were sacked; their persons, violated. Some were tarred and feathered and driven from the town to roam the countryside like homeless curs.

Sir Guy Carleton, doing what little he could to control the patriot mobs, kept redcoat troops on hand until American troops could actually take their places at noon on November 25. As Washington and Hamilton moved in procession down the Broad Way, his oarsmen rowed Carleton over the bay to his waiting ship. On the Battery the Union Jack still fluttered over Fort George. The cavalcade from Cape's Tavern approached. Out on the bay, departing redcoats rested on their oars to watch the last imperial hurrah, prepared for a guffaw. One of their number had nailed the Union Jack to the top of the flagstaff, jammed the halyard, and greased the pole. There was no way the patriot arrangements committee would be able to pull the Union Jack down or run the Stars and Stripes up. The American artillery belched forth a salvo of salute at the appointed time. But it was to the wrong flag. Some patriot dignitaries were for climbing up the slippery mast; others for chopping it down. On the arrangements committee all was dither and disorder. Only Washington remained cool. Then out of the crowd stepped "a short, thickset man in sailor's dress" who proceeded "to shin up the flagstaff." He ripped down the Union Jack and finally unfurled the Stars and Stripes to the New York breeze.

After nine days of tributes and eulogies from all manner of patriot and civic organizations, church congregations, merchants, and trade associations, the time came for Washington's final farewell to the men who had been the officers of his army. It was at noon on Thursday, December 4, at Fraunces Tavern, at the corner of Broad and Pearl Streets in lower Manhattan. As he came in, Hamilton may have pointed out to one or another of the 40 or so officers of the rank of lieutenant colonel and above who were forgathering there the seven-year-old patch on the tavern's roof. He would explain that it covered the gaping hole through which shot from the *Asia's* poorly aimed cannon had crashed the night he and Hercules Mulligan and other stalwart student revolutionists of the Hearts of Oak had hauled other British cannon off the Battery and up the Broad Way to the Liberty Pole at The Fields. Of the officers present besides Washington, only Major Generals Henry Knox, von Steuben, and Alexander McDougall were of exalted rank. Former Colonel Aaron Burr was not among those present.

Washington filled his glass with wine and passed the decanter round. Each of the officers filled his own glass, and a few tentatively sampled the wine. They fell silent, and Washington spoke simply:

> With a heart full of love and gratitude, I now take leave of you. I most devoutly wish that your later days may be as properous and happy as your former ones have been glorious and honorable.

Nothing could be said for a moment more eloquent than the hush that fell. Then, after a silence, as one who was present wrote, Washington's words were answered by "warm expressions and fervent wishes from the gentlemen of the

Army whose truly pathetic feelings it is not in our power to convey to the reader."

In a spirit more like that of a communion than an American Legion convention, the old soldiers raised their glasses. By the time they had drained them to the lees, Washington's emotions had risen so high that tears began to blind his eyes. He did not fumble for his spectacles now. "I cannot come to each of you," he said in a faltering voice, "but shall feel obliged if each of you will come and take me by the hand."

Silently Henry Knox stepped forward and held out his hand. Washington extended his own. But the occasion called for more than a handshake. As he looked into Knox's honest eyes, he remembered what Knox had meant to him through their seven years together—beginning with hauling the Ticonderoga cannons over the ice to surprise the British from the heights of Dorchester—he flung his arms around his stout chief of artillery and, weeping, kissed him. Once done with Knox, the same embrace had to be done with all, starting with the grizzled von Steuben, continuing with Hamilton, and ending with the youngest of the officers. With streaming eyes, each moved up toward Washington, exchanged an affectionate hug with him, and moved on past in silence. None found it fit to utter even a word of admiration or thanks.

Benjamin Tallmadge, who had helped explode Arnold's treason at West Point, wrote long afterward that "the simple thought that we were then about to part from the man who had conducted us through a long and bloody war, and under whose conduct the glory and independence of our country had been achieved, and that we should see his face no more in this world seemed to me utterly insupportable."

Only Hamilton and Knox of all the day's distinguished company at Fraunces would see more active service with Washington in the peace to come than in the war now past.

When the last of the sobbing officers had ended his embrace, Washington walked across the room, raised his arm in an inclusive, silent farewell to them all, turned on his heel, and passed through the door, out of the tavern, between the open ranks of the waiting guard of honor, and along the street to Whitehall, toward the waterside. Hamilton and the other officers filed out after him, but remaining at a distance. At the crowded wharf where Washington took the barge made ready for instant departure for Mount Vernon, mothers held little children up over the heads of the throng to catch a glimpse of the tall man whose firmly set mouth, taut face muscles, and iron composure betrayed no trace of earlier tears. Without a word he boarded the barge. As it shoved off and moved down the harbor, both his arms once again swung wide from the sides of his erect, immobile frame at the stern. It was an all-embracing gesture of farewell, a gesture wide enough even to have encompassed once again the ample circumambience of General Henry Knox.

On the *Ceres*, the last of the British transports, down in the lower harbor now bearing away Sir Guy Carleton and his attendants, the boatswains happily piped "All hands" aloft to make sail; below decks they weighed anchor. The

Ceres caught the breeze in her topsails and rode down through the Narrows and out past Sandy Hook on the evening's ebbing tide for England and home.

Demand for Hamilton's services as a lawyer was strong even before the British had evacuated New York. The "Cash Book," which he maintained meticulously from March 1, 1782 through 1791, contains hundreds of entries, chiefly relating to his law practice, and occupies 60 pages as reproduced in Volume III of the Hamilton Papers. His first paying client seems to have been Isaac Sears, the ardent Son of Liberty who had led the raid on Rivington's *Gazetteer*. In the aftermath of Arnold's treason loyalist publication of an intercepted letter of Hamilton's wartime correspondence with Sears had served as the basis for charges that Hamilton and Washington were conspiring to install Washington as a military dictator.

Sears sent Hamilton a fee of £6 as a retainer for advice in a case one Soderstrom was about to begin. Soon Hamilton was receiving work from relations in the Albany area and drawing a memorial from the manor of "Rensselaerwick" to the legislature. Crusty old Robert Livingston, the lord of the manor, objected to the erection of grist mills on the property by his kinsman, Chancellor Robert R. Livingston, and threatened to tear them down. Another kinsman, Brockholst Livingston, urged the former to retain Hamilton: "His opinion will be well worth having, & in case it be determined to pursue your claims by action, his assistance will be very material."

Old Robert Livingston swore up and down he would smash the trespassing mills. Hamilton did his best to calm his irate client. He warned that "the very act [of pulling down the mills] would have an appearance of passion which might raise prepossessions against his right." An action of trespass *quare clausam fregit*, as explained in Hamilton's *Practical Proceedings*, was the more properly prudent tactic.

Hamilton was one of 35 lawyers listed in David Frank's *New York Directory* for 1786. Others, who were sometimes opposing counsel in one case and on the same side with him in the next, were Robert Troup at 67 Wall Street, Brockholst Livingston at No. 12, and John Laurence at No. 15. Aaron Burr was at No. 10, Little Queen [Cedar] Street and Edward Livingston at No. 51. Richard Varick was at 46 Dock Street and Morgan Lewis at 59 Maiden Lane.

The range of their practice was as broad as the law itself. Hamilton was a specialist in everything, an expert in all fields. He gave advice in his office and prepared deeds, mortgages, wills, contracts, and business charters. He gave opinions on insurance coverages and title deeds to property that created or denied legal rights; he handled civil suits in trial courts and argued appeals. He was not above handling the defense of a criminal charge of rape, like one in which his client, one Murphy, was charged with assault on one Margaret Russell "with force and Arms to wit with Sword and Stones and Knives . . . with intent her said Margaret, an infant . . . to Ravish and Deflour . . . so that her life was greatly despaired of and other enormities." He appeared in the mayor's court, traveled on circuit, drew memorials to the New York legislature and to Congress, and handled affairs for John Barker Church and other clients in Europe.

He had a busy practice in the New York Supreme Court of Judicature, which met alternatively in Albany and in New York City.

His fees at the beginning were small, usually one pound as a retainer; £5 a day plus expenses for trying a case on circuit, with additional contingent fees sometimes based on results obtained for his client. He refused some cases that seemed to go against his professional principles and preferred fees that he thought were excessive. His retainer of $1,000 in one case was endorsed by him "returned as being more than is proper." Relatives often figured in his practice, and so did friends—Robert Morris, John Jay, Timothy Pickering, John Holt, Benjamin Walker, Lewis Pintard, and many others. The Bank of New York, of which he was a founder, would also send along new business. Only Robert Lansing, Burr, and one or two others, who had been practising longer, had more cases. In Hamilton's frequent enforced absences, as at Philadelphia, Annapolis, and Poughkeepsie and in Congress, Hamilton's old friends, like Troup, Laurence, and Balthasar de Haert filled in and substituted for him. He reciprocated by returning the favor for them in their absences.

Leading men besought him to take promising young men into his office as pupil-clerks. Pierre Van Cortlandt and Dirk Ten Broeck commenced in February 1784, paying the usual fee of $150, and Jacob A. Le Roy came in May, but he dropped out and the payment was refunded to his father. John Adams, who at the time did not know Hamilton personally, entered his son July 20, 1789, but the $20 installment of tuition was remitted when Hamilton was called into Washington's cabinet. Joseph Strong served the full three years' clerkship "in the business of an attorney," but Samuel Broome, Jr., could take the grind for only seven months. Hamilton was no easy task master. Dirk Ten Broeck wrote to Simeon Baldwin in 1784, reminiscing about the joys of the jolly college life they had led 'neath the elms of dear old Yale. He confided what he really thought about his apprenticeship with Hamilton: "But now instead of all the happiness once so near to view, I am deeply engaged in the study of law, the attaining of which, requires the sacrifice of every pleasure, demands unremitted application: six long months have passed since my commencing the study of this noble science, heavy for the most part have been the hours to me . . ." Hamilton's office did nothing to impair the renown of Wall Street lawyers for hard work.

Chancellor James Kent spoke with expert knowledge not only of the New York bar but of all American law, and his opportunity for observation commenced at about the time of Hamilton's first appearances in the courts. Eight years younger than Hamilton, he was near enough in age to cherish an intimate friendship and at the same time enough younger to idolize him, a rare enough thing for a judge to do for a practicing lawyer at any age. Describing for young lawyers of another generation the legal personalities and character of law practice during the years after the Revolution, he wrote that the field was left to "a number of ambitious and high spirited young men" most of them fresh from service in the army. Burr was acute, terse; Brockholst Livingston, copious, fluent; Troup, sensible and thorough; Richard Harison, scholarly and lucid; Samuel Jones was a master of older precept and practice. "But among all his brethren, Colonel Hamilton was indisputably pre-eminent," promptly earning recognition for his grasp and frankness. He benefited by the "most active business" in "the claims of real property," which opened with the peace and at the same time helped inform American jurisprudence with reliable English precedents.

Kent also noted that Hamilton "never made any argument in court without displaying his habits of thinking, and resorting at once to some well-founded principle of law, and drawing his deductions logically from his premises. Law was always treated by him as a science founded on established principles. His manners were gentle, affable and kind. He appeared to be frank, liberal, and courteous in all his professional intercourse."

Robert Troup, Hamilton's closest lawyer friend, who had instructed him in the practice when they had shared a house in Albany in the summer of 1782, observed that Hamilton did not parade a knowledge of case law, intending it as a compliment: "But if you stated a Case to him, and allowed him time to examine the Reporters, he would . . . give an opinion that would bear the test of the severest discussion." He did not clutter his mind with citations. Troup put his finger on the secret of Hamilton's success as a winning lawyer: his ability to expand or contract the legal frame of reference to the size that would encompass the winning argument and elevate earnest advocacy into art: "Never failing to be busied . . . in politics, he had only time to read elementary books. Hence he was well grounded in first principles," which he applied "with wonderful facility, to every question he argued."[1]

Many thought that Hamilton's only peer among the lawyers at the postwar New York bar was Aaron Burr. Becoming a member of the New York Assembly, which sat in the city, Burr also took up a lifelong career of speculating in stocks and real estate as well. One contemporary described him as "acute, quick, terse, polished, sententious, and sometimes sarcastic in his forensic discussions." Burr loved the joy of legal combat and reveled in sly courtroom tactics, reconnaissance, strategem, ambuscade, and flanking movements. He liked to raise eyebrows and hackles by smilingly defining law as "whatever is boldly asserted and plausibly maintained." Whether in society or in court, he was *suaviter in modo, fortiter in re.* He was a Lord Chesterfield transplanted to New York, full of precise epigrams that struck to the heart of a jury—or a mistress. He carried all five feet six inches of himself rigidly with a thrusting stride. From under a dark head of hair, a bulging brow rose above a face that sloped down to a chin "rather retreating and voluptuous." His nose jutted strongly forward, slightly bent to his right, giving his demeanor the effect of a hawk about to pounce. His dark eyes "glow[ed] with all the ardor of venereal fire."

Hamilton had never formally joined any church, but he and Betsy must have just walked home from a service at Trinity, a block down Wall Street, that had included the General Confession, when he wrote to Gouverneur Morris, his witty friend from the Bronx, one Sunday in the Spring of 1784: "We are doing those things which we ought not to do, and leaving undone those things which we ought to do. Instead of wholesome regulations for the improvement of our polity and commerce, we are laboring to contrive methods to mortify and punish Tories and to explain away treaties."

The distinctive specialty that set Hamilton apart from Burr and most other

New York lawyers was the series of cases he was handling for former British
sympathizers. Beginning in 1779 with the Confiscation Act, under which "attainted" loyalists were made to forfeit their property, the state legislature had
passed a series of harsh laws aimed at Tories. Under the Trespass Act of 1783,
New Yorkers who had fled their property when the British came could bring
suits for damages against those who had stayed behind and occupied it. Hamilton handled at least 45 cases in all under the Trespass Act and 20 more under
other antiloyalist laws.

When the mayor's court of the city of New York reopened formally for the
first time after the British occupation on February 10, 1784, James M. Hughes,
who had been admitted to the bar in January of that year, described the ceremonies sardonically to his fellow commentator on the New York legal scene, James
Kent:

The gentlemen of the bar of the day "met at Cape's Tavern—and issued
forth like so many devils from their abodes—preceded by Mr. Mayor . . . Proclamation was made commanding silence while his Worship's commission was read
—then his Worship put his parchment in his pocket . . . Then sir, a proclamation
was made for adjournment—and then we did adjourn accordingly to Simmons
Tavern—and guzzled some Hot Punch and wine & bitters at the expense of his
Worship and then, sir, every man went his own way—the lawyers to hunt clients
—the clerk to hunt a printer to print blanks in and his Worship to hunt law—
and so sir—let the devil run a hunting with his Worship, clerk—lawyers and all
—and now sir, as this is as much nonsense as a man of your propriety and
understanding can well bear—I'll have done."

Hamilton and Burr would have been there guzzling and chasing too. His
Worship the Mayor was Hamilton's correspondent and congressional colleague
James Duane, now doubling as presiding jurist of the mayor's court. The moment Hamilton walked out the door, gossip at Cape's and Simmons's must have
buzzed with the question of why a leading patriot and military hero like Alexander Hamilton, the leader of New York's infantry in the winning charge at
Yorktown, who had so many rich patriots as relations and clients, should risk
popularity with them and a bright political future as well by becoming the
defender of these loyalists against suits brought in the name of the patriot cause.
A poem in the New York *Journal* of January 1784, addressed to Hamilton in
the name of "To Lysander," expressed the widespread revulsion at his position:

> Wilt thou Lysander, on this well earned height,
> Forget thy merits and thy thirst of same;
> Descend to learn of law, her arts and slight,
> And for a job to damn your honored name!

In the convivial company at Cape's and Simmons's Taverns, no fellow lawyer, even in his cups, would be so unsophisticated as to say of another that he
was taking a loyalist's cause, or any other, for the sake of a principle. His
colleagues would good-naturedly shrug off Hamilton's aberration by assuming

that he took such cases only for the fees. Hamilton would have smilingly agreed with them. But privately, Hamilton would fall back on principle. It was time to put an end to "Tory baiting" and get on with the business of building a United States. He wrote his friend Gouverneur Morris, "we have assumed an independent station; we ought to feel and to act in a manner consistent with the dignity of that station."

British troops still occupied posts on northern and western frontiers of New York State and remained a constant threat to New York's flourishing fur trade. Hamilton cautioned Governor Clinton that he "ought to take care that nothing is done to furnish a pretext on the other side, even for delaying much less for refusing the execution of the treaty." He reminded the New York Committee of Correspondence of a certain general who had advised his son when the son had the Roman army in his power "either to destroy them utterly or to dismiss them with every mark of honor and respect." By the first method, "you disable the Romans from being your enemies, by the last you make them your friends." The lesson Hamilton drew was that "with respect to the Tories I would either disable them from doing us any injury, or I would endeavor to gain their friendship by clemency. Inflicting trifling punishments only embitters the minds of those on whom they fall, and increases their disposition to do mischief without taking away the power of doing it." Hamilton would check his own convictions against his colleagues' jibes—at what they considered to be either his eccentricity or his greed—by searching classical history for precedents for the anomalous position in which he seemed to place himself by insisting on what he thought was right policy. There was the Athenian general, Phocion, for example, whose loyalty to his city had been certified by valiant services in many battles. But after the crushing defeat of Athens by Philip of Macedon at Chaeronea in 338 B.C., Phocion obtained unusually lenient terms from the conqueror for his city without tricking him and won the confidence of both sides. Under the limited democracy that followed, Phocion became the virtual ruler of the city. Hamilton's moderate position, which was, of course, the essence of good government, made him unpopular with both sides unless a change in popular opinion came. He set to bring about the change by publishing a broadside in the press, a "Letter from Phocion to the Considerate citizens of New York" in January, 1784. In it, he sought to calm fears that the British would reconquer the United States with the help of traitorous loyalists from their fortresses on the northern frontiers. He pointed out calmly that no loyalist threat was imminent. To suppose that the loyalists would take over the government "is to suppose that a majority of the numbers, property and abilities of the United States had been and is in opposition to the Revolution." It was absurd to expel a small number from the city, "which would constitute so insignificant a proportion of the whole, as without diminishing their influence, would only increase their disposition to do mischief . . ."

The idea of having Tories "live among us under disqualifications, is equally mischievous and absurd." It would mean that a large body of citizens in the state would continue to be enemies of the government, ready, at all times, in a moment of commotion, "to throw their weight into that scale which mediates a change whether favorable or unfavorable to public liberty . . ." Hamilton cited the wise policy of the Emperor Augustus, "Who, after conquering his enemies, when the papers of Brutus were brought to him, which would have disclosed all his secret associates, immediately ordered them to be burned." He wanted no enemies' list. "He would not even know his enemies, that they might cease to hate when they had nothing to fear."

Queen Elizabeth, too, "when she was transferred from the prison to the throne, fell upon her knees and thanking heaven, for the deliverance it had granted her, from her bloody persecutors; dismissed her resentment." Hamilton noted that "She buried all offenses in oblivion, and received with affability even those, who had acted with the greatest virulence against her." She did more; she wisely retained many of the opposite party in her councils.

He then drew the political lesson to be learned and relearned by politicians of all places and ages: "The reigns of these two sovereigns are among the most illustrious in history. Their moderation gave a stability to their government, which nothing else could have affected. This was the secret of uniting all parties."

Hamilton's first "Phocion" letter is one of the most one-sided briefs in favor of moderation ever written.

Seriously concerned as he was about Tory-baiting, Hamilton could see as well as any of his colleagues the amusing paradox of advocating on principle a policy from which he stood to profit. Corresponding privately with his friend Gouverneur Morris, he joked, "legislative folly has afforded so plentiful a harvest to us lawyers that we have scarcely a moment to spare from the substantial business of reaping."

Governor Clinton snorted at Phocion's broadside and swore many a popular Populistic oath that he would "rather roast in hell to all eternity than be dependent upon Great Britain or show mercy to a damned Tory." Tories were arrested, imprisoned, fined, and banished. Under the Confiscation Act, goods and estates of "attainted" Tories were placed on an "enemies list" and confiscated and sold.

Clinton's backers like "Mentor," probably Clinton's friend Isaac Ledyard, rushed into print to rebut Hamilton's "Phocion" letter, ending with a furious personal attack on Hamilton for casting aspersions on the personal motives of political opponents like Clinton. Clinton accused Hamilton of displaying "in an eminent degree, that great disqualification for a statesman, an uncontrollable warmth of temper." Of the many different attitudes taken by Hamilton in his expository prose, an apologetic stance is among the rarest. His apology to Clinton and "Mentor" in his second "Phocion" letter is a rare example:

> I shall take occasion to acknowledge, with regret, the injudicious appearance of warmth in my former letter; calculated with many minds, to raise prejudices against the truths it contains . . . I shall only observe an apology . . . that whatever the severity of animadversion may have been indulged, was wholly directed against a *very small* number of men, who are manifestly aiming at nothing, but the acquisition of power and profit to themselves. . . .

"Mentor" and Governor Clinton were not included in this *very small* group.

Despite this apology, the furor grew. Many small farmers, mechanics, artisans, and merchants rallied to crush the Tories and their apologist, Hamilton. Hotheads proposed to challenge him one by one to a series of duels until a bullet should finally erase him. Ledyard, apparently satisfied by Hamilton's apology, heard of this scheme and curbed the hotheads, and they agreed to drop the challenges. When Hamilton heard of Ledyard's intervention, he thanked him for it. Ledyard soon deserted Clinton and reenlisted as an ally of Hamilton, demonstrating the power of a positive apology.

Hamilton's pen names for his public papers seem to expose his otherwise hidden inner thoughts about his public role. Phocion, according to Plutarch, espoused "the cause of those who differed most from him, when they needed his patronage!" Phocion "distinguished himself by advocating the recall and forgiveness of those who had been banished." So far was Phocion from humoring or courting mass public opinion that "he always thwarted and opposed them." Once when he told the people his opinion, and they applauded, Phocion turned to some of his friends and asked, "Have I inadvertently said something foolish?" At first, public acclaim bestowed on Phocion the name of "the Good," but public opinion shifted and condemned him to death without a hearing. A short while later, opinion shifted again, a public burial was decreed, and a statue was erected in Phocion's honor.

When the Mayor's Court of New York City took up the case of *Rutgers versus Waddington* in the spring of 1784, today's indisputable constitutional principle that a treaty is the supreme law of the land had never been heard of.

In time, the case came to stand for the principle that the sanctity of treaties and the good faith of the national government would be upheld by the courts against contrary state legislation. A more momentous constitutional doctrine has never been invented by a less momentous tribunal than Mayor James Duane's, whose jurisdiction was on the judicial ground level where magistrate's courts are found today.

Elizabeth Rutgers, a widow in her seventies, was one of thousands of patriots who had fled New York City when Washington, Hamilton, and the rest of the army had abandoned it to the British in 1776. She left behind a brewery and a malt house on Maiden Lane, which the British Commissary General quickly commandeered "for the use of the Army."

By the time the British Commissary General signed it over to Benjamin Waddington and Evelyn Pierrepont two years later in 1778, it was so "stripped of everything of any value" that before they could begin brewing beer again, they had to spend about £700 on extensive repairs and build a storehouse, a stable, and an enclosure for firewood. Waddington and Pierrepont occupied the brewery without paying rent to anyone until May 1, 1780, when the British commander in chief ordered them to pay rent of £150 per year to John Smythe, the British agent, who, in turn, gave the money to the vestry for the poor. On June 20, 1783, anticipating the British evacuation of New York, General Birch, the British commandant, ordered Waddington to start paying the rent to Mrs.

Rutgers's son Anthony Rutgers, who was acting as her agent, retroactive to May 1, 1783. But Rutgers demanded back rent for all seven years of occupation, not just the past two months; so he refused to accept the 1783 payments in settlement. Waddington argued that all the improvements he had paid for were a full offset to the back rent and offered to settle with Rutgers on that basis. Rutgers refused.

On November 23, 1783, just two days before the British had evacuated the city, the fire that destroyed much of the rest of New York had reduced the brewery "to ashes," causing a loss Waddington estimated at upwards of £4,000. In December, Waddington and Pierrepont handed over the storehouse and stable keys to Rutgers and sought to settle accounts with him. Rutgers again refused. He now brought suit in the Mayor's Court of the city of New York in February 1784 against Waddington and Pierrepont for £8,000 of back rent under the infamous Trespass Act. Passed by the New York legislature at Clinton's urging on March 17, 1783, this short law declared that a refugee from the enemy, like Mrs. Rutgers, might "bring an Action of Trespass against any Person or Persons who may have occupied, injured, or destroyed his . . . Estate . . . within the Power of the Enemy . . . ," as Waddington and Pierrepont had done. The plaintiff's success in such an action was all but guaranteed by the additional provision of the Trespass Act that the "Defendant would not be allowed to plead in Justification," any military order or command whatever, of the enemy, for such occupancy, injury, destruction, purchase, or receipt. The act also provided that a suit like Mrs. Rutgers's might be brought in "any inferior court within this state"—the Mayor's Court was such an "inferior" court. The legislature thought that local magistrates were the tribunals most likely to be sympathetic to aggrieved patriots.

All of this was contrary to the spirit, if not the letter, of Article V of the peace treaty, which provided that Congress should "earnestly recommend" to the states that they restore the rights and possessions of loyalists who had not borne arms against their countrymen.

To the man in the street, *Rutgers* was a melodrama whose plot pitted a forlorn, aged patriot widow who had been hounded out of her home and done out of her rent against two British brewers who had lived high at her expense for the past seven years. When the attorney general of New York State, Egbert Benson, agreed to take the widow Rutgers's side of the case, in association with John Laurence, William Wilcox, and Hamilton's old friend Robert Troup, it took on aspects of a political morality play. It would inflame passions on both sides of the feud that was beginning to smoulder between Whigs and Tories. And when Alexander Hamilton, Brockholst Livingston, and Morgan Lewis agreed to enter the lists as defense counsel for Waddington, the case took on a third dimension—as a battle of the emerging new legal titans as well. Hamilton's co-counsel, Brockholst Livingston, would one day sit on the Supreme Court of the United States, and Morgan Lewis, having married the sister of Chancellor Robert R. Livingston, would have a notable career as a member of the State Assembly, attorney general, justice of the Supreme Court, and chief justice. By defeating Aaron Burr in the hotly contested gubernatorial election of the un-happy spring of 1804, he would contribute to Burr's compulsion to challenge Hamilton to a duel.

Rutgers would be the test case for the new antiloyalist laws. The prospects of recovery by hundreds of other New York patriots rode with Mrs. Rutgers and her son. For them, the able attorney general would defend a perfectly explicit state law, which had the enthusiastic approval of most citizens and politicians.

Whether he won or lost, merely taking Waddington's case exposed Hamil-ton as his champion to social and political odium, at least in the short run. The more effectively Hamilton argued for his client, the deeper the odium would be. If by any chance the verdict should go to Hamilton's client, the public's disgust and sense of outrage would run deep.

Tension ran high in the city when the case came on for argument on June 29, 1784, before Mayor Duane. He presided with a sharp "surveying eye," flanked by recorder Richard Varick, and associate judges Alderman Benjamin Blagge, William W. Gilbert, William Neilson, Thomas Randall, and Thomas Ivers.

Mayor Duane himself was under great political pressure from patriots. They sent him condolences because "the hands of violence and rapacity, have these long years been raging through our State & particularly your City . . . , where thousands have been ruined . . . by these Barbarians. . . ."

The basic facts were not in dispute; so the result would turn on the elo-quence and ingenuity of the lawyers in fashioning arguments based on the applicable law alone. That was the real question—as it usually is in great cases—what was the meaning of applicable law, and how did it fit the facts of this case?

Laurence, followed by Wilcox, opened for the plaintiff and stood on the statute, which was clear and explicit. Elizabeth Rutgers had been an inhabitant of New York City, left it when the British came, and never came back; Wadding-ton occupied her property. She suffered loss and sustained damage, and so on. Given the facts and the law of the Trespass Act, they argued, judgment for plaintiff Elizabeth Rutgers had to follow as the night the day.

Hamilton's defense plea was what lawyers call a demurrer, perhaps to keep a simple thing from sounding too simple to nonlawyers. In plain English, by his demurrer, he simply admitted all the facts of the trespass, but said, in effect, that the law that applied to the facts was different from what the plaintiff claimed or had a different effect and that, accordingly, Mrs. Rutgers was not entitled to recover. He justified Waddington's occupation on the grounds first of the law of nations and second by the treaty of peace. Livingston, Lewis, and Hamilton all argued in turn for the defendant, but Hamilton's argument embraced the other two and made the most powerful impression.

Hamilton argued that New York's Trespass Act was in violation of the law of nations and, therefore, void. New York, by its state constitution, had received and adopted the common law of England as the law of the land in New York; the common law of England included the law of nations, which, in turn, included the laws of war. According to the laws of war, the captors had the right to use real property while that property was under military control. So Waddington had thus derived the right of the captor to use Elizabeth Rutgers's brewhouse. To subject Waddington to liability to Mrs. Rutgers would violate the law of nations, the English common law, and hence the law of New York. No state legislature had the right to alter, or the power to violate, the law of nations. That power must necessarily reside only in Congress, to which each of the states had delegated the exclusive management of its foreign affairs. So, Hamilton concluded with a flourish, the state's Trespass Act, being in violation of the law of nations, was void.

This was strong legal medicine.

Second, the states had delegated to Congress the exclusive power to conclude treaties of peace, including the treaty of peace with England, and thus Congress necessarily possessed the "implied power" to include all reasonable conditions in the treaty. Because the treaty provided that the two countries released each other from all claims for injury or damage to individuals that one or the other might have done to the other—"in consequence of or in any-wise relating to the war"—and because Waddington was a British subject and merchant, "under the protection of the Army and of the said King," this plea argued that Mrs. Rutgers's claim against Waddington had been released or abrogated by the treaty.

Besides, Hamilton went on to argue, the law of nations implies in every final treaty of peace a general amnesty for all public and private injuries arising from the war; therefore, Congress, in approving the treaty, must have consented to a general amnesty. Observance of the treaty was obligatory on the states both by virtue of Congress's implied power and by its specific resolution on the matter. Therefore, no state legislature had the power to violate the treaty and the resolution, and any state law that did so was void.

Hamilton's third argument, interweaving the first two, was that if the Trespass Act were void, either because it was a state law in violation of the law of nations or because it was a state law in violation of the treaty, a state court, even an "inferior" court like the Mayor's Court, had the power and the obligation to declare the statute void and refuse to give it effect. When laws from two different sources came into conflict, a court must apply the law that "relates to" the higher authority in derogation of the law that relates to the lesser authority.

Hamilton shrewdly coupled this lofty third argument, which rested on the broadest possible grounds, with a narrow fourth argument that was more appropriate to a trial court of first impression with no power of review. The Trespass Act simply did not apply to the facts of this case because it failed to say in so many words that it was intended to overrule the peace treaty and the law of nations.

This shrewdly showed the court a narrow way to decide the case in favor of his client without having to strike down the Trespass Act directly.

"Forget the Trespass Act!" Robert Troup pleaded in rebuttal to Hamilton's argument, bringing things back down to earth with a bump out of the legal empyrean into which Hamilton had lifted them.

Even if Hamilton were right and the Trespass Act had given Mrs. Rutgers no right to recover damages, Troup argued, she should still recover from Waddington in the old common law action of trespass *quare clausum fregit.* Under the common law, a man's house is his castle, every man has the right to exclusive possession and use of his property, and every breach or entry of this enclosure, as Waddington had entered Mrs. Rutgers's, carried along with it some damage, if for nothing else than "the treading down and bruising of his herbage." Thus Mrs. Rutgers might win on either of two grounds, Troup argued—the Trespass Act or the action of common law trespass. Troup granted with a chuckle that under the common law, some trespasses were justified, such as, for example, the pursuit of "ravenous beasts of prey as badgers and foxes" onto another man's land. But unfortunately for Hamilton's client, there were no "ravenous beasts of prey" prowling on downtown Maiden Lane that would justify Waddington's trespass.

Hamilton was about to be laughed out of court.

To find a justification for Waddington's trespass that was more plausible than the absurd idea of a "ravenous badger" in Maiden Lane, Hamilton had to dig back again into first principles. According to the law of nations, he argued, the use of abandoned property was justifiable in time of war when authorized by the military commander in charge of occupation forces. Such a justification was also a part of the law of New York, Hamilton urged, because as he had said before, the law of nations was deemed to be a part of the common law, which had been received as New York state law by the state constitution of 1777. Since the Trespass Act of 1783 expressly prohibited pleading military orders and authorizations by way of justification, that act was in direct conflict with the law of nations as incorporated into New York law by New York's own state constitution. The state constitution being a higher authority than an ordinary law like the Trespass Act, it overrode the act, if the act purported to cut off the defense of "justifiable" trespass.

The notes Hamilton spoke from when making the great argument are revealing. At the outset he would pose the "IMPORTANCE of the case . . . from its influence on the national character—May be discussed in Europe; and may make good or ill impressions according to the event." Next was the *"Necessity* of preserving inviolate the rules which regulate the Great Society of Nations." But he was aware that if he announced this too abruptly, it would be much too startling for a mayor's court to swallow. So he had crossed it out and substituted a gradual approach by several steps. He devoted a whole section to the importance of national sovereignty: "As well a County may alter the laws of the State as the State those of the Confederation." The subordination of local to national authority in all matters touching obligations to foreign governments was essential: "Legislation of one State cannot repeal [the] law of [the] United States. All must be construed to stand together." To make the defendant liable "would be to violate the laws of nations . . . a solemn treaty of peace & revive [a] state of hostility." It would be to infringe the Confederation "& endanger [the] peace of the union." He would pause in horror and stare into the face of each judge in turn before posing the rhetorical question: "Can we suppose all of this to have been intended by the Legislature?" and then triumphantly answer his own question: "if it was intended the act is void!"

Chancellor Kent, then only a clerk in the office of Attorney General Egbert Benson, recorded his impressions of some of the lawyers who had been on the case. Livingston, he said, was "copious, fluent, abounding in skillful criticism and beautiful reflections." He had "a cultivated and elegant taste," and his strength lay in "ingenious and sprightly illustration, and in popular and animated addresses to the jury." Robert Troup, "uniting good sense with accurate practice," presented his arguments with "simplicity, earnestness and a winning candor, which commanded invariable attention and respect." Of Benson, his own mentor, Kent commented carefully that, like Samuel Jones, he was a master of the old school of practice. Combining "great quickness and acuteness of mind," Benson "was accustomed to carry his researches back to the recesses and grounds of the law, and to rest his opinion and argument on solid elementary principles." Of Laurence and Hamilton: ". . . Colonel Laurence was graceful, fluent and ingenious; but Colonel Hamilton, by means of his fine melodious voice and dignified deportment, his reasoning powers and persuasive address, soared far above all competition. His pre-eminence was at once universally conceded . . . The audience listened with admiration to his impassioned eloquence. . . ."

Hamilton rested, the defense rested, the court took the case *sub judice*, and Duane and his fellow judges pondered their verdict for more than two months. The anxious lawyers must have sent their clerks up to the court house almost every day to inquire of the clerk there whether a decision had yet been handed down. By now, of course, as often happens in such cases, the humdrum details of the rent dispute between Mrs. Rutgers and Mr. Waddington had all but been forgotten as lawyers and judges soared dizzily out of laymen's sight into murky clouds of legal learning.

While the public and the bar waited anxiously and the judges wrestled with their doubts, other war cases were held up because all recognized that *Rutgers v. Waddington* was the great test case, with international repercussions. There were indications that the British would not relinquish their Western posts at Niagara, at Oswego, on the St. Lawrence, Lake Champlain, and elsewhere in other Western territories until persecutions of loyalists in violation of Articles IV, V, and VI of the treaty were stopped—issues that would continue to reverberate for a decade until after Jay's Treaty.

Politically, *Rutgers v. Waddington* polarized the division between upstate Populist patriots and downstate merchants, businessmen, and small holders who sympathized with the loyalists' plight and feared that British reprisals against trade would be costly to them. For Hamilton, the case was a forge on which he hammered out and refined many important ideas on constitutional national government for which he would fight the rest of his life. For his role as defense counsel, he would never cease to be stamped with guilt by association of "monarchical" and pro-British leanings.

Finally, on Friday, August 27, 1784, the great decision day came. Duane delivered the opinion of the court, which he appeared to have written largely himself. He acknowledged the case to be one "of high importance; from the value of the property, which in this and other actions depends on the same principles; from involving in it questions, which must affect the national character:—questions whose decision will record the spirit of our courts to posterity! Questions which embrace the whole law of nations!"

He saw humor in the fact that a magistrate's court like his should hear a case of such magnitude. As "Magistrates actively engaged in establishing the police of a disordered city, and in other duties," they were "cut off from those studious researches, which great and intricate questions require."

He drily complimented all the attorneys for filling them in, on the "great and intricate question," noting that the "arguments on both sides were elaborate, and the authorities numerous."

As to the period between 1778 and 1780, when Waddington had paid no rent to anyone, while the brewery had been commandeered by the British commissary general, purportedly "for the use of the Army," Waddington owed rent to Mrs. Rutgers. Duane found that the Commissary General was really a civilian official, not directly under orders of the British military occupation forces. But as to the period from May 1, 1780, through March, 1783, Hamilton's plea was "good and sufficient in the law." This meant that during this period, when Waddington had paid rent to the British agent, John Smythe, for the vestry poor box, he had no liability to pay a second time to Mrs. Rutgers. The treaty would protect Waddington because he had been under direct authority from the British commander in chief. An order from a civilian official would be invalid in any event; so the question of whether the Trespass Act forbade pleading it was not reached; on the other hand, an order from the commander in chief was valid under the law of nations; so the Trespass Act did not apply to it, either, Duane reasoned.

Beneath such metaphysical hairsplitting, Duane's actual decision of the rent dispute represented a politic and Solomonic disposition of the case: in a sense, he cut the baby in half by reaching the equitable result that simply excused Waddington from having to pay the same rent twice. On balance, Hamilton's client had won, but the result and Duane's reasoning were sufficiently murky for all sides to take some satisfaction from it.

What did the decision really mean? It straddled Mrs. Rutgers's argument that the authority of the state legislature was supreme; it also straddled Hamilton's argument that the law of nations and the treaty were supreme and that the state legislature was not. It was almost studiously ambiguous, complex, and scholarly. It entirely pleased neither plaintiff nor defendant, patriot nor loyalist. It hinted at things more far-reaching than anything it actually decided.

On the separate question of damages, the jury of twelve citizens met at Simmons's Tavern near City Hall and awarded a verdict of £791 13s. 4d. damages and sixpence costs to Mrs. Rutgers, and this amount was adopted as the judgment of the court. It fell far short of the £8,000 she had sued for; so she appealed to the state supreme court. But in July 1785, while her appeal was still pending, "a voluntary compromise between the parties took place, which superseded its prosecution to a final decision." Waddington paid something additional to her, but it is likely that his final payment was much nearer the £791 verdict than the £8,000 she had sued for. Hamilton's fee for defending the case and securing the settlement? £9 11 s. 3d. It seems absurdly small, even for those days.

But the public sensed that Phocion had won a mysterious victory. The legislature took the decision to be a direct attack upon its power, and the assembly adopted a resolution attacking the decision as "subversive of all law and good order." If a court could "dispense with, and act in direct violation of a plain and known law of the state," it would "end all our dear bought rights and privileges, and legislatures become useless." A committee published an open letter charging that "the mayor's court have assumed and exercised the power to set aside an act of the state." It attacked the decision as "an assumption of power in that court, which is inconsistent with the nature and genius of our government, and threatening to the liberties of the people."

There was a motion to impeach Duane. It called for his ouster and for a new mayor and recorder for the city to be designated who "will govern themselves by the known laws of the land." It lost 31 to 9.

George Washington commented that "reason seems very much in favor of the opinion given by the court, and my judgment yields a hearty assent to it."

For the next decade and beyond, echoes of *Rutgers v. Waddington* would reverberate and rumble through much American foreign and domestic policy.

In 1787 Hamilton successfully argued in New York for repeal of the Trespass Act, Citation Act, and Confiscation Act on the same grounds he had first urged in *Rutgers v. Waddington*. Hamilton's *Federalist Papers* of 1788, particularly number 78, amplified and refined the policy and theory of judicial supremacy that he had introduced in his Mayor's Court argument.

In 1792, when the British minister, George Hammond, claimed that the decision tended to repudiate the peace treaty, Secretary of State Thomas Jefferson, a lawyer himself, asked Hamilton to write to him and explain what the case really meant.

Hamilton's summary, written May 5, 1792, explained that the force of the treaty to overrule the provision of the Trespass Act against pleading a military order "was admitted by the decision, which allowed in fact the validity of such an order, when proceeding from the Commander-in-Chief." On the basis of Hamilton's opinion, Jefferson rebutted Hammond's claim, pointing out that this was "an unequivocal decision of the superior authority of the Treaty over the law." In fact, although Duane's reasoning had left the whole question hanging in midair, Hamilton's analysis as quoted above is correct whereas Jefferson's encapsulation is an overstatement.

In the aftermath of Jay's Treaty and with the passage of time, the facts of the case were forgotten, the persecution of loyalists died down, the British evacuated the Western posts, the immediate passions that gave rise to *Rutgers v. Waddington* subsided, and all that remained was the imprint of the case preserved in the United States Constitution and the law of the land: the supremacy of treaties over local law; the supremacy of national laws in their sphere over state law; and the power of courts to review acts of Congress and legislatures, test them against the law of the Constitution or other higher law, and decide which law prevails.

Writing to his friend Gouverneur Morris in the spring of 1784, Hamilton had adverted to the "Discrimination bills, partial taxes, schemes to engross public property in the hands of those who have present power, to banish the real wealth of the State, and to substitute paper bubbles . . . ," adding with mock resignation that he knew would amuse his nonchalant friend, who often rallied him for his impatience, "Let us . . . erect a temple to time only regretting that we shall not command a longer portion of it to see what will be the event of the American drama."

As Hamilton insisted, a citizen is truly free only in a country whose courts are free, if they choose, to find at his behest that a popular law is unconstitutional and set it aside because an unpopular view is right.

When a swiftly shifting tide of mass popular opinion has pushed legislatures and executives into ill-considered popular measures that threaten the liberties of the people, time after time the doctrine of judicial review and judicial supremacy has made it possible for the courts in America to serve as the last bastion for preservation of individual liberties.

So, from a rent case in a New York City magistrate's court, for a fee of £9 11s. 3d., through the force of his argument for an unpopular client's unpopular cause, Hamilton sent on their way to his great disciple John Marshall, wearing the robes of chief justice of the Supreme Court of the United States, the unique and remarkable legal doctrines that remain the central bulwarks of freedom under law in the American constitutional system today.

20

ANNAPOLIS APOSTROPHE: THE EXIGENCIES OF THE UNION

THE POWER OF REGULATING TRADE IS OF SUCH COMPREHENSIVE EXTENT . . . THAT TO GIVE IT EFFICACY . . . MAY REQUIRE CORRESPONDENT ADJUSTMENT OF OTHER PARTS OF THE FEDERAL SYSTEM . . . [BY] COMMISSIONERS, TO MEET AT PHILADELPHIA ON THE SECOND MONDAY IN MAY . . . TO DEVISE SUCH FURTHER PROVISIONS AS SHALL APPEAR TO THEM NECESSARY TO RENDER THE CONSTITUTION OF THE FEDERAL GOVERNMENT ADEQUATE TO THE EXIGENCIES OF THE "UNION."
—*Address of the Annapolis Convention, September 14, 1786*

A better tribunal in which to adjudicate disputes under foreign treaties than a city magistrate's court like Duane's would have been a federal judicature. The writ of a Supreme Court of last resort on federal questions would prevail over the conflicting writs of separate state legislatures and each separate state's different laws and courts. The lack of such a federal court system was only one of the twelve and more defects in the Articles of Confederation to which Hamilton's Congressional Resolution of July 1783 had pointed to demand the convening of a convention of all the states to make necessary repairs.

Congress's lack of power to borrow and issue credible money, which had left it "at the close of a glorious struggle for independence" without means to pay the army or its suppliers or repay "citizens who have cheerfully lent their money" was another such defect. Issuance of *unfunded* paper by Congress was "pregnant with abuses" and "pernicious to the integrity of the government and to the morals of the people." As a result, "in great national exigencies the public safety may be endangered."

Leaving Princeton, Hamilton had abandoned his constitutional resolution "for want of support in Congress." But returning to private life did not cause him to cease to seek support for his platform for national reconstruction plank by plank. His stand for judicial supremacy and the sanctity of foreign treaties in *Rutgers v. Waddington* had been one such plank.

Another gaping hole in the Articles of Confederation pointed to in Hamilton's resolutions was the fourth clause of the sixth article, which seemed to mean that in time of peace land and sea defense was each state's own responsibility. It "would preclude the United States from raising a single regiment or building a single ship, before a declaration of war, or an actual commencement of hostilities." Furthermore, the lack of effective powers of regulation of trade and taxation and tax collection left the Confederation without resources to prevent "whole states and large parts of others" from being "overrun and ravaged by small bodies of the enemies' forces." The states were destitute of means to pay the army. As a result, troops had been rendered ineffective for military operations and "exposed to sufferings, which nothing but unparalleled patience, perseverance and patriotism could have endured."

Memories of the army's sufferings for the benefit of citizens who had not served and suffered as the officer veterans of the revolution had done remained fresh for Hamilton partly as a result of his active peacetime service in the Society of the Cincinnati. Like him, his fellow war veterans were a powerful force that pressed firmly in the general direction of a stronger national union.

Early in 1783, while Hamilton, as the army's spokesman in the Continental Congress, was desperately trying to rally the states to find money to pay the soldiers, Washington, meeting with the officers at Newburgh and seeking to regain a measure of their confidence, had appointed a committee, headed by General Henry Knox, to draw up a resolution to assure Congress of the "good sense and steady patriotism of the gentlemen of the army."

The loose talk of mutiny that had circulated among the idle officers and men at the last forlorn encampment on the windswept heights at Temple Hill was slowly dispelled. It was a reassertion of leadership by Washington in the crisis. Hamilton had sharply reminded him not to neglect doing so.

General Knox's committee reported that the citizens "who have had so conspicuous an agency in the American Revolution as those who composed the Society of the Cincinnati, should pledge themselves, in a voluntary association, to support by all means consistent with the laws, that noble fabric of united independence, which at so much hazard, and with so many sacrifices they have contributed to erect." Knox's committee proposed "a society to be formed by the American officers" before they separated from the service. This led to the adoption at a meeting on May 10, 1783, with Baron von Steuben presiding, of the constitution of the Society of the Cincinnati. The fundamental purpose of the society was "To promote and cherish between the respective states that union and national honor so essentially necessary, to their happiness and the future dignity of the American empire." The society's original constitution, rather hastily thrown together at the encampment, provided that the members would be "a society of friends, to endure as long as they shall endure, or any of their eldest male posterity, and in failure thereof, the collateral branches, who may be judged worthy of becoming its supporters and members." It probably seemed to the founders at the time this constitution was adopted that if some semiarbitrary limitation were not placed on membership, in a few generations it might come to embrace the whole population and be ipso facto meaningless. Officers of the American army who had served honorably for three years and more were eligible for the national, or general, society, which was subdivided in turn, into state societies in each state. George Washington was elected first president general of the national society and held office until his death, when Hamilton would succeed him. Baron von Steuben was president general of the New York Society. Hamilton, whose active service in Congress had kept him from being an original incorporator at New Windsor, where skillful draftsmanship like his would have been welcome, soon became one of the more active New York members, along with many of his good friends who had also seen service— Robert Troup, Sebastian Baumann, Nicholas Fish, William North, Nathaniel Pendleton, William Popham, and many others. Colonel Aaron Burr was a member too.

Once having served the immediate local purposes for which Knox and Washington had created it—as a sort of safety valve to keep mutinous pressures from building up against and outside their command control structure—the Society of the Cincinnati began pressing Congress for promised back pay, bonuses, and other benefits, much as other veterans' organizations have done during the periods immediately following the ends of the other wars that give them their raison d'être. As years passed, the Cincinnati dwindled down to the status of a genealogical and patriotic society like scores of others. It came to mean little more than a dinner or two a year and an occasional, forlorn-looking, flagstaff-carrying marcher in a small, ill-attended parade.

As time passed, members lost interest, dropped out, and died off. Like those of other members, Hamilton's dues occasionally lapsed into arrears—sometimes by as much as $60.00 or more. After the lobbying of the immediate postwar years has won the usual benefits, such veterans' organizations tend to fade away. In real American life they have never quite lived up to the hobgoblin status that perfervid imaginations of their critics who did not serve credit them with occupying.

As might have been expected, the Society of the Cincinnati immediately drew fierce fire from civilians who had not served in the armed forces. Before the first general meeting of the society in Philadelphia in the spring of 1784, Thomas Jefferson, whose disgraceful war record as governor was the most tragic embarrassment of an otherwise distinguished career, talked earnestly with Washington about the problem long into the night. Jefferson fretted that the society was contrary to the spirit of American political institutions, the foundation of which was "the natural equality of man, and the denial of every pre-eminence but that annexed to legal office, and particularly the denial of a pre-eminence by birth." Jefferson agonized about the Cincinnati with an "anguish of mind" such as he said he had never felt before. He was certain it would never be approved by Congress and that it could not be rendered unobjectionable without changes that "would amount almost to annihilation." He prayed that Washington would avoid compromising himself by refusing membership. The rights of man simply did not include the right to join such a veterans' organization.

John Adams, whose war record as a civilian contained a less tragic, more comical episode of flight than Jefferson's, privately condemned the society and Washington's part in it. So did the popular satirist Hugh H. Brackenridge. So did the egalitarian pamphleteer Mirabeau.

Washington, who had, after all, been instrumental in creating the society and had seen its camaraderie help dispel mutinous talk at Newburgh in 1783, was rather annoyed by all the fuss and pother and silly charges like Jefferson's and Adams's when he wrote to Hamilton on December 11, 1785.

"The Jealousies of, and prejudices against this Society were carried to an unwarrantable length . . ." he fumed. Of anguish like Jefferson's, he added: "It is a matter of little moment whether the alarm which siezed the public mind was the result of foresight—envy & jealousy—or a disordered imagination; . . . I should, on that occasion, as far as my voice would have gone have endeavoured to convince the narrow minded part of our Country men that the Amor Patrie[ae] was much stronger in our breasts than theirs—and that our conduct through the whole of the business was actuated by nobler & more generous sentiments than were apprehended." Neither he nor Hamilton would forget von Steuben's accounts of the complete breakdown of civil government in Virginia confirmed by their own observations following Jefferson's flight from the capital in the critical months before Yorktown.

The society had already served its most important purpose. Washington was so wroth that he would show his purity of intention by abolishing it at once if he thought it would do any good. But he did not think it would. People like Jefferson would go on making the same silly charges anyway, imputing guilt by association to him for associating with other officers who had served their country. Indeed, disbanding the society might be seen as conceding that some basis for such baseless charges existed.

At the society's first general meeting, 15 amendments were offered to the original charter, including one urged by Washington, Hamilton, and others, abolishing the hereditary membership feature. A provision for accumulation of funds in the hands of the society to be given to the poor and the provisions for honorary members also required "alteration in their very essence."

Hamilton argued that such proposals were nonegalitarian and would hold up "an odious difference between men who have served their country in one way and those who have served it in another, a difference ill founded in itself, and improper in a society where the character of patriot ought to be an equal title to all its members." The constitution of the general society thus altered and amended was then circulated to the state organizations for action.

Hamilton also served as chairman of the New York State Society's committee along with his old friend Robert Troup, and their report of July 6, 1786, urged the New York Society to drop the hereditary membership feature. Hamilton found the provision objectionable because "it refers to birth what ought to belong to merit only, a principle inconsistent with the genius of a society founded on friendship and patriotism." Following their urgings, the New York State Society changed the provision.

Consistent with his usual insistence on national solutions rather than separate, state-by-state solutions, Hamilton insisted that there be "uniformity of the institution" by "combining the views and sentiments of the respective societies in some definitive result."

But other states without strong local leadership like Hamilton's and Troup's could not agree on the need for changes, and inertia gradually crept upon the society. It lapsed into quiet obscurity in all but a few lively imaginations like Jefferson's. Year after year innuendos drawn from the fact that an opponent was a card-carrying member of the Cincinnati served him as a simple, mindless, ready-to-hand formula with which to mislead the public by creating the impression that Hamilton favored hereditary class distinctions when he had, in truth, opposed them.

If Jefferson had prevailed and persuaded or forced Washington to dissolve the Cincinnati, such action would have become a precedent of poorly defined outer limits for the proposition that the American peoples' freedoms do not include freedom to form sodalities for self-worship or ancestor worship as they please, at least not if an important patrician who is not eligible for membership pretends to think that their goals are "subversive of liberty." For the useful, contrary precedent that innocuous veterans' or fraternal membership organizations are not "subversive of liberty" the firm stand taken by such common men as the old Virginia surveyor and frontier fighter, the mendicant bogus Prussian general, and the bastard brat of the Scotch peddler from somewhere in the Caribbees has not received the acclaim it deserves for helping to clinch a unique aspect of American freedom.

In the same letter to Hamilton in which he fumed at Jefferson's insinuations against the Cincinnati, Washington agreed to help with the latest of Hamilton's many pleas and do a little lobbying in Congress to get something more for poor old Baron von Steuben. It would not do for the presiding general of the New York Society to go on living on handouts from junior officers like Hamilton forever—as he now was doing.

Baron von Steuben, New York's leading "Knight of the Cincinnati," as

Angelica Church liked to call him, had become a more or less permanent member of the Alexander Hamilton household at number 57 Wall Street. For years Hamilton did his best to put the baron's financial affairs in order and to obtain a pension for him from Congress, often seeking Washington's help. Although the Baron was 27 years older than Hamilton and had been a major general in the war whereas Hamilton was only a lieutenant colonel, peace brought a reversal of roles. The young protégé became guardian, protector, counselor, conservator, and host to the old general, who, once out of uniform, seemed as helpless as a child. Like the Hamiltons, Angelica welcomed von Steuben into her charmed circle of affection. She wrote to her sister Betsy from London:

> I envy you the trio of agreeable men you talk of, my father and my baron and your Hamilton, what pleasant evenings, what agreeable chit-chat, whilst my vivacity must be confined to dull, gloomy Englishmen. Adieu, my dear Eliza; tell Hamilton if he does not send my Father Ambassador, that I shall believe he has no influence at Court, and that I will try not to care for him. Adieu, my dear Eliza, be happy and be gay, and remember me in your mirth as one who desires and wishes to partake of your happiness. Embrace Hamilton and the Baron. Yours, A.C.

Having met the British royal family at the theater, Angelica still pined for America, "but what are Kings and Queens to an American who has seen a Washington!" She looked back fondly: "This day year, my dear Eliza, I had the happiness to see you and receive the affectionate attention of you and my dear Hamilton, and the Gallantries of the Baron."

A jovial, permanent houseguest, a Falstaffian resident jester and butt, von Steuben's extravagant ways kept him embarrassed for money most of the time. Hamilton would lend him large sums on promissory notes, which he never repaid. In later years, when Hamilton was Secretary of the Treasury, von Steuben hugely enjoyed regaling all their friends with a joke on Hamilton. Not only was Hamilton his friend, he said, but the secretary of the treasury was his banker. Tired of retold jokes, and hardpressed for money himself, Hamilton's smile must sometimes have worn a little thin or even grim amid the jolly guffaws.

When the house they were living in was offered him to buy for £2,100, Hamilton did not have the money to pay for it immediately. On March 17, 1785, he instructed Betsy, whose acumen he trusted, to bargain for him while he was out of town: "If you cannot do better you may engage that the whole be paid in three months; but I could wish to pay half in a short time and the other half in a year. Adieu my angel."

Alexander's and Betsy's second child, born on September 25, 1784, was a girl, whom they named Angelica in honor of her glamorous aunt. As six more children followed at fairly regular intervals—Alexander, May 16, 1786; James Alexander, April 14, 1788; John Church, August 22, 1792; William Stephen, August 4, 1797; and Eliza, November 20, 1799, the Hamiltons' household budget would stretch ever tighter over the years. On June 2, 1802, there would be a second Philip, named after the firstborn Philip, who tragically died in a duel at 21, six weeks before the arrival of his namesake.

To his wife, Betsy, and the children as they came along, Hamilton was an affectionate, loving, and tender husband and father. He gave them as much time, warmth, and charm as any practising lawyer at the beck and call of many clients ever could. As the years passed when they were growing up, he would spend an hour or two with them in the nursery, romping with the youngest. Sometimes he would take a ramble in the woods with the older boys. Standing beside slim, sensitive, dark-eyed little Angelica as she accompanied him on the pianoforte that her Aunt Angelica had sent to her all the way from London, he would sing them old songs like "The Drum" from wartime days when he had been courting their mother.

The Hamilton family's tight household budget was also stretched tighter by generous responses to all sorts of outside appeals. In 1785 Hamilton answered a demand from his brother, James Hamilton by agreeing to "cheerfully pay your draft upon me for fifty pounds sterling." He was sorry that he could not afford to send him more at the moment. Brother James, like their father, remained in the Antilles, shiftless and poor. Hamilton asked him:

> What has become of our dear father? It is an age since I have heard from him, or of him, though I have written him several letters. My heart bleeds at the recollection of his misfortunes. Sometimes I flatter myself his brothers have extended their support to him, and that he is now enjoying tranquillity and ease; at other times, I fear he is suffering . . .

Both brother and father kept in touch with Hamilton by repeatedly begging him for money, which they never repaid. He never seemed to mind and helped them out with what he had as best he could. To his brother, Hamilton wrote that if he came to the United States, he would settle him on a farm. He also invited his father to come and make his home with von Steuben and all the rest of them on Wall Street, where "the tender care of your black-eyed daughter will make the blessings of your gray hairs." His brother died the following year, his father never made it up out of the islands, and he never saw either of them again.

From time to time Hamilton also sent small sums of money to his cousin Ann Lytton Venton Mitchell, who had also fallen upon hard times. At about the time he had left St. Croix, Hamilton receipted for advances to Ann by James Lytton's executors, which seem to indicate that she was one who helped him out with money for his passage and earliest days in America. Concerned that he had never done all he should have for her, he made further provision for her in his will. When his half brother, Peter Lavien, died in 1782, Hamilton heard he had been left a small legacy. His hopes rose that some family beneficences would come his way. There is no evidence, however, that he ever received anything from the estate of the half brother who had claimed and taken all the few pitiful possessions their mother, Rachel, had left, leaving nothing for him and his brother James.

Still another who joined the Hamilton household was the daughter of Colonel Edward Antil, formerly of the army's Canadian Corps. Antil had retired penniless from the service, lost his wife, solicited aid from the Society of the Cincinnati, "and there sank under the weight of his sorrows" and died, according to a thumbnail sketch of him by Hamilton's son John Church. Hamilton and Betsy nurtured the orphan daughter of this poor knight-errant of the Cincinnati as one with their own children. Of Betsy's and Alexander's generous gesture in taking on still another dependent Cincinnatian, Angelica Church wrote admiringly to Hamilton on October 2, 1787, "All the graces you have been pleased to adorn me with, fade before the generous and benevolent attitude of my sister in taking the orphan Antle under her protection."

Amid the laughter and scurry and bustle of all the accessions to his household, Hamilton seemed to grow more lonely. While her namesake Angelica was growing up to be the closest and dearest to him of all the Hamilton children, thoughts of the exquisite original Angelica were never further from the front of Hamilton's mind than thoughts of him seemed to be from hers.

John and Angelica Church had made a short visit to America in June 1785 and then returned to England. By August 3 she and Hamilton had already exchanged a number of letters, none of which has been found. On that day he sat down and wrote her yet another, which has. In it, his feelings of love and longing for her come through not less memorably for being understated, yet he never slips over the indistinct line that would mark the margin of verbal impropriety:

> You have been much better to me My Dear friend since you left America, than I have deserved, for you have written to me oftener than I have written to you . . . I am sure you will attribute it to anything else rather than to a defect of pleasure in writing to you.
>
> Now my Dear Sister You have I fear taken a final leave of America and of those that love you here. I saw you depart from Philadelphia with peculiar uneasiness, as if foreboding you were not to return. My apprehensions are confirmed and unless I see you in Europe I expect not to see you again.

Not to see her again—

> This is the impression we all have; judge the bitterness it gives to those who love you with the love of nature and to me who feel an attachment for you not less lively.

Hamilton's love for her is not the "love of nature"; it is a deeper, more exotic, unnatural passion "not less lively."

> I confess for my own part I see one great source of happiness snatched away . . . an ocean is now to separate us.
>
> You will not indeed want friends wherever you are—You will have

no need of them [besides] You have both too many qualities to engage
friendship. But go where you will you will find no such friends as those
you have left behind.

His love for her is different from Betsy's, which is only that of a sister:

Your Good and affectionate sister Betsy feels more than I can say
on this subject. She sends you all a sisters love: I remain as ever Your
Affectionate friend & Brother.

When they could afford it, the Hamiltons kept a hired servant girl or two
around the house to help Betsy cope as best she could with all she had to do—
entertaining friends and clients, childbearing and child rearing, raising the Antil
foster child, and picking up after Baron von Steuben. It is not known whether
either Betsy or Hamilton owned a slave. It is possible Betsy may have been given
or loaned a slave or an indentured servant by her father. For a while the Hamiltons had a girl named Gussie, to whom they paid wages.

Slavery was still legal in New York and closely regulated by law, but usually
it was only the wealthier families who could afford to maintain slaves. Less
affluent families preferred to hire and pay indentured servants for service as
needed. On February 4, 1785, Hamilton was one of the 32 organizers of the
Society for Manumission of Slaves. John Jay, its first president, appointed Hamilton chairman of a committee to devise ways and means to free the slaves by way
of practicing what the society preached. Hamilton forthwith proposed a resolution that the members of the society begin by freeing their own slaves. The
resolution was quashed.

His resolution was an early move to counter the prevailing majority sentiment that he considered wrong in principle. Only the year before, a bill for
gradual grant of freedom to people of "Negro, Mulatto, Indian and mustee blood
born in New York" had been introduced into the legislature. Aaron Burr was for
broadening this to declare that any "person of whatever description, age or
colour, now holden, or claimed as a slave . . . by any inhabitant of this State
. . . hereby are . . . absolutely free," but this was defeated by more than two to
one. Some prohibitions against Negro voting and holding office were added. But
in the legislative confusion, with Burr's bill broadened in scope to include something or other that would offend people on all sides, the whole bill was eventually
killed.

Hamilton remained an active member of the Society for the Manumission
of Slaves until his death and was annually reelected one of its counselors. On
March 13, 1786, Hamilton and others signed a petition to the New York legislature urging the end of the slave trade as "a commerce repugnant to humanity,
and inconsistent with the liberality and justice which should distinguish a free
and enlightened people."

In Philadelphia, where Hamilton's old friend Gouverneur Morris had just
returned, the Pennsylvania Assembly's response to news that the definitive

treaty of peace with England had finally been ratified on January 14, 1784, was a call for a "public demonstration of joy." Morris reported that at the upper end of Market Street between Sixth and Seventh Avenues, a triumphal arch was erected, embellished by illuminated paintings, some by Charles Willson Peale, "with a number of lamps inside and no precautions against flames." Writing while shut in by a raging snowstorm on January 27, Morris added, "If the projectors had intended to fire their city it was an ingenious invention." There were fireworks, too, and "The exhibition would have been perfectly ridiculous" he added, "but for the death of one spectator and the wounds of others," while demonstrating for joy.

The fireworks for peace had touched off a new excitation: "The present influence is the Bank-o-mania," said Morris. He was referring to newspaper announcements of the formation of a new bank, the Bank of Pennsylvania "or, as some call it, the Coalition Bank." That Hamilton might judge of the propriety of the name *coalition*, Morris called off for his friend in New York "the characters of the parties named in the advertisements, as I had them at Breakfast from our friend." It is worth keeping in mind that Morris was a director of the Bank of North America, which the coalition bank would confront with the shock of competition for the first time.

The irrepressible Morris tossed off some irreverent character sketches of the proper Philadelphians whose names on the published list of trustees were intended to convey the appropriate sense of soundness, solidity, sanctity, and stuffiness to all segments of the share buying and depositing public, whose money they solicited. There was "Samuel Howell, a Quaker who would have been Whig, if he had not been afraid . . . he is said to be an honest man which is no bad thing in any Case." As for Archibald McCall, "A good name to him would be a good Purchase." To his labors in spying for the British during the war "his benignity added the charitable trait of supplying small sums to men in distress at moderate interest, such as five or ten per cent per month, according to their necessities." Edward Shippen "has the misfortune to be general Arnold's Father in Law, but he bears no resemblance to his son, except that their political Principles were the same from Arnold's defection till the Treaty of Peace." Jared Ingersoll was ". . . a worthy young Man and his Friends are sorry to see him in such Company."

What had happened was that "the violent Whigs and the violent Tories, who turned their backs on everybody else about two years ago, have each performed a semi-circle and met at the opposite point." Hence the name *coalition*.

Morris noted slyly that "Your friend 'Phocion' has written a book in favor of moderation. He certainly means well, but if he were here he would see what goodly fruit is produced, in the fulness of time, from those seeds of contention which he has labored to destroy, and he would find out the truth of that old proverb, 'the farthest way about is the nearest way home.' "

The reason for the bankomania was that the Bank of North America, the first and at the time only bank in Philadelphia, had been making so much money —14 percent or so a year—that the coalition Morris had described as extremist scoundrels of both factions had been seized with a typically American urge to share the wealth that Morris and his colleagues were enjoying by going into competition with them. Hamilton's brother-in-law John Barker Church was a significant shareholder in the older bank too. The new one could be a serious threat to its profitable monopoly, even to its solvency. This was a simple, obvious point to a businessman like Church, but a point that Hamilton at first overlooked completely.

To Hamilton, there seemed to be no harm in a second bank. Replying to Morris on February 21, 1784, he complimented him on his snowbound letter: "A good theme in good hands could not fail to be amusing." He disagreed with him about the threat: "A new bank in Philadelphia does not appear an evil to the community . . . Competition will cause business to be done on easier and better terms in each to the advancement of trade in general. . . ." Let the two banks "live well together and manage their affairs with good humor and concert."

As a disinterested citizen loftily considering the good of the marketplace as a whole, Hamilton was happy to permit Adam Smith's "invisible hand" in the form of competition from the "coalition" bank to cut into the erstwhile profitable monopoly the Bank of North America had enjoyed for the general good. Not Church.

Neither New York nor Boston yet had a bank, and now that the Bank of North America was to have competition in its hometown, Church saw that New York offered a better prospect for a new and more profitable money monopoly. Hamilton, at least, could not fail to agree that New York was a much more promising place for his brother-in-law's investments, his own law practice, and the prospect of more proximity to his sister-in-law Angelica as well.

Church cared not at all from which country he made his money, and everything he touched seemed to turn to gold, whether he worked for the French army as commissary supplier, the British, or the Americans. Church's splendid, bluff indifference to the political purposes of the war, typical of a rich businessman, contrasted sharply with Hamilton's zeal in fighting it. Now that the war was over, Church's cold eye turned more and more to America as a profitable field of operations. The prospect of a specie bank of his own in prosperous New York had great appeal.

From Paris, on February 7, he wrote Hamilton about the idea and his own plans for the future: "We are taken [sic] measures to vest our Property in America by exporting from here and England a large quantity of ready money Articles and I hope we shall be at New York June or July." As for the family, "Angelica joins me in love to Mrs. Hamilton and yourself. She is very well. The little maid [their daughter Catharine Church] is fat and handsome. Phil [their firstborn, Philip Church] is in Pension he jabbers more French than English." The New York bank would be controlled by Church and his business partner, Jeremiah Wadsworth.

Such a bank as Church—and Hamilton—envisaged would be one based on "established principles," that is, a bank that would do business with merchants and substantial businessmen, with a capital made up of money, bonds, and commercial paper, not mortgages or other interests in land. Its initial capital would be $500,000 in specie—gold or silver—a thousand shares of $500 each. It would receive all payments in gold or silver coin on bank notes only and must never engage in trade.

The problem in New York was that Chancellor Robert R. Livingston, a large upstate landowner, had just petitioned the legislature to grant a charter for another public bank based on wholly different principles. A land bank, it would accept mortgages on land as collateral for subscriptions to its stock and would deal largely with loans based on land as security instead of bills of lading and commercial paper and promissory notes. Its clientele would, therefore, be drawn more from the agrarian and debtor classes.

The farmers, small merchants, and Populist groups in the state who had most fiercely sought reprisals against the loyalists Hamilton championed were suspicious of all money banks and bankers. They feared that money bankers might simply take up where the British had left off by changing the formerly dependent colonist-debtors into free but still dependent mortgator-debtors.

Still another group of New York merchants had the same idea as Church and Hamilton for a New York money bank and came in on the ground floor with them. On February 23, 1784, the following announcement appeared in *The New York Packet* and *The American Advertiser:* "BANK. It appearing to be the disposition of the Gentlemen in this City, to establish a BANK on liberal principles, the stock to consist of specie only; they are therefore hereby invited to meet To-Morrow evening at Six O'Clock at the merchants' Coffee House; where a plan will be submitted to their consideration." Hamilton's old friend General Alexander McDougall was named chairman, plans for the bank were approved, and Hamilton was named a director. As counsel, he drew up a constitution and an outline for the bank's charter, which was adopted at the organizational meeting on March 15, 1784. It became New York's first bank, The Bank of New York.

When he had been asked to act for the Bank of New York group, Hamilton told Church, "I was a little embarrassed how to act" because there might be a conflict of interest between the New York group and his brother-in-law. "But upon the whole I concluded it best to fall in with them, and endeavor to put the business upon such a footing as might enable you with advantage to combine your interests with theirs." Hamilton was always practical enough to see that an intrigue could lead to a marriage of convenience. Church and Wadsworth were practical men too. When they heard of the possible conflict, "it determined Wadsworth and myself to give up all Thought of carrying our banking Plan into execution." A good monopoly would be a good monopoly, and it mattered little whose idea it had been in the first place. Church wanted in on the other group's bank. "I should be glad to be interested in the Shares of that Bank if they are not disposed of," he told Hamilton.

Church wanted a controlling interest, but the Bank of New York's charter had a provision giving a maximum of only seven votes to any individual stockholder, no matter how large his holdings. Hamilton managed to persuade the other subscribers to amend the charter to grant an additional vote for each block of five shares owned above ten. This gave Church and Wadsworth a larger interest as well as seats on the board of directors. Hamilton then introduced and sought to push the constitution and application for a charter through the legislature. Although he remained a director of the Bank of New York until 1788, Hamilton himself owned only a single qualifying share.

In Hamilton's view, Livingston's land bank would interfere with his and Church's Bank of New York, as well as "the commercial interests of the State"; so Hamilton started "an opposition to this scheme." He urged the land bank's "absurdity and inconvenience" on the merchants, who presently began to take measures to defeat the Livingston land bank plan. This marked the beginning of a Hamilton-Livingston rivalry that would raise up a later host of political troubles for Hamilton and Schuyler in New York State politics.

The bank first opened its doors for business at 156 Queen Street in the "Walton Mansion." On May 1, 1784, President McDougall advertised that subscribers to stock of the Bank of New York must pay the first half of their share subscriptions on June 1 to the cashier, William Seton. But it would take Hamilton seven long years to push the bank's charter as a public bank through the New York legislature. He wrote Gouverneur Morris on April 7, 1784:

> You will call our proceedings here *strange doings;* Schemes to engross public property in the hands of those who have present power —to banish the real wealth of the state and substitute paper bubbles are the only dishes that suit the public palate at this time. If some folks were paid to counteract the prosperity of the state, they could not take more effectual measures than they do. But it is in vain to attempt to kick against the Pricks . . .

It was an uphill fight to push through a public bank against the legislature's upstate majority, who feared it was the seed of another part of his program to repair defects in the Confederation that his call for a constitutional convention had pointed out. In the public's mind, the growth of the Bank of North America had been tied to the hard times that followed its formation. The Pennsylvania legislature had tried to withdraw that bank's state charter and raised the question of whether such a public bank "was compatible with the public safety and that equality which ought ever to prevail between the individuals of a republic." Even so, the Bank of North America retained a charter it had received from Congress. Pelatiah Webster and Thomas Paine attacked it and banks in general. James Wilson's patient rebuttals in defending it were hardly a match for the doubts the attackers raised.

Hamilton wrote Jeremiah Wadsworth on October 29, 1785, in alarm at the risks these attacks created for Church's investment in an unchartered bank: "To leave *so considerable a sum* in a Company of this kind not incorporated is too dangerous." Wadsworth made an unsuccessful attempt to get his and Church's money out and suggested that if Pennsylvania continued to deny the bank a charter, the entire bank might be removed to a more hospitable state.

Hamilton's petition to the legislature for the Bank of New York's charter in the autumn of 1784 leaned against the same strong Populist hostility toward all banks that prevailed in Pennsylvania. He argued on broad, fundamental, national grounds that the usefulness of banks in commercial countries had long been demonstrated; in Europe they were "regarded as one of the surest foundations of public and private Credit," which "forms a presumption in their favour, not easily to be outweighed by arguments that rest on speculation and Theory."

Hamilton went on to enumerate the benefits of such a bank. It could assist government with emergency loans, favor industry and commerce by increasing the circulating capital in the safest fashion, offer short credit demanding punctuality, and eventually lower the rate of interest. A bank "By promoting Industry and Commerce . . . necessarily promotes Agriculture and renders landed Property more valuable."

In New York the scarcity of specie, hard money, gold and silver, caused a peculiar need for a bank: "Paper struck by the mere Authority of Government . . . is hardly likely to regain . . . Confidence. . . . The cooperation of a Bank seems the only expedient left to . . . supply the deficiency of Specie by a Paper Circulation."

As in Hamilton's twelve points for a constitution, he saw a public bank not as Church did—merely another profit-making business—but as an institution that would advance the progress of state and nation.

Hamilton's charter application was still pending in the legislature when, in February 1785, almost 300 citizens signed a memorial offering a testimonial in its behalf. The list included the names of the leading men of the city, of all callings and shades of opinion: Philip Livingston, Isaac Sears, John Lamb, William Duer, S. B. Webb, Benjamin Walker, Robert C. Livingston, Wm. Constable, Robert Harpur, Melancton Smith, as well as names from Hamilton's youth like John Cruger, Lawrence Kortright, William Newton, and George Codwise.

The legislature was evenhanded in its Populist prejudices: as it would refuse to incorporate a specie bank, it would also refuse to permit a land bank or an association of tradesmen and mechanics who wished to incorporate. The New York Council of Revision held, contrary to the occasional demand heard in industrialized America that trade unions should incorporate, that they should not incorporate on grounds that New York "may become a community of corporations, influenced by partial views (under the direction of artful men) composing an aristocracy destructive to the constitution and independency of the State." Incorporation of a society for encouraging emigration from Germany was similarly turned down.

While their corporate charter applications languished in Populist legislatures, the Bank of New York and the Bank of North America remained busy private banks.

Another application of the Bank of New York was rejected by the senate in February 1790, but by only one vote, the casting vote of the chairman in a committee of the whole. Returning prosperity, the usefulness of the bank, not to mention the elevation of Hamilton to secretary of the treasury in the meantime all helped beat down the opposition. The following winter William Seton, having patiently inquired when a new petition and bill for incorporation should be filed, finally wrote with confidence that "The Directors . . . repose a firm reliance on the fullest . . . support of the City Members to an Institution whose . . . operations they must be sensible tend to the public good." The new bill was debated from time to time for five weeks, amended in both houses, and finally passed March 21, 1791. It was a final victory for Hamilton scored, typically, only after six long years of defeats. The logic of events more than the force of his arguments had dissolved the majority against him.

Hamilton knew much about the theory and principle of banking, but little about how banks carried on day-to-day business in practice. In 1784 he had dispatched Cashier William Seton to Philadelphia "to procure materials and information in the forms of business," from the Bank of North America. He inquired of Gouverneur Morris for "the best mode of receiving and paying out gold." The Philadelphia method required weighing in quantities, which was certainly inconvenient, but there was no substitute method "unless there could be a coinage." Such would prove to be the answer.

Hamilton almost never confessed to being without a ready answer to a practical problem, but he admitted he could think of no substitute for gold. By "a coinage" he meant coins that would be worth their weight in gold or silver, so that if melted down, their intrinsic value in metal would be equivalent to the denomination stamped on their faces. As all nongold-backed paper currencies of today's world increasingly deteriorate in value from lack of credibility, Hamilton's inability to think of a substitute for a specie-backed currency has contemporary resonance. No one has yet come up with a better answer to the malaise of paper money than Hamilton's reluctant accession to the idea of the indispensability of a gold standard. Gouverneur Morris had the last word on the elusive subject of gold when he replied jokingly to Hamilton's request on June 30, "I meant to have written fully on the Subject of Gold . . . I would say a great Deal on this subject but it would be very useless."

The Bank of North America turned away Seton and his troublesome questions about banking know-how without answers. The coalition bank was threatening to break its monopoly, and there were other troubles besides. The sum of 60,000 pounds sterling of Robert Morris's bills, drawn to cover the Dutch loan, were in default and under protest; because he had founded the Bank of North America, it must support him, or it and the public credit would go down together. In the emergency, Gouverneur Morris suggested making the Bank of New York a branch of the Bank of North America, possibly to help bail out the latter. Finally, the Bank of North America adopted a suggestion of Hamilton that would draw the coalition men back into the fold and restore the banking monopoly that had prevailed in the good old days before competition.

Writing to his bachelor friend Gouverneur Morris of the Bank of North America's proposal to absorb the coalition bank, Hamilton preferred an intrigue to a marriage: "Let the [new bank] be the wife or, still to pursue your propensity, the mistress of the former. As a mistress (or you'll say a wife) it is to be expected she will every now and then be capricious and inconstant; but in the main it will [be to] the interest of both husband and wife that they should live well together and manage their affairs with good humour and concert."

There were the obvious business reasons for such a marriage of convenience that only the "knowing part" of neighbors like Morris and Hamilton would appreciate: "If they quarrel they will not expose themselves to the gibes of their neighbours, but the more knowing part of these will endeavour to keep them by the ears in order to make the favours of each more cheap, and more easily attainable."

Hamilton, like Morris, had known wives who were also mistresses, but, of course, kept clear of their husbands—which made affairs that much easier for the husbands, and the others' wives.

More straight-facedly, Hamilton wrote Thomas FitzSimons that it now seemed "evidently the interest of both" Philadelphia banks to join forces. They finally did so, and all problems were solved.

Seton's report to Hamilton, revealing the damage the threat of competition had done to the Bank of North America had swung Hamilton around to the notion that the two banks should consolidate. When they did, he told Gouverneur Morris, "I am very happy to hear of the union of your two banks . . ." This episode does not prove either that Hamilton was in favor of bank monopolies or all-out competition. If it proves anything at all, which it probably does not, it is that he was against bank failures, much as he was, no doubt, also against sin, but not, necessarily, mistresses.

To Hamilton, the success of the public banks meant more than simply service to an important client or a lawyer's sideline or attention to another moneymaking scheme of his client Church. Central banks were central to the social, political, and economic well-being of the United States he was working to consolidate against everlasting opposition. State legislative hostility to public banks and trade unions were symptoms of deeper public malaise that gripped all the states from New Hampshire to Georgia.

Foreign trade was at a standstill, as was agriculture. Farmers could not pay their debts to city merchants and bankers, interest on public loans was in default, hard money was almost wholly out of circulation, and each state was printing paper money as "legal tender" as fast as presses could run it off. "Stay" laws were passed, declaring a moratorium on the collection of debts. James Madison pointed out to Thomas Jefferson "the present anarchy of our commerces"; he thought "most of our political evils may be traced up to our commercial ones. . . ." States without good harbors "were subject to be taxed by their neighbors, thro' whose parts, their commerce was carried on." New Jersey, lying between Philadelphia and New York, was like a cask tapped at both ends; and North Carolina, between Virginia and South Carolina, was like a patient bleeding at both arms. New York required that every wood boat and shallop from New Jersey of more than 12 tons be regularly entered and cleared out at the custom house, in the same manner as if it had arrived from any foreign port. This ate into the already small profits of Jersey boatmen; so Jersey retaliated by laying a stiff tax of £30 per month on the Sandy Hook Lighthouse and the plot around it, which belonged to the corporation of New York City. Connecticut laid heavier duties on imports from Massachusetts than those from Great Britain.

Like his friend Hamilton in New York, Madison in Virginia was pressing the need for a national solution, but in the summer of 1784 a resolution for a constitutional convention was defeated in the Virginia legislature. On Christmas Day of that year, Madison told Richard Henry Lee that union was necessary to escape foreign danger and internal dissension. He drafted some resolutions dealing with interstate navigation and state jurisdiction over the Potomac basin. Maryland and Virginia commissioners were soon joined by others from Pennsylvania and Delaware in a plan to smooth the commercial relations of all four states.

Ever since 1781, as well as in his 1783 resolutions calling for a convention, Hamilton had been demanding that Congress be given power to regulate trade by imposing duties, granting bounties, and laying embargoes. Finally in 1784, Congress had formally asked the states to invest it with narrow control over commerce by permitting it to lay prohibitions upon the entry of ships and goods from countries that did not have commercial treaties with the United States. Eventually, eleven states agreed to this delegation, but two stood on the Articles of Confederation. The rule of unanimity left all as badly off as if none had approved. Now in 1785 the impost proposed by Congress in 1783 still languished for lack of unanimous approval, and it was in New York, with its great port, that opposition to it was strongest. By 1786 even Rhode Island had approved, leaving Hamilton's New York as the only state that had refused to approve the impost.

During the war New York had suffered more than any of the other states. The British, holding the frontier posts blocked, still posed a constant military threat. They intrigued with the Indians, diverted the fur trade, and limited imports and trade from Connecticut, New Jersey, and Massachusetts. Depression conditions were one reason why 543 leading New York citizens petitioned to suppress a newly opened theatre on John Street: "The private debts in which members were involved—the National debt—the heavy arrears of Taxes—the growing Scarcity of Cash—and the deranged State of Trade . . . evince the high impolicy of suffering the Theatre, which is a school of Dissipation, if not of Vice, to be erected among us at this time." Hamilton, who loved to go to the theater, was not among the signers of this petition.

Governor Clinton and his party were well pleased that the only visible symbol of a national government was the impotent Congress they scornfully called "King Cong." The debt-ridden rural and frontier districts that provided the backbone of Clinton's support saw in a stronger national government more hegemony of the mercantile classes, to whom they were already in debt. It would mean heavy taxes, strict enforcement of the repayment of debts, abolition of easy paper money, and an effective ban on confiscations of Tory property. Clinton's men controlled the state assembly.

The same factors made the merchants and bankers of the seaboard and the landowners of the interior support strengthening the national government. They controlled the state senate—voting for which depended on a heavy property qualification. The result was a deadlock, no action on the impost, and the same practical effect as if the other twelve states had not acted at all. Here was an issue now brought into sharp focus: a victory in the New York State Assembly by Hamilton's nationalists could break the deadlock.

For the effort, Hamilton enlisted the aid of Robert Livingston, the third lord of Livingston Manor. On April 25, 1785, Hamilton wrote that "the state is now governed by a couple of New England adventurers—Ford and Adgate [members of the assembly from Albany] . . . Attempts have been made by this junta to subvert the constitution and destroy the rights of private property; . . . Much depends on the ensuing election . . ." This was the kind of talk to move a man like Livingston, and on June 13, 1785, he reported to Hamilton that he had managed to win over one upstate county:

"I feel happy in finding your sentiments so justly accord with mine, and my Sons . . . we did endeavour the last year for an alteration in the representation, but without the desired Success, while we stood almost alone . . . nor did this failure discourage us, but rather heightened our diligence in this last Election, by Compleating the necessary Junction previous to the day of Election . . . of the Rensselaer, Schuyler, & our family, with other Gent[le]m[en] of property in the County in one Interest." By this means "we carryed this last Election to a man as you must have heard from your friends." There was strength in such unity: "I trust we shall always have the like success provided we stick close to each other."

Hamilton applied the lessons of Livingston's county to New York. Let the merchants, bankers, and similar "Gentlemen of property" in the city likewise combine and elect Robert Troup, William Duer, and Colonel William Malcolm, all loyal followers of Hamilton, to the assembly. The plan worked, and the three won election. Hamilton remained busy offstage with law practice and master strategy.

Thus, when on March 16, 1786, Governor Clinton submitted to the legislature a letter from the governor of Virginia enclosing a resolution appointing commissioners to meet with the commissioners of the different states "for the purpose of framing such regulations of trade as may be necessary to promote the general interest," Hamilton had the necessary votes to make affirmative response in the assembly. Hamilton's men proposed that recalcitrant New York send commissioners to attend and carried the assembly with them, although subject to the express reservation that the convention be limited to commercial objects only and that the commissioners take no final action there but merely report back to the legislature. Hamilton's nationalists then managed, with an assist from Schuyler in the senate, to name all of the commissioners, including Robert Cambridge Livingston, the fourth son of the third lord of Livingston manor, James Duane, Egbert Benson, and, of course, Hamilton himself.

This limited success of Hamilton's men in the legislature was overshadowed by still another defeat for the impost. Hamilton drafted a petition from the people of the city of New York and obtained signatures from supporters—the Clintonians would yield nothing, however, but an emasculated bill that granted the impost to Congress but only on condition that it be handled by state collectors and provided that the depreciated state paper money be acceptable in payment. Such conditions nullified the grant, and Congress turned it down, requesting Clinton to call a special session of the legislature to reconsider its action. Clinton refused, pleading that this was not such "an extraordinary occasion" for a special session as the state constitution required. This provoked Hamilton into a new fight to undo Clinton's refusal. There was one last step he could take: stand for election to the assembly himself. His oratorical powers and quickness of maneuver on the floor might be just enough to tip the balance against the wily old governor in his favorite forum. Because the legislature met in the City Hall at the corner of Broad and Wall Streets, attending sessions would require of him only a short block's walk up the street from his house and office.

Schuyler wrote to Stephen Van Rensselaer that "Colo Hamilton will serve if elected. The Quakers, Merchants and some of the Mechanics are for him, but part of the latter averse; I am inclined however to think he will be returned." After a hard fight, on the list of nine elected, Hamilton received only the fourth highest number of votes. Even with the support stirred up by his election, Hamilton lost the fight to force Clinton to call a special session of the legislature to reconsider the impost.

So his never-ending battle for more power to Congress and more coopera-tion from New York seemed to have been completely crushed when he set out for Annapolis with his friend Egbert Benson for the convention to discuss trade. It did not seem important enough for the other four commissioners appointed by New York to take the trouble to make the trip.

On September 1, 1786, Hamilton broke an engagement with Richard Varick because "Mrs. Hamilton insists on my dining with her today as this is the day of departure and you (who are not a prophane bachelor like Benson) will know that in such a case implicit obedience on my part is proper."

The same day, from Newark, with his "prophane bachelor" friend Egbert Benson, Hamilton wrote that in "obedience to the appointment of the legislature respecting the proposed commercial arrangements, . . . We set out this afternoon on a journey to Annapolis." Their journey to Annapolis for insignificant sounding talks on trade would lead straight out again and on to the Constitutional Conven-tion of 1787, *The Federalist Papers*, and eventually Hamilton's triumphant return to New York as its greatest hero.

Madison had written Jefferson on March 18, 1786, that Annapolis had been selected because "it was thought prudent to avoid the neighborhood of Congress and the large commercial towns, in order to disarm the adversaries to the object of insinuations of influence from either of these quarters." No notice was taken of the arrival of Hamilton and Benson or of the other dozen delegates at George Mann's City Tavern, the best in the town. It had 100 beds and stabling for 50 horses, and its food and service were "elegant and profuse."

Four states, including Maryland, had not even troubled to appoint commis-sioners, and the dozen who finally appeared represented only five states–New York, New Jersey, Pennsylvania, Delaware, and Virginia. They seemed all but lost in the old senate chamber of the State House. Few citizens took notice of the meeting, and there was nothing about it in the press except that on September 14, the last day, as the commissioners adjourned for home, the *Maryland Gazette* reported, "Several Gentlemen, members of the proposed commercial convention, are arrived in this city." Apathy kept state delegates home in droves.

Proponents of state sovereignty were suspicious of the men who had initiated the call. Hamilton and Duane of New York, Robert Morris of Pennsylvania, and Madison of Virginia were men who, they believed, had purposes in mind that ranged far beyond a mere conference on trade. Stephen Higginson of Massachusetts complained to John Adams that "the ostensible object of that convention is the regulation of Commerce; but when I consider the men who are deputed from New York, Pennsylvania and Virginia, and the source from whence the proposition was made, I am strongly inclined to think political Objects are intended to be combined with commercial, if they do not principally engross their Attention."

James Monroe, also suspicious, tried to warn Madison of conspiracy: "The eastern men be assur'd mean it as leading further than the object originally comprehended. If they do not obtain that things shall be arranged to suit them in every respect, their intrigues will extend to the objects I have suggested above." Madison himself was one of the alleged "intriguers."

Discouraged by all the criticism, Madison despaired of accomplishing political results and resigned himself to nothing more than commercial reform. To Jefferson, he wrote on August 12, 1786:

> Many gentlemen, both within and without Congress, wish to make this meeting subservient to a plenipotentiary Convention for amending the Confederation. Tho' my wishes are in favor of such an event, yet I despair so much of its accomplishment at the present crisis that I do not extend my views beyond a commercial Reform.

When the small group of delegates finally assembled, Hamilton noted pointedly that the commissioners appointed by New Hampshire, Massachusetts, Rhode Island, and North Carolina had not even bothered to show up, and that Connecticut, Maryland, South Carolina, and Georgia had not even appointed any. Yet appointments of the commissioners present had been conditioned by their states on meeting with counterparts from all the others, not just the handful present. Without even a quorum, the obvious thing to do was pack up, check out, and go home. Like his congressional resolutions calling for a constitutional convention of 1783, Hamilton felt abandoned for want of support. But he had spent the three years since laying down planks. He seized the moment. Because for lack of a quorum they could not do the small job of talking about trade that they had been sent to do, why not take on a bigger job? Men like Stephen Higginson and James Monroe had charged them with secretly harboring larger designs. If they already bore the onus, why not earn it? Why not report back to their respective states that, it being impossible to proceed without better attendance, they had been obliged to issue a call for all the states to meet in another convention?

Hamilton dusted off his congressional resolutions of 1783 and produced a new draft of a call for a convention that was vigorous, forthright, broad, and sweeping. It provided "That . . . the Matters, intended for the consideration of this Convention, would essentially affect the whole System of Federal Government, and the exigencies of the United States," including "all such measures as may appear necessary to cement the Union of the States, and promote the permanent tranquility, Security, and Happiness."

Governor Edmund Randolph of Virginia and other delegates protested against words like "cement the union," arguing that New York, Pennsylvania, and Virginia had given only narrow authority to their commissioners: to meet merely "to take into consideration the trade and Commerce of the United States, and to report to the several states . . ." and nothing more.

Hamilton, a lifelong diviner of implied powers, scanned the wording of each state's authorizations carefully. He retorted triumphantly that, unlike the three states Randolph had cited, New Jersey had enlarged the authority of her commissioners, empowering them to consider *"other important matters as well."* Another memorable phrase in New Jersey's resolution authorized her commissioners to report out an act that "would enable the United States in Congress assembled, effectually to provide for *the exigencies of the Union."*

From such apparently insignificant niceties of detail and language, much fateful American history has been spun. Randolph insisted that New Jersey was only a minority of one. Hamilton replied coolly that its wording had merit and that, as a matter of fact, the same words could even be read into the authorizations given by the other three states. Their delegates had similar "implied powers." How could anyone disagree with the high-minded generalities that he proposed to include in the call?

The moment cried out for moderation, and Hamilton pressed on, but with circumspection so as not to make enemies of others whose views matched those of the governor of Virginia. Hamilton argued that commerce and trade and economic matters in general undergirded all parts of the federal system, including the political superstructure: "The Idea of extending the powers . . . to other objects than those of Commerce, adopted by New Jersey, was an improvement on the original plan, and will deserve to be incorporated into that of a future convention." An economic foundation underlay all political and social measures: "The power of regulating trade is of such comprehensive extent," he said, "and will enter so far into the general system of the Foederal government, that to give it efficacy, and to obviate questions and doubts concerning its precise value and limits, may require a correspondent adjustment of other parts of the Foederal system."

Before Hamilton could drive Randolph into this corner and an uncompromising refusal, Madison took Hamilton aside to caution him, saying that: "You had better yield to this man, for otherwise all Virginia will be against you."

Without Virginia, the call to other states would lack authority. But with her in favor, even Governor Clinton could not brush it aside. Hamilton yielded. He rewrote the draft call, making its statement of the purposes of the convention less pointed but not altogether absent. The final statement of the Annapolis Convention, addressed to all the states, added to Hamilton's first draft, out of his arguments with Randolph and others, a deeply humble and deferential tone. It also included a low bow in the direction of New Jersey: "your commissioners submit an opinion, that the Idea of extending the powers of their Deputies, to other objects, than those of Commerce, which has been adopted by the State of New Jersey, was an improvement on the original plan."

Trade, commerce, and economics underlie politics and all of Hamilton's policies. Regulation of trade became the root reason for the calling of the Constitutional Convention: "the power of regulating trade is of such comprehensive extent, and will enter so far into the general system of the foederal government, that to give it efficacy, and to obviate questions and doubts concerning its precise nature and limits, may require correspondent adjustment of other parts of the Foederal System."

A date was set; the blanks in Hamilton's 1783 draft were filled in. The commissioners were "to meet at Philadelphia on the second Monday in May next, to take into consideration the situation of the United States . . . to devise such further provisions as shall appear to them necessary to render the Constitution of the Federal Government adequate to the exigencies of the Union."

The call drafted by Hamilton went forth from Annapolis on September 14, 1786. While impatiently awaiting the fruition of his years of so far futile effort to push a routine bank charter through his own state legislature, Hamilton might sooner push through a charter for a nation. It could then issue a national charter to his bank.

The cries of outrage from the likes of Higginson and Monroe when they heard the call that had issued from the runaway rump convention at Annapolis were suddenly drowned out by louder cries of alarm. Farmers in western Massachusetts, not far from the New York line, rose under the leadership of Daniel Shays, a veteran of the Revolution, and took arms against their troubles. They charged that Eastern politicians discriminated against them in levying taxes, distrained their cattle, and, through subservient courts, foreclosed their farms and packed them off to debtors jails when they defaulted on payments of debts and taxes. Great armed bands of Shays' men ranged angrily across the western counties, closing the courts, burning the records, opening jails, forcibly seizing foreclosed property, and disrupting foreclosure sales. They marched on Boston to confront the merchant-controlled legislature.

Conditions of trade and economics, of course, were at the root of this social and political uprising. Interest rates charged farmers ran as high as 40 percent a year. More people were in jail for debt than for all other offenses combined. No wonder the rhetoric of the Shaysites had a frightening pre-Marxist ring to it: "That the property of the United States has been protected from confiscation of Britain by the joint exertions of *all*, and ought to be the *common property* of all."

Fearful commonwealth officials called out the militia under the command of General Benjamin Lincoln. But there was no money in the state treasury, and none was forthcoming from Congress to pay them. The rich merchants themselves had to take up private subscriptions to pay for suppressing the uprising. In the hunting down of Shays' poor, rebellious farmers and backwoodsmen like animals, fright and greed made the suppressors of Shays' Rebellion cruel and merciless. Shays' rebellion was crushed, but fears of other outbreaks like it strengthened the hand of all like Hamilton who favored a strong national government with a powerful standing army that could deal effectively with such terrifying future menaces to peace and order.

Most of the reforms the Shaysites had sought were eventually enacted, and all of the rebels themselves were amnestied. But Shaysites became prize specimens in the natural history of American politics. They served as a common point of reference in argument for Hamilton, Jefferson, Madison, and Thomas Paine. For Hamilton's national purposes, Daniel Shays could not have timed his rebellion better than he did—to fill the pause that followed the Annapolis Address calling the Constitutional Convention to convene the following May.

On February 15, 1787, Hamilton walked out of his front door at 57 Wall Street, picked up papers and briefcase from his office next door at 56, walked one block west to the City Hall building, and took his seat as a member of the tenth session of the New York State Assembly. Although Virginia had voted favorably the previous October 16 to send delegates to the Philadelphia convention, Governor Clinton had been unimpressed; he liked no part of what he had heard from Annapolis and "expressed a strong dislike" to the object of the address, "declaring that . . . no such reform . . . was necessary; that the confederation as it stood was equal to the purposes of the Union . . ." So nothing at all was being done in New York about appointing delegates to go to Philadelphia.

In his opening message to the legislature a month earlier, Clinton had finally laid Congress's request for the impost before it without comment, a committee had been appointed to draft a reply, and Hamilton had managed to wangle appointment to a place on the committee. Clintonians resolved the assembly into a committee of the whole to consider the message. A Clintonian was on his feet at once, proposing "approbation of your Excellency's conduct in not convening the Legislature at an earlier period." This was a slap at Congress and at Hamilton, who had demanded a special session to act on the impost the previous autumn and lost. A large docile majority duly voted approbation to Governor Clinton.

Now, on February 15, Hamilton again pressed the impost issue. The vote on it would also serve as a test of strength on the question of sending delegates to the convention. A bill to grant Congress the duties received on specific items of importation passed: Clintonians did not fight the impost itself—the battle remained over the question of who was to appoint the collectors and who was to control them.

Hamilton rose to his feet to plead on the opposition's ground. He proposed, first, that Congress both appoint and control the collectors; second, he proposed that if this were not acceptable, Congress should have the control of the collectors even if the state should have the right of appointment. With the impost now approved by all the other states and with everything turning on what the New York Assembly would do, the eyes of the nation focused on Hamilton in New York's City Hall. A large audience of visitors in the gallery was noisily sympathetic to him as he rose to speak for the impost. He repeated all the arguments for national revenues he had ever made before and added new ones. New York and Pennsylvania, he pointed out, were the only states making any real contributions to the national treasury, and Pennsylvania was about to quit. Connecticut and New Jersey had already formally refused to make further payments. Did New York then want to shoulder the whole national burden itself or, likewise refusing, see the whole fabric of the nation, which had cost so much blood and tears to raise, perish now because of its own selfishness? Other states had been willing to make an unrestricted grant, but only if all the other states likewise assented; so everything now depended on New York's action. It could make or break the struggling nation. It was not enough to pass the impost. Without congressional control of collectors, the impost itself meant little. Hadn't he, Hamilton, himself been a receiver of taxes under the existing system and seen how futile it was? His own poor performance then reinforced his argument now. Congress had rightly refused New York's empty gesture of approving the impost with state collectors. Now it was all or nothing.

The gallery applauded loudly. The voice of the people, as heard from the gallery, could not fail to shake the proudly Populist Clintonians. No one from their ranks rose to refute him; it seemed that Hamilton alone was speaking in the *vox populi, vox Dei*. When the measure came up for the vote, the galleries bent forward in silence to hear the result.

The vote was announced; party lines held firm; Hamilton's resolutions had been defeated; his eloquence had not changed a single vote. Spectators cried out in shocked disapproval at a typical legislative performance. They filed out muttering imprecations against Clinton, the absent political boss whose puppets had twitched obediently at the end of his string without attempting to argue the issue with Hamilton. Clinton had won a great victory.

But by losing to such a bold demonstration of bossism after none of Clinton's men had stood up to argue against Hamilton, Hamilton and Schuyler built up much sympathy among members of Clinton's majority. Hamilton had learned the lesson of snatching late victories out of sympathies raised by early defeats. The second thoughts that his unopposed argument raised dissolved monolithic opposition. Some Clintonians had listened in silence and voted by Clinton's order, but Hamilton's speech and the indignation of the gallery had made a strong impression on them. Some were ashamed of what they had done and, according to Schuyler, "wished an opportunity to make some atonement."

A group of young Yale graduates called the Hartford (Connecticut) wits, some of whom had had army experiences that left them with a nationalistic bias in favor of being paid, celebrated Hamilton's speech on the impost and his other responses to the exigencies of the times in an epic poem dedicated to their hero, *The Anarchiad*. Hamilton, the young hero of the piece, gives battle to Old Anarch, a distinctly Clintonian type, who favors the happy days "when every rogue shall literally do what is right in his own eyes."

Old Anarch, apprehending that his crushing defeat of Hamilton will serve his young antagonist as a stepping-stone to future victory, soliloquizes:

> Ardent and bold, the sinking land to save
> In council sapient as in action brave,
> I fear'd young HAMILTON'S unshaken soul.
>
> . . . .
> Yet while the Senate with his accents rung
> Fire in his eye, and thunder on his tongue,
> My band of mutes in dumb confusion throng.
>
> . . . .
> And yield an empire to thy wild command.

Now Hamilton and Schuyler made ready to give "Old Anarch" Clinton's "band of mutes" their "opportunity to make some atonement."

They introduced bills simultaneously in the senate and assembly to instruct the New York delegates in Congress to recommend to the other states a convention like that which had been called for at Annapolis, but only "for the purpose of revising the Articles of Confederation." Clinton and some of his mutes still fought the measure, but some of his more independent followers, who had been seen privately by Hamilton and Schuyler, seemed willing to "yield an empire," or, at least, the Empire State, to Hamilton's "wild command" by way of atonement for their earlier opposition. Their votes, now called for publicly, were enough to carry the measure in favor of the Annapolis call for the Constitutional Convention.

Congress had dawdled in confirming the call, but now wasted no time. It quickly adopted the Massachusetts form of approval. The call was rushed back to the states, and Hamilton and Schuyler speedily moved the New York legislature for its approval and appointment of delegates. Their swift tactic caught Clintonian opponents off-balance. Those who had reacted to their boss by committing themselves on the recommendation now found that "it was too late to retract, and they acquiesced with chagrin in a resolution for the appointment of delegates to the convention."

The governor's men in their turn now demanded that the delegates be appointed by both houses, voting together. With the senate almost evenly divided and the assembly heavily antinationalist, this would mean the election of antinationalist delegates. Schuyler quickly saw the problem and prevailed upon the senate to reject this procedure. The assembly favored Clinton's proposal. With a stalemate between the two houses, the opposing factions had to compromise. The names of three delegates were finally agreed on. Two were antinationalist, Robert Yates and John Lansing, Jr. The third was a nationalist, Alexander Hamilton.

The naming of one nationalist did not much trouble Clinton and his followers at the time because at the convention voting would, of course, be by unit rule. The loyal votes of Yates and Lansing could be counted to nullify Hamilton's and keep New York's single vote safely on Clinton's puppet strings. Obscured by the battle over selection of delegates and Clinton's satisfaction at retaining two-to-one control of New York's convention vote was the fact that New York was now formally committed to being represented at the convention. That was the climactic business of the legislative session, and it had gone Hamilton's way.

Hamilton's last speech of his one and only term in the New York State Assembly was a grace note with a pitch from his brief in *Rutgers v. Waddington.* It resonated toward future battles on the floor of the great convention to assemble in Philadelphia the following month. His 1783 resolution calling for a convention had noted as one of the dozen defects of the Confederation that states had in their power the possibility of "defeating the treaties of commerce entered into by the United States."

On March 21 the Continental Congress had resolved that the states should repeal all acts repugnant to the treaty of peace. When the bill to make Congress's resolution effective in the state came up for debate in the assembly on April 17, Hamilton took the floor to make what the New York *Daily Advertiser* described as "a very animated and powerful speech." In broad, general terms, he urged repeal of all the anti-Tory laws. No attempt should be made to itemize specifically just what laws were to be repealed: leave that to the courts and the judges, he said. Treaties were the laws of the land, he insisted, and the bill before the house would confirm this. Now he cited Cicero as authority for the proposition he had urged as his own in *Rutgers v. Waddington:* "that when two laws clash, that which relates to the most important matters ought to be preferred." After his stand, whole new groups of formerly disenfranchised Tories would be staunch Hamilton supporters for life.

Next day, still under the spell of Hamilton's eloquence the assembly passed the bill, sweeping aside all the anti-Tory laws. The senate failed to approve it, and it died. But the assembly's vote, as the legislature adjourned for new elections, gave Hamilton the satisfaction for almost the first time of breaking through Clinton's iron control of the majority's votes in the lower house of the New York legislature. Clintonians were becoming alarmed at such inroads.

The 1786 and 1787 sessions of the New York legislature had met in New York City. As the session adjourned, Hamilton introduced a bill on April 16 that would please his Schuyler and van Rensselaer relatives in Albany and suit his own convenience: in future, the legislature should hold alternate sessions in New York City and Albany. The Clintonians thought they saw one last chance to rid themselves of this freshman assemblyman who had become the chief threat to their monolithic control. They knew that Hamilton and his family divided their time between their house on Wall Street and the Schuylers' at Albany and that Hamilton had many clients in the Albany area. He had few at Poughkeepsie, which was Governor Clinton's bailiwick. John Church Hamilton drily explained the defeat of his father's bill: "It being known that his professional engagements would not permit him to sojourn at Poughkeepsie, that place was selected for the meeting of the next legislature." If Hamilton could not be moved out of their way in the legislature, the legislature would be moved out of his way.

No higher tribute could have been invented. A freshman assemblyman of the minority party is normally considered one of the most insignificant species of all political animals. Having achieved this pinnacle in his first term, Hamilton, in the *Daily Advertiser* of April 23, wryly observing his name being placed in nomination for a second term, informed "such of the fellow citizens as might be inclined to honor him with their choice" in the upcoming election that the decision to meet at Poughkeepsie "renders it impracticable" for him to serve.

To Hamilton, it did not seem illogical to turn down the short trip and limited stay that legislative sessions in Poughkeepsie would have meant as he packed his bags for Philadelphia and a trip twice as long and a stay of indefinite duration beginning May 14. He cleaned up some loose ends of legal business for such clients as John Jay, Augustus van Cortlandt, Mrs. Samuel Bayard, Mary Bryant, and P. I. Moore. He put in an expense reimbursement voucher for expenses of the Annapolis trip of £76 18s. It was twice as much as Egbert Benson had spent. This probably meant that to buck up Madison out of his discouragement and to bring Randolph around to New Jersey's broad language encompassing all federal "exigencies," Hamilton had stood his fellow delegates to some extra rounds of drinks at Mann's. Hamilton probably already felt in his bones that, of all the great state papers he was ever to write, the draft of the Annapolis apostrophe to convene in Philadelphia the following May would be the single most important of his life. Now he gathered up and stuffed into his saddle bags his office file copies of a decade's harvest of unadopted, unsupported, and rejected planks for a constitution, all designed "to render the federal government adequate to the exigencies of the Union."

There was satisfaction in being able to answer a summons he had written himself. And he could smile at the irony that his hostile legislature, partly to rid itself of the threat he posed to its sovereignty, had appointed him a delegate to the convention that he had engineered to take much of its sovereignty away from it and yoke it once and for all into a union of states.

21

AN INVISIBLE HAND GUIDED ALL TOWARD THE GENERAL GOOD

WE ARE NOW TO DECIDE FOREVER THE FATE OF REPUBLICAN GOV-
ERNMENT. IF WE DO NOT GIVE TO THAT FORM DUE STABILITY AND
WISDOM, IT WILL BE DISGRACED . . . AND LOST TO MANKIND
FOREVER. . . . I AM AS ZEALOUS AN ADVOCATE FOR LIBERTY AS ANY
MAN, AND WOULD CHEERFULLY BECOME A MARTYR TO IT. BUT
REAL LIBERTY IS NEITHER FOUND IN DESPOTISM OR THE EXTREMES
OF DEMOCRACY, BUT IN MODERATE GOVERNMENTS.
> —*Speech from the floor of the Constitutional Con-
> vention, June 26, 1787*

HUMAN MIND FOND OF COMPROMISE.
> —*Private Note on a speech of James Madison, June
> 6, 1787*

When Thomas Jefferson, serving comfortably as American minister in
Paris, first read the list of names of delegates to the Constitutional Convention
of 1787, he wrote his friend John Adams, then serving uncomfortably as minister
in London: "It really is an assembly of demigods."

Jefferson was not alone in this view, although no one else expressed it so fulsomely. It was widely held outside the convention and demurely suspected within. The *Daily Advertiser* in New York described the gathering as "the collective wisdom of the Continent"; the *Pennsylvania Herald* found it "a wonderful display of wisdom, eloquence, and patriotism"; and the *New York Journal*, like many other newspapers, identified it as "the Grand Convention." It thought that *august* was the only word that could convey the quality of these 55 men. Benjamin Franklin told a friend that it was truly "une assemblée des notables." Madison remarked that it was "the best contribution of talents the states could make for the occasion." Even crusty George Mason, who was already "heartily tired of the etiquette and nonsense so fashionable in this city," had to admit to his son that "America has certainly, upon this occasion, drawn forth her first characters." The French-American writer Hector St. John de Crèvecoeur informed the Duc de La Rochefoucauld that the convention was "composed of the most enlightened men of the continent." And Louis Guillaume Otto, French chargé d'affaires to the Comte de Montmorin wrote, with patronizing amazement, on April 10, 1787: "If all the delegates named for this Convention at Philadelphia are present, we will never have seen, even in Europe, an assembly more respectable for the talents, knowledge, disinterestedness, and patriotism of those who compose it." The 55 men who finally reached Philadelphia in sufficient numbers to form a quorum by May 25 were of such a temper and quality that a poor, illegitimate, immigrant orphan boy from a backward Antillean island, now just turned 30, had risen far fast to be counted as one of the number. That he would quickly rise further still to establish himself as one of the much smaller inner circle of the fifty-five is still more remarkable unless it be set down to generous tribute that quality pays to genius.

Among the fifty-five were some of the finest political minds of the nation. Virginia had sent a notable delegation: Washington, Madison, Edmund Randolph, George Mason, and George Wythe. Pennsylvania was equally well represented by Franklin, Robert Morris, Gouverneur Morris, and James Wilson. South Carolina sent the two Pinckneys, Charles and Charles Cotesworth, and John Rutledge. Connecticut was represented by Roger Sherman and William S. Johnson; Delaware, by the former Pennsylvanian John Dickinson. The stature of the delegates was a warranty that proposals of the convention would be received and considered everywhere with the greatest respect. During the struggle over ratification that followed in 1788, Melancton Smith of New York grew tired of being told that he ought to approve the Constitution simply because of the extraordinary "character and ability" of its authors. "The favorers of this system," he wrote, were "not very prudent in bringing this forward" because, he added,

> It provokes to an investigation of characters, which is an invidious task. I do not wish to detract from their merits, but I will venture to affirm that twenty assemblies of equal number might be collected, equally respectable both in point of ability, integrity, and patriotism.

Smith was overstating the contrary case, but it was true that, remarkable as the Framers present were, they did not represent the whole nation, nor even all of its best minds. Thomas Jefferson, John Adams, Samuel Adams, John Hancock, and Patrick Henry, who had been prime movers in the Revolution, were not among the Framers. Also absent were such good friends of Hamilton as Oliver Wolcott, Jeremiah Wadsworth, General Philip Schuyler, John Jay, James Duane, R. R. Livingston, Elias Boudinot, and Timothy Pickering. Nor were there present any representatives of poor farmers and debtors like Daniel Shays. During his childhood and teens, Hamilton had probably seen as much hardship, poverty, and slavery from the underside of society as any other man present. None of the others had a mother who had served a term in prison for whoring.

Aside from bibulous Luther Martin of Maryland and Clinton's men Robert Yates and John Lansing, Jr., of New York, there were no self-proclaimed champions of the Populist persuasion present. By and large, the convention delegates represented the propertied people of the country.

Professor Charles A. Beard contended that the motives of the 55 were selfish and that their governing purpose was to rescue and safeguard their own property interests from people like the Shaysites. Beard claimed that at least five-sixths of the delegates "were immediately, directly, and personally interested in the outcome of their labors at Philadelphia, and were . . . economic beneficiaries from the adoption of the Constitution." This does not say much more than that five-sixths of the people in the country-at-large were likewise personally interested in the outcome and would also be economic beneficiaries from it. This was not a bad thing and, on the whole, speaks well for the result. Few were as rich in lands and slaves as Thomas Jefferson. It would have been less misleading for Beard to have taken note that most of the delegates were men who had made their own way in the world as small independent free enterprisers—farmers, merchants, lawyers, bankers, and businessmen—few enjoyed much inherited fortune or the tenured insulation of payrollers. From wide experience of life, they had gained a visceral understanding of the complex economic forces that undergird the loftiest political theories. Such experience is often missing from the lives of payrollers and inheritors.

As nations went, the United States in 1787 was a good one in which to live, work, and aspire. It was not a place for men with the tastes of English dukes, the appetites of French tax collectors, or the memories of Italian bishops, but there was no place like it anywhere else in the world for men with a modest desire to be free, prosperous, and respectable and to own their own homes and farms. "Europe with all its pomp," the French-American Crèvecoeur wrote, "is not to be compared to this continent, for men of middle station, or laborers."

In the opinion of half the philosophers of Europe and most citizens of the United States, even then, there was no better country on the face of the earth. It had extent, resources, and opportunities unbounded; it harbored a "numerous, brave, and hardy people." Crèvecoeur went so far as to say "we are the most perfect society now existing in the world."

The delegates, by and large, felt the same way. Each had been chosen by his state legislature in the same manner prescribed for electing its delegates to Congress. Although property qualifications and certain other limitations on voting make those legislatures seem undemocratic by present-day standards like Beard's, they were by far the most democratic legislatures then existing anywhere in the world. The delegates to the convention were accurate, not wrong, when they called themselves "representatives of the people of the United States." They felt no sense of alienation from the mass of the people of their states. As they trickled into Philadelphia, they could rightly enjoy the feeling of legitimacy that comes to extraordinary bodies that are both legal and popular. Their mood was expansive. They exuded an esprit de corps from the beginning. An auspicious feature of the convention, about which there was approving comment at the time, was the happy reunion of old friends and wartime comrades at the Indian Queen and the Indian King, the Black Bear and Boar's Head, and the other taverns, as well as at the fine private homes of the city, like Robert Morris's and William Bingham's.

By Monday, May 14, the appointed day, only Pennsylvania's and Virginia's delegations had as yet arrived in Philadelphia. Hamilton reached town with his fellow delegate Robert Yates on May 18. After checking in at the Indian Queen Tavern on Fourth Street, between Market and Chestnut, the first thing he did was file his credentials and instructions from President General von Steuben as a delegate from the New York State Society of the Cincinnati to the General Meeting of the Society. It was also convening a convention in Philadelphia that week. The president general of the national society, George Washington, had arrived four days earlier and was lodged at Robert Morris's three-story brick mansion, Lemon Hill, now part of Fairmont Park, which all considered the grandest house in Philadelphia. Within its hospitable mahogany doors, every piece of furniture was a masterpiece of the cabinetmaker's art, fashioned of cherrywood and oak, inlaid with sandalwood, cornered and trimmed with polished silver, and rubbed to a gleam. Lemon Hill was obviously the only suitable headquarters for a national president general.

Many of Washington's former officers saw the Society of the Cincinnati as one of the few effective counterforces left in the country that could be counted on to oppose extremists like those who had stirred up Shays' Rebellion during the terrible winter just past. Stalwart old Henry Knox, secretary general of the Cincinnati, never an alarmist through all the war years, writing to Washington the previous fall of Shays's rebellion, had said that the insurgents, by combining with people of similar sentiments in Rhode Island, Connecticut, and New Hampshire, could "constitute a body of twelve or fifteen thousand desperate and unprincipled men" well adapted by youth for fighting. This was more men than the Continental Army had mustered at most times during the Revolution. Washington had passed Knox's disturbing letter along to James Madison with his own pointed question: "If there exists not a power to check them, what security has a man for life, liberty or property? . . ."

Madison had asked George Washington to come to the Constitutional Convention as head of the Virginia delegation "to give this subject a very solemn dress," as if he were about to place a mute clothes horse in a show window. Washington had responded civilly but tartly that "Influence is no government."

As president general of the Cincinnati, Washington had called the "triennial general meeting" for Philadelphia on the first Monday in May of 1787, but had then told some that he could not attend for reasons of health. Privately, he told Madison what would please him, that his reason for not attending was that the state societies had not yet got around to eliminating genealogical qualifications for membership and certain other features that had drawn civilian fire like Jefferson's.

Washington explained to Madison that he could not attend the federal convention at the same time "with any degree of consistency." He could not appear at the one and not the other "without giving offense to a very worthy and respectable part of the American community, the late officers of the American army." To Madison, the danger of Washington's nonattendance at the one overrode the imagined danger of his presence at the other. By gracefully yielding both to Madison and to Knox and by overcoming his innate reluctance to return to a city of such unhappy wartime memories, Washington won credit and goodwill from people of all shades of opinion across the entire spectrum of American politics. Of his conduct, Madison wrote Jefferson that "To forsake the honorable retreat to which he had retired and risk the reputation he had so deservedly acquired, manifested a zeal for the public interest that could, after so many and illustrious services, scarcely have been expected of him." Knowing Washington better than to patronize him like Madison by saying that it could "scarcely have been expected of him," Knox wrote Lafayette that Washington, "secure as he was in his fame, . . . has again committed it to the mercy of events. Nothing but the critical situation of his country would have induced him to so hazardous a conduct."

After thus carefully paving the political way with both sides, Washington compromised by coming to Philadelphia for both conventions. When he entered the city, crowds gathered, cheering wildly. Madison duly reported to Thomas Jefferson in Paris that Washington had received "the acclamations of the people."

After the formal sessions of both conventions were over for the day, delegates like Hamilton and Washington and the rest would take tea in one place, dine in another, receive and return visits, meet with groups of delegates in various taverns, attend the theater, talk with one another during intermissions, whisper in corridors, and become better acquainted with their counterparts who had come to town from states stretching from New Hampshire to Georgia. Hamilton took tea and dined and drank with Washington and Knox and all the others.

Although nothing could match Washington's lordly lodgings at Robert Morris's Lemon Hill, the Indian Queen Tavern was "kept in elegant style." To George Mason, who had brought his son to town with him, it was "cheap." The proprietor provided his delegate guests—Hamilton, Strong, Gorham, and Gerry

of Massachusetts; Madison and Mason, Martin and Williamson of North
Carolina; John Rutledge and Charles Pinckney of South Carolina—a hall at the
Indian Queen in which they could hold informal gatherings, pass around cigars,
and circulate decanters of wine as they called over each past day's events and
prepared the strategies and surprises of tomorrow's.

The Cincinnati mustered their quorum of state delegates well before a
quorum of state delegates could be mustered for the Constitutional Convention.
The Cincinnati unanimously reelected Washington president general, retold
their war stories, and adjourned; the Constitutional Convention stayed.

On the twenty-fifth, the delegates assembled in the chamber at the State
House, now known as Independence Hall. In the same chamber Hamilton had
sat as a delegate to the Continental Congress, had demanded protection for
Congress from the recalcitrant Pennsylvania Executive Council, and had faced
down the army mutineers.

The original plan of procedure had been for Benjamin Franklin, Washington's only possible rival for the office of president of the Constitutional Convention, to nominate him for the dais, but rain poured down the first day the quorum
was present. The aged philosopher could not attend, even in the shelter of his
customary sedan chair borne on the backs of his two "trusty convicts." In
Franklin's absence, Robert Morris, "on behalf of the deputation from Pennsylvania," rose and nominated his houseguest as president of the convention. John
Rutledge of South Carolina seconded, and Washington's election was made
unanimous. Morris and Rutledge then conducted Washington to the presiding
officer's seat on the low dais. During the Revolution, this same seat had been
occupied by Washington's titular civilian commander, the president of Congress.
When President General Washington finally called the quorum of states to
order, the chamber was quieter than usual inside because loose earth had been
spread on the cobblestones of Chestnut Street outside to deaden the noise of
passing traffic.

From the chair, according to James Madison's notes, Washington "in a very
emphatic manner thanked the Convention for the honor they had conferred on
him, reminded them of the novelty of the scene of business in which he was to
act, lamented his want of better qualifications, and claimed the indulgence of the
house toward the involuntary errors which his inexperience might occasion."

James Wilson of Pennsylvania moved that a permanent secretary be appointed and nominated the absent Benjamin Franklin's grandson, Mr. William
Temple Franklin, for the honor. But George Mason and the powerful Virginia
delegation opposed him. They favored John Beckley of Virginia, who had come
to Philadelphia in the company of Edmund Randolph confident of being elected
with Virginia's support.

Hamilton quickly offered a third name, that of Major William Jackson of
Philadelphia, who had served as assistant secretary of war under the Articles
of Confederation. Jackson had quietly lobbied for the post of secretary and after
a brief struggle was elected by the convention over Franklin and Beckley. For
Hamilton, it was a tactical victory on behalf of a friend and fellow Cincinnatian.

By the same tactical victory, Hamilton established the loser, John Beckley, as one of the most dangerous enemies of the second rank he would have for the rest of his life. Beckley soon became one of Thomas Jefferson's and Madison's most energetic and effective informers and agents provocateurs.

Washington named Hamilton, along with the venerable Chancellor George Wythe of Virginia and Charles Pinckney of South Carolina, to the Committee on Standing Rules and Orders, the first or second most important committee of the convention.

By placing his own man in the key position of secretary of the convention, by obtaining a key committee appointment for himself, and by creating a dangerous enemy, Hamilton won early recognition as a leading member of the convention.

The job of Hamilton's man Jackson, the official secretary, was to keep a simple orderly record of motions and votes. Knowing that posterity would be grateful for much more than the bare bones of journal minutes, for "an exact account of what might pass in the Convention," particularly the text of speeches and debates, Madison appointed himself the amanuensis of the proceedings. The following account of what passed on the floor of the convention is based primarily on his notes. No one kept a record of what was said back at the Indian Queen to make things turn out as they did on the floor. Madison chose a seat in front of the dais, with the other members on his right and left, and from there he said:

> I noted . . . what was read from the chair or spoken by the members; and losing not a moment unnecessarily between the adjournment and reassembling of the Convention, I was enabled to write out my daily notes during the session or within a few finishing days after its close. . . . In the labor and correctness of this I was not a little aided by practice, and by a familiarity with the style and the train of observation and reasoning which characterized the principal speakers.

Anyone who has ever been involved in the inner workings of an important political convention knows that nearly everything that happens on the floor is but the staged sum of an infinite number of backstage maneuvers conceived and rehearsed by small groups off the floor at places like the hall of the Indian Queen. The Constitutional Convention was no exception. If some recorder had taken down all the conversations occurring at the Indian Queen and elsewhere off the floor, posterity would understand far better than it does the real meaning of the happenings on the floor of the Constitutional Convention. Gratitude to Madison for keeping the most complete set of notes of events that took place on the floor should not mislead the reader into believing that they represent more than the onstage events of the convention. The backstage events, the rehearsals, and rewrites that made the onstage events less extemporaneous than they seemed will never be known.

Look back, for example, at the inscrutability of the ostensibly simple opening organizational moves: who decided that Franklin would nominate Washington to preside? Who lined up the winning votes for Hamilton's man William Jackson over such powerful opponents as the deserving and unrewarded Franklin's grandson and the powerful Virginia junta's protégé Beckley? Did not such a coup have to be carefully planned perhaps at a convivial congregation of Cincinnati?

How did Hamilton manage to win a coveted appointment to the Rules Committee, one of the most important committees appointed at any convention? At critical moments of all such conventions, the manner in which the secretary officially records a disputed action or the effect of a standing rule and order on a question of seating a delegate can have a much more significant meaning than a formal speech or the tally of a final vote, or make the final tally a foregone conclusion.

In the case of Hamilton's successes at Philadelphia, it is submitted that the above questions probably had a single, easy answer: Washington's favor to a fellow Cincinnatian. Their complex interpersonal relations going back a dozen years explain some, but, by no means, all of the mysteries of the convention.

Hamilton's rich political experiences at the Annapolis Convention, in the Continental Congress and the New York legislature, and many other conventions, councils, and committees over the years had taught him that notwithstanding the size and importance of the Constitutional Convention of 1787, the methods by which results would be accomplished there were not basically different from methods that had served at lesser conclaves. The process of gaining successful results in deliberative bodies involves dualities that only a man who had seen as many ostensible, early defeats turn into late victories could understand as profoundly as Hamilton did.

He understood that ideas, principles, and policies that are neither defined nor challenged are the most secure. But once challenged, such secure seeming ideas lose their impregnability. A penetrating challenge reaches chinks in the monolith and dissolves the cement. As the French were fond of saying, "Le Dieu défini est le Dieu fini." A thought that, until the challenge came, was unthinkable is transmuted by the challenge into something that is thinkable, then debatable, and finally, over time, winnable or defeatable.

Or at least compromisable. A crushing defeat after a vigorous and brilliant speech from the floor that brings applause from the galleries but changes no votes in favor of a lost cause is not necessarily the whole story, nor even the total defeat that it may seem to be at the time. Experience had also taught him that preplanned parliamentary demonstrations on the floor of control exercised from behind the scenes to convey an impression of irresistible strength are only that. They are not impervious to change or compromise. An initial defeat on the floor for a favored measure is often an essential ingredient of its ultimate victory, which, in such bodies, is almost never total. Positions forcefully stated on the floor, to which adamant objections are interposed, are but the visible "tip of the iceberg" of the backstage, more or less secret life of such conventions. An invisible convention takes place on the periphery of the floor—over tankards at taverns; in smoke-filled rooms, or the hall of the Indian Queen; at gatherings of Cincinnatians, over a quiet dinner, or under cover of a noisy brothel. Accomplishment on the floor of a collective end result that no one could have forseen at the beginning becomes the sum of the interaction of recorded or remembered happenings on the floor with innumerable, mostly unrecorded, happenings off the floor that may be no less well remembered. Such happenings include tentative suggestions, angry rejections, delicate modifications, grudging accommodations, purposeful misunderstandings, crocodile tears, grave forebodings, feelings-out, hurt feelings, abraded egos, gratified greeds, flattering misattributions, intercepted secrets, overheard remarks, and lucky random thoughts: the list is endless. Such events also include ultimate designs and purposeful steps to carry them out.

Few delegates who checked in at the Indian Queen would bring with them traveling bags stuffed as full as Hamilton's with file copies of years of such ultimate designs—and a mind as well stocked with experience of tactical maneuvers for pushing them forward over strong opposition.

He knew the bold postures to strike on the floor to carry forward his program by the visible part of such tactics, as well as the flexible gestures, genialities, and jests needed to smooth their flow by unnoticed tactics on the periphery of the floor. But he could compress the core strategy that underlay all his tactics into the five words that he jotted down privately while listening to a speech of Madison on the floor on June 6. The words were: "Human mind fond of compromise."

This postulate, which would not hold true for all human minds in all times and places, was indisputably true of the human minds represented by the men of the world at this convention. It would probably not have been true of real "demigods," and it was probably less true of Hamilton's mind than any other present. Hamilton's mind did not grasp at compromise except at the last extremity. Like Phocion, he fought with uncompromising, immoderate tenacity for policy that he saw as "moderate." He raised this standard from the floor on June 26, saying, "real liberty is neither found in despotism or the extremes of democracy, but in moderate governments." In order to end up with a constitution that provided "moderate government" it followed that, given the fondness of human minds like those of these delegates for compromise, someone would have to stake out polar positions from which such minds could gratefully recede toward a moderate mean. If fear of loneliness in taking an unpopular stance on the floor prevented all other delegates from staking out such positions, well, Hamilton had stood alone in such stances before.

Even without the help of the senior Cincinnatian presiding from the dais, Hamilton would have been widely recognized at the convention. To fellow delegates he had not already met, Hamilton was pointed out as a prodigy of America —a man of style, skill, ambition, and energy. But because he was a nationalist-minded minority of one in the most strongly Populist and antinationalist delegation any state had sent, it was obvious to all that he would not be able to cast his state's vote where his voice was and that his position was bound to be the most difficult, anomalous, embarrassing, and frustrating of any of the delegates on the floor.

Many of the delegates already knew Hamilton well; and he, them. As his eyes scanned the faces in the meeting room in the State House, they would fall on half-a-dozen men with whom he had served at Trenton, Brandywine, Germantown, Valley Forge, Monmouth, and Yorktown. He had known many from service in Congress and at Annapolis.

More than 30 of the Framers had shared with him the frustrations of service in feckless Congresses, where, like him, they had learned the exigency of a stronger union. Like Hamilton, too, most of them had also served in the legislatures of their states and there had learned well the power of local counterpressures for state sovereignty. In the Pennsylvania delegation, Gouverneur Morris was one of Hamilton's closest friends and wittiest correspondents on such assorted subjects as banks, gold, marriage, and mistresses. And Hamilton had long corresponded with Robert Morris on schemes for bolstering federal credit, improving the fortunes of Robert Morris, and receiving Continental taxes that New Yorkers refused to pay.

The work of Hamilton's Committee on Standing Rules and Orders had much to do with the ultimate success of the convention. Chancellor George Wythe of Virginia reported for the committee on May 28, and the report became the basis of most of the procedures of the convention. For tactical reasons, it was arranged for some of the rules to be introduced from the floor. For the most part, the rules followed those of Congress, but special note should be taken of four.

First, voting was to be, as in Congress, strictly by states, with each state, no matter how large or small, having one vote. Virginia, with a population of 454,983 and 292,627 slaves; Pennsylvania, with 430,636 and 3,737 slaves; Massachusetts, with 387,787; and New York, with 318,796 and 21,324 slaves would have the same single vote as Delaware, with 50,209 and 8,887 slaves.

Although Hamilton and Madison and other nationalist delegates from the large states were determined to do away forever with the confederation principle of one-state, one-vote voting, they recognized that they would have to accomplish this political miracle at a meeting organized on that very principle. Had they not, the meeting would have broken up in angry disorder before it had really begun.

Second, a decorum befitting a gathering of gentlemen was to be maintained. Members were politely forbidden to whisper, read, or pass notes while one of their colleagues was speaking and could be "called to order by any other member as well as by the President."

Third, the proceedings were to be informal, by calls for "yeas and nays" without recording of formal or record votes or roll calls. This made it easier for delegates to feel their way toward solutions they could not immediately anticipate.

Finally, the convention voted, on the prompting of Pierce Butler of South Carolina, to guard "against licentious publications of their proceedings." In search of privacy, which they knew they would need in abundance, the members voted:

That no copy be taken of any entry on the journal during the sitting of the house without leave of the house. That members only be permitted to inspect the journal. That nothing spoken in the house be printed, or otherwise published or communicated without leave.

Few delegates may have clearly grasped the import of their action on May 28–29, but the so-called secrecy rule was the most critical procedural decision the convention was ever to make. At the time, George Mason found this a "necessary precaution to prevent misrepresentations or mistakes;" Madison later insisted that "no Constitution would ever have been adopted by the convention if the debates had been public." The secrecy rule stirred the imaginations and loosened the tongues of delegates on the floor, permitted them to take advanced positions and then to withdraw gracefully under fire, guarded them against careless or willful misinterpretations of their gropings for compromises, allowed one consensus after another to form out of a jumble of half-formed opinions and half-baked prejudices, encouraged them to express honest doubts about such sacred cows as the sovereignty of the states and the glories of the militia, and spared orators like Randolph or Charles Pinckney from the temptation of playing to any gallery but that of posterity. This rule probably had more significance for Hamilton than for any other delegate there. His, too, was the reputation that would suffer most by a breach of it. Without it, the features of the Constitution that we now think of as characteristically Hamiltonian would have been politically impossible.

The secrecy rule was rigidly observed by the delegates and uncomplainingly accepted by the press and public. So careful was Washington in observing it, for example, that he would record nothing in his diary about the sessions. He jotted down notes only of the convivial gatherings he attended afterwards at the Indian Queen and elsewhere. So discreet was Madison, who was keeping the most copious notes of the convention, that when he wrote to a cherished cousin, the president of the College of William and Mary, the latter replied in exasperation: "If you cannot tell us what you are doing, you might at least give us some information of what you are not doing."

Although the newspapers informed their readers that the convention had elected to carry on in "the greatest secrecy," no one seems to have thought it proper until the end of the summer to say openly, as Jefferson wrote privately to Adams, that the "precedent" of "tying up the tongues" of the delegates was "abominable." As a member of Congress, Hamilton had urged that the doors be flung open and the public be allowed in to hear debates. This was a different process, of a higher order. More was at stake than scoring debating points with the populace outside the hall. In an age when "the right to know" was far more restrained in application than it is today—and than it was to be only a few years after the event—Madison reported accurately when he wrote to Jefferson that although "the public mind" was "very impatient" to hear the proposals of the convention, almost no "discontent" was "expressed at the concealment" of the process designed to grind out these proposals. It is a fact of huge consequence for history that the spirit and customs of the age encouraged the men of 1787 to produce "an open covenant, secretly arrived at."

Votes in committee on seemingly unimportant procedural matters, and floor votes as well, seemed to be going Hamilton's way. It is impossible to be certain how important a role he played on the floor or in the hall of the Indian Queen to cause all such votes to turn out as they did. Given the Hamiltonian tone of the end result, however, it is impossible to doubt that his role was important and central.

The call from Annapolis had been framed in terms of exigencies that had to be dealt with in the areas of trade, commerce, and economics. On the face of it, the political overlay was to be adjusted only to the extent that economic exigencies dictated such adjustments. From London Angelica Church had sent her adored brother-in-law a copy of Adam Smith's *The Wealth of Nations* not long after its first publication in 1776. No one at the convention had learned Adam Smith's lessons better than Hamilton. No one knew better than he that an invisible hand could guide all toward the general good.

On May 29 Edmund Randolph rose and presented to the convention 15 resolutions, which constituted the draft of a constitution. This came to be known as the Virginia plan. It provided for a bicameral legislature and a national executive to be appointed by that body. The national legislature would be vested with the right to veto any state law contravening the federal Articles and the power to employ force against a recalcitrant state. The executive, in conjunction with a national judiciary, would have a similar power of veto over both state and federal enactments. Such veto might be overriden by the legislature. There was a departure from the familiar outline when it came to the most important political matter of all; who could vote. Randolph's Virginia plan called not for "one man, one vote," for all offices, but drastically limited the right of suffrage. Voting was proportioned to "the quotas of contribution" or to "the number of free inhabitants, as one or the other rule may seem best in different cases."

The Virginia plan as a whole went far beyond mere tinkering with the Articles of Confederation. So before debate on its provisions could even get under way, the shackles placed on the scope of the convention had to be removed. By the terms of the call from Annapolis, as well as the enabling resolutions of Congress and the state legislatures, most delegates were sent to the convention only for the purpose of amending the Articles of Confederation, not to introduce a whole new form of government.

Randolph moved adoption of the Virginia plan. The question on the floor was whether the United States "were susceptible of one government," that is, whether to frame a new national government or merely to amend the Articles. In the New York delegation, Yates voted "Nay," and Hamilton "Aye." The third delegate, Lansing, had not yet arrived. New York's vote being split, it was not counted either way.

The fundamental resolution finally passed by a vote of 6 to 1: that a *national* government should be established, consisting of a supreme legislature, executive, and judiciary. In favor were Massachusetts, Pennsylvania, Delaware,

ALEXANDER HAMILTON.

John F.E. Prud'homme's engraving of Hamilton after a miniature by
Archibald Robertson (c. 1790) is an arresting study of the country's first
Secretary of the Treasury.

In the person of Elizabeth Schuyler, Hamilton found a lifelong companion whose good nature and even temper nicely balanced his own somber and moody personality.

Hamilton met Lt. Col. John Laurens in 1777 while both were serving as junior officers under Washington's command. Although normally wary of close friendships, Hamilton developed a strong affection for Laurens, which lasted until the latter's death in 1782.

Library of Congress

By Emanuel Leutze: Monmouth County Historical Society

In Emanuel Leutze's stirring canvas *The Battle of Monmouth,* Washington (sword upraised at center) leads his men forward to rally a band of retreating Revolutionary soldiers under the command of General Lee. Hamilton (with white plume hat) and Lafayette (hatless next to Hamilton) rode close behind Washington.

XIX

By Charles Willson Peale: Maryland State House

Charles Willson Peale celebrated Washington's triumph at Yorktown with the above portrait of the general flanked by an aide, Lt. Col. Tench Tilghman (center), and his ally, the Marquis de Lafayette. The work was painted in 1784.

In John Trumbull's famous painting *Surrender of Cornwallis at Yorktown* Hamilton stands at far right next to the gray horse. John Laurens is beside him.

These four men (clockwise from left) John Jay, James Duane, James Madison, and Robert Morris, were among Hamilton's staunchest colleagues in the fight for a strong federal governmental structure.

The Critical Period of American History
by John Fiske

Hamilton was one of New York's representatives to the Annapolis Convention, held at the Maryland State House in 1786 to discuss commercial matters. With only five states attending the meeting, little progress was made, but the convention did issue the call for a meeting of all the states—which was the Constitutional Convention of 1787.

An engraving showing Washington presiding over a session of the momentous convocation of the Constitutional Convention.

The triumph of Hamilton's federalist philosophy was honored when New Yorkers named a float symbolizing the federal "ship of state" for a parade to mark ratification of the Constitution.

In 1788 Hamilton successfully lobbied in the Continental Congress to have New York City named the temporary national capital. The City Hall building was renovated and renamed Federal Hall, and Washington took the oath of office as the first President of the United States from its balcony in 1789. Hamilton's home and law office was just a short walk from this site.

Baron Frederick W.A.H.F. von Steuben was the personification of army professionalism, European style, with which Hamilton sought to imbue continentals at Valley Forge—though some of the Baron's own credentials were bogus.

Life of Alexander Hamilton *by Allan McLane, Hamilton, 1910*

Philip Hamilton, the Hamiltons' eldest and most beloved and brilliant son, at twenty, just before he was shot down in a duel, two and a half years before his father met the same fate. Hamilton called Philip's death "an event, beyond comparison, the most afflicting of my life."

Mrs. Alexander Hamilton
From life, in the Capitol
at Washington
Mch. 1846 —
E. Johnson

Elizabeth Schuyler Hamilton was in her ninetieth year when Eastman Johnson painted this portrait of her from life at Washington, D.C., in March 1846. When she died in 1854, having survived Hamilton by half a century, her knowing eyes, as Johnson shows, were among the last then left to have seen close the demigods—and the disquiets—of the creation of the nation.

XXX

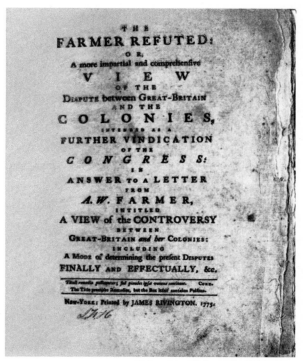

Columbia University Libraries

Title page of "The Farmer Refuted," the second of Hamilton's famous pamphlets of 1774 and
1775 in rebuttal to Reverend Samuel Seabury's pseudonymous Tory, the Westchester Farmer.
In them Hamilton, the self-styled "Sincere Friend to America" and "Vindicator of Congress,"
incited New Yorkers to revolution and full independence a year and a half before the Declaration of Independence.

James Rivington, publisher of *Rivington's New-York Gazetteer,* was the leading Tory news-paperman in New York, but he also published articles like Hamilton's advocating indepen-dence. Hamilton tried but failed to prevent Isaac Sears's Sons of Liberty from destroying his presses and scattering his types, and urged John Jay and Congress to outlaw similar future outrages against opposition papers.

Virginia, North and South Carolina, with only Connecticut opposed. But the winning majority, even with Delaware voting with the large states, represented fewer than half the thirteen. Only Hamilton's "aye" and Lansing's absence prevented New York from being counted with the "nays." If the vote had been taken a few days later, after the rest of the small state delegations had arrived, it would have been much closer. Here at the outset, when many a delegate was barely catching his breath, the convention seemed to have decided, in effect, to scrap the Articles of Confederation and to form a new government that as Gouverneur Morris and George Mason noted portentously, would have "a *compulsive* operation," directly "on individuals."

The following day, May 30, the delegates, having resolved to debate the Virginia plan as "a committee of the whole house," took up the first and most important of its 15 propositions—that dealing with the rights of suffrage in the national legislature.

Legally, slaves were property, chattels like cattle or any other kind of property. Representation proportioned to "quotas of contribution" would mean that as property, slaves would give added weight to white voting representation from slave states. Counting slaves would add to, not dilute, white voting power because only "free inhabitants" could actually vote. There was, of course, no requirement that the white representative vote in the interest of slaves or any other form of property. More than anything else, the extra voting power given to "free inhabitants" by the Virginia plan gave them strong incentive to keep the status quo, including the slavery that produced their great edge in voting power over states whose "free inhabitants" owned fewer slaves.

From his opening remarks to the last day of the convention, Washington presided from the dais without entering the debate. He recognized and refused to recognize speakers and kept order with a firm hand, but only once, on the last day, did he enter into the debate itself. In the sense that a silent conductor is more important to the performance of an orchestra than any single instrumentalist, Washington, although he did not make a single speech, was the most important figure at the convention. With many seeking to be heard, the right of one to speak depended on his being recognized by Washington. Washington seemed to work from an orchestration that contained many striking solo passages for Hamilton.

Hamilton, who has often been pilloried as the champion of the propertied interests, moved to alter Randolph's resolution so as to read "that the rights of suffrage in the national legislature ought to be proportioned to the number of free inhabitants." This struck out representation according to numbers of slaves and other property owned. Hamilton's resolution, seconded by Richard D. Spaight of North Carolina, meant that the "quotas of contribution," or propertied wealth, should have no special weight and should not be equated with the voice of the people of a state. Only people, not property, counted in voting. But consideration of the Hamilton-Spaight resolution was postponed.

During the next two weeks, Hamilton actively urged various proposals that tended to strengthen the power of the central government, particularly the executive branch, by amendments. These were designed to strengthen the Virginia plan.

On June 11 James Wilson and Hamilton moved that "the right of suffrage in the second branch [Senate] ought to be according to the same rule as in the first branch." This meant popular representation—one man, one vote, not one state, one vote, in both houses. This carried.

On June 4, again with Wilson, Hamilton proposed "to give the executive an absolute negative" on all laws, both state and federal," remarking that there was no danger of such a power being too much exercised. (The king of England had not exercised his negative since the Revolution.) All delegates except the two proponents and a Hamilton convert, Rufus King, voted down such sweeping veto power.

When Wilson and Madison immediately moved, as a compromise measure, that a convenient number of judges act with the executive in vetoing acts of the national legislature, Hamilton objected to such dilution of the separation of powers on a point of order. On June 2 he seconded Benjamin Franklin's motion that the chief executive receive an expense allowance, but "no salary, stipend fee or reward whatsoever." This was postponed without debate. On June 5 he proposed that the executive nominate judges and that the Senate have the right of approving or rejecting them.

As small state delegates continued to arrive in Philadelphia and to build up voting strength on the convention floor, it became apparent to Hamilton, in the hall of the Indian Queen, at least, that voting strength on the floor was shifting. The Virginia plan was in trouble. The question was becoming, not whether the Virginia plan could be improved upon, but the much more serious one of whether any plan that went as far as the Virginia plan could survive. As this threat grew, the Virginia plan, as amended, became stronger and more national and more objectionable to the smaller states.

When the committee of the whole rose at the end of the day on Wednesday, June 13, it reported out a set of 19 resolutions that were both a confirmation and an elaboration of the original Virginia plan. The authority to use force against recalcitrant states had been dropped; otherwise, the resolutions were a projection of most of the hopes Hamilton had entertained for a government "truly national." Among the details that had been added in the give-and-take of debate were a three-year term for the lower house and a seven-year term for the upper; payment for members of both houses "out of the national treasury" (a solid blow for nationalism); election of members of the upper house by the state legislatures, not by the people, as Hamilton had proposed; a single executive with a seven-year term (to be chosen by the legislature and ineligible for reelection), who could be removed "on impeachment and conviction of malpractices or neglect of duty"; and a power of veto in the executive, which could be overridden only by a two-thirds majority in both houses. There would also be the "supreme tribunal" which Hamilton had urged for so long, whose judges would be chosen by the upper house. Smooth progress thus far had been deceptive: it had built up powerful countering forces.

By June 15 the small-state delegates had united their forces for full-dress battle against the Virginia plan. On that day William Paterson of New Jersey "laid before the Convention" a set of nine resolutions, a series of amendments to the Articles of Confederation, as "substitutes" for the Virginia plan. It came to be known as the New Jersey plan.

This plan would protect rights of the smaller states against domination by the larger ones. It kept as much as possible of the Articles of Confederation. It provided for a single national legislature, like the old Continental Congress, in which representation was by states, each with a single, equal vote. Powers of Congress would be increased somewhat by grants of imposts and some other revenues, by a grant of the right of regulation of foreign and interstate commerce, and by the significant right to enforce its laws over the objections of the states. It was certainly closer than Randolph's plan to what most of the state legislatures had had in mind when they sent off their delegates to Philadelphia.

By comparison with the Virginia plan, New Jersey's represented merely a tinkering with the old Articles of Confederation, leaving the states clearly sovereign; the Virginia plan looked in the direction of a strong, central, national government. As Hamilton saw it, the latter was the great purpose of the convention, and it needed rescuing.

Delaware switched to the smaller-state group, leaving only five large states of the plurality of six that had originally voted for the Virginia plan. Lansing had arrived on June 2; so now, instead of Yates's vote being canceled out by Hamilton's, the two-to-one majority against him would swing New York into the "small" state column. That meant the possibility of a seven or eight to five vote against the Virginia plan.

"You see the consequences of pushing things too far," John Dickinson, the former Pennsylvanian, now a delegate from Delaware, said in stern reproach to Madison when Madison chided him for Delaware's having switched to make common cause with the antinationalists. He went on:

> Some of the members from the small states wish for two branches in the general legislature, and are friends to a good national government; but we would sooner submit to a foreign power than . . . be deprived of an equality of suffrage in both branches of the legislature, and thereby be thrown under the domination of the large states.

This had been the most intense subject of dispute: whether representation in Congress would be based on population in both the upper and lower houses or only in the lower house. Generally, members from large states and Hamilton, of course, favored representation based on population in both houses, but the smaller states would accept representation based on population only in the lower house. In the upper house, they insisted that all states have an equal vote.

Madison and Wilson still refused to concede an inch to the small-state nationalists. A choice had to be made between the two plans as they stood. This meant that the Virginia plan, with all its other strong features might be voted down, *in toto*, in favor of the New Jersey plan. Or the whole effort to create a national government might simply be abandoned in a breakup of the convention. In either case, the states would be left still operating under the feeble old Articles of Confederation or a somewhat amended version of them. A compromise had to be reached on the single narrow issue of one man, one vote or one state, one vote in the second house of Congress. As the crucial vote approached, it looked as though all of Hamilton's efforts might come to nothing.

Voting was scheduled to take place on Tuesday, June 19; there would, of course, be a day of adjournment for rest and prayer on Sunday, June 17.

As debates grew more heated, Hamilton kept rough notes on the proceedings. His versions of the remarks made by various delegates do not always match those reported by the other principal notetakers—Madison, John Lansing, Robert Yates, and Rufus King. From Hamilton's notes it is not always possible to determine whether a statement is one expressed by the speaker or simply Hamilton's own reaction to the speaker's remarks. When compared with the notes of others, they do make for three- and four-dimensional reading: what was said, what was meant, what had been the purpose of the statement, and what Hamilton's reaction to it was.

On June 6, when Madison was arguing that both branches of the legislature should be elected by the people, Hamilton's record of Madison's ideas bouncing off his own mind is as follows:

> PRINCIPLES
>   I—Human mind fond of compromise—Madison's Theory—Two princi-
>   ples upon which republics ought to be constructed—
>   I—that they have such extent as to render Combinations on the
>   ground of Interest difficult—
>   II—By a process of election calculated to refine the representation of
>   the People—
>   Answer—There is truth in both these principles but they do not con-
>   clude so strongly as he supposes. The Assembly when chosen will meet
>   in one room if they are drawn from half the globe—& will be liable to
>   all the passions of popular assemblies.

Hamilton, in other words, is not as insistent as Madison that no compromise is possible with the smaller states on the issue of voting in one house by states. He is saying that regardless of how the delegates are selected, once they meet together "in one room," they throw off the shackles of the constituency that has appointed them, whether a single state or a numerically determined constituency, and vote independently, subject to "all the passions of popular assemblies." Delegates assembled in the State House had only to consider how far beyond the limits imposed by their legislatures back home their votes for the Virginia plan had already carried them.

Members of such bodies are influenced by many more things than the narrow interests of the constituency that sends them. They are neither Pavlovian dogs nor Clintonian puppets. Hamilton noted:

If more *minute links* are wanting others will supply them. Distinctions of Eastern, middle and Southern states will come into view; between commercial and non-commercial states. Imaginary lines will influence etc. Human mind prone to limit its view by near & local objects. Paper money is capable of giving a general impulse. It is easy to conceive a popular sentiment pervading the E[astern] states.

As Hamilton jotted down these reflections, Madison went on with his argument on the floor. He referred to Roger Sherman's admission that in a very small state, faction and oppression would prevail and that it was to be inferred from this that wherever these feelings prevailed, the state was too small.

Factions had also prevailed in the largest states, he admitted, but less than in the smallest, so that we were "admonished to enlarge the sphere as far as the value of the Government would admit." This was the only defense against the inconveniences of democracy, Madison reasoned, that was consistent with the democratic form of government.

Hamilton recorded this and his reaction, as follows:

Observ. large districts less liable to be influenced by factions demagogues than small.
Note—This is in some degree true but not so generally as may be supposed. Frequently small portions of the large districts carry elections.

Hamilton easily remembered, and foresaw, that a strong campaign or powerfully organized political machine in a single county could carry the vote in a whole state.

Hamilton jotted this down: "An influential demagogue will give an impulse to the whole." It was even possible that such an evil man could spring from Madison's own social class: "Demagogues are not always *inconsiderable* persons. Patricians were frequently demagogues."

Hamilton also foresaw the danger of people developing a distaste for all politicians, plebeian and patrician alike:

I One great defect of our Governments are that they do not present objects sufficiently interesting to the human mind.
II—A reason for leaving little or nothing to the state legislature will be that as their objects are diminished they will be worse composed. Proper men will be less inclined to participate in them.

Jotted down only for himself in rough impressionistic form, these notes show Hamilton's basic agreement with Madison on the problems created by "factions" and demagogues. Far from being in awe of patricians, Hamilton recognized that they could as easily be demagogues as other men. Not a monarchist, he did not truly believe that "the people, sir, is a great beast" or anything of the kind. What he displays here is a generous respect for the ability of elected representatives to ignore the blueprints imposed on them from above and resist the narrow demands of particular constituencies to act freely for the general good. An elected representative was more than a rubber stamp for his constituency.

The three days of debate leading to the crucial vote on June 19 were destined to be long remembered. Lansing of New York and Paterson of New Jersey began on Saturday, June 16, for the antinationalist, small-state coalition. Each man stressed two points: "the want of power in the Convention to discuss and propose" any plan not grounded squarely on "the Confederacy in being" and the "improbability that the states would adopt and ratify a scheme" that they had "never authorized" the delegates to consider. James Wilson rose to meet these arguments head-on the same day, asserting that although the convention was "authorized to conclude nothing," it was "at liberty to propose anything." Randolph followed on cue, suggesting that this was one of those "seasons of a peculiar nature where the ordinary cautions must be dispensed with." Both men denied that "public sentiment" forbade the convention to scrap the Articles of Confederation. The short observation of Charles Pinckney—young, neat, perspicacious—struck to the heart of the matter: if the convention were simply to "give New Jersey an equal vote," she would "dismiss her scruples, and concur in the national system." Would the convention break up in deadlock or struggle on?

When the president general adjourned the delegates for Sunday recess, the question in many minds was who should be recognized by the chair as the speaker on Monday, June 18, the last day of debate before the climactic vote on Tuesday the nineteenth?

One of the most unlikely choices for such an honor at a supreme moment of American history was the man who was a minority of one in his own delegation, the largest state's which had swung over to the small-state side. Repudiated by New York, cut off by the local constituency that had sent him to Philadelphia, Hamilton at the convention would take a uniquely nationalist position. On Monday if the president general of the Cincinnati should beckon in his direction from the dais to solo, the views that would come forth would not be out of harmony with Washington's own.

During the recess Saturday night and all day Sunday, the hall of the Indian Queen, the salons of Lemon Hill, and all the taverns and brothels in between where delegates met buzzed with speculation.

Monday, June 18, was one of the hottest and most humid days of the Philadelphia year.

The delegates, as usual, convened at around eleven. They would sit till about four without a break or any form of air conditioning except as they were fanned by speakers' rhetoric. Washington cast his eye over the room, paused as his glance fell on the New York delegation to his right and at the rear, and nodded recognition to Alexander Hamilton. To many, it was the most peculiar possible choice, but the overwhelming prestige of the president general would frown down any possibility of an overzealous small state delegate eager to speak challenging by calling out for a point of order.

Hamilton rose briskly, without surprise, a sheaf of papers in his hands. Other delegates, also without surprise, settled back in their chairs.

For five hours Hamilton spoke to a silent convention, referring occasionally to the notes he held in his long fingers. He embroidered the severe logic of his argument with sudden flights of fancy. He rarely raised his voice above conversational pitch. He paused at intervals for dramatic emphasis as if probing for the very roots of the argument.

To Major William Pierce of Georgia, who had served as an aide to General Nathanael Greene, his language was at times "didactic like Bolingbroke," but at other times "as light and tripping as Sterne's."

According to James Madison's notes on the speech,

> Hamilton began disarmingly by saying that he had been hitherto silent on the business before the convention, partly from respect to others whose superior abilities, age, and experience rendered him unwilling to bring forward ideas dissimilar to theirs, and partly from his delicate situation with respect to his own state, to whose sentiments, as expressed by his colleagues, he could by no means accede.

But the question was too important; the crisis too serious "to permit any scruples whatever to prevail over the duty imposed on every man to contribute his efforts for the public safety and happiness. . . ."

Hamilton's argument drove straight to first principles. He stated the issue so that the narrow question of state representation in the national legislature became lost within the huge frame he placed around it. Small-state delegates hostile to his views might call them irrelevant, but the president general's ruling on any challenge to cut Hamilton short was a foregone conclusion: It would be "Out of order."

"The great question," Hamilton said, "is what provision shall we make for the happiness of our Country?"

He then artfully set the stage for a "compromise": "He declared himself unfriendly to both plans."

Neither the Virginia plan nor the New Jersey one completely satisfied him because neither established a strong, centralized government that would make the United States an irresistible unity of people instead of a mere alliance among semi-independent states.

It was the New Jersey plan whose substance he attacked: "He was particularly opposed to [it], being fully convinced, that no amendment of the Confederation leaving the states in possession of their Sovereignty could possibly answer the purpose."

"He had no criticism of the Virginia plan on its own merits," but he managed some criticism of it nonetheless: "Too much had already been claimed for it; too much was expected of it." According to Madison, Hamilton "was much discouraged by the amazing extent of the Country in expecting the desired blessings from any general sovereignty that could be substituted."

Then he launched a blistering attack on state sovereignty itself. In spirit this contrasted strikingly with the moderation of the private notes he had jotted down a few days earlier while listening to Madison. He had reflected that it would not be an absolute evil to give equal representation to each state, large or small, in one house.

"I have well considered the subject," he insisted loudly, "and am convinced that no amendment of the Confederation can answer the purpose of a good government, so long as the state sovereignties do, in any shape, exist." No one else would dream of saying such a shocking thing. What good were the states? They gathered to themselves loyalties that should belong to the nation; they constantly pursued internal interests adverse to the interest of the whole; they were not necessary for commerce, revenue, or agriculture; they added vast and useless expenses to the cost of government. In short, if they were reduced to mere local corporations or counties or even altogether extinguished, the nation would be far the better for it.

Hamilton now claimed to be for complete sovereignty in the general government. This, of course, went much further in the direction of reducing the power of the states than anything in the Virginia plan. It went further than anything Hamilton had ever proposed before or would urge afterward. Not only would these views startle and shock William Paterson and the small-state nationalists —as well as Hamilton's fellow New York delegates Yates and Lansing—they went too far for all backers of the Virginia plan. Hamilton stood alone and moved still further apart from the rest:

> All the passions . . . of avarice, ambition, interest which govern most individuals, and all public bodies, fall into the current of the States, and do not flow in the stream of the General Government. The former, therefore, will generally be an overmatch for the General Government and render any confederacy, in its very nature, precarious.

He tossed off historical examples of confederacies that had deluded themselves into believing that they had adequate central powers, including "the power of fining and using force against delinquent members." He cited the Amphictionic League, the German Confederacy, and the Swiss Cantons. But "What was the consequence? Their decrees were signals of war."

He was, of course, using exaggerated terms to state his aversion to leaving a shred of sovereignty in the state governments, in order to set the stage for voting the next day by a room full of human minds fond of compromise. Ridiculous as they might sound in the immediate context, Hamilton's fears that the decrees of sovereign states of a confederacy "were signals of war" demonstrated uncanny foresight to what would happen to the "United" States in 1860, as a result of the convention's ultimate "compromise" of the issue.

Much state governmental apparatus was a waste of money; money could be saved if the states "were extinguished." The only problem would be drawing representatives from the extremes to the center at the capital. Good men would not want to travel too far, and the pay would be bait only to little demagogues.

Three dollars or thereabout, he supposed, would be the salary, and the Senate, he feared, would be filled only by seekers of jobs who could find nothing better.

According to Madison's notes of Hamilton's speech, such things "almost led him to despair that a republican government could be established over so great an extent." But "He was sensible at the same time that it would be unwise to propose one of any other form."

Here followed a passage that Hamilton's enemies would turn to their own political uses against him for the rest of his life.

He had reviewed various forms of government—those of the Germanic Empire, Sparta, Athens, Thebes, Rome, Carthage, Venice, the Hanseatic League, France under Louis XIV, and Austria under the Bourbons. He came at last to England under William and Anne and their successors as a constitutional monarchy beginning to emerge there. He stressed the importance of strong governments to help avoid wars caused by squabbling of petty states. In this context he said, according to his own notes, "The general government must, in this case, not only have a strong soul, but *strong organs* by which that soul is to operate." Then, to illustrate the kind of moderate central government that preserved the liberties of its own people while remaining strong enough to hold complete sway over the local segments that composed it, he cited the British example. According to his notes:

> Here I shall give my sentiments of the best form of government —not as a thing attainable by us, but as a model which we ought to approach as near as possible:
> British constitution best form.

Hamilton was comparing models of governmental forms in as objective a manner as his and his listeners' knowledge of history and philosophy would permit. It was once thought that the power of Congress was amply sufficient to link the states, he noted, but the error of that view was now seen by everyone. "The time would come when others as well as himself would join in the praise bestowed by Mr. Neckar on the British constitution, when he said that it is the only government in the world 'which unites public strength with individual security.' "

Therefore, in the real world, British experience provided a more satisfactory working model for a government of free people than any other. The reason the British model was such a good one for the states in 1787 was that its form provided a strong chief executive. No such figure existed, of course, under the Confederation or in the New Jersey plan.

As one who had fought as long and hard against King George III and his armies as anyone in the room except the silent president general on the dais, Hamilton could make this argument with more force and less fear of false imputation of disloyalty than any other man in the room.

Why was such a chief executive necessary?

Here is the meat of Hamilton's argument from his own notes:

Society naturally divides itself into two political divisions—the *few* and the *many*, who have distinct interests.

If government in the hands of the *few*, they will tyrannize over the many.

If [in] the hands of the many, they will tyrannize over the few. It ought to be in the hands of both; and they should be separated.

This separation must be permanent.

Representation alone will not do.

Without such an executive,

Demagogues will generally prevail.

And if separated, they will need a mutual check.

There must be checks and balances in the system:

This check is a monarch.

Each principle ought to exist in full force, or it will not answer its end.

The democracy must be derived immediately from the people.

'Tis essential there should be a permanent will in a community.

Vox populi, vox Dei. . . .

There ought to be a principle in government capable of resisting the popular current.

There must be a permanent will.

A democratic assembly is to be checked by a democratic senate, and both these by a democratic chief magistrate.

What is to be done?

Answer. Balance inconveniences and dangers, and choose that which seems to have the fewest objections.

Hamilton was saying, as Winston Churchill would later, that "Democracy is the worst possible form of government conceived by man, except for all the others."

What, in the context of his notes, did Hamilton mean by the word *monarch?*

"*Monarch* is an indefinite term" he said. "It marks not either the degree or duration of power."

Whether the "monarch's" term was for seven years, as had been proposed, or for life, "the circumstance of being elective was applicable to both." Robert Yates's notes picked up an important point that Madison failed to put down: Hamilton had given as his opinion that an executive in office for life was less "dangerous to the liberties of the people" than one who was in office for seven years. Both Yates and John Lansing picked up still another important point that Madison had missed. Hamilton said that "By making the executive subject to impeachment, the term monarchy cannot apply." What, then, did Hamilton actually propose? "Let electors be appointed in each of the states to elect the executive."

What Hamilton actually proposed was not a hereditary king, like Britain's, who could not be removed from office, but an executive elected by electors from each state—the general method provided under the Constitution ever since (until the Twenty-fifth Amendment)—subject to removal from office without bloody revolution by the impeachment process. A "monarch" in other words, exactly like the American president as his office was created and has evolved under the Constitution.

Hamilton was speaking in the way a professor of comparative government might speak to a backward class, of the advantages of a political institution of which many members of his class understood little. He was explaining the idea of a limited "monarch" much as another might explain worthwhile institutional features of communism, or socialism, without himself being a Communist. But Madison's notes of Hamilton's remarks subtly seem to transform Hamilton's role into that of a convert exhorting a street crowd to join his fixed faith. Madison reported: "In his private opinion he had no scruple in declaring, supported as he was by the opinions of so many of the wise and good, that the British Government was the best in the world; and that he doubted much whether anything short of it would do in America."

According to Madison, Hamilton advocated the British government as the ultimate solution for America; according to Hamilton's own notes and those of Yates, Lansing, and King, Hamilton was merely citing the British form as a working model for a government with a strong executive whose powers were limited by the legislature. Madison's private misunderstanding became the seed of misleading public charges that Hamilton was a "monarchist"—a charge with which Hamilton's foes would assail him the rest of his life and history.

Having made these observations, Hamilton read the sketch of a plan that he preferred to either the New Jersey or Virginia plan: "He did not mean to offer the paper he had sketched as a proposition to the committee. It was meant only to give a more correct view of his ideas, and to suggest the amendments which he should probably propose to the plan of Mr. Randolph, in the proper stages of its future discussion."

Hamilton's plan shrewdly blunted some of the objections that the small states had raised to the Virginia plan. Hamilton vested "the supreme legislative power of the United States of America" in two houses: the lower house to be elected by the people for a three-year term; the Senate to be elected by electors chosen by the people to serve during good behavior.

This was a master stroke because it bypassed the divisive question of whether there would be one-state, one-vote representation in the Senate, as the small states insisted, or one-man, one-vote representation, as the larger states demanded. Some of the small-state delegates could also perhaps see themselves in the near future as the very senators who would be chosen to sit in the capital "during good behaviour." Hamilton held out a compromise on a narrow, immediate issue that could save the whole convention from breaking up.

His chief executive, to be elected by electors chosen by the people, was to serve during good behavior and to have an absolute veto. If no absolute majority emerged from the balloting, these "first electors" were to choose "second electors" to complete the job.

Supreme judicial authority was to be vested in twelve federal judges, also to hold office during good behavior. All government officials were liable to impeachment before a special court consisting of the chief judges of the highest court of each state. All laws of the particular states contrary to the Constitution or laws of the United States would be void. Exclusive authority over the military and naval forces was to be vested in the federal government. Supreme Court judges would sit on the court of impeachment along with the chief judges of the state courts. In the English model, according to Hamilton, the hereditary interest of the king was so interwoven with that of the nation, and his personal emolument was so great that he was placed above the danger of corruption from abroad, and, at the same time, he was both sufficiently independent and sufficiently controlled to answer the purpose of the institution at home.

There was much to be said for a chief executive elected to serve during good behavior. One of the weak sides of republics was their being liable to foreign influence and corruption. Men of little character, acquiring great power, become easily the tools of intermeddling neighbors and subvert the national interest to schemes by which to insure reelection. If the executive were not elected for life, perhaps a term of seven years would induce the sacrifice of private affairs, which an acceptance of public trust would require, so as to ensure the services of the best citizens in the office.

When Hamilton sat down, the leaves of his plan of government still rustling in his hands, after more than five hours of speaking in the intense heat of the State House chamber, he did not meet with general approbation and applause. There was no occasion to turn to his friends and ask, like Phocion, "Have I inadvertently said something foolish?" No one rose to agree with or confute him; no one offered those additional remarks that were normal in the confidential give-and-take of the convention.[1] Delegates were stunned into quiet, new thought. After a while, someone broke the silence with a remark on a wholly different topic, debate resumed, and the meeting soon adjourned for the momentous vote next day.

Madison came up to Hamilton and asked for a copy of his proposed "Constitution" for entry into his private minutes of the proceedings.

Robert Yates attributed some pungent remarks to Hamilton not recorded by Madison, which tended to show how Hamilton's speech had softened the views even of delegates like Yates who were most adamantly opposed to his.

Yates recorded the confession "that this plan and that from Virginia are very remote from the idea of the people," and that "Perhaps the Jersey plan is nearest their expectation." But Yates did not differ with Hamilton's assessment that "the people are gradually ripening in their opinions of government; they begin to be tired of an excess of democracy; and what even is the Virginia plan, but pork still, with a little change of the sauce."

Lansing's version of Hamilton's remarks has it that instead of the "people" tiring of an excess of democracy, it is only "the principal citizens of every state" who "are tired of democracy."

At such conventions, votes on crucial issues often swing either way, depending on last-minute factors, and men of affairs know that the timing of events may have a more significant influence than any other factor. Hamilton's filibuster had shut out the small-state delegates from offering favorable arguments on their plan as the voting approached and set the delegates thinking hard about the value of a strong government.

His was the longest speech anyone was allowed to make at the convention. He was given the floor and the delegates' undivided attention on its most critical day. The members present heard him out in respectful silence, and many took elaborate notes on what he had said, including, besides Madison and Yates, Lansing, Rufus King, and James McHenry. His speech had the greatest intellectual and historical reach and thrust of any speech made at the convention, even though, strictly speaking, much of it was not germane to the issue before the delegates.

In the buzz of evening gossip outside the Convention Hall and inside the Indian Queen's taproom, where many a huge thirst repaired for slaking, a number of delegates hastened to congratulate the young man of destiny. But as William Samuel Johnson of Connecticut remarked a few days later, "The Gentleman from New York is praised by every gentleman, but supported by no gentleman."

Now the Virginia plan appeared as but a reasonable middle ground between two extreme positions, Hamilton's extreme nationalist position and the New Jersey plan's extreme state-sovereignty position. Hamilton's remarks about abolishing the states had been too provocative. Paterson of New Jersey, Sherman of Connecticut, and even former nationalists from Delaware continued to warn the "large state" men that the small states "would never confederate" on their plan. Nor would Clinton think of letting Yates and Lansing yield any of the local sovereignty his pivotal state enjoyed to national popular sovereignty that was inherent in the large states' plan.

On the day of the vote, Hamilton offered some conciliatory remarks. He declared that "He had not been understood yesterday"; he had not really intended "a total extinguishment of state governments" as some had thought; they could continue as local and police subdivisions. But the "authority of the national government must be indefinite and unlimited, without any hindrance from the states."

But under their conciliatory tone these words created still more constitutional history in favor of strong national government. He added, "a national government ought to be able to support itself without the aid or interference of the state governments. It is necessary to have full sovereignty. Even with corporate rights the states will be dangerous to the national government, and ought to be extinguished, modified, or reduced to a smaller scale. . . ."

James Wilson spoke more to the point:

The declaration of independence preceded the state constitutions. What does this declare? In the name of the people of these states, we are declared to be free and independent. The power of war, peace, alliances and trade are declared to be vested in Congress.

Hamilton rose once more:

I agree to Mr. Wilson's remark. Establish a weak government and you must at times overleap the bounds. Rome was obliged to create dictators. Cannot you make propositions to the people because we before confederated on other principles? The people can yield to them, if they will. The three great objects of government, agriculture, commerce, and revenue, can only be secured by a general government.

Hamilton concluded: "The more close the union of the states, and the more complete the authority of the whole, the less opportunity will be allowed [to] the stronger states to injure the weaker."

The vote was taken. Hamilton was outvoted in his own delegation. New York voted with the small states. The vote could not have been closer: six ayes (Massachusetts, Pennsylvania, Virginia, the Carolinas, and Georgia) to five nays (Connecticut, New York, New Jersey, Delaware, and Maryland). The Virginia plan prevailed. The New Jersey plan lost. The "Hamilton" plan lost. The convention did not break up. The delegates' minds favored "compromise." They now buckled down to working out the details of the constitution of national union that was veiled, but implicit in the Virginia plan.

In the days immediately following, all of Hamilton's actions and votes tended toward strengthening the power of the people to control the national government and to oppose any idea of unfettered kingly power or hereditary monarchs. They tended to reinforce the view that the extreme positions he had set up on Monday had been intended for voting down on Tuesday. On June 21, Charles Cotesworth Pinckney moved that the House of Representatives be elected by state legislatures instead of by the people. Hamilton, in opposition, argued that transfer of voting rights from the people to state legislatures "would essentially vitiate the plan. It would increase the state influence which could not be too watchfully guarded against." In Yates's account, Hamilton asserted that election "directly by the people" is "essential to the democratic rights of the community."

On June 26 Nathaniel Gorham moved for six-year terms for senators, one third to be elected every second year; George Read moved to amend, to make the terms nine years, one third going out triennially. Madison, favoring longer terms for senators, noted with alarm the rise of a "leveling spirit." He argued that longer terms were one way of guarding against such a spirit "on republican principles." Roger Sherman of Connecticut argued for shorter terms and more frequent elections. Hamilton, taking the long view, citing first principles, generally supporting Madison, said, "We are now to decide forever the fate of Republican Government. If we do not give to that form due stability and wisdom, it will be disgraced and lost among ourselves, and disgraced and lost to mankind forever." His paean to liberty and moderation contrasted sharply with the didactic impression made by his speech of the week before. He added, "I am as zealous an advocate for liberty as any man, and would cheerfully become a martyr to it. But real liberty is neither found in despotism or the extremes of democracy, but in moderate governments." Weakness in the government, he pointed out, is what gives rise to the danger of despotic monarchy: "As long as offices are open to all men, and no constitutional rank is established, it is pure republicanism. But if we incline too much to democracy, we shall soon shoot into a monarchy."

He read America's future from Rome's past and saw that, for better or worse, it would hold inequality of property: "The differences in wealth are already great among us, nothing like equality of property exists. Inequality will exist as long as liberty exists, and it unavoidably results from that very liberty itself."

He saw the problem, and faced it with realism:

> In the ordinary progress of things we must look to a period as not very remote when distinctions arising from property will be greater. In Rome, the power of the tribunes had levelled the distinction between the patricians and plebeians. The plebeians instituted the power of the tribunes as a guard against the patricians. But it was not a sufficient check. The distinction between rich and poor was substituted, and this created a greater distinction between the classes than there had ever been before.

On June 22 Hamilton urged that members of the national legislature receive "fixed stipends paid out of the National Treasury," so as not to be "dependent on the legislative rewards of the states" because "Those who pay are the masters of those who are paid." "The feelings and views of the people," he urged, "are different from the governments of the states," and not necessarily "unfriendly to the General Government." The states would be "from personal interests and official inducements."

He argued against express provision making members of the House ineligible to other offices during their term and for one year thereafter: "We must take man as we find him, and if we expect him to serve the public must interest his passions in doing so. A reliance on pure patriotism has been the source of many of our errors."

He added, "I am against all exclusions and refinements, except only in this case; that when a member takes his seat, he should vacate every other office."

The Virginia plan still called for representation in both houses of Congress in proportion to population, and debate on this question went on for days. Luther Martin of Maryland, for the small-state bloc, cited many writers on government to the effect that states entering into a confederacy must of necessity retain equality of votes.

On June 29, his last day on the floor for some time to come, Hamilton rose and attacked Martin's position with new eloquence: "This position cannot be correct: Facts plainly contradict it," he urged. "States are a collection of individual men," he went on. "Which ought we to respect most? The rights of the people composing them, or of the artificial beings resulting from the composition? Nothing could be more absurd than to sacrifice the former to the latter."

He pressed his argument with directness and power: "It has been said that if the smaller states renounce their *equality*, they renounce at the same time their *liberty*. The truth is, it is a contest for power, not for liberty. Men are naturally equal, and societies or states, when fully independent, are also equal."

The simple question: what is the general interest?

It is as reasonable that states should form leagues or compacts, and lessen or part with their national equality, as that men should form the social compact and, in doing so, lessen or surrender the national equality of men. This is done in every society, and the grant to the society affects persons and property.

So, said Hamilton, "Let the people be represented according to numbers, the people will be free: every office will be equally open to all, and the majority of the people are to make the laws."

"Yet it is said," he pointed out, "that the states will be destroyed and the people will be slaves—This is not so. The people are free, at the expense of an artificial and ideal equality of the states."

He had placed seminal ideas before the convention. The "compromise" that rejected them had made the Virginia plan the basis of union. If it were not as strong a Union or as "high toned" as his plan, his plan had served as the horrific "stalking horse" that made it tolerable. It would provide the basis for a workable union. He left Philadelphia the following day for personal reasons. His closing speech to the convention on June 29 declared, "This is a critical moment of American liberty—We are still too weak to exist without union. We must devise a system on the spot—It ought to be strong and nervous, hoping that the good sense, and principally the necessity of our affairs will reconcile the people to it."

In Hamilton's eighteenth-century usage, the word *nervous* for a constitution did not suggest, as it might for us, a "nervous breakdown." To Hamilton, *nervous* meant sinewy, muscular, vigorous, strong, full of energy and courage, and as free from weakness as his tactics and the tactics of his fellow Cincinnatian on the dais could help him to make it.

On June 28, with debate over the suffrage in the lower house growing ever more bitter, Franklin urged that a clergyman be invited to offer prayers at the beginning of each session. But, according to Madison, "Mr. Hamilton said he feared that however proper such a resolution might have been at the beginning of the convention, it might at this late day, in the first place, bring on it some disagreeable animadversions." In the second place, Hamilton said, it might "lead the public to believe that the embarrassments and dissensions within the Convention had suggested this measure."

In the third place, Hamilton added, he was confident the convention could transact the business entrusted to its care without "the necessity of calling in foreign aid"!

The session adjourned without further disquisition or a vote on the subject of prayer.

Hamilton did not see the need of calling in the aid of another, unpredictable, invisible hand. No better result could possibly be expected than had been obtained from the familiar hand that had beckoned to him from the dais to speak all day on June 18—or whenever else he might wish to say something extreme —in the interest of exploiting the human mind's fondness for compromise.

22

WE THE PEOPLE
OF THE UNITED STATES

I AM A FRIEND TO VIGOROUS GOVERNMENT BUT I HOLD IT ESSEN-
TIAL THAT THE POPULAR BRANCH OF IT SHOULD BE ON A BROAD
FOUNDATION.
    —*On the floor of the Constitutional Convention, Sep-
    tember 8, 1787*

Hamilton had seen the convention through its greatest crisis. While it rumbled on without him, he traveled back to New York, talking to people everywhere
along the way, sounding out their opinions on the subject of a national constitution. On July 3 he wrote back to Washington "that there has been an astonishing
revolution for the better in the minds of the people." He added, "This is the
critical opportunity for establishing the prosperity of this country on a solid
foundation." The delegates immured in the State House were out of touch with
the people's mood if they feared to go too far toward "a strong, well-mounted
government" still believing, erroneously, that the people would not stand for
one. Although people might not yet be ready for a plan that went as far as his
own, he was surprised and pleased to find that they would approve "one equally
energetic, if the Convention should think proper to propose it." He expected to
remain in New York ten or twelve days. Then "if I have reason to believe that

my attendance at Philadelphia will not be mere waste of time, I shall, after that period, rejoin the Convention." There was probably no one at the convention whose political views were more closely aligned with Hamilton's than George Washington's, but as presiding officer there was no way for him to express them except by recognizing Hamilton to speak, and now Hamilton was gone. He wrote Hamilton on July 10, "I almost despair of seeing a favorable issue to the proceedings of the Convention, and do, therefore, repent having any agency in the business. The men who oppose a strong and energetic government are in my opinion narrow-minded politicians, or are under the influence of local views." He tactfully reproved Hamilton for his absence: "I am sorry you went away; I wish you were back. The crisis is equally important and alarming, and no opposition under such circumstances should discourage exertions, till the signature is fixed."

When he left Philadelphia, Hamilton had left behind him an able new recruit to the nationalist cause. At the convention he had won over from opposition views, among others, Rufus King, a delegate from Massachusetts, which was now recovering from the aftermath of Shays' Rebellion. Major William Pierce described King as "five feet ten, well formed, handsome, with a sweet, high toned voice." King was sorry he had not left Philadelphia "with our very able and sagacious friend Hamilton," but he remained to hold the floor for the nationalist cause in Hamilton's absence. Of his new friend and disciple King, Hamilton later confided to another friend, "I *revolutionized* his mind."

Hamilton's fellow New York delegates, Yates and Lansing, quit the convention on July 5, never to return. They were discouraged for reasons that were the opposite of Hamilton's and King's. As they explained to Governor Clinton, they had been appointed to revise the Articles of Confederation, not to draw up a wholly new constitution. But ever since Hamilton's speech and the approval of the Virginia plan the following day, the proceedings proved to them that the latter was the true purpose of the convention; so they withdrew. They justified their absence by arguing that with Hamilton also away, there was no need for them to stay to outvote him. The fact of their presence and voting, even voting against union, might imply Clinton's assent to any contrary outcome of the convention that went against New York. On the other hand, it was not lost on Hamilton that with all three delegates absent, no New York vote would be recorded against union; with their presence, New York's vote would be recorded against.

If it took Hamilton's absence to bring Yates and Lansing home, his absence made a significant contribution to removing New York as an obstacle to progress by other large states toward his goal of union. The real reason for his curious absence is not known and can only be guessed at.

The humdrum truth probably is that he simply had to return to New York to earn some fees for a living. Support of a wife and children and the business of a busy lawyer's demanding clients simply cannot be shrugged off for most of a spring and all of a summer.

With Hamilton gone, the convention headed for a showdown on the second great issue: the Connecticut plan, or Great Compromise. This resulted in a second climactic vote on July 16 on the question of equal representation by states in the upper house and by population in the lower. The small states carried the day, five in favor (Connecticut, New Jersey, Delaware, Maryland, and North Carolina) with four against (Pennsylvania, Virginia, South Carolina, and Georgia). Massachusetts was divided; New York, Rhode Island, and New Hampshire were recorded as not voting. After this, the Great Compromise, which Hamilton's private notes had foreshadowed, the success of the new constitution, on the pattern of the Virginia plan, became assured. All that now remained were matters of manageable detail. While Hamilton was still away, the convention recessed two weeks in the depth of Philadelphia summer from July 26 through August 6 to allow its committee of detail to make revisions in the Virginia plan resolutions. Meanwhile, the focus of political significance followed Hamilton, Lansing, and Yates back to New York. Hamilton mediated a private dispute between one of his fellow convention delegates, Major William Pierce of Georgia, and a sometime client, John Auldjo, to prevent their coming to a duel. Pierce had been valuable to Hamilton in helping swing over Georgia's key small-state vote to back the Virginia plan. So when Auldjo asked Hamilton to be his second in a duel with Pierce, Hamilton told him, "I can never take up the character of a second in a duel . . . till I have in vain tried to be a mediator. Be content with *enough* for more ought not to be expected." On July 20 he wrote Pierce's second, Nathaniel Mitchell, that "every man of sensibility must feel [that] extremities [should not] take place if it be in his power to prevent them or until they become an absolutely necessary sacrifice to the prejudices of public opinion." After much delicate negotiating, the ultimate interview was avoided. Honor and the possible casualty of a rare vote from Georgia for union were both spared.

On July 21 an unsigned article written by Hamilton appeared in the *New York Daily Advertiser*. It charged that Governor Clinton had publicly "reprobated the appointment of the Convention," and had "predicted a mischievous issue" of it. It set forth nine "reflections" in favor of the convention, a new constitution, and a stronger union and attacked all opponents of such views. The ninth point was a characteristic Hamiltonian thrust: "Such conduct in a man in high office, argues greater attachment to his *own power* than to the *public good*, and furnishes strong reason to suspect a dangerous predetermination to oppose whatever may tend to diminish the former, however, it may promote the latter."

The harsh, personal tone of Hamilton's attack would win no new support for his position. It would also draw heavy counterfire from Clinton's supporters toward himself. Its general tone of bad temper may reveal Hamilton in one of his recurrent summer illnesses and give a clue to another reason for his absenting himself from Philadelphia. There was still another, more sinister, reason for his ire.

Back in Philadelphia at the Indian Queen as the Convention reconvened on August 6, Hamilton spoke out on August 13. He asserted that "the advantages of encouraging foreigners was obvious and admitted" and that "Persons of

Europe of moderate fortunes will be fond of coming here where they will be on a level with the first citizens." No one could make this argument with more personal conviction drawn from experience than Hamilton. He moved that eligibility be eased and based merely on "citizenship and inhabitancy," but after debate this motion was defeated.

Hamilton was back in New York again late in August for mysterious and inscrutable reasons that must have come up quite suddenly: there is no other way to account for his rushing back to Philadelphia and forth to New York again late in August for only a week or so of not very consequential floor appearances at the convention.

Though the content of the speeches and debates in the State House chamber were supposed to be closely guarded secrets, outside the chamber nothing could prevent chance remarks from slipping out or being slyly muttered or bibulously blurted over tankards at the Indian Queen—or purposefully leaked. On June 19, the very day after Madison had rather misleadingly recorded Hamilton's lecture on comparative government as an emotional commitment to British government for America including a kinglike, nonimpeachable "monarch," an anonymous person in Philadelphia supposedly wrote a deadpan letter to a person in Portsmouth, New Hampshire, saying that the members of the Constitutional Convention wished to invite the second son of King George III "to become King of the United States." Such a young man existed; he was Frederick, duke of York, the secular bishop of Osnaburg, a town in the Prussian province of Hanover. According to the alleged letter, the plan to make him king, which is "so agreeable to the people of America, and so manifestly for their interest," not surprisingly "meets with a favorable reception from the British Court." The members of the convention "have the subject in their deliberations, and are harmonious in their opinions; the means only of accomplishing so great an event, appears principally to occupy their counsels."

In fact, at about this time, in private conjectures, it is known that Hamilton had mentioned as a possibility that if the constitution failed, reunion with Britain might occur, with the duke of York installed as king. Copious extracts from the supposedly private letter were gleefully published in *The Fairfield* [Connecticut] *Gazette* on July 25, in the *Pennsylvania Gazette* on August 15, in the *Pennsylvania Journal* on August 25, and elsewhere. Concerned readers, trying to piece together what had been going on in the secret sessions in Philadelphia from the fragments of such stories, were alarmed. This fantastic scheme to install Frederick as king of the United States was associated with Hamilton's remarkable speech of June 18 and the vote in favor of the Virginia plan the following day.

The date, timing, and artfulness of the accusation by association; the indirectness of the publication; and the smoothly snide literary quality of the letter all might have led Hamilton himself to suspect, without being able to prove, that another invisible hand was at work—that of the shrewd scrivener whose hopes of becoming clerk of the convention had been dashed by Hamilton on the opening day—Randolph's and Madison's friend John Beckley. Publication of the story in

Philadelphia on August 15 broke the story around Hamilton's head. It may have been what sent him rushing back to New York: to run the canard to its source by tracking down the earlier publication in Connecticut.

An alarmed Connecticut reader, Hezekiah Wetmore of Stratford, had supposedly sent a copy of *The Fairfield Gazette*'s story of July 25 to one James Reynolds of New York City, who, in turn, had passed it on to Hamilton.

James Reynolds was the man who later had a complex and mysterious personal relationship with Hamilton that ostensibly began four years later in 1791. Because Hamilton's relationship with Reynolds and his wife was the root cause of Hamilton's ultimate ruin as a public man, few items in Hamilton's story arouse more unsatisfied curiosity than Hamilton's first known mention of Reynolds's name. It occurred in a letter of August 20, 1787, to his friend and client, Jeremiah Wadsworth, who was also the partner of his brother-in-law John Barker Church. Hamilton wrote Wadsworth that an extract from the purported letter from Philadelphia to the person in Portsmouth "was sent by one *Whitmore* of Stratford . . . to a James Reynold [sic] of this City." Hamilton explains that "It has been fabricated to excite jealousy against the Convention" and "opposition to their recommendations." But Hamilton does not further identify "James Reynold" to Wadsworth. This leaves many questions dangling: how and why did Reynolds come to Hamilton with the story if Hamilton's name was not mentioned in it? Convention debates were secret, and Hamilton was supposed to be away in Philadelphia at the time in any event. Did Hamilton come to Reynolds then? If so, why? Why did Hamilton, in writing to Wadsworth, use the article for "a" James Reynold when he mentioned his name? Was it because Reynolds claimed to know Wadsworth but Hamilton doubted that Wadsworth would admit knowing such a man? Were Beckley and Reynolds friends or coadjutors? Who "fabricated" the Philadelphia letter? Beckley, Reynolds, or someone else? Is the "fabrication" based on the leak of a truth? Plausible hypotheses give affirmative answers to most of these questions, but the truth is veiled in mystery that only deepens as the tragic events of Hamilton's later career unfold.

Wadsworth promptly replied that the purpose of the letter was "to scare the anti-federal party" into opposition to the Constitution and that the author can hardly be Hezekiah Wetmore, whom he knows to be a patriot.

A curious fact is that although Jeremiah Wadsworth admits knowing Wetmore, he passes over James Reynolds's name in silence, though it seems certain he knew Reynolds well. Reynolds's father, David, had served under Wadsworth during the war in the commissary department, sometimes aided by son James. David had afterward spent time in jail for various shady business dealings. But Wadsworth's reply volunteers no comment whatsoever about Hamilton's informant, James Reynolds. The information he had received from Reynolds led Hamilton's investigation to a dead end on a false trail.

David Humphreys, a friend of both Wadsworth and Hamilton and a former aide to Washington, wrote directly to Hamilton, tactfully noting that among loyalists the idea of "introducing the Bishop of Osnaburg" has been talked of and wished for and that "where I dined, half jest, half earnest, he was given as the first Toast."

Any who favored the proposal with which Hamilton now was tarred not only was too strong a nationalist, but might also be suspected of being disloyal to America.

Whoever had originated the stories could hardly have struck a harder or lower blow at Hamilton. He enjoined Wadsworth, "Be so good as to attend to this inquiry somewhat particularly, as I have different reasons of some moment [for] setting it on foot."

What those "different reasons of some moment" were are not known. James Reynolds was not a person of consequence or fame or a client of Hamilton. He was a sometime client of Aaron Burr. He spent some time in jail and, after a flash of notoriety, finally disappeared entirely from sight. History offers no explanation of why he would be passing a purported extract from a letter from someone in Philadelphia to someone in New Hampshire to Hamilton in New York during the summer of 1787 unless he or possibly his handsome wife, Maria Reynolds, or both were then already rather well known in some way to Hamilton—or an enemy like Beckley who had reason to hate him.

All that Hamilton's history later recorded was his notorious affair with Maria in 1791 and 1792. It tended to wax most intense during the summer months while Elizabeth and the children were upstate with the Schuylers. The Reynolds's literary style later became well known and was closely analyzed, but it did not encompass the subtlety and literary quality that the bishop of Osnaburg letter displayed. Hamilton's "different reasons of some moment" for inquiry of Wadsworth may have been his effort to trace the letter back to John Beckley in Philadelphia. The latter's presence at its source, political convictions, access to secret information about the debates, capacity for intrigue, literary skill, and good reasons for taking reprisals against Hamilton would all qualify him as a chief object of Hamilton's suspicions.

British-born, but not, as he sometimes claimed, the son of a knight, Beckley had come to Virginia in 1769 as a precocious eleven-year-old. He served as the indentured scribe of John Clayton, the famous Virginia botanist, and attended Jefferson's alma mater, the College of William and Mary. He became mayor of Richmond; and in 1789, at 31, he would be elected first clerk of the national House of Representatives, the first member of the staff to be chosen by the new constitutional Congress. Jefferson called him the "best clerk in the United States."

The same day he had sought Wadsworth's help in tracking down his Philadelphia traducer, Hamilton, feeling somewhat defensive about his second absence from Philadelphia, wrote King that he had told Yates and Lansing that "if either of them would come down I would accompany him to Philadelphia. So Much," he added ironically, "for the sake of propriety and public opinion." Neither came.

Hamilton asked King when he thought the convention would finish its work because he wanted to be present before the end "for certain reasons" that he failed to enumerate. He had also heard whispers "that some late changes in your scheme have taken place which give it a higher tone. Is this the case?"

There had indeed been such changes during Hamilton's absence as he quickly noted when he returned to Philadelphia sometime before September 6. On that day, debate centered on a dispute over the manner of electing the president. Under the report submitted by the Committee of Detail, he was to be elected by ballot by the national legislature and hold office for seven years. Under the report of the Committee of Eleven, consisting of one member from each state, which was to complete the unfinished draftsmanship, he was to be chosen by electors in such manner as the legislature in each state should direct. If the electors gave no candidate a majority of votes, the choice was to devolve on the Senate. To Hamilton, both plans created too powerful a presidency, too much like a hereditary monarch, too far from the people. He argued that under the first plan "the President was a monster elected for seven years, and ineligible afterwards having great powers . . . and continually tempted by this constitutional disqualification to abuse them in order to subvert the government." He insisted that "Some other mode of election should be devised." As for the second plan, "Considering the different views of different states, northern, middle and southern, the states' votes probably will not be concentrated, and appointment would devolve upon the senate. This will perpetuate the President, and aggrandize both him and the senate too much."

What was the remedy?

Let the highest number of ballots of the electors, whether a majority or not, appoint the president without involving the Senate in the process.

What was the objection to this? Merely that too small a number might appoint.

As the plan stood the Senate might take the candidate having the smallest number of votes and make him president against the will of the people expressed through their electors.

Hamilton's plan failed, but later elections in his own lifetime, particularly that of the electoral tie between Burr and Jefferson in 1800, throwing the election into the House of Representatives, demonstrated the wheeling and dealing in smoke-filled rooms and peculiar results that would occur in presidential elections thrown into Congress. But Hamilton's pressure to keep election of the president as close as possible to the people and out of the Senate reinforced the concept of separation of powers in a practical way. The report was amended to give final choice in case of a tie in electoral votes, not to the Senate, but to the House of Representatives, the popularly elected chamber, with each state there having a single vote on the question.

On September 8 Hamilton made still another push for giving more power to the people, supporting with "earnestness and anxiety" the motion of Hugh Williamson "to increase the number of members of the House." Acknowledging that "I am a friend to a vigorous Government," he declared at the same time "I hold it essential that the popular branch of it should be on a broad foundation."

He felt that the House of Representatives "is on so narrow a scale as to be really dangerous, and will warrant a jealousy in the people for their liberties." He warned that "the connection between the President and Senate would tend to perpetuate him, by corrupt influence. It is the more necessary on this account that a numerous representation in the other branch of the legislature should be established." Williamson's motion was voted down, but the defeat was not the end of Hamilton's fight for a larger voice for the people in Congress.

The sting of yet another defeat was partly removed the same day by his appointment to the Committee of Style, which, in light of history, was probably the most important of all convention committees. Charged with molding and arranging the wording of all the drafts and resolutions into the final form of the document, his fellow members, elegant stylists all, were Gouverneur Morris, James Madison, William Samuel Johnson, and Rufus King. Of all the delegates these five men probably had closer personal ties with Hamilton and Washington than any others.

As Hamilton knew, the symmetry, phraseology, form, and style of a document like the Constitution of 1787 in time become its very essence. Innumerable decisions of courts and Congresses and legislatures in the years since the committee met have turned on individual words—their position in each phrase, clause, and sentence—and even on points of punctuation.

Now, in these final weeks, in his work with the Committee of Style, in debates on the floor, and in conversations in the corridors and in the halls of the Indian Queen, Hamilton plied all he knew of the arts of accommodation and compromise. As a result of the fact that earlier he had unforgettably established his preeminence as a student of all forms of government and a position on these matters that remained more truly national than the stand of any other delegate, Hamilton enjoyed a distinct practical advantage. He could forcefully urge compromises and adjustments between proposals, that differed less from each other than they fell short of the high tone of his well-publicized ideal. When he pointed out where middle ground lay or avowed that he would not object, his view in itself, became a strong recommendation for acceptance by others who were more ready to settle for less than he claimed he demanded.

Moreover, he had just returned from travels and talks among the people while the convention stayed in session. He could speak with more authority on current popular opinion in closely divided constituencies than delegates who had remained in Philadelphia all summer. He threw his strength into the fray on a few more key points.

On September 10 Hamilton pointed out that Congress, not the states alone, should be able to call a convention to amend the Constitution: "The lack of an easy mode of amending is a serious flaw in the Articles of Confederation." He proposed that Congress be empowered to call a convention whenever two-thirds of each branch should concur. He then seconded and pleaded for Madison's motion, which led directly to Article V, providing that by a two-thirds vote of both houses or on the application of two-thirds of the legislatures of the several states, Congress shall propose amendments to the Constitution, which shall be valid when ratified by three-fourths of the state legislatures or by conventions in three-fourths of the states. Hamilton was fighting for the maximum possible flexibility and amendability and against rigidity. "An easy mode should be established for supplying defects which will probably appear in the New System," he said.

In later debate the same day, they came down to the mechanics of ratifying the Constitution. Hamilton argued that it would be wrong for nine states, by ratifying, to jam it down the throats of the remaining four. This would be "to institute a new Government on the ruins of the existing one." The plan should be approved by the Continental Congress first, this being "a necessary ingredient in the transaction." Hamilton's motion was defeated, leaving the Constitution to provide only that ratification by nine states, without any action by Congress, would be sufficient.

But if ratification by the states meant ratification by the state legislatures, too many entrenched, vested local interests would remain in control, he warned, remembering well Clinton's monolithic control in his own assembly. Special conventions would at least open up the possibility of new faces, fresh ideas, and more representation of the current wishes of the people at large. Hamilton moved to take the question away from the entrenched interests, to require the legislatures to refer it to a "Convention of Deputies in each state to be chosen by the people thereof." If the peoples' conventions approved, then "such approbation shall be binding and conclusive upon the state."

The Committee of Style recommended that a vote of three-fourths of each house of Congress be required to override a presidential veto. Advocate of the strong executive though he was, Hamilton thought this was going too far. Two-thirds was all that should be required to override a veto, he urged; and, for a change, he won. So the rule has remained to this day in Section 7 of Article I of the Constitution.

The Committee of Style, that inner circle of five within the 55 demigods, produced a masterpiece of draftsmanship. Their most important single contribution came at the beginning. The first version had started off with the words "We the people of the States of New Hampshire, Massachusetts—" and so on, listing each of the thirteen by name, "do ordain, declare and establish the following constitution—". As reported out by the Committee of Style, there was a world of difference: The name of each separate state was omitted. All the names were replaced by the words "United States." Now it read:

> We the people of the United States, in order to form a more perfect Union, establish justice, insure domestic tranquility, provide for the common defense, promote the general welfare, and secure the blessings of liberty to ourselves and our posterity, do ordain and establish this Constitution for the United States of America.

None of the delegates objected immediately to this polished statement of the purposes of the Constitution drawn up by Morris, Hamilton, and the others. But later in the Virginia ratifying convention, Patrick Henry balked with a bellow at the deletion of the names of the sovereign states. Arguably, on narrow grounds, the deletion had been made necessary by the decision of August 31 that the new government should go into operation upon ratification by nine states. Because no one could tell for certain which states would ratify and which would stall or flatly refuse to join, the practical course was to leave out any mention at all of Rhode Island or New Hampshire or their sisters. Thus, perhaps fortuitously or perhaps through Hamilton's urgings in committee that the states be abolished or both, "We the people of the United States," not the states, were acknowledged to be, and became, the nominal as well as real sovereign and source of the Constitution.

This opening acknowledgement of the peoples' direct relation to the national government was balanced by an almost equally important specific restraint on state interference with peoples' property rights. Rufus King, having failed to persuade his colleagues on the floor in late August of the usefulness of restraints on the power of the states to "interfere in private contracts," now persuaded the committee to reinsert just such a clause. On September 14 the convention reconsidered this and accepted it without a murmur, pausing only to tighten it slightly. No state, the Constitution now made clear, was to pass any "law impairing the obligation of contracts." Elbridge Gerry was so impressed by the wisdom of this unauthorized codicil that he tried, without success, to lay Congress "under the like prohibition."

Just before adjournment, the delegates debated enlargements of the powers of the general government. Hamilton's later policies and theories of the powers of the executive owe much to such last-minute enlargements. The delegates agreed to Rutledge's motion to deprive Congress of the power to "appoint a Treasurer," who would be the chief financial officer of the new government. The future secretary of the treasury would be an officer of the executive branch, not an agent of Congress; yet there remained vestiges of a different relationship between Congress and the secretary of the treasury than existed between Congress and other cabinet officers.

The last alteration proposed and accepted on September 15 was an echo of the struggle between the larger states on one side for power, justice, and "one man, one vote" and the smaller, on the other, for power, survival, and "one state, one vote." Gouverneur Morris responded to "the circulating murmurs of the small states" by proposing "to annex a further proviso" to the amending clause, which ordained "that no state, without its consent, shall be deprived of its equal suffrage in the Senate." On this, "No one opposing" the motion "or on the question, saying no," the proviso carried. The small-staters could now relax and look forward to the ridiculously disproportionate voting power they have enjoyed over the large from their one-state, two-vote voice in the Senate ever since.

Three or four leading members of the convention had already expressed serious doubts about the whole scheme. While some delegates sat quietly waiting for the last decisive vote and others tossed more amendments onto the table, William Blount had serious reservations, Gerry, the "Grumbletonian," grumbled, and George Mason prophesied calamity for the lack of a Bill of Rights. Edmund Randolph fell uneasily silent.

The finished document came remarkably close, in terms of general strength and structure, if not in all details of operation, to what Hamilton had urged. No one would have predicted in May that a Constitution with such powerful national institutions as a bicameral Congress, an executive with magisterial power, and a Supreme Court whose writ would be the supreme law of the land would come out of the State House by September. It is a lonely position, but the thesis of this book is that Hamilton's public commitment to a system that was national, centralized, and consolidated and gave less autonomy to the states than any other delegate advocated had more to do with the high tone and nervous strength of the final result than the efforts of any other delegate, except, of course, George Washington's.

Most historians, even those most sympathetic to Hamilton, like Clinton Rossiter, are fond of saying that Hamilton played a disappointing minor role at the convention largely because he gained no converts to his views. True, most of the views he put forward went down to defeat. Rossiter partly excuses him by wondering "if there were not personal reasons for his lackluster showing that have never been revealed?" Auldjo? Beckley? James Reynolds? Maria?

It is this writer's thesis that because he had no concern for personal popularity, but had larger purposes in mind, and because his specific views gained him few converts, they won converts for the kind of constitution that he sought. Because he cared nothing to draw popularity to himself, he gained much for the document that emerged. His role made possible some of the Constitution's most remarkable features as well as the elevation and elegance of tone and style that is its most notable quality.

At every opportunity, at the critical moments, not perversely, not petulantly, not proudly, sometimes taking the stance of a powerful advocate, sometimes of a disinterested judge, Hamilton ostentatiously called attention to how far his views were from those of the majority of the delegates. But when, with a flourish, he signed the finished product on the final day, he was the most active of all in urging every other member to sign. "A few characters of consequence, by opposing or even refusing to sign the Constitution," he said, "might do infinite mischief by kindling the latent sparks which lurk under an enthusiasm . . . which may soon subside." He pointed with a touch of pride to the defeats he had regularly suffered in the convention, in the larger interest now of pressing most forcefully for its unanimous approval.

Despite his long record of vocal objection to various features of the document, Hamilton did not join the bitter-enders like Blount, Mason, Gerry, and Randolph by voicing unalterable objection to the document and refusing to sign.

The president, George Washington, stood to put the two final questions of the day:

On the proposition of Edmund Randolph, that there be a second convention, all the states voted "Nay."

On the question to adopt the Constitution as amended, all the states voted "Aye."

The Constitution was then ordered to be engrossed, and the house adjourned at 6:00 P.M. for a Sunday recess for prayer and rest.

When the convention assembled for the last time on Monday morning, September 17, 41 of the Framers were in their seats, but for New York, only Hamilton was present. His fellow delegates Yates and Lansing had long since

gone home for good. Randolph, Gerry, and Mason, proud of their perfect attendance records, were anxious to see the end with their own eyes and unworried
by the prospect of being recusants at a communion. The sick, exhausted Dickinson had fled home over the weekend after asking Read to sign his name.

Someone, probably Major William Jackson, read the engrossed Constitution
to men who by now knew its every word almost by heart, whereupon Dr. Franklin "rose with a speech in his hand." Unable to remain for long on his feet, he
handed it to Wilson to read and then to Madison to copy into his notes. McHenry
described the speech as "plain, insinuating, and persuasive." It would create a
benign climate for the signing, prevent other dissenters from defecting, and
perhaps lure Blount and Randolph, at least, back into the fold.

It was vintage Benjamin Franklin—wise, gentle, disarming, and politically
realistic. His words must have cast a spell as all listened that morning to the
patriarch of the demigods:

> Mr. President: I confess that there are several parts of this constitution
> which I do not approve, but I am not sure I shall never approve them:
> For having lived long, I have experienced many instances of being
> obliged by better information, or fuller consideration, to change opin-
> ions even on important subjects, which I once thought right, but found
> to be otherwise. It is, therefore, that the older I grow, the more apt I
> am to doubt my own judgment, and to pay more respect to the judgment
> of others. . . . Though many private persons think almost as highly of
> their own infallibility as of that of their sect, few express it so naturally
> as a certain French lady, who in a dispute with her sister, said "I don't
> know how it happens, Sister, but I meet with no body but myself, that's
> always in the right—*Il ny' a que moi qui a toujours raison.*"
>
> On the whole, Sir, I cannot help expressing a wish that every
> member of the Convention who may still have objections to it, would
> with me, on this occasion, doubt a little of his own infallibility, and to
> make manifest our unanimity, put his name to this instrument.

The old fox then offered a motion conceived by a young fox, Gouverneur
Morris, which sought to "gain the dissenting members" by inviting all delegates
to sign as witnesses to the fact of "the unanimous consent of the states" on the
floor. This would create at least an illusion of complete concord.

While the benevolent mood created by Franklin's speech still held the delegates in thrall, one last parliamentary moment remained to give the people more
voting power in the lower house. Nine days earlier, Hamilton had spoken with
great earnestness and anxiety in favor of a motion to broaden direct representation of the people by population in the House, holding that it was "essential that
the popular branch should be on a broad foundation" to prevent any "connection
between the President and Senate" that "would tend to perpetuate him, *by
corrupt influence.*" Then Hamilton's motion had been defeated.

Nathaniel Gorham now moved that the 1:40,000 voting ratio planned for the

House be changed to 1:30,000, thus creating more representatives in the House, each representing a smaller number of people, so that each would be more responsive to popular views.

After King and Carroll had seconded the motion, Washington rose to put the question. Then, to the astonishment of all, after maintaining silence on all debatable issues since the day John Rutledge and Robert Morris had escorted him to the chair on the dais, Washington made his first and only speech of the entire convention.

> Although my situation has hitherto restrained me from offering sentiments on questions depending in the House, and it might be thought, ought now to impose silence on me; yet I cannot forbear expressing my wish that the alteration proposed might take place. ... The smallness of the proportion of Representatives has been considered by many members of the Convention an insufficient security for the rights and interests of the people. I acknowledge that it always appeared to me among the exceptionable parts of the plan; and late as the present moment is for admitting amendments, I think this of so much consequence that it would give me much satisfaction to see it adopted.

Now, at this supreme moment in world history for the cause of free popular government, the president general, whose iron decorum had never been breached, saw fit to breach it one single time in order to support the motion that Hamilton had first urged.

Many would now no longer be in any doubt of the careful prior planning of this and many earlier parliamentary moves that had been worked out by the two men over the tankards at the Indian Queen or at Robert Morris's. This last motion drove home the fact that purposeful planning had had more to do with the success of this and earlier motions than all the speeches exchanged in all the floor debates.

The delegates adopted the amendment unanimously. What else could they do? They then approved the engrossed Constitution and made ready to sign. Blount of North Carolina was still opposed to signing. Of Gerry, one delegate wrote, "he was fond of objecting to everything he did not propose!" The remarks of the two patriarchs had stung rather than soothed Randolph, and once again he rose to explain that by refusing to sign "he meant only to keep himself free to be governed by his duty as it should be prescribed by his future judgment." This was too much for Hamilton, Gouverneur Morris, and Williamson. All resounded Franklin's theme, one that would become familiar in the fight over ratification. "The present plan," Morris said, was "the best that was to be attained," and since "general anarchy" was the "alternative," he would "take it with all its faults." "For himself," Williamson added, "he did not think a better plan was to be expected."

Now came the moment for which Hamilton's speech of June 18, his plan for a government, his draft of a Constitution, even his attack on Clinton had laid the indispensable foundation. His fellow delegates would know that it did not come from him as mere rhetoric when Hamilton rose to speak.

"No man's ideas are more remote from the plan than mine are known to be," he averred, "but is it possible to deliberate between anarchy and convulsion on one side, and the chance of good to be expected from the plan on the other."

That no man's ideas were less remote from the strength and tone of the plan that had emerged might have been said by Hamilton with equal truth and more self-satisfaction. But for him to have done so would not have furthered the purpose that saying the opposite—which came with unique force from him—did. After Hamilton sat down, Blount changed his mind and agreed to sign the document.

Writing in long retrospect in 1831, after 40 years or more in Jefferson's republican and anti-Hamiltonian political camp, Madison was still under the spell of his early collaborator and later political adversary for his everlasting willingness to compromise for the sake of the greater public good:

> If his theory of government deviated from the republican standard, he had the candour to avow it, and the greater merit of co-operating faithfully in maturing and supporting a system which was not his choice.

Franklin's motion on the question of adoption passed ten to zero.

The delegates then came forward to place their signatures on the documents. Like a good lawyer helping a lay client, as each came up, Hamilton wrote in the name of the state before the place each signer was to sign. His hand writing and the strokes of his pen outlining each state's name add the most intimate possible physical flourish any hand was capable of adding to all else he had contributed to the cause of human liberty in a constitutional republic under law. Technically, because of the absence of Yates and Lansing, the state of New York could not be counted as one of the "states present and voting." In the final resolution laying the Constitution before Congress and the states, eleven states are listed plus one individual, "Mr. Hamilton from New York."

Benjamin Franklin got in the last word.

Looking toward the president's chair, on the back of which a rising sun was painted, he said to a few members near him, "Painters find it difficult to distinguish in their art a rising sun from a setting sun. I have often and often in the course of the session, and the vicissitudes of my hopes and fears as to its issue, looked at the sun behind the President without being able to tell whether it was rising or setting: But now at length I have the happiness to know that it is a rising and not a setting sun."

To this famous benediction, Madison added the last words of his precious notes: "The Constitution being signed by all the members except Mr. Randolph, Mr. Mason and Mr. Gerry, who declined giving it the sanction of their names, the convention dissolved itself by an adjournment sine die."

The delegates walked to their lodgings—some to the Indian Queen, some to the City Tavern on Second Street near Walnut—and "dined together, and took a cordial leave of each other." Washington wrote in his diary that "the Constitution received unanimous consent of eleven states and Mr. Hamilton from New York," after which, "I returned to my lodgings, did some business with, and received the papers from the Secretary of the Convention, and retired to meditate on the momentous work which had been executed."

Nothing Hamilton did or supposedly failed to do at the convention caused any of his great colleagues or collaborators there or later in his life to minimize the importance of his role or to concur in the modern conventional assessment that his performance was a disappointment, and they were no mean judges of other men. On the contrary, they saw him named to two of the most important committees; never forgot his speech of June 18; and always spoke, wrote, and acted as if, in matters of political philosophy and constitution building, Hamilton was not only their peer, but also their mentor.

When Hamilton proposed to Madison and Jay that they collaborate with him in writing *The Federalist Papers*, the man whom later historians have called "The Father of the Constitution" followed precepts and outline prepared by Hamilton to expound its meaning. If Madison, Wilson, Washington, and Gouverneur Morris appear nearer the center in group portraits of the Framers, the frame Hamilton provided for them is no less important to the existence of the picture itself.

There is nothing especially unique about a written constitution. In itself it is nothing more than a skeletal outline of old ideas. Since 1787 innumerable fine-sounding constitutions have been composed; Soviet Russia has a fine-sounding one. When the Constitutional Convention adjourned that September 17, 1787, there was a Holy Roman Emperor; Venice was a republic; France was ruled by a king; China, by an emperor; Japan, by a shogun; Russia, by a czar. Great Britain was a monarchy tempered by the barest beginnings of democracy, in which less than 2 percent of the population enjoyed voting representation. All those proud regimes—and scores of others—have passed into history. Among the leading nations of the world, the only government that stands essentially unchanged is the Federal Union put together in 1787 by thirteen states on the East Coast of North America. It has survived foreign wars, a civil war, panics, depressions and recessions, Teapot Dome, Bobby Baker, Watergate, impeachments, and pardons.

Flesh, blood, passion, desire, intellect, experience, force, honor, and moral commitment must come together to bring reality to well-worn skeletal outlines, stay with them, and create institutions that operate according to the words and keep them alive with reverent adherence for years, decades, and centuries to make a constitution worth much more than the paper it is written on.

This writer's thesis is that for the reasons given, and still to come, the unique strength, character, and freedom of the nation that has lived under this one momentous Constitution owes more to Hamilton for what it is, as we see it plain after almost 200 years, than it does to any other man, of his own time or since, notwithstanding his occasional unexplained absences that summer from the floor of the State House—and the hall of the Indian Queen.

23

THE FEDERALIST PAPERS AND OTHER POUGHKEEPSIE PERSUADERS

IT SEEMS TO HAVE BEEN RESERVED TO THE PEOPLE OF THIS COUN-
TRY, BY THEIR CONDUCT AND EXAMPLE, TO DECIDE THE IMPOR-
TANT QUESTION, WHETHER SOCIETIES OF MEN ARE REALLY CAPA-
BLE OR NOT, OF ESTABLISHING GOOD GOVERNMENT FROM
REFLECTION AND CHOICE, OR WHETHER THEY ARE FOREVER DES-
TINED TO DEPEND FOR THEIR POLITICAL CONSTITUTIONS, ON ACCI-
DENT AND FORCE.

—*The Federalist*, No. 1, October 27, 1787

When he arrived home from Philadelphia at Number 57 Wall Street, if he
had spoken of it at all, "Better than nothing" was probably how he described to
Betsy the Constitution that his absence had produced. But to her and the children
after their long summer separations, there were many more important things
to be said. No matter what other affairs may have engaged him during summer
absences, Hamilton always managed to address his Betsy with the most intense
affection that words could convey, even if he did tend to fix on the same expressions as the years went by and repeat them. "Monday at furthest I embrace my

angel . . . Think of me—dream of me and love me, my Betsy, yours my angel, with inviolable fidelity" was typical.

Once past Betsy's adoring embrace, there were the kisses of robust Philip, sweet Angelica, baby Alexander, and the shy touch of Colonel Antil's little orphan child. There would also be a gruff roar and a bristly bear hug from Baron von Steuben.

The summer's work in Philadelphia had left the Hamiltons badly pinched for money; so as soon as he got back to New York, on September 21, Hamilton dunned William Nelson for some, as hard as he thought proper.

"You will recall the cause of *Haydn* against *van Kleeck* put into my hands by you. I hope it will not be inconvenient to you to take care of my costs," he wrote.

His July "reflections" on Clinton and Clinton's policies had helped make him the leading personification of the powerful national constitution; Clintonians held him in large part to blame. On September 6 "A Republican" assailed Hamilton in *The New York Journal*, concluding with some lines of verse "from the works of the celebrated Churchill":

> Smit with love of honor, or the pence,
> O'er run with wit, and destitute of sense,
> Legions of factious authors throng at once;
> Fool becons fool, and dunce awakens dunce.
> To Hamilton's the ready lies repair;
> Ne'er was lie made which was not welcome there.

"Inspector" in *The New York Journal* of September 20 called Hamilton "an upstart attorney" who had "palmed" himself "upon a great and good man." Under such patronage he had made himself known "but being sifted and bolted to the brann, he was at length found to be a superficial, self conceited coxcomb, and was of course turned off and disregarded by his patron."

Clintonians fired off more broadsides in *The New York Journal* signed with the nom de plume Cato. A supporter of Hamilton, perhaps with his prodding, replied with articles in the *Daily Advertiser* signed Caesar. The two ancient Romans refought the old battle of loose confederation versus centralized nation once again, neither with particular originality. Caesar's calling Clinton such names as "designing croaker" won no converts to Hamilton's cause. Hamilton called on Washington for a statement of the facts of their long relationship to rebut the charge that he had "palmed" himself on him. Washington, resting in Mount Vernon from his convention labors, hastened to comply. He affirmed that the charge was unfounded. But he reproved Hamilton: "it is with unfeigned concern I perceive that a political dispute has arisen between Gov. Clinton and yourself. For both of you I have the highest esteem and regard." Washington feared that Hamilton's assaults on Clinton might push that stubborn man into the ranks of the irreconcilables opposed to the Constitution if he were not already there.

The most important thing about these exchanges was that as Hamilton set out upon the difficult work of bringing New York into the fold of the Constitution, he had them before him as object lessons that violent attacks on the opposition would not work. Washington's reproof reminded him that he would lose the backing of the man even his enemies acknowledged to be "great and good" if he kept up such counterproductive tactics. Pride in his accomplishments at Philadelphia and impatience with the necessity of rehearsing the same old arguments all over from the beginning for the instruction of slower minds in upstate New York were no excuse. It was necessary to start all over again with a new tone.

Hamilton's meditations on the future of the "momentous work" of the summer were balanced but not sanguine. In a set of "Conjectures about the new constitution" set down toward the end of September, Hamilton wrote, "Against its success is to be put the dissent of two or three important men in the Convention, who will think their characters pledged to defeat the plan." There were also inconsiderable men in state governments like Clinton, who were fearful of loss of power; there were, too, the disinclination of the people to accept taxes and a strong government, the opposition of debtors to a government that could restrain them from cheating their creditors; and the influence of foreign powers who would not wish to see "an energetic government" established throughout the states.

"If the government be adopted," Hamilton thought, "it is probable General Washington will be the President of the United States." A wise choice of men and a good administration would thus be assured, and the national government would "triumph altogether over the state governments." Everything to be done now must be done in a way to keep Washington's full support. If the Constitution should fail, Hamilton could also foresee "such struggles, animosities and heats in the community that this circumstance conspiring with the *real necessity* of an essential change in our present situation will produce civil war. . . . a dismemberment of the union may be expected. . . . several republican confederacies [may] be established between different combinations of the particular states." The terrible possibility of civil war remained at the front of his mind. Even the possibility of "a reunion with Great Britain, from universal disgust at a state of commotion, is not impossible, though not to be feared." In any event, he thought, if the Constitution failed, "a dissolution of the union seems to be the most likely result."

The most likely cause of dissolution would be the failure to make the necessary "essential change" to eliminate the fatally divisive institution of slavery. Hamilton recalled the inflammatory remarks of Gouverneur Morris at the convention on the subject. They had come close to provoking a walkout by the Southern delegates.

Slavery was "the curse of heaven," Morris had said, on the states where it prevailed. He had compared the free regimes of the middle states "where a rich and noble culture marks the prosperity and happiness of the people" with "the misery and poverty which overspreads the barren wastes of Virginia and other slave states." Morris had spoken most censoriously of "the inhabitant of Georgia and South Carolina who goes to the coast of Africa and in defiance of the most sacred laws of humanity tears away his fellow creatures from dearest connections and damns them to the most cruel bondages." Abraham Lincoln would echo Morris's words in his Cooper Union speech in New York 73 years later, but at the time the only reply John Rutledge of South Carolina could offer to Morris was: "religion and humanity have nothing to do with the question."

Morris, Hamilton, and the others most opposed to slavery were unwilling to sacrifice the Constitution to win debating points for rigid opposition to it at the time; but they had refused to give the Southern states full white representation for their Negroes—as property. This at least would somewhat discourage the slave trade. When the vote went six to four against the South on the three-fifths compromise, Georgia and South Carolina threatened to bolt the convention, but had stayed on. Hamilton remained full of foreboding that without the "essential change"—abolition of slavery—the attempt to compromise the issue would fail and would "produce civil war" between the states.

The details of the covenant "secretly arrived at" during the summer in Philadelphia were now made known to the people of all the states. Early in the morning of September 18, Major William Jackson set out by stage for New York "in order to lay the great result . . . before the United States in Congress" there.

Many of the Framers were also members of Congress. They now followed Major Jackson back to New York, changed hats, took their seats in the New York City Hall, and made ready to welcome warmly the charter they had sent up to themselves from Philadelphia. What the Framers present had wanted from Congress was a strong recommendation from it to the states that the Constitution be ratified; what Congress voted them was much less, a noncommittal declaration providing only that it be transmitted to the states. At least Congress did not reject it or hamstring it with restrictive amendments. On September 28, in the absence of truculent Rhode Island and over the oblique opposition of New York, Congress voted that the Constitution "be transmitted to the several legislatures in order to be submitted to a convention of delegates chosen in each state by the people thereof."

Congress's resolution transmitting the Constitution to the states for ratification launched Hamilton on another long-running political contest. It was a contest that could easily have turned out either way. It consisted of a series of thirteen separate battles for ratification waged up and down the map of the thirteen states. The two most important and decisive battles were to be fought in Virginia and New York. In New York, as at Philadelphia, Hamilton was the visible champion, strategist, tactician, and polemicist for the cause; elsewhere, with Madison's collaboration, Hamilton's views would make themselves felt through correspondence and *The Federalist Papers*.

That the proposed Constitution would require much defending was obvious to Hamilton well before he left the convention, and the strength of the opposition became still plainer to him now that he was back. Chief support came from merchants and businessmen, small shopkeepers and tradesmen and their followers in the towns along the eastern seaboard. People whose livings depended on trade and commerce by and large favored it. But in the hinterlands, among farmers and many landed proprietors too, debtors and frontiersmen, opposition was intense. Favorable or unfavorable economic impact was never far away from what people believed was politically, socially, and morally right. Foreseeing that its chances in state legislatures were slim, at Hamilton's urging, the Constitutional Convention had called instead for state ratifying conventions, popularly elected, to pass on its handiwork. There was also the revolutionary proviso that the consents of only nine of the thirteen states, not unanimity, would be sufficient to start the new nation off as a going concern.

Governor Clinton of New York showed no disposition even to call the legislature into session to devise machinery for the election of a ratifying convention. Tides of opposing opinion rose higher and higher as each day of delay went by. In court corridors during recesses of trials, at luncheons, with groups of friends and rivals at Fraunces or Cape's Tavern, or over coffee or tankards of ale in the late afternoon at the Tontine, Hamilton's ironic smile flickered with the humor of the thing as he explained over and over again with quicksilver charm that "no man's ideas were more remote from the plan" than his. Even so, he now ardently urged all to support it. No one could be a more powerful persuader in private conversations with small groups of men. Private dinners were part of the tactics too, and the Hamiltons entertained frequently.

Few wives could have been better fitted than Elizabeth Hamilton for the part she now was called upon to play. She had, after all, been accustomed to helping her mother as hostess to distinguished people from everywhere in her father's houses at Albany and Old Saratoga. And she had been trained by her careful mother to preside over a large household.

With her own large family, the Antil child, and Baron von Steuben to look after and usually only Gussie, the cross and impudent hired girl, to help her (in place of the squads of servants her mother had taught her to deploy), Elizabeth may have comforted herself with the thought that here on Wall Street there was at least no need to worry about night raids by tomahawk-throwing Indians.

After dinner, when the ladies had withdrawn with Mrs. Hamilton to the parlor, her husband's voice could be overheard among the men, as the port and walnuts passed round, discoursing on the virtues of "better than nothing." The quiet voice of James Madison, a frequent visitor those fall and winter evenings, harmonized with that of his host in infinite variations on the same theme.

The young patroon, Stephen van Rensselaer III, now settled down with Elizabeth's sister Peggy, was happy to hear, he wrote Betsy, "that you are so good a *housewife, housekeeper,* etc. The General [Schuyler] talks of nothing but you & the Esquire & says you and he will be models for us all."

Late at night, by candlelight, after the guests had gone, Betsy would lend her hand to Hamilton's by making neat copies of his drafts of *The Federalist*, as her husband, and sometimes Madison, scribbled on. Sometimes, very late, she would grow faint, for she was now pregnant with the child of one of Hamilton's compassionate absences from Philadelphia. When he was born April 14, 1788, they would christen their third son James Alexander.

As Hamilton's plan for *The Federalist Papers* unfolded, it became obvious that it was too vast for any one man to carry out, even a writer as facile as Hamilton. John Jay agreed to help write some of the papers, but he was a slow, methodical writer with a somewhat tedious style. Besides, he soon fell ill.

James Madison, who had been one of the chief architects of the Constitution, agreed with Hamilton's desire for a strong union and other fundamentals. A scholarly writer, with a mind well-stocked with precedents and logical arguments, he had taken notes at all stages of the unfolding of the floor debates. Virginia's approval was as crucial as New York's in the impending struggle, and the opposition forces there were just as strong. Now in New York as a Virginia delegate to Congress preparing for the desperate fight over ratification there, Madison agreed to collaborate with Hamilton on the *Federalist* scheme.

Gouverneur Morris later said that Hamilton had pressed him to help, too. A good friend of Hamilton, William Duer, also helped out with three essays in defense of the Constitution, which he signed "Philo-Publius," but they were not incorporated in *The Federalist* itself. Duer soon dropped out of the faster intellectual company.

Speed was essential. Pennsylvania, New Jersey, and Delaware had already made provision for holding their conventions; other states were preparing to follow suit. If *The Federalist Papers* were to influence decisions of the delegates, they must appear in swift, consecutive order.

The purpose of Federalists, as the men who had fought hardest for the new, national Constitution somewhat paradoxically came to be called, was much the same in every state: to push ratification of the Constitution through promptly and unconditionally. Delay in state ratifications had drained all vitality from the Articles of Confederation before they had gone into force. Thin margins of victory over bitter men would not be enough. If the Constitution were to last, even those who opposed it most vigorously would have to concede its legitimacy. Ratifications by nine small states would not be good enough to bring the Constitution to life. The geographical and political position of any one of the four largest states—New York, Virginia, Pennsylvania, or Massachusetts—was such that it would make the Constitution a dead letter if it should vote to stay out.

In every state, Anti-Federalists made forceful cause against the Constitution in speeches, letters, pamphlets, and newspaper broadsides, repeating endlessly that the Federalists were trying to stampede the country into an untested new system by painting a picture of troubles that did not exist and horrors that might not arise. "To say that a bad government must be established for fear of anarchy," Richard Henry Lee wrote publicly to the still unsure Edmund Randolph, "is really saying that we should kill ourselves for fear of dying."

Anti-Federalists charged that the Framers had acted contrary to both the law and spirit of the Articles of Confederation. They had done this—a damning and symbolic piece of evidence—as a "Dark Conclave" under a "thick veil of secrecy." The Constitution, they felt, was a long step toward monarchy and aristocracy and a repudiation of the Revolution of 1776. Four features drew fire in every state, even from men who wished it well: the failure to include a bill of rights ("Should not such a thing have preceded the model?" Adams asked Jefferson); the creation of a powerful and virtually irresponsible executive ("A bad edition of a Polish king," Jefferson warned Adams); the provision for "one state, two votes" in the upper house ("this host of influence and power," George Clinton described it); and the narrow scale of representation in the House of Representatives (which would make it simply an "assistant aristocratical branch," wrote one outraged Bostonian).

In Patrick Henry's angry words, the Constitution doomed the states to decline and death by creating "one national government." The taxation clause, George Mason warned softly, "clearly discovers that it is a national government, and no longer a confederation." The supremacy clause, Robert Whitehill of Pennsylvania echoed angrily, "eradicates every vestige of state government—and was intended so—it was deliberated." Thomas Wait of Maine, one of many Anti-Federalists who summoned Montesquieu to witness, held that the "vast continent of America" could not be ruled on principles of freedom if "consolidated into one government." He wrote a friend, "You might as well attempt to rule Hell by prayer."

So Hamilton took on a mighty task of advocacy when he sat down at 57 Wall Street and took up his quill to write *The Federalist, No. 1*. When he had finished it, he signed it with the name of "Publius."

The pen name of the mime was the one he had used in 1778 as an army officer to attack venal congressmen like Samuel Chase. It may still have seemed appropriate to conceal the identity of three men who were writing as one—a prize-winning mime could quickly switch identity from one character to another during a single performance. Besides, as a proper name, *Publius* called to mind the common noun *publisher* and its Latin root in *publicare*, "to proclaim," "to bring before the public." Other connotations that clustered around the name for educated men of Hamilton's day recalled the early Roman hero, Publius Valerius, who, according to Plutarch, after the fall of Tarquin, "resolved to render the government, as well as himself, familiar and pleasant to the people instead of terrible." A late Roman, Publius Valerianus, was proclaimed emperor by rebellious soldiers at a time of imperial bankruptcy. At any rate, the signature *Publius* for the whole series of 85 papers served to keep the attention of readers focused firmly on the points being made rather than on the personalities or peccadillos of individual authors.

The *Federalist No. 1*, datelined New York, addressed to "The People of the State of New York," appeared in *The* [New York] *Independent Journal: or The General Advertiser* on October 27, 1787, and reappeared in both *The New York Packet* and *The* [New York] *Daily Advertiser* on October 30. Readers of these newspapers were immediately aware that here was no ordinary polemicist like Cato or Caesar.

Gone was the "designing croaker" style of earlier attacks on Clinton. The first paragraph elevated the hectic earlier forms of abuse to lofty heights of Olympian calm and orderly exposition. Washington would not reprove.

"The subject speaks its own importance," Publius announced. "Nothing less than the existence of the UNION, the safety and welfare of the parts of which it is composed, the fate of an empire, in many respects the most interesting in the world."

He was speaking not for himself nor for a faction or a party, but for all mankind:

> It has been frequently remarked that it seems to have been reserved to the people of this country, by their conduct and example, to decide the important question, whether societies of men are really capable or not, of establishing good government from reflection and choice, or whether they are forever destined to depend for their political constitutions, on accident and force.

All mankind was now at a political continental divide:

> If there be any truth in the remark, the crisis at which we are arrived may with propriety be regarded as the era in which that decision is to be made; and a wrong election of the part we shall act may, in this view, deserve to be considered as the general misfortune of mankind.

Although it was true that much of the opposition to the new Constitution came from men whose obvious interest it was to resist any diminution in the power they wielded under the present state governments, Publius would refuse to dwell on critical "observations of this nature." With a fairness that would strike a new high note in American pamphleteering, a pitch to which he would too seldom rise, Hamilton agreed that much of the opposition was honest, if wrongheaded, in intent. To this honest opposition he addressed himself. "We are not always sure," he admitted, "that those who advocate the truth are influenced by purer principles than their antagonists."

He warned his fellow citizens to be on their guard against attempts to influence their judgment "by any impressions other than those which may result from the evidence of truth." He frankly avowed that he was in favor of the new Constitution while "my motives must remain in the depository of my own breast. My arguments will be open to all, and may be judged of by all. They shall at least be offered in a spirit which will not disgrace the cause of truth."

He called attention to universal truths of human nature: "Jealousy is the usual concomitant of violent love, and the noble enthusiasm of liberty is too apt to be infected with a spirit of narrow and illiberal distrust."

He sounded his lifelong theme, a painful truth about human nature in politics that haunts us still:

> A dangerous ambition more often lurks behind the specious mask of zeal for the rights of the people, than under the forbidding appearance of zeal for the firmness and efficiency of government . . . of those men

who have overturned the liberties of republics the greatest number
have begun their career, by paying an obsequious court to the people,
commencing Demagogues and ending Tyrants.

He concluded with a survey of the points that Publius intended to discuss
in future papers: the utility of the Union to political prosperity, the necessity of
an "energetic" government, "the conformity of the proposed constitution to the
true principles of republican government," and "the additional security which its
adoption will afford to [republican] government, to liberty and to property."

At its simplest level, *The Federalist* was a series of papers defending the
proposed Constitution and urging its adoption by the people of New York. But
as the series unfolded, it became something larger and more philosophical. From
its methodical analysis of the clauses and sections of the Constitution, there
emerged a coherent essay on the purposes and nature of all government, a
universal political philosophy adapted to the American scene. That such a plan
of composition was plainly visible to Madison or Jay at the beginning is unlikely;
yet as the work proceeded and paper after paper was signed, rescanned, blotted
with sand, and tossed to the impatient printer's devil to run to the printer who
was holding open his type sticks and presses, the whole took on an organic form
that transmuted its immediate purpose of serving as a brief in favor of the
Constitution into a great essay on the subject of free government.

Though Hamilton and Madison were both in New York most of the time
during the first four months of publication, roughly from October 27, 1787,
through March 4, 1788, the date of No. 61, there was little time for cross-
checking against inconsistencies, overlaps, repetition, and disproportion.

Madison said, "Though [publication] is carried on in concert," whatever that
might mean, "the writers are not mutually answerable, for all the ideas of each
other, there being seldom time even for a perusal of the pieces by any but the
writer before they are wanted at the press, and sometimes hardly by the writer
himself."

But had they brooded over *The Federalist* for years before carefully putting the first word on paper, the three busy men who were Publius could hardly
have created a more unified architectonic structure. The stately, magisterial,
serene tone Hamilton set for the series in No. 1 lent credibility to a story that
went the rounds that he had written it while sitting on the deck of a sloop sailing
up the Hudson to Albany.

In accordance with Hamilton's overall plan, John Jay, the former secretary
for foreign affairs of the Confederation, next took up pen and wrote Nos. 2
through 5, dealing with relations with foreign powers. The same thread of
argument runs through all—the indispensable necessity of a firmly united nation
to defend against foreign aggression and prevent a breakup into rival confederacies. With these four papers, Jay's contribution halted until he wrote Number
64, a defense of the Senate's role in the treaty-making process. Hamilton and
Madison shared the rest of the labor with Hamilton writing more than 50 papers
in all. Madison's papers made up in substance, however, much of what they
lacked in number.

New essays appeared two, three, and sometimes four times a week, rotating among the New York papers. Hamilton wrote in haste, snatching scraps of composition time from between interviewing clients and trying law suits. Often the printer waited in Hamilton's office to catch the sheets unsanded from his racing pen to rush them into galleys.

In four vigorous numbers, 6 through 9, Hamilton called attention to the perils of disunion that would ensue if the Constitution were not ratified; signs and portents of civil war were already visible: "Let the point of extreme depression to which our national dignity and credibility have sunk, let the inconveniences felt everywhere from a lax and ill administration of government, let the revolt of a part of the State of North Carolina, the late menacing disturbances in Pennsylvania, and the actual insurrections and rebellions in Massachusetts, declare—!" the need for union. Hamilton employed such references with telling effect to argue for strong authority that could deal with uprisings promptly and forcefully.

In No. 10, the first of the series written by Madison, and one of the most famous of all, Madison anticipated a major thesis of Karl Marx. With plain speaking untempered by moral judgments that echoed some of the observations Hamilton had made at the convention, Madison argued that "A well-constructed union" is necessary "to break and control the violence of faction, the most common and durable source of which is the various and unequal distribution of property. Those who hold and those who are without property are always separate and distinct interests in society." Nothing that Hamilton ever wrote sounded more typically Hamiltonian than Madison's first essay as Publius.

In the philosophy of John Locke, which was the then prevailing philosophical mode for thinking about governmental systems, protection of property emerged as the principal purpose of government. This was a consequence of natural law and a mandate of municipal law and had an ethical foundation. Property was derived from labor, and each person had a different value because his ability and industry differed from that of every other person. Madison put it this way: It is "The diversity in the faculties of men, from which the rights of property originate.... The protection of these faculties is the first object of government. From the protection of different and unequal faculties of acquiring property, the possession of different degrees and kinds of property immediately results...."

Nowhere in his own writings did Hamilton lock people and property into any such a rigidly doctrinaire and simplistic equation as Madison insisted on here.

Madison added that a majority in a small area, governing directly under a "pure democracy," could and would ride roughshod over the interests and liberties of a minority. He insisted that "Neither moral nor religious motives can be relied on as an adequate control." Hence a republic, such as the Constitution envisaged, was the best form to protect minority rights. The delegation of authority to a small group of citizens chosen for wisdom, patriotism, and love of justice might avoid such madnesses as "a rage for paper money, for abolition of debts, for an equal division of property, or for any other improper or wicked project."

Hamilton at the Constitutional Convention had summed up the idea that the government must assure liberty and order by mediating between warring classes: "Give all power to the many, they will oppress the few. Give all power to the few; they will oppress the many. Both therefore, ought to have power, that each may defend itself against the other."

In later papers of *The Federalist*, Hamilton followed up Madison's economic arguments by emphasizing the commercial importance of a union that could meet European nations on an equal footing and enforce respect for its trade and commerce by a powerful army and navy. The prosperity of commerce was the "most useful as well as the most productive source of national wealth."

Hamilton's views closely followed those of Thomas Hobbes in *The Leviathan* that the national state should not be limited in its functions to police powers or to keeping of the peace, but should help promote general prosperity by positive means. Hobbes believed that "a generall Providence" must overcome poverty. The weak, the poor, the handicapped, those unable to work, "ought not to be left to the Charity of private persons; but to be provided for . . . by the Lawes of the Common-wealth." Those with strong bodies should work "and to avoyd the excuse of not finding employment, there ought to be such Lawes, as may encourage all manner of Arts; as Navigation, Agriculture, Fishing, and all manner of Manifacture that requires labour." Because ". . . the Passions of men, are commonly more potent than their Reason," as Hobbes observed, "it follows, that where the publique and private interest are most closely united, there is the publique most advanced." Hamilton's sentiments exactly.

Liberty was in law; only a powerful state could enforce the law; due process was the means to private and public happiness.

Hamilton parted company with Madison and the other Virginians in his opposition to the fiction of giving voting power in proportion to property. Slaves were people, not property, and should be allowed to vote for themselves, not solely through the voices of their white owners. Jefferson, relying on his own experience of chattel slavery, considered agriculture the only sound basis for a national economy. Hamilton valiantly attempted to win such slave-state interests to his side by appealing to their high regard for property values. He argued that a strong government that aided commerce would help large land and slave owners too: "It has been found in various countries that, in proportion as commerce has flourished, land has risen in value."

In 1787 and 1788, while Madison was filling in the outlines of *Federalist Papers* suggested to him by Hamilton, most of his writing reads like vintage Hamilton. But two years later, having fallen under the aegis of his fellow Virginian Jefferson, Madison swung around to an almost opposite set of views; Hamilton hewed for the rest of his life to those Madison had earlier shared with him. As Hamilton had said of Rufus King, Jefferson could say of Madison, "I revolutionized his mind." It is fair to ask whether, without Hamilton's serving as his aegis in 1787 and 1788, Madison would have contributed as much as he did to the creation of a national Constitution and to seeking its ratification by his contributions to *The Federalist* and by his work at the Virginia ratifying convention.

The great series rolled on in the newspapers, continuing through No. 77, published on April 2, 1788. The last eight numbers, ending with 85, were first printed in the second volume of J. and A. McLean's edition of *The Federalist* of May 28, 1788. Then beginning on June 14, the papers were reprinted at invervals of several days, first in *The Independent Journal* and then in *The New York Packet*.

When Hamilton had first contracted with Archibald McLean, the printer, for printing and binding *The Federalist*, he had planned only 20 or at most 25 essays. McLean estimated the cost would be £30. With the beginning of the busy term of the New York Supreme Court, Hamilton had to take a vacation from Publius to get back to his law practice and his duties as a member of the Continental Congress, to which he had just been elected again. After writing Nos. 1 and 6 through 9, 11 through 13, 15 through 17, 21 through 36, and coauthoring 18 through 20 with Madison, he took a break through the end of February, and Madison wrote Nos. 37 through 48 and 53. There is a scholarly dispute over which of the two, or both, wrote Nos. 49 through 58, 62 and 63, although Madison's claim to authorship of them is the stronger. With Madison's departure for Virginia at the end of February, it fell to Hamilton alone to complete the important papers that remained, including the detailed exposition of the meaning of particular sections of the Constitution in all the remaining papers through No. 85. As a result, it is to Hamilton that lawyers and courts, as well as historians and philosophers, have chiefly looked since 1787 for the roots of precedental authority on the meaning of the most important parts of the Constitution.

Take, for example, the question of abuse of presidential power and impeachment. Is the abuse of power by an imperial presidency a threat to our liberties? No, Hamilton reassures us with humorous tolerance in No. 67, even though the institution of the presidency sometimes "has been shown to us with the diadem sparkling on his brow . . . the imperial purple flowing in his train . . . seated on a throne surrounded with minions and mistresses . . . murdering janizaries" and a "future seraglio."

But might not an unscrupulous president's abuse of his role as commander in chief of the army and navy make him a threat? Not really, Hamilton explained in No. 69, because the powers of declaring war and raising and regulating armies and fleets are reserved to the legislature; so in this if "there be a resemblance to the King of Great Britain, there is not less a resemblance to the Grand Seigneur, to the Khan of Tartary, to the Man of the Seven Mountains, or to the Governor of New York."

Don't you understand, pleaded Hamilton—striving to train the public's attention on the important differences between an American president and an English king—"the President of the United States would be an officer elected by the people for *four* years; the King of Great Britain is a perpetual and *hereditary* prince. The one would be amenable to personal punishment and disgrace; the person of the other is sacred and inviolable."

It is "The practice of impeachments" Hamilton explained in No. 65 that serves "as a bridle in the hands of the legislative body upon the executive servants of the government." He goes on to explain how the whole impeachment process works. Must the president be impeached before he can be tried for an ordinary crime? Yes, Hamilton advises in Nos. 65 and 69, "the punishment of conviction upon impeachment is not to terminate the chastisement of the offender. After having been sentenced to personal ostracism from the esteem and honors and emoluments of his country, he will still be liable to prosecution and punishment in the ordinary course of law."

Could the president escape punishment for a conspiracy and screen himself and his coconspirators "by the interposition of the prerogative of pardoning" them? No, says Hamilton in No. 69; the president, "though he may even pardon treason, when prosecuted in the ordinary course of law, could shelter no offender, in any degree, from the effects of impeachment and conviction."

But is not impeachment just a political charge by which the party that has lost the presidential election can stir up passions and win it another way? Yes, says Hamilton in No. 65, that is unfortunately true, at least to some extent. "The prosecution of them . . . will seldom fail to agitate the passions of the whole community, and to divide it," but this cannot be helped. Impeachments "are of a nature which may with peculiar propriety be denominated POLITICAL, as they relate chiefly to the injuries done immediately to the society itself. . . ."

But does there not have to be a violation of some specific criminal law? No, explains Hamilton in No. 65, impeachments "are those offenses which proceed from the misconduct of public men, or, in other words, from the abuse or violation of some public trust." It is not really proper to try to define an impeachable offense with the precision required for ordinary crimes because, he explains in No. 70, "Men in public trust will oftener act in such a manner as to render them unworthy of being any longer trusted, than in such a manner as to make them obnoxious to legal punishment." Besides, he adds, there may be cover-ups. "It often becomes impossible, amidst mutual accusations, to determine on whom the blame or the punishment of a pernicious measure, or a series of pernicious measures, ought really to fall." The president or an unscrupulous group around him may shift blame "from one to another with so much dexterity and under such plausible appearances, that the public opinion is left in suspense about the real author." This is especially true, he adds, where the guilty president works through two or three underlings. "If there happened to be a collusion between [them], how easy it is to clothe the circumstances with so much ambiguity as to render it uncertain what was the precise conduct of any of those parties."

Can the courts force the president to comply with a subpoena to surrender papers or tapes? Can they judicially review the legality and validity of an impeachment proceeding? See Nos. 78 and 79, says Hamilton. When the president admits that free transportation and improvements to property he owns constitute additional income to him, does he thereby admit violating the constitutional prohibition against extra emoluments while in office and so commit a new impeachable offense? According to newspaper accounts of late twentieth-century presidential misbehavior when the legal staffs of the Internal Revenue Service and the Judiciary Committee of the House of Representatives did not know the answer to this abstruse question, the most pertinent authority they were able to find, was Hamilton's *Federalist Paper No. 73*.

Can the president unilaterally grant pardons to anyone he pleases, without the consent of the Senate, the courts, or anyone else? Yes, Hamilton said in No. 74. But can it be right to permit a man charged with subverting the government, if he resigns before being impeached to be pardoned? Yes, even then, Hamilton said. There are times when a well-timed offer of a pardon to the insurgent or rebel may restore the "tranquillity of the commonwealth." He added that "Humanity and good policy conspire to dictate that the benign prerogative of pardoning should be as little as possible fettered or embarrassed." Of course, it is not available in cases of impeachment. Should not the power be in Congress or a committee rather than just one man? No, said Hamilton. "The reflection that the fate of a fellow creature depended on his *sole fiat* would naturally inspire scrupulousness and caution . . . a body of men might encourage each other in obduracy. . . . One man appears to be a more eligible dispenser of the mercy of government, than a body of men."

Then sir, is it true, as de Tocqueville predicted that "when the American republic begins to degenerate," it will be easy to tell "by remarking whether the number of political impeachments is increased"? Possibly, Hamilton believed, but probably not. He is confident of the durability of the Framers' handiwork, reminding us serenely in No. 9 that "The science of politics . . . like most other sciences, has received great improvement. The regular distribution of power into distinct departments; the introduction of legislative balances and checks; the institution of courts composed of judges holding their offices during good behavior; the representation of the people in the legislature by deputies of their own election: these are wholly new discoveries, or have made their principal progress towards perfection in modern times." America, not Rome or any great nation of the past, had made these great contributions. "They are means, and powerful means, by which the excellencies of republican government may be retained and its imperfections lessened and avoided."

The above extracts demonstrate the amazing precision and prescience of Hamilton's many answers to the knottiest problems the nation has faced for two centuries, but they are only a small sampling. Hamilton as Publius also explained with similar perspicacity the constitutional provisions for regulating elections (Nos. 59–61), for qualification and representation of senators (62 with Madison), the general powers of the president (No. 67), the president's appointive power (Nos. 68 and 76), the importance of "energy in the executive" (No. 70), the reasons for and against a four-year term for presidents and unlimited eligibility for reelection (Nos. 71 and 72), the president's veto power (No. 73), the role of president and Senate in the treaty-making process (No. 75), and the doctrine of judicial supremacy and judicial review by extension of the doctrine of *Rutgers v. Waddington*.

This was perhaps Hamilton's greatest contribution of all. It was in *The*

Federalist No. 78 that the American people for the first time received the news that the Constitution had incorporated the thesis of Hamilton's brief No. 6 to the Mayor's Court. Neither the Constitution itself nor Hamilton had baldly stated that "we are under a Constitution, but the Constitution is what the judges say it is." But as a member of the Committee of Style of the Constitution, he had helped see to it that the power of interpreting the Constitution would fall logically on the Supreme Court. From this felicity of style, it was but a short step to *The Federalist No. 78*, in which Hamilton wrote that judicial review "only supposes that the power of the people is superior to both" judicial power and legislative power; it follows that "where the will of the legislature, declared in the statutes, stands in opposition to that of the people, declared in the Constitution, the judges ought to be governed by the latter rather than by the former." Largely on the strength of these words, constitutionalism became "one of the most persistent and pervasive characteristics of American democracy."

The concluding series of papers discuss further reaches of the judicial power, the powers of the Supreme Court and of the inferior federal courts, the relations between federal and state courts, trial by jury as the "palladium of free governments" (Nos. 79–83), and the question of the need for a Bill of Rights (No. 84).

There were important things that Publius failed to foresee. In No. 84, Hamilton said that a bill of rights was unnecessary because such protections were sufficiently provided in the Constitution as drawn and that further specification might lead to unforeseen invasions of freedom at the margins of the rights that were specifically guaranteed. Publius did not envisage the two-party system, nominating conventions, and boss rule. But Publius' fears of insufficient strength in the federal government were well founded, as Jefferson's Kentucky and Virginia Resolutions of ten years later, threats of New England secession 15 years later, the Hartford Convention, South Carolina nullification, Southern secession, and the Civil War were all to demonstrate. Even with such omissions, it is not surprising that Archibald McLean's printing bill overran the £30 estimate more than seven times. It came to £220.

Hamilton closed the great brief for his ailing client with a dose of "better than nothing" for "human minds fond of compromise": "I never expect to see a perfect work from imperfect man. . . . The compacts which are to embrace thirteen distinct States in a common bond of amity and union, must as necessarily be a compromise of as many dissimilar interests and inclinations. How can perfection spring from such materials?"

His call for compromise was the more forceful because, as he insisted, "no man's ideas were more remote from the plan" than his. He tossed off a small private joke to his collaborator Madison in Philadelphia when he wrote him on April 3, 1788, enclosing copies of *The Federalist* from the beginning through essay No. 77: "If our suspicions of the author be right, he must be too much engaged to make a rapid progress in what remains. The Court of Chancery and Circuit Court are now sitting." Sending a copy to Benjamin Rush in Philadelphia, he said modestly that "they appear evidently to be written by different hands."

Much ink has been spilled by scholars on the question of which of the two wrote which of the disputed papers. Madison was meticulous in claiming credit for all of his own authorship, but once the job had been done and the result accomplished, Hamilton was characteristically casual about claiming personal credit for his—until the day before his duel with Burr. Then, perhaps full of a presentiment of death, Hamilton walked into the office of his old friend Judge Egbert Benson, where he learned from the judge's nephew, Robert Benson, that the judge and Rufus King had gone to Massachusetts for a few days. While the two spoke quietly, Hamilton took down a volume of Pliny's letters from one of the bookshelves in the office and held it in his hand. A few days later, after Hamilton was dead, Robert Benson remembered his visit, looked in the Pliny, and found a scrap of paper, unsigned but in Hamilton's hand, listing the *Federalist Papers* that he had written. Judge Benson pasted the list inside the cover of his own copy of *The Federalist* and deposited it with the New York Society Library for safekeeping. From there the original was stolen in 1818 and never recovered.

The episode, which only adds to the confusion over authorship, somehow serves to symbolize the often partial, qualified, and grudging thanks that has been accorded Hamilton by the United States and other free peoples of the world and those aspiring to be free for his priceless, nonroyalty-paying, nontax-deductible gift of *The Federalist Papers* to all of them.

To receive Washington's praise was some reward. He wrote, "As the perusal of the political papers under the signature of Publius has afforded me great satisfaction, I shall certainly consider them as claiming a most distinguished place in my library.—I have read every performance which has been printed on one side and the other of the great question lately agitated . . . and, without an unmeaning compliment, I will say that I have seen no other so well calculated [in my judgment] to produce conviction in an unbiased mind, as the Production of your Triumvirate."

Jefferson, still in Paris, declared to Madison that he had read *The Federalist* "with care, pleasure & improvement" and warmly commended it as "the best commentary on the principles of government which ever was written." Jefferson assigned the lion's share of credit to his friend Madison, credited Hamilton with a minor portion, and denied any at all to Jay.

After the battle over ratification was finished, William Maclay, the fiercely democratic senator from Pennsylvania, made an entry in his journal on June 12, 1789: "Mem. Get, if I can, the Federalist, without buying. It is not worth it." Hostile to it as he was, he conceded that "it truly was instrumental in procuring the adoption of the Constitution."

The Federalist appeared in five or six editions during Hamilton's lifetime and has been republished innumerable times since. It is the basic commentary on the fundamental law of the United States. Constant citation by the courts from that day to this has made it an authority on the Constitution second only to the Constitution itself. Young James Kent, later chancellor of New York, wrote in December 1787, "I think 'Publius' is a most admirable writer and wields the sword of party dispute with justice, energy and inconceivable dexterity. The author must be Alexander Hamilton who . . . in genius and political research, is not inferior to Gibbon, Hume and Montesquieu."

Guizot, the French foreign minister, wrote, "In the application of elementary principles of government to practical administration, it was the greatest work known" to him. And Charles A. Beard, that great Populist among historians, acknowledged that "In my opinion it is the most instructive work on political science ever written in the United States; and owing to its practical character, it ranks first in the world's literature of that subject."

In all thirteen states, in every town and village, on farm and plantation, the political controversy over ratification of the Constitution raged with a fury unexampled in previous American experience.

The pivotal states of Massachusetts, South Carolina, Virginia, New Hampshire, and New York had ample time to read and digest much of *The Federalist* before coming to final decisions, and proponents of ratification found it an inexhaustible arsenal of arguments for use in debate.

In state conventions Delaware, Pennsylvania, and New Jersey ratified before the end of 1787. Georgia and Connecticut followed early in 1788. These five had been expected; the real opposition was in the great states of Massachusetts, South Carolina, Virginia, and New York. Hamilton led the Federalist forces in New York; his collaborator Madison was the party whip in Virginia; Hamilton's disciple Rufus King worked for the cause in Massachusetts; his good friends the Pinckneys were active in South Carolina. Federalist leaders wrote to each other continually, advising, exhorting, planning, keeping one another in immediate touch with the ebb and flow of Federalist fortunes in each of their states.

The opposition was just as well organized. Using tactics that had served well during the Revolution, the Anti-Federalists spread a network of committees of correspondence out from New York to rally all forces against the Constitution. John Lamb, the collector of customs, was chairman of the New York Republican Committee, and his expresses went out to Richard Henry Lee, Patrick Henry, and George Mason of Virginia; to Aedanus Burke of South Carolina; to other cohorts in Massachusetts and Maryland. Lee's pamphlets known as "Letters of the Federal Farmer" contained some of the most cogent arguments against ratification. As in revolutionary days, the letters were sent clandestinely and under false names and covers.

In New York, Governor Clinton showed no disposition even to call for an election of delegates to a ratifying convention. As 1788 began, he still had made no move. Hamilton determined to force his hand. On January 31, 1788, he arranged for a resolution to be introduced in the assembly to call a convention; on February first, a similar resolution came before the senate. They squeaked by in both houses, 27 to 25 in the assembly; 11 to 8 in the senate.

The election for delegates to the convention was held on April 3 and for five days thereafter. Both sides had agreed on universal adult male suffrage for the election, thereby insuring that the New York convention would be the most democratically chosen of any of the thirteen states. The Anti-Federalists believed that such broad suffrage was in their interest, feeling certain that the poor and unpropertied yeomanry would vote overwhelmingly against the Constitution.

The Federalists feared they were right. Unlike many other Federalists, Hamilton, too, urged the broadest possible base for suffrage so that the legitimacy of constitutional government would come directly from the people. Since the convention had finally been called only after Federalists' urging, Hamilton's party deserved major credit for fostering the broadest possible base for suffrage in the convention.

In the voting, Clinton and the Anti-Federalists won an overwhelming victory, 46 delegates to the Federalists' 19. Clintonians swept the entire state except the four lower counties, New York, Kings, Richmond, and Westchester. Even Queens went Anti-Federal. But in New York City, within Hamilton's ambiance, the Federal majority was immense. Of a total of 2,836 ballots cast, the nine Federal candidates received a minimum of 2,651 votes and a maximum of 2,735 to 134 for the chief Anti-Federalist candidate, Governor Clinton. This extraordinary show of power by Hamilton's local machine led some to dub the city Hamiltonopolis out of derisory respect.

From the debacle Hamilton had saved what he had to save—a power base in his home county and the adjacent counties—but little else. The Anti-Federalist majority was four-sevenths of the state at large, and two-thirds in the convention.

The city Federalists who had been elected included some of the ablest men in the state, Hamilton, John Jay, Richard Morris, John Sloss Hobart, Robert R. Livingston, Isaac Roosevelt, James Duane, Richard Harrison, and Nicholas Low. The Clintonians had Clinton himself, John Lansing, Melancton Smith, Robert Yates, and 42 others.

But the Clintonian majority was not quite as overwhelming as it first appeared to be. Not all of Clinton's delegates were opposed to the Constitution *in extremis.* Some objected chiefly on the grounds that no Bill of Rights (as later provided by the first ten amendments) had been written into the document. Few were diehards like young De Witt Clinton, the nephew of the governor, who declared that "if the Constitution is adopted, I am convinced that several people who now warmly advocate its adoption will exclaim—'From the insolence of great men—from the tyranny of the rich—from the unfeeling rapacity of the excise-men and Tax-gatherers—from the misery of despotism—from the expence of supporting standing Armies, Navies, Placemen, sinecures, federal cities, Senators, Presidents and a long train of et ceteras, Good Lord deliver us.' " He added with nervous self-reassurance, "There is yet no prospect of its being ratified." Not many felt as strongly as Hamilton's old enemy Abraham Yates, Jr., brother of delegate Robert Yates, that "rather than to adopt the Constitution I would risk a government of Jew, Turk or Infidle [*sic*]." Such extremists were an embarrassment to the more moderate members of Clinton's majority. These latter were the men Hamilton hoped to win over.

Far from being crushed by upstate Clintonians, Hamilton briskly set about making up for lack of votes with energy, brains, and eloquence.

Thinking continentally, Hamilton turned his repudiation by New York to good use in other states by writing friends there to point out that if they wished to avoid civil war, and so forth, they must speed through ratification in their own conventions. On February 16, Massachusetts joined the procession; on April 26, Maryland ratified; on May 23, South Carolina finally approved. With these eight states already decided, only one more was required to put the new union on a going basis. But Rhode Island was hopeless, North Carolina seemingly as bad, and New York firmly opposed. Thus either New Hampshire or Virginia must come in or Hamilton's constitutional labors would be for nothing. Without Virginia, remote New Hampshire would mean little as a practical matter.

So the battle for the Constitution came down to battles for the two great states, Virginia and New York. A nine-state union without these two would be but a paper union, no union at all, a geographical monstrosity of two separated confederacies. Anti-Federalists like George Mason, Richard Henry Lee, James Monroe, William Grayson, Theodorick Bland, and Patrick Henry seemed to be winning the war of words in Virginia, and they came into the June convention at Richmond with at least half of the 170 delegates. James Madison led the Federalist side there, with the backing of George Wythe, John Marshall, Henry Lee, Edmund Pendleton, and Governor Edmund Randolph, who had at last made up his inconstant mind.

Talents and numbers were so closely divided in the Homeric struggle in Virginia that Madison thought that if the Constitution were to obtain a majority at all, it would not exceed three or four. New Hampshire's convention had met on February 19 with a decisive majority of the delegates opposed to ratification. Only the tactics of the proponents in obtaining an adjournment for four months while *The Federalist*'s arguments (and some less high-toned efforts at arm twisting) were allowed to do their work had saved the Constitution from immediate repudiation there.

Hamilton wrote to Madison in Virginia, "It will be of vast importance that an exact communication should be kept up between us while the two conventions are in session. The moment any decisive question is taken, if favorable, I request you to dispatch an express to me, with pointed orders to make all possible diligence, by changing horses, etc. All expense shall be thankfully and liberally paid."

To John Sullivan of New Hampshire, Hamilton wrote in similar vein: "The Anti-Federal party has prevailed in this State by a large majority. . . . all external circumstances should be made use of to influence their conduct. This will suggest to you the great advantage of a speedy decision in your State, if you can be sure of the question, and a prompt communication of the event to us." Sullivan was to send an express to Hamilton at Poughkeepsie, if any vote should prove favorable. Rufus King in Boston told John Langdon in New Hampshire to send him the news too, so that he could forward it to Hamilton by a relay of horses.

Someone had arranged for cannons on the Battery to honor the New York

City delegates as they departed for Poughkeepsie by firing a thirteen-gun salute as their sloop sailed past. Throughout all the time the convention remained sitting, the Federalists of Hamiltonopolis kept up the same sort of jubilant obbligato. For any good news that arrived by express or river sloop, they rang church bells and fired off more cannon salutes. The citizens were made conscious that their city had an identity separate from, and independent of, the rest of the state.

When Hamilton and his little band of Federalists—John Jay, James Duane, Robert R. Livingston among them—arrived in Poughkeepsie, they found Main Street, which was the local interruption of the post road, and East Street, which was the terminus of the Dutchess turnpike, gaily decorated with flags and sprigs of greenery. Pavements and windows of houses were crowded with people whose faces reflected the nervous excitement with which the whole country throbbed. The original village had spread over the hills into a sprawling town. Governor Clinton had his official residence on the Dutchess turnpike nearby, and the town was his stronghold. Conscious of the dignity reposed upon it as the political hub of the state, it had put down violent demonstrations like those that had erupted in other towns like Albany. There Hamilton had already been burned in effigy.

The courthouse, halfway up the hill on the corner of Main and East Streets, surrounded by a stand of maples, was a two-story building of rough local stone with a sloping roof crowned by a belfry. The convention met on the upper story in a bare room unbroken by partitions, whose open windows looked out on the trees and let in sounds of the singing of birds, the keening of crickets, and the murmur of leaves in the breeze. The alert-looking men, with their powdered hair held back in queues, their lawn and ruffles, their elaborately cut corded-silk coats of many colors, completed an Arcadian scene as they gathered in the little town in mid-June.

James Kent later recorded with his usual gusto that the New York convention "formed the most splendid constellation of the sages and patriots of the Revolution which I had ever witnessed, and the intense interest with which the meeting . . . was anticipated and regarded can now scarcely be conceived. . . ."

Seeing the Federalist delegates sally forth from their New York City stronghold to the thirteen-gun salute, James M. Hughes, an observer from Clinton's camp, thought they were being cannonaded to keep up their courage. "I believe," he remarked, "there has not been a Time since the Revolution in which, the Well Born, who are the Leaders of that Party, have felt and appeared so uninfluential, as they feel and appear at this Time and Place." He added, "the Numbers of the Antis astonish the Federalists and they look on their Case as desperate."

General Knox told Rufus King that "the majority of the antis is so great at Poughkeepsie, that I ask no questions." To Madison, things looked black in Virginia too: "I fear that overwhelming torrent Patrick Henry."

Poughkeepsie's newspaper, *The Country Journal*, published a letter from "Turtle Dove" to "Mr. Soaring Lark" in the style of the day, which related that

"The Hawks, Owls, Ravens, Vultures, Kites, & c. are gathering all the sour, nautious, obscene, and offensive matters . . . to burn our Phoenix, and out of her ashes is to arise an enormous big Eagle, that is to prey upon us as long as there is feather, skin, flesh, muscle, fiber, entrail, & c. left . . . but let us destroy their eggs sir. . . ."

Hamilton exuded brisk cheer, circulating widely among the leaders of the other side, and using every contact he could make to persuade all of the inevitability of ratification elsewhere.

One Anti-Federalist assured a friend in New York that "all the acts of a Hamilton et cetera will have no effect"; but, he added significantly, "the latter's manners and mode of address would probably do much mischief, were the members not as firm as they are."

When the convention opened on June 17, Hamilton and his men enthusiastically joined in supporting the election of George Clinton as presiding officer. The perennial governor of New York State, a brigadier general of New York militia with a long record of fighting popular battles and losing them, the tall, erect 49-year-old Clinton was a well-liked, energetic Populist who would be a formidable adversary in any political battle. If the Federalists could not elect one of their own to preside, they could at least neutralize the opposition's most forceful leader by imposing on him the silence, or at least restraint, that parliamentary decorum requires of a chairman. The Anti-Federalists showed unexpected moderation, or overconfidence, by giving the Hamiltonians two out of five appointments to the important Committee on Rules.

Near the central table from which Clinton looked down his long martinet's nose sat his 45 henchmen. Melancton Smith, the Clinton floor leader, one of the most astute and brilliant debaters of the time, was well to the front. Farther away, nearer the open windows, sat Hamilton and General Schuyler, Jay, Duane, and Robert R. Livingston and their small coterie, knowing that if through the windows they heard horses' hooves below, bringing news from afar, it would probably be more important for their cause than any of the noisy speeches made in debate.

Beyond the railing, invited guests crowded, many of them women, as elegantly dressed as they might later have been for a summer race meeting at Saratoga.

Hamilton's tactics would necessarily be based on what happened in Virginia and New Hampshire. Any quick ballot would mean a crushing defeat for the Constitution. So would an adjournment. Hamilton had to prevent both these outcomes by holding the convention in session, marking time with debates and speeches, avoiding a defeat until word of an improvement in the situation came in from elsewhere.

The Federalist was still appearing; copies had been passed from hand to hand; arguments from it passed from speech to speech. A seismic shift in popular consciousness seemed to be slowly getting underway. But because none of this had been reflected in the voting of upstate New York, Hamilton would again have to win the war by arranging to lose many small battles to avoid losing one big one.

On a less exalted political level, the veiled threat that Hamiltonopolis might sever itself from the rest of the state was beginning to be heard. John Jay wrote to Washington on May 29, 1788, that "An idea has taken root that the southern part of the state will at all Events, adhere to the Union; and if necessary to that end, seek a separation from the northern." This would leave Clinton's hinterland cut off from its great port and chief source of tax and trade revenue. News of ratifications by other states, leaving New York State out in the cold, would also have a chilling impact on the more moderate among Clinton's Anti-Federalists.

Clinton would have been satisfied to adjourn the convention without a vote. If other states failed to ratify, well and good. If they did ratify and the union began to operate, he could still adopt a policy of watchful waiting. As Hamilton pointed out to Madison, Clinton would "see how the government works and . . . act according to circumstances." Should any considerable discontent arise, "they will stand ready to head the opposition. If on the contrary the thing should go on smoothly and the sentiments of our own people should change they can then elect to come into the Union." But to advocates of the Constitution now, a vote to adjourn would be as bad as a vote to deny.

In the ordinary course of procedure, at such a convention, there would be debate on the pros and cons of the Constitution, the chairman would put the simple question—for or against ratification, aye or nay—the two-thirds majority of Clintonians would carry the question for the "nays," the Constitution would be dead, and the convention would adjourn.

Hamilton would have to arrange moves to take events out of such an ordinary course. So he and Robert R. Livingston drafted and arranged to introduce a resolution to the effect that no vote be taken on the Constitution itself until each of its provisions had been considered by the convention, sitting as a committee of the whole, clause by clause. Thus, the issue on which each delegate would first be called upon to vote would not be the question of whether he was for or against the Constitution itself, but whether he was for or against free speech and discussion or for cutting off of discussion. If self-proclaimed Populists were called to vote for or against free speech, there was only one way the Populist vote could go. As Hamilton noted to Madison, "I imagine the minor partisans have their scruples, and an air of moderation is now assumed."

Besides, to Melancton Smith and other moderates, Hamilton's resolution would seem but a minor point of procedure; to have voted down his request summarily would have made the Populist majority appear to be too monolithic, inflexible, and boss-controlled. Robert Yates, another Clintonian leader, commented, "Fully relying on the Steadiness of our Friends we see no Danger in this Mode and we came into it to prevent the Opposition from charging us with Precipitation."

But despite the large Clintonian majority, Yates had misgivings: "We yielded to a Proposal made by our Opponents to discuss the Constitution in a Committee of the whole, without putting a Question on any Part, provided that in the Course of Discussion, we should suggest the Amendments . . . which we deemed necessary. . . ."

Hamilton's procedural motion carried. His exultance was quietly understated when he wrote to Madison that "Tomorrow we go into a committee of the whole . . . a full discussion will take place, which will keep us together at least a fortnight. So far the thing is not to be despaired of." Clinton later remarked bitterly of Melancton Smith and his overconfidence when he let Hamilton's procedural motion slide through without much resistance, "his vanity lost the state."

The procedural decision to discuss the Constitution clause by clause as a committee of the whole turned the convention into a debating society in which "Antis" and "Feds" rose in turn to deliver long orations to urge their points. Arguments from *The Federalist Papers* were endlessly rehashed.

Chancellor Livingston led off for the Federalists with a general discussion of the advantages of a well-ordered government. Hamilton, keeping notes of the various speeches, wrote of Livingston's effort: "Bravo! As far as it went one of the most excellent energetic speeches that ever heard." *Energy* was his favorite word and highest form of praise.

Melancton Smith rose for the opposition. Kent called him "the most prominent and . . . responsible speaker on the Anti-Federal side. . . . There was no person to be compared to him in his powers of acute and logical discussion. He was Mr. Hamilton's most persevering and formidable antagonist. . . . The style . . . of Smith's speaking was dry, plain and syllogistic, and it behooved his adversary to examine well the ground on which they started . . . or he would find it . . . embarrassing to extricate himself from a subtle web. . . ." Smith refuted the general reasoning of Chancellor Livingston, who, he thought, had overdrawn the perils of the Confederation: "If a war with our neighbors was to be the result of not acceding, there was no use in debating here; we had better receive their dictates, if we were unable to resist them. The defects of the old Confederation needed as little proof as the necessity of an Union: But there was no proof in all this that the proposed Constitution was a good one." With sarcasm, he was pleased to hear Livingston candidly admit that the Constitution was no confederacy, but a consolidated government.

Smith considered the rule of apportionment unjust because it embraced three-fifths of the slaves, who could have no part in government. Like Hamilton, he thought the number of representatives in the House ought to be still higher —say, one for every 20,000 inhabitants.

The next day, June 21, Hamilton rose to answer Smith, and the delegates and spectators settled back in their chairs to listen to Publius in person. As Hamilton spoke, Clinton's cold eye scanned the faces of his delegates intently for any signs that Hamilton's oratory might be softening up their opposition.

"Although I am persuaded this convention will be resolved to adopt nothing that is bad," Hamilton began smoothly, "yet I think every prudent man will consider the merits of the plan in connection with the circumstances of our country; and that a rejection of the Constitution may involve most fatal consequences." He proceeded to consider, point by point, the objections to particular provisions.

"I will not agree," he said, "with gentlemen, who trifle with the weaknesses of our country; and suppose, that they are enumerated to answer a party purpose, and to terrify with ideal dangers. No, I believe these weaknesses to be real, and pregnant with destruction." It was necessary "to dwell upon the imbecility of our Union; and to consider whether we, as a State, could stand alone."

He skillfully appealed to New Yorkers' memories of 1779 and 1780, when they had complied with requisitions of taxes and been "compelled by the delinquency of others, to bear most unusual burdens. . . . Sir, if we have national objects to pursue, we must have national revenues. . . . The national laws must operate on individuals, in the same manner as those of the states do."

He concluded: "The fundamental principle of the old Confederation is defective. We must totally eradicate and discard this principle before we can expect an efficient government." During the war, common danger had obscured the ruinous weakness, "But since the peace, . . . we have felt the poison of the system in its unmingled purity."

He explained that compromises at Philadelphia had been necessary to accommodate clashing interests and defended the apportionment of representatives as reasonable and sound. His treatment of the last question was a model of persuasion: New York had 65 members in the state assembly—the same number that would form the first national House of Representatives; so he challenged the opposition to give a better rule than that provided by the New York example.

Melancton Smith rose to rebut him. He wanted representation in Congress to be large enough to embrace principally "men in the middling class" rather than members of the "natural aristocracy" of "birth, education, talents and wealth." Otherwise, "This will be a government of oppression."

Not at all, Hamilton argued. "I rely more on the interests and opinions of men, than on any speculative parchment provisions whatever." Despotic governments, too, depend in a great degree on opinion, but "In free republics . . . the will of the people makes the essential principle of the government; and the laws which control the community receive their tone and spirit from the public wishes. It is the fortunate situation of our country, that the minds of the people are exceedingly enlightened and refined." In the ancient pure democracies, where the people assembled, "the field of debate presented an ungovernable mob, not only incapable of deliberation, but prepared for every enormity." There, "the enemies of the people brought forward their plans of ambition systematically."

Furthermore, Hamilton went on, it was not true that popular assemblies demanded a numerous representation: "The confidence of the people will easily be obtained by a good administration. This is the true touchstone." The kind of knowledge required for regulation of commerce and taxation in the general government did not hang upon specialized knowledge, but "is that which is open to every intelligent inquirer; and of which, five men may be as perfectly possessed as fifty. . . ." Hamilton denied favoring an aristocracy. "Why . . . are we told so often of an aristocracy?" he asked. "For my part, I hardly know the meaning of this word as it is applied. . . . The image is a phantom. Does the new government render a rich man more eligible than a poor one? No. . . . It is bottomed on the broad and equal principle of your state constitution." He demanded to know whether "if the people have it in their option, to elect their most meritorious men; is this to be considered as an objection? . . . It is a harsh doctrine that men grow wicked in proportion as they . . . enlighten their minds. . . . The difference . . . consists, not in the quantity but kind of vices, which are incident to the various classes." He candidly acknowledged the probability that "here the advantage of character belongs to the wealthy. Their vices are probably more favorable to the prosperity of the state, than those of the indigent; and partake less of moral depravity. . . . the true principle of a republic is, that the people should choose whom they please to govern them. Representation is imperfect, in proportion as the current of popular favour is checked. This great source of free government, popular election, should be perfectly pure, and the most unbounded liberty allowed."

He spoke with earnestness and energy and much gesture day after day, repeating arguments straight from *The Federalist* or employing classical and historical examples to prove the necessity of strong government. "Men will pursue their interests," he remarked. "It is as easy to change human nature as to oppose the strong current of selfish passions. A wise legislator will gently divert the channel and direct it, if possible, to the public good."

His long-windedness and his repetitions and recitations from *The Federalist* were an early filibuster, marking time, preventing the convention from voting until hoped-for news arrived from New Hampshire or Virginia. There was not much thought that all the oratory by itself would change many votes. He shaped his tactics to counter Governor Clinton's strategy and Melancton Smith's "vanity." Kent wrote that Hamilton "spoke with . . . energy and considerable gestures. His language was clear, nervous. . . . He . . . brought to the debate a mind filled with all the learning and precedents applicable to the subject . . . His candor was magnanimous. . . . His temper was spirited but courteous . . . and he frequently made pathetic and powerful appeals to the moral sense and patriotism, the fears and hopes of the assembly."

Gilbert Livingston, a Clintonian, introduced an amendment that would prevent any senator from serving more than six years in twelve and subjecting senators to recall by their legislatures. His flowery speech in support provided some welcome comic relief; he ranted in mixed metaphors that provided sharp contrast to the careful, logical styles of both Hamilton and Melancton Smith. "What," he cried, "what will be their situation in a Federal town? Hallowed ground! Nothing so unclean as State laws to enter there, surrounded as they will be by an impenetrable wall of adamant and gold, the wealth of the whole country flowing into it!"

"*What?* What WALL?" cried a Federalist.

"A wall of gold, of adamant, which will flow in from all parts of the continent." The reporter noted that here arose "a great laugh in the house."

Hamilton leaped back to his feet, urging that the senate should have dignity and independence: "There should be in every republic some permanent body" like the senate "to correct the prejudices . . . check the passions, and regulate the fluctuation of a popular assembly."

The mails from Virginia and New Hampshire to New York had been full of daily accounts of progress in the conventions there. Now, at last through the open windows were heard the sounds of an express rider galloping into town, lashing the last weary horse of the relay of horses he had worn out on the long journey to Poughkeepsie from New Hampshire. The tired messenger thrust an envelope from John Sullivan, president of the New Hampshire convention, into Hamilton's hands. He ripped it open and read the enclosures with joy. On June 21, New Hampshire had ratified the Constitution! That made nine. The United States of America as a nation and not a mere aggregation of states had just been born.

Hamilton surely smiled broadly as he announced the news to the convention, and Clinton surely scowled. The Federalists in New York City set church bells happily ringing. But remote New Hampshire was not enough. Without mighty Virginia there could only be a paper union, and Madison's expresses to Hamilton from there were increasingly gloomy. His opponents were demanding amendments in the form of a Bill of Rights as a condition precedent to ratification. There was talk of adjournment or even secession without it. Madison was fighting for ratification first and a "recommendation" of amendments to be submitted afterward.

Hamilton sent an express to Madison, passing on the good news from New Hampshire and adding, "There are some slight symptoms of relaxation in some of the leaders, which authorizes a gleam of hope, if you do well, but certainly I think not otherwise." Clinton asserted in a private letter that "the News from New Hampshire has not had the least Effect on our Friends at this Place."

Smith insisted, like Clinton, that he was not influenced by the fact that union was now officially in effect. Lansing remarked acidly, "Since nine states have acceded to it, let them make the experiment." Hamilton, nevertheless, had a powerful new argument to press on them.

"The local interests of a state ought, in every case, to give way to the interests of the Union," he cried. The Constitution made the states "essential, component parts of the union; and therefore the idea of sacrificing the former to the latter is totally inadmissible."

Debate took a crucial turn when John Williams, of remote Washington and Clinton counties, objected that the authority of Congress "to provide for the common defence, and general welfare" gave it too great power in the laying of taxes. He proposed a crippling amendment, a variant of Mason's in the Virginia convention, that would forbid an excise on any article of growth or manufacture of the United States, except when proceeds of the impost and excise on foreign goods were insufficient.

Melancton Smith followed up, insisting that the national government ought to rest on the state governments; otherwise, "The individual states in time will be allowed to raise no money at all. . . ."

Hamilton's authorship is evident in Chancellor Livingston's reply, followed by Hamilton's own impatient remonstrance. It is easier for the human mind, he swore, "to calculate the evils, than the advantages of a measure . . . to apprehend the danger, than to see the necessity of giving powers to our rulers." The

Constitution was skillfully designed to ensure free representation and mutual checks: "Now what do gentlemen mean by . . . declaiming against this government? Why do they say we ought to limit its powers, to disable it, and to destroy its capacity of blessing the people? . . . Sir, when you have divided and nicely balanced the departments of government; when you have strongly connected the virtue of your rulers with their interest; when, in short, you have rendered your system as perfect as human forms can be;—you must place confidence; you must give power."

Hamilton reassured his hearers that he was the friend of scope and permanence for the state governments. It could never be the desire of the national legislature to cut off the states: "The blow aimed at the members, must give a fatal wound to the head; and the destruction of the states must be at once a political suicide. Can the national government be guilty of this madness?" There must be "mutual dependence between state and central authorities, which forms the essence of union."

Tempers grew short. John Lansing recalled that Hamilton, now saying that the states must be preserved as repositories of the people's liberties, had said the opposite at Philadelphia; Lansing had kept notes on Hamilton's argument there "with much decision and . . . plausibility, that the state governments ought to be subverted. . . ." Hamilton jumped to his feet to deny such duplicity. "A warm personal altercation" between the two occupied the remainder of that day and much of the next, the reporter notes. In the uproar, Smith threatened to call for a vote on the crippling tax amendment, still confident of his overwhelming majority.

Hamilton and his friends remembered and shrewdly called upon the secretary to read from an old speech of Governor Clinton's to the legislature of 1780–1782, lamenting the feebleness of Congress and the burdens this threw on a state that voluntarily met its revenue obligations. Clinton and Smith were furious. Clinton was forced to declare himself "a friend to a strong and efficient government." Hamilton waded in. No, Clinton was an obstructionist; else why did he say he approved a strong federal government, but opposed the Constitution, insisting on substitute provisions? Why did he say he had favored granting Congress power during the war to lay an import duty, when he had in fact disapproved the only practicable mode of collection? Clinton's system was "rotten, and ought forever to be banished from our government." Now the more moderate Clintonians were shocked and repelled by Hamilton's rough tactics and the violence of his language.

Passions rose high between the two parties. There was a riot and bloodshed in Albany, of which Hamilton with grim satisfaction wrote Madison "the Anti-Federalists were the aggressors, the Federalists the victors."

Clinton saw an opening, changed his tactics, and moved to take command of the moderates' middle ground.

He would be willing to accept the Constitution, he declared, provided it was revised. To that end he offered a series of no fewer than 55 amendments, arranged under three categories: explanatory, recommendatory, and conditional.

He had hit upon a formula on which he could reasonably go to the people of the state; reserved rights, he insisted, were vital. He was willing to enter the union, but he wished to reserve the right to withdraw if the amendments failed of later passage. Hamilton and Jay would soon exploit this reasonable sounding "compromise" to unravel the Clintonians' whole logical position, but first Hamilton had to make a tactical retreat and an ostentatious personal admission of error. He apologized if he had hurt the feelings of any opponent. He confessed that he had a vehement nature, which condemned "those indifferent mortals, who either never form opinions, or never make them known."

"If such has been my language," he went on, "it was from the habit of using strong language to express my ideas . . . and on no subject has my breast been filled with stronger emotion, or more anxious concern." He would never aid the rich by grinding down the poor. "I declare I know not any set of men who are to derive peculiar advantages from this constitution," he said, adding, "If today I am among the favored few, my children tomorrow may be among the oppressed."

Just after noon on July 2, as Clinton was launching into a speech on the power of Congress to contract loans, the silent respect accorded the governor and president suddenly erupted into "such a bug through the House, that little of His Excellency's speech was heard." Through the open windows delegates could hear and see the uproar down below. From a horse, whose muzzle was flecked with foam, a rider had dismounted. He delivered his dispatch to Barclay, the courthouse doorkeeper, for Hamilton's eyes only. It was a letter from Madison, with an official certification by Edmund Pendleton, announcing that on June 25 Virginia had ratified the Constitution. Outside, jubilant Federalists crowded around and then, as a fife and drum struck up, marched in a happy throng around the convention house.[1]

The good news of Madison's letter contained some cautionary words to the effect that Virginia's ratification carried some "highly objectionable" recommendations for amendments.[2] Patrick Henry had announced "he should wait with impatience for the favorable moment of regaining in a constitutional way, the lost liberties of his country."

As Hamilton spread word of Madison's letter to the delegates, and Clinton stood speechless, James Kent noted that "a visible change took place in the disposition of the House." The problem of how to keep out of the union and still keep their power, prosperity, and New York City now had to be faced by all Clintonians.

On July 8 Hamilton wrote Madison to ask how the crippling amendments had been dealt with in Virginia, saying that at Poughkeepsie he would yield to "constructive declarations" as far as possible, without invalidating the act, and would "concur in rational recommendations." He was regaining the middle ground he had almost lost, while leaving all "the rest for our opponents." But he was standing firm on the point that a "conditional" ratification would have no effect.

Clinton was now pressing for an immediate vote, fearing a further swing of moderate opinion against him. Hamilton pleaded with him not to call the question, "but retire and consider." Hamilton was ready, he said, to go as far as he thought safe in "recommendatory and explanatory Amendments." He pledged his party "to endeavor for their adoption," but he begged the Clintonians not to listen to "Jealousy" or put "Liberty to the hazard" by insisting that ratification be "upon conditions." The story went round that Hamilton had sent a message to the city, "Tell them that the convention shall never rise until the Constitution is adopted!"

During the following days, word poured in to Poughkeepsie from New York City of the ringing of church bells and of rallies favoring the Constitution, lending credibility to threats like Jay's that the city intended to secede and join the Union however the convention might vote. Then there came word of a huge parade of all the tradesmen, merchants, and businessmen of the city, with a float honoring Hamilton as the centerpiece. It was planned for Wednesday, July 23.

The Federalist parade planned for the twenty-third was to be the greatest anyone could recall since Evacuation Day. Carpenters would build a replica of a 32-gun frigate, 27 feet long, with a ten-foot beam. She would be full rigged as if for sea and drawn by ten white horses; she would fire her cannons as she rolled along. There would be 30 seamen arrayed on her deck under the authentic command of Commodore James Nicholson. Her figurehead would be a carved statue of Hamilton, and *Hamilton* was her name.

Not to be outdone, the sailmakers were building a four-horse stage on which another ship, the *New Constitution*, would sail along proudly bearing the figure of Hamilton holding the "Constitution" in his right hand and the "Confederation" in his left. Fame with a trumpet would hold a crown of laurel to press upon his amiable brow.

After weeks of noisy preparation and mounting excitement, reports of all of which were duly relayed to the tense delegates at Poughkeepsie, the ten sections of the parade, each honoring one of ten ratifying states, began forming in The Fields early on the morning of the twenty-third, where only a dozen years before Hamilton had made his first public speech. At ten o'clock, a thirteen-gun salute was fired from the cannons of the good ship *Hamilton*, and the grand march began to roll down the wide Broad Way.

The coopers' float was led by thirteen apprentice boys, each thirteen years old. On the rear of their float was a barrel whose ill-joined staves stood for the old Confederation. Turning their backs on the wreckage, diligent workmen on the float fashioned a snug new constitutional cask as the procession got under way.

The float of the "artificial florists" featured a gorgeous garland from which disconsolately drooped three broken blossoms, representing the states that had not ratified the Constitution. The block and pump makers finished a pump and made thirteen blocks, sheaved and pruned complete, on their stage during the march. Then came the crash and blare of a marching band.

As the good ship *Hamilton* rode the artificial waves toward Wall Street, she made "a fine appearance, sailing with flowing sheets and full sails, the canvas waves dashing against her sides." Glum Anti-Federalists in the throng looked "as sour as the devil." Naturally, Betsy and von Steuben and Philip and Angelica and little Alexander and the Antil orphan cheered wildly as the *Hamilton* sailed past.

A slight accident, it is true, probably caused by some disgruntled Anti, marred the sailmakers' float: the right arm of the figure "Hamilton" had been broken off—it was the arm that had held the symbolic "Constitution." Few noticed because next came the tailors, holding aloft an oversized banner on which Adam and Eve sat naked except for figleaf aprons, illustrating the motto "And they sew'd fig leaves together." The furriers displayed an Indian delivering pelts. The draymen dragged a 300-gallon cask of ale with a living Bacchus on top—a handsome boy sewn from chin to toe into flesh-colored silk, wearing a cap adorned with hop vines and barley and drinking daintily from a silver goblet in his hand. His attendant Silenus sat beside him on a hogshead of porter soberly labeled, "Ale, proper drink for Americans." On other floats, printers at their presses were actually striking off and then distributing copies of an ode. Blacksmiths hammered out a symbolic constitutional anchor. Marching along behind came hatters, peruke makers, and shipwrights, nailers, paper stainers, and upholsterers, as well as representatives of all the other urban crafts of the great city. Nicholas Cruger, Esq., guided a plow drawn by six oxen. As he looked up ahead at the *Hamilton*'s rigging riffling in the breeze, Cruger probably thought back in some wonder to the morning 16 years before when he had seen his former clerk sail off from St. Croix to the continent. A quick, diligent boy, yes, with good training in the counting house. He was far along now on his way to transmuting New York City into the national as well as the commercial capital of a new empire. Yes, young Alexander had well repaid Cruger's contribution to the expense of an ocean passage to the mainland.

The parade moved amid cheering and surging throngs down the Broad Way, through Great Dock Street, into Hanover Square, and up Queen Street, where its members halted and disbanded until the evening.

Brissot de Warville, the urbane French traveler, after standing beside the line of march, described that night's huge outdoor feast in The Fields, where at ten long tables members of Congress were served bullock and mutton roasted whole. "Magnificent," or possibly "Magnifique," was what he said. Five or six thousand lesser citizens joined the celebration and watched the fireworks. That night a popular toast was to "The whole gradation of Heroes and Benefactors of mankind, from the first of the human race to the immortal Washington, and all the sons of wisdom, from Solon to the invincible Hamilton."

Some of the cartmen and sailors who had served as the *Hamilton*'s ship's crew still proudly carried the standards bearing the legend "The Federal Ship *Hamilton*." When they turned the standards around, in the glare of the blazing torches and occasional rocket bursts, on the reverse side could be read:

Behold the federal ship of fame;
The *Hamilton* we call her name;

> To every craft she gives employ;
> Sure cartmen have their share of joy.

The great parade and celebration could not have been better timed for psychological impact on Clinton's delegates upriver at Poughkeepsie. On the same Wednesday, July 23, Melancton Smith wavered and switched. Instead of continuing to insist on ratification "upon conditions," Smith moved for ratification "in confidence" that the recital of the bill of rights and other amendments "will receive an early consideration." The moderates in Clinton's forces swung with Smith. His motion carried, 40 to 19. Among the "antis" voting with Smith and all the jubilant Federalists were Clinton, Lansing, and Yates.

To explain his new position, Melancton Smith declared that until Virginia came in, he had hoped amendments could be made previous to the operation of the government, but now "he was satisfied they could not, and it was equally the dictate of reason and duty to quit his first ground, and advance so far as that they might be received into the Union." Now he argued that the best way to serve "the great end of the opposition" that he had led was to vote against any proposition that would not be received as a ratification of the Constitution. Otherwise, his own party, too weak to amend the Constitution, would "be dispersed like sheep on a mountain."

Next day, Thursday, July 24, Lansing, still groping toward the way to contingent ratification, moved to add that the state reserved the right to withdraw from the Union if after a fixed number of years the amendments had not "been submitted to a convention in the mode prescribed in the fifth article of the Constitution."

Hamilton and Jay, rebutting Lansing, argued that adoption, subject to the right to withdraw, implied a distrust of the other states. Hamilton read from Madison's reply of July 20 that "a conditioned ratification does not make New York a member of the new Union." Conditional ratification was voted down, 31–28. An overwhelming majority of two to one against ratification had been transformed in six strenuous weeks into a majority of three in favor of unconditional ratification. A thankful Federalist wrote, "The Constitution has . . . undergone an ordeal torture, and been preserved, as by fire."

The rest was formal. The body resolved itself from a Committee of the Whole back into convention, and on Saturday, July 26, the engrossed ratification, with a proposed Bill of Rights and added amendments only recommended, was approved, 30–27, and signed by the president and two secretaries. Jay's circular letter pressing for conventions for changes was given unanimous approval, and the convention adjourned *sine die.*

When all was done, Clinton, from the chair, offered a qualified benediction. Until a convention should be called to consider amendments, "The probability was, that the body of the people who are opposed to the constitution, would not be satisfied"; he would however "endeavour to keep up peace and good order among them. . . ." After this generous statement of Clinton, it was reported that upon the countenances of delegates and spectators alike "more than a common pleasantness appeared."

In Boston, Federalist merchant Andrew Craigie received the news of New York's ratification, which should have brightened his countenance with political joy, with deep economic gloom. Outstanding certificates of Continental public indebtedness shot up in value on the news of New York's ratification.

Craigie dispatched a letter full of self-reproach to a business partner. "Had it been certain that the Constitution would be adopted by New York," he wrote, "or even probable, I should have been more anxious to secure the Certificates at the going price, but knowing that they would not probably rise higher than 5/. should all the States come in, & would fall in consequence of its rejection by that State I thought it best to take the chance [of not purchasing]." Craigie had missed the boat on a good thing. Holders already in on the ground floor would not sell out now. He added ruefully, "The greater part of the public Debt is held by rich people who can afford to keep their Interest."

The union was an accomplished fact. Though North Carolina and Rhode Island still refused to ratify, they could not remain out indefinitely. North Carolina ratified on November 21, 1789, and pugnacious perverse Rhode Island finally came in on May 29, 1790.

It was common talk that Hamilton, more than anyone else, had been the man who somehow reversed what had seemed to be insurmountable odds. "Col. H——," said the *New York Journal* in a story July 4, 1788, "stands the political porcupine, armed at all points and brandishes a shaft to every opposer: a shaft powerful to repel and keen to wound." It was said that his arguments had brought about Melancton Smith's eleventh-hour conversion.

What actually caused the sudden break in the ranks of the Clintonians has never been fully explained. Several factors weighed heavily. Once Virginia ratified, New York had lost a powerful state to stand with it outside the union. The threat—and it was, in fact, no idle one—that lower New York would break away and leave the upper state without the city that made the state rich and powerful worried the moderates. The parade featuring the good ship *Hamilton* made visible the threat. Clinton's offer to ratify with reservations exposed a weakness in his earlier all-or-nothing position. Once he admitted that the document might be ratified, Madison's letter, which Hamilton read to the delegates, cut what remained of that position from under him. With that lost, he had nothing to do but surrender. It is worth noting that even with all these points in his favor, Hamilton's great victory was not exactly a landslide—just three votes.

The New York City convention delegates reached home the following Monday, two days after adjournment. Hamilton brought with him New York's signed and engrossed ratification of the Constitution, which he forthwith proudly presented to the expiring Continental Congress. While resting at home at No. 57 Wall Street for a few hours after the rough ride down from Poughkeepsie, before bathing and dressing to walk up Wall Street to City Hall to make the official presentation, Hamilton with elaborate offhandedness would let Betsy and von Steuben and young Phil and wide-eyed Angelica and little Alexander and the Antil orphan crowd around and examine the impressive document. In the excitement of their often absent father's homecoming, some of them may have even been allowed to touch it. Perhaps Betsy held up four-month-old James Alexander so he could say someday that he had seen it too. Hamilton's offhand manner could not hide from his children the glint of proprietary pride that flickered in their father's eyes.

They would vie to regale him with stories of the great parade of the Wednesday just past and the banqueting and fireworks the same night and allow no detail of it all to be dimmed in the retelling. No words were left to convey the magnificence of the good ship *Hamilton* as she rolled by the crowds to the blare of the bands or the excitement of their cries of applause. When they quieted down a little, one of them, Angelica perhaps, would recite for her doting father the verses she had memorized from the waving standards held aloft by the *Hamilton*'s crew!

Behold the Federal ship of fame,
The *Hamilton* we call her name!

The greatest parade New York had ever seen since Evacuation Day, as everyone said, was in her sweet father's honor. It made her a little sad that he had been so busy he had missed it except in the presence of his name. It would be almost sixteen years before New York City saw another parade that was as great again. It would also be in Hamilton's honor, with him also absent in all but name inside the flag-draped coffin in the train of his funeral cortege.

24

THE SECRETARY
OF THE TREASURY WEPT

THE VIGOUR OF HIS GENIUS CORRESPONDING WITH THE IMPOR-
TANCE OF THE PRIZE . . . OVERCAME THE NATURAL MODERATION
OF HIS TEMPER . . . ANIMATED BY AN ENLIGHTENED SENSE OF THE
VALUE OF FREE GOVERNMENT, HE CHEERFULLY RESOLVED TO
STAKE HIS FORTUNE HIS HOPES HIS LIFE AND HIS HONOR UPON AN
ENTERPRISE OF THE DANGER OF WHICH HE KNEW THE WHOLE
MAGNITUDE IN A CAUSE WHICH WAS WORTHY OF THE TOILS AND
THE BLOOD OF HEROES.
 —*Eulogium on General Nathanael Greene*, July 4,
  1789

Going into the Poughkeepsie convention underdogs by a head count of 19
to 46, Hamilton's dedicated minority had by hook or by crook come out winners
by a margin of three. No one claimed that tactics like the threat of New York
City's secession were not rough. Such a stunning political reversal leaves losers
ordinarily used to winning nursing wounds that bleed for a long time before
scarring over and never fade away. The historian H. S. Randall once noted that
Aaron Burr "had in his interest a motley band of scouts and spies, male and
female, who helped him succeed in some surprising intrigues". In imaginative

literary efforts and much historical speculation, Hamilton, too, has been charged with using all manner of illicit female assistance to woo Clinton's moderate delegates to the Federalist cause. None of such plausible surmises withstands a historian's demand for documentary proof, but that is not to say such wooing did not occur. In political struggles of the magnitude of the struggle for ratification, history and experience tell us again and again that no holds are barred, including embraces of deplorable lubricity. Wounds of some Clintonians were still suppurating the spring of 1789, when Clinton, or one of his supporters, purporting to tell all under the name of *William Tell*, replied to a series of anti-Clinton broadsides—probably written by Hamilton over the initials H. G. (perhaps meaning "Hamilton of Grange"). Of Hamilton, *William Tell* said threateningly, "Your private character is still worse than your public one, and it will yet be exposed by your own works, for [you] will not be bound by the *most solemn* of all obligations! *******" In the tone and context of *William Tell*'s abuse, few alert readers would have much difficulty understanding that each of the seven asterisks that completed his indictment of Hamilton stood for one letter of the then more or less sacred word *wedlock*.

Over and above all of the demands of the busy Wall Street law practice that generated the fees to support his growing family, all during the years 1786, 1787, and 1788, Hamilton had been superimposing a seemingly monomanic frenzy of payless *pro bono* activity in the cause of union of the states. The Annapolis Convention; the Constitutional Convention; *The Federalist Papers;* Federalist party leadership in the battle for ratification at Poughkeepsie and throughout the thirteen states; authorship of uncounted broadsides, bills, petitions, and polemics; reelection as a delegate to the Continental Congress on January 22, 1788, where he would be able to shepherd in the new government, consumed his days and nights. The inference is irresistible that a secret loneliness, somewhere near the center of his soul, an unrequited passion that even his own acierating realism would not acknowledge, drove him on and onward.

"I seldom write to a lady without fancying the relation of lover and mistress," he wrote to his sister-in-law, Angelica Church, the wife of his most important client, on December 6, 1787. "It has a very inspiring effect." He added, "In your case the dullest materials could not help feeding that propensity." He asks her to "Imagine, *if you are able* the pleasure" she gives him, and underscores the question. He is thanking her for her "invaluable letter by the last packet" of October 2, in which she had written him, "Indeed my dear, Sir if my path was strewed with as many roses as you have filled your letter with compliments, I should not now lament my absence from America."

Instead of addressing him conventionally—"Indeed, my dear sir"—her delicate hand rewarded his roses by omitting from the phrase the commas that would ordinarily follow the words *indeed* and *sir*, and by inserting a special, secret, improper comma for him after the word *dear*. She thus magically transformed a conventional salutation into an endearment of unguessable depths. At least, in the ache of his loneliness, he read it that way.

Angelica's tiny, misplaced pen prick pierced his heart. With a characteristic mixture of scoffing and emotional outpouring (before resuming the magisterial tone of *Federalist Paper* No. 18, on which he and Madison were putting the finishing touches that day) he assured her that she had not failed to cause his heart an exquisite pang.

"You ladies despise the pedantry of punctuation," he wrote her. "There was a most critical *comma* in your last letter. It is my interest that it should have been designed; but I presume it was accidental." If her "most critical comma" had really been accidental and she had not kept an exact copy of her letter, she would, of course, have had no idea what he was raving about. Despite his "presuming" that her comma was accidental, he really was certain that it had not been and that her lonely passion for him matched his for her. "I have a great opinion of your *discernment* and, therefore, I venture to rant," he confided, but "If you read this letter in a certain mood you will easily divine that in which I write it." All the roses he has strewn in her path "could give you but a feeble image of what I should wish to convey." At the end, he adds, "Betsy sends her love. I do not choose to say *joins in mine*. Tis old fashioned."

Hamilton closes to Angelica by matching her endearing and pointed error of punctuation with one of his own: "Adieu ma chere, Soeur. A. Hamilton."

Though this preoccupation with commas has comical overtones, it serves to draw into the tiny focus of two discreet scratches of their quills the whole range of frustrated, sublimated passion that seemed to consume this handsome, intense gentleman and his beautiful, brilliant, witty, sister-in-law separated from each other by an Atlantic. It had smoldered for years. When he was on her mind, her intensity of focus on him easily matched his on her, even when she was writing to his wife, her sister Betsy.

Taking time away from a brilliant swirl of parties and balls in Paris, she complained to Betsy on January 27, 1784, of not having had a separate letter from Hamilton. She resolutely gives news of others, but her thoughts keep turning back to Betsy's "lord":

> I should like Paris if it was nearer to America, for I have a very agreeable set of acquaintances. Mrs. Jay lives in a small house, about half a mile from Paris. The Americans have the pleasure to drink tea with her once a week. Mr. [Benjamin] Franklin has the gravel and desires to return to America. They talk of Papa or Col. Hamilton as his successor. How would you like to cross the Atlantic? Is your lord a Knight of the Cincinnati? It has made a wonderful noise here, but the order will probably exist in France when it will be neglected in America.

There are other things she wants from America, but most on her mind is the embrace of Betsy's lord. She says his name or a pronoun or other word that stands for his name over and over again, no fewer than 14 times in three short sentences. In the sentence before her close, he crops up no less than nine times:

> Will you send me the newspapers regularly instead of sending me fruit, for it is generally spoiled, and the trouble getting it thro. the custom house is immense. But the papers must be those that contain

your husband's writings. Adieu, my dear embrace your *master* for me, and tell him that I envy you the fame of so clever a husband, one who writes so well: God bless him, and may he long continue to be the friend and brother of your affectionate

Angelica

Her postscript reverts to her obsession:

P.S. Tell Colonel Hamilton, if he does not write to me, I shall be very angry. A.C.

In the many letters that passed between Alexander and Angelica over the years that have never been found, many other secret intimacies are lost. Her spell hovers over the few that are extant like a rare perfume.

"All the graces you have been pleased to adorn me with," she writes Hamilton in October 1787, would fade before the good works of her sister. But Betsy was no rival to her in their kind of passion, any more than her husband, Church, was to Hamilton. She jeered to Hamilton that Church's "head is full politics," as if her love were blind to Hamilton's other obsession.

Church was "desirous of making [it] once in the British House of Commons where I should be happy to see him if he possessed your eloquence." But by Church, "I am now no longer heard."

Now she was confident that she had no rival for the kind of passion her sister's husband had for her. But that did not keep her from being suspicious that once there had been one. Angelica, from strength, added a nervous postscript: "Is Kitty Livingston married?"

Amid the jumble of events of December 1787, with new numbers of *The Federalist* due at the printer's two or three or four times a week, Kitty's name in Angelica's hand must have released a flood of memories in Hamilton's mind.

They carried him all the way back to his first winter in America 15 years before, to Elizabethtown, where the 17-year-old guest of the William Livingstons had at first worshiped their 23-year-old daughter Catharine, their Lady Kitty, as a votary might worship a chaste Diana on her pedestal. At 20, as he whirled with her through the rigadoons and reels and sleigh rides of the winter quarters at Morristown or sauntered beside her on summer picnics at The Pastures, keeping only a step or two ahead of the packs of other swains who ardently pursued her, year after year, Kitty had been the darling of them all, Hamilton, Tilghman, Troup, Meade, Humphreys, Laurens—poor Laurens—and all the rest.

At 20, a still adoring Hamilton had written her from Morristown in 1777 that "woman is not a *simple*, but a most complex, intricate and enigmatical being." He chided her that "if you would choose to be a goddess, and to be worshiped as such," he would offer poems "at your goddesship's shrine."

He had shown one of the letters she had written him to Laurens and reported to her how his dearest friend had been smitten with her too: "The liveliest emotions of approbation were pictured in his face, 'Hamilton,' cries he, 'when you write to this divine girl again, it must be in the style of adoration: none but a goddess, I am sure, could have penned so fine a letter.' " He could hear again gallant Laurens's Carolina drawl as he set down his words.

He told Kitty he had risked Washington's wrath—"being anathematized by grave censors"—for "dedicating" as much precious time to Kitty then as he was now spending dawdling dreamily over memories to answer Angelica's post-script, "Is Kitty Livingston married?" He ought not to be wasting so much precious time over "so trifling and insignificant a toy as—woman." Besides, as he had told Kitty long ago, danger from the jealousy of a dear friend gave their own romance a special savor.

There was the risk "of being run through the body by saucy inamorato's who will envy me the prodigious favor, forsooth, of your correspondence." But "between the morose apathy of some and the envious sensibility of others," Kitty's love-struck young correspondent had remained unworried about being run through by any lances but Cupid's or pricks of her pen. He had proclaimed to Kitty, in capital letters, "ALL FOR LOVE is my motto."

Angelica would remember that even Gouverneur Morris's most eloquent sallies had failed to sweep Kitty off her chaste pedestal.

Courting her one bright May morning when both were 18, Morris had written her,

> Know then, dearest Kitty, thy note I received
>
> . . . .
> For thee every Beauty more fair shall be seen
> more blooming the blossoms, more verdant the green.

Morris had even gone so far as to offer her "any part of me which you think proper."

Six years later, Hamilton had tried another tack, writing Kitty owlishly that "I know you have an invincible aversion to all flattery and extravagance" like Morris's. Hamilton was not "afraid that a Quixote, capable of uttering himself perfectly in the language of Knight-errantry, will ever be able to supplant me in the good graces of a lady of your sober understanding."

Ten years later, Kitty's father, William Livingston, still governor of New Jersey, had written in March 1787 that "my daughter, Kitty," now serving as his "principal Secretary of State," was off to New York "to kick up her heels at the balls and assemblies of a metropolis." It was hard to realize that La Kitty, the onetime darling of them all, had ripened or withered, into a spinster of 36, with nothing better to do.

On December 6, 1787, Hamilton finally got around to answering Angelica's question: "You ask if your friend Kitty Livingston is married? You recollect the proverb. She was ready, with as much eagerness as can be ascribed to the chaste wishes of a virgin heart, to sip the blissful cup, when alas! it slipped through her fingers—at least for a time, if not for ever."

Now, ten years after Hamilton had projected onto Gouverneur Morris or others of Kitty's swains his image of himself as a sort of Quixote, the well-ordered circuitry of Hamilton's mind completed for Angelica the quixotic metaphor it had begun then. He fills Angelica in on the sad fate of Quixote's mistress: "Her lover a buxom widower of five and forty braving summer heats and wintry [blasts] exerted himself with so much zeal in the service of his Dulcinea that there is every appearance it will cost him his lungs. He is gone to the South of France, if possible, to preserve them," leaving Dulcinea waiting at the church.

Hamilton's own rueful reflections on Kitty's imperviousness to his finest knight-errantry allowed him to share with Angelica the faintly malicious pleasure he knew his report would give her. He lightheartedly pleaded his innocence of any such ungentlemanly pleasure: "This method of speaking of the *misfortune of your friend* proceeds from pure levity not a particle of malice. I beg your pardon for it; and I hope you will be able to tell me in your next that you have not by the least propensity to a smile verified the maxim of that scurvy defamer of human nature—. Rochefoucault."

"Not by the least propensity of her smile"—Hamilton mused as his own smile flickered briefly before a new onset of his loneliness: "Despairing of seeing you here my only hope is that the jumble of events will bring us together in Europe."

Nothing he would put in writing to his sister-in-law slipped over the edge of an impropriety to a client's wife except the private code of their eccentric punctuation. He closed: "Wherever I am believe always that there is no one can pay a more sincere or affectionate tribute to your deserts than I do—adieu ma chere, Soeur."

The "jumble of events" swirling around him in America now demanded of Hamilton his most ardent attention to drafting a new president to preside over the newly drafted and ratified Constitution. He was also kept from idle mischief by deep involvement in drawing or not drawing new lines on the map to carve new states out of old—Kentucky out of Virginia and Vermont out of New York—and in trying to prevent Congress from snatching the honor and importance of becoming the first capital of the nation away from New York City.

On March 4, 1788, the Continental Congress, sitting as a committee of the whole, took up the motion of Virginia delegates for the erection of the District of Kentucky into a separate state. Hamilton had opposed the measure as having a diversionary effect on the critical battle for ratification of the Constitution then pending. It would also add another vote to the Southern Anti-Federalist bloc.

Kentuckians and other Westerners feared that negotiations with Spain, then also pending, might result in closing the Mississippi to their trade and navigation. If Kentucky were not taken into the union, the rugged Kentuckians might declare themselves independent, try to force Spain to open up the river by fighting, and provoke an unwanted war on the western frontier. Part of Hamilton's parliamentary tactics was to set a backfire against the strong drive for Kentucky statehood by igniting a counterproposal against it. He proposed to create a new state out of the disputed territory of Vermont. If the tactic were successful, this would keep both states out while debate rumbled on and still keep the Kentuckians from coming to a rebellious boil until the battle for ratification of the Constitution was safely behind him.[1]

As a member of the New York Assembly the year before, Hamilton had done as much as any member to earn himself the title of Father of Vermont against the strong opposition of New Yorkers who owned property there. Richard Harison, an attorney friend of Hamilton who represented one group of New Yorkers with large Vermont real estate interests, allowed to speak in opposition to Hamilton's motion, argued that "The social compact, to which all the members of society are parties, and by which all of them are bound" was a "sacred compact" that would suffer "the grossest violation, whenever the rights and properties even of the meanest individual, are sacrificed without the most pressing and apparent necessity."

Hamilton's answer in the assembly in April 1787 had not denied the basic principle of the social compact to protect property. However, Hamilton pointed out, "It must be taken with this limitation: the united strength of the community ought to be exerted for the protection of individuals so far as there is a rational prospect of success; so far as is consistent with the safety and well being of the whole."

Ethan Allen's Green Mountain Boys, who had seized Fort Ticonderoga from the British, had proved that Vermonters were no less ruggedly individualistic than Kentuckians. Hamilton pointed out that Vermonters had enjoyed actual independence for several years under a regular form of government without taxes and also without the debts that burdened New York. From the floor of the assembly, Hamilton demanded to know "Where are our resources, where our public credit to enable us to carry on an offensive war against Vermont?" With its own finances in such poor shape, New York might not even be able to beat Vermont in a war: "We ought to recollect, that in war, to defend or attack, are very different things—to the first, the mountains, the wildernesses, the militia, sometimes even the poverty of a country will suffice; the latter requires an *army* and a *treasury.*" Such Hamiltonian common sense might have prevented rich twentieth-century nations from thrusting troops into poverty-stricken nations whose minds and hearts and once verdant mountains could not be won by any amount of deficit spending on offensives. Hamilton pointed out that it would be necessary to obtain the consent of the Vermonters to be governed and that "the scheme of coercion would ill suit even the disposition of our own citizens; the habits of thinking, to which the Revolution has given birth, are not adapted to the idea of a contest for dominion over a people disinclined to live under our government."

If Vermont were allowed to be free and then taken into the union, it would have to bear its own share of expenses as a state. It would also be detached from any possibility of making an alliance with the British in Canada. Hamilton sarcastically pointed out that such an alliance "may enter into the head of a British Minister" because, he noted, in "the government lately established in Canada—the splendid title of Viceroy—seems to look beyond the dreary regions of Canada and Nova Scotia." Hamilton's bill made it an express condition of Vermont's independence from New York that it be incorporated into the American union. This would keep its verdant regions out of the shade of any viceregal parasol.

Richard Harison scornfully asked what the Romans would have done if, like the Vermonters who belonged to the Empire State, "an inconsiderable part of their citizens had presumed to declare themselves a separate and independent state." Hamilton rejoined that "neither the manners nor the genius of Rome are suited to the republic or age we live in. All her maxims and habits were military, her government was constituted for war." Our peace-loving Republic "is unfit for it, and our situation, still less our Constitution, does not invite us to emulate the conduct of Rome" or to attempt "a display of unprofitable heroism." Hamilton would disapprove twentieth-century displays of American superpower, world police power as displays of "unprofitable heroism." Such hegemony should not extend beyond Vermont.

The congressional committee of which Hamilton was a member reported out in favor of making Kentucky a state on June 2, 1788, just as Hamilton was making preparations to go to Poughkeepsie for the ratifying convention. His spadework in the legislature the year before had brought Vermont far enough along the road to statehood to serve as a counterploy. John Brown, the Virginia delegate who was Kentucky's chief advocate, had said: "Colo. Hamilton heads the Opposition from an apprehension that a compliance might embarrass the new Constitution. He is supported by all the eastern States least it might add to the Southern Interest." Madison, too, had surmised that Hamilton had been willing to "throw obstacles in the way, till Vermont can be let in at the same time. . . ." Madison had been anxious to avoid angering Kentuckians because their opposition might tilt Virginia against ratifying the Constitution.

When New Hampshire finally became the required ninth state to ratify the Constitution, pressure abated, the grand committee was discharged, and Kentucky's application was bucked over to the incoming government with a favorable recommendation.

If Hamilton had lost any favor with expansive Westerners by delaying tactics against Kentucky statehood, he regained it many times over as chairman of the committee that reviewed John Jay's equivocal report on freedom of Mississippi River navigation. Hamilton reported out on September 15 a series of forthright resolves that upheld "the clear and essential right" of the United States to free navigation of the river.

Having taken a stand for popular self-determination for Vermont, Hamilton took a firm stand against the imperial hegemony of Spain. Congress backed him by affirming his free navigation resolutions.

Although sessions of the Continental Congress convened in City Hall, only a short block west on Wall Street from Hamilton's home and office, his attendance record was spotty after he returned to his seat on July 30, back from the Poughkeepsie convention.

Debate on the question of time and place for commencing the new government occupied the spacious floor of the chamber. The committee for putting the Constitution in operation had recommended that electors be chosen the first

Wednesday in January 1789 and that government under the Constitution begin the first Wednesday in February. To suit the convenience of Southern states, these dates had been moved to a month later. The city in which the government would begin remained undecided.

The question was, Where should the capital be put?

New York City was an unlikely choice for the permanent capital, for if it were, there would be only eight senators north, or "eastward," of it, as New Englanders said, and 16 to the southward; there would be only 17 members of the House east of it, and 42 south. The distance from New York to New Hampshire was hardly a third of the distance from New York to Georgia. Even as a temporary location, New York was objectionable to Madison, "for . . . it tends to stop the final . . . seat short of the Potomac . . . and probably in . . . N. Jersey." He sniffed suspiciously, "I *know* this to be one of the views of the advocates of N. York."

None of this, of course, kept Hamilton from playing his advocacy of New York City as a pawn on the great national chessboard for everything it might be worth and more. When he heard a report that New Jersey delegates would be instructed to favor Philadelphia, Hamilton remonstrated with his old friend Governor William Livingston. Admitting that the "exposed and eccentric position [of New York] will necessitate the early establishment of a permanent seat," he insisted that "The Northern States do not wish to increase Pennsylvania by an accession of all the wealth and population of the federal city. Pennsylvania herself, when not seduced by *immediate possession*, will . . . concur on the Jersey side of the Delaware." But, "place the government once down in Pennsylvania and that state and Delaware would hold fast." It was a "question of very great importance," Hamilton insisted, "not only to this state but to the northern states in general" to marshal all possible votes now in support of New York. He offered to pay out of his own pocket the traveling expenses of an absent Rhode Island delegate if he would come and vote in favor of New York.

With Hamilton's support, Jonathan Dayton of New Jersey and Huger of South Carolina moved in favor of New York. Henry Lee of Virginia and Clark of New Jersey moved to substitute in the resolution the words "at such place as shall hereafter be appointed by Congress." Both motions failed.

After further politicking, to general surprise, Baltimore was resolved as the new capital. Hamilton picked up more support for New York from Southern states that hoped to have the capital ultimately placed still farther south on the Potomac. They felt that "The only chance the Potomac has is . . . that the final seat may be undecided for two or three years, within which period the Western and S. Western population may enter more into the estimate."

Hamilton argued that choice of a second temporary location would entail two moves instead of one. That would be expensive and "indicative of instability in the national councils. . . ." With the support of South Carolina's Thomas Tucker and Virginia's Henry Lee, it was finally moved that the temporary seat remain in New York, leaving it up to the new Congress to determine the permanent capital.

Madison explained that this "was the result of the dilemma to which the opponents of N. York were reduced of yielding to its advocates or strangling the Government in its birth." He testily called the initial victory of New York "as at once a proof of the preponderancy of the Eastern strength, and of a disposition to make an unfair use of it."

Countermotions failed; Hamilton's prevailed. New York was to be the first capital. By his strenuous efforts to win what would at best be only a brief tenure for New York as the national capital, Hamilton had built up the importance of an apparently weak pawn in an exposed position. The value he brought it now made it much more valuable later when thrown in as a sacrifice to Thomas Jefferson's wishes as part of the famous bargain to gain Jefferson's support for Hamilton's program of assumption and funding. It helped to make possible Hamilton's entire economic program in the first national administration.

Although New York's eminence as the capital ended by the autumn of 1790, its beginnings as the capital helped make it the center of the nation's banking and securities business, as well as the chief market for investment capital and for trading and speculation. In August of 1788, the Common Council of the City voted to appropriate £35 to repair the leaky copper roof of City Hall; in September, the whole building was appropriated to the use of the federal government and Major Pierre L'Enfant was hired to remodel the structure to serve as the first capitol of America. If the first capital had been Philadelphia or Baltimore, instead of just a block down the street from Hamilton's home and office in New York, no young lawyer like him with a large family and without private means could have played the central part in forming and shaping the character of the first national administration that Hamilton did.

The Constitution adopted after so much labor was, like any plan or blueprint, in itself only a piece of paper. In private conversation, Hamilton sometimes facetiously commented that it was, as such, only "frail and worthless fabric" if not stiffened by solid and energetic administration. Gouverneur Morris would say later, rather misleadingly, that Hamilton considered "all republican government to be radically defective, because he confounded it with democratical government," which, he believed, "would end in despotism and be destructive to public Morality." Hamilton often cited the British government as a good example of the kind of stable government he sought to build. In it the monarch was balanced by a prime minister and parliament whose modern outlines were just beginning to emerge. According to Morris, Hamilton supported the Constitution, imperfect as it might be, because "he considered it as a band which might hold us together for some time, and he knew that national sentiment is the offspring of national existence." Laws, institutions, and a government had to be built; gaps between the words of the Constitution had to be filled in with practice and precedent. A national president, a senate, a house of representatives, a cabinet, courts, and a host of underofficers had to be chosen before the people and ratifying states would become parts of an organic union. As "national sentiment" took hold and Americans became used to the idea that they were part of one nation living under one Constitution and that they were Americans, as

Englishmen were Englishmen and Frenchmen were French, and not New Yorkers or Virginians or Pennsylvanians first, the blueprint would become the foundation of a true nation.

Only three weeks after New York had ratified the Constitution, on August 13, 1788, Hamilton returned to his familiar role of giving advice and counsel
to Washington. He was sending him, by Madison, "a set of papers under the
signature of Publius—I presume you have understood that the writers of these
papers are chiefly Mr. Madison and myself with some aid from Mr. Jay."

But the real burden of the letter was that Washington must agree to be the
first president:

> I take it for granted, sir, you have concluded to comply with what
> no doubt will be the general call of your country in relation to the new
> government. It is indispensable you should lend yourself to its first
> operations—It is to little purpose to have *introduced* a system, if the
> weightiest influence is not given to its firm *establishment* at the outset.

Washington replied that his election "may never happen," but that in any
event "It is my great and sole desire to live and die, in peace and retirement, on
my own farm."

Hamilton took an almost peremptory tone as he pressed Washington to
change his mind. "I should be deeply pained my dear sir," he replied in September, "if your scruples in regard to a certain station should be matured into a
resolution to decline it."

Hamilton's tone is that of a patient Dutch uncle. He sounds more like an
older man counseling a younger (Washington was 56 to his 31):

> The caution you observe in deferring an ultimate determination is
> prudent. I have however reflected maturely on the subject and have
> come to a conclusion that every public and personal consideration will
> demand from you an acquiescence in what will *certainly* be the unani-
> mous wish of your country. The absolute retreat which you meditated
> at the close of the late war was natural and proper. . . . but the crisis
> which brought you again into public view left you no alternative but to
> comply. . . . You are by that act *pledged* to take part in the execution
> of the government. . . . a regard to your own reputation as well as to
> the public good, calls upon you in the strongest manner to run that risk.

There were also "considerations that might have a more personal application," but Hamilton spared him those. He went on to insist that "A citizen of so
much consequence as yourself to its success has no option but to lend his services
if called for. . . . It would be inglorious in such a situation not to hazard the glory
however great, which he might have previously acquired."

If the new government miscarried, the Framers would suffer the disrepute
of having "pulled down one utopia without substituting anything that was

worthy of the effort." This would be a "greater hazard" to Washington's fame. Washington's aid was "indispensable."

Except for Washington's mother, no one but Hamilton ever dared to use such a tone with Washington; yet Hamilton used it often. When he did, the former commanding general usually obeyed his former aide. Hamilton assumed Washington's acquiesence without waiting for it and moved on to the question of who should be the vice-president. The Anti-Federalists were set on putting up Clinton of New York. In Massachusetts the Federalists had split on whether to choose presidential electors by the legislature, in which case John Adams would win, or by popular vote, which would see John Hancock the probable winner.

In reply to a question about John Adams, then representing the United States as minister to Britain, from Theodore Sedgwick, a Massachusetts leader, Hamilton replied on October 9, 1788; "I believe Mr. Adams will have the votes of this state." But, he added, "the only hesitation in my mind has arisen from a suggestion that he is unfriendly in his sentiments to General Washington."

Richard Henry Lee and the Lees of Virginia and the Adamses "have been in the habit of uniting; and hence may spring up a Cabal very embarrassing to the executive," Hamilton said. "Consider this, sound the reality of it and let me hear from you. What think you of [Benjamin] Lincoln or [Henry] Knox? This is a flying thought."

Sedgwick, though no particular friend of Adams, replied that Adams "formerly infinitely more democratical than at present," would be all right. He appeared to have "an ardent love for the public good" and "a knowledge of the world." He had "corrected those jealousies" that once had governed him.

Neither Hamilton nor George Washington would forget those "jealousies" of Adams during the Revolution; he had overestimated the army's strength and kept its organization temporary and weak, claiming to fear that a strong army would dominate the government or that Washington at its head would make himself a monarch. Madison, recalling Adams's "cabal during the war against General Washington" and considering his "extravagant self-importance," had confided to Jefferson that Washington's attitude toward having Adams as his "second" would hardly be "cordial."

Asked for his own opinion, Washington declared that he did not want to be accused of "electioneering." He assumed that the vice-president would come from Massachusetts, that the electors would choose "a true Federalist," and that anyone the states chose would not be disagreeable to him. He avoided mentioning Adams by name, saying only, "If I had any predilection, I flatter myself I possess patriotism enough to sacrifice it at the shrine of my country." Washington sacrificed his predilection. As Hamilton saw it, Washington agreed. Swallowing Adams was "the only certain way to prevent the election of an Anti-Federalist."

Despite Adams's petty vanity, Hamilton readily acknowledged his qualifications. "I see not," he concluded, after scanning all the possibilities in various states, "how any person can come near Mr. Adams."

On the other hand, if one considered the good of the nation as a whole, there would be no harm done if Adams did not gain the vice-presidency. Hamilton explained to Madison that political capital for the nation might be made from Clinton's candidacy and, indeed, his election. "I should imagine, if pains are taken, the dangers of an Anti-Federal Vice-President might itself be rendered the instrument of Union," he said. The Union was the point. Obviously, the presence of a leading representative of both Federalist and Anti-Federalist factions in the first national government would be the most powerful kind of cement the new union could have. If it fostered "national sentiment," Hamilton would view a setback to his own party, and incidentally Adams, with the same equanimity as Washington.

What worried him more was a defect of draftsmanship in the Constitution that was now exposed! The Framers had failed to make a distinction between ballots cast for president and vice-president. Because the voting was for two men, an obvious vice-presidential choice like a Clinton or an Adams might, through the action of one elector withholding his vote for president, defeat an obvious presidential choice like Washington. Then, too, there was always the possibility of a tie, which would throw the decision into the House of Representatives. If the worst can happen, it might happen. It did happen twelve years later in the election of 1800. A tie in electoral votes then confronted Hamilton with a choice between Jefferson and Burr. This gaping hole in the "worthless fabric" demonstrated that even "demigods," including Hamilton, could occasionally suffer lapses as legal draftsmen.

To avoid the possibility of a tie between Washington and Adams in the first election or even a sneak victory by Adams, Hamilton suggested that some of the Federalist electors withhold their votes from Adams. This would do Adams no harm unless he was indeed secretly hoping to snatch the first place away from Washington. For some reason, Adams never forgot and never forgave Hamilton for this, even though Hamilton had never rated any man higher than Adams— for second place.

Adams's seemingly inexplicable bitterness, despite Hamilton's frank support, smoldered like a time fuse for the next decade—before touching off the explosion that finished both their political careers and the Federalist party they had led.

The Electoral College met on February 4, 1789, in New York and unanimously elected Washington president and, by withholding a few votes at Hamilton's suggestion, chose Adams for vice-president. A sense of political parties was now beginning to emerge, and the man emerging as leader of the one that put forward the winning national ticket was Hamilton.

Unfortunately, he did not do as well in his own state, where Anti-Federalists, led by his old nemesis George Clinton, still had the strength to push through the legislature a full slate of five Anti-Federalist delegates to the last moribund Continental Congress of 1789, thereby ousting Hamilton from the seat he had held in Congress the year before.

Hamilton and the Federalists, sensing a favoring tide of enthusiasm for the new Constitution, had thought that this might be the year to unseat Clinton, the perennial governor. John Jay declined to run; so they hit upon Robert Yates, an Anti-Federalist who might be expected to bring moderate Anti-Federalists into the Federalist column.

As Federalist party leader (to friends) and boss (to enemies), Hamilton rallied support for John Laurance, a lawyer, against Jacob Broome, a merchant, for election to the new Congress from the city. Hamilton argued in meetings at Bardin's Tavern and the Coffee House and City Tavern and in campaign broadsides that it was important for the city to have its own man in the House, one who "would be disposed to withstand every attempt to *destroy* or *weaken* the national government." He should be "of *early* and *decided* attachment to the federal constitution," which "cannot yet be regarded as entirely out of danger."

Hamilton served as chairman of the all-important committee—which included Robert Troup, William Duer, William Constable, John Murray, Richard Platt, and Robert Bowne—to correspond with other counties to solicit their votes.

In a circular letter of February 18 to the supervisors of Albany, which was sent to other towns as well, Hamilton asserted that the state's chief magistrate should be free from temptation "wantonly to perplex . . . the national Government, whether . . . from a preference of partial confederacies, from a spirit of competition with the national rulers for personal preeminence, from an impatience of the restraints of national authority, or fear of a diminution of power and emoluments."

In his series of letters to the newspapers signed "H. G.," Hamilton declared that Clinton was too deeply committed in opposition to the new government, whereas Yates would work harmoniously with it to win federal favor, jobs, and patronage for New York. When Clintonians counterattacked, Hamilton's earlier moderate tone grew biting, harsh, and personal.

Admitting that Clinton was "fair on the score of probity," he denounced him as an "artful man," cunning and obstinate, who had "betrayed a stronger attachment to his own power, influence and advantage than to the dignity, respectability and prosperity of the people." He was a hypocrite to cry out against the "men of property" in Federalist ranks when everyone knew that Clinton himself was rich. During the Revolution he had commanded but once, at Fort Montgomery, where he had "made a well-timed retreat (I mean personally, for the greatest part of the garrison were captured)."

Clinton or one of his closest supporters shot back under the name of "William Tell," asking, "Who tells us every day, 'that we have not common sense sufficient to judge or act for ourselves?' I will tell you who. . . . Start not, thou well known Machiavel, wince not thou galled horse. For well I know thee and thy compacted band. Puffed up . . . by an expecting band of sycophants, a train of ambitious relations, and a few rich men . . . didst thou vainly *conceit* that no man dared attack thee?" Hamilton was called Clinton's "bitterest enemy" and accused of wanting to be governor himself. He was also accused of having recently told a friend "that his first . . . love, Alexander like, is that of fame." Hamilton wanted Congress to be poorly entertained in New York City by the prudent, poor Yates, so that the national capital would then be removed to Albany, "where the interest of the family with which he is immediately connected . . . is . . . established."

Hamilton's broadsides were almost, but not quite, enough to finish off Clinton, who won the election by a margin of only 429 votes. Hamilton's candidate, John Laurance, won election to the House, and for the first time the Federalists won control of both houses of the New York legislature, so that it would now be possible for them to elect two Federalists to the United States Senate. After much maneuvering, stretching over many days of the special session, the assembly nominated for the Senate Philip Schuyler and James Duane. The state senate nominated Schuyler and Ezra L'Hommedieu, but the assembly rejected the latter in favor of Rufus King. Hamilton insisted that Schuyler and Rufus King be chosen. The dispute narrowed down to dropping either King or Duane.

Hamilton "immediately set about circulating an idea that it would be injurious to the city to have Duane elected, as the probability was some very unfit character would be his successor. . . ." Here Aaron Burr rose, as a Federalist, and announced that the Federalists of both houses had agreed upon Schuyler and Duane in a manner that could not now be changed. Hamilton accepted Burr's challenge to a test of strength.

Duane had married a Livingston daughter; so the Livingstons would go along with Hamilton's own in-law Schuyler for one Senate seat as long as he allowed one of *their* in-laws, Duane, to have the other. Besides, Hamilton's close friend and new disciple, Rufus King, was only a recent arrival in New York from Massachusetts, not, like the Livingstons, descended from three or four generations of Hudson River lords of the manor aristocracy. But Hamilton's power was now so great that he was able to overbear the alliance of Duane, all the Livingstons, and Burr. The senate accepted Rufus King and rejected Duane—and a legion of powerful former friends switched to the ranks of the enemies already arrayed against Hamilton.

As a result of his total victory in 1789 an astute commentator wrote, "The Livingstons were hopelessly . . . alienated, the State became doubtful, and was finally lost to the Federalists." Hamilton's overreaching here at the pinnacle of his power had "led him into a fatal error as a politician."

It also helped to provide Burr his foothold on the first rung of the ladder of his own political rise. Only eleven years later he would vault past Hamilton into a tie for the rung at the top that would always remain beyond Hamilton's grasp. One of the wily Clinton's first moves in his fourth term as governor, as leader of the shattered party that had just lost both houses of the legislature, was to appoint the nominally Federalist Burr to the office of attorney general. This would help to bring disaffected Federalists into the Antis' fold. It would also solidify the defection of the Livingstons from Hamilton's momentarily all-powerful Federalist camp.

While Hamilton awaited the New York election returns, Washington and the rest of the new national government were being inaugurated on April 30. After receiving word of his election to the presidency and then trying to borrow some cash from friends to pay for the trip to New York, George Washington set off from Mount Vernon. Along the way there were lavish triumphal receptions at Baltimore, Chester, Philadelphia, and Trenton. At Philadelphia Washington's escort was the ever suavely smiling General Thomas Mifflin, who once had helped organize the Conway Cabal against him. On the sumptuous welcoming barge that picked up the new president at Elizabethtown Point, New Jersey, to ferry him the 15 miles through the upper bay to the tip of Manhattan at the Battery, Hamilton was among the notables. They greeted the chief under an awning festooned with red side curtains stretched above the deck. Batteries of cannon boomed a thirteen-gun salute from Staten Island as they passed, and from still heavier guns a Spanish galleon in the North River belched reply. Lesser vessels made all the noise of which they were capable and ran up whatever flags and bunting could be found stowed in their lockers.

Porpoises leaped and frolicked in the frothy prow waves as a sloop under full sail swung alongside Washington's barge. On board the sloop two gentlemen and two ladies stood on deck facing Washington, singing loud and clear across the water new words to "God Save the King":

> . . . Joy to our native land,
> Let every heart expand,
> For Washington's at hand,
> With glory crowned.

Washington disembarked at Murray's Wharf at the foot of Wall Street and climbed the carpeted steps flanked by railings upholstered in crimson. There, before tightly packed crowds and the thunder of deafening huzzahs, he was formally greeted by Governor Clinton. He made his way slowly through the huge crowd from the wharf to the presidential house a half mile north in Cherry Street, about where Fulton Fish Market now stands. Some in the crowds pressed close to touch the tall gentlemen in the cocked hat, blue suit, and buff underdress. One spectator remembered that as he slowly made his way, "The General was obliged to wipe his eyes several times before he got to Queen Street."

Into New York City flocked an army of journalists, lawmakers, wives, families, domestics, and camp followers. Boarding houses, taverns, and real estate brokers did thriving business. Prices rose; business boomed. On April 30, 1789, crowds filled up Broad and Wall Streets in front of the old City Hall, now rebuilt by Pierre L'Enfant and renamed Federal Hall, to suit the grandeur of the new presidential and congressional parties and the formal Constitutional inaugural ceremonies that were just about to begin.

A week after his arrival, from the second floor balcony, George Washington looked down on the excited throng, solemnly held up his right hand, and swore to the Speaker of the House of Representatives, Frederick A. C. Muhlenberg, the presidential oath that is part of Section I of Article II of the Constitution: "I do solemnly swear that I will faithfully execute the Office of President of the United States, and will to the best of my ability, preserve, protect and defend the Constitution of the United States." Washington did not much like the vice-president, and kept as much distance between himself and the short stocky figure of John Adams as the proprieties of the situation on the cramped balcony would permit. Adams, in his turn, swore to execute faithfully the duties of vice-president although neither the Constitution, *The Federalist*, or anybody else could tell him quite what they were beyond presiding over the Senate.

The most urgent questions confronting the new nation were not grave constitutional issues, but points of etiquette. Washington turned to Hamilton for advice, and five days after the inauguration, on May 5, Hamilton replied. Addressing Washington as "Dear Sir," and referring to his office as simply "President," or the "Executive," Hamilton left the exact form of address to Congress. "Men's minds are prepared for a pretty high tone in the demeanor of the executive," he said, "but I doubt whether for so high a tone as in the abstract might be desirable. The notions of equality are yet, in my opinion, too general and too strong to admit of such a distance being placed between the President and other branches of the government as might even be consistent with a due proportion."

For a president elected by the entire nation to pretend to be nothing more than just another common man would have struck Hamilton as demagoguery and humbug, not "consistent with a due proportion," a phrase that was one of Hamilton's watchwords.

Hamilton called for a far more "open" chief executive than any other country of that time had yet established and one who was far more open to the people, except for staged public appearances, than any American presidency has been in recent times.

"The public good requires as a primary object that the dignity of the office should be supported . . ." Hamilton wrote. He called for a levee once a week for receiving visits, "the President to remain half an hour, in which time he may converse cursorily on indifferent matters with such persons as shall strike his attention, and at the end of that half hour disappear."

Unlike modern presidents, most of whose "informal" appearances are staged, the president should "give formal entertainments only twice or four times on the anniversaries of important events in the revolution . . ."—the day of the Declaration of Independence, the inauguration of the President, the day of the treaty with France, and of the definitive treaty with Britain.

Hamilton added, "I believe it will be necessary to remove the idea of too immense an equality which I fear would excite dissatisfaction and cabal." There is some danger of jealousy and overexposure, too. "The thing may be so managed as neither to occasion much waste of time, nor to infringe on dignity."

Hamilton suggested that those who might be invited to formal functions should include senators but not representatives, because "the Senate are coupled with the President in certain executive functions; treaties and appointments" and "have a right of continual communications with the President as a safeguard against secret communications to deceive him." This called for much more openness in communications between president and Congress than has obtained since.

Hamilton's frank suggestions for openness in the chief executive contrasted sharply with the ideas of Adams and a majority of the Senate.

The House of Representatives paralleled Hamilton's idea that the president be called merely "the President of the United States," but the Senate rejected the recommendation. As the presiding officer, not supposed to inject himself into the debates, John Adams's sense of self-importance overbore decorum. He sought to exalt much higher the office to which he saw himself as heir apparent. "What," Adams demanded, "will the common people of foreign countries, what will the sailors and soldiers say" when asked to speak of "George Washington, the President of the United States?" They will despise him. Adams thought the president should be called "His Most Benign Highness."

The vice-president and his Abigail had rented the impressive but somewhat rundown estate known as Richmond Hill just north of town, where they often entertained hundreds of guests a day in courtly splendor. However, the status of his office fell far short of the pomp that Richmond Hill implied. Adams seemed to feel the disparity keenly. He described his office with disgust as "the most insignificant . . . that ever invention of man contrived, or his imagination conceived." When a Senate committee voted to call the president "His Highness the President of the United States of America and Protector of the Rights of the Same," this came closer to what Adams had urged.

Somewhat quixotically, Adams admitted "This is all nonsense to the philosopher, but so is all government whatsoever."

Although Washington's own predilections were probably more closely aligned with Adams's preference for dignity and solemn investitures than Hamilton's suggestions for openness, he feared that the Antis would greet any excess solemnity with charges of monarchy and the like. He followed Hamilton's suggestions in the main. An imagined look in at one of his levees suggests that the results of following Hamilton's advice were, at best, mixed.

The president's "levee" was for men only every Tuesday from three to four, and there were dinners on Thursdays at four o'clock in the afternoon. Martha Washington held a tea party for both men and women on Fridays. The levees were stiffly formal, but at the tea parties Washington became known for his attentions to the ladies. The levees exposed him, as he explained it himself, to "foreign characters, strangers and others who from motives of curiosity . . . or any other cause are induced to call upon me." No one could imagine "what pomp there is in all this . . . perhaps it consists in not sitting." Like typical politicians in any age, "Gentlemen, often in great numbers, come and go, chat with each other, and act as they please. A porter shows them into the room and they retire from it when they please and without ceremony. At their *first* entrance, they salute me and I them, and as many of them as I can talk to I do."

Resuming the closeness he had to Washington during the war years, Hamilton again became "the principal and most confidential aid of the Commander in Chief." He continued to counsel Washington on every imaginable subject besides etiquette. Their relationship was easy and natural, though Hamilton, knowing his chief as he did, always treated his older friend in public and private with deference and reserve. A story is told that in the presence of a large group, out of Washington's hearing, Hamilton once said that Washington "was reserved and aristocratic even to his intimate friends, and allowed no one to be familiar with him."

Gouverneur Morris disputed this and said that *he* could be "as familiar with Washington as with any of his other friends."

"At the next reception evening," Hamilton replied, "gently slap him on the shoulder and say, 'My dear General, how happy I am to see you look so well.' " If Morris would really do so, Hamilton promised to treat him and a dozen of his friends to a supper with wine.

Taking Hamilton up on the bet at the next levee, Morris publicly slapped Washington on the back.

Washington stepped back and "fixed his eye on Morris with an angry frown, until the latter retreated abashed, and sought refuge in the crowd."

The rest of the company (with Hamilton, no doubt, doing his best to suppress a guffaw) looked on in shocked silence. Over wine glasses at the free dinner for thirteen, which Hamilton cheerfully bought him, Morris is said to have avowed, "I have won the bet, but dearly paid for it, and nothing could induce me to repeat it."

Washington's reply to Hamilton's "etiquette" letter on the same day conveyed "unfeigned thanks" for his "friendly communications," and a discreet hint of things to come: "Permit me to entreat a continuation of them as occasions may arise."

In the organization of the new Congress in the tapestried chamber of Federal Hall, nothing could be done by Hamilton to prevent the election of Madison's protégé and Hamilton's enemy, John Beckley, as chief clerk. Elias Boudinot then moved the House into a committee of the whole to take up the creation of executive departments for foreign affairs, war, and finance.

First and most controversial for debate would be the Department of Finance.

Robert Morris had closed out his accounts as superintendent of finance on November 1, 1784, and turned the books over to a new Board of Treasury. A committee, of which Nathan Dane was chairman, after reviewing the board's records, reported back to Congress on September 30, 1787, that the records of Robert Morris and the board were disorderly, inconclusive, and full of shortages and imbalances, if not outright proof of wrongdoing and embezzlement.

The charges against Morris compelled return of the Treasury to a board, whose management had been even worse than Morris's.

Should the Treasury Department now be placed under a single head or under a board of three commissioners? It was no mere routine debate.

Elbridge Gerry of Massachusetts was for a three-man board, arguing that by putting "all this power into the hands of one great man, who is to be the head of the department . . . we shall establish an office giving one person a greater influence than the President of the United States, and more than is proper for any person to have in a republican government." He pointed out that for one man to occupy this office "is as much as his reputation is worth . . . he can hardly

548 HAMILTON I

preserve his integrity." Gerry doubted whether a fit person could be found in the whole country.

Hamilton's close friends in Congress knew better and insisted that a single head would be better than a board. Jeremiah Wadsworth let fly a broadside against the irresponsibility and inefficiency of the Boards of Treasury. He had dealt with Morris, too, as the single financier; and, by contrast with the board, Morris was a "master of the science in which he was engaged," serving the needs of the war and publishing clear accounts that would have been settled long ere this but for the ineptitude of the board that had succeeded him. To show how one member of a board could be expected to hide behind another, Egbert Benson recalled that more than 20 had applied for appointment to the board that replaced Morris: "If this trust had been . . . reposed in one responsible individual, not perhaps more than three of the candidates would have had confidence to come forward . . . for the office." Madison and others professed themselves at a loss to see where the danger of a single head lay. The bill finally passed, preserving the Treasury Department, ranking with War and Foreign Affairs, under a single all powerful secretary, as one of the three great departments.

Hamilton's name was kept out of the debates as much as possible by his friends, but his presence just below the surface as the likely appointee brought an extra edge of sound and fury to consideration of such abstractions as that of a single head versus board. The first great debate on the subject of greatest importance to the new Congress had as its implicit focus the subject of Hamilton himself.

When Washington had asked Robert Morris for suggestions for a man to occupy the great office, Morris replied "There is but one man in the United States": Alexander Hamilton. He added, "I am glad you have given me this opportunity to declare to you, the extent of the obligations I am under to him." Robert Troup recalled that Washington, immediately after his inauguration, "called on Hamilton, and told him it was his intention to nominate him to the charge of the financial department" as soon as it should be organized. The next day, Hamilton asked Troup to take over his law practice if he should be appointed. Willing to oblige, Troup duly pointed out the financial sacrifice it would mean for Hamilton's family. Hamilton readily admitted this, but said he could not refuse an assignment in which he "could essentially promote the welfare of the country."

When Hamilton confided a hope of appointment to Gouverneur Morris and Morris remonstrated that the Treasury post would earn him only calumny, Hamilton retorted, "It is the situation in which I can do most good."

Only a few weeks after Washington's inauguration, Madison confided to Jefferson, with critical passages in cipher, that John Jay or Hamilton would be proposed for the Treasury: "The latter is perhaps the best qualified for that species of business and on that account would be preferred to those who know him personally." Madison added that "Chancellor Livingston wishes this department, but will not succeed."

Jay, who wanted to be chief justice, said that those who mentioned his name for the Treasury "do me more Honor than my Qualifications for that place merit; nor have I the least wish or Room, to expect, to be employed in affairs of that kind. . . ."

It became an open secret that summer that Hamilton was Washington's choice. Vice-President John Adams, almost three months in office, had tolerable knowledge that Hamilton would be appointed to the Treasury, but was not certain when he wrote to Hamilton on July 21, 1789. He introduced his second son, Charles, who had just taken his degree "at our University of Cambridge" and was destined for the law. "I wish to get him into some office in New York, and should give the preference to yours," Adams wrote. Two contingencies were in the way. Congress might force Adams "to Philadelphia or the Lord knows where: the other that you may become a Minister of State, or some other Thing better or worse than the Practice of the Bar, but . . . incompatible with it." Any political resentment Adams may have harbored against Hamilton for withholding electoral votes did not put him above asking a practical favor for his son.

Testimonials to an unnamed person exactly like Hamilton emerged from support by friends and attacks by foes in the debates that were going on in Congress.

Fisher Ames of Massachusetts, a friend in the House, noted that governmental finance "presents to the imagination a deep, dark, and dreary chaos; impossible to be reduced to order without the mind of the architect is clear and capacious, and his power commensurate to the occasion; he must not be the flitting creature of a day. . . . it is with an intention to let a little sunshine into the business that the present arrangement is proposed. . . ."

John Page of Virginia, a foe, feared that the duty of the secretary to "digest and report plans for the improvement and management of the revenue, and the support of the public credit," was not only "a dangerous innovation upon the constitutional privilege of his House," but might even lay "a foundation for an aristocracy or a detestable monarchy." He feared that "Members might be led, by the deference commonly paid to men of abilities . . . to support the minister's plan, even against their own judgment."

Egbert Benson, a friend, pointed out that the representatives in Congress, there for brief tenure and uninformed except by local views, would flounder with fiscal matters, whereas the secretary, with superior and comprehensive knowledge, could bring things to a focus by presenting plans that could be amended or corrected as legislative wisdom required.

The most important work of the secretary would be "that of digesting and reporting plans for the improvement of the revenue, supporting public credit," and drawing forth the riches of the country. Such business must be "submitted into the hands of an able individual."

James Madison now brought winning support to his former partner Publius. The danger of his exercising undue influence, Madison insisted, was far less than the injury from the House's bungling without his guidance. "From a bad administration of the Government, more detriment will arise than from any other source," he pointed out.

There had been no objection to the secretary's working up a plan "and giving it in when it was called for." Therefore, by merely changing the word *report* to *prepare*, the House could protect itself from its own presumed weakness before a powerful secretary. Thomas FitzSimons's amendment to this effect carried the day.

The final question was whether the head of one of the great departments, whose appointment had to be with the "advice and consent" of the Senate, could be removed by the president at will, or only with "advice and consent" of the Senate once again. The Constitution and *The Federalist* left room for doubt.

In foreign affairs and war, it seemed clearer that the President should have a free hand, but with revenue powers vested in the House, Jackson of Georgia charged, "if the President has the power of removing all officers who may be virtuous enough to oppose his measures . . . Your Treasury would fall into his hands; for nobody in that department would dare to oppose him. Having then the army and the treasury at his command, we might bid a farewell to the liberties of America forever."

Thomas Scott of Pennsylvania made fun of these "frightful pictures," "that the Treasurer must be the mere creature of the President," who "arbitrarily removes him from office, and lays his hands violently upon the money chest. . . ." Even a virtuous Treasurer could not halt a wicked President who, supported by army and navy, "would . . . carry away the money and the Treasurer too. . . ."

Wide suspicion that the Treasury would fall to the powerful Federalist party leader, who would work hand in glove with the Federalist president, lent fierce personal intensity to the whole abstract subject of ministerial powers. Benson finally brought both sides together by amendments that would leave the president's power of removal of the head of a department to construction of the Constitution, not to legislation by the House. The bill passed, 31–19. It was left that the president could remove cabinet ministers at will without the further advice and consent of the Senate.

The Treasury Department bill passed the House on July 2, 1789. Senate concurrence was voted on July 31, it took effect September 2, and Hamilton was commissioned secretary of the treasury on the eleventh.

The legislative history that now lay behind the creation of the department indicated that the secretary was to have the widest and most significant powers in the government, including even broad jurisdiction over western lands. Debates had rejected the idea of subjecting him to control of Congress as inconsistent with the theory of separation of powers. The department was firmly within the executive branch, despite arguments by responsible members like Elbridge Gerry that this would give the secretary greater power and influence than the president. Yet charged with reporting to the House of Representatives on all proposals affecting finance, he would have more intimate access to the people's branch of the tripartite government than any other member of the executive branch.

Few aspects of foreign affairs or war could be imagined that would not significantly involve finances. It was, after all, a government supported largely by import duties, under constant threat from warlike Indians and great powers on northern, western, and southern borders and everywhere on the high seas. As the longest and closest intimate of a reluctant, aging and remote president, who saw it as his duty to remain above all partisan dispute, Hamilton would be the cabinet minister who in practice would hold the office most resembling that of an American prime minister.

With powers so vast, it is not particularly surprising that the secretary of the treasury shunted aside warnings of the dangers of calumny he had heard or insufficiently noted—dangers implied by specifically penal provisions of the Treasury's enabling legislation to the effect that anyone employed in the Treasury who was concerned in commerce or speculated in public funds should be held guilty of a high crime. Suspicion of inattention to such strictures would ultimately lead to his disgrace.

Inauguration of the new government roughly coincided with an upturn in the economy. Short grain crops in Europe created brisk demand in America. One newspaper reported the "pleasing reflection, that whilst America is enriching herself by her exports, she at the same time is feeding starving millions abroad." President Washington wrote Lafayette of the gratifying manifestations of prosperity on every hand: "In the last year, the plentiful crops and great prices of grain have vastly augmented our remittances. The rate of exchange is . . . much in our favor." People could afford to import more European goods so the "duties payable into the public treasury" had increased. Trade with the West Indies flourished. There was reason to hope that being secretary of the treasury would not be as disastrous for Hamilton as it had been for his predecessors Robert Morris and William Duer and the Board of Treasury. Even so, Hamilton's mood was more somber than usual on the Fourth of July, 1789, thirteen years after the nation's first Independence Day, as he and Baron von Steuben bade farewell to the family and went off to join fellow members of the New York Society of the Cincinnati and friends and brethren from the other state societies who were in town that day for a preprandial collation at the City Tavern.

Even after he had exchanged toasts to independence and congratulations of the day with the perennial national president general, who had also just been made the nation's president, Hamilton could not shake off his anxious mood. General Nathanael Greene had died more than three years before, on June 19, 1786. His widow, Catherine Littlefield Greene, had called upon Hamilton as her attorney to help her sort out the tangled affairs of the apparently insolvent estate.

The Cincinnati had called upon Hamilton, their greatest orator, to deliver an eulogium this afternoon to the memory of the man who had recommended him to be Washington's aide. The weight of this solemn honor on his mind did not entirely account for his deep melancholy. Greene had once written Hamilton, "Poor Laurens is dead," and Hamilton had replied, "I feel the deepest affliction" at "the loss of a friend I truly and most tenderly loved, and one of a very small number." Another absent friend he had loved was Francis Barber, his schoolmaster at Elizabethtown, who had led a column beside his to the last redoubt at Yorktown—and then been killed by a falling tree at the Newburgh encampment. Alexander Scammell had died at Yorktown, and Captain-Lieutenant Thomas Thompson, whom he had first promoted from the ranks, was dead at Springfield. Many other old friends were absent from the day's ranks as those of the Cincinnati present jovially fell into irregular formation behind Colonel Sebastian Baumann's well-drilled regular artillery regiment. With a crash and blare a band of music struck up a revolutionary air. The old soldiers marched off stiffly in cadence up Broadway to St. Paul's Chapel on Vesey Street, a few of the older ones taking a skip or two before getting into step.

The brilliant audience assembled in the church pews there included Vice-President Adams, members of the Senate, the Speaker and members of the House of Representatives, and all their ladies. Hamilton looked down on the crowded rows from the lectern for a long moment of silence. He spoke in a low, intense voice. His eulogium recounted at first hand major actions in which both he and Greene had played a part—Trenton, Princeton, Springfield, and Monmouth. In all perils, Greene's "calm intrepidity and unshaken presence of mind [served] to arrest the progress of the disorder and retrieve the fortune of the day." Hamilton went on to describe Greene's brilliant campaigns in the South —replacing General Horatio Gates after the debacle at Camden—Greene's strategy and tactics at places like Hick's Creek; Guilford Court House; the river crossings of the Catawba, the Yadkin, and the Dan; and the Battle of Eutaw Springs had saved the South for the nation and finally forced the British to evacuate Charleston and Savannah.

As he described the despair Greene had found in the Southern states as he arrived to inspirit them, Hamilton's thoughts must have dwelt on his lost friend Laurens's plan to free the slaves by enlisting them in the army, as well as his own hatred of slavery, hypocrisy, and cowardice. Otherwise, he would not have inserted in Greene's eulogium a striking but rather irrelevant reference to prostrate Virginia before Yorktown with Governor Jefferson in hiding, "incumbered by a numerous body of slaves bound by all the laws of *injured* humanity to hate their masters," a Virginia "deficient in order and vigour in its administration."

In St. Paul's Chapel on this thirteenth national Independence Day, Cruger's former clerk and Neddy Stevens's "constant projector" looked down from the lectern on Martha Washington as she listened from the pew that is marked with her and Washington's names today, on John and Abigail Adams, and on a congregation of other notables as distinguished as any that had gathered under one roof since the adjournment of the Constitutional Convention. Hamilton made no mention of his own role where he and Greene had been in the same battles —he rarely spoke about himself—but in another striking passage he made the ascending arch of Greene's life story sound remarkably like the arch of Hamilton's own to date. Not loudly, nor with rhetorical flourishes, but with the precise phrasing and peculiar ardor that he brought to his finest efforts, Hamilton told the brilliant gathering, with simple, understated intensity:

Nathanael Greene descended from reputable parents, but not placed by birth in that elevated rank, which under a monarchy is the only sure road to those employments, that give activity and scope to abilities, must in all probability have contented himself with the humble lot of a private citizen, or at most with the contracted sphere of an elective office, in a colonial and dependent government, scarcely conscious of the resources of his own mind, had not the violated rights of his country called him to act a part on a more splendid and ample theater. . . .

Removed from St. Croix's "contracted sphere" to the continent, "the resources of his own mind" had been brought to full consciousness by the part Hamilton had been called upon to act by Greene's recommendation in "a more splendid and ample theater." There was no mistaking the pride he projected on Greene for having done it all without having been placed by birth in the "elevated rank" that gives "activity and scope to abilities." Hamilton added, telling more about his unmentioned self than about Greene:

The vigor of his genius corresponding with the importance of the prize to be contended for overcame the natural moderation of his temper [and] though not hurried on by enthusiasm, but Animated by an enlightened sense of the value of free government, he cheerfully resolved to stake his fortune his hopes his life and his honor upon an enterprise of the danger of which he knew the whole magnitude in a cause which was worthy of the toils and of the blood of heroes.

Since writing Neddy Stevens 20 years ago, Hamilton, like Greene, had often "willingly risk[ed] my life tho not my character to exalt my station." From then "being jusly said to Build Castles in the air," Hamilton now had risen to a civil station, if not army rank, more exalted than Greene's. Indeed, as he spoke there from the lectern in St. Paul's Chapel, his was a station more exalted than that of any political man of his age and youth except the younger William Pitt's— Napoleon Bonaparte was still a sublieutenant in Ajaccio—in everything that mattered but personal wealth.

It remained a source of sorrow to Hamilton's friends that just as he was beginning to build a law practice that would soon have repaired this one deficiency, Hamilton was turning his best clients over to Robert Troup and arranging stipulations for Troup and others to be substituted for him as their attorney of record in pending court cases, while he briskly set to work to create the precedental legal, economic, and administrative foundations for enduring free republican government on its salary of $3,500 a year.

Again and again his friends had warned him that no official concerned with the Treasury—as the experience of Robert Morris and William Duer had shown —could preserve his honor, integrity, and public credit or, if he did, remain in office unsmeared by calumny and scandal. Lacking the personal wealth of his ill-fated predecessors, he was willingly putting his honor and his character to even greater risk than they had run in a cause that would prove more perilous than the war that he and Greene had found, and would eventually cost him his life.

As he took up his duties of office in September, Hamilton quickly became the most newsworthy figure of the new government, as much by default of others as through any conscious effort of his own. The public followed all developments closely in the newspapers. There was popular interest in Congress because the lawmakers directly represented the people. The federal judiciary, under John Jay, at first did little but wait for cases to work their way up to the highest court, though later, under John Marshall, who followed so many of Hamilton's prescripts, it would gather to itself supreme power. The executive department was new, had operative responsibility, and a proliferation of active appointive agents, some with senatorial sanction. The War Department was anemic; the State Department seemed to deal with foreign relations remote in place and time. Hamilton's Treasury Department, by contrast, was domestic, vital, and immediate. It extracted taxes, gave out jobs, turned down worthy applicants, and was a chief target of criticism. Its activities clothed every action of the secretary with political blessing or bane.

After taking up the tumultuous tasks of his secretariat, Hamilton continued to post entries in the clients' Cash Book he had maintained since 1782 in the meticulous manner of Cruger's careful bookkeeper. Under each of more than 150 names, left- and right-hand columns record in the Cash Book every receipt and disbursement as a debit or credit to the client's account. He also kept a few personal ledgers in the Cash Book under such heads as "House Expenses," an account showing a debit to his wife as "Mrs. Hamilton." The ledgers for John B. Church are extensive, showing credits for dividends and other items received for his account, as well as debits for disbursements made on his behalf to others. One fascinating feature of Church's (and some other ledgers) is the practiced ease with which Hamilton automatically converts sums of money from pounds, shillings, and pence, and sometimes guineas, to dollars and cents and back again as he posts within a single ledger, creating a bookkeeping system more like quadruple entry than double entry.

From late May through early November of 1789, Angelica Church was on a visit to New York without her husband, John. He had just won long-sought election from Westover to a seat in the British Parliament, where he would be busier than ever and hear her still less. So there is also fascination in comparing the debit entries in Church's ledger as he pays for Angelica's absence in New York—at the climax of Hamilton's life—with the entries Hamilton posts to a separate account headed "Angelica Church" (on the same page Hamilton posts another ledger for his wife as "Mrs. Elizabeth Hamilton"). From the comparison it appears that out of a total of £1705.9.3 spent for Angelica's lodging, coachman, valet de chambre, servants, coach hire, and miscellaneous, Church and Angelica paid only about half themselves. The other half seems to have been defrayed out of Hamilton's own flat pocket. Three of the most intriguing items paid by Hamilton for Angelica are for money she took back with her, for a mysterious unnamed "last" landlady (different from the Mrs. Cuyler Church paid), and for her "Music Master." These are posted as follows:

Angelica Church   Dr.

Monies paid to Yourself

1789			
May	Cash dld you myself	500 Dollars	£200
15	ditto by Mrs. Hamilton	200 do	80
June	paid your valet De Chambre ℔ order		21.12
Aug. 12	Paid Mrs. Cuyler for your lodgings from May 10 to Oct 7. 21 weeks		162.
Nov. 2	Cash paid for passages of yourself & servant 370 Dollars & 66 Cents or		148. 5
4	This sum advanced to take with you 200 Dollars		80
10	paid account of your last landlady for rooms & some damage done by your servants in removing		23. 9.3
	This sum paid your former Music Master		40

Angelica's ledger is untypical of the Cash Book because it contains only debit and no credit entries and is posted in a more disorderly manner than any of the others. It is buried amid the dreary regularity of the skilled bookkeeper's pages after businesslike pages of names, notations, and figure postings. Unlike any of the more than 150 other accounts, Angelica's is subdivided into two uniquely labeled subheads which are "Monies paid to Yourself" and "For You." They leap off the page to strike an auditor's eye much the way the words "I love you" tucked randomly into a logarithm table might strike an arithmetician's.

Amid the kaleidoscopic "jumble of events," the secret lonely passion the exalted bookkeeper felt "For You," and she for him, seemed to go on consuming them both, year after year, whether she is in New York or an Atlantic away, in the pages of books of account or letters full of stifled passion. When Angelica took ship to return to England early in November, her poor heart was undone as she wrote back to him from shipboard having just sailed out of his sight.

> Me voila mon très cher bien en mer et le pauvre coeur bien effligé
> de vous avoir quitté. I have almost vowed not to stay three weeks in
> England. . . .

She was *"efflige"*—the word could mean "griefstricken" as well as
"afflicted" and, at the same time, by elision, "unraveled" and "distraught" and
"undone." Hamilton well knew Angelica's orthography to be more breathless
and impassioned than exact, and more intensely poetic and affecting for him on
that account. She seemed *"efflige"* by the rush of emotion that had overcome her
at their parting after being with Hamilton for so little precious time. She cannot
seem to wring thoughts of him out of her sentences, solicitous as she tries to
be for ailing sister Betsy:

> I am not much disposed for gaiety, and yet I endeavour already to
> make myself tolerable to my fellow passengers, that my sweet friends
> advice may not be lost on me. Do my dear Brother endeavour to sooth
> my poor Betsey, comfort her with the assurances that I will certainly
> return to take care of her soon. Remember this also yourself my dearest
> Brother and let neither politics or ambition drive your Angelica from
> your affections.
> . . . Adieu my dear Brother, may God bless and protect you, prays
> your ever affectionate Angelica ever ever yours.

Alone on the wintry passage after spring, summer, and early autumn in
New York, she seemed to unravel in an attack of despairing anxiety:

> Bitter whilst in sight of my friend, thus far my dear Brother I am
> content with my company, and apparently they with me, but how can
> I be content when I leave my best and most valuable invaluable friends.
> Adieu my dear Hamilton, you said I was as dear to you as a sister keep
> your word, and let me have the consolation to believe that you will never
> forget the promise of friendship you have vowed. A thousand embraces
> to my dear Betsey, she will not have so bad a night as the last, *but poor
> Angelica* adieu mine plus cher
>   my best affectionate wishes to my Baron.
>   Same to Van Berckal and l'Enfant
>   packet, six O'Clock, all well on board.

Anything but drily matter-of-fact like his meticulous ledger entries memori-
alizing her visit—except those posted under the subhead "For You"—was the
letter Hamilton wrote Angelica that crossed hers of the same date sent *"efflige"*
from her packet. His yearning was a match for hers. After seeing her up the

gangplank and going home for a little while, he had walked back down to the Battery with Baron von Steuben and his son Philip to wave to her ship as it sailed past the tip of the island and out of sight toward the Narrows and wept:

[New York, November 8, 1789]

My dear Sister

After taking leave of you on board of the Packet, I hastened home to sooth and console your sister. I found her in bitter distress; though much recovered from the agony, in which she had been. After composing her by a flattering picture of your prospects for the voyage, and a *strong infusion* of hope, that she had not taken a last farewell of you; The Baron little Philip and myself, with her consent, walked down to the Battery; where with aching hearts and anxious eyes we saw your vessel, in full sail, swiftly bearing our loved friend from our embraces. Imagine what we felt. We gazed, we sighed, we *wept;* and casting "many a lingering longing look behind" returned home to give scope to our sorrows, and mingle without restraint our tears and our regrets. . . .

The Vergilian tag from his favorite poet but hinted at the depths of his sadness:

Amiable Angelica! how much you are formed to endear yourself to every good heart! How deeply you have rooted yourself in the affections of your friends on this side the Atlantic! *Some* of us are and must continue inconsolable for your absence.

His sentences try to be as full of Betsy as Angelica's are; he and Betsy are dutifully serving out a life term of fruitful wedlock to each other. But

Betsey and myself make you the last theme of our conversation at night and the first in the morning. We talk of you; we praise you and we pray for you. We dwell with peculiar interest on the little incidents that preceded your departure. Precious and never to be forgotten scenes!

He is open in courtship, but checks his ardor:

But let me check, My dear Sister, these effusions of regretful friendship. Why should I alloy the Happiness that courts you in the bosom of your family by images that must wound your sensibility? It shall not be. However difficult, or little natural it is to me to suppress what the fulness of my heart would utter, the sacrifice shall be made to your ease and satisfaction.

Gentlemanly understatement can hardly speak more eloquent volumes of mixed but deep emotion:

> I shall not fail to execute any commission you gave me nor neglect any of your charges . . . already have I addressed the consolation, I mentioned to you, to your Father. I have no doubt the arguments I have used with him will go far towards reconciling his mind to the unexpected step you took. I hope the inclosed letters may not be such as to give you pain. They arrived the day after you set sail.

What was the "unexpected step you took" that had so displeased her father and her mother? Why was Betsy in such distress? Hamilton's "For You" entry shows he paid for her separate lodgings the last month of her stay. Neither in his busy household nor in the Schuylers' nor at Mrs. Cuyler's were they likely to have been able to spend an hour alone together. In separate lodgings with the "last" unnamed landlady during the last weeks of her lone visit, it may be comforting to some, although shocking to others, to suppose that these two indiscreet, emotion-wracked souls lived with each other through at least a few precious hours and nights. Or perhaps his unreimbursed payment to her music master means no more than that in her separate lodgings once in a while she played her pianoforte for him and joined her voice with his in some old wartime tunes like "The Drum" and "A Successful Campaign." He had but few moments to spare amid the "jumble of events" that always beset them.

Angelica's father and mother would, no doubt, begrudge her these absent hours—hence their reproofs. Perhaps they would soften them a little in their letters he now was forwarding to her.

". . . Kiss your children for me," he charges her. "Teach them to consider me as your and their father's friend. I shall by the first *direct* opportunity begin a correspondence with Philip. [Angelica's eldest was Philip, too.] I have serious designs upon his heart and I flatter myself I am not a bad marksman. Adieu Dear Angelica! Remember us always as you ought to do—Remember us as we shall you."

With his letter to Angelica, Hamilton enclosed another to her from his wife. Few of Betsy's letters have survived; none of hers to her husband has. But hers to Angelica joins her to both of them in a triangle of yearning hearts. All three are embraced by Betsy's closing benediction:

[Enclosure]
<u>Elizabeth Hamilton to Angelica Church</u>

[New York, November 8, 1789]

> My Very Dear Beloved Angelica—I have seated myself to write to you, but my heart is so saddened by your Absence that it can scarcely dictate, my Eyes so filled with tears that I shall not be able to write you much but *Remember Remember*, my dear sister of the Assurances of

your returning to us, and do all you can to make your Absence short. Tell Mr. Church for me of the happiness he will give me, in bringing you to me, not to me alone but to fond parents sisters friends and to my Hamilton who has for you all the Affection of a fond own Brother. I can no more

Adieu Adieu.   E.H.

heaven <u>protect</u> <u>you.</u>

To their three yearning hearts must be subjoined those of young Philip Hamilton and the gruff old lord of the Cincinnati standing there on the Battery beside Hamilton gazing out to sea as the sails of her packet slid below the horizon, and weeping with him. It was a kind of recessional fugue in five parts for warm and anxious hearts—Angelica's, Alexander's, Betsy's, von Steuben's, and Philip's—hauntingly played on black keys behind the crash and blare of the band celebrating Hamilton's arrival at the most exalted station of his rise.

Heaven protect them all! They would need more than it could provide.

Autumn in New York is sometimes shadowed with tears.

HAMILTON CHRONOLOGY
1757–1804
HAMILTON'S TIMES

1755

Jan. 11   H born, according to some authorities.

?   James Hamilton, Jr., H's brother, who was two years older than H, born [or in 1753].

1756

May 4   Mary Uppington Fawcett, H's maternal grandmother, deeds three slaves to Archibald Hamm for life, then to Rachel Fawcett; dies on St. Eustatius shortly after.

Aug. 29   Seven Years' War begins, pitting Britain and Prussia against France, Austria, Sweden, and Saxony and leading to founding of British Empire and modern Germany.

1757

Jan. 11   H born, Charlestown, Nevis, British West Indies; mother: Rachel Fawcett Lavien, daughter of Dr. John Fawcett and Mary Uppington Fawcett, his wife; father: James Hamilton, son of Alexander Hamilton, laird of The Grange, Ayrshire, Scotland, and Elizabeth Pollock Hamilton, his wife.

1758

Oct. 1   Rachel Fawcett Lavien and James Hamilton on St. Eustatius as godparents to Alexander Fraser, son of Alexander Fraser and Elizabeth Thornton.

1759

Feb. 26   H's mother, Rachel Fawcett Lavien, sued by John Michael Lavien for absolute divorce in Temperret, or divorce court, Christiansted, St. Croix.

1760

H, age three, taken by James Hamilton and Rachel Fawcett Lavien with James, Jr., age five, from Nevis to St. Kitts about this year.

Oct. 25   King George III becomes king of England, succeeding George II.

1761

Oct.   William Pitt the Elder resigns as British prime minister.

1763

Feb. 15   Seven Years' War ends by Treaty of Hubertusberg.

1765

April   H, age eight, taken by father, James Hamilton and mother, Rachel, with brother James, Jr., from St. Kitts to St. Croix.

July   Stamp Act Congress, New York City, first major organized protest against British.

Aug.   H with mother, Rachel Fawcett Lavien, lives in house and shop at 34 Company's Lane, Christiansted, St. Croix, where H clerks for her.

1766

Jan. 8   H, Rachel, and James, Jr., left by James Hamilton after he collects judgment on St. Croix for employer, Archibald Ingram, and returns to St. Kitts.

March   British repeal the Stamp Act.

1767

H, age ten, clerks in Rachel's store, 34 Company's Lane, Christiansted; perhaps works also at Beekman and Cruger's, 7 and 8 King's Street, Christiansted.

1768

H clerks in Rachel's store, perhaps also at Beekman and Cruger's.

Feb. 19   H's mother, Rachel Fawcett Lavien, dies, Christiansted.

H clerks at Beekman and Cruger's.

1769

July   H's uncle James Lytton, of The Grange, St. Croix, and cousin Peter Lytton, his closest relatives on St. Croix, die.

Nov. 11   H writes his first extant letter to Edward Stevens: "I contemn the groveling condition of a clerk . . . and would willingly risk my life, though not my character, to exalt my station."

1770

Britain removes American import duties, except for the tax on tea.

March 5   Boston Massacre.

1771

April 6   H verses "In Yonder Mead My Love I Found" and "Coelia's an Artful Little Slut" published in *The Royal Danish American Gazette*, Christiansted, St. Croix.

April 10   "Rules for Statesmen," attributed to H, published in *The Royal Danish American Gazette*.

Oct. 15   H left in charge of Cruger's business while Nicholas Cruger is in New York City.

1772

Jan. 1   H manages Nicholas Cruger's business until Cruger returns March 15.

May 16   H gives receipt to cousin Ann Lytton Venton for remittances.

H meets Reverend Hugh Knox, who begins Presbyterian ministry on St. Croix.

Aug. 31   Devastating hurricane strikes St. Croix.

Sept. 6	H writes so-called Hurricane Letter to his father, James Hamilton, on St. Kitts.
Oct. 3	H's Hurricane Letter published in *The Royal Danish American Gazette.*
Oct. 17	H's poem "The Soul Ascending into Bliss, In Humble Imitation of Popes Dying Christian to His Soul," published in *The Royal Danish American Gazette.*
Oct.	H sails from St. Croix to Boston about this date.
Nov.	H reaches New York City about this time.
	Samuel Adams organizes new committees of correspondence.

1773

Jan.	H boards with William Livingston's family at Liberty Hall, Elizabethtown, New Jersey, while attending Francis Barber's grammar school. Becomes acquainted with Elias Boudinot's family.
May	H gives cousin Ann Lytton Venton receipts for remittances, including one for proceeds of sale of 15 hogsheads of sugar, indicating that she helped pay for his board and schooling at Elizabethtown.
June	H writes out quotations and paraphrases from Book of Genesis, Book of Revelation, translations from Homer's *Iliad,* notes on geography of the eastern Mediterranean, and a numbered list of 27 books on ancient and medieval history and philosophy at about this time, probably as part of his school exercises.
Oct.	H's application for admission to Princeton turned down. H matriculates at King's College, now Columbia University, New York City.
Dec. 16	Boston Tea Party destroys 340 chests of tea.

1774

May	Boston Port Act closes port of Boston.
July 6	H makes "Speech in the Fields" in New York City.
Sept. 4	H writes "Poem on the Death of Elias Boudinot's Child."
Dec. 15	H publishes first pamphlet *A Full Vindication of the Measures of the Continental Congress* in reply to "Free Thoughts on Congress" by A. W. Farmer (Samuel Seabury).
Dec.	H begins drilling with militia company (Corsicans or Hearts of Oak) in St. George's Churchyard.

1775

Feb. 23   H publishes pamphlet *The Farmer Refuted* as a reply to Seabury's "A View of the Controversy."

April 19   Battles of Lexington and Concord.

May 10   H and Robert Troup stand off riotous mob at King's College gates.

June 15   H publishes "Remarks on the Quebec Bill, Parts One and Two" in Rivington's New York *Gazetteer.*

June 17   Battle of Breed's Hill and Bunker Hill in Boston.

Aug. 23   H with Hearts of Oak militia removes cannon from fort at Battery under bombardment from the battleship *Asia*'s guns.

Nov. 23   H stands against Isaac Sears's raiders when they seek to destroy Rivington's printshop and press.

Nov. 26   H writes John Jay in Congress to take measures to prevent raids like that of Sears.

1776

March 14   H commissioned as captain of New York provincial artillery company by Alexander McDougall.

June 29   British begin invasion of New York.

July 4   Declaration of Independence signed in Philadelphia.

Aug. 29   H offers Washington plan for evacuation after Battle of Long Island.

Sept. 16   H's encampment at Harlem Heights; H first comes under Washington's eye and meets him.

Oct. 28   H's artillery at Battle of White Plains helps to hold off Hessian battalion.

Nov. 29   H's artillery covers Washington's Raritan crossing at Brunswick.

Dec. 25   H crosses Delaware with Washington and attacks Trenton.

Dec. 25   Adam Smith's *The Wealth of Nations* published.

1777

Jan. 3   H at Princeton fires round from battery of two fourpounders into Nassau Hall.

March 1   H appointed aide-de-camp to Washington; promoted to rank of lieutenant colonel.

April 20   H begins corresponding with Gouverneur Morris, George Clinton, Robert R. Livingston, and others of New York Committee of Correspondence.

Sept. 11   H at Battle of Brandywine.

Sept. 18   After Daverser's Ferry H warns Congress to leave Philadelphia.

Sept. 26   Cornwallis's army occupies Philadelphia.

Oct. 3   H at Battle of Germantown.

Oct. 17   Burgoyne surrenders to Horatio Gates at Saratoga.

Oct. 30   H sets out on mission to obtain reinforcements from Gates for Washington.

Nov. 5   H arrives in Albany to see Gates, Troup, perhaps General Philip Schuyler.

Nov. 12   H, returning from Albany, falls ill at New Windsor.

Nov.   Congress adopts draft of Articles of Confederation and recommends it to states for adoption.

1778

Jan. 17   H and Captain Caleb Gibbs return to Valley Forge from mission to Gates.

Jan. 29   H submits "Report on Army" to Congressional Committee to Supervise Army.

            H assists von Steuben with professional training of army and writing *Rules for the Order and Discipline of the Troops.*

May 5   Alliance with France announced at Valley Forge.

May 12   H swears congressional oath abjuring allegiance to King George III and promising to defend United States against him.

June 28   H issues and delivers orders to field commanders at Battle of Monmouth in Washington's name. On battlefield H tells Major General Charles Lee, "Let us all die here, rather than retreat."

July 4   At Brunswick court martial of Major General Charles Lee, H begins testimony as witness for the prosecution.

July 13   H continues testimony against Lee and is cross-examined by Lee, who charges H with "a frenzy of valor."

July 19   H meets Comte d'Estaing to plan joint American-French operation against Newport.

Oct. 19   H's Publius letter No. I attacks Congressman Samuel Chase for
           profiteering from secret information about grain purchases. Pub-
           lius II on October 26 and Publius III on November 16 continue
           attacks.

Dec. 22   H serves as second for John Laurens in his duel with Charles Lee.

1779

Feb.   H with Washington in Philadelphia confers with congressmen, in-
           cluding Robert Morris and others.

March 14   H writes John Jay to urge on Congress raising battalions of Negro
           troops "to give them their freedom with their muskets."

July 4   H receives word from Lieutenant Colonel John Brooks of charge
           that H had said it was "high time for the people to rise, join General
           Washington, and turn Congress out of doors."

Oct. 7   H goes to Lewes, Delaware, and Great Egg Harbor, New Jersey,
           to meet d'Estaing and give orders for joint operation against New
           York.

Oct. 9   French-American amphibious expedition to retake Savannah fails.

Dec.   H writes long letter to member of Congress, probably Robert Mor-
           ris, calling for plan to strengthen currency, enlist "moneyed men"
           in support of government, and establish a national bank.

Aug.   Spain declares war on Britain.

Aug.   Iroquois confederacy subdued by John Sullivan's expedition.

           John Paul Jones wins naval victory.

Nov.   British evacuate Newport; bring garrison back to New York.

1780

May   John Paul Jones drives British frigates to take cover.

May   British under Henry Clinton capture Charleston, South Carolina.

July 10   French under Comte de Rochambeau arrive at Newport.

Aug. 16   Cornwallis routs Gates at Battle of Camden, South Carolina.

Sept. 3   H writes long letter from Liberty Pole, New Jersey, to James
           Duane: "The fundamental defect is a want of power in Congress
           . . . another defect is want of method and energy in the administra-
           tion . . . a convention would revive the hopes of the people."

Sept. 22   H at Hartford conference with Washington, Comte de Rocham-
           beau, Chevalier de Ternay, Chevalier de Chastellux.

Sept. 25   H with Washington discovers Benedict Arnold's "treason of the deepest dye . . . to sacrifice West Point" and pursues Arnold. Peggy Shippen Arnold accuses Washington of a plot to murder her child.

Oct. 2   Major John André hanged at Washington's insistence against André's and H's protest that he should be shot instead.

Nov. 15   H with Washington and army in winter quarters at New Windsor.

Oct.–Dec.   H rebuffed in several efforts to obtain transfer to a field command.

Dec. 14   H marries Elizabeth, daughter of General Philip Schuyler, in elaborate ceremony at The Pastures, Albany, New York.

1781

Feb. 6   H writes letter for Washington to Governor Thomas Jefferson of Virginia responding to report of British incursions; requests Virginia to help reinforce southern army.

Feb. 16   H breaks with Washington.

Feb. 18   H writes Schuyler from New Windsor describing circumstances of break with Washington.

March 1   H goes to Newport with Washington.

April 30   H resigns officially as aide-de-camp to Washington.

April 30   H writes long letter to Robert Morris urging an "executive ministry," financial reforms, plan for a national bank.

                 Articles of Confederation ratified; executive departments created.

July 12   H publishes first "Continentalist" essay in *The New York Packet and the American Advertiser*, Fishkill, N. Y. Five more issues of "The Continentalist" follow on July 19, August 9, and August 30, 1780, and on April 18 and July 4, 1782.

July 31   At Dobbs Ferry, H is given command of New York and Connecticut light infantry battalion for Yorktown campaign.

Aug. 7   Tories and Indians raid The Pastures, leaving tomahawk scar on stairway bannister.

Oct. 14   H at Yorktown commands and leads bayonet assault on British Redoubt No. 10.

Oct. 19   H, as officer of the day, helps arrange British surrender ceremony at Yorktown.

Dec.   H returns to The Pastures; suffers spells of illness.

1782

Jan. 22   Philip Hamilton, H's eldest son, born.

May 2   H appointed Continental receiver of taxes for New York.

Jan.–July   H studies law in Albany; writes practice manual *Practical Proceedings in the Supreme Court of the State of New York.*

July 21   H urges New York legislature to pass a resolution calling for a general convention of the states to amend the Articles of Confederation.

July 22   H appointed delegate to Continental Congress from New York.

Oct. 30   H resigns as Continental receiver of taxes for New York.

Nov. 25   H takes seat in Continental Congress.

Nov. 30   Preliminary articles of peace treaty signed in Paris.

1783

Jan.–March   H participates in congressional debates for strengthening finances of the Confederation.

Feb. 13   H advises Washington of dangers of troop mutiny and suggests measures to forfend it: "The claims of the army urged with moderation, but with firmness may operate on those weak minds."

March 11   Washington addresses officers and men at Newburgh and regains influence over disaffected members.

June 17   Units of Anthony Wayne's troops mutiny at Lancaster and march on Congress in Philadelphia.

June 19–22   H heads committees of Congress dealing with mutineers and Pennsylvania Executive Council. H recommends removal of Congress to Princeton June 26.

July 16   H leaves Congress in Princeton and returns to The Pastures at Albany to rejoin family.

Nov. 25   British evacuate New York City, and Americans make triumphal entry.

             H takes house at 57 Wall Street and opens law office at No. 56.

Dec. 4   H attends Washington's farewell to his officers in Fraunces Tavern.

1784

Jan. 1   H writes pamphlet "Letter from Phocion to the Considerate Citizens of New York" criticizing the legislature's violation of Articles

IV, V and VI of the peace treaty by refusing to restore confiscated loyalist property and ignoring provision against further confiscations.

Jan. 14   Definitive treaty of peace signed in Paris.

Feb. 24   H attends Bank of New York founders' meeting and draws constitution, charter, and incorporation papers for New York's first bank.

April   "Phocion II" appears.

June 29   H argues case of *Rutgers v. Waddington,* raising question of judicial supremacy of United States law and treaties over state law provisions.

Sept. 25   H's second child, Angelica, born.

Congress makes New York City temporary capital of United States.

1785

Feb. 4   H is founding member of Society for Promoting the Manumission of Slaves, and chairman of a committee to recommend to the society the "line of conduct" to be followed by members in respect of their own slaves. Also, he is to make a register for those who manumit slaves to record the names and identification of manumitted slaves that "the society be the better enabled to detect attempts to deprive such manumitted persons of their liberty."

1786

March   H is elected to New York Assembly.

March 13   H joins petition to New York legislature urging the end of the slave trade, "a commerce so repugnant to humanity, and so inconsistent with the liberality and justice which should distinguish a free and enlightened people."

March 16   H after legislative struggle is named one of six commissioners to meet at Annapolis for the ostensible purpose of framing trade regulations in the general interest.

May 16   Son, Alexander Hamilton, Jr., born.

Sept. 14   H as New York delegate to Annapolis Convention drafts resolution calling for a general convention to enlarge the powers of the federal government.

Nov.   Shays' Rebellion erupts in Western Massachusetts.

1787

Jan. 12	H takes seat in New York State Assembly.
May 25–June 29	H at Constitutional Convention in Philadelphia.
June 18	H holds floor all day prior to vote on Virginia and New Jersey plans in the longest speech delivered at the convention.
Aug. 6	H at Constitutional Convention after a visit to New York.
Sept. 17	Constitution adopted; convention adjourns.
Oct. 27	Publication of H's *The Federalist*, No. 1.

1788

Jan. 22	H reappointed a New York delegate to the Continental Congress.
April 14	Son, James Alexander Hamilton, born.
June 17–July 26	H leads fight for ratification of the Constitution in New York at convention, Poughkeepsie, New York.
July 23	Parade in New York City in support of Constitution with the federal ship *Hamilton* as centerpiece.
July 27	Constitution ratified by New York State.

1789

April 30	George Washington elected president; government organized at New York City, the first capital.
Sept. 11	H appointed secretary of the treasury.
Nov. 5	H with son Philip and Baron von Steuben sees Angelica Church off to England after her summer in New York and weeps.

HAMILTON II
1789–1804

1790

Jan. 14	H sends first "Report on the Public Credit" to Congress.
Feb. 14	Thomas Jefferson accepts appointment as secretary of state.
April 12	H's assumption legislation defeated in the House.
June 20	H, Jefferson, and James Madison make "a deal by candlelight" for assumption and location of national capital; assumption measures pass Congress.

Sept.	H moves to Philadelphia with wife and four children.
Dec. 13	H submits "Second Report on the Public Credit"; leads campaign for assumption measures.

1791

Jan. 28	H submits "Report on the Mint."
Feb. 23	H gives Washington opinion upholding constitutionality of national bank under "implied powers."
May 17–August 25	Jefferson and Madison make trip to New York and New England to hunt the Hessian fly.
July	H begins affair with Maria Reynolds about this time.
Nov. 5	H submits "Report on Manufactures" to House.

1792

March 9	William Duer defaults on payments and is arrested in time of financial panic.
July 25	H writes defense of his policies in newspapers; attacks on Jefferson and Philip Freneau.
Aug. 3	Jefferson writes 21 objections to Hamilton's "system," and Washington refers them to H for reply.
Aug. 10	Suspension of French king.
Aug. 22	Son, John Church Hamilton, born.
Sept. 15	H publishes first "Catullus" paper.
Sept. 21–25	Creation of the French Republic; National Convention replaces legislative assembly; onset of war of the First Coalition of European powers against France.
Dec. 15	James Monroe, Frederick A. C. Muhlenberg, and Abraham Venable confront H with evidence of his affairs with Maria and James Reynolds.
Dec. 27	Congress adopts resolutions to inquire into H's administration of the Treasury.

1793

Jan. 4	H submits report on loans.
Jan. 21	King Louis XVI is executed, a fact that does not become generally known in U.S. until March.
Jan. 23	H is impeached by Giles Resolutions introduced into House.

Feb. 27   Second set of Giles Resolutions is introduced.

March 2   Giles Resolutions defeated.

March 4   Second inauguration of Washington and Adams.

April 7   French declaration of war on Britain, Holland, and Spain becomes known in U.S.

April 8   Citizen Genêt lands at Charleston.

April 22   H advises Washington on Proclamation of Neutrality.

June 21   H tells Washington of intention to resign.

June 29   H publishes first "Pacificus" letter.

July 10   H advises cabinet in crisis of the *Little Democrat.*

July 31   H publishes "No Jacobin" letter revealing Genêt's threat to appeal over the head of the president directly to the people.

August   H and wife, Elizabeth, stricken in yellow fever epidemic in Philadelphia.

Nov.   H helps to raise funds to keep Fenno's *Gazette of the United States* alive.

Dec. 31   Jefferson officially resigns as secretary of state.

1794

Jan. 6–13   H drafts presidential message on Genêt's diplomatic status.

Jan. 14   H advises Washington on request to king of Prussia for release of Marquis de Lafayette from prison.

Jan. 31   H publishes "Americanus," No. 1, urging neutrality in dealings with France.

March 8   H recommends that Washington fortify ports and raise troops in preparation for hostilities with Britain.

March 18   H submits report to House on all receipts and expenditures from commencement of government through 1793.

April 23   After withdrawing his own name from consideration for appointment, H urges John Jay for special mission to Britain and writes detailed instructions for Jay.

1795

Jan. 31   H resigns as secretary of the treasury; returns to New York law practice.

March	After this time H works on complicated law cases involving debts of Robert Morris to H, to John B. Church, to William Pulteney, William Hornby, and others.
April 13	H writes Robert Troup, "It has been the rule of my life to do nothing for my own emolument *under cover* . . . it is pride. But this pride makes it part of my plan to *appear truly what I am.*"
June 24	Jay's Treaty approved by U.S. Senate.
July 18	H is stoned by a Wall Street mob.
July 22	H publishes first of 38 articles entitled "The Defense" and signed Camillus in defense of Jay's Treaty.
July 25	H writes Robert Troup concerning his will.
July 27	H publishes "Philo Camillus," No. I.
July 30	H writes essay "Defense of the Funding System."
July	H publishes "Horatius II" essay in defense of Jay's Treaty.
August	Edmund Randolph is forced to resign as secretary of state after suspicious financial dealings with French minister.
Oct. 16	H advises Washington concerning treatment to be given to Lafayette's son in U.S.
Oct. 26	H defends Washington against newspaper charges that he has overdrawn his pay and allowances.
Nov. 28	H drafts Washington's Seventh Annual Address to Congress.
Dec.	H writes essay attacking "American Jacobins."

1796

Feb. 24	H argues in support of carriage tax in U.S. Supreme Court.
March 3	Thomas Pinckney's Spanish Treaty approved by Senate.
April 30	House votes provisions necessary to carry Jay's Treaty into effect.
May 15–August 25	H drafts Washington's Farewell Address, delivered September 19, followed by active presidential campaign.
Nov. 10	H drafts Washington's Eighth Annual Message to Congress, calling for a national university, a military academy, and a board of agriculture.
Dec. 5	Electors meet and elect Adams president, Jefferson vice-president.
Dec. 8	H publishes "The Answer," signed Americanus, to rebut Adet's criticisms of American policy toward France.

1797

Jan. 27   H publishes "The Warning," signed Americanus, first of six essays setting forth his view of Franco-American relations.

March 4   Adams and Jefferson inaugurated.

1797

June 20   Adams appoints Elbridge Gerry to serve with Charles C. Pinckney and John Marshall on mission to France.

July 5   H discloses his 1791–1792 liaison with Mrs. James Reynolds and begins quarrel with Monroe.

July   H buys house at No. 58 Partition Street, New York, N. Y.

August 4   Son, William Stephen Hamilton, born.

August 25   H publishes "Reynolds Pamphlet."

1798

March 30   H publishes "The Stand," signed Titus Manlius, attacking the Paris Directory.

April 3   Adams reports XYZ Affair to House.

June 25–
July 14   Alien and Sedition Acts approved. H is critical of them.

July 25   H appointed inspector general of the army with rank of major general.

July   Quasi war with France has been going on for some time.

1799

March 16   H gives orders for suppression of Fries's rebellion.

June 3   Death of H's father, James Hamilton, on St. Vincent, British West Indies.

Oct.   Adams, overriding cabinet recommendations, orders commissioners to France.

Oct. 1   Francisco Miranda letter proposes expedition for liberation of Spanish colonies.

Nov. 9   Napoleon overthrows Directory in coup and installs Consulate with himself as first consul.

Nov. 20   Daughter, Eliza Hamilton, born.

Dec. 19   George Washington dies at Mount Vernon.

1800

May 6   Adams discovers H's influence on his cabinet and demands McHenry's resignation.

May 7   H requests Jay to revise method of choosing electors to reverse Federalist New York election defeat by Republicans.

July 1   H resigns as inspector general after disbanding troops.

Oct. 3   Treaty of Mortefontaine ends Quasi-War with France.

Oct. 22   H publishes attack on John Adams in Bache's *Aurora* and elsewhere.

Nov.   H supports Federalists John Adams and Charles C. Pinckney in election campaign against Jefferson and Burr.

Dec. 16   H supports Jefferson over Burr after electoral tie.

December   Capital moved to District of Columbia.

1801

Jan. 15   Federalists in caucus decide to support Burr over Jefferson.

Jan. 16   H writes Bayard, characterizing Jefferson.

Jan. 24   Senate approves nomination of John Marshall as chief justice.

Feb. 17   H is instrumental in Jefferson's election over Burr on thirty-sixth tie-breaking ballot in House.

July 1   H plans house for Grange.

Nov. 16   H founds *The New York Evening Post*.

Nov. 23   H's eldest son, Philip, mortally wounded in duel with George Eacker, a supporter of Aaron Burr.

Dec. 17   H publishes first of 18 installments of "The Examination," attacking Jefferson's program, as "a performance which . . . makes a prodigal sacrifice of constitutional energy, of sound principle, and of public interest to the popularity of one man."

Dec. 19   Senate approves treaty with France.

1802

Feb. 27   H writes Gouverneur Morris "Mine is an odd destiny" letter.

April 16–18   H advises Federalists to adopt Republican methods to achieve goals, including establishment of the Christian Constitutional Society.

Dec. 29   Hamiltons move into Grange and H writes Charles C. Pinckney "A garden, you know, is a very usual refuge of a disappointed politician."

1803

Feb. 24   Supreme Court issues decision in *Marbury v. Madison*.

April 30   Treaty ceding Louisiana to United States signed in Paris.

1804

Feb. 13   H argues in defense of freedom of the press in *People v. Croswell*.

April   H opposes separatist movement threatened by New England.

April 25   Burr defeated in New York gubernatorial election.

July 11   H mortally wounded in duel with Burr at Weehawken.

July 12   H dies at house of William Bayard, New York City.

July 14   H buried in Trinity Churchyard, New York City, with full military honors.

A NOTE ABOUT SOURCES, NOTES, AND BIBLIOGRAPHY

The principal source for this book that was not available to earlier Hamilton biographers is *The Papers of Alexander Hamilton*, Volumes I through VI, of which Harold C. Syrett is the editor and Jacob E. Cooke the associate editor and which was published by Columbia University Press (Volumes I and II in 1961 and Volumes III, IV, V, and VI in 1962). These are referred to herein as the Hamilton Papers, or PAH. The other important source that has become available only recently is *The Law Practice of Alexander Hamilton*, Volumes I and II, edited by Julius Goebel, Jr., and published by Columbia University Press (Volume I in 1964 and Volume II in 1969), herein referred to as the Hamilton Law Papers, or LPAH.

All significant letters and other documents written by Hamilton, all significant letters and other documents written by others to him, and all other significant documents that directly concern him (commissions, certificates, and so on) for the years covered by *Hamilton I* (1757–1789), are printed in chronological order in Volumes I through VI of the Hamilton Papers.

The Hamilton Papers and the Hamilton Law Papers relate back and refer to the principal earlier sources of Hamilton material. These include John C. Hamilton's *Life of Alexander Hamilton*, Volume I, New York, 1834, and Volume II, Philadelphia, 1840 (Hamilton, *Life*); his *Life of Alexander Hamilton, A History of the United States as Traced in the Writings of Alexander Hamilton and His Contemporaries*, seven volumes, 1857–1864 (Hamilton, *History*); and his *The Works of Alexander Hamilton*, edited by John C. Hamilton, New York 1851 (JCHW); Allan McLane Hamilton's *The Intimate Life of Alexander Hamilton*, New York, 1910 (Hamilton, *Intimate Life*); and other printed sources of primary importance, as well as to the manuscripts or printed or other sources reprinted in such works. The Hamilton Papers and Hamilton Law Papers also refer to other primary and some important secondary sources, including John C. Fitzpatrick's *Calendar of the Correspondence of George Washington, Commander in Chief of the Continental Army, with the Officers*, Washington, D.C., 1915 (Fitzpatrick, *Calendar*); his *The Writings of George Washington*, Washington, D.C., 1931–1944, edited by John C. Fitzpatrick (GW); Broadus Mitchell's *Alexander Hamilton, Youth to Maturity, 1755–1788*, New York, 1957 (Mitchell, *Hamilton*), the first volume of the best two-volume biography —its 465-page text is buttressed by 180 pages of notes—and John C. Miller's *Alexander Hamilton, A Portrait in Paradox*, New York, 1959 (Miller, *Hamilton*), the best one-volume biography.

My debt to the scholars who produced these works as well as to the writers and editors of the other books listed in my bibliography is great.

Annotations and commentary in the Hamilton Papers and the Hamilton Law Papers give full information concerning the nature and location of each Hamilton document reproduced. They tell whether it is an autograph document, whether signed or a draft or a letter book copy or taken from a printed source, and so forth; identify Hamilton's correspondent and the individuals mentioned in the text, explain events and ideas referred to in the text, cross-reference to related documents and events, point out textual variations and mistakes, inform whether the original is cropped or has been mutilated or bowdlerized in an earlier edition, and supply historical background material. In the case of some important documents, both Hamilton's first draft and final version are reproduced.

Routine letters and documents by Hamilton, routine letters to Hamilton, most letters and documents written by Hamilton for someone else (such as the letters he wrote for Washington as his aide-de-camp), letters and documents that have not been found but that are known to have existed, letters and documents erroneously attributed to Hamilton, and letters that deal exclusively with his legal practice have been chronologically calendared in the Hamilton Papers and, where possible, a citation is given to another source for the full text of the document and other information about it. The list of "Short titles and abbreviations" in each Hamilton Papers volume serves as a limited bibliography for source material, and each volume also contains an exhaustive index to names of persons, places, events, and other things.

In *Hamilton I* (1757–1789) and in *Hamilton II* (1789–1804), which is shortly to follow, nothing is presented as fact that I have invented or that lacks a basis in documentary evidence. Where documentary evidence is conflicting or admits of more than one interpretation, I have usually resolved doubts in the manner more fully explained in Chapter 1 of *Hamilton I* consistently with my view of Hamilton as a flawed hero. In the few instances where surmises or suppositions of fact are presented—as in Chapter 11 on the subject of the place where

Elizabeth Schuyler and Hamilton first met—they are indicated to be such. For unconvincing inferences, implications, insights, conclusions, and opinions, I assume full responsibility.

When one considers the comprehensive and authoritative quality of the Hamilton Papers and other accessible source material mentioned above and in my bibliography, it has become more and more apparent to me as I have proceeded that a full apparatus of footnotes, source notes, citations, and so forth here, although perhaps impressive-looking to nonscholars, would provide specialists with little or nothing not readily available to them in more complete form elsewhere. Yet for the nonspecialist reader such an apparatus would increase the bulk, weight, and cost of the book and might needlessly impede or break the stride of the story of Hamilton's rise. Accordingly, in lieu of such an apparatus I have given or indicated in the text the dates of documents, events, and actions with more frequency than is usual in books of this kind and have supplied a brief set of chapter notes at the end.

If further information is desired about a document, name, place, event, or other thing mentioned in the text, the reader should first refer to the volume of the Hamilton Papers covering its time period; turn to the date in that volume; read and follow up the references found there; and then look up the related names, places, events, and things in the volume index. Volume I covers 1768 through 1778; II covers 1779 through 1781; III, 1782 through 1786; IV, 1787 through May 1788; V, June 1788 through November 1789; and VI, December 1789 through August 1790.

The Hamilton Legal Papers are not arranged chronologically, but by legal topics. Volume I contains practice and procedure, war cases, interstate boundary disputes, and criminal cases. Volume II contains commercial transactions, maritime affairs, and admiralty and maritime jurisdiction. The indexes of these volumes are complete and will quickly bring the reader to almost any Hamilton document, name, place, thing, or case he seeks.

If still more information is desired, the books and articles listed in the bibliography and the bibliographies and indexes contained in them may be consulted. The period and subject matter are all but inexhaustible.

NOTES

FOREWORD: THE GRANGE AND MONTICELLO

[1] Page xi Clinton Rossiter, *Alexander Hamilton and the Constitution*, 4: "Almost lost from view (except by a handful of spiritual and flesh-and-blood descendants) in the first half of the nineteenth century, taken up thereafter by historians and statesmen who were busy grinding right-handed axes, portrayed too conveniently in the mythology of democracy as the spoiler of the dreams of the faultless Jefferson, Hamilton has never been given a full and fair shake by most of the men who write American history or most of those who teach it to our children. In these years of crisis, to be sure, we have all become tougher and braver, more open-eyed and less sentimental—in a word, more Hamiltonian and he has been granted a new measure of respect. . . . he remains the one important Founding Father about whom it is considered bad form to be too enthusiastic."

[2] Page xi The Marquis de Talleyrand-Périgord is supposed to have said, "I consider Napoleon, Pitt and Hamilton as the three greatest men of our age, and if I had to choose among the three, I would without hesitation give the first place to Hamilton." (*Étude sur la république des États-Unis d'Amérique in New York* (1876), 192; Duc de Broglie, ed., *Memoirs of the Prince de Talleyrand* (New York, 1891, I, 181–187).)

[3] Page xii Rossiter, *Constitution*, p. 259, note 1. Authority for the durability of the Manichean view of the struggle between Jefferson and Hamilton is found in Malone, *Jefferson;* Bowers, *Jefferson and Hamilton;* and the poem "Hamil-

ton" in Rosemary and Stephen Vincent Benét, *A Book of Americans*, (New York, 1933), pp. 42–43, which begins:

> Jefferson said, "the many!"
> Hamilton said, "the few!"
> Like opposite sides of a penny
> Were these exalted two.

[4] Page xii For a recent account of Hamilton and his family at The Grange, see Eric Sloane and Edward Anthony, *Mr. Daniels and The Grange* New York: Funk & Wagnalls, 1968.

For the best account of the building of The Grange and family life there, see Allan McLane Hamilton, *The Intimate Life of Alexander Hamilton*, pp. 348, 350, 404, 414, 444.

[5] Page xii See section "The Marketing Orientation" from *Character, from Man for Himself: An Inquiry into the Psychology of Ethics* by Erich Fromm, reprinted in *An Outline of Psychoanalysis* New York: The Modern Library, 1955, pp. 349, 351: "One experienced oneself as a commodity or rather simultaneously as the seller and the commodity to be sold. A person is not concerned for his life and happiness but with becoming salable." See also Fromm, *Character*, p. 339: "The behavior trait covers numerous and entirely different character traits. Courageous behavior may be motivated by ambition so that a person will risk his life in certain situations in order to satisfy his craving for being admired; it may be motivated by suicidal impulses which drive a person to seek danger because, consciously or unconsciously, he doesn't value his life and wants to destroy himself; it may be motivated by sheer lack of imagination so that a person acts courageously because he is not aware of the danger awaiting him; finally, it may be determined by genuine devotion to the idea or aim for which a person acts, a motivation which is conventionally assumed to be the basis of courage."

[6] Page xiii The best biographies of Hamilton are *Alexander Hamilton: A Biography in His Own Words*, ed. by Mary-Jo Kline; Broadus Mitchell, *Alexander Hamilton*, two volumes, the most thoroughly documented and accurate account of Hamilton's life; John C. Miller, *Alexander Hamilton, Portrait in Paradox* (New York, 1959), the best one-volume life.

Notes for Chapter 1
RESTLESS LOVE IN THE LESSER ANTILLES

[1] Page 1 Hamilton, *Life*, p. 1.

[2] Page 1 The reference is to Gertrude Atherton, *The Conqueror*, and also to *Adventures*, and *Letters*.

[3] Page 1 For crumbling state of documentary evidence, see Mitchell, *Hamilton*, I, p. 471, note 29: "Ramsing said record, on last page of protocol, crumbled between time he noted it, 1902 and 1936, when he wanted to refer to it again."

See also Mitchell, *Hamilton*, I, Chapter I, pp. 1–14, and his Notes to Chapter I, pp. 468–477, for most complete account of state of available evidence.

[4] Page 2 All accounts of Hamilton's origin, forbears, and early environment in the West Indies, including Gertrude Atherton's, are based on information in the monograph by H. U. Ramsing, *Alexander Hamilton og hans modrene sloegt Tidsbillider fra Dansk Vest—Indies Barndom*, English translation by Solvejg Vahl (microfilm in New York Public Library). The account in this chapter is based on a new translation made for me by Inger Marie Hansen and Vibeke Jensen of the Danish Consulate in New York.

Statement that the probate court document of 1768 is the first extant document in which Hamilton is mentioned is disputed by George Bancroft, *History of the United States* (Boston, 1858), VII, 79, and Henry Cabot Lodge, *Alexander Hamilton* (Boston, 1899), 283–285. Both refer to an earlier document dated 1766, of which Bancroft states: "The first written trace of [Hamilton's] existence is in 1766, when his name appears as a witness to a legal paper executed in the Danish island of Santa Cruz." In PAH I, note, p. 3, it is stated that this document has not been found.

[5] Page 5 For topography of Nevis and Charlestown, 2 *Caribbeana* 6; for island records, see 2 *Caribbeana* 55, 269, 270, 328; 3 *Caribbeana* 78, 80, 216, 220 ff.

[6] Page 5 There were about 73 families in the parish as reported by Henry Pope, rector of St. George's Church, Gingerland Parish, Nevis, 3 *Caribbeana*, 216; 2 *Caribbeana*, 269.

[7] Page 6 John Adams, filled with a sense of unredressed wrong, sneered at Hamilton in private letters as "the bastard brat of a Scotch pedlar," Adams to Jefferson, July 12, 1813; *Historical Magazine*, July 1870. James T. Callender, the journalist, referred to him in public print as "the son of a camp girl" in *The Prospect Before Us*, I (1800), p. 82.

[8] Page 6 For the ancestry of James Hamilton, see Atherton, *Conqueror*, p. 537; James Paterson, 2 *History of Ayrshire*, 201–203; James A. Hamilton, *Reminiscences*, 302.

[9] Page 6 For a history of the British West Indies, see *The United States Magazine*, I (Philadelphia, 1779), 81–83; W. C. Westergaard, *The Danish West Indies under Company Rule* (New York, 1917), pp. 222, 227, 236, 250, 253; F. W. Pitman, *The Development of the British West Indies* (New Haven, 1917),

pp. 28–282, 313, 316; Bryan Edwards, *The History, Civil and Commercial, of the British Colonies in The West Indies* (Philadelphia, 1805), II, 184.

[10] Page 7 See Mitchell, *Hamilton,* I, 4–5.

[11] Page 8 The will of Dr. John Fawcett recorded on St. Croix, found by Mitchell in Notarialprotocol, f. St. Croix, M. 316, f. 15 Rigsarkivet, that is, Danish National Archives, Copenhagen. Mitchell states that "Protocol is moldering, but the fragment of will is doubtless a piece of f. 15, as there are four leaves between that and first, where folio number, 20, is preserved." Mitchell concludes that Dr. Fawcett's will was executed on Nevis because Robert Huggins, Jr., one of the witnesses, with Joseph Burke, was a planter on Nevis. Mitchell, *Hamilton I,* p. 470–71, note 21.

[12] Page 12 Allegations that Negro blood flowed in Rachel's veins may be found: Buell Gallagher, *Color and Conscience,* 125 n; M. R. Davie, *Negroes in American Society,* 391.

[13] Page 15 For another recent account, see Dorothie Bobbe, "The Boyhood of Alexander Hamilton," 6 *American Heritage,* number 4 (June 1955), p. 4.

[14] Page 15 Mitchell, *Hamilton,* I, pp. 477–478, notes 2 and 3, speculates that the cottage at Number 23 Company's Lane, Christiansted, St. Croix, may be the one that Rachel occupied.

Notes for Chapter 2
ISLAND PROPAEDEUTICS:
MR. CRUGER'S COUNTINGHOUSE
AND DR. KNOX'S PRESCRIPTS

[1] Page 20 For history of St. Croix, see Florence Lewisohn, *St. Croix Under Seven Flags.* See also Hans West, *Beyträge zur Beschreibung von St. Croix* (translated from Danish; Copenhagen, 1794, 274 pages, New York Public Library), which describes life on St. Croix and nearby islands during period shortly after Hamilton's departure.

[2] Page 22 Little is known of the history of Hamilton's older brother, James. Both Alexander and James were living with Rachel in 1767. Alexander wrote a letter to James in June 1783 offering to help him by settling him on a farm, but no more is heard of him thereafter. Ramsing speculates that he had died by 1786 (pp. 249–250).

Reference to Hamilton's knowledge of Hebrew Decalogue appears in Hamilton's *Life,* I, 3.

[3] Page 22 Nicholas Cruger was born in New York 1743 died in St. Croix 1801. Hamilton's employer and patron, he had close family and business ties with New York City. He was of the third generation of merchants, his grandfather being John Cruger, an immigrant who began business in New York as a merchant shipper in 1700 and became alderman and later mayor. He was German, had lived in England before he came to America, and married the eldest daughter of Hendrick Cuyler of Albany, who was Dutch. Their sons, Tileman and Henry, went as merchants to the Caribbean, and Henry afterwards settled in England. The younger son, John, was mayor of New York, speaker of the assembly, delegate to the Stamp Act Congress of 1765, and a founder and first president (1768–1770) of the New York Chamber of Commerce. Nicholas Cruger was the fourth and youngest son of Henry. He married Anna N. De Nully, daughter of town captain Bertram Pieter De Nully and his wife, Catherine, on April 15, 1772, six months before Hamilton left Cruger's employ for America. On the Cruger family generally, see Delancey, *New York Genealogical and Biographical Record* (April 1785). In January 1784 Nicholas Cruger gave "a violent beating in the street" to James Rivington, claiming that during the war, when he had been a prisoner in New York, the Tory printer had published aspersions against him (letter of Benjamin Walker to Frederick W. von Steuben, January 12, 1783, 10 Steuben Papers NYHS).

[4] Page 28 For an account of Hugh Knox, see Mitchell, *Hamilton*, I, 31 ff., and Mitchell, "The Man Who Discovered Hamilton," 69 *New Jersey Historical Society Proceedings*, 88–114.

Notes for Chapter 3
THE IMPORTANCE OF STRICT COLLEGE ENTRANCE REQUIREMENTS

[1] Page 41 On John Rodgers, see Miller, *Rodgers*. For accounts of Hamilton's early years by his friends Hercules Mulligan and Robert Troup, see 4, *William and Mary Quarterly*, 3d Series (1947), pp. 205 ff.

[2] Page 43 For information about William Livingston, see Sedgwick, *Livingston*. For information about Elizabethtown, New Jersey, see Murray, *Notes Concerning Elizabethtown* (ed. 1941), p. 75.

[3] Page 45 Boudinot, Rodgers, and others were founders of the American Society for Promoting Religious Knowledge among the Poor in British Colonies. This was the forerunner of the American Bible Society, of which Boudinot was the first president.

[4] Page 51 Many Tory pamphlets were credited to President Myles Cooper. Philip Freneau is supposed to have written "last words, dying speech, and

confession of J–S R–G–N [James Rivington] . . . supposed . . . written by himself
. . . the night preceding . . . his execution" (in effigy):

> Behold grim Pluto from the infernal plains,
> See how he drags with him my massy chain . . .
> My reverend friends! O Cooper! Where art thou
> No Seabury, Chandler to assist me now!

[5] Page 54 For the jurisprudential basis of Hamilton's arguments for revolution, see Charles F. Mullett, *Fundamental Law and the American Revolution* (New York, 1933).

[6] Page 54 For New York at the time of the Revolution, see Jones, *History*.

[7] Page 54 For Hamilton's speechmaking ability, see Ally, *Rhetoric*.

[8] Page 54 For information about Samuel Seabury, see Beardsley, *Seabury;* Cross, *Anglican Episcopate and American Colonies*.

[9] Page 55 Controversy between Tories and Whigs prior to the Revolution conducted in pamphlets was widely argued by public exchanges. See Myles Cooper's "Friendly Address . . . on . . . Our Political Confusions," answered by Phillip Livingston's "The Other Side of the Question," both 1774; Charles Lee's "Strictures on . . . a Friendly Address, 1775" and "The General Attacked by a Subaltern," *American Querist* (1774), attributed to Cooper.

During this period of mob violence there were a number of attacks on loyalists and loyalist sympathizers. In Hercules Mulligan's account, Mulligan described Dr. Cooper as follows: "Dr. Cooper was a Tory and an obnoxious man and the mob went to the college with the intention of tarring and feathering him or riding him upon a rail." However, Robert Troup and Hamilton feared that something worse might happen, "that if Dr. Cooper should be taken hold of by the mob his life would be endangered; as he was a most obnoxious Tory."

Notes for Chapter 4
TO FREE THE SLAVES HELD THRALL BY THE *ASIA*'S GUNS

[1] Page 57 For Hamilton's intervention with another mob, see Hamilton, *Life*, I, 38, describing his interposition with the "Travis mob in behalf of Ralph Thurman who was threatened by his fellow merchant Robert Harding for sending military supplies to General Gage during the siege of Boston."

[2] Page 87 There are numerous accounts of the *Asia*'s broadside on New York. See Bliven, *Guns*, 36, 37; Hamilton, *Life*, I, 48.

[3] Page 88 For an account of Isaac Sears's raid, see Dawson, *Westchester During the American Revolution*, 136–139.

John Jay reacted to the raid on Rivington just as Hamilton did. On November 26, 1775, Jay wrote Nathaniel Woodhull, president of the New York Provincial Congress, that "I think [the raid] neither argues wisdom nor bravery, if it was to have been done, I wish our own people, and not strangers had taken the liberty of doing it." (I *Journal of the New York Provincial Congress*, 218; Johnston, I *Correspondence of John Jay*, 41)

Notes for Chapter 5
COVERING THE BEATEN RETREAT OF AN ESSENTIAL AEGIS TO BE

[1] Page 92 St. George's Chapel of Ease, Trinity Parish, built 1748–1752, was notable for its high steeple and stood on the northwest corner of Beekman and Cliff Streets (4 Stokes 633–634). A song of the title "Hearts of Oak" was a favorite during the Revolution and may have been one that Hamilton later sang to his family. Hamilton, *Life*, I, 47; Hamilton, *History*, I, 99.

[2] Page 93 Commissions to officers in New York companies for Continental service were conditional on recruiting 72 men. Until then, warrants for recruiting, not commissions, were issued. (15 *N.Y. Col. Docs.*, 11–12; cf. 18, 94; cf. Graydon, *Memoirs*, 117–118.)

[3] Page 94 In 1775 the state of New York loaned the Continental Army six brass fieldpieces (six pounders), which were delivered to Captains Hamilton and Sebastian Baumann; later they were returned (cf. Washington to Governor George Clinton, June 13, 1779, 15 *GW*, 276. In their accounts, Mulligan (pp. 214–215) and Troup (p. 210) described the zeal with which Hamilton trained his men.

[4] Page 96 John Little, of Hamilton's company, was sentenced by court-martial to 39 lashes for abusing and striking adjutant Henley. (6 *GW*, 37, September 8, 1776.)

[5] Page 98 Bayard's Hill Redoubt was also known as Independence Battery and Montgomery's Hill and Bunkers' Hill.

[6] Page 101 Hamilton's son described the Battle of Long Island and Washington's withdrawal across the East River, adding that Hamilton "brought up the rear, having lost his baggage and a field piece." Hamilton, *Life*, I, p. 54.

⁷ Page 101 A council of Washington's general officers on August 29 agreed to leave Long Island. (5 *GW,* 496, 508–509.) Washington informed the New York legislature of the unanimous advice of his council of war "to give up Long Island; and not, by dividing our force, be unable to resist the enemy in any one point of attack." (5 *GW,* 498–499, 502, 506–508.)

For an account of retreat northwards, see Livingston, *Putnam,* 311, and Humphreys, *Putnam,* 120–121.

⁸ Page 105 Hamilton's paybook indicates that his artillery company was at Kings Ferry, North Castle, Peekskill, and on his way there he would have been at White Plains. Hamilton's son says only that "at the Battle of White Plains . . . his conduct was remarked." (Hamilton, *Life,* I, 56)

Notes for Chapter 6
HEADQUARTERS INTELLIGENCER

¹ Page 118 Hamilton probably served as an acting aide to Washington prior to his official appointment and commission. He suffered a lengthy period of sickness at Morristown, and this may have given him time to do the extensive reading that is reflected in the notes he jotted down in the back of his paybook of the New York Artillery Company. PAH I, 373–411. The quotations show that the principal books he read were Malachy Postlethwayt's *The Universal Dictionary of Trade and Commerce,* "translated from the French of Monsieur [Jacques] Savary [des Bluons] with large additions and improvements," London, Volume I (1751), 1017 pages and Volume II (1755), 356 pages, both volumes with tables and maps. During this period he also apparently read extensively and jotted down excerpts from Plutarch's *Lives* and Demosthenes' *Orations.* Postlethwayt particularly provided Hamilton with systematic discussion, facts, and examples relating to areas of national geography, economy, products, agriculture, manufacturing, mining, shipping, and fisheries. Hamilton analyzed what he read and set down critical observations on certain of Postlethwayt's generalizations.

² Page 121 For accounts of informal life of aides at headquarters, see Graydon, *Memoirs,* 275–277.

³ Page 126 The New York Committee of Correspondence consisted of Gouverneur Morris, Robert R. Livingston, and William Allison. The New York Provincial Convention authorized designation of a person at headquarters to send them intelligence on March 13, 1777 (I *Journals of the Continental Congress,* 835), and Hamilton accepted.

⁴ Page 131 For Hamilton's toast after supper at headquarters in 1780, see Chastellux, *Travels,* 67–68.

Notes for Chapter 7
THE IDOL OF AMERICA GOVERNED BY
BY ONE OF HIS AIDES

[1] Page 140 For discussion of reasons for New Englanders' antipathy to Schuyler, see Hamilton, *History*, I, 225.

[2] Page 144 For Enoch Anderson's recollections, "Personal Recollections," 26 *Papers Historical Society of Delaware*, 44; for accounts of the Battle at Germantown, see Lee I *Southern Department*, 28–29.

[3] Page 147 For Adams's exclamation, Charles Francis Adams, 1 *Life of John Adams*, 267; John Adams 2 *Diary*, 439.

[4] Page 148 Hamilton took pride in his efforts to prepare Philadelphia citizens for the invaders and to requisition supplies for the army. (Hamilton, *History*, I, 284.)

[5] Page 153 Washington knew that he had enemies scheming against him, as he indicated writing on Gates to Lafayette, December 31, 1777 (10 *GW*, 236–237) and that Conway was involved, that "a malignant faction . . . for some time forming to my prejudice" to Henry Laurens, January 31, 1778 (10 *GW*, 410) and to Patrick Henry that "General Gates was to be exalted on the ruin of my reputation and influence," March 28, 1778 (11 *GW*, 164).

Note for Chapter 9
MISBEHAVIOR AT MONMOUTH

[1] Page 200 For account of the trial, see "Proceedings of a General Court-Martial . . . for Trial of Major General Lee, 1778," p. 66, for Hamilton's testimony. In Hamilton, *History*, I, 473, his son says that Hamilton had gone forward with Lafayette "before break of day." In the court-martial proceedings (pp. 12, 13, and 22), the testimony of Lafayette, Colonel David Forman, John Laurens, and others supported Hamilton's testimony that Washington had intended an attack, which Lee failed to make. A review of the evidence at the trial is contained in Stryker-Myers, *Monmouth*, 188–192.

Notes for Chapter 10
EMANCIPATION—OR A GOLDEN CHAIN?

[1] Page 220 Beginning in 1779, army headquarters made secret preparations for a punitive march into Indian country. Washington would have preferred

Schuyler to command the expedition (14 *GW*, 198–201, March 1779), but asked Gates instead, who refused.

[2] Page 225 During the spring and summer of 1779, public clamor was reflected in newspaper accounts demanding measures to stop inflation and issuance of printing press money. (Burnett, *Continental Congress*, 410–411.)

For a critical analysis of Hamilton's stature as an economist and his knowledge of classical economics, see Sumner, pp. 108 and 110–113, and C. F. Dunbar, "Some Precedents Followed by Hamilton," in *Economic Essays*, edited by O. M. W. Sprague. Hamilton's insight that "the fundamental defect is a want of power in Congress" is cited by Broadus Mitchell as announcing the historic division between adherents of liberal or "loose" construction and adherents of "strict" construction of the Constitution, between advocates of retaining local powers and of central authority in government and between partisans of states' rights and partisans of nationalism.

Notes for Chapter 11
ELIZABETH SCHUYLER COMES TO MORRISTOWN

[1] Page 246 The Schuyler mansion was built in 1760–1762. It is a large foursquare house in the Georgian style of orange brick on top of a hill looking eastward toward the Hudson. It was originally surrounded by a large yard, farm buildings, and a 90-acre farm. An account of life in the Schuyler mansion is given in Baroness Riedesel, *Letters and Journals*, 134–136; Riedesel, *Memoirs*, I, 171, 211, 214; Chastellux, *Travels*, 371.

[2] Page 251 On January 15, 1780, Hamilton was a member of Lord Stirling's party, which crossed to Staten Island over the ice with 2,500 troops. Hamilton had warned of a stone house that the British defenders of Staten Island would turn into a fort. Reinforcements from New York relieved the British defenders, and the Americans returned to the mainland and Morristown with no success. See Hamilton, *History*, II, 5, and Duer, *Stirling*, 206. Writing to George Washington from Crane's Mills, New Jersey, the day before the attack, Hamilton predicted unsuccess. The artillery was insufficient, and the stone house proved a formidable defense. Hamilton lost another horse in the attack, writing Nathanael Greene on January 22, 1780, that "the horse I borrowed of you the other day giving out while we were on Staten Island, my servant exchanged him there for another. The one he took in lieu of him I now return. I believe the public will lose nothing by the exchange." His letter of January 1780 to Catharine Livingston and Elizabeth Schuyler may have owed its vagueness to his efforts to create a cover story for the attack on Staten Island rather than for his date with Cornelia Lott.

Note for Chapter 12
TREASON!

[1] Page 271 The way the plan to capture Washington was to have worked was that when Washington returned with his aides from Hartford and the meeting with Rochambeau and lodged at the Beverly Robinson house, Robinson would collect a party of armed troops from the *Vulture*, lead them to his own house —Arnold's headquarters—and capture the entire top command of the American army before they moved on to West Point. Immediately thereafter, West Point would be attacked.

Notes for Chapter 13
RECONCILED TO HIS BEING SHOT,
BUT NOT TO HIS BEING HANGED

[1] Page 280 For an account of the trial, see Dawson, *Trial of Smith*, 20 ff.; for Joshua Hett Smith's version of the trial, see Joshua Hett Smith, *Narrative of Death of Major André* (London 1808), 133.

[2] Page 284 The inn that became André's prison during the week before his execution on October 2, 1780, is described in Heusser, *Footsteps.*

[3] Page 287 For listing of conflicting authorities on whether or not Hamilton wrote the "AB" letter, see Mitchell, *Hamilton*, I, 563–564.

Note for Chapter 14
I AM NO LONGER A MEMBER OF THE
GENERAL'S FAMILY

[1] Page 298 Washington agreed with Hamilton's position that an aide was eligible for a field command. Washington wrote to the Board of War that "it is clearly my opinion, that those appointed before the 27th May, 1778 and now in service as aides, and who are not admissible into any state line, are eligible to command . . ." otherwise, "the rank given these officers would be a mere sound" and meaningless. January 15, 1780, 17 *GW*, 402–404.

Notes for Chapter 18
FORFENDING MUTINEERS

[1] Page 377 For an account of the events at the end of 1782 and the beginning of 1783 that came together to burden the Continental Congress, see Mitchell,

Hamilton, I, 293 ff. These events included the official news that Great Britain had commissioned Richard Oswald to conclude peace with the "13 United States of America," that the deputation to Rhode Island to appeal to her legislature to supply reliable funds for Congress had failed, and that Virginia had retracted its consent to the impost. On December 29 the delegation from the army made fresh demands for pay. They circulated among members of the Congress, preparing them for the memorial drawn by General Henry Knox and a dozen other officers. The committee from camp at Newburgh consisted of General Alexander McDougall and Colonels Mathias Ogden and John Brooks. Robert Morris had overdrawn the funds borrowed in Europe to the extent of 3,500,000 livres. The only hope was that France might stand behind further Continental drafts.

[2] Page 389 In February 1783 James Madison wrote Edmund Randolph in cipher that "the arms which have secured the liberties of this country will not be laid down until justice is secured to those who have wielded them and that dangerous convulsions would be hazarded by orders for that purpose." (7 Burnett, 44.) Hamilton drew up the resolutions of Congress thanking Washington for "his prudence and attachment to the welfare of the community" in resisting the attempts to create disturbances in the army and praising the officers for their patriotism (24 *Journals of the Continental Congress,* 306 n.).

Note for Chapter 19
JUDICIAL SUPREMACY

[1] Page 411 A revealing insight into the press of Hamilton's legal business is gained from his letter to Gouverneur Morris of March 21, 1784, in which he explains that his inattention to a particular client was "owing to the continual hurry in which my engagements for a long time past, have kept me. . . ." He had been "out of town on indispensable business. In the intervals I have been occupied about objects of immediate and absolute necessity, which could not have been delayed without letting my business run into utter confusion." See letter of November 8, 1785, to John Wilkes.

Note for Chapter 21
AN INVISIBLE HAND GUIDED ALL
TOWARD THE GENERAL GOOD

[1] Page 474 Commenting on Hamilton's speech at the Constitutional Convention on June 18, Gouverneur Morris noted that he "promoted the views of his opponents, who, with the fondness for wealth and power which he had not, affected a love for the people which he had and . . . they had not." 2 *Diary and Letters of Gouverneur Morris,* 525–526.

Note for Chapter 23
THE FEDERALIST PAPERS AND OTHER
POUGHKEEPSIE PERSUADERS

[1] Page 523 Nicholas Power, publisher of the *Country Journal and Pough-keepsie Advertiser,* July 5, No. 154, struck off an "extra" giving the form of Virginia's ratification. A week after Virginia's action on June 25, bells began ringing at dawn in New York City, a salute was fired from ten 24-pounders at sunrise, and at night bonfires were lit. William Duer was the orator at a dinner of the Society of the Cincinnati at St. Paul's Church when Steuben was elected president of the society and Hamilton was elected vice-president. One of the toasts "drank" at dinner was "Wisdom to our Convention, and may they pursue the true interests of our country."

Note for Chapter 24
THE SECRETARY OF THE TREASURY WEPT

[1] Page 535 Hamilton was intimately involved with the question of admission of Vermont as a state, which became tied up with the ratification of the Constitution by New York. A group of Vermont leaders gathered at the house of Nathaniel Chipman at Tinmouth, Vermont, and issued an appeal to New Yorkers like Hamilton who favored a strong union for admission of Vermont as a state.

BIBLIOGRAPHY

SELECTED BOOKS AND ARTICLES

Abbott, William. *The Crisis of the Revolution.* New York, 1899.

Abernethy, T. P. *Western Lands and the American Revolution.* New York, 1937.

Adair, Douglass. "The Authorship of the Disputed Federalist Papers." 3d ser., 1 *William and Mary Quarterly,* 97–122.

_____ and Hamilton, Walton, *The Power to Govern.* New York, 1914.

Adams, Abigail. *Letters of Mrs. Adams.* Charles F. Adams, ed. 2 vols. Boston, 1848.

Adams, John. *Adams Family Correspondence.* Edited by Lyman H. Butterfield. Vols. I–IV. Cambridge, Mass., 1963.

_____ *Works of . . . , with a Life of the Author, . . .* by Charles Francis Adams. 10 vols. Boston: Little, Brown, 1850–1856.

_____ *Correspondence of the Late President Adams. Originally Published in the Boston Patriot.* Boston: Everett & Munroe, 1809.

_____ *Correspondence between . . . John Adams . . . and the late Wm. Cunningham . . . , 1803–12.* Boston: E. M. Cunningham, 1823. See, in connection, Timothy Pickering, *A Review of the Correspondence between . . . Adams . . . and Cunningham.* Salem, Mass.: Joshua & J. D. Cushing, 1824.

Adams, John Quincy. *Memoirs.* Charles F. Adams, ed. 12 vols. Philadelphia 1874–1877.

Adams, Randolph G. *The Burned Letter of Chastellux.* New York, 1935.

Adams, S. A. *The Episcopal Church in the American Colonies. The History*

of St. John's Church, Elizabethtown, N.J., 1703. Philadelphia: Lippincott;
New York: T. N. Stanford, 1857.

Alden, John R. *General Charles Lee, Traitor or Patriot?* Baton Rouge: Louisiana State University Press, 1951.

Alexander, D. S. *Political History of New York.* 3 vols. New York: Henry Holt,
1906–1909; continued in *Four Famous New Yorkers.* New York: Henry
Holt, 1925.

Alexander, Holmes. *Aaron Burr: The Proud Pretender.* New York: Harper,
1937.

Alexander, S. D. *The Presbytery of New York, 1738–1788.* New York: A. D. F.
Randolph & Co., 1888.

Aly, Bower. *The Rhetoric of Alexander Hamilton.* New York: Russell & Russell, 1965.

*American Archives: . . . A Collection of Authentic Records, State Papers,
. . . forming a Documentary History of . . . Origin and Progress of the
North American Colonies.* 4 vols. Washington, D.C.: M. St. Clair Clarke &
Peter Force, 1836–1846.

Anburey, Thomas. *Travels through . . . Interior Parts of North America.* 2
vols. London: W. Lane, 1791.

Anderson, Enoch. "Personal Recollections of an Officer in the Delaware Regiments in the Revolutionary War," in *16 Historical and Biographical Papers of Delaware.* Wilmington: Historical Society of Delaware, 1896.

Anderson, John. *Memoirs of House of Hamilton.* Edinburgh: J. Anderson, Jr.,
1825.

Anderson, Troyer S. *The Command of the Howe Brothers During the American Revolution.* New York and London, 1936.

André, John. *André's Journal. An Authentic Record of the Movements . . . of
the British Army in America, June 1777 to Nov. 1778.* Boston: H. A.
Houghton & Co., 1903.

André, John (1751–1780), Defendant. *Minutes of Court of Inquiry upon Case
of . . . André, with . . . Documents.* Albany: J. Munsell, 1865.

————— *Proceedings of a Board of General Officers . . . Respecting Major John
André, Sept. 29, 1780.* Philadelphia: F. Bailey, 1780.

————— *Proceedings of . . . Trial of . . . André, and Letters Pertaining to
. . . Treason of . . . Arnold.* photographed from originals, 1908; copy in New
York Public Library.

*Arguments and Judgment of . . . Mayor's Court . . . in a Cause between
. . . Rutgers and Waddington.* New York: S. Loudon, 1784; see also H. B.
Dawson's reprint with historical introduction, Morrisania, N.Y., 1866.

Aptheker, Herbert. *The Negro in the American Revolution.* New York: International Publishers, 1940.

Armstrong, John. "Review of Sketches of the Life and Correspondence of General Nathanael Greene . . . by William Johnson," *United States Magazine*
1 (1823), 3–44.

Atherton, Gertrude. *Adventures of a Novelist.* New York: Liveright, 1932.

———— *The Conqueror.* New York: Macmillan, 1902.

———— *A Few of Hamilton's Letters.* New York: Macmillan, 1903.

———— "The Hunt for Hamilton's Mother," in 175 *North American Review* (1902), 229–242.

Bailey, Ralph E. *An American Colossus: The Singular Career of Alexander Hamilton.* Boston: Lothrop Lee & Shepard, 1933.

Bailyn, Bernard. *Ideological Origins of the American Revolution.* Cambridge, Mass., 1967.

Bakeless, John. *Turncoats, Traitors and Heroes.* Philadelphia and New York, 1959.

Bancroft, George. *History of the Formation of the Constitution of the United States.* 2 vols. New York, 1882.

———— *History of the United States.* 6 vols. New York: Appleton, 1888.

Bast, Homer. "Tench Tilghman—Maryland Patriot," in 42 *Maryland Historical Magazine*, 71–94.

Baxter, Katharine Schuyler. *A Godchild of Washington* [Catharine Van Rensselaer Schuyler]. New York: F. T. Neely, 1897.

Beard, Charles A. *An Economic Interpretation of the Constitution.* New York: Macmillan, 1935.

———— *The Republic; Conversations on Fundamentals.* New York: Viking, 1943.

Beard, C. A., ed. *The Enduring Federalist.* New York: Doubleday, 1948.

Beardsley, E. E. *Life and Correspondence of Samuel Seabury.* Boston: Houghton Mifflin, 1881.

Bein, Alex. *Die Staatsidei Alexander Hamilton in ihrer Entstehung und Entwicklung.* Munich and Berlin: Oldenbourg, 1927.

Bemis, Samuel Flagg. *The Diplomacy of the American Revolution.* Bloomington, Ind.: Indiana University Press, 1965.

Benedict, W. H. *New Brunswick in History.* New Brunswick, N. J.: privately printed, 1925.

Benson, Egbert. *Vindication of . . . Captors of André.* New York: F. S. Hoffman, 1865.

Beveridge, A. J. *Life of John Marshall.* 4 vols. Boston and New York: Houghton Mifflin, 1916–1919.

Bezanson, A. *Prices and Inflation During the American Revolution.* Philadelphia, 1951.

Bill, A. H. *The Campaign of Princeton, 1776–1777.* Princeton, N.J.: Princeton University Press, 1948.

Blackstone, Sir William. *Commentaries on the Laws of England.* 4 vols. Oxford, 1765–1769.

Bliven, Bruce. *Battle for Manhattan.* New York: Henry Holt & Co., 1956.

Bolton, Robert. *History of County of Westchester.* 2 vols. New York: Alexander S. Gould, 1848.

Boudinot, Elias. *Journal or Historical Recollections of American Events during the Revolutionary War.* Philadelphia: F. Bourquin, 1894.

Boudinot, J. J. *Life of Elias Boudinot.* 2 vols. Boston and New York: Houghton Mifflin, 1896.

Bourg, Cromot du, "Diary," in 4 *Magazine of American History,* 205 ff.; Vol. 7, 283 ff.

Boutell, Lewis H. *Alexander Hamilton, Constructive Statesman.* Chicago: S. Thompson, 1890.

Bowen, Catherine Drinker. *Miracle at Philadelphia.* Boston, 1966.

Bowers, Claude G. *Jefferson and Hamilton: The Struggle for Democracy in America.* Boston: Houghton Mifflin, 1929.

Boyd, G. A. *Elias Boudinot.* Princeton, N.J.: Princeton University Press, 1952.

Boynton, E. C. *History of West Point.* New York: D. Van Nostrand, 1863.

Brant, Irving. *James Madison, Father of the Constitution, 1787–1800.* Indianapolis, Bobbs-Merrill: 1941.

Breck, Samuel. *Historical Sketch of Continental Paper Money.* Philadelphia, 1843.

Brissot de Warville, J. P. *New Travels in the United States.* New York: T. and J. Swords, 1792.

Brodie, Fawn M. *Thomas Jefferson: An Intimate History.* New York: W. W. Norton, 1974.

Brown, Stuart G. *Alexander Hamilton.* New York: Washington Square Press, 1967.

Brunhouse, R. L. *The Counter-Revolution in Pennsylvania 1776–1790.* Philadelphia, 1942.

Bryce, James. *The American Commonwealth.* 2 vols. London: Macmillan, 1888.
———— *The Predictions of Hamilton and De Tocqueville.* Baltimore: Johns Hopkins University, 1887.

Burgess, J. W. *Political Science and Comparative Constitutional Law.* 2 vols. Boston and London: Ginn, 1902.

Burnett, Edmund C. *The Continental Congress.* New York: Macmillan, 1941.

Burnett, E. C., ed. *Letters of the Members of the Continental Congress, 1774–1789.* 8 vols. Washington, D.C.: Carnegie Institution of Washington, 1921–1936.

Burr, Aaron. *Memoirs of, with . . . Selections from His Correspondence.* Edited by M. L. Davis. 2 vols. New York: Harper, 1836–1838.

Butler, Richard. "Journal of the Siege of Yorktown," *Historical Magazine,* VIII (1864), 102–112.

Caldwell, Lynton K. *Public Administration: Hamilton and Jefferson.* Chicago, 1943.

Callahan, North. *Henry Knox: General Washington's General.* New York: American Book Co., 1968.
———— *Daniel Morgan, Ranger of the Revolution.* New York: Holt Rinehart & Winston, 1961.

Canton, Milton, comp. *Hamilton* (Great Lives Observed). Englewood Cliffs, N.J.: Prentice Hall, 1971.

Carey, Mathew, ed. *Debates and Proceedings of General Assembly of Pennsyl-*

vania on Repeal or Suspension of Law Annulling Charter of Bank. Philadelphia: Carey & Co., 1786.

Caribbeana ("being miscellaneous papers relating to the history . . . , genealogy, topography and antiquities of the British West Indies"). Edited by V. L. Oliver. London: Mitchell, Hughes and Clarke, vols. 1–6, Jan. 1909–Oct. 1919; no more published.

"Cassius" (Aedanus Burke). *Considerations on the Society or Order of Cincinnati, Proving that it Creates . . . Hereditary Patricians.* Philadelphia: Robert Bell, 1783.

Chadwick, Mrs. French E. "The Visit of General Washington to Newport," *Bulletin Newport Historical Society,* No. 6 (1913).

Chamber of Commerce of State of New York. *The Charter and By-Laws, with a History of the Chamber* by Charles King. New York: The Chamber, 1855.

——— *Colonial Records of the New York Chamber of Commerce, 1768–1784.* New York: J. F. Trow & Co., 1867.

——— *Catalogue of Portraits in the Chamber of Commerce.* New York, 1924.

Chase, Eugene Parker. *Our Revolutionary Forefathers; The Letters of François Marquis de Barbé-Marbois.* New York, 1929.

Chastellux, François Jean, Marquis de. *Travels in North America, 1780–82.* 2 vols. London: G. G. J. & J. Robinson, 1787.

Chinard, Gilbert. *Honest John Adams.* Boston: Little Brown, 1933.

Chipman, Daniel. *Life of . . . Nathaniel Chipman . . . with Selections from his . . . Papers.* Boston: C. C. Little & J. Brown, 1846.

Clark, Victor S. *History of Manufactures in the United States, 1607–1860.* Washington, D.C., 1916.

Clinton, DeWitt. "Address . . . to Alumni of Columbia College," in W. W. Campbell, *Life and Writings of DeWitt Clinton.* New York: Baker and Scribner, 1849.

Clinton, George. *Public Papers.* Compiled by Hugh Hastings. 10 vols. New York and Albany: published by State of New York, 1899–1914.

Clinton, Sir Henry. *The American Rebellion.* Edited by W. Willcox. New Haven: Yale University Press, 1954.

——— *Narrative.* London, 1783.

Closen, Baron Ludwig von. *Revolutionary Journal.* Translated and edited by Evelyn A. Acomb. Chapel Hill, N. C., 1958.

Colden, Cadwalader. *Letters and Papers of . . . , 1711–1775.* 9 vols. New York: NYHS, 1918–1937.

Collins, V. L. *The Continental Congress at Princeton.* Princeton, N.J., 1908.

——— *President Witherspoon: A Biography.* 2 vols. Princeton, N.J.: Princeton University Press, 1925.

Columbia University. *Columbia University Officers and Alumni 1754–1857.* Compiled by M. H. Thomas. New York: Columbia University Press, 1936.

Continental Congress. *Journals 1774–1789.* 8 vols. Washington, D. C., 1921–1926.

Cook, Lewis D. *The Boudinot Mansion*. Elizabeth, N. J.: for New Jersey Commission on Historic Sites, 1943.

Cooke, Jacob E., ed. *The Federalist*. Middletown, Conn.: Wesleyan University Press, 1961.

―――― ed. *Alexander Hamilton: A Profile*. New York: Hill and Wang, 1967.

Cooper, Myles. "Sketch of the Life and Literary Character of the late President Cooper," in 14 *Analectic Magazine*, 73–76. Philadelphia: M. Thomas, 1813+.

―――― *A Friendly Address to All Reasonable Americans, on . . . Our Political Confusions*. New York: James Rivington, 1774.

―――― *Poems on Several Occasions*. Oxford: W. Jackson, 1761.

―――― "An Exile from America," stanzas in 46 *Gentleman's Magazine* (London), 326–327.

Corwin, Edwin S. *Court over Constitution*. Princeton, N. J.: Princeton University Press, 1938.

―――― *The President, Office and Powers*. New York, 1940.

Cresson, William P. *James Monroe*. Chapel Hill: University of North Carolina Press, 1946.

Cronau, Rudolf. *The Army of the American Revolution and Its Organization*. New York: R. Cronau, 1923.

Cross, A. L. *The Anglican Episcopate and the American Colonies*. New York: Longmans, Green, 1902.

Crosskey, William. *Politics and the Constitution*. 2 vols. Chicago, 1952.

Curtis, Charles P. *Lions Under the Throne*. Boston, 1947.

Custis, G. W. P. *Recollections and Private Memoirs of Washington*. Philadelphia: J. W. Bradley, 1861.

Cutler, Manasseh. *Life, Journals, and Correspondence*. Cincinnati: R. Clarke & Co., 1888.

Davie, M. R. *Negroes in American Society*. New York: Whittlesey House, 1949.

Davis, Matthew L. *Memoirs of Aaron Burr*. 2 vols. New York, 1836.

Dawson, H. B., ed. *The Foederalist*. Vol. I only. New York: Scribner, 1863.

Dawson, H. R., ed. *Record of Trial of Joshua Hett Smith . . . for alleged complicity in . . . Treason of . . . Arnold*. Morrisania, 1966.

Dayton, Elias. "Papers," in 1st. ser., Vol. 9, *New Jersey Historical Society Proceed.*, 175–194.

De Ford, Miriam A. *Love-Children; A Book of Illustrious Illegitimates*. New York: Dial Press, 1931.

De Lancey, E. F. "Original Family Records, Cruger," in 6 *New York Genealogical and Biographical Record*, 74–80.

De Pauw, Linda G. *The Eleventh Pillar: New York State and The Federal Constitution*. Ithaca: Cornell University Press, 1966.

Desmond, Alice Curtis. *Alexander Hamilton's Wife, a Novel*. New York: Dodd, Mead, 1953.

Deux-Ponts, W. de. *My Campaigns in America*. Translated and edited by S. A. Green. Boston: J. K. Wiggin and W. P. Lunt, 1868.

DeWitt, Cornelis. *Histoire de Washington et de la fondation de la République des États-Unis.* Paris: E. Perrin, 1884.

Dickinson, John. "Report to Assembly," in 4th ser., *3 Pennsylvania Archives,* 905 ff.

[Dickinson, John] *Letters from a Farmer in Pennsylvania.* Philadelphia: Hall & Sellers, 1768.

Dillon, Dorothy R. *The New York Triumvirate.* New York, 1949.

Dix, W. R., "Old Houses of Elizabethtown," in new series, 8 *New Jersey Historical Society Proceed.,* 169–185.

Domett, H. W. *A History of the Bank of New York, 1784–1884.* Cambridge, Mass.: Riverside Press, 1902.

Doniol, Henri. *Histoire de la participation de la France . . . à l'establissement des États-Unis.* 5 vols. Paris: Librairie des Archives et de la Société de L'École des Chartes, 1886–1892.

Dorfman, Joseph. *The Economic Mind in American Civilization.* 2 vols. New York, 1946–1949.

Drake, F. S. *Life and Correspondence of Henry Knox.* Boston: S. G. Drake, 1873.

Duer, W. A. *Life of William Alexander, Earl of Stirling.* New York: Wiley & Putnam, 1847.

Duer, William A. *Reminiscences of an Old Yorker.* New York: W. L. Andrews, 1867.

Dunbar, C. F. "Some Precedents Followed by Hamilton," in his *Economic Essays.* Edited by O. M. W. Sprague. New York: Macmillan, 1904.

Dunbar, Louise A. *Study of Monarchical Tendencies in the United States 1776–1801.* New York, 1923.

Dunlop, William. *History of the Province of New York.* New York, 1840.

Dupuy, R. Ernest, and Trevor N. Dupuy. *The Compact History of the Revolution.* New York, 1963.

Duval, Ruby R. *Guide to Historic Annapolis.* Baltimore: Norman, Remington, 1926.

Earle, Edward Meade. *Makers of Modern Strategy.* Princeton, N. J., 1943.

Earle, Edwin M., ed. *The Federalist.* New York, 1937.

East, Robert A. *Business Enterprise in the American Revolutionary Period.* New York, 1938.

Edwards, Bryan. *The History, Civil and Commercial, of the British Colonies in the West Indies.* 2 vols. Philadelphia, 1805.

Elliot, Jonathan, ed. *Debates in . . . State Conventions on Adoption of The Federal Constitution.* 5 vols. Washington, D. C., 1836–1846.

Evans, Charles. *American Bibliography.* 13 vols. Chicago: printer varies, 1903–1955.

Ewald, J. von. *Belehrungen uber den Krieg.* Schleswig, 1798.

Farrand, Max, ed., *Records of the Federal Convention of 1787.* 3 vols. New Haven, Yale University Press, 1911.

The Federalist: a Collection of Essays written in Favour of the New Constitu-

tion. 2 vols. New York: J. and A. M'Lean, 1788, 2 vols.; the first edition.

Feltman, William. *Journal . . . 1781–82, including the Siege of Yorktown.* Philadelphia: H. C. Baird, 1853.

Ferguson, Elmer James. *The Power of the Purse.* Chapel Hill, N.C., 1961.

Field, Thomas Warren. *The Battle of Long Island.* Brooklyn, N. Y., 1869.

Finn, Percy T. *The Development of the Constitution.* New York, 1940.

First Presbyterian Church, Elizabeth, N.J. *Record Book of the Sextons . . . , 1766–1800.* Elizabeth, 1891.

Fiske, John. *The Critical Period of American History, 1783–1789.* Boston: Houghton Mifflin, 1888.

Fithian, P. V. *Journal and Letters, 1767–74.* 2 vols. Vol. 1 edited by J. R. Williams; Vol. 2, by R. G. Albion and L. Dodson. Princeton, N. J.: Princeton University Press, 1904–1934.

Fleming, T. J. *Beat the Last Drum, The Siege of Yorktown, 1781.* New York: St. Martin's Press, 1963.

Flexner, James T. *The Traitor and the Spy.* New York: Harcourt, Brace, 1953.

—— *George Washington in the American Revolution (1775–1783).* New York: Little, Brown & Co., Vol. II, 1967.

—— *George Washington and the New Nation (1783–1793).* New York: Little, Brown & Co., Vol. III, 1969.

Ford, Henry Jones. *Alexander Hamilton.* New York: C. Scribner's Sons, 1920.

Ford, P. L. *Bibliography . . . Relating to the Adoption of the Constitution.* Brooklyn, N. Y.: no pub., 1896.

—— *Bibliotheca Hamiltoniana.* New York: Knickerbocker Press, 1886.

Ford, P. L., ed. *Essays on the Constitution . . . Published during its Discussion by the People.* Brooklyn, N. Y.: New York Historical Printing Club, 1892.

—— *Pamphlets on the Constitution.* Brooklyn, N. Y., 1888.

Ford, P. L. *The True George Washington.* Philadelphia: J. B. Lippincott, 1896.

—— and E. G. Bourne. *The Authorship of The Federalist.* Brooklyn, N. Y.: Historical Printing Co., 1897; reprinted from *Am. Hist. Rev.*, Vol. 2, No. 4, 675–687.

Ford, W. C. "Alexander Hamilton's Notes in the Federal Convention of 1787," in 10 *American Historical Review*, 97–109.

Forman, Sidney. *West Point: A History of the United States Military Academy.* New York: Columbia University Press, 1956.

Franks, David C. *The New York Directory.* New York: Kollock, 1786.

Freeman, D. S., and J. A. Carroll and M. W. Ashworth. *George Washington, a Biography.* 7 vols. New York: Scribner, 1948–1957.

Freneau, Philip. *Poems . . . Written chiefly during the late War.* Philadelphia: F. Bailey, 1786.

Friederich, Carl J. *Constitutional Government and Democracy.* Boston, 1941.

Gallagher, B. G. *Color and Conscience.* New York: Harper, 1946.

Gallatin, Gaspard de. *Journal of Siege of York-Town.* Washington, D. C.: Government Printing Office, 1931.

Ganoe, W. A. *The History of the United States Army.* New York: Appleton, rev. ed., 1942.

Gavin, Frank. "Chandler in Light of His Diary," in *Church History*, June 1932, 3–19.

Gideon, Jacob, Jr., ed. *The Federalist*. Washington, D. C.: Gideon, 1818.

Ginzberg, Eli. *The House of Adam Smith*. New York, 1934.

Goddard, William. *To Friends of Freedom in the City of New York*. New York, May 2, 1775; broadside in New York Public Library.

Gordon, William. *History of the Rise, Progress, and Establishment of the Independence of the United States*. London, privately printed, 1788, 4 vols.; New York, Hodge, Allen, & Campbell, 1789, 3 vols.

Gottschalk, Louis R. *Lafayette and the Close of the American Revolution*. Chicago: University of Chicago Press, 1942.

———— *Lafayette Joins the American Army*. Chicago, 1937.

Graydon, Alexander. *Memoirs of His Own Time*. Harrisburg: John Wyeth, 1811; Philadelphia: Lindsay and Blackiston, 1846.

Greene, G. W. *The Life of Nathanael Greene*. 3 vols. New York: Putnam, 1867–1871.

Guedalla, Philip. *Fathers of the Revolution*. London: Putnam, 1926.

Gugler, et al. *Architectural History of First Presbyterian Church, Elizabeth*. First Presbyterian Church Building Fund, 1947.

Hacker, Louis M. *Alexander Hamilton in the American Tradition*. New York: McGraw Hill, 1957.

Hague, J. T. *Parks and Other Public Properties of the City of Elizabeth*. City of Elizabeth, 1921.

Haines, Charles G. *The American Doctrine of Judicial Supremacy*. New York, 1914.

Hamilton, Alexander. *A Biography in His Own Words*. Edited by Mary-Jo Kline. New York: Newsweek, 1973. An excellent introduction to Hamilton by a scholar.

———— *The Farmer Refuted: or, A More Impartial and Comprehensive View of the Dispute between Great-Britain and the Colonies*. New York: James Rivington, 1775.

———— *The Founding of the Nation*. Edited by Richard B. Morris. New York: Dial Press, 1957.

———— *The Law Practice of Alexander Hamilton: Documents and Commentary*. Edited by Julius Goebel, Jr., et al. 3 vols. New York: Columbia University Press, 1964.

———— *The Papers of Alexander Hamilton*. Edited by Harold C. Syrett et al. 21 vols. New York: Columbia University Press, 1961–1975. An indispensable source. Vol. I (1768–1778); Vol. II (1779–1781); Vol. III (1782–1786); Vol. IV (1787–May 1788); Vol. V (June 1788–November 1789); Vol. VI (Dec. 1789–Nov. 1790).

———— *The Works of Alexander Hamilton*. Edited by John C. Hamilton. 7 vols. New York: J. F. Trow, 1850–1851.

———— *Works*. Edited by H. C. Lodge. 12 vols. New York and London: Putnam, Federal Edition, 1904.

———— *A Full Vindication of the Measures of the Congress.* New York: James Rivington, 1774.

Hamilton, Allan McLane. *Intimate Life of Alexander Hamilton.* New York: Scribner, 1910.

Hamilton, James A. *Reminiscences.* New York: Scribner, 1869.

Hamilton, John C. *Life of Alexander Hamilton.* Vol. 1, New York: Halsted & Voorhies, 1834; Vol. 2, Philadelphia: Appleton, 1840. No more published. Valuable for firsthand insights.

———— *A History of the Republic of the United States of America ... as Traced in the Writings of Alexander Hamilton and of his Contemporaries.* 7 vols. New York: Appleton, 1857–1864.

Hamilton, John C., ed. *The Federalist.* 2 vols. Philadelphia: Lippincott, 1964.

Hamilton, Walton, and Douglas Adair. *The Power to Govern.* New York, 1914.

Hammond, Bray. *Banks and Politics in Early America.* Princeton, N. J.: Princeton University Press, 1957.

Hammond, O. G. *Letters and Papers of General John Sullivan.* 3 vols. Concord, N.H.: 1930–1931.

Harbison, W. A. and A. H. Kelly. *The American Constitution, its Origins and Development.* New York, 1948.

Hart, A. B., ed. *The Varick Court of Inquiry.* Boston: Bibliophile Society, 1907.

Hasell, B. D. "The Cruger Family in America." MS. 1892, in New York Public Library.

Hatfield, E. F. *History of Elizabeth, New Jersey.* New York: Carlton & Lanahan, 1868.

Haven, C. C. *Thirty Days in New Jersey Ninety Years Ago.* Trenton: State Gazette Office, 1867.

Hawkins, Ernest. *Historical Notices of Missions of Church of England in the North American Colonies.* London: B. Fellowes, 1845.

Heath, William. *Memoirs of the American War.* Edited by R. R. Wilson. New York: A. Wessels Co., 1904.

Heckscher, Eli. *Mercantilism.* 2 vols. London, 1935.

Heitman, F. B. *Historical Register of Officers of the Continental Army ... 1775–83.* Washington, D. C.: Rare Book Shop Publishing Co., revised ed., 1914.

Henry, William Wirt. *Patrick Henry's Life, Correspondence and Speeches.* 3 vols. New York, 1891.

Heusser, A. H. *In the Footsteps of Washington.* Paterson, N.J.: privately printed, 1921.

Hobbes, Thomas. *Leviathan.* London: Dent, Everyman's Library, 1914.

Hofstadter, Richard. *The American Political Tradition and the Men Who Made It.* New York, 1948.

Holcomb, Thomas. *Sketch of Early Ecclesiastical Affairs in New Castle, Delaware.* Wilmington: Delaware Printing Co., 1890.

Hopkins, Joseph R. *Hamiltoniad: or, The Effects of Discord,* a poem. Philadelphia: privately printed, 1804.

Horton, James T. *James Kent, A Study in Conservatism.* New York, 1934.

Hoyt, A. H. Sketch of T. B. Chandler in 27 *New England Historical and Genealogical Register,* 227–236.

Hoyt, Edwin P. *Lost Statesmen.* Chicago: Reilly & Lee, 1961.

Hufeland, Otto. *Westchester County During the . . . Revolution.* New York: Knickerbocker Press, 1926.

Hume, David. *Essays, Moral and Political.* London: A. Millar, 1748.

―――― *History of England.* 6 vols. London: A. Millar, 1754–1762.

Hume, Edgar E. "Early Opposition to the Cincinnati," in 30 *Americana,* 597–638.

Humphreys, David. *Life of . . . Israel Putnam.* Philadelphia: W. McCarthy, 1811.

―――― *Conduct of Washington Respecting Asgill.* New York: Holland Club, 1859.

Humphreys, Frank Landon. *The Life and Times of David Humphreys.* 2 vols. New York, 1917.

Humphreys, Mary G. *Catherine Schuyler.* New York: Scribner, 1897.

Hutcheson, Harold. *Tench Coxe.* Philadelphia, 1938.

Inglis, Charles. *The Case of Major John André, . . . who was put to Death by the Rebels.* New York: James Rivington, 1780.

Irving, Washington. *Life of George Washington.* 5 vols. New York: Putnam, 1856–1859.

Ives, Mabel Lorenz. *Washington's Headquarters.* Upper Montclair, N. J., 1932.

Jacobs, James R. *Tarnished Warrior: Major General James Wilkinson.* New York, 1938.

Jameson, J. F. *Studies in the History of the Federal Convention of 1787.* Washington, D. C.: Government Printing Office, 1903.

Jay, John. *An Address to the People of the State of New York.* New York: S. & J. Loudon, 1788.

Jay, John. *Correspondence and Public Papers.* Edited by H. P. Johnston. 4 vols. New York: Putnam, 1890–1893.

Jay, John (1817–1894). *Correspondence between John Jay and Henry B. Dawson, and between James A. Hamilton and . . . Dawson, concerning the Federalist.* New York: J. M. Bradstreet & Son, 1864.

Jefferson, Thomas. *Papers.* Edited by Julian Boyd. Vols. I–VI. Princeton, N. J., 1950–1952.

―――― *Writings.* Edited by Paul Leicester Ford. Vols. I–III. New York, 1892–1894.

Jensen, Merrill. *The New Nation: A History of the United States During the Confederation, 1781–89.* New York: Knopf, 1950.

Johnson, E. A. J. *Predecessors of Adam Smith: The Growth of British Economic Thought.* New York, 1926.

Johnson, W. *Sketches of the Life and Correspondence of Nathanael Greene.* Charleston: privately printed, 1822.

Johnston, H. P. *The Campaign of 1776 around New York and Brooklyn.* Long Island Hist. Soc., *Memoirs,* Vol. 3. Brooklyn, N. Y., 1878.

_____ *The Yorktown Campaign and the Surrender of Cornwallis.* New York: Harper, 1881.

Jones, Thomas. *The History of New York During the Revolutionary War.* 2 vols. New York, 1789.

Kalm, Peter. *The America of 1750; Peter Kalm's Travels,* in John Pinkerton, 13 *Collection of Travels* 374–700. London: Longman, Hurst, Rees and Orme, 1808–1814.

Kalmer, P. *The Island of St. Croix as a Winter Residence for Invalids.* St. Croix: C. Dahl, 1871.

Kapp, Friedrich. *Life of Frederick William von Steuben.* New York: Mason Brothers, 1859.

Kelley, F. B., compiler; W. R. Dix, ed. *Historic Elizabeth, 1664–1914. Elizabeth Daily Journal,* ca. 1914.

Kelly, A. H., and W. A. Harbison. *The American Constitution, Its Origins and Development.* New York, 1948.

Kemble, Stephen. *Journals 1773–1789.* 2 vols. New York, N. Y., 1884–1886.

Kent, James. *An Address . . . before the Law Association of the City of New York.* New York: G. & C. Carvill, 1836.

_____ *Commentaries on American Law.* 4 vols. New York: Halsted, 1826–1830.

Kent, James. *Memoirs and Letters.* Edited by Wm. Kent. Boston: Little, Brown, 1898.

King, Charles R. *The Life and Correspondence of Rufus King.* 6 vols. New York, 1895.

King's College. "Matricula or Register." MS., Columbia University.

_____ "Book of Misdemeanours" in King's College, 1771–1775. MS. Published as *Black Book . . . in King's College,* Columbia University Press, 1931.

Kirk, Russell. *The Conservative Mind.* Chicago, 1953.

Kirkland, Edward C. *A History of American Economic Life.* New York, 1933.

Klein, M. M. *William Livingston: Exponent of Education in New York.* Typescript, College of City of New York, 223 pp.

Knollenberg, Bernhard. *Washington and the Revolution: A Reappraisal.* New York: Macmillan, 1940.

Kohn, Richard H. *Eagle and Sword: The Federalists and the Creation of the American Military Establishment, 1783–1802.* New York: Free Press, 1975.

Konefsky, Samuel J. *John Marshall and Alexander Hamilton, Architects of the American Constitution.* New York: Macmillan, 1964.

Kouwenhoven, John A., ed. *Columbia Historical Portrait of New York.* New York: Harper & Row, 1972.

Krafft, J. C. von. "Hessian Military Journal, May 1776–Jan. 1784," in 15 *NYHS Collections,* 1–200.

Knox, Hugh. *The Dignity and Importance of the Gospel Ministry.* New York: Hugh Gaine, 1755.

_____ *Discourses on the Truth of Revealed Religion.* 2 vols. London: T. Cadell, 1768.

———— *A Discourse . . . on Occasion of the Hurricane.* St. Croix: Daniel Thibou, 1772.

———— *Letter to Rev. Jacob Green.* New York: T. & J. Swords, 1809.

———— *Moral and Religious Miscellany.* New York: Hooge & Shober, 1775.

———— *The Probable Sources of Our Saviour's Tears.* No place or publisher, 1765.

———— Select Sermons. Glasgow: R. & A. Foulis, 1782.

———— *Transitory Nature . . . of all Sublunary Things.* Glasgow: A. Foulis, 1782.

Kulsrud, Carl J. *Maritime Neutrality to 1780.* Boston, 1936.

Lafayette, Marquis de. *Letters . . . to Washington, 1777–1799.* Edited by Louis Gottschalk. New York, privately printed by Helen F. Hubbard, 1944.

———— *Memoirs, Correspondence, and Manuscripts.* 3 vols. Published by his family. London: Saunders & Otley, 1837.

Larkin, Paschal. *Property in the Eighteenth Century.* New York, 1930.

Larrabee, Harold Atkins. *Decision at the Chesapeake.* New York, 1964.

Larson, Harold. "Alexander Hamilton; the Fact and Fiction of His Early Years," in 3d ser., 9 *William and Mary Quarterly*, 139–151.

———— "The Birth and Parentage of Alexander Hamilton," in 21 *American Genealogist*, 161–167.

Laurens, John. *Army Correspondence . . . , 1777–78.* Edited with memoir by William Gilmore Simms. New York: Bradford Club, 1867.

Leake, Isaac Q. *Memoir of the Life and Times of . . . John Lamb.* Albany: J. Munsell, 1850.

[Ledyard, Isaac] *Mentor's Reply . . . with some Observations on Trade.* New York: Sheppard Kollock, 1784.

Lee, Charles. *The Lee Papers, 1754–1811.* New York, New York Historical Society Collections, vols. 4, 5, 6, 7, 1871–1874.

———— *The Lee Papers.* 4 vols. New York, 1872–1875.

———— Strictures on a Pamphlet, entitled a *"Friendly Address . . ."* Philadelphia: W. & T. Bradford, 1774.

Lee, Henry. *Memoirs of the War in the Southern Department of the United States.* New York: University Publishing Co., 1869.

Lewisohn, Florence. *St. Croix Under Seven Flags.* Hollywood, Fla.: Dukane Press, 1970.

Livingston, Edwin Brockholst. *The Livingstons of Livingston Manor.* New York, 1910.

Livingston, W. F. *Israel Putnam.* New York and London: Putnam, 1901.

Livingston, William. *The Independent Reflector.* New York: J. Parker, 1753.

———— "The American Whig," in *New York Gazette*, 1768–1769.

———— "The Sentinel," in *New York Post-Boy*, 1765.

———— "The Watch Tower," in *New York Mercury*, 1754–1755.

———— "The Watchman," in *New York Journal*, 1770.

Locke, John. *An Essay Concerning the True Origin, Extent and End of Civil Government.* Boston: reprinted by Edes & Gill, 1773.

Lodge, Henry Cabot. *Alexander Hamilton*. New York: Arlington House, 1970. Originally published 1882.

Lossing, B. J. *Life and Times of Philip Schuyler*. 2 vols. New York: Sheldon & Co., 1873.

_____ *Pictorial Field Book of the American Revolution*. 2 vols. New York: Harper, 1850–1851.

Loth, David G. *Alexander Hamilton: Portrait of a Prodigy*. New York: Carrick & Evans, 1939.

Lowell, E. J. *The Hessians and Other German Auxiliaries . . . in the Revolutionary War*. New York: Harper, 1884.

Lycan, Gilbert L. *Alexander Hamilton and American Foreign Policy: A Design for Greatness*. Norman, Okla.: University of Oklahoma Press, 1970. A fine study of Hamilton's often overlooked contributions to American foreign policy.

Lynch, D. T. "The Growth of Political Parties, 1777–1828," in New York State Historical Association, 6 *History of State of New York*, 37 ff.

MacElree, Wilmer W. *Along the Western Brandywine*. Chester, Pa., 1912.

Machiavelli, Niccolo. *The Prince*. Translated by W. K. Marriott. London: Dent, 1908.

Mackesy, Piers. *The War for America 1775–1783*. Cambridge, Mass., 1964.

Maclay, William. *Journal*. Edited by E. S. Maclay. New York: Appleton, 1890.

Madison, James. *Autobiography*. Edited by Douglass Adair. In 3d ser., 2 *William and Mary Quarterly*, 191–209.

_____ *Writings*. Edited by Gaillard Hunt. 10 vols. New York: Putnam, 1900–1910.

Magi, Sobei. *The Problem of Federalism*. New York, 1951.

Malone, Dumas. *Jefferson the Virginian*. [to 1784] Boston: Little, Brown, 1948.

_____. *Jefferson and the Rights of Man*. [1784–1792] Boston: Little, Brown, 1951.

Manchester, Kathleen D. *Historic Heritage of St. Kitts, Nevis, Anguilla*. Port of Spain, Trinidad, 1971.

Manucy, Albert. *Artillery Through the Ages*. National Park Service Interpretive Series, History No. 3, Washington, D. C., U.S. Government Printing Office, 1949, p. 42.

Marshall, John. *Life of George Washington*. 5 vols. Philadelphia: C. P. Wayne, 1804–1807.

McCarthy, E. J. "Lieut. Col. Francis Barber of Elizabethtown," in 50 *New Jersey Historical Society Proceed.*, 273–284.

McLaughlin, Andrew C. *The Confederation and the Constitution*. New York, 1905.

McConnell, Matthew. *An Essay on the Domestic Debts of the United States*. Philadelphia, 1787.

McMaster, John B. *A History of the People of the United States from the Revolution to the Civil War*. 2 vols. New York, 1879.

[Michener, John H.] *Bank of North America*. New York, 1906.

Miller, John C. *Alexander Hamilton: Portrait in Paradox*. New York: Harper

& Row, 1959. The best one-volume biography of Hamilton.

_____ *The Federalist Era 1789–1801.* New York: Harper & Row, 1960.

Miller, Samuel. *Memoir of the Rev. John Rodgers.* New York: Whiting & Watson, 1813.

Miner, C. E. *Ratification of the Federal Constitution in New York.* New York, 1921.

Mintz, Max, M. "Gouverneur Morris: The Emergence of a Naturalist." Ph.D. dissertation. New York University, 1957.

Mirabeau, H. G. R., Comte de. *Considérations sur l'ordre de Cincinnatus.* London: J. Johnson, 1784; English trans., London: J. Johnson, 1785.

Mitchell, Broadus. *Alexander Hamilton.* 2 vols. New York: Macmillan, 1957–1962. The most authoritative biography to date.

_____ *Heritage from Hamilton.* New York: Columbia University Press, 1957.

_____ "The Man Who Discovered Hamilton," in 69 *New Jersey Historical Society Proceed.,* 88–114.

_____ "Practical Proceedings in the Supreme Court of . . . New York," in *Record of Association of Bar of City of New York,* 210–211.

Monaghan, Frank. *John Jay, Defender of Liberty.* Indianapolis: Bobbs, Merrill, 1935.

Monroe, James. *Writings of James Monroe.* Edited by Stanislaus Murray Hamilton. 7 vols. New York, 1850–1851.

Montesquieu, C. L. *De L'Esprit des Loix.* Leiden, Les Libraires Associés, 1749.

Moon, Robert C. *The Morris Family of Philadelphia.* Philadelphia, 1898, 3 vols.; suppl. 2 vols., 1908.

Moore, C. C. *The Early History of Columbia College.* Edited by M. H. Thomas. New York: Columbia University Press, 1940.

Morris, Gouverneur. *Diary and Letters.* Edited by Anne C. Morris. 2 vols. New York: Scribner, 1888.

Morris, Richard B., ed. *Alexander Hamilton and the Founding of the Nation.* New edition. New York, 1969.

_____ "Insurrection in Massachusetts," *America in Crisis.* Edited by Daniel Aaron. New York, 1952, 21–49.

_____ "Washington and Hamilton: a Great Collaboration," in *Proceedings of the American Philosophical Society,* c. II (1958), 107–116.

Morris, Robert. *Confidential Correspondence.* Philadelphia: S. V. Henkels, 1917.

Morrison, Samuel Eliot. *By Land and Sea.* New York, 1955.

Morse, J. T. *Life of Alexander Hamilton.* 2 vols. Boston: Little, Brown, 1876.

Mullett, Charles F. *Fundamental Law and the American Revolution.* New York, 1933.

Mullin, Gerald W. *Flight and Rebellion: Slave Resistance in Eighteenth Century Virginia.* New York, 1972.

Murray, Nicholas. *Notes, Historical and Biographical, Concerning Elizabethtown.* New York: Columbia University Press, 1941. Reprint from ed. of 1844.

Myers, W. S. *The Battle of Monmouth.* Edited by W. S. Stryker. Princeton, N. J., 1927.

Nevins, Allan. *History of Bank of New York and Trust Company 1784 to 1934.* New York: privately printed, 1934.

——— *The New York Evening Post.* New York, 1922.

New York. *Debates and Proceedings of . . . Convention of . . . State of New York assembled at Poughkeepsie, . . . 17th June, 1788. . . . Taken in Shorthand.* New York: F. Childs, 1788.

New York, Documents Illustrative of Colonial History of. Albany: various publishers, 1853–1857; see especially Vol. 15.

New York, Journal of Assembly of State of (also called *Votes and Proceedings*). Seventh sess., Jan. 1784, through eleventh sess., Jan. 1788; publisher and place vary.

New York. *Journal of . . . Convention of . . . State of New York: Held at Poughkeepsie, 17th June, 1788.* Poughkeepsie: Nicholas Power, 1788. This supplements *Debates and Proceedings,* of Childs, cited earlier.

New York. *Journal of the Provincial Congress, Provincial Convention, Committee of Safety, etc., 1775–1776–1777.* Albany: Thurlow Weed, 1842.

New York, Journal of Senate of State of. Same dates as *New York, Journal of Assembly of State of.*

New York. *Laws of . . . Legislature of . . . New York, in force against Loyalists.* London: H. Reynell, 1786.

New York, Office of State Comptroller. *New York in the Revolution as Colony and State.* Compiled by J. A. Roberts. Albany: Brandow Print Co., 1898.

New York City. *Minutes of Common Council, 1675–1776.* New York: Dodd, Mead, 1905; *Minutes of Common Council, 1784–1831* published by City of New York, 1917; see analytical index by D. M. Matteson.

New York Directory and Register, 1789–96. New York: Hodge, Allen, and Campbell, 1789–1796; after 1796 publisher varies.

New York Society Library. *Catalogue of Books Belonging to the Society, 1813, with Supplement.* New York: C. S. Van Winkle, 1825.

North, William. "Baron Steuben," *Magazine of American History,* VIII (1882), 187–199.

"North-American" [Myles Cooper]. *American Querist.* New York: James Rivington, 1774.

Oberholtzer, E. P. *Robert Morris.* New York: Macmillan, 1903.

O'Brien, Michael, Jr. *Hercules Mulligan.* New York: P. J. Kennedy, 1937.

Ogden, Aaron. *Autobiography.* Annotated by Wm. Nelson. Paterson, N.J.: Press Printing Co., 1893.

Oliver, F. S. *Alexander Hamilton: An Essay on American Union.* London: Constable, 1915.

Padover, Saul K., ed. *The Complete Madison.* New York: Harper, 1953.

Paine, Thomas. *Dissertations on Government Affairs of Bank and Paper Money.* Philadelphia: Charles Cist, 1786.

Palmer, J. M. *General von Steuben.* Port Washington, N. Y.: Kennikat Press, 1966.

Panagopoulos, E. P. *Alexander Hamilton's Pay Book* [of his New York Artillery Company]. Detroit: Wayne State University Press, 1961.

Parkes, H. B. *The American Experience.* New York: Knopf, 1947.

Parrington, V. L. *Main Currents in American Thought.* 3 vols. New York: Harcourt, Brace, 1927–1930.

Paston, James. *The Life and Times of Aaron Burr.* 2 vols. New York, 1864.

Paterson, James. *History of the Counties of Ayr and Wigton.* 3 vols. Edinburgh: J. Stillie, 1863–1866.

Patterson, S. W. *Horatio Gates.* New York: Columbia University Press, 1941.

Pennsylvania, Records of. *Minutes of Executive Council.* Harrisburg: Theodore Penn & Co., 1853.

Pickering, Octavius. *The Life of Timothy Pickering.* 4 vols. Boston: Little, Brown, 1867–1873.

Pinckney, Charles C. *The Life of General Thomas Pinckney.* Boston, 1895.

Pine, J. B. *King's College and the Early Days of Columbia College.* New York: Columbia University Printing Office, 1917.

Pitman, F. W. *The Development of the British West Indies.* New Haven, 1917.

Platt, Edmund. *The Eagle's History of Poughkeepsie . . . , 1683 to 1905.* Poughkeepsie: Platt & Platt, 1905.

Pomerantz, Sidney I. *New York: An American City.* New York, 1938.

Pomeroy, Mary. *The Island of Neors, the Birthplace of Alexander Hamilton.* n. p., 1956.

Postlethwayt, Malachy. *Britain's Commercial Interest Explained and Improved.* 2 vols. London: D. Browne, 1757.

———— *Great-Britain's True System.* London: A. Millar, 1757.

———— *The Universal Dictionary of Trade and Commerce.* Translated from French of [Jacques] Savary [des Brulons]. 2 vols. London, 1751, 1755.

Presbyterian Church in the United States, General Assembly. *Records of the Presbyterian Church . . . , embracing the Minutes of the Presbytery of Philadelphia, 1706–1788.* Philadelphia: Presbyterian Board of Publication, 1841.

Price, Richard. *Additional Observations on the Nature and Value of Civil Liberty.* London, 1777.

Pufendorf, Samuel von. *Of the Law of Nature and Nations.* London: J. Walthoe, R. Wilkin, 1729.

Quarles, Benjamin. *The Negro in the American Revolution.* Chapel Hill: U. of N. Carolina Press, 1961.

Ramsing, H. U. "Alexander Hamilton og hans modrene Slaegt. Tidsbilleder fra Dansk Vest-Indiens Barndom" (Hamilton's early days in the West Indies), in *Personalhistorisk Tidsskrift,* 59 de Aargang, 10 Rekke, 6 Bind, 1939.

Ratner, Sidney. *American Taxation, Its History as a Social Force in Democracy.* New York, 1942.

Redlech, Fritz. *The Molding of American Banking.* 2 vols. New York, 1951.

Reed, W. B. *Life and Correspondence of Joseph Reed.* 2 vols. Philadelphia: Lindsay & Blackiston, 1847.

Reynolds, Helen W. *Dutch Houses in the Hudson Valley ... before 1776*. New York: Payson and Clarke, 1929.

―――― *Dutchess County Doorways*. New York: W. F. Payson, 1931.

Riedesel, Baroness von. *Letters and Journals Relating to the War of American Independence*. New York: G. & C. Carvill, 1827.

Riedesel, Major General. *Memoirs during Residence in America*. Translated by W. L. Stone. 2 vols. Albany: J. Munsell, 1868.

Riker, James. *Harlem, Its Origin and Early Annals*. New York: privately printed, 1881.

Robertson, George. *A Genealogical Account of the Principal Families in Ayrshire*. 3 vols. Irvine, Scotland: Cunninghame Press, 1923–1925.

Rochambeau, Comte de. *Memoires militaires, historiques et politiques*. 2 vols. Paris: Fain, 1809.

Rochefoucauld-Liancourt, F. A. F. Duc de. *Voyage dans les États-Unis d'Amérique, 1795–97*. 8 vols. Paris: Du Pont, 1799.

Rodell, Fred. *Fifty-Five Men*. New York, 1936.

Rodney, Caesar. *Letters to and from Caesar Rodney, 1756–84*. Philadelphia: University of Pennsylvania Press, 1933.

Rodney, Thomas. *Diary of ... , Dec. 1776-Jan. 1777*. Edited by Caesar A. Rodney. Wilmington: Historical Society of Delaware, 1888.

Roosevelt, Theodore. *Gouverneur Morris*. Boston, 1888.

Root, Elihu. "Address at Hamilton College," *New York Sun*, June 17, 1918.

Rossiter, Clinton L. *Alexander Hamilton and the Constitution*. New York: Harcourt, Brace & World, 1964.

―――― *1787: The Grand Convention*. New York: Macmillan, 1966.

Rossman, Kenneth R. *Thomas Mifflin*. Chapel Hill, N.C., 1952.

Rowe, John. *Letters and Diary*. Edited by Anne R. Cunningham. Boston: W. B. Clarke Co., 1930.

Rowland, Kate Mason. *Life of George Mason*. 2 vols. New York, 1892.

Rush, Benjamin. *Autobiography*. Edited by G. W. Corner. Princeton, N. J.: Princeton University Press, 1948.

―――― *Letters*. Edited by Lyman H. Butterfield. 2 vols. Princeton, 1951.

Sabin, Joseph. *Bibliotheca Americana*. 29 vols. New York: Bibliographical Society of America, 1868–1936.

Sabine, Lorenzo. *The American Loyalists*. Boston: C. C. Little & J. Brown, 1847.

St. Christopher. *Acts of Assembly ... of St. Christopher, 1711–1735*. London: J. Baskett, 1739–1740. See also abridgment of same, 1711–1740, and *Acts of Assembly in ... Leeward Islands, 1690–1730*. Same publisher, 1740.

The St. Croixian Pocket Companion. Copenhagen: privately printed, 1780.

Salley, A. S., Jr., ed. *Minutes of the Vestry of St. Helena's Parish, South Carolina ... , 1726–1812*. Columbia, S.C.: The State Co., 1919.

Sanders, J. B. *The Evolution of the Executive Departments of the Continental Congress*. Chapel Hill, University of North Carolina Press, 1939.

Sawyer, R. C., ed. Wills for New York County. Typescript, New York Public Library.

Schachner, Nathan. *Aaron Burr*. New York, 1937.

_____. *Alexander Hamilton*. New York: Appleton-Century, 1946. A lively one-volume biography, but outdated and full of errors.

_____, ed. "Alexander Hamilton Viewed by His Friends. The Narratives of Robert Troup and Hercules Mulligan," in 3d. ser., 4 *William and Mary Quarterly*, 203–225.

_____ *The Founding Fathers*. New York, 1954.

Scharf, J. Thomas, and Thompson Westcott. *History of Philadelphia*. 3 vols. Philadelphia, 1884.

Scheer, George F., and Hugh F. Tankin. *Rebels and Redcoats*. Cleveland, 1957.

Schlesinger, Arthur M., Jr., *The Imperial Presidency*. Boston: Houghton Mifflin, 1973.

Schneider, H. and C., eds. *Samuel Johnson, President of King's College*. 4 vols. New York: Columbia University Press, 1929.

Schneider, H. W. *A History of American Philosophy*. New York, 1946.

Schuyler, G. W. *Colonial New York, Philip Schuyler and His Family*. 2 vols. New York: Scribner, 1885.

[Schuyler, Georgina] *The Schuyler Mansion at Albany*. New York: DeVinne Press, 1911.

Schuyler, Robert L. *The Constitution of the United States*. New York, 1923.

Scott, James Brown. *De Grasse at Yorktown*. Baltimore, 1931.

"A Farmer" [Samuel Seabury]. *Free Thoughts on Proceedings of the Continental Congress*. New York: James Rivington, 1774.

"A. W. Farmer" [Samuel Seabury]. *A View of the Controversy between Great Britain and her Colonies*. New York: James Rivington, 1774.

_____ *The Congress Canvassed: or, an Examination into the Conduct of the . . . Grand Convention . . . held in Philadelphia, 1774*. New York: James Rivington, 1774.

Sedgwick, Theodore, Jr. *Life of William Livingston*. New York: J. & J. Harper, 1833.

Shea, George. *Life and Epoch of Alexander Hamilton*. Boston: Houghton, Osgood, 1879.

Simcoe, J. G. *A Journal of Operations of . . . the Queen's Rangers*. Exeter: privately printed, 1787.

Sloane, Eric, and Edward Anthony. *Mr. Daniels and The Grange*. New York: Funk & Wagnalls, 1968.

Smertenko, J. J. *Alexander Hamilton*. New York: Greenberg, 1932.

Smith, Adam. *Wealth of Nations*. New York, 1942.

Smith, Elias D. *The School Interests of Elizabeth, 1664–1910*. Elizabeth, N.J., 1911.

Smith, J. Eugene. *One Hundred Years of Hartford's History*. New York, 1947.

Smith, Joshua Hett. *An Authentic Narrative of . . . Death of Major André*. London: Mathews & Leigh, 1808; New York: E. Duyckinck, 1809.

Smith, Samuel Stelle. *The Battle of Monmouth*. Monmouth Beach, N.J.: Philip Freneau Press, 1964.

———— *The Battle of Princeton.* Monmouth Beach, N.J.: Philip Freneau Press, 1967.

Society of the Cincinnati, Institution of, with List of Members of New York State Society. New York: M. M. Elliott, 1851.

Sparks, Jared. *Correspondence of the American Revolution; being Letters of Eminent Men to . . . Washington.* 4 vols. Boston: Little, Brown, 1853.

———— *Life of Gouverneur Morris.* Boston: Gray & Bowen, 1832.

Spaulding, E. W. *His Excellency George Clinton, Critic of the Constitution.* New York: Macmillan, 1938.

———— *New York in the Critical Period, 1783–1789.* New York: Columbia University Press, 1932.

Steiner, Bernard C. *The Life and Correspondence of James McHenry.* Cleveland, 1907.

Stevens, B. F., compiler. *The Campaign in Virginia.* 2 vols. London, 1888.

———— *The Clinton-Cornwallis Controversy.* London, 1888.

Stevens, John A. *The French in Rhode Island.* n. p., 1928.

Stevens, W. O. *Annapolis.* New York: Dodd, Mead, 1927.

Stiles, Ezra. *Literary Diary.* Edited by F. B. Dexter. New York: Scribner, 1901.

Stillé, C. J., *Wayne and the Pennsylvania Line.* Philadelphia: Lippincott, 1893.

Stokes, I. N. Phelps. *Iconography of Manhattan Island.* 6 vols. New York: R. H. Dodd, 1915–1928.

Story, Joseph. *Commentaries on the Constitution of the United States.* 2 vols. Boston, 1858.

Stourzh, Gerald. *Alexander Hamilton and the Idea of Republican Government.* Stanford: Stanford University Press, 1970.

Strayer, J. R., ed. *The Delegate from New York, or Proceedings of the Federal Convention . . . from the Notes of John Lansing, Jr.* Princeton, N. J.: Princeton University Press, 1939.

Stryker, W. S. *The Battle of Monmouth.* Edited by W. S. Myers. Princeton, N. J.: Princeton University Press, 1927.

———— *The Battles of Trenton and Princeton.* Boston and New York: Houghton Mifflin, 1898.

Studenski, Paul, and Herman E. Krooss. *Financial History of the United States.* New York, 1952.

Sullivan, John. *Letters and Papers.* Edited by O. G. Hammond. Concord, *New Hampshire Historical Society Collections*, vols. 13, 14, 15; 1930–1939.

Sullivan, William. *Familiar Letters on Public Characters and Public Events . . . 1783–1815.* Boston: Russell, Odiorne, & Metcalf, 1834.

Sumner, William Graham. *Finances and Financiers of the American Revolution.* 2 vols. New York, 1891.

Swiggett, Howard. *War Out of Niagara.* New York, 1933.

———— *The Extraordinary Mr. [Gouverneur] Morris.* New York: Doubleday, 1952.

Tansell, C. C., ed. *Documents Illustrative of the Formation of the Union of the American States.* Washington, D. C.: 1927.

Tarleton, Banastre. *A History of the Campaign of 1780 and 1781 in the Southern Provinces of North America.* London: T. Cadell, 1787.

Thacher, Charles C. *The Creation of the Presidency, 1775–1789.* Baltimore, 1922.

Thacher, James. *A Military Journal during the American Revolutionary War.* Boston: Richardson & Lord, 1825.

Thayer, Theodore. *Nathanael Greene, Strategist of the American Revolution.* New York: Twayne Publishers, 1960.

Thorp, Willard, ed. *The Lives of Eighteen from Princeton.* Princeton: Princeton University Press, 1946.

Tilghman, Oswald. *Annapolis.* Annapolis, 1925?

————— *Memoir of Lieutenant Colonel Tench Tilghman.* Albany: J. Munsell, 1876.

Tousard, Louis. *American Artillerist's Companion.* 2 vols. Philadelphia: C. and A. Conrad, 1809–1813.

Tower, Charlemagne. *The Marquis de Lafayette.* 2 vols. Philadelphia, 1895.

Townsend, Joseph. *The British Army and the Battle of Brandywine.* Philadelphia, 1846.

Trevelyan, G. O. *The American Revolution.* 4 vols. New York and London: Longmans, Green, 1926–1929. Extends to 1778; continued in his *George the Third and Charles Fox,* 2 vols., same pub., 1921–1927.

Trumbull, John. *The Autobiography of Colonel John Trumbull.* Edited by Theodore Sizer. New Haven, 1953.

Trumbull, Jonathan, Jr. "Minutes of Occurrences Respecting the Siege and Capture of York in Virginia . . . ," in ser. 1, Vol. 14 *MHS Proceed.,* 331–338.

Tuckerman, Arthur. *When Rochambeau Stepped Ashore.* Newport, R.I., 1955.

Tuckerman, Bayard. *Life of . . . Philip Schuyler, 1733–1804.* New York: Dodd, Mead, 1903.

United States. *Proceedings of a General Court Martial . . . for Trial of Major-General Lee, July 4, 1778.* Philadelphia: J. Dunlap, 1778.

United States Bureau of Rolls and Library. *Documentary History of the Constitution.* 3 vols. Washington, D. C.: Department of State, 1894.

United States Continental Congress. *Journals, 1774–1789.* 34 vols. Washington, D. C.: Government Printing Office, 1904–1937.

————— *Secret Journals of the Acts and Proceedings of the Continental Congress.* 4 vols. Boston: Thomas B. Wait, 1820–1821.

United States Department of State. *Diplomatic Correspondence of the American Revolution.* Edited by Jared Sparks. 12 vols. Boston: N. Hale, Gray & Bowen; New York: Carvill, 1829–1830.

United States House of Representatives. *Revolutionary Diplomatic Correspondence of the United States.* Edited by Francis Wharton. 6 vols. Washington, D. C.: Government Printing Office, 1889.

United States Inspector General [Steuben, F. W. von]. *Regulations for . . . the Order and Discipline of the Troops of the United States, Part I.* Philadelphia: Stymer and Cist, 1779.

United States Superintendent of Finance [Robert Morris]. *Statement of Accounts of United States, Feb. 20, 1781, to Nov. 1, 1784*. Philadelphia: R. Aitken, 1785.

Valentine, D. T. *Manual of the Corporation of the City of New York*. New York, 1842–1870.

Van Doren, C. C. *Secret History of the American Revolution*. New York: Viking, 1941.

—— *Meeting in January*. New York, 1943.

Vandenberg, Arthur H. *The Greatest American: Alexander Hamilton*. New York: G. P. Putnam, 1921.

—— *If Hamilton Were Here Today*. New York: G. P. Putnam, 1923.

Vandewater, R. J. *The Tourist, or Pocket Manual for Travellers on the Hudson River*. New York: Harper, 1841.

Vattel, Emmerich de. *Le Droit des Gens*. Londres, 1758; another edition at Neuchâtel: Société Typographique, 1773.

Vermont. *Records of Governor and Council*. Edited by E. P. Walton. 8 vols. Montpelier: J. & J. M. Poland, 1873–1880.

Ver Steeg, Clarence Lester. *Robert Morris: Revolutionary Financier*. Philadelphia, 1954.

Vrooman, J. J. *Historic Sites of New York State*. Albany: New York State Education Department, 1949.

Waldo, Albigence. "Diary, Valley Forge, 1777–1778," *Pennsylvania Magazine of History and Biography*, XXI (1897), 299–323.

Wallace, D. P. *Life of Henry Laurens, with a Sketch of the Life of . . . John Laurens*. New York: Putnam, 1915.

Ward, Christopher. *The War of the Revolution*. Edited by John Richard Alden. 2 vols. New York: Macmillan, 1952.

Warren, Charles. *The Making of the Constitution*. Boston, 1937.

—— *Jacobin or Juno: or Early American Politics as Viewed in the Diary of Dr. Nathanael Ames 1758–1822*. Cambridge, Mass., 1931.

Warren, Winslow. *The Society of the Cincinnati, A History*. Boston: Massachusetts Society of Cincinnati, 1929.

Washington, George. *Correspondence Concerning the Society of the Cincinnati*. Edited by E. E. Hume. Baltimore: Johns Hopkins Press, 1941.

—— *Correspondence of . . . and Comte De Grasse, Aug. 17–Nov. 4, 1781*. Institut français de Washington. Washington, D. C.: Government Printing Office, 1931.

—— *Diaries*. Edited by John C. Fitzpatrick. 4 vols. Boston: Houghton Mifflin, 1925.

—— *Writings*. Edited by John C. Fitzpatrick. 39 vols. Washington, D. C.: Government Printing Office, Bicentennial Edition, 1931–1944.

—— *Writings*. Edited by W. C. Ford. 14 vols. New York: Putnam, 1889–1893.

—— *Writings*. Edited by Jared Sparks. 12 vols. Boston: American Stationers' Co., 1834–1837.

Webb, Samuel B. *Correspondence and Journals*. Edited by W. C. Ford. 3 vols. New York: Wickersham Press, 1893–1894.

"A Citizen of Philadelphia" [Pelatiah Webster]. *An Essay on Credit, in which . . . some Remarks are made on present State of Bank of North-America.* Philadelphia: E. Oswald, 1786.

Webster, Pelatiah. *Political Essays on . . . Money, Public Finance.* Philadelphia: J. Crukshank, 1791.

Webster, Richard. *A History of the Presbyterian Church in America.* Philadelphia: J. M. Wilson, 1857.

Wecter, Dixon. *The Hero in America.* New York, 1945.

Weedon, George. *Valley Forge Orderly Book.* New York, 1902.

Wertenbaker, T. J. "The Battle of Princeton." in *The Princeton Battle Monument.* Princeton, N. J.: Princeton University Press, 1922.

———— *Father Knickerbocker Rebels.* New York, 1948.

West, Hans. *Beytrage zur Beschreibung von St. Croix.* Translated from Danish. Copenhagen: C. G. Proft Sohn und Co., 1794.

Westergaard, Waldemar C. *The Danish West Indies under Company Rule (1671–1754), with a Supplementary Chapter, 1755–1917.* New York: Macmillan, 1917.

Wheeler, Richard. *Voices of 1776.* Greenwich, Conn.: Fawcett, 1972.

Wheeler, W. O., and E. D. Halsey. *Inscriptions on Tombstones and Monuments in Burying grounds of . . . First Presbyterian Church and St. John's Church at Elizabeth, N.J., 1664–1892.* New Haven: Tuttle, Morehouse, & Taylor, 1892.

White, Leonard D. *The Federalists: A Study in Administrative History.* New York: Macmillan, 1948.

Whiteley, Emily S. *Washington and His Aides-de-Camp.* New York: Macmillan, 1936.

Whitridge, Arnold. *Rochambeau.* New York, 1965.

Wildes, Harry E. *Anthony Wayne.* New York, 1941.

Wilkins, Isaac. *My Services and Losses in Aid of the King's Cause during the American Revolution.* Brooklyn, N. Y.: Historical Printing Club, 1890.

Wilkinson, James. *Memoirs of My Own Times.* 3 vols. Philadelphia: A. Small, 1816.

Wilkinson, Norman B. "The Forgotten Founder of West Point" [Louis Tousard], in *Military Affairs*, Vol. 24, No. 4, (Winter 1960–1961), pp. 177–188.

Willard, Margaret Wheeler. *Letters of the American Revolution, 1774–1776.* Boston and New York, 1925.

Willey, Basil. *The Eighteenth Century Background.* New York, 1956.

Willcox, William B. *Portrait of a General: Sir Henry Clinton.* New York, 1964.

William and Mary Quarterly, 3d ser., Vol. 12, No. 2 (April 1955, Bicentennial Number): *Alexander Hamilton, 1755–1804.*

Williams, John. *Life of Alexander Hamilton.* New York, 1805.

Williams, Catherine. *Revolutionary Heroes.* Providence, 1839.

[Wilson, James]. *Considerations on Bank of North-America.* Philadelphia: Hall & Sellers, 1785.

Wood, Gordon S. *The Creation of the American Republic, 1776–1787.* Chapel Hill, N. C., 1969.

Woodhull, A. A. *The Battle of Princeton*. Princeton, N. J.: W. C. Sinclair, 1913.
Yoshee, Harry B., and James F. Zimmerman. *Impressment of American Sea-men*. New York, 1925.
Young, Eleanor. *Forgotten Patriot: Robert Morris*. New York, 1950.

MANUSCRIPT COLLECTIONS

Library of Congress, Washington, D.C.
    The largest collection of Hamilton documents; large collections of Jefferson,
    Washington, Madison, and so forth, documents.
New York Public Library, New York, New York
    Bancroft transcripts, Elias Boudinot, George Clinton, William Constable,
    Emmet Collection, Hamilton, Thomas Jefferson, James Kent, Gilbert Living-
    ston, William Livingston, James Madison, James McHenry, James Monroe,
    Robert Morris, Philip Schuyler, William Smith, Robert Troup, Noah Web-
    ster, Marinus Willett, Abraham Yates.
New York Historical Society, New York, New York
    William Alexander (Lord Stirling), John and Henry Cruger, James Duane,
    William Duer, Horatio Gates, Rufus King, John Lamb, Robert Livingston,
    Robert R. Livingston, Nicholas Low, Alexander McDougall, Joseph Reed,
    F. W. von Steuben.
Columbia University Library, New York, New York
    Nicholas Fish, Hamilton, John C. Hamilton Transcripts, Robert Harpur.
Yale University Library, New Haven, Connecticut
    Hamilton
Hamilton College Library, Clinton, New York
    Hamilton
Long Island Historical Society, Brooklyn, New York
    Hamilton, Henry and John Laurens.
Massachusetts Historical Society, Boston, Massachusetts
    Hamilton, Henry Knox, William Livingston, Timothy Pickering, Theodore
    Sedgwick.
National Archives, Washington, D.C.
    Military records, Virgin Islands records.
Henry E. Huntington Library, San Marino, California
Pennsylvania Archives, Harrisburg, Pennsylvania
Historical Society of Pennsylvania, Philadelphia, Pennsylvania
The Bank of New York, New York, New York

ACKNOWLEDGMENTS

Unless otherwise credited below, Hamilton documents quoted in the text are from *The Papers of Alexander Hamilton,* edited by Harold C. Syrett et al, 22 volumes to date. New York, Columbia University Press, 1961– and *The Law Practice of Alexander Hamilton,* edited by Julius Goebel, Jr., Joseph H. Smith, et al, 2 volumes to date. New York, Columbia University Press, 1964– . In general, all documents cited are traceable (except as otherwise noted) to the Manuscript Division, Library of Congress, Washington, D.C., and other collections of the Library of Congress, as set forth in detail in the notes of the editors to *The Papers of Alexander Hamilton* and *The Law Practice of Alexander Hamilton.* The following are also gratefully thanked for permissions given for use of material in their possession:

	Letters	*By permission of*
Nov. 26, 1775	Hamilton to John Jay	Hamilton Personal Papers, Manuscripts and Archives Division, The New York Public Library, Astor, Lenox and Tilden Foundations
April 11, 1777	Hamilton to Catharine Livingston	Massachusetts Historical Society
April 14, 1777	Hamilton to New York Committee of Correspondence	Haverford College Library

April 20, 1777	Hamilton to New York Committee of Correspondence	New-York Historical Society
August 10, 1777	Robert R. Livingston to Hamilton	The British Museum
August 18, 1777	Hamilton to Robert R. Livingston	New-York Historical Society
Sept. 1, 1777	Hamilton to Gouverneur Morris	New-York Historical Society
Nov. 21, 1777	Anthony Wayne to Horatio Gates	New-York Historical Society
Dec. 22, 1777	Hamilton to George Clinton	Harvard College Library, Harvard University
March 14, 1779	Hamilton to John Jay	Windsor Castle
May 22, 1779	Hamilton to John Laurens	Massachusetts Historical Society
Sept. 11, 1779	Hamilton to John Laurens	Historical Society of Pennsylvania
July 6, 1780	Hamilton to Anthony Wayne	Manuscripts and Archives Division, The New York Public Library, Astor, Lenox and Tilden Foundations
Sept. 6, 1780	Hamilton to James Duane	Columbia University Library
Sept. 30, 1780	Hamilton to Sir Henry Clinton	William L. Clements Library (University of Michigan)
Feb. 4, 1781	Hamilton to John Laurens	South Carolina Historical Society, Miscellaneous Manuscripts
Feb. 18, 1781	Hamilton to Philip Schuyler	Morristown National Historical Park
Oct. 12, 1781	Hamilton to Elizabeth Schuyler	Andre de Coppet Collection (Princeton University Library)
August 15, 1782	Hamilton to John Laurens	The Pierpont Morgan Library
July 25, 1783	Hamilton to John Jay	Windsor Castle
August 5, 1783	Hamilton to James Duane	New-York Historical Society
August 13, 1783	Hamilton to Robert R. Livingston	New-York Historical Society
August 30, 1783	Hamilton to Robert R. Livingston	New-York Historical Society
Jan. 27, 1784	Gouverneur Morris to Hamilton	Columbia University Library

Other acknowledgments are made to

Dodd, Mead and Company for *Alexander Hamilton's Wife* by Alice Curtis Desmond (1953).

Historical Society of Pennsylvania for excerpts from Benjamin Rush's notebook.

New Jersey Historical Society for "The Man Who Discovered Hamilton" by Broadus Mitchell from *Proceedings, New Jersey Historical Society*, LXIX, April 1951, 88–114.

New York Public Library, Astor, Lenox and Tilden Foundations for *Alexander Hamilton og hans modrene slaegt. Tidsbilleder fra Dansk Vest Indiens barndom,* by H.U. Ramsing.

Danish National Archives for information from Probate Court Transaction on the estate of Rachel Lavien.

INDEX

Abouville, d' 323
Adams, Abigail (Mrs. John) 225, 546, 552
Adams, Charles 549
Adams, John 59, 68, 82, 83, 132, 141, 147, 148, 153, 410, 427, 443, 453, 461, 502, 540, 546, 549, 552
  chosen for vice-presidency 541
  low opinion of H 6, 12, 35
  views on "taxation without representation" 60
Adams, Samuel 38, 61, 64, 68, 154, 453
Addison, Joseph 66, 348
Adgate, Mr. 441
Albany, New York 45, 59, 139, 156, 157, 162, 168, 169
Alexander, Catherine (Mrs. William) 49, 186
Alexander, James 45
Alexander, William 49, 98, 105, 106, 107, 111, 119, 125, 137, 145, 169, 170, 188, 193, 196, 197, 198, 200, 206, 208
Alexander Hamilton's Wife, A Romance of the Hudson (Desmond) 244
Alison, Francis 29
Allen, Ethan 84, 184, 535
Alsop, John 92
Ambler, Betsy 315
American Advertiser, The 346, 435, 502
Americanus (pseudonym of H) 62, 63
Ames, Fisher 549

Amsterdam, Holland 35
Anarchiad, The 448
Anderson, Enoch 144, 150
"Anderson, John" 272, 273, 280
André, John 97, 223, 268, 269, 272, 276, 295, 310, 314, 322, 383
  acknowledges complicity 275
  British propaganda use of his case 284
  captured 273
  H intercedes 284, 286–291
  manner 286, 291–292
  meeting with Arnold 272
  trial and execution 283–284, 291–292
Annapolis, Convention of 1786 442, 443, 530
  H addresses 444–445
  sets date for Constitutional Convention 445
Anti-Federalists 501–502, 513, 516, 517, 518, 525, 534, 540, 541, 542
Antigua 45
Antil, Edward 46, 431, 497, 500, 525
Arawak Indians 13, 28
Argentina 231
Armstrong, John 389, 396
Army
  H's plan 399, 400
Arnold, Benedict 84, 125, 153, 154, 190, 192, 199, 223–224, 280, 281, 283, 284, 285, 287, 288, 290, 291, 292, 295, 306, 307, 314, 325, 377, 408, 409, 433

eve of treason 268–271
flight 274–276
letter to Washington 276–277, 278, 279
meeting with André 272
Arnold, Peggy Shippen (Mrs. Benedict) 223–
224, 268, 274, 276–277, 279, 285, 292
guilt in treason plot 278
ravings described by H 274–275
Arnold Tavern, Morristown, N.J. 121
Articles of Confederation 177, 262, 342, 345,
346, 359, 363, 448, 462, 463, 465, 466, 468,
481, 487, 501
defects 401, 424–425
Asgill, Charles 383–385
Asia, H.M.S. 58, 62, 66, 84, 92, 94, 214, 407
fires on New York City 86–87
Atherton, Gertrude 1, 8, 10, 19, 47, 246
Augustus (Rom. emp.) 414
Auldjo, John 482, 490
Ayrshire, Scotland 6, 39

Badlam, Stephen 92–93
Bailey, Colonel 164
Baker, Bobby 494
Baldwin, Simeon 410
Bank of England 230, 264, 342
Bank of New York 300
applies for incorporation 437
charter granted 438
constitution drawn by H 437
founding 435–436
Bank of North America 394, 433, 434, 436
founded 345
Bank of Pennsylvania 433
Bank of the United States 230–231, 264
Barbados 12, 20
Barbé-Marbois, François de 340, 341
Barber, Francis 43, 182, 330, 336, 380, 551
influence on H 44, 49
Bard, Samuel 352
Barney, Joshua 399
Barras, Louis de 327, 335
Basking Ridge, New Jersey 108, 191
Baumann, Sebastian 93, 426, 552
Baurmeister, Major 102
Bayard, Mrs. Samuel 450
Baylor, George 118
Bean, Lieutenant 120
Beard, Charles 453, 512
Beaumarchais, Pierre Augustin Caron de 187
Beawe, Mr. 351
Beckley, John 456, 457, 483, 484, 485, 490,
547
Beckman, David 16, 22

Benson, Egbert 103, 119, 416, 420, 441, 442,
450, 511, 549, 550
Benson, Robert 511
Bermuda 407
Bethlehem, Pennsylvania 147
Betts, Stephen 332
Bicameral legislature 462, 466
Bill of Rights 489, 510, 521, 526
Birch, General 415
Blackstone, William 52, 76, 351, 353
Blagge, Benjamin 417
Bland, Martha Dangerfield 131–132
Bland, Theodorick 386
Blount, William 489, 490, 491, 492, 493
Blue Book 182
Board of War 167, 172, 178, 179
Boardman, John 37
Bonetta, H.M.S. 335
Book of Misdemeanours 52
Boston 35, 36, 40, 58, 59, 61, 62, 64, 96, 97, 98,
153, 218, 284
Boston Massacre 60
Boston Port Bill (1774) 63, 66
Boston Tea Party 60, 61, 62, 63, 83
Boudinot, Anna Maria 45, 46
Boudinot, Elias 41, 43, 56, 61, 87, 119, 184, 185,
186, 191, 193, 204, 210, 218, 334, 359, 376,
394, 395, 396, 453, 547
influence on H 44, 45–46
Boudinot, Elisha 45
Boudinot, Hannah (Mrs. Elias) 46, 186
Boudinot, Susanna Vergereau 45
Bowne, Robert 542
Boycott, Colonial 64, 68
Brandywine Creek, Battle of 143–145, 152, 153,
192
Brant, Joseph 220
Brazil 231
Breckenridge, Hugh H. 427
British monarchy 471, 473, 538
British Parliament: *see* Great Britain (Parlia-
ment)
Broeck, Dick Ten 410
Brooklyn, New York 42, 98, 100, 143
Brooklyn Heights, New York 98, 100, 101, 110,
289
Brooks, John 182, 238, 380, 381
Brooks's Club (London) 153
Broome, Jacob 542
Broome, Samuel, Jr. 410
Brown, Miss 131
Brown, John 536
Brown, Joseph 354
Brutus, Marcus Junius 414

Bryant, Mary 450
Buller, Mr. 351
Bunker Hill, Battle of 58, 59, 83, 84, 96
Burgoyne, John 84, 139, 140, 142, 153, 154, 155, 157, 166, 190, 215, 244, 246
    surrenders to Gates in Saratoga 154
Burke, Aedanus 512
Burke, Edmund 78
Burlamaquis, Jean Jacques 52, 351
Burr, Aaron 103, 122, 278, 353–354, 355, 407, 409, 410, 411, 412, 417, 426, 432, 485, 486, 511, 529, 541, 543
    first meeting with H 102
Burr, Theodosia Prevost (Mrs. Aaron) 354
Burwell, Rebecca 315
Butler, Richard 196, 393
Butler, Walter 220
Buus, Hans 25

Cadwalader, John 113, 193
Caesar, Julius 28, 214, 502
Cahoon brothers 272
Caldwell, James 46
Cambridge, Massachusetts 85, 97
Camden, Battle of (S.C.) 265–267, 283
Campbell, Archibald 124, 226
Campbell, Patrick 332, 334
Canada 63, 72, 73, 83, 84, 96, 97, 135, 139, 377, 407, 535
Carib Indians 13, 21, 28
Carleton, Guy 153, 384, 407, 408
Caron, Pierre Augustin 128
Carpenter's Hall 68
Carrington, Edward 314
Carroll, Daniel 376, 492
Carter, John: *see* Church, John Barker
Cato 502
Causes of Depreciation of the Continental Currency (Schuyler) 253
Cedar Street Church (New York City) 41
Ceres, H.M.S. 408–409
Chambers, Captain 63
Chandler, T.B. 52, 53
Channing, William Ellery 316
Charles II (Eng. k.) 59, 62
Charles XII (Swed. k.) 52
Charleston, South Carolina 96, 99, 139, 226, 256, 266, 270, 377
Charlestown, Nevis 5
Charon, H.M.S. 329
Chase, Samuel 212–214, 225, 370, 502
Chastellux, François de 240–241
Checks and balances 472
Chew, Benjamin 149

Chief executive 464, 471–472
    election 472–473, 474, 486
    impeachment 464, 472, 474, 507–509
China 59
Choisy, Mr. 328, 331
Chouin, Marquis de (André Michel Victor) 219
Christiansted, St. Croix 2, 8, 10, 11, 15, 25, 26, 34, 41
Church, Angelica Schuyler 244, 247, 250, 252, 254, 255, 257, 258, 302, 320, 326, 348, 349, 352, 373, 376, 403, 429, 430, 431, 434, 462, 530–534, 554–559
Church, Catherine 434
Church, John Barker 254, 319, 328, 354, 373, 409, 434, 435, 439, 484, 532, 554, 559
Church, Philip 326, 348, 352, 369, 370, 434, 558
Churchill, Winston 472
Cicero, Marcus Tullius 40, 449
Cincinnati, Society of the 425, 426–428, 454–455, 456, 458, 468, 531, 551
Citation Act 422
Civil rights 73, 74, 77
Clark, Mr. 537
Clausewitz, Carl von 137
Clayton, John 485
Clinton, De Witt 513
Clinton, George 68, 97, 164, 165, 171, 173–174, 175, 176, 177, 187, 221, 360, 361, 362, 363, 364, 366, 379, 381, 385, 386, 399, 402, 406, 413, 414, 415, 416, 440, 445, 446, 447, 449, 475, 481, 488, 493, 498, 500, 502, 512, 513, 515, 530, 540, 541, 542, 543
    impost 441–442
    Poughkeepsie Constitutional Convention 516–526
Clinton, Henry 84, 94, 139, 141, 142, 154, 157, 158, 163, 166, 191, 192, 193, 195, 196, 197, 210, 211, 213, 215, 219, 220, 225, 260, 262, 268, 269, 271, 276, 280, 283, 284, 285, 286, 288, 289, 290, 314, 319, 321, 324, 325, 327, 328, 329, 333, 334, 335, 362, 383, 384
Clinton, James 327
Clintonians 446–449
    Poughkeepsie convention 517–526, 530
Closen, Jean von 311
Coalition Bank: *see* Bank of Pennsylvania
Coates, Elizabeth 143
Cochran, Mrs. John 247
Codwise, George 437
Coercive Acts: *see* Intolerable Acts
Coke, Edward 351
Colden, Cadwallader 86
College of New Jersey: *see* Princeton University

College of William and Mary 461, 485
Columbia University 26, 34, 41, 42, 43, 45, 56, 57, 58, 59, 61, 64, 67, 74, 75, 82, 84, 85, 88, 92, 93, 244, 350
    Barnard College 104
    discipline 53
    H at 50–56, 57
Columbus, Christopher 13, 21
Commentaries on the Laws of England (Blackstone) 76, 351
Commerce 346–347, 439, 506
Committee of Correspondence (New York) 126–127, 136, 173, 413
Committee of 51, 64, 67
Committee of Mechanics 64
Committee of Safety 86
Concord, Battle of 54, 58, 59, 83, 96
Confederation Congress: *see* Congress of the Confederation
Confiscation 422
Congress, U.S.
    powers of 487–488
    see also Continental Congress
Congress of the Confederation 46
Connecticut 38, 174, 365, 440, 443, 447, 454, 463, 476, 482, 512
Connecticut Plan 482
    see also Constitutional Convention; New Jersey Plan; Virginia Plan
Conqueror, The 1, 246
Constable, William 437, 542
Constitution, U.S. 46, 60, 177, 473, 474, 487, 488, 490, 491, 493, 494, 495, 496, 497, 498, 502, 503, 506, 510, 527, 534, 535, 536, 537, 538, 539, 541, 550
    adopted by Convention 493
    ratification 488–489, 499, 501, 512–527
    Twenty-fifth Amendment 473
Constitutional Convention 500, 506, 530, 552
    adopts constitution 493
    Committee of Detail 486
    Committee of Eleven 486
    Committee of Style 487–488, 510
    Committee on Standing Rules and Orders 457, 460
    economic motives 445
    "Great Compromise" of July 16 482
    H calls for 263, 345, 363, 385–386, 402
    Hamilton-Spaight resolution 463
    rules 460–461
    secrecy rule 461–462
    slavery 463
    see also Connecticut Plan; New Jersey Plan; Virginia Plan

Continental Army 93, 94, 142–143
    demands for pay 123, 164, 165, 374, 377, 380–382, 389–395
    dissatisfaction among officers 268, 380–385
    H's reorganization plan 262–265
    low morale 108–109, 123, 174–175, 380
    Morristown, winter quarters at 118, 121, 122, 131–132, 134
    mutiny 232, 306, 380, 389–390, 392–397
    Negro slaves 232–234, 368
    ragged condition 96, 107, 108, 110, 174–175, 240, 380
    reorganization 178–182
    suffering 145, 174–175, 190, 240, 380
    Valley Forge, winter at 173–189
    weaknesses 101–103, 106, 109, 134, 261
Continental Association 58, 60, 61, 68, 92, 96, 153
Continental Congress, First 51, 58, 60, 83, 92, 93, 94, 96, 101, 125, 128, 488, 507, 534
    Articles of Confederation 177
    Claims by the army 374, 377, 380–382, 389–395
    Committee on Finance 305
    Committee on the War 109
    Declaration of Independence 99–100
    defended by H 70–73, 74, 75, 82
    divided 376–397
    Gates, Horatio 154–155
    import taxes 359–360, 374, 377–379, 388
    incapacity 176–178, 262
    Laurens, J. 295–296
    mutineers 392–397
    Princeton 395
    rebuked by H 212–214
    recruiting foreign officers 128–130
    Seabury's attack 69–70
    taxation authority 224–225, 228–229, 344–345
    warned by H to leave Philadelphia 146
    Washington 101, 102, 106, 107–108, 112, 122–123, 151, 176, 178; (criticized) 151
    weakened 403
    see also Congress, U.S.
Continental Congress, Second 82, 84, 89, 118
Continentalist, The 318, 346, 347, 348, 357, 359, 378
Conway cabal 152, 161–162, 167, 168–172, 176, 179, 184, 190, 198, 204, 237, 238, 245
Conway, Thomas 152, 155, 161, 167, 168, 172, 179, 181, 207, 245
Cooper, Myles 51, 52, 53, 57, 58, 62, 66, 67, 69, 74, 75, 82, 83, 85, 88
    rescued by H 54–55

Cooper Union for the Advancement of Science
    and Art 499
Cornwallis, Charles 100, 107, 109, 110, 112, 114,
    142, 143, 148, 186, 200, 265, 266, 270, 306,
    314, 315, 322, 327, 328, 329, 330, 333, 334,
    336, 359, 383, 385
  surrenders at Yorktown 334–337
Coronaro, Luigi 217
Corsicans, The: *see* Hearts of Oak (volunteer
    company)
Cortlandt, Augustus van 450
Country Journal, The 515
Craigie, Andrew 527
Crèvecoeur, Hector St. John de 452
Cromot du Bourg, General 324
Cruger, Henry, Jr. 22, 24
Cruger, John H. 22, 437
Cruger, Nicholas 16, 26, 27, 28, 38, 40, 43, 354,
    525, 554
  character and career 22
  H in his employ 16, 22–25
  leaves affairs to H 23–25
  patron of H 22, 34, 40, 44
  return to St. Croix 25
Cruger, Tileman 24
Curaçao 22, 24
Currency
  depreciation 224–225, 261, 376
  national 376
Curtennies 93
Curtis, Jack 381
Custis, G.W.P. 108, 122

Dana, William 238
Dane, Nathan 547
Davis, William 182
Dayton, Elias 327
Dayton, Jonathan 49, 537
Deane, Silas 187
Dearborn, Henry 174, 176
Declaration of Independence 69, 72, 99–100,
    347
Defense of the Destruction of the Tea, A (H)
    62
Delaware 29, 39, 365, 442, 463, 465, 476, 482,
    501, 512, 537
Delaware River 108
  crossing 109, 112
Democracy in America (Tocqueville) 954
Demosthenes 116–117, 234
Denmark 38
  Virgin Islands 2, 15, 21–22
Dennis, Patrick 216
De Nully, Nancy 24

Desmond, Alice Curtis 244
Destouches, Admiral 316
Deux-Ponts, Guillaume de 331
Dickinson, John 60, 177, 202, 204, 393, 394, 395,
    396, 452, 465, 491
Dipnall, Thomas 16–17
Dobbs Ferry, New York 289, 319, 323
Donop, Mr. 112
Douglass, William 95
Duane, James 65, 68, 227, 255, 261, 262, 295,
    305, 336, 340, 342, 344, 360, 361, 402, 405,
    412, 415, 417, 420, 421, 422, 424, 441, 443,
    453, 513, 515, 516, 543
Dudley, Dorothy 97–98
Duer, Catherine 49
Duer, William 49, 128, 180, 181, 204, 437, 441,
    501, 542, 551, 553
Dundas, Alexander 335
Dundas, Thomas 314

East India Company 60
  Dutch 59
Eclogues (Virgil) 18, 26
Edgeworth, R.L. 285
Edict of Nantes (1658) 7
Edwards, Evan 195, 202, 209
Egan, William 16, 17
Electoral College 541
Elizabeth I (Eng. q.) 414
Elizabeth, New Jersey 40, 41, 47, 49, 56, 132,
    182, 245, 532
  schooling 43–44, 46
Elizabethtown, New Jersey: *see* Elizabeth,
    New Jersey
Elizabethtown Academy 44, 45, 46
Elliot, Andrew 289
Ellsworth, Oliver 376, 393, 394
England, Church of 45, 51, 62
Epithalamium (McHenry) 302–304, 368
Erskine, William 112
Essay Concerning Human Understanding
    (Locke) 62–63
Estaing, Comte d' 212–213, 216–217, 218, 219,
    226, 227–228, 237
Eulogium on General Nathanael Greene
    116, 193, 552–553
Eustace, John S. 208
Evidence (Gilbert) 351
Evidence, Historical 2–4

Fairfield Gazette, The (Conn.) 483, 484
Farmer Refuted, The (H) 53, 75–82, 83, 84, 99,
    187
Fawcett, John 7, 8, 10

Fawcett, Mary Uppington 7, 8, 15
  St. Eustatius 10
  separation from husband 7–8
Fawcett, Rachel 2, 4, 5, 10, 11, 19, 21, 430
  bequest of slaves 17
  birth 7
  death 16–17
  divorced 6, 11–13
  estate settled 17–18
  keeps store 16
  marriage 6, 9
  St. Croix 8–9, 15–16
  St. Eustatius 10, 11
  separation from James Hamilton 15
Federalist, The 26, 214, 345, 354, 422, 442, 494,
  514, 516, 518, 520, 530, 531, 532, 550
  authorship 499–500, 507, 510–511
  first issue 502
  principal themes 502–511
  purpose 500
  significance 511–512
Federalists 521, 523, 524, 526, 529, 530, 541,
  543, 544
Financial planning and national government
  342–344
First Philippic (Demosthenes) 116
Fish, Nicholas 52, 64, 66, 84, 98, 187, 320, 330,
  332, 426
Fishkill, New York 157, 273, 346
FitzPatrick, Richard 183
Fitz Simmons, Thomas 376, 378, 388, 439,
  550
Fleming, Edward 84, 92
Fleury, Francis Louis T. (Marquis de Fleury)
  226, 255, 260, 314, 328, 336, 349
Flexner, James T. 197
Florida 40
Floyd, William 388, 402
Ford, Mr. 441
Ford, Jacob 121, 240, 247
Forman, David 207, 269
Fort Albany, New York 59
Fort George, New York 87, 94, 407
Fort Lee, New Jersey 106, 107, 108, 149, 262
Fort Mercer, New Jersey 151, 152, 155, 157,
  166, 167, 172, 192, 245
Fort Mifflin, Pennsylvania 151, 152, 155, 157,
  166, 167, 172, 179, 192, 245
Fort Montgomery, New York 220, 542
Fort Orange, New York 59
Fort Stanwix, New York 154
Fort Ticonderoga, New York 84, 97, 135, 138,
  140, 141, 153, 154, 163, 172, 220, 244, 247,
  301, 535

Fort Washington, New York 98, 105, 106, 107,
  108, 109, 149, 215
Fox, Charles James 153, 183
France 14, 21, 38, 60, 132, 260, 264, 342, 345,
  399, 400
  ally of U.S. 187–188, 191, 212–213, 224, 269,
  316, 399–400
  interests in North America 39–40
  supplies and munitions 128–129
Franklin, Benjamin 60, 68, 151, 179–180, 187,
  341, 398, 452, 456, 458, 464, 478, 491, 493,
  531
Franklin, William Temple 456
Franks, David 274, 277, 279, 409
Fraser, Alexander and Elizabeth (Thornton) 11
Fraunces Tavern 87, 407, 408
Frederica (princess of Wurttemberg) 180
Frederick (duke of York) 483
Frederick the Great (Prus. k.) 179
Frederiksted, St. Croix 11, 34
Free Thoughts on Congress (Seabury) 69–70, 74
French, Susannah 45
French and Indian War 40, 97, 116
*Full Vindication of the Measures of Con-
  gress, A* (H) 53, 70–73, 75, 82, 83, 84, 99,
  187

Gadsden, Christopher 60, 99
Gage, Thomas 69, 88
Galloway, Joseph 68
Gates, Horatio 124, 125, 174, 175, 176, 178, 190,
  199, 203, 214, 215, 238, 244, 245, 246, 253,
  270, 276, 314, 362, 389, 392, 552
  Camden 265–267
  congratulated by Congress 154–155
  Conway cabal 152, 161–162, 168–172
  influence in Congress 152, 153
  popularity 141
  president of Board of War 167
  reluctant to release troops 158–160
  succeeds Schuyler in northern command 141
  Washington, George 152–153, 154
Gentleman's Magazine of London 55
George II (Eng. k.) 113
George III (Eng. k.) 42, 60, 96, 99, 183, 188, 198,
  214, 220, 398, 471, 483
George Washington (Flexner) 197
Georgia 39, 226, 234, 365, 443, 476, 482, 499,
  512
Germantown, Battle of 148–151, 152, 153, 168,
  192, 207
Gerry, Elbridge 455, 489, 490, 491, 492, 493,
  547, 548, 550
Gibbon, Edward 512

Gibbs, Caleb 160, 176, 246
Gilbert, Mr. 351
Gilbert, William W. 417
Gililand, John 330
Gimat, John Joseph 330, 332, 333
"Gingerland," Nevis 5, 6, 9
Gist, Mordecai 327
Glover, John 101, 110, 111, 112, 160, 162, 218
God and nature 76–77
God-child of Washington, A (Schuyler) 246
Goodchild, Cecil Wray 17
Gordon, William 238–239
Gorham, Nathaniel 376, 455, 476, 491
Government credit
    national debt 342–344
    restoration 367
Government, National: *see* National government
"Grange," The (Ayrshire, Scotland) 6, 39
"Grange," The (New York City) 56, 103, 369
"Grange" plantation (St. Croix) 6, 7
Grant, James 112
Grasse, Francois Joseph Paul de 322, 326, 328, 329, 334
Graves, Thomas 327
Graydon, Alexander 131
Grayson, William 185, 186, 197, 202
Great Britain 29, 38, 231, 407, 440
    American colonies 38–40, 58–61
    Parliament 22, 52, 60, 62, 63, 69, 72, 73, 77–78, 99, 100, 183, 254, 554
    peace treaty 392, 399, 401
    Rome 72
    trade 38–39, 60–61, 84
    West Indies 14, 15, 21
"Great Meeting in the Fields" 64–67, 68, 69, 82, 92, 99, 262
    H addresses 65–67
Green, Jacob 30
Green, Nicholas 37, 38
Green Mountain Boys 84, 153, 184, 535
Greene, Catherine Littlefield (Mrs. Nathanael) 186, 551
Greene, Christopher 152
Greene, Nathanael 98, 100, 105, 106, 107, 119, 143, 144, 145, 149, 150, 186, 187, 193, 196, 197, 198, 208, 218, 270, 276, 279, 283, 289, 290, 297, 298, 306, 314, 315, 316, 321, 322, 333, 372, 377, 403, 469, 551, 552–553, 554
Greyhound 289
Grotius, Hugo 52, 351
Guarda Costas 24, 28
Guichen, Luc Urbain de B. 269
Guizot, Francois P.G. 512

Hackensack, New Jersey 106, 107
Haert, Balthasar de 410
Hale, Nathan 38, 286
Half Moon 59
Hamilton 524–525, 527
Hamilton, Alexander (great grandfather of H) 6
Hamilton, Alexander 11, 13, 14, 39
    abolition of slavery 432
    Adams, John 6, 12, 35
    America, faith in 138
    André, John 284, 285, 286–291, 292–293
    Annapolis convention 444–445
    anti-Tory laws in New York 449
    appearance 15, 41, 65–66, 108
    army, discontent in the 380–385, 392–397
    army, peacetime 399, 400
    army supplies 178–182, 223, 320
    Arnold, Benedict 274–276
    Arnold, Peggy 277
    Asgill 384–385
    authority, respect for 61
    Bank of New York 435–436
    Bank of the United States 230–231, 264, 305
    bar 354
    Barber, Francis 43, 44, 39
    birth 1–2, 18
    birthdate 2–4
    Bland, Mrs. 131–132
    bookkeeper 16
    Boston 40
    Boston Tea Party 61
    Boudinot, Elias 41, 43, 44, 45–46, 56, 61
    boyhood 16, 17, 18, 19, 22–36, 233–234
    British monarchy 471, 473, 538
    Burr, Aaron 102
    business experience 16, 35
    cash book 409, 554, 557
    Chase, Samuel and Congress 212–214
    Church, Angelica 530–534, 554–559
    civil rights 73, 74, 77, 126
    Clinton criticized for opposing Convention 482, 497
    college rules observed 53
    colonial independence 61
    colonial union and Continental Congress 66, 70–71, 74
    Congress 66, 70–71, 74, 75, 82, 146
    Congress, member of 263–264, 267, 370, 374
    Congressional debates, public admission 387–388
    Congressional powers 487–488, 489
    conscription urged by H 263
    Constitution 487

Constitution, signer of 493
Constitutional Convention 263, 345, 363, 385–386, 402, 456–495
Continental Congress 403
Cooper, Myles 51, 52, 53, 54–55, 57, 58, 62
Convention for New York 480
courtship and marriage 242–259, 298–304
Cruger 16, 22–25, 34, 40, 44
d'Estaing 216
disinherited 13, 18
Duane, James 262–265
economic philosophy 80, 224–225, 229–231, 342–344
education 18, 25–26, 43
Elizabethtown preparatory school 43–44, 46
English-speaking union 83
father, concern for 7, 15–16, 430
federal judicial power 418–420
federal republic 262–263
Federalist, The 504
Foreign Affairs, Secretary of 306
foreign loans 295, 296–297
French aid 187–188
Gates, Horatio 156–166
Germantown, Battle of 149–151
Gordon's libeling 238–239
government reorganization 262–265
Great Britain, rebellion against 66–67
Harpur 51–52
"hurricane" letter 32–34
illegitimacy 6, 18
inflation, fears of 136, 224–225, 261
Jefferson, Thomas 6, 12
King's College 50–51, 52–56, 57
Knox, Hugh 28–30, 33–35, 36, 41, 43, 44, 45, 51, 77
Laurens 209, 372
law practice 405, 409–423
law studies 351–352
Lee court-martial 200–207
Livingston, Kitty 47, 131–132
Livingston, William 41, 43, 44, 45, 46–47, 51, 56, 61
Long Island 101
manners 47, 131, 258
matrimony 348–349
military career 91–337
mobs 54–55, 61, 89–90
Monmouth campaign 192–200
Morris, Robert 229–231, 253, 362–364
mother 19
national government 262–263, 305, 345, 346, 362, 369, 462–463, 464, 465, 476, 477, 481
national sovereignty 402

Negro slaves in army 232–234
New York Assembly 446–447
New York City, plan for attack on 270
New York legislature 450; (letters to) 126–128
New York politicians 366–367
Newport, Rhode Island 215–216, 217–218
"numerous representation" in the House 486–487, 519
oath of allegiance to U.S. 188–189
"open" presidency 545–546
personality 26–28
Philadelphia 392–397
piety 17, 51
polemical powers 62–63, 65–67, 71, 75
political philosophy 62–63, 65–67, 70–84, 262–265, 342–347
Poughkeepsie Constitutional Convention 516
precocity 22, 26, 82
Princeton University 50
prisoners' exchange 183–186, 375
profiteering deplored 212, 224
pseudonyms 62, 63, 212, 413, 415, 542
Quebec Act 72–73, 85
religious freedom 72, 85–86
"sacred rights of mankind" 76–77
St. Croix newspaper pieces 30–31
Schuyler, Elizabeth 244–248
Schuyler, Philip, support of 141
Seabury, pamphlet controversy with 69–84
separation of powers 464
slavery 20–21, 22, 24, 71–72, 77, 233–235, 368, 506, 552
Smith, Joshua 281–283
Stevens, Edward 12, 26–27
tax collector for New York 360–364
taxation 224–225, 228–229, 305, 344–345, 359–360
Tories 412–423
Treasury, Secretary of the 550
treaties as "supreme law of land" 418–423, 449
Troup, Robert 51, 52, 53, 54, 56, 57
Valley Forge, winter at 173–189
volunteer company, drills in 84, 86
Waddington and Trespass Act 416–423
Washington 118–133, 123–126, 172, 270, 284, 294–295, 297, 307, 308–310, 319, 380, 539–540, 546–547
West Florida boundary 399
Wilson, James 386
writings 31, 32–34, 36, 46, 48–49, 52–53, 62, 63, 212, 229–231, 262–265, 318, 346–347,

351–352, 356, 357, 359, 413, 482, 498, 500–501, 502–504, 542, 552–553
Yorktown, Battle of 321, 337
Hamilton, Alexander, Jr. (son of H) 429, 497, 525, 527, 528
Hamilton, Allan McLane 9, 18
Hamilton, Angelica 429, 430, 431, 497, 525, 527
Hamilton, Eliza 429
Hamilton, Elizabeth 6
Hamilton, Elizabeth Schuyler 2, 19, 132, 266, 270, 274, 277, 285, 286, 287, 290, 295, 306, 311, 319, 320, 325, 326, 338, 339, 349, 352, 357, 368, 379, 398, 401, 405, 411, 429, 430, 485, 496–497, 500, 525, 527, 528, 531, 532, 554, 556, 557, 558, 559
  character 249, 257, 258–259
  courtship and marriage 242–259, 298–304
  first meeting with H 244–248
  love for H 258–259, 277–278
Hamilton, Gilbert de 6
Hamilton, Isabelle Erskine 6
Hamilton, James (brother of H) 2, 12, 15, 17, 18, 22, 26, 430
Hamilton, James, Sr. (father of H) 5, 6–7, 8, 10, 11, 12, 13, 15, 31–32, 39
Hamilton, James Alexander 429
Hamilton, John Church 2, 3, 19, 25, 26, 28–29, 43, 61, 88, 90, 101, 103, 106, 119, 120, 125, 146, 166, 193, 429, 431, 449
Hamilton, Philip 352, 357, 358, 405, 497, 525, 527, 557, 559
Hamilton, Walton de 6
Hamilton, William Leslie 6, 12
Hamilton, William Stephen 429
Hamiltonapolis 43, 515
Hamiltons of Ayrshire (Scotland) 6
Hamm, Archibald 10
Hammond, George 422
Hampton, Wade 314
Hancock, John 147, 148, 453, 540
Harding, Robert 88
Harison, Richard 410, 513, 535, 536
Harlem Heights, Battle of 102–105, 119
Harpur, Robert 51–52, 92, 437
Harrison, Robert Hanson 118, 122, 124, 184, 185, 186, 196, 280, 311, 313
Haverstraw, New York 106, 215, 216, 220, 272, 324
Hearts of Oak (volunteer company) 84, 85, 86, 92
Heath, William 124
Heister, General 100
Henly, Adjutant 96

Henry, Patrick 38, 61, 68, 171, 174, 453, 488, 502, 512, 514, 523
Henry, William 393
Herkimer, Nicholas 154
Herring, Dr. 16
Hessians 99, 100, 105, 106, 110, 111, 112, 118, 136, 143, 148
H.G. (pseudonym of H) 542
Higginson, Stephen 443, 445
Hobart, John Sloss 513
Hobbes, Thomas 52, 506
Holland 21, 38, 59, 231, 341, 342, 345, 385
Holt, John 53, 62, 212, 410
Homer 45
Hood, Samuel 327
Hoogland, Jeronimus 275
Horace 29, 44
Hortalez et Cie 128, 187
House of Representatives, U.S. 49, 464, 485, 486, 502, 519, 541, 550, 552
  H's plan 476
  Judiciary, Committee of 508–509
  proportional representation 477–478, 491–492
Howard, John Eager 314
Howe, Richard 99, 100, 101, 102, 217
Howe, Robert 306
Howe, William 84, 97, 99, 100, 102, 104, 105, 106, 109, 113, 131, 135, 136, 137, 138, 139, 141, 142, 143, 146, 147, 148, 151, 152, 154, 156, 157, 158, 166, 167, 175, 185, 191, 192, 210, 211
Howell, Samuel 433
Huddy, Joshua 383
Hudson, Henry 59
Huger, Mr. 537
Hughes, Hugh 165
Hughes, James M. 412, 515
Hume, David 17, 52, 78, 512
Humphrey, Mr. 311
Humphreys, David 122, 261, 484, 532
Hunt, Thomas 332
Huntington, Mr. 328
Hurricane of 1772 32–34

Import duty 359–360, 377–378, 441–442
Independence Hall 38, 456
Independent Journal, The 502, 507
Indonesia 231
Inflation
  H's fear of 136
  wartime 224–225, 261
Ingersoll, Jared 433
Ingram, Archibald 15

Internal Revenue Service, U.S. 508
Intolerable Acts (1774) 63
Instructions for the Captain (Steuben) 94
Ireland 39
Iroquois Indians 59, 84
Italy 45
Ivers, Thomas 417
Izard, Ralph 377

Jackson, Mr. 158, 550
Jackson, William 393, 456, 457, 458, 491, 499
Jamaica, B.W.I. 13
James II (Eng. k.) 59
Jameson, John 273, 274, 275
Jay, John 47, 49, 65, 68, 82, 89, 90, 91, 92, 94,
    214, 233, 234, 262, 403, 404, 410, 432, 450,
    453, 494, 504, 513, 515, 516, 523, 524, 539,
    542, 548, 554
  collaborates with H on *The Federalist* 501
Jay, Sarah Livingston (Mrs. John) 242, 531
Jay's Treaty (1794) 401, 423
Jefferson, Martha Wayles (Mrs. Thomas) 241–
    242
Jefferson, Thomas 59, 83, 234, 258, 307, 314,
    315, 327, 376, 388, 422, 427, 439, 442, 443,
    446, 451, 452, 453, 455, 457, 461, 485, 486,
    493, 502, 506, 510, 511, 538, 541, 548, 552
  low opinion of H 6, 12, 68
Johnson, Lieutenant 95
Johnson, Samuel 52, 53, 75
Johnson, William S. 452, 475, 487
Jones, John 165
Jones, Joseph 389
Jones, Samuel 410, 420
Journals of the Continental Congress 1774–
    1779 147
Judicial review 509
Jumel Mansion 105
Jungkenn, Baron von 102

Kalb, Johann de 177, 186
Kennedy, Dennis 165
Kent, James 353, 410, 412, 420, 511, 515, 518,
    520, 523
  describes H 411
Kentucky 534–535
Kilpatrick, Lieutenant Captain 332
King, Rufus 464, 466, 473, 475, 481, 485, 487,
    489, 492, 506, 512, 514, 515, 543
King's College: *see* Columbia University
King's College (Oxford University) 51
King's Ferry, New York 272, 273, 279, 324
Kingfisher, H.M.S. 55, 57, 58, 85, 88
Kingston, New York 94, 128, 154, 157

Kissinger, Henry A. 116
Knowlton, Thomas 103–104
Knox, Henry 97, 102, 103, 105, 113, 114, 119,
    142, 149, 150, 268, 280, 311, 324, 327, 333,
    383, 384, 385, 406, 407, 408, 425, 426, 454,
    455, 515, 540
Knox, Hugh 28–30, 31, 33–35, 36, 41, 43, 44, 45,
    51, 76, 130–131, 135–136, 142, 174, 237
Knox, Lucy 186
Knyphausen, William von 261, 263, 289
Kortright, Cornelius 22, 34, 40, 41
Kortright, Lawrence 437
Kortright & Company 44
Kosciuszko, Thaddeus 177, 186, 269

Laberius (Decimus) 214
Lafayette, Marquis de 38, 129, 130, 139, 142,
    144, 171, 177, 183, 187, 192, 193, 194, 195,
    196, 198, 200, 218, 268, 277, 280, 283, 288,
    297, 301, 302, 307, 308, 309, 312, 313, 315–
    316, 318, 321, 322, 326, 327, 328, 330, 333,
    369, 455, 551
  following Arnold's treason 275
  recommends H's promotion 297–298
Lamb, John 65, 93, 324, 512
Lancaster, Pennsylvania 147, 148, 392–393
Land bank 435, 436
Langdon, John 514
Lansing, John, Jr. 448, 453, 462, 463, 465, 466,
    468, 470, 472, 473, 475, 481, 482, 485, 490,
    493, 513, 521, 522, 526
Lansing, Robert 366, 410
Lasher, John 85, 86, 87, 98
Laurence, John 409, 410, 416, 417, 420, 542, 543
Laurens, Henry 171, 209, 213, 232, 295
Laurens, John 122, 131, 150, 171, 199, 207, 208–
    209, 213, 214, 231–232, 235, 238, 239, 241,
    242–243, 244, 249, 256, 257, 260, 267, 268,
    271, 283, 285, 286, 291, 298, 300, 305, 306,
    309, 317, 318, 320, 324, 330, 332, 333, 334,
    335, 336, 341, 345, 368, 370, 371, 389, 532,
    552
  appointed minister to France 295–296
  death 371–372
  duel with Lee 208–210
  H prepares letter 296
  H helps enlist slaves 232–234
  secures foreign loan 341
Lauzan, Mr. 329
Lavien, John Michael 2, 11, 18
  marriage to Rachel Fawcett 6, 9
  obtains divorce 6, 11–13, 18
Lavien, Peter 2, 11, 12, 13, 18, 258, 430
Law, John 264

Learned, Ebenezer 163, 164

Ledyard, Isaac 414, 415

Lee, Charles 94, 97, 98, 105, 107, 108, 122, 125,
    128, 152, 155, 158, 167, 168, 171, 183, 184,
    185, 191, 199, 212, 213, 214, 215, 220, 280,
    337, 354, 371
  court martial 195, 197, 200–207
  dismissed from army 210
  Laurens duel 218–210
  Monmouth 192–198

Lee, Henry ("Light-Horse Harry") 146–147,
    151, 314, 514, 537

Lee, Richard Henry 68, 177, 386, 440, 501, 512,
    514, 540

L'Enfant, Pierre 538

Le Roy, Jacob A. 410

L' Estrade, Colonel 331

*Letter from Phocion to the Considerate Citi-
    zens of New York* (H) 413–414

Letters of the Federal Farmer (Lee) 512

Leviathan, The (Hobbes) 506

Levine, Alexander: *see* Lavien, John Michael

Lewine, John Michael: *see* Lavien, John Mi-
    chael

Lewine, Peter: *see* Lavien, Peter

Lewis, Morgan 409, 416

Lex Mercatoria (Beawe) 351

Lexington, Battle of 54, 58, 59, 83, 96

L'Hommedien, Ezra 543

Lightbourn, Captain 28

Lincoln, Abraham 71, 235, 499

Lincoln, Benjamin 125, 226, 319, 323, 324, 335,
    380, 446, 540

Lippincott, Richard 383

Little, John 96

Livermore, David 319

Livingston, Brockholst 46, 409, 410, 416

Livingston, Catherine (Kitty) 221, 245, 251,
    532–534
  courted by H 47–49, 131–132

Livingston, Catherine Van Brugh (Mrs. Philip)
    45, 221, 339, 341

Livingston, Edward 409

Livingston, Gilbert 520

Livingston, James 95, 272

Livingston, Judity 47

Livingston, Peter 65

Livingston, Philip 42–44, 65, 92, 437

Livingston, Robert 42, 409, 441

Livingston, Robert C. 437, 441

Livingston, Robert R. 136, 137, 140, 405, 409,
    416, 420, 435, 436, 453, 513, 515, 516, 517,
    518, 521

Livingstoń, Sarah 47, 49

Livingston, Susan 47

Livingston, Susannah ("Suki") 46–47, 221–223,
    237, 243, 245, 261

Livingston, William 41, 43, 45, 56, 61, 82, 261,
    532, 533, 537
  influence on Hamilton 44, 46–47, 51

Livingston Manor, New York 45

Livy 29

Locke, John 52, 62–63, 83, 351, 505

Lockyer, Captain 63

London 63

Long Island, New York 98, 99, 104, 105, 110,
    113

Long Island, Battle of 100–102

Longinus, Dionysius Cassius 117

Lott, Abraham 251

Lott, Cornelia 251

Loudon, Samuel 346

Louis XIV (Fr. k.) 13, 471

Louis XVI (Fr. k.) 406

Louisiana Territory 40

Lovell, James 154, 296

Low, Isaac 65

Low, Nicholas 513

Lowndes, Captain 28

Lucian 44

Luzerne, Chevalier de la 273

Lytton, Ann: *see* Mitchell, Ann Venton

Lytton, Ann Fawcett 7, 8, 17

Lytton, James 8, 9, 11, 17, 18, 19, 430
  purchases "Grange" plantation 7

Lytton, James, Jr. 19

Lytton, Josia 8

Lytton, Peter 16, 19, 35
  appointed guardian of H 17, 18

McCall, Archibald 433

McCurtin, Daniel 98–99

McDonnell, Ann 16

McDougall, Alexander 52, 62, 64–65, 67, 68, 69,
    82, 92, 105, 151, 158, 220, 263, 270, 353,
    380, 381, 407, 435, 436
  speaks at "Great Meeting in the Field" 65

McHenry, James 122, 124, 192, 199, 217, 252,
    270, 274, 275, 279, 295, 302–304, 309, 311,
    325, 368, 369, 373, 376, 379, 403, 475, 491

McLean, Archibald 507, 510

McNobeny, Thomas 22

McWilliams, William 169

Machiavelli, Niccoló 31

Maclay, William 511

Macon, John 41, 101

Madison, James 50, 83, 214, 376, 377, 378, 380,
    381, 386, 387, 388, 392, 396, 397, 439, 440,

442, 443, 446, 452, 454, 455, 456, 457, 460, 461, 464, 465, 466, 467, 469, 470, 471, 473, 474, 475, 476, 478, 483, 487, 491, 493, 494, 500, 504, 505, 506, 507, 510, 511, 512, 514, 517, 518, 521, 523, 527, 531, 536, 538, 539, 540, 541, 547, 548, 549, 550

collaborates with H on *The Federalist* 501

Maecenas, Gaius 29

Magna Charta 39

Maine 39

Malcolm, William 367, 441

Malmedi, M. 128

Malone, Dumas 315

Manduit du Plessis, Chevalier de 150, 152

Manhattan Island, New York City 39, 40, 42, 43

Manning, Martha 241

Mansfield, Lord 214

Mansfield, Mr. 331

Manumission of Slaves, Society for 432

Marion, Francis 314

Marshall, John 423, 514, 554

Martin, Joseph 150

Martin, Luther 453, 456, 477–478

Marx, Karl 445, 505

Maryland 443, 476, 482, 514

Maryland Gazette 443

Mason, George 452, 456, 461, 463, 489, 490, 491, 493, 512, 512, 514

Massachusetts 38, 39, 61, 63, 65, 97, 365, 397, 440, 448, 462, 476, 482, 501, 512, 514
  Assembly 107

Mawhood, Charles 113

Maxwell, "Scotch Willie" 143

Meade, Richard Kidder 122, 207, 256, 268, 357, 358, 370, 532

Meigs, Mr. 276

Memoirs (Rochambeau) 322

Mendy, W. 221

Mentor (sobriquet of Isaac Ledyard) 414

Mercer, Hugh 111, 113

Mercer, John Francis 195, 202, 396, 397

Mercury 128

Mercury, H.M.S. 94

Mifflin, Thomas 122, 125, 155, 167, 168, 190, 376

Military conscription urged by H 263

Miller, John C. 2

Minuit, Peter 59

Mirabeau, Comte de (Honoré Gabrièl Victor Riquetti) 427

Mitchell, Ann Venton 8, 19, 34, 430

Mitchell, Broadus 2, 19

Mitchell, John 236

Mitchell, Nathaniel 482

Mob rule
  distrust of by H 54–55, 61, 89–90

Mohawk Indians 63

Moir & Gordon 15

Monitor (pseudonym of H) 62

Monmouth, Battle of 122, 210
  indecision concerning 192–194
  terrain 196

Monroe, James 111, 232, 443, 445, 514

Montague, James 55

"Montague, James" 228, 253, 340

Montesquieu, Baron de La Brède et de (Charles de Secondab) 52, 63, 351, 502, 512

Montgomery, Richard 85, 97, 128

Montmorin, Comte de 452

Montreal 96, 97

Moore, James 120

Moore, P.L. 450

Morgan, Daniel 140, 156, 157, 193, 195, 201, 202, 314

Morris, Chief Justice 353

Morris, Gouverneur 47, 85, 121, 126, 127, 128, 135, 139, 140, 143, 225, 228, 341, 342, 411, 413, 423, 432, 433, 434, 436, 438, 439, 452, 460, 463, 487, 488, 491, 492, 494, 498–499, 501, 534, 538, 547, 548

Morris, Robert 109, 121, 223, 224, 225, 228, 263, 305, 322, 340, 341, 342, 344, 347, 359, 360, 362, 364, 365, 366, 367, 379, 388, 392, 393, 410, 438, 443, 452, 454, 455, 456, 460, 463, 492, 513, 547, 548, 551, 553

appoints H tax receiver 360

Morris, Roger 87

Morristown, New Jersey 47, 114
  winter quarters for Continental Army 118, 121, 122, 131–132, 135, 136, 137, 236, 239–240

Morristown National Historical Park 121

Mulligan, Hercules 40, 41, 87, 92, 94, 101, 102, 407

introduces H to Witherspoon 50

Mulligan, Hugh 40

Murnan, John Barnard 319

Murray, Mr. 289, 290

Murray, John 542

Musgrave, Colonel 149

Nancy 63

Nantes, Edict of: *see* Edict of Nantes

National debt
  H's view of 344, 387

National government
  H's views 262–263, 305, 345, 346, 362, 369, 462–463, 464, 465–476, 477, 481, 498

Neckar, Mr. 471
Negro slaves: *see* Slaves, Negro; Slavery
Neilson, William 417
Nelson, Thomas 327, 329
Nelson, William 497
Netherlands, The: *see* Holland
Nevis, B.W.I. 1, 4, 5, 6, 7, 8, 10, 11, 12, 13, 14,
     28, 39, 40, 233
New Amsterdam 59
New Brunswick, New Jersey 107, 108, 112,
     114, 137, 139
New Castle, Delaware 29
New England 84, 85, 107
   convention for appointing a dictator 270
New Hampshire 443, 454, 482, 512, 516, 520,
     536
   Constitution ratification 521
New Haven, Connecticut 88
New Jersey 45, 84, 101, 106, 109, 112, 114, 129,
     191, 192, 261, 266, 365, 439, 440, 442, 444,
     445, 447, 476, 482, 501, 512
New Jersey Plan 465–476
   vs. Virginia Plan 465–476
   See also Connecticut Plan; Constitutional
     Convention; Virginia Plan
New London, Pennsylvania 29
New Netherlands 39, 59
New Sweden 39
New Windsor, New York 157, 163, 166, 168
New York, state 38, 442, 443, 444, 476, 482,
     499, 501, 512, 514
   Assembly 52, 60, 65, 70, 84, 88, 91, 441, 446
   British operations 58–59
   British goods boycotted 64
   Constitution ratification 526
   constitution, state 127
   Constitutional Convention 362, 363, 449
   H tax receiver 360–364
   impost, veto of 446–447
   political temper on eve of Revolution 60–62,
     65–67
   Trespass Act 412, 416, 417, 418, 421
New York, city 22, 24, 26, 30, 34, 35, 37, 45, 49,
     55, 56
   agitation on eve of Revolution 54–55, 57–58,
     64–66
   British domination 58–59
   British occupation 99
   capital of U.S. 538
   celebrates adoption of Constitution 524–526
   Common Council 538
   Constitution 524
   fortifications 96, 98, 100
   H's first arrival 40–43
   Manhattan 39, 40, 42, 43
   mob riots 54–55, 57–58, 85, 88–90
   shelled by H.M.S. *Asia* 86–87
   Staten Island 42, 98, 99, 135
   Tories, attacks on 54–55, 57–58, 85, 88–90
New York Civil Practice Acts, Laws, and Rules
     351
New York Council of Revision 437
New York Daily Advertiser 449, 450, 452, 482
New York Directory (Frank) 409
New York Gazette, The 42
New York *Gazetteer* 57, 58, 70–71, 85, 409
*New York Journal and General Advertiser,
     The* 53, 62, 212, 412, 452, 497, 527
New York Liberty Boys 305
New York Packet 346, 357, 435, 507
New York Provincial Congress 60, 61, 70, 84,
     85, 86, 88, 92, 93, 94, 95, 97, 101, 103, 120
   commends H's artillery company 94
New York Provincial Convention 126, 127, 136
New York Regiment, First 92, 94
New York Society Library 511
New York Stock Exchange 42
Newark, New Jersey 107
Newburgh, New York 44, 163
"Newburgh Addresses" 389, 390, 392
Newport, Rhode Island 215
   Franco-American attack 217–218, 227
Newton, William 24, 28, 437
Nicholson, James 524
Nicola, Lewis 381
Nicoll, Delancey 52
Nicoll, Samuel 52
Nicolls, Richard 59
Nisi Prius (Buller) 351
Nixon, General 160
Noailles, Louis Marie de 328, 335
Norse, William 426
North, Frederick 63, 71, 181, 183
North Carolina 270, 365, 439, 443, 463, 476, 482,
     514
   Constitution ratification 527

Ogden, Aaron 197, 288–289, 290
O'Hara, Charles 335, 336
Olney, Jeremiah 199
Ossining, New York 272
Otis, James 38, 59
Otto, Louis Guillaume 452

Page, John 549
Paine, Thomas 71, 150, 379, 436, 446
Paoli, Pennsylvania 147, 148, 151, 178
Paracelsus 217

Paris, Treaty of (1763) 40
Paris, Treaty of (1783) 392, 399, 401
Paterson, John 158, 162, 163
Paterson, William 353, 465, 468, 470, 475
Paulding, John 268, 292
Paxton, Mr. 59
Pay Book (H) 116, 117
Peale, Charles Wilson 434
Peekskill, New York 140, 165, 173, 215
Pendleton, Edmund 68, 514, 523
Pendleton, Nathaniel 426
Penn, William 68, 351
Pennsylvania 29, 64, 109, 365, 442, 444, 447, 476, 482, 501, 512, 537
   army mutiny 392–397
   Executive Council 393–395, 396, 456
Pennsylvania Gazette 483
Pennsylvania Herald 452
Pennsylvania Journal 483
Percy, Lord 100
Peru 231
Peter the Great (Russ. czar) 52
Peters, Richard 377, 401
Pettit, Charles 219
Philadelphia 23, 35, 40, 54, 84, 96, 99, 100, 108, 109, 118, 130, 135–136, 140, 141, 142, 143, 145, 147, 151, 157, 166, 167, 175, 191
   British capture 148
   Congress flees 148
   mutinous troops 393–395
   see also Constitutional Convention
Philip of Macedon 413
Phillips, William 140
Phocion (pseudonym of H) 413, 433, 459
Phoenix, H.M.S. 94
Pickens, Andrew 314
Pickering, Timothy 122, 144, 149, 150, 321, 410, 453
Pierce, William 469, 481, 482
Pierrepont, Evelyn 415, 416
Pinckney, Charles 452, 456, 457, 461, 468, 512
Pinckney, Charles Cotesworth 99, 452, 476, 512
Pintard, Lewis 410
Pitt, William (earl of Chatham) 101, 553
Platt, Richard 542
Plutarch 26, 28, 502
Poems on Several Occasions (Johnson) 53
Poland 97
Poor, Mr. 163, 164
Pope, Alexander 26, 36, 75
Popham, William 426
Portail, Louis Le Beque du 226, 227, 228, 236, 269, 324
Portsmouth, New Hampshire 128

Postlethwayt, Malachy 52
Poughkeepsie, New York
   Constitutional Convention 514–526
Power
   abuse 474, 476, 507
   fear 464
   shared 463
Practical Proceedings in the Supreme Court of the State of New York (H) 351–352, 356, 357, 409
Practice Manual (Wyche) 351
Princeton, New Jersey 44, 108, 112, 113
Princeton, Battle of 112–114, 158
Princeton University 29, 49, 55, 56, 376
   H not admitted 50
Prisoners, exchange of 183–186
Proeck, Baron von 11
Profiteering 212, 224
Property rights 505
Providence, Rhode Island 217
Provincial Artillery Company (New York) 93, 96, 99, 102, 108, 114, 120, 200, 253
Public Advertiser (London) 214
Public credit: *see* Government credit
Publicus (pseudonym of H) 212, 214, 239, 354, 370, 502
Publius Syrus 214
Publius Valerianus 502
Publius Valerius 502
Puerto Rico 4
Pufendorf, Samuel von 31, 52, 351
Pulaski, Casimir 149, 150, 177, 186, 226
Putnam, Israel 97, 102, 103, 158, 163, 164, 165, 166, 176, 273
Putnam, Rufus 98, 100, 101

Quebec 96, 97
Quebec Act (1774) 63, 139
   H's attack on 72–73, 85

Rall, Johann Gottlieb 110, 111
Randall, H.S. 529
Randall, Thomas 417
Randolph, Edmund 444, 445, 450, 452, 456, 461, 462, 463, 468, 473, 483, 489, 490, 491, 493, 501, 514
Randolph, Mary Fitzhugh Grimes 358
Read, George 476, 491
Reed, Joseph 104, 109, 110, 155, 240, 291, 292
Reeve, Sally 354
Religion, Freedom of
   advocated by H 72, 85–86
Remarks on the Quebec Bill (H) 85
Rennselaer, Angelica Livingston Van 302

Rensselaer, Stephen Van 442, 500
Reports (Coke) 351
Revere, Paul 38
Revolutionary Army: *see* Continental Army
Revolutionary War
  Boston 97–98
  Brandywine Creek, Battle of 143–145, 152, 153, 192
  British legislation restricting American economic activities 38–40, 58–61
  Camden, Battle of 265–267, 283
  Franco-American attack 217–218, 227
  French aid 212–213
  Germantown, Battle of 149–151, 152, 153, 168, 192, 207
  H's changing views 61, 62–63, 65–67, 70–84
  Harlem Heights, Battle of 102–105, 119
  Long Island, Battle of 100–102
  Monmouth, Battle of 122, 192–200, 210
  New York City 86–87, 99
  Philadelphia 148
  popular support 63
  Quebec expedition 97
  Princeton, Battle of 112–114, 158
  prisoners, exchange of 183–186
  Saratoga, Battle of 154, 187
  Savannah, Ga. 226
  Tories 69–70, 88–90
  Trenton, Battle of 110–111, 289
  Washington's retreat from lower Manhattan 105
  White Plains, Battle of 105–106, 196
  Yorktown, Battle of 328–334
Reynolds, David 484, 485
Reynolds, James 232, 484, 490
Reynolds, Maria 485, 490
Rhinelander, Phillip 40
Rhode Island 38, 125, 128, 135, 365, 377, 378–379, 388, 440, 443, 454, 482, 499, 514
  Constitution ratification 527
Richmond, Virginia 306
Rivington, James 57–58, 59, 70–71, 75, 85, 88, 90, 284, 316, 409
Roach, John 10
Robertson, James 289, 290, 322
Robinson, Beverly 271, 272, 273, 274, 275, 277, 279
Rochambeau, Comte de 254, 268, 270, 284, 289, 297, 307, 316, 317, 321, 322, 324, 328, 330, 335, 373
Rochefoucauld, Duc de La 452, 534
Rodgers, John 29, 33, 41
Rodney, George 270
Roepstorff, Ulrich Wilhelm 32

Roosevelt, Isaac 513
Ross, Alexander 335
Rossiter, Clinton 490
Rousseau, Jean-Jacques 63
Royal Danish American Gazette, The 30–31, 33–34, 36, 48
Royal Gazette 284, 316
Rules for the Order and Discipline of the Troops (Steuben) 182
Rules of Practice (Kent) 353
Rush, Benjamin 107, 144–145, 156, 168, 395, 510
Russell, Margaret 409
Russia 494
Rutgers, Anthony 416
Rutgers, Elizabeth 415, 416, 417, 418, 419, 420, 421, 422
Rutgers University 107
Rutgers vs. Waddington 415–423, 425, 449
  protest against decision 422
Rutledge, John 68, 376, 452, 456, 489, 492–499

Saba 29, 30
St. Augustine, Florida 191
St. Christopher: *see* St. Kitts
St. Clair, Arthur 111, 125, 140, 141, 175, 393, 394, 395
St. Croix 2, 4, 6, 10, 11, 12, 13, 26, 28, 29, 31, 34, 35, 36, 38, 41, 44, 48, 93, 233, 430, 525, 553
  hurricane 31–32
  Knox, Hugh 29
  slavery 20–21, 22
  social conditions 20–22, 25
St. Eustatius 10, 11
St. Johns Anglican Church (Christiansted) 16, 18, 29
St. Kitts 2, 4, 6, 8, 10, 11, 13, 14, 15, 28, 29, 39, 40, 233
St. Leger, Barry 139, 154
St. Lucia, F.W.I. 191, 215
Saint-Simon, Comte de 331
St. Vincent 7, 11
Saratoga, New York 140, 152, 153
Saratoga, Battle of 154, 187
Savannah, Georgia 226, 227, 266
Scammell, Alexander 297, 298, 328, 332, 333, 552
Schuyler, Catherine van Rennselaer (d. Philip Schuyler) 246, 348
Schuyler, Catherine van Rennselaer (Mrs. Philip) 241, 243, 246, 253, 254, 301, 302, 343, 349
Schuyler, Margarita (Peggy) 244, 248, 252, 255, 258, 302, 320, 348, 349, 350, 500

Schuyler, Philip 65, 84, 85, 97, 132, 139, 141, 153, 154, 161, 176, 220, 241, 243, 244, 245, 247, 266, 270, 291, 292, 295, 296, 301, 302, 308, 310, 312, 317, 321, 326, 340, 348, 349, 350, 362, 363, 364, 366, 367, 379, 386, 441, 442, 448, 453, 500, 516, 543
    satisfaction in H 257–258
Scotch Plains, New Jersey 137
Scott, Charles 193, 195, 196, 197
Scott, John Morin 65, 367
Scott, Thomas 550
Seabury, Samuel ("Westchester Farmer") 53, 54, 58, 88
    pamphlet controversy with H 69–84
Sears, Isaac 82, 84, 88–89, 91, 284, 305, 409, 437
Secker, Thomas 51
Secret Journals 296
Sedgwick, Theodore 540
Senate, U.S. 464, 476, 486, 504, 545, 546
Separation of powers at Constitutional Convention 54
Seton, William 436, 437, 438
Seven Years' War 60
Shaw, Samuel 209, 274, 389
Shays, Daniel 445, 446, 453
Shays' rebellion 445–446, 454, 481
Sherman, Roger 452, 467, 475, 476
Shippen, Edward 433
Simcoe, John Graves 288, 289, 314
Slavery 498–499
    Constitutional Convention 463
    H advocates abolition 432, 499
    H's hatred of 21, 71–72, 77, 233–235, 368, 506, 552
    St. Croix 20–21, 22, 24
Slaves, Negro
    enlistment in Continental Army 232–234, 368
Smith, Adam 344, 434, 462
Smith, Joshua Hett 271, 272, 273, 279, 280–283, 287, 354
Smith, Melancton 437, 452, 513, 516, 517, 518, 519, 520, 521, 522, 526
Smith, Samuel 152
Smith, William 27
Smith, William 150
Smith, William (Tory) 268, 271, 280, 289
Smith, William Livingston 199
Smythe, John 415, 421
Smythe's Journal 237
Sneyd, Honora 285
Society for Establishing Useful Manufactures (SUM) 215, 300
Society of the Cincinnati: see Cincinnati, Society of the

Soderstrom, Mr. 409
Solzhenitsyn, Alexander 78
Sons of Liberty 60, 62, 64, 88, 89, 284
South Carolina 2, 13, 18, 64, 130, 233, 234, 235, 265, 365, 397, 439, 443, 476, 482, 499, 512, 514
Spaight, Richard D. 463
Spain 21, 260, 342, 398
    Mississippi navigation rights 534, 536
Spectator, The (Addison) 52, 66
Spencer, Joseph 125
Spirit of Laws (Montesquieu) 63
Springfield, Battle of 46, 96
Stamp Act (1765) 60, 64
Stamp Act Congress 22, 60, 64
Stark, John 111
State, Department of (U.S.) 554
State sovereignty
    vs. federal government 402
    foreign commerce 439–440
    national currency 376, 439
    Virginia Plan vs. New Jersey Plan 465–476
Staten Island, New York City 42, 98, 99, 135
States' rights vs. federal government 418, 469, 522
States, Small vs. large 465–476, 478, 482, 489
Statute of Westminster (1731) 83
Stephen, Adam 125, 150
Steuben, F.W.A. von 94, 177, 179, 191, 199, 207, 208, 212, 213, 219, 220, 231, 240, 247, 315, 327, 407, 408, 426, 427, 428–429, 497, 500, 525, 527, 551, 557, 559
    friendship with H 180
    prepares regulations for troops 182
    services as inspector-general 180–182
Stevens, Ebenezer 106, 324
Stevens, Edward 12, 26–27, 28, 34, 37, 41, 51, 52, 294, 552, 553
    earliest letter of H 27
Stevens, Thomas 12, 26, 34
Stewart, Walter 389
Stirling, Lord: see Alexander, William
Stony Point, New York 220, 225, 271, 280
    captured by Anthony Wayne 226
Strong, Mr. 455
Strong, Joseph 410
Stuyvesant, Peter 55, 59
Suffrage, Right of
    Constitutional Convention 463–464
Sugar Act (1764) 60
Sullivan, John 100, 101, 105, 110, 111, 144, 145, 149, 150, 153, 186, 215, 217, 218, 219, 305, 514, 521
Sumter, Thomas 314

Supreme Court, N.Y. 507

Supreme Court, U.S. 417, 423, 424, 464, 474, 490, 510

Supreme Court of Judicature (New York) 352, 353

"Swamp Fox": *see* Marion, Francis

Sweden 38

Switzerland 231

Tappan, New York 280, 288

Tarleton, Banastre 314, 315, 328, 329

Tarquin 502

Taxation
  Adams, John 60
  British 60, 61
  Continental Congress 224–225, 228–229, 344–345
  farmers 231
  H's plan 342, 367–368
  public opinion 231
  right of 62

Teapot Dome 494

Ten Eyck, Tobias 42

Ternant, Jean Baptiste 182

Ternay, Charles Louis d'Arsac 270

Thacher, James 325

Thayer, Simeon 152, 177

Thompson, Thomas 95–96, 120, 552

Thoughts for Conducting the War from the Side of Canada (Burgoyne) 153

"Three Millions" 54

Throg's Neck, New York 104

Thunderbolt 24, 28

Thurman, Ralph 88

Tilghman, Tench 104, 121, 122, 124, 126, 131, 142, 166, 244, 249, 251, 307, 311, 316, 320, 321, 358, 532

Tilghman, William 252

Tillotson, Thomas 365

Tobago 11

Tocqueville, Alexis de 354, 355, 509

Tories 45, 53, 60, 96, 125, 136, 143, 166, 226, 349, 355, 365, 366, 383, 433
  hated 88–90, 383, 404–405, 406
  property rights 401, 412, 415–423

Tousard, Louis 218

Towers, John 17

Townshend Acts 60, 65

Trade: *see* Commerce

Travis mob 88

Treasury Department (U.S.) 25, 49, 547–551, 554

Treat, Samuel 166

Trenton, New Jersey 109, 112, 114, 118, 119

Trenton, Battle of 110–111, 289

Trespass Act (1783) 412, 416, 417, 418, 421
  annulment 422

Trinity Church 42

Troup, Robert 52, 53, 54, 56, 57, 64, 66, 84, 92, 100, 160, 162, 169, 170–171, 176, 246, 352, 353, 354, 409, 410, 411, 416, 418, 420, 426, 428, 441, 532, 542, 548, 553
  memories of H at King's 51

Tryon, William 65, 85, 86, 88, 91

Tucker, Thomas 537

Two Treatises of Government (Locke) 83

Unit rule at Constitutional Convention 464, 473

United States, Bank of: *see* Bank of the United States

Valley Forge 146, 147, 148, 167, 168, 173–189, 192, 196, 199
  Conway cabal 176, 179, 184

Van Cortlandt, Philip 321

Van Cortlandt, Pierre 410

Vanderput, Captain 86, 87

Van Wart, Isaac 268, 292

Varick, Richard 274, 277, 279, 409, 417, 442

Varnum, James 199

Vattel, Emeric de 351

Venus 24

Vergennes, Comte de (Charles Gravier) 297

Vermont 534–536

Verplanck's Point, New York 225, 226, 273, 275, 276, 279, 280, 325

View of the Controversy, A (Seabury) 75

Violence 54–55, 61, 89–90

Viomenil, A.C. du Houx 330, 332

Virgil 18, 26, 30

Virgin Islands 2
  Danish 2, 15, 21–22

Virginia 19, 39, 61, 64, 266, 270, 365, 401, 439, 442, 444, 446, 463, 476, 482, 499, 501, 506, 512, 514, 516, 520, 521, 526, 534
  Constitution ratification 523
  House of Burgesses 63

Virginia Plan 462–464, 477, 478, 481, 482, 483
  vs. New Jersey Plan 465–476
  opposed 465–476
  see also Connecticut Plan; Constitutional Convention; New Jersey Plan

Visme, Catherine de 354

Vulture, H.M.S. 268, 271, 272, 273, 274, 275, 276, 280, 325

Waddington, Benjamin 415, 416, 417, 418, 419, 420, 421, 422

Wadsworth, Jeremiah 213, 254, 373, 403, 434, 435, 453, 484, 485, 548
Wait, Thomas 502
Waldo, Albigence 175
Walker, Benjamin 181, 208, 247, 410, 437
Walker, John 122
Wall Street Presbyterian Church 41
Waltemeyer, John 349
War, Department of (U.S.) 554
War of 1812 182
Ward, Artemus 124
Ward, Christopher 176
Warner, Seth 158, 164
Warville, Brissot de 525
Washington, George 12, 22, 41, 64, 94, 96, 98, 99, 107, 109, 110, 111, 115, 116, 119, 120, 136, 348, 452, 454–455, 458, 481, 484, 490, 492, 494, 502, 517, 551
    "aegis" of H 310
    aides 121–128
    André, John 284
    Arnold, Peggy 278
    Arnold's treason at West Point 271–278
    Constitutional Convention 456
    Continental Army 85, 97
    Continental Congress 101, 102, 106, 107–108, 112, 122–123, 151, 176, 178
    Fabian tactics 139, 226
    "Farewell Address" 132
    Federalist, The 511
    French, slur on 316–317
    Gates, Horatio 152–153, 154
    Gates and Conway 161–162
    H advises on Army discontent 380–385
    H and the presidency 539–540
    H–Clinton dispute 497
    H field command, unable to give 318
    H's quarrel 307–308
    H sent to Gates 156
    Harlem Heights, Battle of 103, 104
    Hartford, French at 270–272
    Lee court-martial 200–207
    Monmouth campaign 192–200
    New York City 319, 321; (after election) 544
    Newburgh Addresses 389–391
    Newport 215–216, 217–218
    presidency 541
    prisoner exchange 183–186
    Society of the Cincinnati 426, 454–455
    Steuben 180
    supplies, appeals for 219, 223, 270
    Valley Forge 173–189
Washington, Lund 105, 316
Washington, Martha 97, 121, 131, 186, 236–237, 240, 241, 247, 248, 305, 348, 546, 552
Washington, William 111, 314
Watergate 494
Waters of St. Croix, The 35
Wayne, Anthony 147, 150, 151, 155, 178, 186, 192, 193, 195, 196, 197, 198, 199, 221, 225, 255, 322, 327, 330, 380, 389, 392
    West Point captured 226
Wealth of Nations (Smith) 462
Webb, Samuel Blatchley 101, 250–251, 437
Webster, Daniel 245
Webster, Noah 322
Webster, Pelatiah 436
Weedon, George 111
West Indies 83, 191, 212, 215, 218, 258, 322, 377
    Danish 9
West Point 215, 220, 225, 238, 267, 271–277, 279, 283, 291, 292
Westchester County, New York 105, 220, 273
Westerlo, Eilardus 348
Westfield, New Jersey 137
Westminster, Treaty of (1724) 59
Westmore, Hezekiah 484
"Whaleboat War" 220
Whigs 45, 70, 89, 416, 433
White, Colonel 193
White, Philip 383
White Plains, Battle of 105–106, 196
Whitehill, Robert 502
Wiederhold, Andreas 111
Wilcox, William 416, 417
Wilkins, Isaac 53
Wilkinson, James 113, 155, 168–170
    Conway cabal 237
Willett, Marinus 65, 82, 84, 154
William and Mary, College of: see College of William and Mary
Williams, David 268, 292
Williamson, Hugh 377, 456, 486, 492
Willing (Morris) & Company 341
Willing & Taylor 24
Wilmington, Delaware 142, 143
Wilmington, North Carolina 377
Wilson, James 376, 386, 387, 388, 392, 452, 456, 464, 465, 468, 475, 476, 491, 494
Windham, Connecticut 64
Witherspoon, John 49–50, 55
Wolcott, Oliver 376, 453
Wooster, General 101
Wyche, Mr. 351
Wythe, George 452, 457, 460, 514

Xenophon 44

Yale University 45, 69
Yates, Abraham, Jr. 360–361, 364–365, 366, 386
Yates, Robert 448, 453, 454, 462, 465, 466, 470, 472, 473, 475, 476, 481, 482, 485, 490, 493, 513, 526, 542, 543

York, Pennsylvania 148, 152, 153, 176
York Island: *see* Manhattan Island
Yorktown, Battle of 44, 130, 186, 328–337
    preparations 321–328